SUBSTANCE USE AMONG WOMEN

SUBSTANCE USE AMONG WOMEN

A Reference and Resource Guide

Ann Marie Pagliaro
Professor and Director

and

Louis A. Pagliaro
Professor and Associate Director

Substance Abusology Research Unit
University of Alberta

USA	Publishing Office:	BRUNNER/MAZEL
A member of the Taylor & Francis Group
325 Chestnut Street
Philadelphia, PA 19106
Tel: (215) 625–8900
Fax: (215) 625–2940
	Distribution Center:	BRUNNER/MAZEL
A member of the Taylor & Francis Group
47 Runway Road, Suite G
Levittown, PA 19057
Tel: (215) 269–0400
Fax: (215) 269–0363
UK		BRUNNER/MAZEL
A member of the Taylor & Francis Group
11 New Fetter Lane
London EC4P 4EE, UK
Tel: +44 171 583 9855
Fax: +44 171 842 2298

SUBSTANCE USE AMONG WOMEN: A Reference and Resource Guide

Copyright © 2000 Taylor & Francis. All rights reserved. Printed in the United States of America. Except as permitted under the United States Copyright Act of 1976, no part of this publication may be reproduced or distributed in any form or by any means, or stored in a database or retrieval system, without prior written permission of the publisher.

1 2 3 4 5 6 7 8 9 0

Printed by Edwards Brothers, Lillington, NC, 1999.
Cover design by Ellen Seguin.

A CIP catalog record for this book is available from the British Library.
The paper in this publication meets the requirements of the ANSI Standard Z39.48–1984 (Permanence of Paper).

Library of Congress Cataloging-in-Publication Data

Pagliaro, Ann Marie
    Substance use among women: a reference and resource guide / Ann Marie Pagliaro and Louis A. Pagliaro.
        p. cm.
    Includes bibliographical references and index.
    ISBN 1-58391-035-2 (case)
    1. Women—Substance use—United States. 2. Substance abuse—United States. I. Pagliaro, Louis A. II. Title.
RC564.5.W65P34   1999
362.29'082'0973—dc21   99-41873
                                                                    CIP

ISBN 1-58391-035-2 (case)

To all those women, whose hearts have been killed and whose souls have been murdered by substance use, and to the health and social care professionals, whose dedication and assistance have provided healing and solace for these women.

CONTENTS

List of Figures · xi
List of Tables · xiii
Acknowledgments · xv
Preface · xvii

I. INTRODUCTION

Chapter 1   **An Overview of Substance Use Among Women** · 3
The Mega Interactive Model of Substance Use
    Among Women · 6
The Substance Dimension · 10
Treatment · 24
Conclusion · 26

Chapter 2   **Explaining Substance Use Among Women** · 28
Why Women Use Alcohol and Other Substances of Abuse · 28
Conclusion · 58

II. DEVELOPMENTAL CONSIDERATIONS

Chapter 3   **Substance Use During Pregnancy and Lactation: Effects on the Developing Fetus, Neonate, and Infant** · 65
Substance Use During Pregnancy · 65
Maternal Substance Use · 66
Maternal Substance Use and Teratogenesis · 68
Substance Use and Breast Feeding · 80
Conclusion · 81

Chapter 4 Effects of Maternal Substance Use on Mothering and Child Rearing — 87

Mother-Infant Dyads — 87
Issues of Separation, Loss, and Abandonment — 88
Physical Abuse and Neglect — 89
Concerns for the School-Aged Child — 93
Consequences for the Next Generation of Mothers — 94
Conclusion — 94

Chapter 5 Substance Use Among Elderly Women: Effects on Healthy Aging — 97

Identifying Problematic Patterns of Substance Use Among Elderly Women — 97
Problematic Patterns of Substance Use Among Elderly Women — 102
Treating Problematic Patterns of Substance Use Among Elderly Women — 109
The Mega Interactive Model of Substance Use Among Elderly Women — 110
Conclusion — 119

III. SOCIAL CONSIDERATIONS

Chapter 6 Women as Victims of Substance Use Related Violence — 123

Accidents and Acts of Violence — 123
Suicide — 128
Conclusion — 130

Chapter 7 Women as Perpetrators of Substance Use Related Violence — 133

Substance Use and Crime — 133
Substance Use and Commerce- and Pharmacopsychologic-Related Crime — 138
Examples of Substance Use Related Violence Perpetrated by Women — 142
Conclusion — 145

Chapter 8 Women, Substance Use, HIV Infection, and AIDS — 149

HIV/AIDS Incidence Among Women — 151
Intravenous Drug Use and AIDS — 151
Sex for Drugs — 155
Conclusion — 157

IV. CLINICAL CONSIDERATIONS

Chapter 9	**Assessing and Diagnosing Substance Use Disorders Among Women**	165
	Psychometric Instruments	*167*
	Conclusion	*180*
Chapter 10	**Dual Diagnoses Among Women**	182
	Substance Use and Mood Disorders	*185*
	Substance Use and Anxiety Disorders	*186*
	Substance Use and Psychotic Disorders	*187*
	Substance Use and Personality Disorders	*187*
	Substance Use and Sexual or Gender Identity Disorders	*187*
	Treatment	*188*
	Conclusion	*189*
Chapter 11	**Preventing and Treating Substance Use Disorders Among Women**	191
	Primary Prevention	*192*
	Secondary Prevention	*194*
	Tertiary Prevention	*194*
	Relapse	*210*
	Conclusion	*210*

V. RESOURCES AND REFERENCES

Appendix I	**Abbreviations and Symbols Used in the Text**	219
Appendix II	**Substances of Abuse: Generic, Trade, and Common Names**	222
Appendix III	**Directory of Major North American Substance Use Treatment Centers, Referral Agencies, and Related Information Sources for Women**	238
References		287
Index		335

LIST OF FIGURES

1-1 The abusable and nonabusable psychotropics
1-2 Patterns of substance use
1-3 The Mega Interactive Model of Substance Use Among Women (MIMSUAW)
1-4 Acute opiate overdose: Sequence of events
1-5 Amphetamines: Physical and psychological effects
3-1 Multivariate determinants of teratogenesis
3-2 Organogenetic variation in human teratogenic susceptibility
3-3 Common craniofacial characteristics associated with FAS
5-1 The Mega Interactive Model of Substance Use Among Elderly Women (MIMSUAEW)
5-2 Patterns of substance use
5-3 The MIMSUAEW flowchart
6-1 Risk of motor vehicle crash: Relationship to BAC, age, driving experience, and drinking experience
7-1 Substance use and crime: Proposed relationships
8-1 Transmission of HIV among IVDUs and their family members, friends, and other contacts
9-1 Type I and Type II diagnostic errors
10-1 Transmission of HIV among women intravenous drug users and their family members, friends, and other contacts
11-1 Prevention in relation to patterns of substance use
11-2 Typical relapse rates following treatment for problematic patterns of substance use

LIST OF TABLES

1-1	Major substances of abuse: The abusable psychotropics
1-2	Alcohol use among women: Acute and chronic adverse effects
1-3	Opiate use among women: Short-term physiologic effects
1-4	Acute opiate overdose among women: Signs and symptoms
1-5	Caffeine content of selected beverages
1-6	Caffeine use among women: Acute effects of high doses
1-7	Cocaine use among women: Adverse effects
1-8	Nicotine use among women: Adverse effects
1-9	Cannabis use among women: Acute and chronic adverse effects
3-1	Criteria for neonatal urine tests
3-2	Abnormalities originally associated with FAS
3-3	Reported incidence of FAS
3-4	Obstetrical complications among pregnant women who use cocaine
3-5	Substances of abuse excreted in human breast milk
4-1	Mental and physical disorders associated with the abuse or neglect of children by their mothers
4-2	High risk factors for child abuse and neglect
5-1	Reasons why geriatric clinicians avoid or are resistant to diagnosing and treating elderly women who have problematic patterns of substance use
5-2	Nonpathognomonic symptoms of problematic patterns of substance use commonly misdiagnosed by health and social care professionals
5-3	Life events and lifestyle changes associated with aging
5-4	Adverse effects related to chronic alcohol abuse among elderly women
5-5	Factors specifically associated with problematic patterns of benzodiazepine use among elderly nursing home residents
6-1	Substance use related violent physical injuries among women
6-2	Major risk factors associated with suicide ideation and attempts by women
7-1	Alcohol use and criminal behavior: Methodologic limitations
7-2	Situational factors that may significantly affect the relationship between alcohol use and crime
7-3	Types of substance use-related crime

List of Tables

8-1	Demographics of women IVDUs
8-2	Drug use history for women
8-3	Knowledge of HIV infection and AIDS among women IVDUs
8-4	Findings in relation to unsafe injection drug use
8-5	Self-perception of risk for HIV infection among women IVDUs
8-6	Behaviors of hard-core IVDUs that contravene the intended efficacy of needle exchange programs
9-1	Alcohol Use Disorders Identification Test (AUDIT)
9-2	Brief MAST (B-MAST)
9-3	CAGE: An alcohol screening test
9-4	Drug Abuse Screening Test (DAST)
9-5	Index of Alcohol Involvement (IAI)
9-6	MacAndrew Alcoholism Scale (MAC)
9-7	Malmo Modified Michigan Alcoholism Screening Test (Mm-MAST)
9-8	Maternal Short-MAST (M-MAST)
9-9	Maternal substance use screening questionnaire
9-10	Michigan Alcoholism Screening Test (MAST)
9-11	Rapid Alcohol Problems Screen (RAPS)
9-12	Short Michigan Alcoholism Screening Test (SMAST)
9-13	TWEAK: An alcoholism screening test developed for women
10-1	Diagnoses, in addition to addiction and habituation, that are commonly associated with substance use
10-2	Substance use and sexual behavior
11-1	Variables associated with substance use and amenability to primary, secondary, or tertiary prevention strategies
11-2	An example of a comprehensive alternatives model
11-3	Intrapersonal and interpersonal skills training elements
11-4	General guidelines for the family therapist
11-5	Types of family therapy and their major components or focus
11-6	The 12 steps of Alcoholics Anonymous
11-7	The 13 affirmations of Women for Sobriety
11-8	Characteristics of a woman-oriented substance use treatment program
11-9	Overview of the program objectives and elements in a typical short-term residential treatment program
11-10	Performance goals/criterion in relation to the evaluation of treatment success and relapse prevention
11-11	General guidelines for treatment of women who have a substance use disorder

ACKNOWLEDGMENTS

We wish to acknowledge and thank Bernadette Capelle, our acquisitions editor at Taylor and Francis, Brunner/Mazel, and Herb Reich, our publishing agent, for their continued faith and support. We also would like to thank Stephanie Weidel and her staff for the design and production of this text. Thanks also goes to Leona Laird for preparing the manuscript drafts and revisions, John Williamson for his assistance in retrieving needed references and other resource materials, and John Driedger for preparing the figures used in the various chapters. In addition, we would like to express our sincere appreciation for the women whose experiences have been shared in this text. We have learned much from their stories and continue to learn from them as we have come to appreciate the unique ability of the human heart and soul for overcoming seemingly overwhelming adversity when provided with genuine respect, kindness, and hope.

PREFACE

An increasing number of health and social care professionals, including counselors, family therapists, nurses, occupational therapists, pharmacists, physicians, psychologists, and social workers, are concerned about substance use among women and its effects on their health and well-being. Many health and social care professionals also are concerned about its consequences on the families and communities of these women. This text is written for these concerned health and social care professionals and for students who are assimilating knowledge in their respective fields of professional study. It also is written for health and social policy makers, who must increasingly address substance use among women and its impact on our society.

In an effort to meet the needs of these health and social care professionals, students, and policy makers, this text, in five parts, presents an integrated compilation and synthesis of theoretical, empirical, and clinical knowledge concerning several important topics associated with substance use among women. Attention is given to both current and historical research, which has been contributed from a variety of disciplines, and reflects diverse positivist, post-positivist, and postmodern philosophical and theoretical orientations. Although reference citations within the text predominantly focus upon recent original research studies that examine substance use among women and its antecedents and consequences, citations for general review articles and significant textbooks also have been included to encourage further study by interested readers.

Part I, "Introduction," is comprised of two chapters. Chapter 1, "An Overview of Substance Use Among Women," provides an overview of substance use among women and presents the Mega Interactive Model of Substance Use Among Women as a framework for approaching this complex phenomenon. Special attention is given to this model's substance dimension so that readers will have a better understanding of various substances of abuse used by women, their actions in the human body, and their patterns of use. Chapter 2, "Explaining Substance Use Among Women," presents contemporary explanations of why women use alcohol and other substances of abuse.

Part II, "Developmental Considerations," presents three chapters that consider the effects of substance use by women who are pregnant or may become pregnant, breast feeding, child rearing, or aging. Thus, Chapter 3, "Substance Use During Pregnancy and Lactation: Effects on the Developing Fetus, Neonate, and Infant," provides detailed information regarding maternal substance use during pregnancy and its effects on the developing fetus and neonate. This chapter also provides information on the potential effects of maternal substance use on breast-fed neonates and infants. Chapter 4, "Effects of Maternal Substance Use on Mothering and Child Rearing," explores the effects of maternal substance use on the development of healthy bonds between mothers and their infants and children; separation, loss, and abandonment; and physical abuse and neglect. This chapter also gives attention to the consequences of inadequate mothering and child rearing for the next generation of mothers. Part II concludes with Chapter 5, "Substance Use Among Elderly Women: Effects on Healthy Aging." This chapter considers the identification and treatment of problematic patterns of substance use among aging women and presents the Mega Interactive Model of Substance Use Among Elderly Women, a useful guide for assessing substance use among elderly women and planning appropriate treatment.

Part III, "Social Considerations," is comprised of three chapters. Chapter 6, "Women as Victims of Substance Use Related Violence," presents current data for and discussion of accidents, acts of violence, and suicide among women as related to substance use. Chapter 7, "Women as Perpetrators of Substance Use Related Violence," considers the varied factors associated with acts of violence by women against their spouses, other women, and their infants and children. This chapter also presents an overview of substance use and commerce- and pharmacologic-related crime, including crimes committed as a result of drug-induced automatism. Chapter 8, "Substance Use, Women, HIV Infection, and AIDS," presents an overview of the characteristics and prevalence of HIV infection and AIDS among women. Particular attention is given to the relationship between intravenous drug use and the phenomenon of "sex-for-drug-exchanges."

Part IV, "Clinical Considerations," concludes the didactic parts of the text with three chapters. Chapter 9, "Assessing and Diagnosing Substance Use Disorders Among Women," describes the various psychometric instruments commonly used for assessing substance use disorders among women. Attention also is given to the validity and reliability of these instruments. Chapter 10, "Dual Diagnosis Among Women," presents an overview of the dual diagnoses that are often identified among women, including substance use disorders and mental disorders such as mood, anxiety, and psychotic disorders. Attention also is given to substance use disorders and sexual or gender identity disorders. Chapter 11, "Preventing and Treating Substance Use Disorders Among Women," focuses on preventing and treating substance use disorders among women. Attention is given to primary, secondary, and tertiary prevention as well as relapse prevention.

Part V, "Resources and References," is comprised of three appendices and the references used for the preparation of this text. Appendix I, "Abbreviations Used in the Text," provides an alphabetical listing and corresponding definitions for all the abbreviations and symbols used in this text. Appendix II, "Substances of Abuse: Generic, Trade, and Common Names," presents a comprehensive table that lists the generic names for substances of abuse in alphabetical order, along with their corresponding trade names (if available), pharmacologic classification, and subclassification, and common street names. Appendix III, "Directory of Major North American Substance Use Treatment Centers, Referral Agencies, and Related Information Sources for Women," is arranged in three sections to facilitate access to needed information. The first section provides a directory of substance use treatment centers, referral agencies, and related information sources for women arranged in alphabetical order by organizational name. This section provides an initial source of contact for interested health and social care professionals. The second section of this appendix provides a directory of substance use treatment centers, referral agencies, and related information sources for women is arranged in alphabetical order by the state or province in which they are located. The third section provides a separate directory of major North American AIDS hotlines, listed in alphabetical order by state or province. Following these appendices is an alphabetical list of the references cited in this text, arranged by author, and a comprehensive subject index.

It is hoped that, by applying the information presented in this text, health and social care professionals, students, and policy makers will be able to better understand the nature and extent of substance use among women and its impact on their families and communities. It also is hoped that these health and social care professionals and policy makers will be better able to develop and provide appropriate and effective prevention and treatment services for women who engage in problematic patterns of substance use. Working together with women and their families and communities, and by using the information presented in this text, it is hoped that optimal health and well-being may be achieved for women who may, in various ways, use the substances of abuse.

Ann Marie Pagliaro
Louis A. Pagliaro
2000

PART

I

INTRODUCTION

CHAPTER 1

An Overview of Substance Use Among Women

Substance use affects all North American women directly or indirectly, regardless of age, culture, ethnicity, education, race, or socioeconomic status (Clemenger, 1993; Hoffman & Goldfrank, 1990; Johnson, 1990). Even women in rural America, who were once thought to be protected from the scourges of substance use, find themselves affected in a variety of ways and demonstrate patterns of use similar to those observed among women in urban settings (Chaiken, 1995; Morra, 1992).

Substance use is a phenomenon shared by women worldwide (Araya, 1994; Deen, 1996; Deshpande & Nagpal, 1993; Dreher, 1984; Gotoh, 1994; Ikuesan, 1994; Kua, 1994; Medina-Mora, 1994; Mphi, 1994; Park, 1993; Senay, Kozel, & Gonzalez, 1991). In addition, it has been prevalent throughout recorded history and is expected to continue. The use of various substances of abuse appears to begin at increasingly younger ages (A. M. Pagliaro & L. A. Pagliaro, 1996; Senay, Kozel, & Gonzalez, 1991; Westermeyer, 1992) and although patterns of use for some women may wax and wane, it may continue, or even begin, in middle or old age (L. A. Pagliaro & A. M. Pagliaro, 1992) (see Chapter 5, Substance Use Among Elderly Women: Effects on Healthy Aging).

Although some published reports seem to indicate that the use of various substances of abuse (Table 1-1 and Figure 1-1) is decreasing and that women, like men, "mature out" of substance use (Harrison, 1992; Miller-Tutzauer, Leonard, & Windle, 1991), these reports may be misleading and require careful interpretation. In fact, the careful scrutiny of these reports reveals that polysubstance use (i.e., the concurrent or concomitant use of more than one substance of abuse) is pervasive and appears to be increasing (Senay, Kozel, & Gonzalez, 1991; Shaw & Gray, 1996). The frequency of more serious patterns of use, such as abuse and compulsive use (Figure 1-2), and their associated morbidity and mortality, also are increasing (Bullows & Penfold, 1993; Moore, 1994). This increase in substance use by women is taxing the ability of established health and social care services to meet the increasing demands (Bullows & Penfold, 1993; Curtis & McCullough, 1993).

Morbidity related to substance use among women in North America is significant (Lee, 1995). Substance use is involved in most cases of child abuse (Child Abuse, 1991;

TABLE 1-1. Major substances of abuse: The abusable psychotropics*

Central Nervous System Depressants
  Opiates (e.g., codeine, heroin, meperidine, morphine, pentazocine)
  Sedative-Hypnotics (e.g., alcohol [beer, wine, distilled spirits]; barbiturates; benzodiazepines; miscellaneous)
  Volatile Solvents and Inhalants (e.g., gasoline; glue)
Central Nervous System Stimulants
  Amphetamines (e.g., dextroamphetamine)
  Caffeine (e.g., caffeinated soft drinks; coffee, tea)
  Cocaine (e.g., cocaine hydrochloride; crack cocaine)
  Nicotine (e.g., tobacco cigarettes, cigars)
Psychedelics (partial list)
  Lysergic acid diethylamide (LSD)
  Mescaline (peyote)
  Phencyclidine (PCP)
  Psilocybin (hallucinogenic mushrooms)
  Tetrahydrocannabinol (THC) (e.g., hashish; hashish oil; marijuana)

*Classification scheme from A.M. Pagliaro (1990, 1991).

Pribor & Dinwiddie, 1992; Rose, Peabody, & Stratigeas, 1991). It also commonly is associated with physical trauma involving women (Lindenbaum, Carroll, Daskal, & Kapusnick, 1989; Sloan, Zalenski, Smith, Sheaff, Chen, Keys, Crescenzo, Barrett, & Berman, 1989; U.S. Department of Justice, 1994; see Chapter 6, Women as Victims of Substance Use Related Violence) and is a significant factor in urban and rural crime (DeWitt, O'Neil, & Baldau, 1991; see Chapter 7, Women as Perpetrators of Substance Use Related Violence).

The chronic abuse of alcohol by women of childbearing age has increased the potential for, and frequency of, fetal alcohol syndrome, the most common preventable cause of mental retardation in North America (Pagliaro & Pagliaro, 1996; Pietrantoni & Knuppel, 1991; Streissguth, Aase, Clarren, Randels, LaDue, & Smith, 1991). Cocaine use among women of childbearing age also has increased over the past decade and attention is only recently focusing on the learning deficits and other developmental delays observed among infants, toddlers, preschoolers, and young school-aged children that may be possibly related to inutero cocaine exposure (i.e., crack babies) (Adler, 1992, see Chapter 3, Substance Use During Pregnancy and Lactation: Effects on the Developing Fetus, Neonate, and Infant, for additional details).

Substance use by women who have children tends to effect their mothering and child rearing adversely. For example, tragic cases of infants and toddlers being left alone in their cribs for days while their mothers are out drinking or partying have been reported. Other tragedies, such as the death of children left alone for hours in a locked car in very hot weather have been reported. In addition, crying infants have been sedated by their mothers placing a gasoline-soaked rag over the infants' faces without apparent attention to any possible harmful effects (Hickl-Szabo, 1987, see Chapter 4, Effects of Maternal Substance Use on Mothering and Child Rearing). Substance use by women also is associated with an increased incidence of sexually transmitted diseases, such as

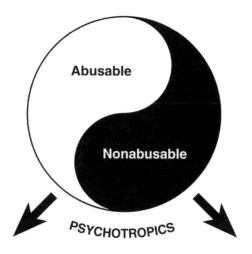

Central Nervous System Depressants:
OPIATES (Codeine, Heroin, Meperidine, Morphine, Pentazocine)
SEDATIVE HYPNOTICS (Alcohol [Beer, Wine, Distilled Liquor], Barbiturates, Benzodiazepines, Miscellaneous)
VOLATILE SOLVENTS & INHALANTS (Gasoline, Glue)

Central Nervous System Stimulants:
AMPHETAMINES, CAFFEINE, COCAINE, NICOTINE (Tobacco)

Psychedelics:
LSD, MESCALINE (Peyote), PCP, PSILOCYBIN, THC (Marijuana, Hashish, Hash Oil)

Anticonvulsants:
(Carbamazepine, Phenytoin, Primidone, Valproic Acid)

Antidepressants:
MONOAMINE OXIDASE INHIBITORS (Moclobemide, Phenelzine, Tranylcypromine)
SELECTIVE SEROTONIN REUPTAKE INHIBITORS (Fluoxetine, Paroxetine, Sertraline)
TRICYCLIC ANTIDEPRESSANTS (Amitriptyline, Desipramine, Imipramine, Nortriptyline)
MISCELLANEOUS (Amoxapine, Bupropion, Maprotiline, Trazodone)

Antiparkinsonians:
(Amantadine, Levodopa, Trihexyphenidyl)

Antipsychotics:
(Chlorpromazine, Clozapine, Haloperidol)

FIGURE 1-1. The abusable and nonabusable psychotropics.

syphilis and AIDS (Hibbs & Gunn, 1991; Nwanyanwu, Chu, Green, Buehler, & Berkelman, 1993, see Chapter 8, Women, Substance Use, HIV Infection, and AIDS).

Mortality associated with substance use by women is significant (Rehm, Fichter, & Elton, 1993). For example, the majority of fatal motor vehicle crashes involving women are the result of alcohol intoxication (Alcohol-Related, 1991; Ward, Flynn, Miller, & Blaisdell, 1982) and the number of impaired driving charges against women is increasing nationally (U.S. Department of Justice, 1991). Of equally serious concern is the noted relationship between substance use and suicide among women. Although traditionally significantly lower than for men, the incidence of suicide can be increased up to six-fold for women who are heavy drinkers (Klatsky & Armstrong, 1993). The number of murders related to substance use also has grown dramatically. The numbers of murders are particularly increased among inner city women and account for a significant percentage of the annual deaths reported for women (see Chapter 6, Women as Victims of Substance Use Related Violence, and Chapter 7, Women as Perpetrators of Substance Use Related Violence).

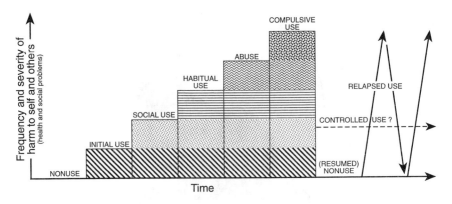

FIGURE 1-2. Patterns of substance use.

☐ The Mega Interactive Model of Substance Use Among Women

The Mega Interactive Model of Substance Use Among Women (MIMSUAW), extended from a model originally proposed by L.A. Pagliaro (1985a), and A.M. Pagliaro and L.A. Pagliaro (1996), has been developed to help clinical psychologists, counselors, family therapists, and other health and social care professionals concerned about substance use among women to better understand and deal with this complex phenomenon (Figure 1–3). The MIMSUAW can be used for assessing, developing, delivering, and evaluating individualized prevention and treatment programs for women who present with actual or potential problems related to substance use.

The model consists of four interacting variable dimensions. These dimensions are the: 1) Woman Dimension, 2) Societal Dimension, 3) Substance Dimension, and 4) Time Dimension. These dimensions comprise a number of interacting subsets or unit coteries. Each unit coterie represents a particular woman and her substance use at a particular time in her life. A collection of unit coteries represents the larger social group or community to which a woman belongs (e.g., a senior citizens association, a particular gang, women's swim team, professional association, Women for Sobriety). Thus, the model is useful for both individual and group assessment and intervention.

MIMSUAW accounts for the multidimensional etiology of substance use without the imposition of a singular, restrictive theoretical focus (e.g., illness/disease, psychoanalytical, social learning, family system) or classification system (e.g., *DSM-IV, Diagnostic and Statistical Manual of Mental Disorders*, 1994), which have been found to be inadequate by many clinicians and researchers.[1] This approach is important for providing comprehensive health and social care services. Thus, the MIMSUAW can be used as a theoretical framework by professionals from a variety of theoretical orientations when diagnosing substance use and planning, implementing, and evaluating pluralistic and multimodal therapy, which is often required in order to achieve optimal therapeutic benefit in this clinical context.

An Overview of Substance Use

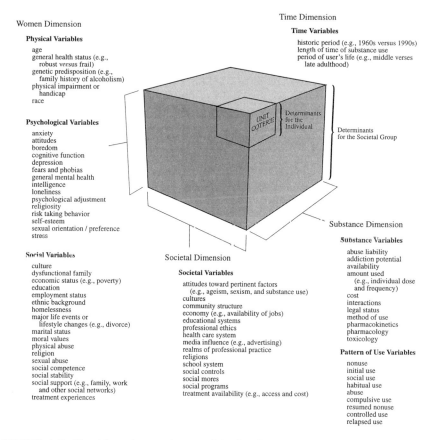

FIGURE 1-3. The Mega Interactive Model of Substance Use Among Women (MIMSUAW).

The complexity of MIMSUAW reflects the complex nature of substance use among women of all ages. Substance use always has been and always will be a complex phenomenon (see Chapter 2, Explaining Substance Use Among Women). Thus, a single simple solution should not be expected to be found. The multifactorial etiology of substance use and the myriad of possible interacting and confounding variables that must be considered for the provision of optimal prevention and treatment programs have been identified and are incorporated into the MIMSUAW. As illustrated in the following example using MIMSUAW, clinical psychologists, family therapists, psychiatrists, and other health and social care providers should attempt to abandon stereotypic and unidimensional thinking in relation to the etiology and treatment of substance use and should develop broad perspectives in regard to the possibilities that exist for a more diverse and varied approach for dealing with this complex problem.

Allison, a 24-year-old woman, consumes alcoholic beverages in excess on a regular basis. When encountered in a clinical context, it is not unlikely that she would be simply labeled as an alcoholic and referred to a generic treatment program for alcoholics. Alternatively, Allison's alcohol consuming behavior could be characterized in the context of the four variable dimensions of MIMSUAW. The health or social care professional would identify relevant variables to address when developing and implementing an individualized treatment plan. Let's say Allison had developed an alcohol problem as a preadolescent after the death of her father from alcohol-related cardiopathology, received bereavement counseling and had abstained from alcohol use until six months ago when her boyfriend broke up with her. Then, attention to the previously successful treatment, which involved resolution of grief, the development and strengthening of coping abilities, and the provision of alternative support systems, may do much to alleviate the current problem (see Chapter 11, Preventing and Treating Substance Use Disorders Among Women, for further discussion of various treatment approaches).

MIMSUAW serves as a heuristic device to help in the identification of the variables associated with substance use among women. It also encourages a better understanding of the complexity of the phenomenon. MIMSUAW offers a means for health and social care providers to focus on the important factors involving the woman, societal, time, and substance dimensions. Although the primary focus of this chapter will be on the substance dimension, a brief overview of the other three dimensions will be presented first so that the substance dimension can be considered in its proper context.

Variable Dimensions

Almost two decades ago Andrew Weil (1983) noted that, "It's a real problem when you classify drugs as good and bad . . . Drugs are drugs [i.e., inanimate objects without any inherent goodness or badness]. The only point that good and bad comes in is in the individual use of drugs" (p. 22). Thus, the use of morphine to relieve severe cancer pain for a terminally ill woman is considered good. However, the use of morphine at the invitation of a boyfriend that results in overdose and death is considered bad. The MIMSUAW perspective encourages an approach to substance use that goes beyond the substance dimension to include the physical, psychological, and social characteristics of the user with attention to the possible interactions of the various factors inherent in the "woman" dimension.

Woman Dimension The influence of the physical, psychological, and social variables of the woman dimension is significant (see Chapter 2, Explaining Substance Use Among Women). These variables must be addressed fully when assessing women for problematic patterns of substance use and when planning and implementing prevention and treatment programs for them. For example, a treatment program for an alcoholic woman would differ greatly for: 1) a 23-year-old, middle class, native American woman who previously performed well academically in college and is living in a stable, supportive family unit with her lesbian partner and her two school-aged children, but who has a family history of alcoholism in both maternal and paternal parents and grandparents; 2) a 32-year-old caucasian woman who is clinically depressed and is being sexually abused at her residential treatment facility; 3) a 20-year-old Jamaican woman who has recently immigrated to the United States, uses sex-for-drug-exchanges to maintain her cocaine addiction, and is currently pregnant and living in a crack house; 4) a 48-year-old Hispanic woman, a previous gang member now paroled and living in the inner city with her teenaged daughter and new grandson; 5) a 64-year-old Chinese woman, who has above-average intelligence, has recently immigrated to the United States, does not speak English well, and is unhappy in her new country where she lives with her oldest son and his wife; and 6) an 81-year-old homeless Haitian woman, who is an illegal immigrant without any family or social support and is positive for the human immunodeficiency virus (HIV). Clearly, all women alcoholics are *not* alike. Consideration of the variables associated with the woman dimension can assist in differentiating the unique aspects of each woman. This differentiation will help to encourage individualized assessment and treatment, which will optimize therapeutic outcomes.

Societal Dimension The societal dimension is sometimes given less attention than the other dimensions. This dimension reflects the "law of the land" (legal restrictions), professional ethics, realms of professional practice, attitudes toward substance use, and a myriad of other variables. As such, the societal dimension has a significant influence on the prevention and treatment programs available for and provided to women. For example, the availability of prenatal and postnatal treatment programs for mothers who use crack cocaine in terms of access and cost (i.e., Is the program available only to the affluent, who have the necessary finances or insurance?) needs to be considered when planning or recommending intervention at the local, state, or provincial, and national levels. Other societal variables, such as the dominant culture of a community,[2] also can have a significant impact on treatment outcomes for women. Women are more likely to seek, enter, and complete treatment if the treatment program is consonant with their cultural and social needs (Baker, 1992; Del Boca, 1994).[3] For example, membership in certain societal classes, cultures, or groups may have a positive moderating effect upon alcohol consumption rates. For example, among Hispanics excessive drinking is deemed to be predominantly a male or machismo activity. Thus, a low prevalence of alcoholism is typically observed among most groups of Hispanic women (Canino, 1994). However, these societal or culturally defined mores (for example, the Yiddish saying *a shikker is a goy* [*a drunk is a non-Jew*]) may make it more difficult for those who are the exception to the rule to seek and receive treatment. Consider the following woman:

> Hello, my name is Janet. I am an alcoholic, an addict, a woman, and a Jew. Put those things together and it almost killed me. Out there I couldn't be an alcoholic because I am a woman and a Jew. Even when I was drinking around the clock I thought it was a disease for men on park benches. (Perlman, 1996, p. 1)

These socially defined mores also can be found in the whole of the dominant society. For example, in North America (and most other parts of the world) alcoholism is traditionally deemed to be less acceptable among women than men. This socially constructed value has resulted in significant consequences for women who have drinking problems. As noted for Janet, it fosters denial of the problem and, hence, forestalls attempts at therapeutic intervention. It also encourages concealment of the unacceptable behavior and, in support of this contention, it has been noted that women drink at home alone more often than do men (Clemenger, 1993; Gearhart et al., 1991; Lex, 1994; Wilsnack, Wilsnack, & Hiller-Sturmhofel, 1994).

As noted by Woodhouse (1992), another theme reported by most of the women in her study was that of male dominance. The women saw themselves as having no identity without men and as being dependent on men. This theme was reflected in the vignette of a 28 year old woman who was a cocaine addict:

> I thought I was ugly, with an ugly shape. I still think that sometimes. I am married to a very dominant and demanding man now because I thought also that I was weak and I needed someone to make decisions for me. I constantly need to be reminded that I am pretty or nice. My mother used drugs with me and we slept together with the men who brought us drugs. (pp. 273–274)

The women who participated as subjects in Woodhouse's (1992) study "reported that every aspect of their lives is dependent on men. They are dependent on men for money, entertainment, sex, and drugs" (p. 275).

Although the variables in the societal dimension of MIMSUAW are generally not amenable to immediate change, they significantly affect patterns of substance use among women and the availability and comprehensiveness of treatment. Therefore, they must be realistically and appropriately addressed at the local and national levels as necessary.

Time Dimension The time dimension also often receives insufficient attention. The time dimension includes variables such as the historic period during which a particular substance of abuse is available for use, the length of time during which it is used in relation to its pattern of use, and the specific period of the user's life (e.g., early, middle, or late adulthood). The time dimension plays a significant role in terms of the historic context of substance use in relation to each of the other dimensions. It also affects the consequences associated with the use of a particular substance. For example, the legal consequences of cannabis use in North America 100 years ago were significantly different than they are today. The use of cannabis was legal during the late 1800s and was widely used. Women often used cannabis and various opiate-containing tonics for the treatment of "female complaints."

Although cocaine was available in various forms for nasal insufflation and injection and could be found in popular "invigorating" beverages (e.g., Vin Mariani® and, later, Coca Cola®) during the late 19th and early 20th centuries, the crack form of cocaine, now widely used by women in North America, was not used. This is because of the simple fact that it had not yet been formulated and made available for use. Similarly, new substances of abuse (e.g., various new designer drugs), and new methods for using currently available substances of abuse (i.e., smoking pure heroin or "chasing the dragon") can be expected to become prominent in the future.

☐ **The Substance Dimension**

The substance dimension is comprised of two major types of variables: 1) the substance variables; and 2) the pattern of use variables (Figure 1–2). This dimension has obvious relevance. The pharmacology, pharmacokinetics, toxicology, abuse liability, addiction potential, and related parameters of a particular substance of abuse are critical factors that continue to receive a great deal of attention in relation to the prevention and treatment of substance use.

Substance Variables

North American women are exposed to and use a variety of substances of abuse including alcohol, amphetamines, benzodiazepines, caffeine, cannabis (i.e., marijuana), cocaine, nicotine (i.e., tobacco), and opiate analgesics (Brady, Grice, Dustan, & Randall, 1993; E. L. Gomberg, 1986; Senay, Kozel, & Gonzalez, 1991). This discussion addresses the common use patterns and the social trends associated with substance use by women.

The substances of abuse described in this chapter, and the statistics presented concerning their use, generally reflect the behavior of women in North America. However, there are regional differences with annual fluctuations (DeWitt, 1991). The use of various substances of abuse by certain subpopulations of women (e.g., incarcerated, inner city, Native American, or homeless women) is significantly higher than what is reported in this chapter for the general population (Johnson, 1990; Swartz, 1991a). For example, a study of inner city women found that more than 90% used both alcohol and illicit drugs. Although studies have suggested, sometimes seemingly for political reasons, that substance use among particular groups of women or within particular geographic regions in North America has decreased (Hauschildt, 1992), reports of serious substance use patterns (i.e., use patterns associated with a high frequency and severity of harm to self and others) ("Coke Emergencies," 1992), and admissions to alcohol and drug treatment centers are currently at an all time high (L. A. Pagliaro & A. M. Pagliaro, 1995b; A. M. Pagliaro & L. A. Pagliaro, 1996; L. A. Pagliaro & A. M. Pagliaro, in press).

Central Nervous System (CNS) Depressants The CNS depressants include alcohol and other sedative-hypnotics, opiate analgesics, and volatile solvents and inhalants (e.g., gasoline, glue). However, alcohol is by far the CNS depressant most commonly used by women.

Alcohol. The use of alcohol is a common part of adult socializing. Women who develop problematic patterns of alcohol use generally began drinking alcoholic beverages in the form of beer, wine, or distilled spirits during their mid- or late teen years. The major factors contributing to their alcohol use are thought to include: 1) a desire to be more feminine; 2) social pressure; 3) risk taking behavior; 4) a desire for sexual activity (alcohol decreases social inhibitions as a direct pharmacologic effect); 5) availability; and 6) societal attitudes that encourage the use of alcohol (i.e., media advertisements) (Beckman & Ackerman, 1995; Bullows & Penfold, 1993; Shore & Batt, 1991; Wilsnack & Wilsnack, 1991; Wilsnack & Wilsnack, 1995) (see Chapter 2, Explaining Substance Use Among Women).

Problematic patterns of alcohol use by women is responsible for more physiologic, psychologic, and sociologic harm than are all other substances of abuse combined (Clemenger, 1993; Hill, 1995a; Wolfgang, 1997). Inappropriate alcohol use has reportedly been associated with up to 70% of criminal assaults, armed robberies, drownings, and murders and 50% of all traffic crash fatalities. It also has been associated with up to 50% of cases of child abuse, rapes, and suicides or suicide attempts (Klatsky & Armstrong, 1993; Prevention Plus II, 1989). The net effects are staggering not only in terms of economic costs (e.g., lost productivity and direct health care costs), but also in terms of social and emotional costs (see Chapter 6, Women as Victims of Substance Use Related Violence, and Chapter 7, Women as Perpetrators of Substance Use Related Violence).

Alcoholism. The concept of alcoholism is rooted in the classic disease theory. As such, it may be defined as the sporadic or continuous inappropriate use of alcohol that harms or interferes with a woman's physical or mental health, work, family responsibilities, and/or social life. Alcoholism is characterized as being: 1) progressive (i.e., the condition slowly becomes more serious over time); 2) chronic (i.e., whether use of alcohol is sporadic or continuous, the pattern of inappropriate use occurs over long periods and, in some cases, over a lifetime); and 3) insidious (i.e., even though most friends, relatives, or employers may be aware of a drinking problem, women who have alcoholism are usually unable to recognize themselves, without the help of others, as alcoholics) (Seixas, 1982a). Women who appear to be at the greatest risk for excessive problem drinking (i.e., alcoholism) are generally single and under 25 years of age (Bullows & Penfold, 1993). Many of these women are college students who drink deliberately to get drunk (Gleason, 1994). Physical and/or sexual abuse during childhood also are highly correlated with risk for excessive problem drinking among women (El-Bassel et al., 1995; Holmstrom, 1990; Wilsnack, Wilsnack, & Hiller-Sturmhofel, 1994).

The classic signs and symptoms of alcoholism include: 1) starting the day with a drink; 2) drinking alone; 3) gulping down drinks (i.e., as is commonly done with shooters); 4) having an increased tolerance to alcohol; 5) experiencing blackouts; and 6) displaying personality changes (Segal & Sisson, 1985; Seixas, 1982b). Once identified as a disease primarily affecting men, these signs and symptoms are increasingly observed among women (Bullows & Penfold, 1993; Clemenger, 1993). "Overall, the course of the disease of alcoholism seems to develop somewhat more rapidly among women than men, though the progression of symptoms is quite similar" (Schuckit, Anthenelli, Bucholz, Hesselbrock, & Tripp, 1995).

For women who began drinking during their adolescent years, problems associated with inappropriate alcohol use become clearly recognizable by 20 years of age (Swartz, 1991b). For some women problems may be documented in late childhood and early adolescence (A. M. Pagliaro & L. A. Pagliaro, 1996). In fact, alcoholism has been identified as the "third leading cause of death" among American women 35 to 55 years of age (Gearhart, Beebe, Milhorn, & Meeks, 1991, p. 907).

Like alcoholic men, there are two major types of alcoholic women: 1) bender or binge drinkers and 2) daily or chronic drinkers. Bender drinkers drink heavily for short periods of time, such as on weekends (i.e., "TGIF") or during and after a sporting event (e.g., golf tournaments).[4,5] Daily or chronic drinkers drink heavily every day or whenever alcohol is available (Wallace, 1982). Significant problems can be associated with alcohol use among women of all age groups. However, accidents and violence related injuries are more frequently encountered among younger women than alcohol cirrhosis or late stage alcoholism because of their shorter number of years of alcohol use and the nature of their alcohol use, which tends to be more episodic (Schuckit et al., 1995).[6] Arrests for impaired driving (Moore, 1994), aggressive or violent behavior, often involving family members such as spouses, children, or an older parent living in the home (Schuckit et al., 1995), and being fired from a job are common among women who are alcoholics.

The major adverse effects related to acute alcohol intoxication among women are listed in Table 1–2 (Beckman & Ackerman, 1995; Gavaler et al., 1993; Harper & Kril, 1990; Korsten & Lieber, 1985; Lindberg & Oyler, 1990; L. A. Pagliaro & A. M. Pagliaro,

TABLE 1-2. Alcohol use among women: Acute and chronic adverse effects*

absenteeism from work	Korsakoff's psychosis
accidents, general (e.g., drownings, falls)	malnutrition
	memory dysfunction
abusive and aggressive behavior, physical and psychological	motor vehicle crashes
	neuropathy
addiction (physical dependence)	osteoporosis
alcoholic ketoacidosis	pancreatitis
anemia	psychomotor impairment
ascites	psychosis (alcoholic hallucinosis)
breast cancer	reproductive dysfunction
child abuse, physical and psychological	respiratory depression
cirrhosis of the liver	self-neglect
cognitive dysfunction	sexual function, impaired
coma	sexual inhibitions, decreased
criminal behavior	social problems (e.g., absence from work, arguments with family members, divorce)
depression	
dysfunctional parenting	
dysmenorrhea	spousal abuse, physical and psychological
elder abuse, physical and psychological	
fetal alcohol syndrome	suicide
gastritis	victimization (e.g., physical assault, sexual assault)
guilt	
hangovers	violent behavior, including physical assault and rape
heart disease	
hypertriglyceridemia	Wernicke-Korsakoff syndrome
hypoglycemia	work productivity, decreased

*See also Table 5–4, Adverse Effects Related to Chronic Abuse of Alcohol Among Elderly Women.

1992c; A. M. & L. A. Pagliaro, 1996; L. A. & A. M. Pagliaro, in press; Van Natta, Malin, Bertolucci, & Kaelber, 1985)[7]. (See also *Polysubstance Use.*) Much research (e.g., Ashley et al., 1977; Gavaler, 1982; Jones & Jones, 1976; Klatsky & Armstrong, 1993; Rehm, Fichter, & Elton, 1993; Schuckit et al., 1995) has demonstrated that women generally appear to be more susceptible than men to the adverse physiological effects of alcohol[8] at equal and even *lower* levels of use.

Women have a higher percentage of body fat and a lower percentage of body water than men. Thus, the ingestion of the same amount of alcohol results in higher blood alcohol concentrations and more severe toxic effects in women than in men (Bullows & Penfold, 1993; Gearhart, Beebe, Milhom, & Meeks, 1991).

Opiates. The opiates comprise a group of natural (e.g., morphine) and synthetic (e.g., heroin [diacetylmorphine]) derivatives of opium (i.e., resin derived from the unripe seed pod of the plant, *Papaver somniferum* [i.e., "poppy that causes sleep"]). When women who used intravenous drugs were asked to name the first drug that they injected and their age at the time when they first injected, they generally reported that they first injected cocaine or heroin when they were about 16 or 17 years of age

TABLE 1-3. Opiate use among women: Short-term physiological effects

- central nervous system depression*
- constriction of the pupils of the eyes
- decreased gastrointestinal activity*
- depression of the cough reflex*
- dilation of superficial blood vessels and a warming of the skin (rush)
- increased perspiration
- nausea
- reduced respiratory rate
- reduced cardiovascular activity

*These effects are used for their therapeutic properties. The *other* physiological effects can be considered adverse drug reactions.

(Pagliaro, Pagliaro, Thauberger, Hewitt, & Reddon, 1993). Over the past two decades the use of heroin has remained fairly stable (i.e., ~0.5%) (U.S. Department of Justice, 1994). However, this figure is now increasing as more women begin to "chase the dragon." "Chasing the dragon" refers to heating high purity heroin (alone or in combination with crack cocaine) and inhaling the trail of smoke through a tube. The increased purity of heroin now available at the street level (an increase from ~7% to ~30% purity during the last two decades) and the decreased cost have contributed to a renewed interest in heroin and this noninjectable method of heroin use (Gettman, 1994).

The short-term physiological effects of opiates are listed in Table 1–3. The signs and symptoms of acute opiate overdose are presented in Table 1–4 and the sequence of events related to acute overdose are presented in Figure 1–4. Acute overdoses are treated with the opiate antagonist, naloxone [Narcan®] along with appropriate supportive emergency medical care (L. A. Pagliaro & A. M. Pagliaro, 1999a; 1999b).

CNS Stimulants The CNS stimulants include amphetamines (e.g., amphetamine, dextroamphetamine, methamphetamine), caffeine, cocaine, and nicotine. The use of these substances of abuse by women are briefly discussed.

TABLE 1-4. Acute opiate overdose among women: Signs and symptoms

Pupils	Generally constricted (pinpoint pupils). However, with meperidine, or extreme hypoxia, the pupils may be dilated
Blood Pressure	Decreased (shock)
Body Temperature	Subnormal
Respirations	Decreased, or absent with cyanosis
Reflexes	Diminished or absent
CNS Status	Stupor or coma. However, with meperidine or propoxyphene may cause convulsions (convulsions also may be associated with anoxia)
Miscellaneous	Constipation, pulmonary edema

An Overview of Substance Use   15

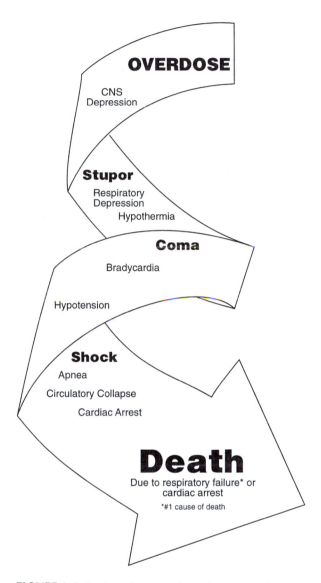

FIGURE 1-4. Acute opiate overdose: Sequence of events.

Amphetamines. The amphetamines (e.g., amphetamine [Benzedrine®], dextroamphetamine [Dexedrine®], methamphetamine [Desoxyn®]), their derivatives (e.g., chlorphentermine [Pre-Sate®], phentermine [Fastin®]) and closely related compounds (e.g., methylphenidate [Ritalin®]) are CNS stimulants that elicit their pharmacologic actions presumably by increasing the release of norepinephrine by directly stimulating the postsynaptic norepinephrine receptors (L. A. Pagliaro & A. M. Pagliaro, 1999b). Amphetamines and their related derivatives have been, and continue to be, commonly prescribed for the treatment of eating disorders among women (i.e., obesity). It has been estimated that 20% to 40% of women who are diagnosed with eating disorders develop problematic patterns of amphetamine use (Wilens, Biederman, Spencer, & Frances, 1994). Women also use amphetamines illicitly, usually by intravenous injection. Although the use of the amphetamines has been largely replaced in North America over the past three decades by cocaine (see Cocaine section, following), renewed interest in intravenous and smokable forms of amphetamine (i.e., "Ice") has been reported (see discussion, below).

Women who use the amphetamines (~10% within the past year [U.S. Department of Justice, 1994]) generally do so in order to increase their physical performance (e.g., stay awake at night to study for university examinations, maintain professional performance [airline pilots, surgeons]), or assist with weight reduction (i.e., appetite control). In regard to the latter group of users, these women have reportedly been more likely to be white and to also smoke cigarettes (Gritz & Crane, 1991).

In the late 1980s a new form of amphetamine called Ice or Crystal Meth (i.e., the street names for the rock-like crystal form of methamphetamine [speed, crank]) was introduced. Ice is available on the street in virtually pure form (i.e., 92% to 98%) and can be injected or smoked in virtually the same manner as the crack form of cocaine because of its high purity. Smoking Ice gives the user a high that is reportedly similar to that obtained from crack cocaine, except that the high typically lasts for hours instead of minutes. Ice had the real potential to become the drug of the 1990s (Pagliaro, 1988a) because of its prolonged action and the fact that it could be produced domestically at low cost. However, widespread use did not occur, most likely because of the ready availability and decreased cost of cocaine. The physical and psychological effects of the amphetamines in relation to the amount used are listed in Figure 1–5.

Caffeine. Caffeine (1,3,7-trimethylxanthine) is a natural product found in over 60 different plants. Its major natural sources include the coffee plants (i.e., *Coffea arabica, Coffea robusta*) that are native to Ethiopia and Saudi Arabia, respectively, and the tea plants (i.e., *Camellia sinensis*) that are native to China and India. Due to its natural presence in these popular beverage plants, as well as its addition to many other commonly consumed beverages (e.g., many caffeine-containing soft drinks) (see Table 1–5), caffeine is currently the most widely consumed substance of abuse in the world (Iancu, Dolberg, & Zohar, 1994; Lelo, Miners, Robson, & Birkett, 1986) and is regularly used by over 90% of North Americans.

Caffeine may be used to increase vigilance or physical endurance, or less consciously, to refresh oneself mentally or wake-up. The average daily caffeine consumption in North America is approximately 250 mg per day with over 80% coming from the use of coffee or tea. The remainder comes from soft drinks, chocolate, and prescription and nonprescription drugs (e.g., combination nonopiate analgesic products, such as Anacin®, which contain caffeine).

The adverse effects associated with caffeine use include a moderate degree of addiction or physical dependence and an associated withdrawal syndrome. The caffeine withdrawal syndrome generally has its onset within 12 to 24 hours after the discontinuation of caffeine use. The withdrawal syndrome can last for up to one week. Signs and symptoms include drowsiness, fatigue, and headache (Hughes, Oliveto, Helzer, Higgins, & Bickel, 1992). Additional effects are listed in Table 1–6.

Cocaine. Cocaine has been used by approximately 15% of North American women (Lex, 1994). However, this percentage is expected to increase significantly, primarily

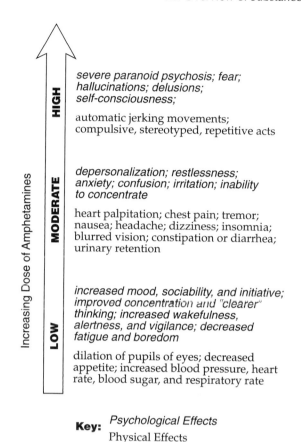

FIGURE 1-5. Amphetamines: Physical and psychological effects.

because of the continually increasing availability and low cost of the smokable form of crack cocaine (L.A. Pagliaro, 1992d; "Survey Finds", 1995). Currently, approximately 21% of college students, and 30% of young adult women in the U.S. have reported a lifetime prevalence of cocaine use (O'Malley, Johnston, & Bachman, 1991). Other data indicate that the use of cocaine by women is significantly related to the incidence of actual and attempted suicides (Marzuk, Tardiff, Leon, Stajic, Morgan, & Mann, 1992).

The adverse effects associated with cocaine use are listed in Table 1 7. The intravenous use of cocaine and its association with high risk behaviors for infection with HIV (e.g., sharing used needles; unprotected sex with multiple partners) has been an increasing and alarming trend over the last decade (Pagliaro, Pagliaro, Thauberger, Hewitt, & Reddon, 1993; A. M. Pagliaro & L. A. Pagliaro, 1996). This trend comes at a time when the transmission of HIV is increasing among intravenous drug users (IVDUs) in North America and poses one of the greatest risks for the transmission of infection among heterosexuals. In addition, the relationship between cocaine and other substance use (e.g., alcohol use) and an increase in sexual experimentation have important health implications with respect to the current AIDS pandemic (Carlson &

TABLE 1-5. Caffeine content of selected beverages[a,b]

Product	Caffeine Content
Brewed Coffee	80 to 175 mg per 6 ounces (i.e., a typical cup)
Chocolate Milk	1 to 2 mg per ounce (8 to 160 mg per typical 8 ounce glass)
Instant Coffee	60 to 100 mg per 6 ounces (i.e., a typical cup)
Soft Drinks	30 to 65 mg per typical 12 ounce bottle or can
Tea	30 to 80 mg per 6 ounces (i.e., a typical cup)

[a]Note that these are average values and that the actual amount of caffeine may vary significantly according to product manufacturer or brand.
[b]Modified from Wickens and Wood, 1994.

Siegal, 1991; Gibb, 1987; Sex Tied To, 1988) and the spread of other sexually transmitted diseases (STDs) (e.g., genital ulcers and syphilis) (Balshem, Oxman, van Rooyen, & Girod, 1992; Chirgwin, DeHovitz, Dillon, & McCormack, 1991; Farley, Hadler, & Gunn, 1990; Hibbs & Gunn, 1991).

Cocaine use by women has increased at a faster rate than cocaine use by men. Sexual favors are commonly exchanged for cocaine (i.e., sex-for-drug-exchanges), which also has increased the risk for STDs and physical and psychological abuse (Ratner, 1993; Rolfs, Goldberg, & Sharrar, 1990). Sex-for-drug-exchanges to support cocaine use, particularly crack cocaine use, usually involve women ("strawberries"), but may also involve men ("raspberries") (Pagliaro, Pagliaro, Thauberger, Hewitt, & Reddon, 1992, 1993; Ratner, 1993). (See Chapter 8, Women, Substance Use, HIV Infection, and AIDS)[9]

Nicotine (Tobacco Smoke). Nicotine, an autonomic ganglionic stimulant, is one of more than 4,000 chemicals inhaled with tobacco smoke (Dawson & Vestal, 1982; Hoff-

TABLE 1-6. Caffeine[a] use among women: Acute effects of high doses[b]

- anxiety
- gastrointestinal upset
- headaches
- heart palpitations
- insomnia
- irritability

[a]Other adverse effects (e.g., cancer of the lower urinary tract) have been reportedly associated with coffee drinking, but currently available data do not support these additional toxicities (Viscoli, Lachs, & Horwitz, 1993).
[b]Generally considered to be in excess of the equivalent of 10 cups of coffee daily, although considerable variability is noted among women, particularly in relation to age (i.e., increasing age is generally correlated with increasing sensitivity to the adverse effects associated with caffeine use).

TABLE 1-7. Cocaine use among women: Adverse effects

General (independent of method of use)
cardiac dysrhythmias
compulsive use, development of
convulsions
habituation (psychological dependence), development of
hyperpyrexia (body temperature exceeding 100°F or 40°C)
pseudo hallucinations (e.g., seeing "cocaine bugs" and "snow lights")
psychosis (e.g., hypervigilance and paranoia)
respiratory depression
Crack Cocaine Inhalation
irritation of the respiratory tract
Cocaine Hydrochloride Injection
abscess formation at injection site(s)
embolism
infection (e.g., septicemia, hepatitis, and HIV)
phlebitis at injection site(s)
Cocaine Hydrochloride Insufflation
erosion of the nasal septum
nasal congestion

man & Wynder, 1986). It also is absorbed buccally as a constituent of chewing tobacco, nicotine chewing gum, and cigars[10] (Benowitz, 1988; Gori, Benowitz, & Lynch, 1986). In addition, nicotine has been formulated for transdermal absorption by various therapeutic transdermal drug delivery systems (e.g., Habitrol®, Nicoderm®) which have been developed as a component of smoking cessation programs (Generali, 1992a; 1992b; Nicotine Patches, 1992; L. A. Pagliaro & A. M. Pagliaro, 1999b). It also is available for this use as a nasal spray (e.g., Nicotrol NS®).

Nicotine is regularly used in the form of cigarettes by millions of North American women (~30%) (Federal, 1996). In fact, due to changing demographic use patterns (i.e., increasingly, young girls more than young boys begin to smoke tobacco [Federal, 1996; A. M. Pagliaro & L. A. Pagliaro, 1996]) it has been predicted that the prevalence of smoking among women in North America will exceed smoking among men by 2005 (Berman & Gritz, 1991; Murray, Pirie, & Luepker, 1991). Although more research needs to be completed, it appears that some occupations (e.g., military) carry a greater risk of smoking for women.[11] As noted by Whitlock, Ferry, Burchette, and Abbey (1995):

> A high proportion (32.5%) of our sample of female veterans were current smokers, and 67% of female veteran smokers reported smoking at least one pack daily. More than one-third of ever-smokers began smoking during military service. (p. 409)

Tobacco smoking is the largest single preventable cause of illness in North America and is responsible for approximately 15% of all deaths. A large number of deaths from coronary heart disease (25%) and cancer (30% of all cancer deaths and 87% of lung cancer deaths) are attributed to tobacco smoking (Collishaw & Leahy, 1991; Smoking-Attributable Mortality, 1991; Smoking Control, 1983). Women exposed to passive or second-hand smoke by their partners, children, and coworkers also are at risk for the

TABLE 1-8. Nicotine use among women: Adverse effects

- addiction (physical dependence), development of
- blood pressure, increase
- heart rate, increase
- nausea
- tremor
- vomiting

adverse effects of smoking including alterations in lipid profiles, atherosclerosis, and lung cancer (Lesmes & Donofrio, 1992). Impaired respiratory function, including respiratory infections and bronchitis, occur significantly more often among women whose partners smoke than among women whose partners never smoked (Masi, Hanley, Ernst, & Becklaki, 1988; Stone, 1992; Weitzman, Gortmaker, Walker, & Sobol, 1990). The majority of the adverse effects associated with tobacco smoking (e.g., respiratory tract irritation, lung cancer) are not directly related to nicotine. These adverse effects generally are related to the other constituents found in tobacco smoke (see Table 1–8 for a list of adverse effects directly related to nicotine).

Psychedelics The psychedelics include cannabis in its various forms (e.g., hashish, hash oil, marijuana), lysergic acid diethylamide (LSD), mescaline (peyote), and psylocibin (magic mushrooms). Cannabis is by far the psychedelic most used by women.

Cannabis. *Cannabis sativa* in its plant form (marijuana), resin form (hashish), or extracted oil form (hashish oil) has been used by approximately 40% of North American women. In fact, marijuana is the illicit drug that is most frequently used by younger women. Although use statistics vary by state, province, and city, it is generally estimated that approximately 10% of North American women have used marijuana within the previous year and 5% used it within the previous month (Lex, 1994). Younger women (i.e., between 25 and 50 years of age) who heavily use marijuana reportedly are more likely to: have obtained post-secondary trade or technical training; be craft workers; be current or past users of alcohol and tobacco; and be living alone or in a cohabitating relationship (Bourque, Tashkin, Clark, Schuler, 1991; Wilsnack & Wilsnack, 1995).

The adverse effects associated with cannabis use are listed in Table 1–9. Contrary to popular beliefs about cannabis, its use does *not* cause permanent brain damage as depicted, for example, in the classic cult movie, *Reefer Madness* (Dewey, 1986; Meade, Hirliman, & Gasnier, 1937). However, several well-defined toxicities have been related to cannabis use. These toxic effects are particularly significant for women and include adverse effects on the respiratory and the central nervous systems (L. A. Pagliaro, 1983; L. A. Pagliaro & A. M. Pagliaro, 1995b; A. M. Pagliaro & L. A. Pagliaro, 1996). Other CNS toxicities include habituation (psychological dependence), panic attacks, and paranoia (Hollister, 1988). These CNS toxicities have been clearly associated with cannabis use, but also appear to depend on genetic and psychological predisposition (see Chapter 2, Explaining Substance Use Among Women).

TABLE 1-9. Cannabis use among women: Acute and chronic adverse effects

Acute
  Paranoia
  Panic reaction
  Psychomotor impairment and related motor vehicle crashes
  Short-term memory impairment
  Tachycardia
  Toxic delirium
Chronic*
  Habituation (psychological dependence), development of
  Lung irritation and disease (e.g., asthma and bronchitis)

*Although not listed because of a paucity of formal, reliable available data, lung cancer would be an expected adverse effect associated with long-term cannabis smoking. This effect would be expected because of the presence of known human carcinogens in cannabis in concentrations significantly higher than that found in tobacco cigarettes (Pagliaro, 1983).

Respiratory Toxicities. A number of studies have documented the direct irritant effects (e.g., coughing, dry mouth, sore throat) of cannabis smoke on the respiratory tract and its associated negative effects on pulmonary function including chronic obstructive pulmonary diseases such as asthma and bronchitis (Fligiel, Venkat, Gong, & Tashkin, 1988; Kalant, Fehr, Arras, & Anglin, 1983; Negative Pulmonary Effects, 1987). The severity of these respiratory toxicities appears to be clearly related to the smoking techniques used by women who are cannabis smokers (i.e., inhaling deeply and holding the smoke in the respiratory tract for several seconds to obtain optimal psychotropic effects) (Agurell et al., 1986). Many researchers have reported an increased risk for lung cancer among cannabis users and also have noted that, in terms of respiratory toxicity, smoking one marijuana joint is roughly equivalent to smoking a package of 20 tobacco cigarettes (L. A. Pagliaro, 1988d).

CNS Toxicities. The use of even moderate amounts of cannabis produces an acute state of intoxication. A dose-related impairment of the CNS may affect the user's ability to drive a motor vehicle or to operate other complex and hazardous machinery (L.A. Pagliaro, 1983). This impairment is primarily related to the following effects of tetrahydrocannabinol (THC), the principle active psychotropic ingredient in cannabis: 1) time-space distortion; 2) impaired visual accommodation; 3) decreased muscular coordination; and 4) impaired short-term memory (Gettman, 1995). These effects impair perceptual-motor skills and performance on decision-making tasks and, hence, the ability to supervise children or to operate a motor vehicle or other hazardous machinery. These adverse effects are significantly exacerbated by the concurrent ingestion of alcohol, a commonly observed phenomenon among women who are cannabis smokers (Poklis, Maginn, & Barr, 1987; Smiley, Moskowitz, & Ziedman, 1985).

Polysubstance Use

During the 1980s, the trend of using several different substances of abuse concurrently or concomitantly (i.e., polysubstance use) became firmly established among women. This trend has continued into the 1990s (Lex, 1994). Polysubstance use is characterized by the: 1) concurrent use of more than one substance of abuse (e.g., drinking alcoholic beverages while smoking tobacco cigarettes); and 2) concomitant use of different substances of abuse at different times predicated primarily upon availability and cost (L. A. Pagliaro & A. M. Pagliaro, 1995b; A. M. Pagliaro & L. A. Pagliaro, 1996; L. A. Pagliaro & A. M. Pagliaro, in press).

Polysubstance use also is associated with producing various synergistic and interactive effects among the different substances of abuse. For example, the use of alcohol, cannabis, and nicotine are highly correlated with each other and with the use of other substances of abuse. Many specific patterns of polysubstance use have been identified.

Other examples of common patterns of polysubstance use include putting hash oil on a tobacco cigarette, mixing marijuana or hashish with tobacco and rolling the mixture into a cigarette or placing it in a pipe, and mixing cocaine in tobacco or marijuana before rolling it into a cigarette (i.e., "coolie" or "woolie," respectively) (A. M. Pagliaro & L. A. Pagliaro, 1996). Polysubstance use by women appears to be significantly influenced by social pressure and behavioral group norms.

The importance of the substance of abuse dimension and its associated variables cannot be denied. However, quantitative, as well as qualitative, descriptions of substance use behavior are required to better reflect varying degrees of use and associated consequences. The Patterns of Use Variable is particularly useful in this regard (L. A. Pagliaro & A. M. Pagliaro, 1993; L. A. Pagliaro & A. M. Pagliaro, 1995b; A. M. Pagliaro & L. A. Pagliaro, 1996).

Patterns of Use Variable

Over the last decade of the 20th century, women have come to widely use such substances of abuse as alcohol, cannabis, and cocaine. Today's women are perhaps not unlike previous generations of women who used these and other substances of abuse, including caffeine and opiates. However, current patterns of use have been increasingly associated with serious and harmful effects (L. A. Pagliaro, 1993b; L. A. Pagliaro, 1991c; L. A. Pagliaro, 1990a; L. A. Pagliaro, 1986) (see Chapter 3, Substance Use During Pregnancy and Lactation, and Chapter 6, Woman as Victims of Substance Use Related Violence). This situation is expected to worsen as the next century begins and the use of substances of abuse continues to increase annually.

There are eight well-defined patterns of use that represent a continuum of increasingly more compulsive and harmful substance use: 1) initial use; 2) social use; 3) habitual use; 4) abuse; 5) compulsive use; 6) resumed nonuse; 7) controlled use; and 8) relapsed use (Figure 1–2). Obviously, initial and social use do not always progress to abuse and compulsive use. However, this conceptualization offers a means for identifying the nature and severity of actual or potential problems associated with substance use that may require different treatment approaches. The focus of this approach is on the overall pattern of substance use and not only on the characteristics of a specific substance of abuse.

Initial Use The first-time use of a particular substance of abuse generally involves some degree of curiosity and experimentation and usually does not develop into a pattern of abuse or compulsive use. However, as many emergency room personnel know, admission to a hospital or morgue can result from the initial use of a particular substance of abuse by a particular woman. Fortunately, this occurrence is not encountered commonly. Most women are curious about the effects of a particular substance of abuse and use it only once when the opportunity presents itself and suffer no long-term adverse effects. For example, a university student may try a marijuana cigarette, or take a puff of crack cocaine at a party with the encouragement of another student.

Social Use The second pattern of use is social use. Although a substance of abuse typically is actively sought out, the use of the substance of abuse is limited and generally, there are no major adverse effects associated with its use. An example of this pattern of use is drinking an alcoholic beverage at a favorite restaurant "to celebrate the end of a hectic work week." In these situations, the woman did not go to the restaurant primarily for the alcohol, but once there, sought it and used it.

Habitual Use Habitual use involves the establishment of a definite pattern of substance use (e.g., smoking marijuana every weekend or "drinking with the girls" every Friday and Saturday night). The characteristics of this pattern of use include the absence of addiction (i.e., physical dependence) and the infrequent occurrence of major adverse effects. However, habituation (i.e., psychological dependence) is an integral feature of this pattern of substance use.

Abuse In the pattern of abuse, the substance of abuse is actively sought and continues to be used despite well recognized harmful effects. Examples of this pattern of substance use include a middle-aged woman, who has been charged with driving under the influence of alcohol, who continues to drink alcohol and drive; an elderly woman with chronic obstructive pulmonary disease controlled by bronchodilators, who continues to smoke cigarettes; and a young pregnant mother who continues to use crack cocaine, even though she has been warned about the possible dangers to her unborn baby. In this pattern of use, the negative consequences of substance use generally are recognized, but the substance continues to be actively sought and used.

Compulsive Use The most serious pattern of substance use is compulsive use. This pattern of use is characterized by a complete lack of control over the use of the substance of abuse. For example, alcohol may be taken to work in a Thermos® so it will be available at break times. Women who display this pattern of use, generally indicate that they "just cannot help themselves." The substance of abuse, regardless of whether it is alcohol, cocaine, nicotine, or gasoline, becomes the major focus of concern. Women who are compulsive users spend most of their time thinking about, obtaining, and using the substance of abuse. These women feel a lack of control over the use of the substance of abuse and continue to use it despite expected and predictable harmful effects (e.g., fetal alcohol syndrome).

Resumed Nonuse, Controlled Use, and Relapsed Use Once the pattern of compulsive use is reached, a return to previous and less severe patterns of use (i.e., social use) has been thought to be virtually impossible. Complete abstinence has been the accepted therapeutic approach for the treatment of women who use the substances of abuse compulsively. This traditional approach has been challenged and continues to be debated (Levy, 1992; Littrell, 1991; Sobell & Sobell, 1972). However, until further research produces clear evidence to the contrary, complete abstinence is probably the best way to prevent the return to compulsive use. This therapeutic caveat appears to apply to all women and to the use of all substances of abuse.

The eight patterns of substance use depict steps in the progressive development of addiction and habituation (i.e., physical and psychological dependence, respectively). A better understanding of these patterns of substance use will help to encourage better assessment of women for potential and actual problems related to their use of various substances of abuse. They also will help to guide the development of prevention strategies and treatment programs that are tailored to meet the needs of women who have not yet begun to use substances of abuse, are developing patterns of abuse or compulsive use, or are trying to achieve resumed nonuse or prevent relapsed use. Attention to the latter patterns of use also encourages increased attention to the development of abstinence and relapse prevention programs specifically designed for women for whom extremely high recidivism rates are usually encountered (i.e., in excess of 70% over 12 months post treatment) (see Chapter 11, Preventing and Treating Substance Use Disorders Among Women).

☐ Treatment

Pharmacologic advances for the prevention and treatment of substance use have been significant and include: methadone maintenance programs (Dole, 1971; Dole & Nyswander, 1980; L. A. Pagliaro, 1985b) and the use of naltrexone (Crabtree, 1984; Greenstein, Arndt, McLellan, O'Brien, & Evans, 1984) for the treatment of opiate addiction; clonidine-aided opiate detoxification (Gold & Dackis, 1984; Washton, Gold, & Pottash, 1985); naloxone for the treatment of opiate overdose (Handal, Schauben, & Salamone, 1983); flumazenil for the treatment of benzodiazepine overdose (Flumazenil, 1992; Karavokiros & Tsipis, 1990); and disulfiram (Antabuse®) for the management of alcoholism (Chick et al., 1992) and naltrexone (ReVia®) as an adjunct to psychotherapy in the treatment of alcohol withdrawal (Pagliaro & Pagliaro, 1999b).

Pharmaceutical advances also include the development of dosage forms that can prevent or help reduce the illicit intravenous use of substances of abuse such as pentazocine (Talwin®), the use of which has now been all but eliminated in the United States, by the development of combination pentazocine/naloxone tablets (Talwin-Nx®) (Pagliaro & Pagliaro, 1999b; Poklik, 1984). The development of transdermal nicotine delivery systems and nicotine nasal sprays have become important adjuncts to smoking cessation programs (Pagliaro & Pagliaro, 1999b; Tonnesen, Norregaard, Simonsen, & Sawe, 1991). Attention also has been given to pharmacologic management of the withdrawal phenomenon associated with the use of several substances of abuse (e.g., bromocriptine-aided cocaine withdrawal [Herridge & Gold, 1988] and buspirone-aided nicotine withdrawal [Hilleman, Mohiuddin, Del Core, & Sketch, 1992]). A number of promising pharmacologic interventions are under development, including several aimed at the pharmacologic prevention and treatment of cocaine addiction (Lacombe, Stanislav, & Marken, 1991).

Although researchers have been successful in accumulating general knowledge regarding the pharmacology, toxicology, abuse potential, and addiction liability of the substances of abuse, increased attention must be directed toward accumulating knowledge specifically for women with attention to the prevention and treatment of substance use. Thus, it must be recognized that:

1. certain substances of abuse (e.g., cocaine, tobacco [nicotine]) are particularly attractive to women and are preferentially used for a variety of reasons (e.g., major psychotropic effect, availability, and social norms);
2. women are at particular risk for personal and social problems associated with their substance use (e.g., overdose death; morbidity and mortality related to automobile crashes; child custody problems; incarceration for drug related offenses, such as possession of illicit substances, breaking and entering, and prostitution; family violence and incest; unwanted pregnancy; suicide attempts; and infection with sexually transmitted diseases (STDs), including gonorrhea, syphilis, and HIV); and
3. because of their heterogeneity, women require individualized and diverse prevention and treatment approaches (i.e., what works for a 20-year-old pregnant white woman habituated to crack cocaine who is living in a large inner city probably will not work for a 32-year-old Hispanic lawyer addicted to alcohol who is from an upper-middle class, extended family living in the suburbs).

Although it is generally agreed that multimodal prevention and treatment approaches have the greatest potential for success, further research is required in order to deter or curtail problematic patterns of substance use by women.

Obviously the best treatment for problematic patterns of substance use is prevention, and considerable effort has been made in this regard. To achieve maximum success in the treatment of women, the approach must be tailored to meet their individual needs (Shaw & Gray, 1996). Efforts must be made to more widely disseminate available knowledge about the prevention and treatment of substance use by women and to apply it in clinical practice. Attempts at preventing and treating problematic patterns of substance use among women fail more often than they succeed, but such failures are rarely reported in the literature. Thus, development of efficacious prevention and treatment strategies must address methods that have failed in the past as well as those that have been successful with particular groups. MIMSUAW can facilitate this endeavor.

MIMSUAW can help in the planning of treatment by identifying the variables in each dimension that are amenable to change. For example, if in the substance dimension, the substance of abuse is identified as particularly harmful, a less harmful substance from the same pharmacologic classification might be substituted (e.g., methadone for heroin). If the method of use is identified as particularly dangerous, a less dangerous method might be used (e.g., substituting heroin cigarettes for heroin injections) as part of a treatment plan.

Similarly, if specific stresses and maladaptive coping mechanisms are identified among the psychological variables in the woman dimension, techniques for stress reduction and the development of better coping abilities would be an integral component of the treatment plan. If a lack of family support is identified as a major contributing factor to substance use among the social variables in the woman dimension, intervention might include attempts to increase family or other support (i.e., couples or family therapy might be considered). If a lack of adequate health care resources (e.g., women's programs with appropriately trained staff) is identified as a major factor contributing to substance use in the societal dimension, intervention may include attempts to increase social assistance (i.e., develop specific social programs for women) and the training of clinical psychologists, counselors, family therapists, social workers, and other health and social care professionals.

Evaluation of treatment is one of the most crucial steps and, yet perhaps the most frequently overlooked step in the treatment process. It is useless to prescribe treatment, or for a woman to follow a plan of treatment, if the treatment is ineffective. Evaluation can be readily performed using MIMSUAW by comparing the variables before treatment (i.e., baseline assessment), during treatment (i.e., formative evaluation), and at a predetermined interval(s) after treatment is completed (i.e., summative evaluation).

For example, if unemployment is a social variable in the individual dimension that is identified as a major contributory factor to the history of substance use and if sufficient attention is not given to appropriate job training and employment strategies, the prognosis is bleak in spite of other treatment interventions. Although program evaluators and researchers are often particularly interested in the summative evaluation in terms of program success and recidivism rates, others may be most interested in the formative evaluation because an ineffective treatment plan can be modified midstream to optimize therapy.

MIMSUAW also is useful because it can reveal factors that may, for a particular woman contribute to relapse if not addressed. Such factors include substance use related to inadequate coping when the young woman is faced with significant stressors such as the death of a parent, spouse, or child; a diagnosis of cancer; or an arrest. In addition, MIMSUAW can be useful as a framework for helping women understand the factors affecting their substance use and, thus, enable them to become better participants in their treatment planning and implementation. See Chapter 11, Preventing and Treating Substance Use Disorders Among Women, for a more comprehensive discussion.

☐ Conclusion

The use of the substances of abuse is a significant problem among North American women and is expected to worsen as we begin the 21st century. The major substances of abuse used by women include alcohol and other sedative hypnotics, amphetamines, caffeine, cannabis, cocaine, nicotine, and opiate analgesics. The Mega Interactive Model of Substance Use Among Women (MIMSUAW) is a heuristic device that can encourage the identification and analysis of the myriad of variables associated with substance use. The MIMSUAW can be used to improve understanding of the complex phenomenon of substance use among women and encourage the provision of more effective prevention and treatment strategies.

☐ Notes

1. For example, in commenting on the alcoholic family, S. Brown and V. Lewis (1995) noted:

    These dual or even multiple frameworks raise critical, more complicated questions than we have ever before addressed. If parental alcoholism is also a "family disease," does every individual suffer the consequences of the traumatic environment and family systems pathology, and if so, how? When do we focus on the family as a whole, and when do we address the individuals? Do we need to do both? If so, when? What is the diagnosis? Do we incorporate the complexities of these multiple tracks into the dominant, individually based DSM-IV, or do we push for additional tracks, which would require separate assessment and diagnosis? We argue for the latter. (p. 282)

We too, in this case, would argue for "the latter." However, where DSM-IV taxonomy can make a significant contribution (e.g., for extricating clinical diagnoses from semantic debate) we recommend its use.
2. Several feminist authors, particularly radical feminists like Laura S. Brown (1994), have commented on their views regarding the paternalism that is predominant in North America and its negative influence upon the diagnosis and treatment of women who have substance use disorders (see also Chapter 11, Preventing and Treating Substance Use Disorders Among Women).
3. In this regard, cultural and social biases also can forestall treatment intervention and contribute to negative stereotyping. As noted by Erickson and Murray (1989), "findings suggest that women who use cocaine are subject to more negative stereotyping and social repercussions than are men who engage in the same behavior" (p. 135). In addition, as noted by Clemenger (1993), ". . . moral double standards still exist. One example is that drunken men are accepted more easily than their female counterparts" (p. 24). This lack of societal acceptance has resulted in women alcoholics experiencing significantly more guilt and embarrassment related to their drinking and considerable lower self-esteem than their male counterparts (Gearhart, Beebe, Milhorn, & Meeks, 1991). These effects, in turn, can contribute to continued substance use like cocaine use: "Women reported that crack [cocaine] increases their self-esteem" (Coachman, 1996, p. 2).
4. This pattern of alcohol use also has been referred to in the published literature as "episodic".
5. Several studies, summarized by Gleason (1994), have reported an incidence of ~ 35% of women college students engaging in heavy or binge drinking (i.e., five or more drinks in a row) within the previous 2-week period.
6. Long-term use among older women can have significantly different effects than those noted among younger women. For example, in their 20-year follow-up study of alcoholic women, Smith et al. (1994) noted that: "The literature has indicated that liver damage is more related to a continuous drinking pattern, and our data indicated that binges on top of this pattern were particularly lethal for women" (p. 185).
7. Alcohol is a demonstrated risk factor for additional serious adverse effects such as cancer of the gastrointestinal tract (Cullen, 1982) and heart disease.
8. These adverse effects include anemia, cirrhosis of the liver, and gastrointestinal hemorrhage.
9. In this context, it is interesting to note the observation made by Erickson and Murray over a decade ago in 1989: "Findings suggest that women who use cocaine are subject to more negative stereotyping and social repercussions than are men who engage in the same behavior" (p. 135). However, this negative stereotyping may be contextual in that Oprah Winfrey, a noted television talk show hostess, did not appear to receive any of this type of "social repercussion" after admitting that she had used cocaine (Twigg, 1995). "I had a perfect round little Afro, I went to church every Sunday and I went to Wednesday prayer meeting when I could . . . and I did drugs." (Winfrey admits, 1995, p. A7)
10. Cigar and pipe tobacco, having generally been air-cured, have an alkaline pH that enhances buccal absorption.
11. It also has been suggested that women who have experienced physical violence as a young girl are significantly more likely to smoke tobacco (DeFronzo & Pawlak, 1993).

CHAPTER 2

Explaining Substance Use Among Women

Explaining why women use the various substances of abuse has received increased attention over the last decade as mounting concerns have been raised regarding women's personal health and safety, mothering abilities, employment performance, and incarceration for drug-related criminal offenses. Concern also has been directed at the effects of short- and long-term maternal substance use during pregnancy and its effects on the developing embryo/fetus, neonate, infant, and child (A. M. Pagliaro & L. A. Pagliaro, 1996). Attention, too, has been given to the effects of maternal substance use on breast fed neonates and infants (L. A. Pagliaro & A. M. Pagliaro, 1995b, in press).

Although several hundred theories have been produced over the last 150 years in an effort to explain why people use the various substances of abuse, a comprehensive search of relevant computerized and noncomputerized databases revealed relatively few formalized theories that specifically addressed women (A. M. Pagliaro, 1997). Given the excellent theoretical reviews by such theorists as Beckman (1975), Forth-Finegan, 1991; Wilsnack and Wilsnack (1991), Lisansky Gomberg (1991), and others, the purpose of this chapter is to highlight contemporary theories that have been published over the last decade in an effort to explain why women use alcohol and other substances of abuse. It is hoped that this review will encourage a better understanding of the varied explanations that have been advanced over the last decade and the need for increased formal choice, testing, and use of these published theories for research and practice as we seek to understand why women use the various substances of abuse.

☐ Why Women Use Alcohol and Other Substances of Abuse

In a pioneering study published in 1937, Wall identified several possible antecedent variables related to problematic patterns of alcohol use among 50 women who were receiving treatment for their alcoholism at the Bloomington Hospital in White Plains, New York. As noted by Wall:

> The family background of these patients was not unusual. One-half of them showed alcoholic individuals in the two preceding generations. There were 12 fathers and only two mothers who drank to excess. In 13 instances there were friction and unhappiness in the home. The parents were incompatible and contributed much toward an unwholesome environment....
>
> In infancy there were no outstanding feeding problems, and as a group the patients were robust, healthy children. Of striking interest was the frequent occurrence of temper tantrums ... during infancy and early childhood they were given to outbursts of rage, oftentimes elicited by the slightest frustration or denial ... and in adult life they were inclined to react to difficult life situations by throwing things and displaying a childish tantrum. A state of alcoholic intoxication served as an excuse for such outbursts.
>
> Prior to puberty they were active and energetic; 30 of them (60%) were described as tomboyish. They were fond of boys' games and sports, frequently expressing openly their intolerance of the interests of their female associates. Masturbation was a concomitant factor in this type of development. Noticeable was the absence of strong attachment to any member of the family.... In their school work, as a group, they were above the average. The average age for menarche was 13. Dysmenorrhea was present in 40 of these patients (80%), and continued throughout the period of hospitalization.... In addition, there was an associated premenstrual depression of spirits.... the menstrual period became associated with excessive drinking. In the six patients who began to overindulge before the age of 20 the heaviest drinking occurred at this time....
>
> The average age at first marriage was 23.... Many of the patients married men who were alcoholic and psychopathic, or men who were many years older or younger than themselves. Divorce occurred in 20 cases (40%), while fully as many were estranged. Only 23 of the patients had children.... Their attitude toward their children was either one of indifference or neglect. In most instances the children were unwanted, or unhappily planned for as a means of saving a marriage from the rocks....
>
> For the entire group, the average age when drinking began was 28. There were six who started before the age of 20, 22 between the ages of 20 and 30, 17 between 30 and 40, and five after 40. The patients who began to drink before the age of 20 used alcohol from the first as an escape from unpleasant feelings and situations.... A definite personal problem such as dysmenorrhea, an abortion, or desertion by a lover marked the beginning. The excessive drinking in those who began in the third or fourth decades of life was preceded by a period of the moderate social type of drinking. In this particular group were factors such as an incompatible marriage, guilt and conflict over an extramarital affair, jealousy, childbirth, physical disease, and deaths of relatives. The five patients who began to drink after 40 were passing through the menopause. Insomnia, restlessness and unpleasant physical sensations were given as the causes for inebriety. The fear of growing old was disturbing to those in the climacterium, and one of these patients became profoundly intoxicated for the first time when she was becoming accustomed to dental plates.... Proportionately there were more cases of delirium tremens and Korsakoff's psychosis among the women patients   (pp. 943–952)

The findings noted by Wall (1937) can be conveniently grouped into the following 11 factors:

Factor 1, generational effects—the role of genetics;
Factor 2, friction and unhappiness in the childhood home—emotional, physical, and sexual abuse;
Factor 3, problematic marriages and other relational problems;

Factor 4, childhood temper tantrums and adult alcoholic outbursts—personality disorders;
Factor 5, tomboyishness—femininity, masculinity, and sexual identity crisis;
Factor 6, lack of maternal and family attachment—problems with object relations;
Factor 7, intelligence;
Factor 8, women's biology—menarche, menopause, and reproductive health;
Factor 9, gender role;
Factor 10, depression; and
Factor 11, age.

These factors continued to be explored in various ways by later theorists over the last decade of the twentieth century. They also will be used to organize the discussion of the theories presented, with the addition of another factor, not specifically addressed by Wall, **Factor 12,** other factors—race, culture, and ethnicity, which also has been found to be important in regard to explaining substance use among women.

Factor 1: Generational Effects—The Role of Genetics

Recovering alcoholic Marcia Mae Jones, a successful child actress in the 1930s, was "pushed into the motion picture industry" by her mother. . . . Marcia told me that her father, a telegraph operator, was an alcoholic who apparently quit drinking on his own before Marcia was born. Marcia told me that both her parents "thought like alcoholics," even though her mother was a teetotaler. This was doubtless because her mother's own father's alcoholism had been severe enough for him to put all his children—including Marcia's mother—in an orphanage. . . . Marcia Mae Jones stopped making films in her late twenties. Divorced, living with her parents, with two little boys to support, she ran the switchboard for [a Hollywood attorney] . . . and did some TV shows. She began to drink. . . . "I used it to escape, to kill that well of loneliness, that emptiness in your gut that you want to fill up."

"I was always a sneaky drinker," Marcia told me. "I'd buy that half-pint, sit on this cold tile bathroom floor, and drink that half-pint just to keep myself from screaming. I never drank to have fun. I drank because I didn't want to feel anything. I just wanted to die. . . ." Later she attempted suicide. "I hadn't called anybody for help, I didn't leave a note, I felt that my kids would be better off without me . . ."

Marcia Mae Jones firmly believes that alcoholism runs in families, as it did in hers, and that "somebody in that family has to seek help or it will go from one generation to another. I'm so happy that I did something about it, and hope that my little grandson will never have the problem." (Barry Robe,[1] 1986, p. 206)

Three studies were identified that illustrate very different theoretical directions for examining familial influences on women's drinking. Each of these studies will be briefly presented.

In the first study, Kendler, Neale, Heath, Kessler, and Eaves (1994) used a new methodological approach, the personal interview of a large population-based sample of female twins and their parents, to examine the contribution of genetic and environmental factors in regard to the development of alcoholism among women. As explained by the researchers, "While rarely used in psychiatric research, the twin-family design, and specifically twins and their parents, compares favorably with adoption designs in its ability to discriminate vertical cultural transmission from parent-offspring genetic transmission" (p. 708).[2]

As noted by Kendler, Neale, Heath, Kessler, and Eaves (1994), "The past decade has seen an increasing interest in the impact of parental alcoholism on children. While children of alcoholic parents may differ from other children in a variety of ways, the best demonstrated effect is that they themselves have an increased risk for alcoholism" (p. 707). Thus, in an effort to more clearly identify how parents transmit the vulnerability to alcoholism to their daughters, the theorists interviewed 1,030 pairs of female twins of known zygosity and 1,468 of their parents, who were classified as having one of three levels of severity of alcohol-related problems. The sample was obtained from the population-based Virginia Twin Registry. The analyses of these data indicated that: 1) the familial resemblance for alcoholism was due to genetic factors; 2) genetic vulnerability to alcoholism was equally transmitted to daughters from their fathers and from their mothers; and 3) alcoholism in parents was not environmentally transmitted to their children. As concluded by the theorists, "The transmission of the vulnerability to alcoholism from parents to their daughters is due largely or entirely to genetic factors. . . . Our results provide substantial evidence that the heritability of alcoholism in women is substantial, similar for narrow and broad definitions, and comparable to what has been previously reported in other studies in men" (pp. 707, 712).

Following another direction of research, Hill and Steinhauer (1993) assessed alcoholic women (n = 25), their high-risk nonalcoholic sisters (n = 31), and control women from low-risk families (n = 30) for differences in event-related potentials (ERPs).[3] All of the women were Caucasian and were in reasonably good health. They were well matched in regard to age (all the women were approximately 35 years of age) and socioeconomic status. Prior to testing, they were screened for the absence of alcohol or other substance use during the previous 48 hours and, to control for possible menstrual cycle effects, a determination was made of menstrual cycle day by self-report and/or plasma progesterone levels (54% of the women were in the follicular phase, 26% were in the luteal phase, and 20% were not cycling).

Substantial differences in the magnitude of the P300 component of the ERP were identified between the groups of women. As summarized by Hill and Steinhauer (1993):

> The present findings provide the strongest evidence obtained to date that P300 amplitude reduction may be an important neurobiological marker of alcoholism risks in women. Differences between high- and low-risk groups could not be attributed to differences in behavioral performance of the tasks, age, socioeconomic status, or menstrual cycle effects. . . . In view of the recent report that as much as 50% of the variance in outcome with regard to adult alcoholism can be attributed to genetic factors, these results hold promise for screening young girls to determine possible risk status. Completion of longitudinal studies to fully assess this possibility are needed. (p. 353)

The third study reflected the increasing interest over the last decade of research on children of alcoholics (COAs),[4] which, as noted by the authors of the study, is "one of the most active study areas within the alcohol research arena" (Jacob, Windle, Seilhamer, & Bost, 1999, p. 3). In an effort to address several of the identified limitations in the research studies published to date, the major objective of their study was "to conduct a broad-based assessment of the drinking, psychiatric, and psychosocial status of adult children of alcoholics and to identify family-of-origin moderators [i.e., variables that serve to attenuate or exacerbate the relationship between family history of alcoholism and offspring outcome—gender, parental personality characteristics, characteristics of the family environment] that qualify the impact of paternal alcoholism on offspring outcomes" (p. 14).

As summarized by the researchers:

> Present findings indicated that COAs exhibited disturbance in the realms of drinking, drug use, behavioral control, and educational achievement. In addition, the impact of paternal alcoholism on offspring nondrinking outcome was found to be importantly moderated by FSES (father's socioeconomic status). Most important, however, was the finding that female versus male COAs were most clearly differentiated from normal and psychiatric controls [suggesting that they are at increased risk for developing problematic patterns of alcohol use]. The importance of current findings is threefold: First, our replication of other findings in this area is noteworthy insofar as our design involved a carefully selected sample of COAs who were reared within intact family structures and whose alcoholic parent did not exhibit psychiatric disturbances in addition to alcoholism. That these offspring still exhibited greater impairment than non-COAs across several important outcome domains provides further evidence for the specific and potent effects of family history of alcoholism on both drinking and nondrinking outcomes. Second, our sample of young adult COAs provides an important link in a literature that has been dominated by the study of adolescent age samples and the discussion of how these children are likely to develop during their adult years. Although a longitudinal assessment was not undertaken—data that would have been more directly relevant to assessing issues of the continuity of effects—our single time assessment of a carefully studied sample of young adult COAs provides important support for such continuity assumptions when evaluated within the larger COA literature. Third, our assessment of moderator effects provides some evidence for the contention that the risk associated with a family history of alcoholism is qualified by variations in family-of-origin characteristics; in particular, that lower FSES significantly increases risk for adverse offspring outcomes. (Jacob, Windle, Seilhamer, & Bost, 1999, pp.17–18)

Factor 2: Friction and Unhappiness in the Childhood Home—Emotional, Physical, & Sexual Abuse

> One morning they [Jim Bishop's wife and his mother-in-law] awakened not knowing where they had been or how they got home . . . the drinking, I felt, had gone far enough for all of us . . . Virginia Lee, my favorite [child] (aged 13) shouted at me to shut up; that if there was a problem I ought to study my own behavior. My left hand, coming hard, caught her open-palmed on the side of the face and her features seemed to shatter into a grotesque mask. She sobbed. "All my life," she said, holding her face, "I have known nothing but drinking in my house and parents screaming and arguing. I just can't stand it."
>
> "I had hurt the child I loved and made a vow to stop drinking . . ." (Barry Robe, 1986, p. 229)
>
> "It is the greatest moment of my life," declared Joan [Crawford] when the news was announced on the radio [that she had won her Oscar]. Three decades later, she told Newquist that her "drinking problem" had begun in the late 1930s. "I used to have a few before I had to meet the press, way back at Metro (MGM) . . . we all drank—it was part of going to a club, parties at home, lunches off the set. The film community drinks its share—probably more than its share."
>
> But according to David Houston's *Jazz Baby: The Shocking Story of Joan Crawford's Tormented Childhood,* she began drinking heavily some years before this in the 1920s, as a Kansas City teenager and a student at Stephens College.
>
> Joan attributed her first career decline to MGM's assigning all the big pictures to newcomers Judy Garland, Lana Turner, Elizabeth Taylor, and Ava Gardner. "I had money

problems, personal problems, career problems, and having a few drinks didn't solve any of them."

Dropped by MGM in 1943, Joan Crawford was devastated. For 18 years that powerful studio had employed, advised, protected, and made most major decisions for her. Now, at 39, she was on her own.

Daughter Christina Crawford related in *Mommie Dearest,* one of the first books to give a voice to children of alcoholics, that by 1946 her mother's drinking problem was serious enough to trigger violent behavior—her notorious "night raids" in which she physically abused her two oldest children. (Barry Robe, 1986, p. 49)

Although Wilsnack and Wilsnack (1991) found little evidence of major changes in drinking levels or drinking problems among women in general in their review of U.S. and Canadian surveys conducted over the past two decades, they did note that change may be occurring within certain subgroups of women based on age, ethnicity, employment, or marital status. They also noted that: "One potentially important antecedent of problem drinking in women is the experience of incest or other childhood sexual abuse" (p. 149). Childhood sexual abuse and other related factors were addressed by several theorists over the 1990s who generally found evidence in support of this factor. For example, Velleman and Orford (1993) examined the importance of family discord in explaining childhood problems among children of problem drinkers. As summarized by the theorists:

> Two hundred and forty-four 16- to 35-year-olds were recruited from a variety of clinical and community sources. One hundred and sixty-four were offspring of parents with drinking problems; eighty were comparison respondents of similar ages and from similar sources. Each was interviewed at length using a semi-structured interview which focussed on, among other things, carefully reconstructed recollections of childhood family environments. [The results of their study] shows that the children of problem drinkers reported very much more disharmonious family environments, and much higher levels of childhood difficulties, than did the comparisons.
>
> The degree of disharmony reported by both offspring and comparison respondents ranged from negligible to extreme; thus allowing a test of whether family disharmony or parental problem drinking was a more harmful influence on the incidence of childhood difficulties. It is shown, using path analysis, that all the covariance of childhood difficulties and parental problem drinking can be explained in terms of the effect of family disharmony.... the negative effects of parental drinking problems are seen only indirectly via their effects on family disharmony: once the effect of parental drinking on disharmony is partialled out, there is almost no residual effect on childhood difficulties [regardless of gender]. (pp. 39, 51)

Focusing on parent-to-child violence and familial and nonfamilial childhood sexual abuse, Miller, Downs, and Testa (1993) explored the interrelationships between experiences of childhood victimization and the development of problematic patterns of alcohol use among women. This focus was continued in another study by Miller and Downs (1993) where they hypothesized that being the victim of violence by a family member during childhood or adulthood affected a woman's use of alcohol. As explained by the theorists:

> To date, our explorations of the links between victimization and women's alcohol problems have focused on the impact of childhood victimization on the development of those problems. We have postulated two theoretical connections. First the experiences of childhood victimization may result in feelings of low self-esteem, which may lead to women using alcohol as a way of coping with negative feelings about themselves. Second, childhood victimization often results in girls feeling that their experiences (particularly sexual)

have made them distinctly different from other girls their age. These feelings may lead them to join adolescent groups, such as a group of delinquent adolescents, where alcohol and other drug use is accepted as part of the social activities. Thus, women may learn to drink heavily and subsequently to develop drinking problems from this socialization experience ... our data indicate that many women with alcohol problems have endured severe violence from fathers as well as childhood sexual abuse by another male. The impact of having multiple perpetrators and having multiple experiences of violent victimization must be considered. (p. 142)

Extending their work and the work of other theorists, Miller and Downs (1995) and Miller, Maguire, and Downs (1995) reviewed existing studies that suggest a significant and important link between childhood victimization and the later development of a woman's alcohol problems. In order to provide a framework for understanding how prevention and intervention programs might benefit from this knowledge, they provided several explanations for how and why these events are linked (see Chapter 11, Preventing and Treating Substance Use Disorders Among Women).

Following a different theoretical orientation, DeFronzo and Pawlak (1993b) analyzed data from a national sample of 595 adults in an effort to simultaneously evaluate the potential effects of social bonds and childhood characteristics on smoking and alcohol use. Religious belief and belief in the importance of conformity with shared moral principles had significant negative effects on smoking, alcohol use, and alcohol abuse. In addition, commitment (satisfaction with one's socioeconomic status) inhibited smoking and attachment (strong emotional bonds to family and friends) deterred alcohol abuse. However, childhood trauma was found to promote both smoking and alcohol abuse. (See also Factor 6, lack of maternal and family attachment— problems with object relations.)

In another study, DeFronzo and Pawlak (1993a) explored the deviance gender gap in relation to alcohol abuse and tobacco smoking with a national sample of adults. Extending sex role theory, they hypothesized that much of the influence of gender on deviance is conveyed through the relationship of gender to social bonds (see Factor 9, gender role) and to the experiences of physical violence in childhood. The results of their study indicated that being female was: 1) positively associated with belief and attachment bonds that inhibited alcohol abuse and smoking; and 2) negatively associated with the experience of physical violence as child, which promoted alcohol abuse and smoking.

In a study of incarcerated women, who were identified as problem drinkers, El-Bassel, Ivanoff, Schilling, Gilbert, & Chen (1995) noted that childhood sexual abuse as well as negative coping skills and familial alcohol abuse were related to problem drinking. When these women were compared to incarcerated women who were identified as nonproblem drinkers, they also were found to comprise a higher proportion of women who had been incarcerated prior to being 17 years of age and who were currently incarcerated for violent offenses. These women also had less education than the women who were nonproblem drinkers and they were more likely to have histories of homelessness. In addition to these findings, the incarcerated women who were problem drinkers reported 1) earlier onset and longer periods of alcohol abuse than the incarcerated women who were nonproblem drinkers (age: 19 years, 8.45 years of abuse, versus age: 21 years, 3.26 years of abuse); and 2) the use of crack cocaine and heroin 3 or more days per week during the month prior to arrest.

Although both groups of women had higher levels of depression than would be found in the general population, the mean depression score for the incarcerated women who were problem drinkers was higher and, in fact, similar to the score reported for psychiatric populations. (See also Factor 10, depression.)

Finally, Langeland and Hartgers (1998) reviewed published prospective and retrospective studies addressing the prevalence of child sexual or physical abuse among alcoholics and nonalcoholics. They also reviewed the published retrospective studies of mental health clients and population samples comparing the prevalence of alcohol use disorders in abused and nonabused subjects. The results of their review of these published studies indicated that: 1) a significant association between child sexual or physical abuse and alcoholism was not supported by prospective studies, although studies addressing alcoholic women do suggest a relationship; 2) population studies revealed a significantly higher prevalence of alcohol problems among abused women when compared to nonabused women; and 3) the results in regard to mental health clients were inconclusive. Although the researchers acknowledged that the evidence they reviewed was insufficient to draw conclusions about the relationship between child sexual or physical abuse and alcoholism among men, their review did provide evidence that supported a higher likelihood of alcohol problems among women if they were sexually or physically abused as children.

Factor 3: Problematic Marriages & Other Relational Problems

Ironically, two of alcoholic actress Susan Hayward's best roles were portrayals of alcoholic women: singer Lillian Roth in *I'll Cry Tomorrow* and a character rumoured to be based on Dixie Lee Crosby in *Smash-up, The Story of a Woman*.

For *I'll Cry Tomorrow*, Susan and the director went to AA meetings, hospitals, and jails to learn about alcoholic women. Lillian Roth served as the technical adviser to the film. Another ironic twist: in her next-to-last film, Susan replaced ailing alcoholic Judy Garland in the role of Helen Lawson, another addicted woman, in *Valley of the Dolls*. At the time, in my opinion, Susan was deep in alcoholism herself.

Susan was considered a fine actress. She made fifty-seven movies in thirty-five years, was nominated four times for Academy Awards and won an Oscar in 1958 for *I Want to Live*.

Her regular—and heavy—drinking reportedly began when she was twenty and new to Hollywood. She was twenty-six when she married actor Jess Barker. Their 1953 divorce trial included descriptions of Susan drinking heavily and of alcohol-related physical violence. Susan won custody of their twin sons.

In 1955 Susan was hospitalized after a widely publicized suicide attempt; she mixed grapefruit juice and gin with handfuls of sleeping pills . . .

Susan married her second husband, Georgia businessman Floyd Eaton Chalkley, in 1957. They moved to a small town in Georgia and also had a house in Fort Lauderdale. Chalkley was reported to be a heavy drinker. Susan adored him, and was devastated when he died in 1966 of hepatitis and cirrhosis of the liver.

She moved to Florida to mourn, and there began the downward spiral of around-the-clock drinking that lasted for most of the rest of her life. She bought liquor by the case and drank martinis from enormous brandy snifters. (Barry Robe, 1986, pp. 403–404)

Several theorists have identified an unhappy marriage to an alcoholic husband as an important factor associated with the development of depression, poor self-esteem, and problematic patterns of alcohol use among women. As noted by Tax (1993), women who are alcoholic, or who are at risk for developing problematic patterns of alcohol use, also appear to be attracted to alcoholic men, marry them, and remain married to them even if they are abusive. Lambert (1991) developed a study to examine, within the context of sex role stereotypes, the psychological functioning (i.e., depression, state and trait anxiety, self-esteem, coping) of women married to chemically dependent men. Data were collected from two groups of women. The Affected Group was comprised of 32 women married to chemically dependent men who were attending groups offered by the Affected Persons Program of the Alcoholism Foundation of Manitoba. The Contrast Group was comprised of 28 women married to nonchemically dependent men who were attending parenting programs in Winnipeg. The women were paid for their voluntary participation in the study.

Lambert (1991) found that the Affected Group did not identify more with the feminine sex role, as measured by the Bem Sex Role Inventory, than the Contrast Group. Results also indicated that both feminine and masculine scores correlated at a low to moderate level with good mental health. However, as predicted, the Affected Group was more depressed and more anxious in regard to both state and trait anxiety, had lower self-esteem, and used more reactive coping strategies than did the Contrast Group. Addressing the finding that women in the Affected Group did not identify with the feminine sex role, Lambert (1991) argued that the concept of codependency was, in essence, refuted—the Affected Group was not more traditionally feminine (i.e., passive, dependent, and overly sensitive to the needs of others) than women in the Contrast Group. In fact, they were significantly more active in seeking help for themselves and used more proactive coping skills than did the Contrast Group. (See also Factor 9, gender role.)

Using semistructured interviews covering the respondent's life and drinking history, Lammers, Schippers, and van der Staak (1995) examined the functionality of alcohol as a means for coping with unhappy heterosexual partner relationships among a group of 45 Dutch women, 30 to 55 years of age (the study was completed in the Netherlands). The women were alcohol-dependent. During the interviews, the women were encouraged to talk about the various aspects of their drinking focusing on functionality—the effects and meanings associated with alcohol use. The theorists were interested in how each woman evaluated the effects of her alcohol use; how she perceived others viewed these effects, and whether, and how, these effects were related to coping with the problems she experienced. More specifically, the theorists were interested in answering the following questions: Do women hide their drinking from their partners? Do they feel that their partners have any advantages associated with their drinking? And, if so, what are these advantages?

As concluded by Lammers, Schippers, and van der Staak (1995):

> Differences were observed in functions of alcohol use between women who started excessive drinking largely as a response to a problematic (heterosexual) relationship and women for whom relationship problems were not an important factor in the development of excessive drinking. Alcohol consumption in the first group primarily seemed to be a means to adjust: to keeping in the relationship by suppressing undesired emotions and to adjust sexuality. On the other hand, alcohol enabled resistance: the first group used "alcoholic" behavior more often as a signal or a sign of rebellion toward the partner.... Compared with group 2, the partner was more often viewed as dominant, as not understanding the respondent, and furthermore as having less often a realistic image of her drinking behavior and as having a greater number of advantages from her drinking. (pp. 912–913)

Allan and Cooke (1986) offered an alternative explanation:

> Unfortunately, research directed at this problem [problem drinking among middle age women] has been limited to asking alcoholic patients to recall events which *they* considered may have precipitated their heavy drinking. However, there are significant problems

with this approach. . . . many of the events are as likely to be the consequence, as the cause of heavy drinking . . . job loss, domestic disharmony, or divorce. . . . the link between life events and alcohol consumption may be spurious, reflecting the activities of a sizable [sic] sub-group of socio-pathic alcoholics, who, because of their impulsive and aggressive behaviour, are likely to generate both excessive drinking and life events . . . the apparent association may merely reflect reporting biases. Arguably, women are more likely to *attribute* their heavy drinking to causes which may elicit sympathy [e.g., an unhappy marriage] rather than censure, particularly since heavy drinking is still a stigmatised [sic] condition, especially for females. . . . (p. 462)

As identified by Gleason (1984), relationships are integral to the psychological development and identity of women. In fact, many women use alcohol to facilitate relationships and to self-medicate when relationships are not mutual or are abusive. Henderson and Boyd (1997) also emphasized the importance of women's relationships in regard to problematic patterns of substance use, including relationships to self and relationships with men and other women, including mother-daughter relationships. Following another line of theoretical development, Bepko (1989/1991) addressed the subjective relationship between an addicted woman and her "drug":

Our hypothesis is that addiction reflects a disordered power arrangement embedded in gender. Not only do patterns of addiction depend on gender, but addiction also mirrors, on an internal, subjective level, the interactional power imbalances and hierarchical constraints imposed by gender arrangements in our culture. . . . addiction represents a complex process that occurs on many levels within the system. It is, at its roots, a subjective process that occurs between the addict and . . . her drug or compulsive behavior. A fundamental failure to understand the nature and intensity of this subjective relationship has led us to assume that rebalancing a system will eliminate the need for addictive behavior. However, the addiction takes on a life of its own within the individual that, although affecting and affected by the system, cannot be entirely addressed by shifting the system. The relationship between the addict and the drug needs to be disrupted as well. (pp. 406–407)

In a more recent qualitative study of substance abuse among Latina lesbian women, Reyes (1998) identified the importance of women's relationships with their families, valued social groups, communities in which they lived, and other women. As shared by Reyes (1998), many of the women in her study expressed a "tremendous feeling of loneliness," particularly when they made the decision to make their preferred sexual orientation known. For some of the women, this loneliness was associated with a loss of family kinship and loss of their ethnic communities. Loneliness also was associated with difficulties fitting or being accepted into the mainstream gay and lesbian community. Being in a relationship with another woman also was an important theme. As explained by Reyes (1998), because women have been traditionally socialized to be attached in relationship to others, lesbian women may find it hard not to be in a relationship. Some of the women, especially those who identified themselves as moderate users of alcohol, shared that they "drank the most when they found themselves out of a relationship" (p. 187). (See also Factor 5, tomboyishness—femininity, masculinity, and sexual identity crisis; and Factor 9, gender role.)

Factor 4: Childhood Temper Tantrums & Adult Alcoholic Outbursts—Personality Disorders

At age twenty, rock groupie Nancy Spungen finally achieved the kind of publicity she had so frantically and naively sought as a teenager. But she never knew about it, for her notoriety came late—when she was murdered by punk rock performer Sid Vicious, her boyfriend.

Nancy had been a heavy drinker and drug (including heroin) addict for years. Her tragic story was told by her mother, Deborah Spungen, in the book, *And I Don't Want to Live This Life*.

According to her mother, Nancy showed seriously disturbed behavior during childhood, and there were continual searches by her parents for a medical solution. Doctors prescribed mood-changing drugs, including phenobarbital, Atarax, and Thorazine. By age nine, Nancy was obsessed with rock music. By thirteen, she was taking illicit drugs in boarding schools for unmanageable kids.

"Drugs were a natural outgrowth of her life," wrote her mother. "Drugs were a badge of rebellion and, for a thirteen-year-old, of maturity. They offered her a passport to a different, 'better' reality. Drugs would take her somewhere else, take her where her beloved hard rock music was. She had continually been on prescription drugs since her infancy—to mask discomfort, restlessness, anger. It was only natural for her to move on to the illegal means to the same end." (Barry Robe, 1986, p. 322)

Beckman (1975) noted in her comprehensive review of published studies examining the various factors associated with alcohol use among women, which dated back to 1950, that:

> Data from the MMPI and other personality tests show that, apparently, the pathology associated with excessive drinking decreases differences in personality characteristics between the sexes. Tentative longitudinal evidence supports the contention that in women distinct clusters of personality traits can be traced as far back as early adolescence in those with different drinking patterns and that these clusters of traits continue into adulthood. (p. 807)

Considering antipersonality disorder and legal infractions among incarcerated women identified as having drinking problems, Lex, Goldberg, Mendelson, Lawler, and Bower (1993) extended to women Cloninger and colleagues' Swedish adoption studies, which identified two types of genetic/familial alcoholism in men. Type I, milieu-limited, occurred after 25 years of age and appeared to be shaped by environmental factors. Type II, male limited, occurred prior to 25 years of age and was generally associated with antisocial personality disorder (ASPD) and legal infractions. Based on these types of alcoholism identified for men, the theorists hypothesized that alcohol-dependent women with Type II alcoholism characteristics or ASPD could be found among a population of women incarcerated for alcohol-related driving offenses (pp. 49–50).

As reported by Lex et al. (1993), the results of their study supported their initial hypothesis:

> All women in the sample who met the criteria for ASPD also showed onset of alcohol dependence before age 21. These women appear to fit the description of Type II alcoholism, although the high percentage of parental alcoholism in this sample obscures the effects of heritability in any group. However, behaviors characteristic of ASPD occurred mainly in connection with drinking. . . . Age 25 was established as the cut-off for early onset in men. Our findings suggest that age 21 may be more appropriate for women with early onset. . . . This downward shift may be an artifact of the legal drinking age or might reflect a secular trend toward earlier use of alcohol and other drugs and concomitant oppositional behavior. Both of these interpretations may also apply to men. Finally, this effect could be influenced by cultural patterns whereby males date younger females and dating is a primary vector of alcohol and drug use in women. . . . behaviors diagnostic of ASPD

were largely consequent to substance abuse, and childhood behaviors were limited predictors of ASPD. Relationships among gender, prodromal behaviors, and substance abuse appear more complex than anticipated, and they indicate the need to recognize adult onset ASPD associated with substance abuse as a legitimate diagnosis manifested differently by women and men. (pp. 55–56) (See also Factor 11, age.)

Factor 5: Tomboyishness—Femininity, Masculinity, and Sexual Identity Crisis

Joan Crawford's mother "could not understand why Billie (Joan's childhood nickname) would not behave. Why couldn't the girl be like her brother, Hal, who never talked back to his mother and was always willing to run errands and help around the house?" . . .

Billie never felt close to her mother. They tangled constantly for Billie was a rebellious tomboy with characteristics that reminded her mother of herself. . . . (Barry Robe, 1986, p. 198)

Meg Christian is a singer, songwriter, guitarist, and co-founder in 1973 of Olivia Records, "the largest and oldest women's recording company" according to an *Aquarian* article. She is also a lesbian and a recovering alcoholic who shares her story in hopes that other lesbian alcoholics will seek help.

Meg knew she was a lesbian from an early age, according to Linda R. Schwartz's pamphlet, *Alcoholism Among Lesbians/Gay Men*. Feeling alienated, isolated, and persecuted, she drank to relieve stress. For fourteen years, as her alcoholism progressed and she became more involved in the women's movement, she was the ironic contrast between the freedoms she espoused and the drinking which enslaved her. "I had dedicated my life to fighting oppression, the forces in the world which were trying to kill me as a woman, as a lesbian. And at the same time I was using alcohol to destroy myself."

She knew that the Alcoholism Center for Women (ACW) in Los Angeles included a special program for lesbians. Her recovery began there. "Starting with ACW, I met a group of women who were just like me and the more I was in groups with them, the more I realized all my most awful experiences with alcohol, all the things I did that I was so ghastly ashamed of while I was drunk, or in order to get drunk, and all the worst feelings I had about myself, were shared by every woman there.

"What they did was validate me. I had been validated before as a lesbian and now I was getting validated as an alcoholic."

On her concert tours, she meets "more and more women who are recovering . . . which gives me a lot of encouragement." (Barry Robe, 1986, pp. 332–333)

An effort to explain alcoholism recovery among lesbian women was offered by Hall (1990) in her "theory-in-development." As noted by the theorist, lesbian women comprise approximately 10% of the female population and alcoholism affects lesbian women at three times the rate found in the general public:

Though there may be nondrinking alternatives to the "bar scene" for lesbians in many locales, the lesbian alcoholic who arrives for help may not know about these. She may conceptualize recovery as a demand that she give up her lesbian culture and identity. This tension (self) was resolved by one woman who quoted a well-known lesbian song: "They always said 'Wild women don't get the blues,' so drink up. But I know now that they do get the blues, and a lot of other pain besides. . . . So I don't drink today and I've discovered there are a lot of sober lesbians. I just didn't know they were around before." (p. 119)

As described by Hall (1990), the theory-in-development addresses the recovery process and the core experiences of recovery as a dimension of health. As such it clarifies help-seeking in the transition from drinking to abstinence, and transitional issues within the recovery process, including failure and relapse. Although the theory does not account for stages of recovery, it posits that the same tensions are actually faced over and over in different ways by the same recovering woman. In this way, as noted by Hall (1990), it allows for individual variability within the patterns of recovery while acknowledging the continuing familiar repetitive qualities of addictive problems. As such, this theory has the potential to stimulate the development of a meaningful knowledge base about lesbian health and alcoholism recovery.

In an effort to disentangle contradictory research findings regarding the relationships among self-esteem, sex role identification, and alcoholism among women, Sorell, Silvia, and Busch-Rossnagel (1993) studied these factors in a sample of 60 alcoholic and 60 nonalcoholic women. The results of their study indicated that the two groups of women differed in regard to levels of masculinity, femininity, and self-esteem. According to the theorists, women who see themselves as high in socially valued masculine psychological attributes (e.g., competitiveness, independence, and self-confidence) are self-oriented and associated with assertive action—as opposed to feminine psychological attributes (e.g., gentleness, compassion, and kindness), which are other-oriented and associated with responsive passivity, and are less likely to be alcoholic than those who are low in these attributes.

Factor 6: Lack of Maternal and Family Attachment— Problems with Object Relations[5]

> Actress-singer Jan Clayton crossed the line into alcoholism after her teenage daughter, Sandy, died.
>
> Jan had begun drinking regularly in her late twenties, when she played Julie in the original (1945) production of Rodgers and Hammerstein's *Carousel*. As a new Broadway star, she was invited to parties every night. She later believed that she "got by with the drinking for years because I was in a group where hangovers were fun."
>
> In 1954 Jan started her long Hollywood stint as the first mother in TV's *Lassie*. The show involved "working six days a week and trying to be a wife and mother [to Sandy, and to three more children born in three years] at the same time. It can't be done," she told *Good Housekeeping* magazine. "During four frantic years on that schedule, alcohol was my crutch." However, she told *People* magazine that she was still a social drinker during that period, although "even then, after a few drinks, I'd get the sillies, then the cries, finally the meanies."
>
> Meanwhile, daughter Sandy was like another mother to the three younger children. Then in 1956, sixteen-year-old Sandy was killed in an auto accident. "I was devastated," Jan told me in 1982. "Sandy's death threw me into active alcoholism. I think many women begin drinking alcoholically after some sort of crisis. I suffered the most incredible grief— I even made an aborted attempt at suicide. One night I drove fast down a highway, hoping that an accident would happen to me."
>
> Fourteen more years of drinking lay ahead, including some drinking around the clock, two divorces, her children's move to Mexico to join their father, and a career slump.
>
> After she stopped drinking in 1970, Jan threw her energies into the alcoholism field. For thirteen years, she publicly deplored the stigma against women alcoholics, and inspired others all over the country to get sober and stay sober. (Barry Robe, 1986, pp. 354–355)

Tax (1993), focussing on the proclivity of female offspring of alcoholic parents to marry alcoholic men and the factors (other than financial factors or familial factors) that account for wives of alcoholics remaining in marriages in which they are often physically or emotionally abused, found fear of abandonment was the core issue. As explained by the theorist:

None of the women appeared to have experienced consistent parental nurturing in their families, and they all appeared to have been emotionally abandoned as children. They unconsciously seemed to seek husbands, alcoholics, who were less than perfect, whom they believed would be less likely to abandon them. It was observed that wives of alcoholics seemed to use one of two major projective identifications in their relationships with their husbands. The first group (7 out of 10 women) appeared to identify with their passive parents (usually the mother) and unconsciously sought men, controlling alcoholics, with whom they could work through their issues with their fathers. These women used the projective identification of ingratiation, using self-sacrificing, caretaking behavior in order to influence feelings of appreciation in their husbands. The second group of women (3 out of 10 women) seemed to identify with the controlling parent and unconsciously sought alcoholics who generally appeared weak and ineffectual. This group of women used the projective identification of power, inducing feelings of incompetency in their husbands. The unconscious motive of both groups of women, however, is the same, i.e., prevention of abandonment. (p. 497)

The classic work of John Bowlby (1973a, 1973b) focused attention on the concepts of mother-infant attachment and separation behaviors and the importance of considering the effects of poor attachment, painful or prolonged separation, and experiences of loss on later psychological development and parenting. Although these concepts have been generally neglected over the last several decades as other concepts and theoretical directions have been given more attention, themes of separation, loss, and abandonment seem to be resurfacing in the substance abuse literature. Reflecting this change are an increasing number of studies focussing on mother-infant relationships where mothers used various substances of abuse during their pregnancies.

For example, Heller, Sobel, and Tanaka-Matsumi (1996) used sequential analysis to conduct a functional analysis of positive and negative behaviors of five prenatally drug-exposed preschoolers while interacting with their mothers and with an unrelated adult on separate occasions. Two mother-child dyads engaged in extended sequences of negative-coercive interactions whereas the unrelated adult terminated negative exchanges quickly. As noted by Heller et al. (1996), the results of their study suggest the need for the development of specific behavioral training programs for mothers of drug-exposed children and other significant adults.

In a somewhat related study, Miller (1997) examined the literature from a variety of disciplines on in utero cocaine exposure and mother-infant interaction and attachment. Of concern to the researcher were the effects of maternal cocaine use and the associated neurobehavioral deficits among the neonates that may adversely affect mother-infant interactions. As noted by Miller (1997), knowledge of child development, sensory regulation, and infant cues will enable therapists to assist mothers to create positive interactive experiences between themselves and their infants and children.

In another study, Fineman, Beckwith, Howard, and Espinosa (1997) explored the relationships between maternal characteristics and mother infant interactions in a sample of women who had histories of substance abuse. The researchers were interested in determining whether the level of ego development among drug-addicted mothers affected mother-infant interactions at 1 month postpartum. Data collection procedures included a clinical interview, self-report measure of the woman's addiction severity, clinical personality inventory, measurement of ego development, and videotaped observations of mother-infant feeding interactions. As noted by the researchers, only ego development, and to a lesser degree psychological symptoms associated with substance abuse, were found to be a significant predictor of maternal-infant interactions at 1 month. This finding suggested that treatment and other related services should focus on developing the internal resources of substance-abusing mothers.

Focusing on maternal-infant interactions of older infants—8 to 12 months of age—and their mothers who had histories of substance abuse during pregnancy, Burns, Chethik, Burns, and Clark (1997) provided preliminary evidence for the characteristics that may be most problematic for such dyads of infants and mothers. Ten mother-infant dyads where substance abuse occurred during pregnancy were compared to 10 matched drug-free dyads. The short form of the Parent-Child Early Relational Assessment instrument was used to analyze videotaped mother-infant interactions. There was a consistent tendency for the mean scores of the drug abusing group to separate from the controls—"drug abusing dyads had significantly lower scores in the unstructured play situation for items that measured enthusiasm, responsivity to infant cues, and infant happiness" (p. 279).

Attention also is being given to parent interaction behaviors between mothers and their older children and adolescents. For example, in regard to parent-child interactions, Moser (1997) compared parents and children from alcoholic and nonalcoholic families (n = 137) in regard to quality of interactions, child outcomes, and the possible moderating effects of parenting behavior on child outcome. Attention also was given to the effect that gender of alcoholic parents has on parent-child interactions and child outcomes as measured by the Child Behavior Checklist. The results of the study indicated that dual and mother-only alcoholic families exhibited the most impaired interactions. Where fathers were alcoholic, nonalcoholic mothers appeared to have a protective effect on child outcomes.

Finally, in a study considering the impact of maternal and adolescent factors on initial and increased levels of substance use by adolescents, Brook, Cohen, and Jaeger (1998) examined two groups of adolescents, a group of younger adolescents—12 to 14 years of age (n = 210)—and a group of older adolescents—15 to 18 years of age (n = 199). The adolescents and their mothers were interviewed at two points in time, three years apart. The results of the study suggested that adolescent unconventionality is a crucial determinant for both initial and increased levels of substance use for both age groups. However, it also was found that intrapsychic distress is more important for the younger adolescent's initial substance use. As concluded by the theorists:

> Lack of maternal attachment and poor control techniques were associated with initial levels of drug use for both groups. However, the mother-child relationship and models of the mother's conventionality had a greater impact on the older than on the younger group's increased involvement.... Interactive results suggest that adolescents from both age groups who are well adjusted can offset the potential risks of maternal models of drug use. (p. 179)

Factor 7: Intelligence

Many alcoholics are known to be high achievers. When Leclair Bissell, M.D., conducted long-term studies on recovered alcoholics in "high status occupations" (doctors, dentists, nurses, attorneys, social workers), she found that the majority were high achievers in graduate school.... Add to these the ingredient of charm or charisma, the special mix of winning qualities that gathers friends and fans. Alcoholics, whether they are on stage or not, often are gifted with particular personal appeal and charm, a charm that turns manipulative when it helps convince others to accept their imaginative excuses for chaotic alcoholic behavior.... Actress Jan Clayton, also a recovered alcoholic, said that a crucial element of her own denial was her recognized intelligence: "Me? An alcoholic? How could I be? I'm a Phi Beta Kappa!" (Barry Robe, 1986, pp. 36–37)

Both high and low levels of intelligence have been related to various patterns of substance use among women (Bissell & Haberman, 1984; Saunders, Bailey, Phillips, & Allsop, 1993). For example, Nace (1995) noted that nurses who have problematic patterns of alcohol use, in addition to other related factors, had a history of better than average academic and career achievement. They usually were in the top one third of their class, held demanding and responsible jobs, had advanced degrees, and had been recognized as excellent nurses long after they had begun patterns of heavy drinking.

Factor 8: Women's Biology—Menarche, Menopause, and Reproductive Health[6]

Marilyn [Monroe] got pregnant during filming.... [On] her return to New York City ... [she] "tried to avoid her normal routine of champagne and sleeping pills" to protect her unborn baby, "yet without these, she was terribly nervous."
Marilyn miscarried shortly before Christmas, leaving her severely depressed all winter, according to photographer David Conover in *Finding Marilyn: A Romance*. "While Miller worked on the final draft of *The Misfits*, she consumed quantities of alcohol and barbiturates to reduce her feeling of emptiness and inadequacy. During the winter.... Marilyn was never more unhappy; her favorite companions were champagne and sleeping pills." (Barry Robe, 1986, p. 3)

As noted by Beckman (1975), in her review of the social and psychological research examining alcoholism among women, "the available evidence indicates that women alcoholics, as compared with nonalcoholic women, have gynecological difficulties and high sterility rates. Some studies suggest a close relationship between premenstrual tension and onset of drinking episodes, whereas others provide conflicting evidence" (p. 818).

Wilsnack, Klassen, and Wilsnack (1986) analyzed how women's experiences with reproductive problems and depression are related to lifetime maximum drinking levels as compared with current drinking levels. They also analyzed how heavy drinking precedes and follows adverse reproductive experiences and depression among women who report both heavy drinking and these experiences. As summarized by the theorists:

> Experience with depression was associated with higher levels of alcohol consumption in women's drinking histories, although heavy drinking was more likely to follow the onset of depression than to precede it. Heavy drinking was also more likely to follow than to precede initial experiences with reproductive problems, and typically developed a decade or so after these problems began. These findings do not mean that heavy drinking never causes or contributes to depression or reproductive disorders; there is ample evidence from animal and human studies, for example, that heavy drinking can lead to a variety of adverse reproductive consequences. The findings presented here do suggest, however, that the reverse temporal sequence also occurs, perhaps even more often—that is, a sequence in which problems with depression or reproductive disorders precede and possibly contribute to the onset of heavy drinking.... It is important to discover some of the more immediate precipitants of changes in women's drinking, and to learn to what extent the influences of life experiences on drinking depend on other characteristics of a woman's environment (such as her family, income, work, friends, etc.). And it is important to investigate how the dynamics of women's drinking and its consequences vary as

women's ages vary ... (Wilsnack, Klassen, & Wilsnack, 1986, pp. 25–26) (See also Factor 10, depression, and Factor 11, age.)

In a more recent study, Lindenberg, Solorzano, Kelley, Darrow, Gendrop, and Strickland (1998) explored the use of the Social Stress Model of Substance Abuse[7] for explaining parameters that may influence alcohol and other substance use among low-income Hispanic women of childbearing age. This model was selected by the theorists because it emphasized both risks (stressors) and protective factors (social networks, personal and social competencies, and availability and use of community resources) and incorporated and integrated variables from several psychosocial theories and models. As such, it was thought to provide a broad and flexible model for both building and testing theory related to substance abuse and other risk behaviors (p. 118).

The theorists identified one of the central constructs of the model, competence, as being vital for modifying the effects of stress and key to motivation and effective decision-making relative to drug use and other high risk behaviors. Based on theoretical and empirical studies, eight domains of drug protective competence were identified and conceptually defined. Using subscales from existing instruments that had demonstrated validity and reliability, a multiscale, self-report, 44-item instrument was developed. The instrument, the Drug Protective Competence (DPC), was designed to measure eight domains of drug protective competence among low income, young, Hispanic, childbearing women.

Hypothesis testing was used to assess construct validity. Four drug protective competence domains (i.e., social influence, sociability, self-worth, and control/responsibility) were found to be statistically associated with drug use behaviors. Although not statistically significant, expected trends were observed between drug use and the other four domains of drug protective competence (intimacy, nurturance, goal directedness, and spiritual directedness). Study limitations and suggestions for further psychometric testing of the instrument are described. (See also Factor 9, gender role.)

Factor 9: Gender Role

> "The woman with the big-time politician is permitted no complaints.... Instead they play the devoted couple for the sake of a career that inevitably takes the man away from home most of the time. The Washington wife may not look bad, talk bad, or behave conspicuously at any time. She is always second to her husband, captive to his drives. She is always on display, and she dare not take a lover. She can never pack up her children for a life more suited to her temperament, unless, of course she is prepared to destroy a political career. She survives on the glamour that surrounds the candidate's wife, the senator's lady, the president's consort. She has no privacy..." (Barry Robe, 1986, p. 281)
>
> In 1978 twenty-year old Susan Ford became concerned about her mother's drinking.... "Susan saw how I was withdrawing from my activities, my friends, practically all my interests, ... One morning, I was sitting around in my robe trying to decide whether to take another handful of pills or to get dressed. This good doctor friend appeared at my front door, unannounced.... He mentioned pills, he mentioned alcohol. He was a gentleman: very kind, very nice. I can assure you that I *wasn't*. I was incensed!"
>
> "I asked him to mind his own business and get out of my house. You might even say that I threw him out!"
>
> "I thought: 'Who in the world does he think he is?' I mean—suggesting that I have a problem? Didn't he have any idea who I was?"
>
> "He was right, of course. I did have a problem. Two in fact: I *had* become chemically dependent, and both my family and I were suffering from the disease of alcoholism."

"Their hardest problem was getting me to admit that I *had* a problem. As far as I was concerned, my life was going along just fine. But fortunately for me, my good doctor friend was not about to accept this rejection. He looked for reinforcements.

"One morning a few days later, I was unexpectedly confronted not by one doctor, but two; as well as by my husband (former President Gerald Ford), my three sons, my daughter, and my daughter-in-law. They were wonderful, because they came to me as a family unit, with professional counseling, and professional people who could help them as well as help me.

"With a great deal of love, they told me what my disease was doing, not only to me, but to our whole family. How it was destroying all of our lives."

A good intervention focuses on the alcoholic's drinking, and how it has affected her and her loved ones. . . . The Ford family confronted Betty's alcoholism as a group. . . .

"Their total love and concern convinced me that I did have a problem. . . . Then they suggested that we seek help professionally, which we all did together . . ." (Barry Robe, 1986, pp. 233–234)

As described by Shore and Batt (1991):

With the increase in attention by researchers and practitioners has come a number of theories concerning the antecedents and correlates of women's drinking, including hypotheses about stress, biological and gynecological disorders, self-esteem, sex-role discomfort, role conflict and overload, and the influence of others on women's drinking.

Investigation of the effect of women's roles on their drinking has evolved over the years from earlier studies of masculinity and femininity, women's fantasies, and unconscious sex-role conflicts to consideration of actual roles, role conflicts, and role overload as correlates of heavy or abusive drinking. Variables such as marital and employment status have been found to be related to drinking levels and adverse consequences of use. Although role conflict and overload is suggested as a cause of abusive drinking among women, research does not support the putative connection.

The drinking behavior of women's friends and significant others has been viewed as providing a social inducement to, or protection from, heavy drinking. . . . women's drinking was like that of their husbands or domestic partners as well as like that of their close friends and siblings. The idea that women are vulnerable to social influence raises concerns that those working outside the home may begin drinking like their male colleagues. . . . social context [also] may be important in understanding women's drinking. Variables directly related to drinking, such as time spent in drinking situations, are correlated with increased drinking, while other contextual variables, such as membership in organizations, may play a preventive role. (pp. 171–172)

A role-related hypothesis was advanced by Burns (1980) to explain the use of alcohol among women:

Why do women drink in ways which are destructive? Is it reasonable to expect that there may be common denominator(s) in their life histories or current circumstances? If we reject the unsupported clinical impressions, the negative comparisons with men, and the trivial conjecture, and if methodologically sound studies are going to be undertaken, a first essential task is to develop alternate hypotheses. . . . *Alcohol abuse by women as a self-destructive behavior is related to the role of women.*

The woman's role is often a limiting, second-class role. A social and economic system and interpersonal relationships within that system which restrict the development of the full self, tend to develop, instead, the characteristics of despair, dependency, helplessness, hopelessness, passivity, and rage. These in turn, for some women serve to initiate and sustain the addictive, destructive use of alcohol. (pp. 226–227)

Recognizing that new research methodologies must reflect a feminist orientation, Burns (1980) argued that:

> Although insecurity in the feminine role may contribute to the misuse of alcohol, it is dissatisfaction with the feminine role, as it is constituted in modern, urban society, which is of major significance for many women. Though it is difficult indeed to cope with a fragile sense of feminine adequacy, the more fundamental problem is to develop and sustain a sense of adequacy as a human being, and women must do so within a system that fosters their passivity and dependency and severely limits opportunities for full development.... Women, as women, are further limited by a circumscribed *role*. It is suggested that *for some women* this leads to feelings of helplessness and hopelessness, which in turn produce the deep depression that may finally lead to alcohol abuse.... It is vitally important to examine women's use of alcohol not only in comparison to that of men but as a socially significant behavior which may relate to and evolve with their changing role. (p. 230) (See also Factor 10, depression.)

Addressing this theory, Wilsnack and Cheloha (1987) noted that specific patterns of role deprivation, including lack of paid employment and recent emptying of the nest, predicted greater risks of problem drinking among specific age groups or cohorts of women drinkers (e.g., white middle-class women). Other theorists claimed that lack of employment may harm women and that more probably, paid employment offered multiple role responsibilities and may improve women's health because of its association with higher self-esteem, personal value, greater sense of purpose in life, and increased social support and social resources. Being able to use multiple responsibilities limits the demands of any one role. Thus, for some women, paid employment outside of the home increased performance demands and social monitoring in ways that could inhibit the use of alcohol and was actually, for some women, beneficial (Wilsnack & Wilsnack, 1992).

As explained by Wilsnack and Wilsnack (1992), where paid employment is considered traditionally masculine or requires traditionally masculine behavior, taking on such roles were hypothesized as clashing with a woman's socialized feminine behavior patterns or with social expectations about how women should behave. These clashes were thought to lead to psychological and social conflicts and tensions that could adversely affect a woman's mental health. In turn, women would self-medicate with alcohol in order to alleviate the bad feelings associated with psychological and social conflicts, including those bad feelings related to overloads of role demands (i.e., housekeeper, mother, paid employee outside the home).

Another related line of argument proposed that women developed problematic patterns of alcohol use as a result of being exposed to conditions that facilitate alcohol use (e.g., increased income to buy beverages more easily; greater opportunities to drink while spending longer periods of time away from home; conforming to job-related drinking norms established by men). For example, Winchester-Vega (1992) surveyed 205 attorneys to examine gender differences in regard to level of stress, coping, job satisfaction, social support, and substance use. Results demonstrated that there are significant gender differences in the areas of alcohol use, primary child care responsibility, and income. For both men and women, social support was the most significant factor associated with level of stress.

However, as emphasized by Wilsnack and Wilsnack (1992), although employment may adversely affect women's drinking patterns when their work is unpleasant, stressful, or dissatisfying (i.e., overloads, time pressures, powerlessness, inequities, conflicts on the job, subjective tension levels, self-estrangement, social isolation, or a lack of social support on the job), no research to date could support a theory that paid employment inherently makes women more likely to become problem drinkers.

As summarized by Shore (1992):

> Early theories and predictions about the drinking behavior of women in paid employment may have been based more on reactions to societal changes in women's roles and responsibilities than on any documented increase in alcohol abuse or related threats to women's health. More sophisticated theories are now being developed that deal with the complex ways in which drinking norms, values, accessibility, stress, age, job type, and other factors may combine to influence alcohol consumption and alcohol-related problems in women. Areas that remain to be addressed include the drinking patterns and drinking problems of women in jobs other than white-collar professional positions, and the possible relationship between paid employment, alcohol use, and rising highway death and injury rates among women. Continued work may provide greater understanding of the relationship between the workplace and alcohol consumption and may contribute to the prevention of alcohol problems among women and men. (pp. 160, 163–164)

As noted by Saunders, Bailey, Phillips, and Allsop (1993), when compared to men, recovering women may have very different reasons for relapse. As explained by the theorists:

> ... most of these women were independent, with relatively successful careers or independent means, and approaching middle age. It is possible to speculate that their use of alcohol was reflective of dissatisfaction with their lifestyle, particularly loss of, or lack of, a parenting role. The finding that the lower the number of children living at home the more likely the female subjects were to return to heavy drinking raises the important issue of role loss or role absence. (p. 1419) (See also Factor 11, age.)

However, in an earlier retrospective and outcome study of 72 women admitted to an Addiction Recovery Unit at an inpatient psychiatric hospital, Herr and Pettinati (1984) found that homemakers (n = 48) had been drinking for significantly more years than working women (n = 24). All the women had been in treatment for a minimum of 10 days. Demographic, drinking, marital, and employment histories were obtained at admission from the patients and confirmed subsequently by a social worker who was experienced in working with alcoholic women. The women's ages ranged from 21 to 65 years of age (mean age: 43 years of age) and all but one were Caucasian. The date of discharge was recorded and the social worker visited each woman for a personal interview at four consecutive anniversaries following discharge. The interview, although based on a structured format of questions, was informal so that the social worker could assess, using clinical judgment, the woman's drinking status and her adjustment back into the community. At least one, but typically two or three additional sources (e.g., relative, employer) were contacted by the same social worker to corroborate the information obtained for the women over the preceding year. As summarized by the researchers:

> Upon admission ... proportionately more homemaking than working women came to treatment, and homemaking women had been drinking heavily for significantly more years. These two groups of women did not differ in age, indicating that the homemaking women began drinking heavily at an earlier age than the working women. Significantly more homemaking women were married while more working women were divorced. Long term outcome based on adjustment in the community did not differ for homemakers compared to workers 4 years following treatment, even when marital status was accounted for. Although overall, a change in occupation following treatment did not directly relate to outcome, women who actually improved status following discharge over

the 4-year follow-up period were more likely to have made a change in occupation. (Herr & Pettinati, 1984, p. 578)

Using data from the 1991 National Employment Survey conducted by the Survey Research Center of the Institute for Behavioral Research at the University of Georgia, which contained both male and female data, Kraft, Blum, Martin, and Roman (1993) provided support for Wilsnack and Wilsnack's 1991 finding that the gender mix of occupations can be linked to drinking patterns. However, Kraft et al. (1993) found that the processes linking the gender mix of occupations and drinking behaviors are essentially the same for men and women:

> The analysis of drinking patterns and problem drinking support the argument that gender mix alters drinking behavior by shaping opportunities to drink. Although gender mix does not significantly influence how much respondents drink, who they are with when they drink, or problem drinking once a control for opportunities to drink with coworkers is included, gender mix does affect opportunities to drink with coworkers, and opportunities to drink with coworkers predict drinking patterns and problem drinking; gender mix indirectly influences these outcomes. (Kraft et al., 1993, p. 172)

Given the limitations of their study, the researchers identified that their results were important enough to warrant further investigation, particularly aimed at more carefully examining the causal mechanisms underlying the associations among the gender mix of occupations, opportunities to drink, and drinking practices.

As emphasized by Wilke (1994):

> The male-as-norm bias describes male alcoholic behavior as the norm and the standard by which female alcoholic behavior is judged. This bias suggests that alcoholic women are sicker and harder to treat than are alcoholic men and defines women as a special population in the alcoholism field. . . . The special population framework is used to incorporate the unexpected experiences of women, when what is necessary is to revise the fundamental assumptions of the male model of alcoholism. There is an inherent contradiction in that women's alcoholism is viewed as abnormal or different when compared to men's but women are researched as if their alcoholism was the same. . . .
> An alternative framework in which to do research is a women's health perspective, which begins with the belief that women's health is distinct from men's and that "imbalances in social roles, and subsequently in power, equality, and control, are likely to affect women's health adversely." . . . "Research conducted with unexamined assumptions derived from traditional scientific models ultimately may be more harmful to women than no research at all." . . . Therefore, a male-as-norm bias in addiction models not only affects the theoretical questions in research, but also ultimately affects assessment techniques, treatment interventions, and follow-up care. (pp. 29–30)

And, as concluded by Wilsnack and Wilsnack (1992):

> When trying to explain how women's employment affects their drinking behavior, oversimplified theories produced weak and inconsistent results. Recent research casts doubt on any simple ideas that paid employment is hazardous for women's mental health and drinking, or that paid employment is beneficial for women's mental health and drinking, or that stressful jobs increase women's risks of problem drinking. Improved, more complex theories could specify which women will modify their drinking behavior as a result of particular employment conditions with other aspects of women's lives, and explain how employment may create a context where other variables may increase or reduce risks of problem drinking. (p. 172) (See also Chapter 11, Preventing and Treating Substance Use Disorders Among Women.)

Factor 10: Depression

> At age eighteen, actress Jean Seberg catapulted to prominence after winning a nation wide search for a "new face" to star in Otto Preminger's 1957 film *Saint Joan*. Following her second film, a flop, she moved permanently to France in the 1960s. There she starred in many French films....
>
> Jean reportedly married four times. She was widely publicized because of her involvement with members of the Black Panther party; one of them may have fathered her infant daughter, who died in 1960, according to three *New York Times* articles in 1979 and 1980. Husband Romain Gary claimed that Jean—depressed as a result of a smear campaign by the FBI—tried to commit suicide annually on the child's birthday....
>
> According to David Richards' biography, *The Jean Seberg Story*, Jean drank extremely heavily and also took tranquilizers, particularly in the last eleven years of her life.... Yet the *Times* report of her death mentioned no drinking; only prescribed drug use, and "psychiatric treatment for serious depressions" and a "crack-up" after her daughter's death. (Barry Robe, 1986, p. 387)

A relationship among depression, problematic patterns of substance use, and suicide was suggested as early as 1938 when Karl Menninger published his text, *Man Against Himself*. Although this factor received some attention during the 1970s, it has received surprisingly little attention over the last decade.

In a study exploring the relationship among self-esteem, drinking behavior, and depression among alcoholic women in treatment, Turner (1995) sought to answer two questions: 1) Does low self-esteem in women alcoholics pertain more to their alcoholism or to their gender? and 2) Why is the self-esteem of women alcoholics so low, and, for some, so entrenched that even making an improvement in drinking behavior does not help raise it? As suggested by the theorists, the answers to these questions may be related to recent literature on girls' self-esteem:[8]

> Girls' self-esteem begins to fall in early adolescence, which is the same time that alcohol- and other drug-using behavior often begins. In contrast, pre-adolescent girls show striking capacities for self-confidence, courage and resistance to harmful norms of feminine behavior ... and are quite clear and candid about what they think and feel and know. What happens to girls at eleven or twelve is that they lose their sense of self-confidence and self-esteem—they literally lose their voices, particularly in the classroom. This decline in self-esteem and emergence of negative attitudes toward oneself does not disappear as they mature.... Recent research has linked depression in late adolescent young women to the ineffective coping strategies that they learned to use in dealing with stress and to the fall in self-esteem that they endured in early adolescence. In fact, a recent study has shown that greater numbers of both males and females are becoming depressed in late adolescence, but females outnumber males in rates of depression, and severely depressed young women have higher rates of substance abuse than similarly depressed young men. (p. 111)

As noted by Turner (1995), the results of her study emphasize the need to promote self-esteem, and, thus, break the cycle of diminished self-esteem among adolescent girls if alcoholism among women is to be curtailed. As explained by the theorist: "Enhancing the self-esteem and resilience of adolescent young women by teaching them positive coping skills in environments where they feel valued, might have positive effects on the prevention of depression as well as alcoholic drinking" (p. 115).

In addition to depression, women are frequently diagnosed with other mental disorders for which they are prescribed various substances of abuse (e.g., benzodiazepines, [Ativan®, Valium®]).[9] These prescription practices often result in problematic patterns of use (see also, Factor 9, gender role). As noted by Bepko (1989/1991), women are at higher risk than men for the development of problematic patterns of polysubstance use:

> They are twice as likely to abuse tranquillizers and sedatives and are consequently at greater risk for accidental overdose. It is hypothesized that while men are more likely to abuse illicit drugs . . . women suffer more from polydrug use because they are routinely tranquillized and sedated by doctors. Symptoms of addiction in women are frequently misdiagnosed as depression, "hysteria," or, as a local doctor termed one client's problem, "husbanditis." (p. 416)

Factor 11: Age

> Alcoholism knows no age boundaries. But at both ends of the age spectrum—and in women—alcoholism experts often see a telescoping of the disease's onset and progression. Recovering writer and artist Joan Donlan (her real name is Mimi Noland), who shared her diary about becoming alcoholic/chemically dependent in her book, *I Never Saw the Sun Rise*, told me that she became addicted in a matter of weeks at the age of fourteen. Alice, a widow in her seventies, started drinking alcoholically and taking pills during her husband's final illness and found that suddenly, or so it seemed to her, she had a problem with alcohol and other drugs. (Barry Robe, 1986, p. 333)

Lisansky Gomberg (1994) reviewed risk factors associated with alcohol use over the lifespan of women:

> First, although most risk factors characterize all age groups, some are unique to each stage in the life cycle. For example, inadequate control over impulses characterizes *adolescents* at risk for problem drinking, and patterns of distress are more closely tied to female than to male drinking in this age group. *Middle age* historically has been associated for women experiencing loss, depression, the "empty nest," and menopause. Although most women in their forties and fifties handle these challenges well, for some, the events of middle age are overwhelming and distressful and may lead to problem drinking. Second, in light of the presence of more than one risk factor for each life stage, it is important to remember that the more risk factors that are present, the greater the likelihood that problem drinking will develop. (pp. 225–226)

Schuckit, Anthenelli, Bucholz, Hesselbrock, and Tipp (1995), replicating and expanding an earlier investigation of alcohol-related life events among men, evaluated the time course of development of 44 relatively objective alcohol-related life experiences in men (n = 317) and women (n = 161) who had alcohol dependence. All respondents were free of intoxication at the time they were interviewed by a trained interviewer using the Semi-Structured Assessment for the Genetics of Alcoholism (SSAGA) research instrument. The alcohol section of the instrument extensively reviews the history of alcohol-related events and establishes for each positive response the age at which the problem first occurred.

The researchers identified that for both alcohol-dependent men and women (mean age 37.8 years, average of 12.8 years of education, 46% married, 22% separated or divorced, 31% single, and 1% widowed; 77% white, 11% black, 9% brown, and 3% other), their data demonstrate:

> . . . an earlier appearance of experiences with more minor alcohol-related job and interpersonal problems along with reversible physical/psychological events such as blackouts that occurred in the later teens to early 20s. By the mid-20s, persons who developed alcohol dependence reported they had begun to demonstrate tolerance, established rules to

attempt to control their intake in the face of binges, and developed more serious legal problems. Between ages 25 and 28 alcohol intake patterns were felt to have become more rigid with a greater tendency to drink in the morning, and the subjects reported experiencing repeated problems in attempting to cut back on drinking, expressed remembering feelings of guilt, noted psychological impairment and recognized that he or she had become "an excessive drinker." Evidence of withdrawal, use despite consequences and efforts to abstain for periods of time were felt to have been first observed between ages 28 and 31, followed by a recognition of the need to seek help along with more serious health and withdrawal problems by the mid-30s. Thus, 11.31 years elapsed between the development of any alcohol-related problem and seeking help. It is interesting to note that the proportion of individuals experiencing most of these problems remained relatively high (i.e., one third or more of the sample) through most of the course of alcohol dependence. However, the less serious life events were generally more frequently experienced. . . .

While men and women generally reported having experienced the same progression of problems, there were some interesting trends relating to potential differences. For example, the 69 women (43% of the 161 alcohol-dependent women) who reported that they hit inanimate objects or threw things while intoxicated experienced this event later in the progression of their problems related to alcohol than was true for the 180 of the 317 (57%) alcohol-dependent men who also reported this symptom. Similarly, women appeared more likely to report binges, craving alcohol when unable to drink and striking a family member at a later point in the course of their problems than men. In contrast, alcohol-dependent women reported experiencing driving and nondriving arrests, feelings of guilt and the formation of rigid drinking patterns earlier in their development of problems than their male counterparts. . . . It is interesting to note that the retrospective report of other age of onset of regular drinking for men in this sample was 17.5 + 4.83 years, but for women the onset was reported as having occurred a bit later at 18.5 + 5.3 years. . . . Despite the later age of onset of regular drinking, among those women who went on to experience alcohol inpatient rehabilitation, their first experience with formal treatment was reported to have occurred at 30.1 + 8.99 years, slightly earlier than the 32.5 + 11.72 year age of first treatment reported by the alcohol-dependent men who had ever received inpatient care. (p. 220)

In the late 1980s, the United States legal drinking age was increased to 21 years in an effort to reduce the number of negative outcomes associated with the irresponsible use of alcohol by adolescents and young adults. However, according to reactance theory, a theory advanced by Brehm in 1966, raising the legal drinking age to 21 years may actually cause an increase in the rate of drinking among underage students because of the belief that their behavioral freedom was lost. As explained by Allen, Sprenkel, and Vitale (1994), who sought to test the veracity of this theory with a sample of 2,142 college students (53.8% of whom were women) sampled from 10 midwestern colleges:

. . . raising the legal alcohol consumption and purchasing age could be seen as potentially causing psychological reactance in underage students. This is because alcohol consumption is, and has traditionally been, highly associated with college life and activities, with the large majority of students consuming at least some alcohol. . . . Denying students the opportunity to make choices in this area may be perceived by students as a coercive attempt to limit their behavioral freedom. According to reactance theory, students under the legal drinking age may then try to regain this lost behavioral freedom by making an even greater effort to acquire and consume alcoholic beverages. (p. 34)

The researchers also hypothesized that there would be no differences between the underage and legal-age groups in the use of illegal substances of abuse, which were unaffected by the legal changes.

The students who participated in the study were asked to respond to the Alcohol and Other Drug Use Needs Assessment Survey. Most of the students (66.2%) ranged in age from 17 to 20 years of age while the remainder (33.8%) were 21 years of age or older. As predicted by reactance theory, significant differences were found between groups in regard to the use of alcohol, but not in regard to the use of illegal substances of abuse. Gender effects were not reported.

Grover and Thomas (1993), using the conceptualization of social stress as advanced by Pearlin and Lieberman in 1981,[10] examined individual and social network variables and modes of anger expression as potential explanations for alcohol and over-the-counter (OTC) drug use among 87 mid-life women, ranging in age from 35 to 55 years of age, who were participating in a longitudinal study of health. The study was based on a secondary data analysis of third-phase data. They found that alcohol and OTC users reported higher anger symptomatology than nonusers and had different profiles in terms of age as well as education (i.e., the drinkers were better educated, whereas the high OTC users were less educated and older in age—however, both groups were comparable in that both experienced a high degree of anger symptomatology as evidenced in physiological symptoms. The researchers identified that these symptoms may have precipitated self-medication through either alcohol or OTC medications). Social network variables were unrelated to substance use.

Over a decade earlier, Schuckit and Morrissey (1979) reported that:

> Of 293 women in an alcoholic treatment center, two-thirds had received prescriptions for drugs of potential abuse, usually hypnotic and antianxiety drugs. One-third of the women admitted abusing substances; 80% of these subjects got prescriptions for potential drugs of abuse while actively abusing. These figures are alarming in light of the lack of evidence that antianxiety drugs, hypnotics, and stimulants are effective in treating alcoholics and drug abusers. Drug-misusing women in this sample reported more suicide attempts and early antisocial problems and had received more psychiatric care than nonabusers. The authors urge that hypnotics, antianxiety drugs, and stimulants almost never be prescribed to outpatient alcoholics and that analgesics be prescribed only with great care. (p. 607)

Factor 12: Other Factors—Race, Culture, & Ethnicity

Chaney Allen, daughter of an Alabama minister, was the first recovering black woman alcoholic to tell her story in book form. Her autobiography, *I'm Black & I'm Sober*, was published in 1978, ten years after this turning point experience she described in her book:

> 1968, San Diego: "My head had cleared enough for me to know that I was going into DTs and convulsions . . . I knew I had one can [of beer] left in the refrigerator. I staggered to the kitchen, holding onto the walls . . . My hands shook so that I could hardly open it . . . I prayed 'Dear GOD make this the LAST drink!' I spilled some, but got most of it down . . .
>
> "This was the summer of 1968, and Blacks all over the nation were . . . listening to the one and only James Brown sing *I'M BLACK AND I'M PROUD* . . . I turned the radio on . . . And there it was again. *I'M BLACK AND I'M PROUD*, say it aloud, I'm Black and I'm proud, *I'M BLACK AND I'M PROUD*. . . . I quickly snapped the radio off and moaned out loud, "Stop singing that song. *I'M BLACK AND I'M DRUNK!* I don't feel proud. I'm nothing but a drunken bitch. I am Black but I am not proud. I had reached *MY* bottom. I had reached *MY* skid row." (Barry Robe, 1986, pp. 330–331)

Gerald Gregory Jackson (1980a) proposed the *Backlash Theory of Substance Abuse*, a sociological (sociocultural) theory explaining substance use among African American women. Rejecting Euro-American explanations of substance use, Jackson (1980a) offered the "Afro-behavioral approach," which specifically dealt with one antecedent to substance abuse, identity. As argued by Jackson (1980a), "past failure to conceptualize differences in terms of differences in antecedent cultures and contemporary circumstances has aborted a number of fruitful lines of inquiry in the substance abuse field. Specifically, the individualist motif in the conceptualization of treatment and prognosis has fostered a number of problems . . . and furthermore collides with the communal orientation of Afro-American culture" (pp. 98, 101).

As further argued by Jackson (1980b),

> . . . most of the recent studies of female substance abusers either have excluded the variable of subculture or considered it in passing but not as an independent variable. . . . The most obvious implication. . . . is that researchers and theoreticians should not level differences between Afro- and Euro-American females but seek to understand the nature of the differences between them. The latter recommendation does not mean that they are opposites, it merely recognizes and acknowledges the possibility that they are not identical. . . . Despite what might be regarded as the workings of institutional racism and professional elitism, very few researchers have expanded upon the relevance of these factors in subsequent research on the subject of female substance abuse. What one witnesses is the dangerous extension of ideas and concern from traditional mental health research into the area of substance abuse or what this writer has discussed elsewhere as the "backlash theory." One example of this theory is the use of income level as a deciding factor in substance abuse problems and solutions. In the folklore of the mental health establishment, the absence of Afro-Americans in therapy was related to their inability to afford the cost of therapy and not to such factors as the racial bias of therapists and institutional racism. . . . It is the contention of this writer, therefore, that even when researchers compliment facets of Afro-American behavior, if the method used is based upon a dichotomous mode of thought, then negative implications for Afro-Americans result. . . . The dichotomous mode of thinking underlying a social class paradigm, therefore, is not appropriate for an Afro-American solution. In short, we find little relief for the Afro-American female when the basis for decision-making is a dichotomous mode of reasoning. (pp. 84–87)

Rejecting social psychological explanations of deviance,[11] Dreher (1984) argued that the concept of intracultural diversity would be a better framework for understanding the nonconforming behavior observed among Jamaican women living in two rural communities in regard to culturally approved sex roles for marijuana use.[12] As explained by the theorist:

> In collecting data from thirty households about the consumption of ganja by their constituent children and adults, it was discovered that despite the prevailing norms which mitigate against the smoking of marijuana by women, there are indeed women who smoke ganja in a manner not unlike their male counterparts . . . (p. 51)

Although one group of women prepared ganja teas and medicinal remedies as expected by social norms, the other group of women did not—even when ganja was readily available for this purpose. The latter group also exchanged and used ganja socially among themselves or with their husbands or male partners. The two groups of women varied little in relation to their personal characteristics and activities of daily living. Thus, as concluded by the theorist, differences in ganja-linked behavior, as observed among the two groups of thirty African-Jamaican women, are best explained as being embedded in the social fabric of community life and in the structural position of women rather than in the personal characteristics of the women themselves (Dreher, 1984, p. 63).

Lillie-Blanton, MacKenzie, and Anthony (1991) noted that empirical data regarding the nature and extent of alcohol problems among black women, although limited, suggested that alcohol use was associated with more serious health consequences (e.g., cirrhosis of the liver, heart disease) among black women than among white women. As noted by Lillie-Blanton, MacKenzie, and Anthony (1991), citing the 1965–1979 national surveys of Adult Drinking Practices, "a larger percentage of black women than white women abstain from drinking, but among women who do drink, a larger percentage of black women are heavy drinkers" (p. 124).

In an effort to characterize the nature of the problem more precisely so that effective interventions could be planned, the researchers completed a secondary analysis of interview survey responses from 809 black women and 1,291 white women, 18 to 59 years old, obtained from the Baltimore Epidemiologic Catchment Area household survey. The analyses were designed to test the hypothesis that patterns of alcohol consumption differ for black and white women. The researchers also were interested in testing 3 subhypotheses: 1) black women are more likely to be nondrinkers than white women, 2) black women are more likely to be heavy drinkers than white women, and 3) black women are more likely than white women to meet criteria for an alcohol use disorder, as defined by the third edition of the *Diagnostic and Statistical Manual* of the American Psychiatric Association. As noted by the researchers, "To our knowledge, this is the first study to examine both drinking patterns and the diagnosis of alcohol abuse-dependence within the same population" (p. 125).

The black and white women differed significantly in regard to their distributions of age, income, education, and marital status. "Black women were younger, had fewer years of formal education, and less income. Also, while a similar percentage of black women and white women were separated, divorced, or widowed, considerably fewer black women were married" (Lillie-Blanton, MacKenzie, & Anthony, 1991, p. 129).

In regard to drinking patterns, black women and white women were similar with 48% of black women and 40% of white women reporting no alcohol use in the month prior to the interview. On average, black women and white women consumed less than one drink per day and the percentage of heavy drinkers among black women and white women also was similar (5% and 4%). "Race, however, was associated with a history of a DIS[13] alcohol use disorder. A larger percentage of black women than white had a history of a DIS alcohol use disorder (6% and 3%, respectively), but not a current alcohol use disorder (3% and 2%, respectively). Multivariate techniques used to assess the degree of association between sociodemographic characteristics and drinking, found significant racial differences in the nondrinking and heavy drinking categories (p. 129). Other results are summarized by Lillie-Blanton, MacKenzie, and Anthony (1991):

> This study provides strong evidence that black women and white women in the Baltimore ECA did not differ significantly in the proportion with an alcohol use disorder. However, racial differences were observed in the likelihood of nondrinking and heavy drinking. The differences detected were a result of the joint effects of race with sociodemographic characteristics of age, education, and marital status. Black women who were ages 18–24, 60 or older, or married were more likely to be nondrinkers than were white women. Among drinkers, women of each race drank on average similar amounts of alcohol, but the likelihood of being a heavy drinker was less for blacks than whites with 11 or more years of education. Of the sociodemographic characteristics examined, only education

differed in its association with heavy drinking among black women compared with white women.

Findings regarding racial differences in heavy drinking among women ages 60 or older deserved further investigation. While the largest percentage of heavy drinkers was among black women ages 45–59, no black women ages 60 or older were identified as heavy drinkers. Moreover, about twice as many black women as white women ages 60 or older were diagnosed with a current alcohol use disorder. Thus, there were no older black women consuming alcohol in large enough amounts to be classified as heavy drinkers, but some met criteria for current alcohol abuse or dependence. It is possible that older black women perceive and report their impairment in social or occupational functioning differently than whites. Further research will be required to clarify whether the dramatic drop in heavy drinkers is real or a function of the measurement tool used in this study. . . . Explanations other than drinking patterns, such as later detection of symptoms, less effective treatment modalities, or the presence of other illnesses, should [also] be investigated as possible factors that account for racial differences in alcohol-related morbidity and mortality. (pp. 131–132)

More recently, Caetano (1994) compared drinking practices and alcohol-related problems among women comprising three ethnic groups—black women, brown women, and white women—for which national data were available. The database used was from the 1984 National Alcohol Survey (ANAS-84) and its 1992 follow-up survey conducted by the Alcohol Research Group. A total of 1,947 blacks, 1,453 browns, and 1,777 whites were interviewed. In regard to drinking patterns, abstention was higher among black women and brown women than among white women. Results from the 1984 study indicated that most women who drank in all three groups were light drinkers. The proportion of more frequent drinkers was higher among white than among black and brown women. The results from the 1992 survey revealed a decrease in drinking, which was more pronounced among white women than among black and brown women—perhaps as a result of aging of the sample. As explained by Caetano (1994):

Results by age for the NAS-84 survey show that drinking decreases with age among women in all three ethnic groups. The variation is such that rates of abstention are two times higher among women who are 60 years of age and older than among women 18 to 29 years of age. However, black and Hispanic women have higher rates of abstention than do white women in almost all age groups. . . . Only in the middle-age group (ages 40 to 59) do Hispanic drinkers consume more than white drinkers consume. This higher rate of . . . drinking among middle-age Hispanic women could be examined in terms of an increase in independence among women who are older and have a central role in their family but who also may hold jobs and therefore are able to adopt less traditional roles in the household and in the family. (p. 236)

Other areas that were addressed by the surveys included the effects of acculturation and problems associated with alcohol use. In regard to acculturation,[14] which was examined in the NAS-84, it was found that it was a powerful force shaping women's drinking patterns. For example, brown women who are highly acculturated are more likely to drink than those who are less acculturated. In regard to alcohol-related problems in general, the proportion of white women who reported alcohol-related problems was higher than the proportion of black and brown women who reported problems. The most frequently reported problems across women in the three groups were salience of drinking (i.e., when other aspects of life take a secondary place to drinking); belligerence; health problems; and other drinking-related problems, such as arguments with people other than the spouse.

Toward the mid-1990s, attention focused increasingly on explaining various patterns of alcohol and other substance use among women of various ethnic and cultural backgrounds who had recently immigrated to North America. For example, Adrian, Dini, MacGregor, and Stoduto (1995), through an analysis of Canadian data from the 1989 National Alcohol and Drugs Survey (NADS), sought to support their hypotheses that women from ethnocultural groups that had high or low rates of alcohol and other substances of abuse in their country of origin would tend to continue their old world patterns of use in Canada. Thus, it was expected that the patterns of substance use observed among women who had recently immigrated to Canada would exceed or fall below the Canadian mainstream patterns of use.

The NADS survey provided information on 110 variables that measured different aspects of substance use behaviors, including frequency of consumption, quantities consumed, and circumstances surrounding consumption. Questions on drug-taking behavior, reasons for drinking or not drinking, and opinions regarding appropriate drinking or drug taking behavior also were included. Findings from an analysis of these data indicated that alcohol, tobacco, and other substance use behavior differed among ethnocultural groups and the mainstream national average for substance use.

The amount of difference between each ethnocultural group and the national average was related to the period of arrival and the length of time that a particular group had been present in Canada. Women of ethnocultural groups that have been in Canada the longest are those whose substance use is closest to the national average, and women from groups that have been in Canada for the shortest time are those whose substance use differs most from the national average. Whereas the NADS survey data did not allow measurement of cultural tensions that have been related to patterns of substance use among ethnocultural groups immigrating to North America, the theorists suggested that their study provided evidence that "the degree of similarity or differences between each ethnocultural group and the mainstream national average of alcohol, tobacco, and drug use may be used to measure the degree of social integration of each ethnocultural group and the degree of acculturation of women of specific ethnocultural groups into the mainstream Canadian society" (p. 725).

In an effort to address the impact of culture and gender on alcohol problems, Mora (1998) explored the meaning of culturally competent and gender specific programming for Latinas.[15] A theoretical framework for the treatment of problematic patterns of alcohol use among Latinas based on feminist, cultural, and community perspectives was developed because of the lack of attention to this area over the last decade. As summarized by Mora (1998):

> There are few empirical studies detailing the efficacy of various treatment approaches or modalities with this population. It is not known, for example, which forms of alcohol treatment are most effective or desirable for Latinas in general and for specific groups of Latinas, including Latina adolescents, Latina lesbians, and other Latinas who may be at risk for developing alcohol dependency problems. (p. 164)

As noted by Reyes (1998), "because of ethnocentrism, racism, androcentrism, and lesbophobia, Latina lesbians are an invisible substance abuse population that risk facing social and emotional problems" (p. 179). Latinas display various patterns of substance use in regard to their drugs of choice and have tendencies toward polysubstance use. Their patterns of use may be affected by their exposure to neighborhoods, schools, and bars that are characterized by high rates of substance use and crime. Family dysfunction, especially physical and sexual abuse, and culturally mediated child rearing practices may be related to substance abuse among this group of women. As identified by Reyes (1998), many Latina women begin to use alcohol and other drugs once they have had the opportunity to become more independent (e.g., obtain employment, move away from home to attend college). Becoming involved with partners who consume alcohol and other drugs also is an important factor for Latina women as it is for other women.

As further explained by Reyes (1998), both *Marianismo* and *Familismo* are important factors in regard to the development of substance use among Latina women, including Latina lesbian women:

> *Familismo* is a distinctive cultural tradition of Latino populations that places the family at the center. . . . loyalty, emotional closeness and interdependence are common overriding descriptors of the Latino family. This kinship network poses issues for women, especially lesbians who encounter family conflict because of sexism and lesbophobia. Moreover, the historical heritage of cultural androcentric values and traditions and practices of *machismo* and *Marianismo*, play a major role regarding the substance abuse practices of Latina women. A salient characteristic of the Latino culture assumes rigid delineations in how males and females are socialized. For example, one manifestation of machismo is that males tend to be socialized to be dominant and independent, while gender role expectations for women are different. For example, socialization of females falls within the *good-bad* dichotomy of Marianismo, which ultimately attempts to model behavior to harmonize with and represent the virtues of the Virgin Mary. This value system places women in a position of power regarding the assumption that women are spiritually superior to men. As such, Marianismo is intricately linked to the cultural expectations of women marrying, having children in a heterosexual relationship and taking care of others in spite of their personal needs and requirements. Marianismo may also be conceptually applied to the parent's protective position in regard to their daughter's abuse of alcohol and other drugs in order to maintain the honor of the family. Moreover, *Marianismo* is key to understanding lesbophobic values and doctrines of the Catholic church. (pp. 182–183)

Another component of Marianismo is *hembrismo*. The concept of hembrismo has been reclaimed by some Latina feminists as a healthy challenge to Marianismo. Although the term has been generally used in a negative way to describe women who take on some of the male characteristics of machismo in order to demonstrate that they, too, can be independent, resilient, and strong, the term also has been used to describe Latina women who are involved in various patterns of substance abuse. As described by Reyes (1998):

> One manifestation of *hembrismo* is when women prove their toughness by measuring how tolerant they are to alcohol and other drugs. In Puerto Rican folklore, the term *jodedora* is often used to describe this manifestation, as well as women who are in an integral part of the illegal drug culture. *Chola* lifestyles, which may include gang, and alcohol and drug involvement tend to be more specific to the Chicano (Mexican-American) experience. This lifestyle often promotes a reaction to *Marianismo* and a counterculture street socialization experience "which pushes the individual to adopt a *locura* mind set (thinking and acting in a daring, courageous manner, and especially crazy fashion in the face of adversity) in order to manage many of the fearful and stressful situations they encounter on a daily basis."
>
> It is difficult to arrive at a complete understanding of the complex and often devastating effects that androcentric and heterocentric traditional Latino cultural values and norms have on Latina lesbian women, and how this population group is additionally impacted by USA racism, ethnocentrism and classism. Moreover, the paucity of research on this population does not adequately provide information on the complex interactions between ethnic, racial and sexual minority status and the abuse of alcohol and other drugs.

(pp. 183–184) (See also Factor 5, tomboyishness—femininity, masculinity, and sexual identity crisis, and Factor 9, gender role.)

☐ Conclusion

This chapter has presented, in broad brush strokes, several themes of selected modern theories advanced in a effort to explain why women use alcohol and other substances of abuse. While these theories are rich and diverse in their contributions, causal understanding remains out of reach. Obviously we have come far, but not far enough, in our quest for understanding why women use the substances of abuse. As noted by Lisansky Gomberg (1991) almost a decade ago:

> There has been a continuous production of reviews of literature about women and alcoholism for more than 30 years. . . . This list does not even include the many popular writings, annotated bibliographies, and articles in journals and in books on alcohol-related problems. Reviews have been published in Canada, in the United Kingdom, and in other countries. A complete list of all the works published in the last 30 years about women's drinking and women's alcohol-related problems would look impressive until compared with a similar list about male drinking behavior and problems. . . . The point that women are under represented in the scientific literature about alcoholism has been made many times. . . . In dealing with women's drinking behaviors and alcoholism, one is confronted by interface of two challenging research issues: female biology, psychology, and social role on the one hand, and the effects of alcohol, intoxication, and heavy drinking on the other. . . . If alcoholism or any other psychopathological behavior is the same for men and women, why study women at all? As for the effects of alcohol, intoxication, and heavy drinking, there are research questions fraught with conflicting views and we are still arguing about the definition and diagnosis of alcoholism and whether alcoholism is or is not a disease. (pp. 263–264)

As yet another decade comes to a close and a new century and millenium begins, we seek to support through research evidence these published theories and await new theoretical directions. Our quest continues into a new decade, new century, and new millenium as we endeavor to disentangle a multitude of interacting factors related to understanding why women use in various ways the substances of abuse.

☐ Notes

1. Lucy Barry Robe (1986) read over 500 books and thousands of articles, seeking alcohol-related information about well-known women in this century. She conducted dozens of personal interviews with writers, performers, society leaders, wives of politicians, celebrities in the arts, and people who knew them. Selected excerpts from her text, *Co-Starring Famous Women and Alcohol*, have been used to illustrate the heterogeneity of women's experiences with alcohol and the various factors that have been related to substance use among women.
2. Two basic mechanisms have been postulated for the transmission of alcoholism from parents to offspring: 1. genetic mechanisms (i.e., heredity or parent-offspring genetic transmission); and 2. environmental mechanisms (i.e., vertical cultural transmission—children "learn" alcoholism, or behaviors that increase their vulnerability for developing alcoholism, from their parents in the same way that they learn language, social attitudes, or religious affiliation). Arguments regarding the contribution of these two mechanisms in regard to explaining causation or variability in observed target behaviors have been generally referred to as the nature or nurture controversy.

3. As explained by Hill (1993), ERPs recorded at the scalp could be a useful marker for screening high risk girls for alcoholism. ERPs have been associated with particular sensory and cognitive aspects of information processing and the ERP waveform appears to be under genetic control. Thus, it is minimally affected by environmental factors (e.g., exposure to an alcoholic parent, sibling, or other family member). ERP studies using information processing models have been used to study the relative contribution of genetic factors to alcoholism vulnerability. Although little attention has been given to women, studies of male subjects who have chronic alcoholism or who were presumed to be at high risk for alcoholism, demonstrated deficits in the P300 component of the ERP.
4. The Children of Alcoholics (COAs) or Adult Children of Alcoholics (ACOAs) literature reflects a self-help movement that focused increased attention on the possible detrimental effects alcoholic parents could have on their children, both during childhood and adulthood. Popularized by the authors of several self-help books and given extensive media coverage, the early aims of the movement were to identify adult offspring of alcoholics in order to characterize the effects of alcoholic parenting and to provide support and treatment. Generally, it has been found that ACOAs have significantly higher rates of problematic patterns of alcohol use, depression, and other psychological symptomatology, including self-depreciation and decreased self-esteem.

    Concurrently, attention also was focused on a related phenomenon, codependency. Codependency refers to a syndrome of pathological effects displayed by a person that have been generally attributed to that person having a parent or significant other who is addicted to alcohol or other substances of abuse. The person, regardless of gender, engages in denying, ignoring, tolerating, and enabling behaviors that have been associated with encouraging the alcoholic's problematic patterns of drinking. Codependency also has been formulated as a person displaying "over-responsibility" or "under-responsibility" in her or his interactions with others (Krestan & Bepko, 1991). In turn, the person who is codependent suffers the consequences of being in a relationship with an alcoholic or substance user, which may generally include physical and psychological abuse. Although there may be two distinct subtypes of codependency based on whether a person is raised by, or married to, an alcoholic or substance user, living with an alcoholic or substance user is associated with increased psychological difficulty (Beattie, 1987, 1990; George, La Marr, Barrett, & McKinnon, 1999; Hinkin & Kahn, 1995).
5. As explained by Volkan (1994), people who have strong ego formation and mature object relations will probably not feel the need to compulsively use drugs, much as normal adults no longer need transitional objects from their childhood. However, people who have poor object relations, a weak ego formation, narcissistic disturbances, and a history of introjective depression are likely to begin to use drugs as reactivated transitional objects in an attempt to repair early object relations deficits. Based on psychoanalytic theory, these deficits can be traced to specific dynamics between infants and their parents. As further explained:

    > The mothers of compulsive drug users generally appear weak and depressed and have many unmet needs of their own. Their children are starved emotionally and the transitional object phase is not successfully negotiated. Yet, these mothers cling to their children with the hope that their offspring will somehow magically take care of them and alleviate their pain. This effectively prevents the separation of the child from its mother. . . .
    >
    > Nevertheless, the blame does not entirely rest with the mother. In many instances the mother's problems are caused or exacerbated by the fathers. These men are often physically or emotionally unavailable. When they are present, they are often narcissistic, expecting both mother and child to gratify their needs. The fathers, therefore, do not fulfill their role in helping their children separate from the mother. In some cases, the father takes over the mothering role for the child, but usually is emotionally distant or uses the role to get the child to gratify his narcissistic needs. . . . the child tries to resolve its object relations needs (caused by inadequate mothering) through a relationship with the father. When this fails, the

child (or possibly by now young adult) may turn to other people or fetish-like objects to mediate his or her internal object relations conflicts.

Clearly, environmental influences come into play during this time. If the child is in an environment where the use of drugs is accepted or tolerated, he or she will be more likely to use drugs to compensate for his or her problems. (pp. 111–112)

6. Heavy drinking has been associated with several gynecological problems including painful menstruation, heavy menstrual flow, absence of menses, and early menopause. Drinking episodes have been related to premenstrual tension among 65% of premenopausal women. In addition, women who have histories of alcoholism have a higher rate of gynecologic surgery (excluding hysterectomy) and have more chronic medical disorders associated with their drinking, such as cirrhosis of the liver, inflammation of the pancreas, and malnutrition. These medical disorders also contribute to gynecologic problems. On the other side of the coin, sexual dysfunction has been related to heavy drinking among women (70% of alcoholic women report sexual dysfunction) and many women experience decreased sexual satisfaction once their drinking problems begin. In addition, women often are targets of sexual aggression when they are drinking (Gore Gearhart, Beebee, Milhorn, & Meeks, 1991, p. 909).

7. The Social Stress Model of Substance Abuse was proposed by Rhodes and Jason in 1988 to explain parameters that influence drug use. According to the model, which was extended from Albee's 1982 theory of psychopathology, the likelihood of an individual engaging in drug use is seen as a function of the stress level and the extent to which it is offset by stress modifiers (e.g., social competencies, social networks, social resources). It emphasizes individual and family system variables and social networks, with attention to the social influences of family and peers. The theory also incorporates research on competence and coping. The variables in the denominator of the model (i.e., social network, social competencies, and stress modifiers) are viewed as interacting with each other to buffer the impact of stress (Strachan Lindenberg et al., 1998).

8. Building on her previous research and that of others in the area of women's health, women's psychology, and substance abuse, Turner (1995) defined self-esteem as the ability to think well of oneself at any given period in time and the ability to maintain a coherent and positive sense of well-being when dealing with change or other stressful situations. To have self-esteem is to value one's self, based upon self-perception of strengths, regardless of perceived shortcomings. Low self-esteem is characterized by a discrepancy between one's ideal self-concept and actual self-concept. While evidence has shown that many American women in general, and women alcoholics in particular, experience this discrepancy, it also has been found that the self-esteem of alcoholics is lower than that of nonalcoholics and the self-esteem of women alcoholics is the lowest of all (p. 110).

9. In our professional opinions, this prescribing behavior is, for the most part, inappropriate and professionally irresponsible.

10. As explained by Grover and Thomas (1993), these theorists perceived the process of social stress as the culmination of the interaction between three major concepts: the source, the mediators, and the manifestations of stress. For this study, the source of stress was defined as mid-life (a life event); the concept of social network support, measured by the Norbeck Social Support Questionnaire, was explored as a mediating resource; and the manifestations of social stress were anger expression and substance use as measured by means of scores on the Framington Anger Scales and self-reports of alcohol and OTC use.

11. Three general directions of explanation have been advanced from this theoretical stance: 1) women who use marijuana or other substances of abuse possess personality characteristics that are typically identified as masculine—they are aggressive, competitive, dominant, rebellious, and tough—that make them more likely to transgress social norms; 2) women who smoke marijuana tend to be educated, independent, and have high social status as compared to women who do not smoke marijuana who tend to display high religiosity and commitment to home and family; and 3) women who smoke marijuana have been initiated into marijuana smoking by men (i.e., agents of contagion), who also supply them with their marijuana (Dreher, 1984, pp. 51–52).

12. As noted by Dreher (1984): "... the regular smoking of cannabis in Jamaica is a predominantly male activity. Even though women, like their male counterparts, may have been exposed to ganja through the ingestion of teas and tonics as infants and small children and even though they may have experimented with smoking ganja with their friends as adolescents, women are not included in the adult male social groupings in which cannabis is routinely exchanged and smoked; nor do they generally smoke with peers of their own sex. This exclusivity based on sex is rationalized by the widely held belief (among men) that women 'don't have the brains' for smoking and should either abstain from or restrict smoking to no more than occasional use—and then only in the company of their mates. Women who do smoke, socially, often are regarded as brawling and unrespectable" (p. 54).
13. The DIS, or Diagnostic Interview Schedule, is a standardized interview schedule designed to make mental disorder diagnoses according to criteria of the DSM-III. The core of the ECA survey was the National Institute of Mental Health (NIMH) Diagnostic Interview Schedule (Lillie-Blanton, MacKenzie, & Anthony, 1991, p. 125).
14. Acculturation can be defined as "the process by which immigrants adopt the norms, social values, and overall culture of the host country. Because drinking norms vary greatly for women among different cultures, acculturation is studied to determine how women's drinking habits may change as they adapt to a new culture" (Caetano, 1994, p. 237).
15. Latinas comprise a heterogenous population of women who can trace their ancestry to one or more of the 25 countries comprising Latin America: Mexico, Central America, South America, and the Caribbean. As explained by Reyes (1998), the essential feature of what is today Latin America originated in pre-Columbian, indigenous cultures along with the Spanish colonial social formation of the 1500s to the 1800s. These cultural, linguistic, and racial heritages contribute to the widely diverse formation of present Latin American national characteristics. Although diverse in their characteristics, Latina women as a group are reported to have the highest poverty levels when compared to other marginalized populations.

PART II

DEVELOPMENTAL CONSIDERATIONS

CHAPTER 3

Substance Use During Pregnancy and Lactation: Effects on the Developing Fetus, Neonate, and Infant

This chapter focuses on substance use during pregnancy and lactation and its effects on the developing fetus, neonate, and infant. The specific effects of substance use by pregnant women or women who are breast feeding upon the developing fetus, neonate, or infant are reviewed and discussed. We begin, in temporal order, with the effects of substance use during pregnancy.[1]

☐ Substance Use During Pregnancy

The focus of this section is on maternal substance use and human teratogenesis. A teratogen is broadly defined as any factor (e.g., drug) associated with the production of physical or mental abnormalities in the developing embryo or fetus. The word teratogen is derived from the Greek words "terato," monster, and "genesis," origin or beginning. It is estimated that some type of teratogenic effect can be found among 2% to 3% of all live births and that teratogenic effects, at least in part, account for 20% of the deaths that occur during the first five years of life. These effects, which can be acute and self-limiting, or irreversible and long-term, may be displayed in a variety of ways (L. A. Pagliaro & A. M. Pagliaro, 1995a; A. M. Pagliaro & L. A. Pagliaro, 1996).

The type and degree of human teratogenesis has been associated with many factors, including unknown factors, genetic factors, and maternal/fetal environmental factors (Pajer, 1992). The maternal/fetal environmental factors can be divided into radiation, disease, infections, and drugs. Although many prescribers and other health and social care providers are paying closer attention to the potential teratogenic effects associated with the use of selected drugs during pregnancy (see L. A. Pagliaro & A. M. Pagliaro, in press; A. M. Pagliaro & L. A. Pagliaro, 1997), their general knowledge and understanding of the possible teratogenic effects associated with the substances of abuse may be limited.

This section summarizes the published literature examining the teratogenic effects associated with the maternal use of the various substances of abuse during pregnancy. Attention is given to human studies only because of the inherent difficulties associated with extrapolating data from animal studies to humans. These difficulties include determining physiologic and genetic differences in teratogenic susceptibility and establishing comparable doses, stages of pregnancy, environmental conditions, ages, and maternal health status (Hemminki & Vineis, 1985; Hoyme, 1990). A classic example of the problems associated with the extrapolation of the results of animal studies to humans is the thalidomide tragedy. When thalidomide, a sedative-hypnotic and substance of abuse, was tested among several pregnant rodent species, no teratogenic effects were noted. However, when thalidomide was prescribed for women to treat anxiety and insomnia during the first trimester of pregnancy, devastating teratogenic effects (ie., phocomelia or major limb reduction) were produced (Lenz, 1962; McBride, 1961).[2]

☐ Maternal Substance Use

According to a recent survey conducted for the National Association for Perinatal Addiction Research and Education,[3] 11 percent of all American babies are born with evidence of drug exposure. We know that we are seeing just the first few months and years in the lives of an entire generation of children who are maimed and deformed physically, emotionally, and mentally by the drug addictions of their mothers. We will be mourning for decades if not generations the waste of human and financial resources that these children represent. (Gore, 1991, p. 99)

Some authors (e.g., Gilchrist, Gillmore, & Lohr, 1990; Higgins et al., 1995; Lohr, Gillmore, Gilchrist, & Butler, 1992) suggest that substance use declines "voluntarily and substantially during pregnancy." However, the preponderance of available data suggest that most women still use one or more of the substances of abuse at some time during their pregnancies (Abma & Mott, 1991; Deren, Frank, & Schmeidler, 1990; Kokotailo, Adger, Duggan, Repke, & Joffe, 1992; Lee, 1995; Marques & McKnight, 1991; Merrick, 1993; Newman & Buka, 1991; L. A. Pagliaro & A. M. Pagliaro, 1995a; A. M. Pagliaro & L. A. Pagliaro, 1996; Sarvela & Ford, 1992).[4] The substances of abuse and the extent of their use appears to be determined primarily by such factors as age, race, and socioeconomic status (Cornelius, Richardson, Day, Cornelius, Geva, & Taylor, 1994; Jorgensen, 1992; Wheeler, 1993).[5] Research also has identified additional risk factors associated with substance use during pregnancy, including previous physical or sexual abuse during childhood (A. M. Pagliaro & L. A. Pagliaro, 1996).

Unfortunately, a reliable estimate of the nature and extent of substance use among pregnant women is not available. There are many reasons for this lack of data including the fact that many substances of abuse (e.g., cocaine, heroin, marijuana) are illegal and, thus, their use is hidden or underreported. However, although variance is reported in specific percentages of use of the various illicit substances by pregnant women, all studies agree on one conclusion—that a significant number of pregnant women use illicit drugs. For example, the NIDA's 1984 National Pregnancy and Health Survey found that "an estimated 113,000 white women, 75,000 African-American women, and 28,000 Hispanic women used illicit drugs during pregnancy" (Mathias, 1995, p. 1). Of concern is the fact that although the moderate use of a particular substance of abuse may have limited harmful effects for the mother, it may be extremely toxic and pose high teratogenic risk to the developing embryo or fetus as a result of differences in maternal and fetal metabolism, blood and tissue concentrations, tissue sensitivity, and a variety of other factors that preclude a single direct cause-effect relationship (Griffith, Azuma, & Chasnoff, 1994).[6]

Attention to the types of substances of abuse used by women during pregnancy and their patterns of use before and during pregnancy are important in order to retrospectively identify teratogenic risk to the developing embryo and fetus.[7] Although there are limitations to this type of research, human teratogenic experiments cannot be ethically performed, and the results of experiments involving animal models, as previously noted, cannot be relied upon to determine human teratogenic potential. In order to better identify the teratogenic risk associated with maternal substance use during pregnancy, attention also must be given to the interaction of several factors including maternal factors (e.g., general health, maternal dose), placental factors, fetal factors (e.g., stage of fetal development), environmental factors, and specific substance of abuse factors (Cordier, Ha, Ayme, & Goujard, 1992; L. A. Pagliaro & A. M. Pagliaro, 1995a; A. M. Pagliaro & L. A. Paliaro, 1996; Van Allen, 1992) (Figure 3-1).

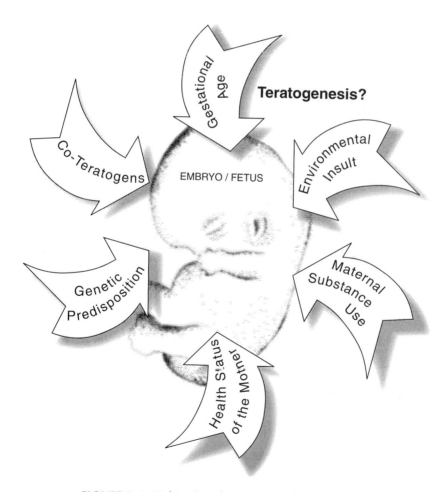

FIGURE 3–1. Multivariate determinants of teratogenesis.

Maternal factors include uterine blood flow, concomitant medical conditions (e.g., diabetes, epilepsy, infections, thyroid disorders), and general health. Placental factors include the size and thickness of the placenta, placental blood flow, ability of the placenta to metabolize the substance of abuse to an inactive, active, or teratogenic metabolite; and placental age. Fetal factors include the stage of fetal development, the status of hepatic metabolizing systems, the amount of hepatic blood flow through the ductus venosus, fetal blood pH, genetic predisposition, and concomitant exposure to other potential teratogens. Environmental factors include food additives (e.g., aspartame, nitrates), pesticides (e.g., chlordane), air and water pollutants, radiation, and toxins (e.g., mercury, organic solvents). The substance of abuse factors include the amount, frequency, and method of maternal use during pregnancy; distribution (concentration), metabolism, and excretion; lipid solubility; degree of ionization; molecular weight; concentration of free or nonprotein bound drug; and the pharmacologic effects of the particular substance of abuse (Gilbody, 1991; L. A. Pagliaro & A. M. Pagliaro, 1995a; A. M. Pagliaro & L. A. Pagliaro, 1996).

Of all the factors identified as being involved in producing a particular teratogenic effect, the most important factor is timing in regard to organogenesis (Figure 3-2). There is a critical period of greatest teratogenic susceptibility. Although this critical period of susceptibility varies slightly among different organ systems, teratogenic effects associated with major physical malformations are generally induced during the first trimester. It is important to note that teratogenic effects will not occur if exposure to a particular substance, which is a known teratogen, occurs after organogenesis is complete. For example, the maternal use of diazepam (Valium®) during pregnancy has been implicated in cleft palate anomaly. However, this teratogenic effect would not be observed if diazepam was used during pregnancy after fusion of the fetal palate. Thus, when evaluating the possible teratogenic potential of a particular substance of abuse, it is essential to identify if the substance of abuse, or another in the same class, has been implicated in producing a human teratogenic effect *and* the stage of embryo and fetal development at which time the exposure occurred.

☐ Maternal Substance Use and Teratogenesis

The potential teratogenic effects associated with the various substances of abuse are summarized in the following sections. The use of any substance of abuse during pregnancy always involves some degree of risk to the developing embryo or fetus. Therefore, regardless of how safe a substance of abuse may appear to be, it should *not* be used during pregnancy unless it is clearly indicated and its benefits outweigh its potential risks. Women who are pregnant or considering pregnancy should be advised to limit their use of the substances of abuse. Women who display problematic patterns of substance use (e.g., abuse or compulsive use) should be referred to treatment programs aimed at promoting resumed nonuse or, in the event that use has been discontinued, preventing relapsed use.

In this regard, it also is important to note that although not a direct teratogenic effect of substance use, mother-to-infant transmission of the HIV infection is a significant problem associated with intravenous and other substance use by pregnant women (Deren, Beardsley, Davis, & Tortu, 1993; Risk factors for . . . , 1992; Hoegerman, Wilson, Thurmond, & Schnoll, 1990; Lyman, 1993; Nwanyanwu, Chu, Green, Buehler, & Berkelman, 1993; Pagliaro & Pagliaro, 1993; VanDyke, 1991) (see Chapter 8, Women, Substance Use, HIV Infection, and AIDS). As noted by Gabiano et al. (1992): "Intra-

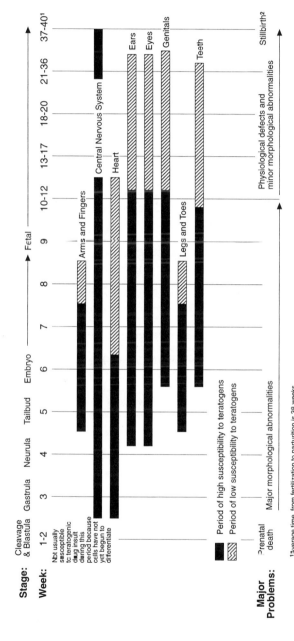

FIGURE 3–2. Organogenic variation in human teratogenic susceptibility.

[1]Average time from fertilization to parturition is 38 weeks.
[2]Drugs administered during this period may cause neonatal depression at birth (or other effects directly related to the pharmacological effect of the administered drug)

venous drug use was the most frequent maternal risk factor [for mother-to-child intrauterine transmission of HIV]" (p. 369). This risk underscores the increased need for: 1) prevention and treatment programs specifically tailored to meet the needs of women who are pregnant or thinking about becoming pregnant (see Chapter 11, Preventing and Treating Substance Use Disorders Among Women); and 2) early intervention for neonates and infants who have been prenatally exposed to the substances of abuse (Russell & Free, 1991).

Bays (1992) has developed a useful set of guidelines to assist in determining the need to test newborn infants' urine in order to identify maternal substance use during the antepartum period and consequent need for attention to the neonate (see Table 3-1).

TABLE 3-1. Criteria for neonatal urine tests*

The following criteria may be used to assist health and social care providers to determine the need to test a neonate's urine for substances of abuse possibly used by the mother during the antepartum period.

Mother who has a history of:
- No, infrequent (<5 visits), or late (after 28 weeks) prenatal care
- Undocumented prenatal care or care in clinics accessed in areas characterized by a high incidence of substance use
- Alcohol, amphetamine, cocaine, heroin, marijuana, or other substance use anytime during the antepartum period or physical evidence of substance use (e.g., needle marks; hepatitis)
- Previous birth of an infant exposed to substances of abuse prenatally
- Participation in a substance use treatment program
- Substance use in the home by family members or other people residing in the home
- Prostitution
- Multiple sexually transmitted diseases, including infection with HIV
- Multiple abortions and stillbirths, placental abruption, placenta previa, precipitous delivery, premature rupture of the membranes, or premature births
- Poor maternal weight gain

Neonate who is:
- microcephalic
- premature
- retarded
- small for gestational age

Other:
- Abnormal maternal or neonatal neurobehavioral activity (e.g., signs of intoxication or withdrawal)
- Abnormal neurobehavioral activity among other family members or friends (e.g., signs of intoxication or withdrawal)

Usually several criteria are present among neonates affected by maternal substance use. It is important that the mother is informed that a urine collection bag will be placed on the baby for a urine drug test to determine possible maternal substance use during the antenatal period. The primary care provider should discuss the reasons for this test with the mother. It is recommended that urine collection bags *not* be placed on neonates in the delivery room.

*Modified from Bays (1992, p. 486)

Central Nervous System Depressants

The central nervous system (CNS) depressants discussed in this section include the opiates and sedative-hypnotics. Although the CNS depressants have been associated with various levels of teratogenic risk, data accumulated over the last several decades only support a particularly strong relationship for the sedative-hypnotic, alcohol (L. A. Pagliaro & A. M. Pagliaro, 1995a; A. M. Pagliaro & L. A. Pagliaro, 1996; L. A. Pagliaro & A. M. Pagliaro, in press). For this reason, a more comprehensive discussion of alcohol has been included in this section.

Opiates Several cases have been reported implicating teratogenic insult with maternal opiate use during pregnancy. However, a review of this literature only provides weak support for teratogenic effects involving such opiates as codeine, heroin, meperidine (Demerol®), methadone, morphine, and pentazocine (Talwin®). Although not strongly implicated in regard to teratogenic insult, the use of these opiates near term may result in neonatal CNS depression, as indicated by decreased Apgar scores, and the neonatal opiate withdrawal syndrome, particularly when chronic high-doses have been used by the mother (L. A. Pagliaro & A. M. Pagliaro, 1995a, 1999b).

Convulsions during unmedicated opiate withdrawal occur most frequently among neonates exposed in utero to methadone. Whenever possible, women who use methadone, including those enrolled in methadone maintenance programs, should undergo detoxification before becoming pregnant. Methadone detoxification during the first and third trimesters has been associated with an increased incidence of spontaneous abortions and fetal distress, respectively. If methadone detoxification is to be implemented during pregnancy, it should be attempted between the 14th and 28th weeks of gestation with a slow tapering of the dosage. Intrauterine growth retardation may be noted, but appears to be related to confounding variables such as poor maternal nutrition and concurrent alcohol and nicotine use (L. A. Pagliaro & A. M. Pagliaro, 1995a; A. M. Pagliaro & L. A. Pagliaro, 1996; L. A. Pagliaro & A. M. Pagliaro, in press).

Sedative-Hypnotics The sedative-hypnotics include alcohol, barbiturates, benzodiazepines, and miscellaneous sedative-hypnotics (e.g., chloral hydrate [Noctec®]). A more comprehensive discussion of alcohol is included in this section because of the increased accumulation of data regarding its teratogenic effects and related sequelae among fetuses and neonates.[8]

Alcohol. Alcohol (ethanol; ethyl alcohol) is a known human teratogen. As such, it has the potential to affect all fetuses of mothers who consume it during their pregnancies (Day & Richardson, 1991; Larroque, 1992; Pietrantoni & Knuppel, 1991; Schenker, Becker, Randall, Phillips, Baskin, & Henderson, 1990). Once ingested and absorbed into the maternal bloodstream, alcohol readily crosses into the fetal circulation (L. A. Pagliaro & A. M. Pagliaro, 1995a). It also is found in significant levels in the amniotic fluid even after the maternal ingestion of a single moderate dose. Alcohol is eliminated from the amniotic fluid at a rate that is one-half the rate that it is eliminated from the maternal blood. Thus, it remains in the amniotic fluid and fetal circulation after it is no longer present in the mother's blood stream. The effects of alcohol on neuroendocrine function have been well documented (Mello, Mendelson, & Teoh, 1993) and may contribute mechanistically to the development of the fetal alcohol syndrome (FAS). As noted by Gabriel, Hofmann, Glavas, & Weinberg (1998): "Some of the effects of maternal alcohol consumption on fetal hormone systems may contribute to the adverse effects observed in children with fetal alcohol syndrome and related disorders" (p. 170).

Unfortunately, many women drink quantities of alcohol that are known to be harmful to their unborn babies (Cornelius, Richardson, Day, Cornelius, Geva, & Taylor, 1994; Substance Abuse, 1994). It is estimated that approximately 1 out of every 3 to 4 mothers expose their fetuses to the harmful effects of alcohol (A. M. Pagliaro & L. A. Pagliaro, 1996; L. A. Pagliaro & A. M. Pagliaro, in press). However, even if there is a lack of agreement regarding the exact percentage of mothers who use alcohol during pregnancy, there is consensus that the FAS is currently the leading cause of mental retardation and neurobehavioral deficits in North America and that it is totally preventable (L. A. Pagliaro & A. M. Pagliaro, 1995a; A. M. Pagliaro & L. A. Pagliaro, 1996; L. A. Pagliaro & A. M. Pagliaro, in press; Smith, 1997).[9]

Fetal Alcohol Syndrome. The harmful effects associated with the use of alcohol during pregnancy have been long recognized (L. A. Pagliaro & A. M. Pagliaro, 1995a). However, the specific physical, mental, and developmental characteristics associated with the FAS were not formally identified until the early 1970s (Lemoine, Harousseau, & Borteyru, 1968; Jones & Smith, 1973) (Table 3-2). Subsequently, clinicians and scientists have used this list of physical characteristics, particularly the associated craniofacial features (Figure 3-3), to assist them with the identification of affected infants and children. Although the characteristic features of the FAS vary among affected infants and children and can present difficulties in clinical identification (Little, Snell, &

TABLE 3-2. Abnormalities originally associated with FAS*

Category	Abnormality	Percentage of occurrence
Growth	Prenatal Growth Deficiency	100
Craniofacies	Short Palpebral Fissures	100
	Microcephaly	91
	Maxillary Hypoplasia	64
	Epicanthal Folds	36
	Micrognathia	27
	Cleft Palate	18
Development	Developmental Delay	100
	Postnatal Growth Deficiency	100
Limbs	Altered Palmar Crease Pattern	73
	Joint Anomalies	73
Heart	Cardiac Anomalies	70
Other	Fine-Motor Dysfunction	80
	Anomalous External Genitalia	36
	Capillary Hemangiomata	36

*This original list from Jones et al. (1977), has been expanded by several authors (e.g., American Academy of Pediatrics, 1993; L. A. Pagliaro & A. M. Pagliaro, 1995a; A. M. Pagliaro & L. A. Pagliaro, 1996) in order to account for the additional features (e.g., asymmetrical or low-set ears; flat or absent philtrum; hypoplastic, flat midface; short nose; and thin vermilion of the upper lip) commonly noted by other researchers (e.g., Clarren & Smith, 1978; Haddad & Messer, 1994).

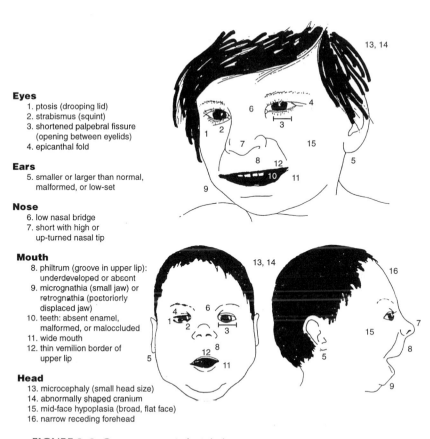

FIGURE 3-3. Common craniofacial characteristics associated with FAS.

Eyes
1. ptosis (drooping lid)
2. strabismus (squint)
3. shortened palpebral fissure (opening between eyelids)
4. epicanthal fold

Ears
5. smaller or larger than normal, malformed, or low-set

Nose
6. low nasal bridge
7. short with high or up-turned nasal tip

Mouth
8. philtrum (groove in upper lip): underdeveloped or absent
9. micrognathia (small jaw) or retrognathia (posteriorly displaced jaw)
10. teeth: absent enamel, malformed, or maloccluded
11. wide mouth
12. thin vermilion border of upper lip

Head
13. microcephaly (small head size)
14. abnormally shaped cranium
15. mid-face hypoplasia (broad, flat face)
16. narrow receding forehead

Rosenfeld, 1990), the consistent use of these characteristic features has been found to be generally reliable (Abel, Martier, Kruger, Ager, & Sokol, 1993).

In addition to the use of these characteristic features, a consensus case definition for FAS was established by the Fetal Alcohol Study Group of the Research Society on Alcoholism (L. A. Pagliaro & A. M. Pagliaro, 1995a; A. M. Pagliaro & L. A. Pagliaro, 1996; L. A. Pagliaro & A. M. Pagliaro, in press). This consensus case definition includes the following three major criteria:

1. prenatal and/or postnatal growth retardation (weight and/or length or height below the 10th percentile when corrected for gestational age);
2. central nervous system involvement (including neurological abnormality, developmental delay, behavioral dysfunction or deficit, intellectual impairment and/or structural abnormalities, such as microcephaly [head circumference below the third percentile] or brain malformations found on imaging studies or autopsy); and
3. a characteristic face qualitatively described as including short palpebral fissures, an elongated mid-face, a long and flattened philtrum, thin upper lip, and flattened maxilla.

The incidence of the FAS in North America varies among cultural, ethnic, and socioeconomic groups (Spagnolo, 1993) with the highest incidence reported among blacks and Native American Indians (Abel & Sokol, 1991; Burd & Moffatt, 1994; Duimstra et al., 1993; Fetal Alcohol Syndrome, 1991; Gordis & Alexander, 1992; May, 1991) (Table 3-3). The incidence increases directly in relation to the magnitude of alcohol use by women during pregnancy (Eliason & Williams, 1990). However, its actual incidence is difficult to specify for a number of reasons. These reasons include the unreliability of self-reports of maternal drinking (i.e., consistently biased underreporting); qualitative and quasi-experimental research methods (e.g., case report, retrospective studies); and possible confusion, or overlap, with Fetal Alcohol Effects (FAE, see discussion below) (Remkes, 1993; Wallace, 1991).

FAE and FAS. Fetal alcohol effects is a term that is used to identify neonates and children who exhibit fewer of the characteristics deemed necessary, by definition or convention, for the establishment of a conclusive diagnosis of the FAS (Caruso & Bensel, 1993; Ginsberg, Blacker, Abel, & Sokol, 1991; Smitherman, 1994). Other terminologies also have been suggested and have been used in the clinical literature (e.g., alcohol-related birth defects [ARBD] and alcohol-related neurodevelopmental disorder [ARND] [Gabriel et al., 1998; Harris, Osborn, Weinberg, Loock, & Junaid, 1993; Jacobson, Jacobson, Sokol, Martier, Ager, & Kaplan-Estrin, 1993]). We strongly disagree with the use of these terminologies and have argued that the infants and children who display more specifically clustered or fewer of the classic characteristics of the FAS be diagnosed more appropriately as having a less severe form of FAS and not a different syndrome (L. A. Pagliaro & A. M. Pagliaro, 1995a; A. M. Pagliaro & L. A. Pagliaro, 1996).[10]

We continue to argue that this approach to diagnosing the FAS would: 1) more accurately reflect the anticipated normal distribution of the effects of the FAS among affected infants and children in the general population or its subpopulations; 2) indicate more completely the extent of the FAS in the general population; 3) represent more fully the nature of the FAS; 4) clearly identify that even modest social drinking during

TABLE 3-3. Reported incidence of FAS

Incidence*	Country (group)	Reference
1 : 8	Canada (Native American Indians)	Robinson et al., 1987
1 : 20–40	Canada (Native American Indians)	Asante & Nelms-Matzke, 1985
1 : 33–200	U.S.A. (Native American Indians)	May 1991
1 : 125–250	U.S.A. (Native American Indians)	Duimstra et al., 1993
1 : 333–500	Europe (mixed)	Hill et al., 1989
1 : 500	World Wide (mixed)	Abel & Sokol, 1987
1 : 500–1000	Western World (mixed)	Clarren & Smith, 1978
1 : 700	U.S.A. (mixed)	Bertucci & Krafchik, 1994
1 : 1000	U.S.A. (mixed)	Rosett et al., 1983
1 : 1500–3000	Western World (mixed)	Abel & Sokol, 1991
1 : 3000	U.S.A. (mixed)	Shoemaker, 1993

*per number of live births

pregnancy places the exposed fetus at significant risk for the FAS; 5) reflect the relationship of other factors in regard to the severity of the teratogenic effects associated with maternal alcohol use (Figure 3-1); and 6) encourage the development of more rational and comprehensive prevention strategies and treatment programs aimed at promoting the development of infants and children affected by maternal alcohol use.

Long-Term Sequelae of the FAS. The effects associated with the FAS do not end in infancy, but persist into childhood, adolescence, and, unfortunately, throughout adulthood (Dorris, 1990; A. M. Pagliaro & L. A. Pagliaro, 1996; Smitherman, 1994; Spohr, Wilms, & Steinhausen, 1993). "The growth and neurological disabilities associated with alcohol consumption in pregnancy persist even when the child grows up in a good home" (Karp, Qazi, Hittleman, & Chabrier, 1993). The life-long effects of FAS on human growth and development are troubling and should not be ignored. In this regard, we concur with Streissguth, Randels, and Smith (1992) that, for infants and children affected with the FAS and their parents and caregivers, more realistic expectations for performance during childhood and adolescence may result in the availability of more appropriate services, less frustration, and improved behavioral outcomes in later adolescence and adulthood.

Recommendations. Alcohol is a known human teratogen that can cause significant, life-long deficits in relation to physical growth, cognitive functioning, psychomotor skills, and psychological health. Although some authors (e.g., Knupfer, 1991; Koren, 1991; Walpole, Zubrick, Pontré, & Lawrence, 1991) disagree, we concur with the recommendation made by the National Institute of Child Health and Human Development, the American Academy of Pediatrics, and the U.S. Surgeon General (American Academy, 1993; Schydlower & Perrin, 1993), and others (e.g., Caruso & Bensel, 1993; Olson, Sampson, Barr, Steissguth, & Bookstein, 1992; Olson, 1994; Streissguth, Barr, Olson, Sampson, Bookstein, & Burgess, 1994), that women who are pregnant or planning to become pregnant totally abstain from alcohol use. This recommendation is based on the observations that 1) no safe level of alcohol use has been demonstrated; and 2) there is no known cure for the FAS. As noted by Karp, Qazi, Hittleman, & Chabrier (1993), the FAS is not a treatable disease in the literal sense. In this regard, it is essential that prevention and treatment programs be developed to assist women who are, or who may become, pregnant to abstain from alcohol use. Specifically, attention must be given to women for whom abstinence may be difficult to achieve or maintain (i.e., women who compulsively use alcohol).

Barbiturates The barbiturates discussed in this section include mephobarbital [Mebaral®], pentobarbital [Nembutal®], phenobarbital [Luminal®], and secobarbital [Seconal®]. Although the use of the barbiturates has decreased dramatically over the past three decades as a result of the synthesis and use of the benzodiazepines, they are still generally available and may be used therapeutically for the treatment of seizure disorders among women who are unresponsive to other anticonvulsant therapy. The use of the barbiturates during pregnancy has been generally associated with a number of teratogenic effects. However, confounding variables, particularly maternal epilepsy, have not yet been completely ruled out as principal or cofactors for teratogenic risk. The use of the barbiturates near term, particularly chronic, high doses, may result in neonatal respiratory depression and the barbiturate withdrawal syndrome (L. A. Pagliaro & A. M. Pagliaro, 1998; 1999b).

Benzodiazepines The benzodiazepines include chlordiazepoxide [Librium®], diazepam [Valium®], lorazepam, nitrazepam, and oxazepam [Serax®]. The use of these substances of abuse during pregnancy has been associated with various degrees of teratogenic effects, particularly cleft lip and palate. However, data are conflicting and heavy benzodiazepine use in this context has been generally associated with multiple exposure to alcohol and other substances (Bergman, Rosa, Baum, Wiholm, & Faich, 1992; DuPont & Saylor, 1992). Overall, the use of benzodiazepines during pregnancy appears to have a low teratogenic risk (L. A. Pagliaro & A. M. Pagliaro, 1995a; A. M. Pagliaro & L. A. Pagliaro, 1996; L. A. Pagliaro & A. M. Pagliaro, in press). Maternal use of the benzodiazepines near term has resulted in lethargy, poor muscle tone, and respiratory depression among neonates. Fortunately, these effects are generally fully reversible with proper recognition and care (Chesley, Lumpkin, Schatzki, Galpern, Greenblatt, Shader, & Miller, 1991; Sanchis, Rosique, & Catala, 1991).

Volatile Solvents and Inhalants Although volatile solvents and inhalants (e.g., gasoline, glue) are not commonly used by pregnant women, their potential teratogenic effects should be considered. Only four studies were found in a review of the published literature. One report (Wilkins-Haug & Gabow, 1991) contained data on 30 pregnancies in ten women with chronic glue- and paint-sniffing abuse and another (Arnold, Kirby, Langendoerfer, & Wilkins-Haug, 1994) reviewed the case records of 35 deliveries with antenatal exposure to toluene (a volatile solvent found in many different products, including glues and spray paint). Based on these studies, the teratogenic effects possibly related to the use of these volatile solvents and inhalants include: preterm delivery; neonatal electrolyte imbalances (i.e., hypobicarbonatemia, hypokalemia); low birth weight; microcephaly; and postnatal growth retardation.

Toluene embryopathy associated with maternal toluene use was first described among five children by Hersh in 1989. The reported embryopathy, which has since been supported by Arnold, Kirby, Langendoerfer, and Wilkins-Haug (1994) and Pearson, Hoyme, Seaver, and Rimsza (1994), includes growth retardation, developmental delays, and minor craniofacial anomalies (e.g., short palpebral fissures, flat [wide] nasal bridge, deficient philtrum, and micrognathia). These teratogenic features are extremely similar to those associated with the FAS. This similarity of features may be due to the pharmacologic similarity between alcohol and the volatile solvents and inhalants or to the mother's possible concomitant use of alcohol. Pearson, Hoyme, Seaver, and Rimsza (1994) have proposed "a common mechanism of craniofacial teratogenesis for toluene and alcohol, namely a deficiency of craniofacial neuroepithelium and mesodermal components due to increased embryonic cell death" (p. 211). More data are needed.

Central Nervous System Stimulants

The central nervous system stimulants discussed in this section include caffeine, cocaine, dextroamphetamine [Dexedrine®], methylphenidate [Ritalin®], and nicotine (tobacco smoking). Research results are mixed in regard to the teratogenic effects associated with this group of substances of abuse, particularly dextroamphetamine and methylphenidate. These substances of abuse and caffeine, cocaine, and nicotine, because of their widespread use, are discussed separately in the following sections.

Caffeine Caffeine, in the form of coffee, tea, and other beverages (e.g., caffeinated soft drinks), is probably consumed to a greater extent by pregnant women than any other substance of abuse, including alcohol. Although research has not been as prolific as that for alcohol, some studies have associated caffeine consumption with birth defects. The consumption of eight or more cups of coffee per day was related to fetal limb defects in three case reports, but more recent studies have shown that the only teratogenic effect associated with maternal caffeine use during pregnancy is reduced birth weight (Olsen, Overvad, & Frische, 1991; L. A. Pagliaro & A. M. Pagliaro, 1995a; A. M. Pagliaro & L. A. Pagliaro, 1996; L. A. Pagliaro & A. M. Pagliaro, in press). This effect was associated with the consumption of three or more cups of coffee per day and appears to be most significant among women who smoke (i.e., as a likely cofactor). However, a significant correlation between increased caffeine consumption during pregnancy and fetal loss also has been reported (Infante-Rivard, Fernandez, Gauthier, David, & Rivard, 1993). Although these data would generally support the relative safety of the use of caffeine during pregnancy, pregnant women should be encouraged to minimize their caffeine use, particularly if they smoke tobacco cigarettes. Tobacco smoking, which is significantly correlated with coffee consumption, is an obvious confounding factor in the interpretation of data supporting the possible teratogenic effects of caffeine. (See also the section, Nicotine: Tobacco Smoking)

Cocaine

> Cocaine's $pK_{[a]}$ is alkaline. Thus the drug would tend to accumulate in the ionized form on the side of a membrane where protons abound. Because fetal pH is normally lower than maternal, and is even lower during asphyxial episodes, cocaine can accumulate in the fetus. Therefore, at equilibrium fetal tissue levels may exceed maternal concentrations. Demethylation, a hepatic enzyme activity, may also be developmentally reduced, resulting in prolonged fetal exposure. (Scanlon, 1991, pp. 89–90)

Cocaine use during pregnancy, in injectable, nasal insufflation, and inhalation (crack) forms, increased significantly during the last two decades and continues to be, after marijuana, the most commonly used *illicit* substance of abuse among pregnant women, particularly in North American inner cities (Das, 1994; Forman, Klein, Meta, Barks, Greenwald, & Koren, 1993; Hume, Gingras, Martin, Hertzberg, O'Donnell, & Killam, 1994; Volpe, 1992).

> The typical cocaine user abuses cocaine repeatedly prior to conception, continues to use the drug repeatedly throughout pregnancy, and often combines it with other drugs. (Plessinger & Woods, 1991, p. 112)

Cocaine use during pregnancy has been associated with intrauterine death (including spontaneous abortions); low birth weight; preterm delivery; neonatal seizures; neonatal tachycardia; intrauterine growth retardation; hypoxemia; a variety of fetal physical anomalies, particularly affecting the ocular and urogenital systems; and limb reduction defects (Bandstra & Burkett, 1991; Brouhard, 1994; Calhoun & Watson, 1991; Chasnoff, 1992; Hannig & Phillips, 1991; Hume, Gingras, Martin, Hertzberg, O'Donnell, & Killam, 1994; Nucci & Brancato, 1994; Offidani et al., 1995; Plessinger & Woods, 1991; Scanlon, 1991; Sheinbaum & Badell, 1992; Singer, Arendt, Song, Warshawsky, & Kliegman 1994; Stafford, Rosen, Zaider, & Merriam, 1994; Van den Anker & Sauer, 1992; Zimmerman, 1991).

Autopsies of fetuses exposed to cocaine in utero often reveal cerebral hemorrhages (Gieron-Korthals, Helal, & Martinez, 1994; Kapur, Cheng, & Shephard, 1991) presumably due to a rapid and significant rise in systemic and cerebral blood pressure and hyperthermia (Jones, 1991). However, some researchers have attributed these effects

TABLE 3-4. Obstetrical complications noted among pregnant women who use cocaine*

- Abortion
- Abruptio placentae
- Breech presentation
- Previous Cesarean section
- Chorioamnionitis
- Eclampsia
- Gestational diabetes
- Intrauterine death
- Intrauterine growth retardation
- Placental insufficiency
- Post-partum hemorrhage
- Pre-eclampsia
- Preterm labor
- Premature rupture of membranes
- Septic thrombophlebitis

*Modified from Lesar, 1992, p. 38.

to confounding factors associated with maternal cocaine use (e.g., poor nutrition; inadequate prenatal care) (Church, 1993; Hutchings, 1993; Koren, 1993; Neuspiel, 1992; Racine, Joyce, & Anderson, 1993; Snodgrass, 1994). (See Table 3-4 for a list of obstetrical complications noted among pregnant women who use cocaine).

There also appears to be a significantly higher incidence of behavioral and learning disorders (e.g., attention-deficit/hyperactivity disorder; delays in receptive and expressive language skills) among preschoolers and school-aged children exposed to cocaine in utero (Jones, 1991; Pagliaro, 1992b; Rivers & Hedrick, 1992; Van Dyke & Fox, 1990). However, the teratogenic effects associated with the maternal use of cocaine during pregnancy remain inconclusive because of the difficulties associated with interpreting and evaluating research data. For example, the retrospective case report methodology generally used has several inherent limitations, including the possible inaccuracy of reported information. These limitations make definitive conclusions highly speculative (Dow-Edwards, 1991, 1993; Frank & Zuckerman, 1993; Hume, Gingras, Martin, Hertzberg, O'Donnell, & Killam, 1994; Konkol, 1994; Neuspiel, 1993; Slutsker, 1992; Spear, 1993).

In addition, women who use cocaine also commonly use alcohol, a known teratogen, to come down from a cocaine high. This additional risk factor and similar risk factors, further confound the interpretation of data (Rizk, Atterbury, & Groome, 1996; Snodgrass, 1994). In addition, residual amounts of the organic solvents (e.g., benzene) that are used in the extraction of cocaine from *Erythroxylon coca* leaves are commonly found in cocaine street samples. These organic solvents may contribute to the teratogenic effects associated with maternal cocaine use, particularly neuroteratogenic effects (Scanlon, 1991).

Thus, a general consensus seems to be that the use of high doses of cocaine (i.e., intravenous and smokable crack or "rock" forms of cocaine usage) probably has a significant, but low, potential for inducing teratogenic effects (Coles, 1993; Koren, Gladstone, Robeson, & Robieux, 1992; Martin, Khoury, Cordero, & Waters, 1992; Martin & Khoury, 1992). In addition, when used by the mother near term, the neonate may experience CNS excitation with insomnia, irritability, and poor feeding response. However, as noted by Plessinger and Woods (1993), "a well-defined 'fetal cocaine syndrome' does not exist" (p. 275).

Dextroamphetamine (Dexedrine®) Dextroamphetamine (i.e., crystal meth), used intravenously, is receiving renewed interest among young women. It also has been commonly prescribed for women as a means for weight control. Although data are contradictory regarding the teratogenic effects of dextroamphetamine exposure in utero, it appears that there is a moderate risk for human teratogenesis. Various case reports (e.g., Tsai, Lee, Chao, & Chai, 1993) have suggested that the maternal use of dextroamphetamine during the first trimester of pregnancy is associated with abnormal brain development, biliary atresia, cleft lip and palate, congenital heart disease, and prematurity among neonates, who also may be small for their gestational age. However, a prospective study found no increase in fetal malformations. More data are needed. During the interim, it appears prudent to advise women *not* to use dextroamphetamine during pregnancy (L. A. Pagliaro & A. M. Pagliaro, 1995a; A. M. Pagliaro & L. A. Pagliaro, 1996; L. A. Pagliaro & A. M. Pagliaro, in press).

Methylphenidate (Ritalin®) No teratogenic effects have been reported in regard to the maternal use during pregnancy of methylphenidate, a substance of abuse commonly prescribed for children and adolescents diagnosed with A-D/HD. However, as A-D/HD is increasingly being conceptualized and, in many cases, treated as a life-long disorder, increasing numbers of young women are being prescribed and continue to use methylphenidate during their childbearing years. Some women also may use methylphenidate (Ritalin®) in conjunction with pentazocine (Talwin®) as a "poor woman's speedball." However, only one study, which included 11 neonates exposed prenatally to methylphenidate, could be found in the published literature. More data are needed.

Nicotine: Tobacco Smoking The modal reported rate of tobacco use among pregnant women appears to be approximately 35% (Gupton, Thompson, Arnason, Dalke, & Ashcroft, 1995; Haug, Aaro, & Fuelli, 1992), although significant variation is noted among certain ethnic groups, geographic regions, and races (Castro et al., 1993; L. A. Pagliaro & A. M. Pagliaro, 1995a; A. M. Pagliaro & L. A. Pagliaro, 1996; L. A. Pagliaro & A. M. Pagliaro, in press). Unfortunately, tobacco smoking during pregnancy is teratogenic to the fetus. There also is an inverse relationship between the number of cigarettes smoked per day and the birth weight of neonates. Neonates born to mothers who smoke weigh an average of 200 grams[11] (range: 100 to 400 grams) less than neonates born to mothers who did not smoke. They also have a shorter body length (Nash & Persaud, 1988; Yawn, Thompson, Lupo, Googins, & Yawn, 1994). Fortunately, a period of accelerated growth occurs during the first year of life and, generally, no differences in body weight or length are observed among these infants at one year of age. Women who cease smoking during the first trimester of their pregnancy generally have infants of normal size (L. A. Pagliaro & A. M. Pagliaro, 1995a; A. M. Pagliaro & L. A. Pagliaro, 1996; L. A. Pagliaro & A. M. Pagliaro, in press).

Women who continue to smoke during pregnancy also have higher rates of spontaneous abortions, abruptio placentae, placenta previa, uterine bleeding, and perinatal mortality rates (DiFranza & Lew, 1995; Gupton, Thompson, Arnason, Dalke, &

Ashcroft, 1995; Handler, Mason, Rosenberg, & Davis, 1994). In addition, mothers who smoke also may have a higher fetal malformation rate (Seidman, Ever-Hadani, & Gale, 1990). The risk for the sudden infant death syndrome (SIDS) is estimated to be 4.4 times higher for infants born to mothers who smoke during pregnancy than for infants born to mothers who do not smoke during pregnancy and may account for over 2,000 SIDS deaths annually (DiFranza & Lew, 1995). Some studies (e.g., Olds, Henderson, & Tatelbaum, 1994) suggest that maternal smoking may cause among their children a neurodevelopmental impairment resulting in a reduction in IQ scores by 4 to 8 points. Another study (Milberger, Biederman, Faraone, Chen, & Jones, 1996) suggests that maternal smoking during pregnancy may be a risk factor for the development of A-D/HD. However, as with other substances of abuse, the teratogenic effects of heavy tobacco smoking are confounded by the concurrent use of alcohol (see discussion of Alcohol earlier in this chapter). Based on the available data, and as a precaution, women should be advised *not* to smoke during pregnancy.[12,13]

Psychedelics

The psychedelics comprise a variety of substances of abuse, which are generally used for their hallucinatory and consciousness expanding effects. No studies were found that reported teratogenic effects associated with the maternal use of psilocybin (magic mushrooms) or peyote (mescaline) during pregnancy. Several publications were found for lysergic acid diethylamide (LSD), tetrahydrocannabinol (THC), and phencyclidine (PCP). For example, Fried and Watkinson (1990) noted that, "at 48 months [of age], significantly lower scores in verbal and memory domains [among children] were associated with maternal marijuana use" (p. 49). However, the use of LSD, THC, and PCP during pregnancy has not been clearly and consistently associated with major physical or developmental teratogenic effects in humans (Day et al., 1991; L. A. Pagliaro 1991a; Tabor, Smith-Wallace, & Yonekura, 1990). Given the widespread use of the psychedelics by women of childbearing age and the relative paucity of reported teratogenic effects, the teratogenic potential of the psychedelics, if it does exist, appears to be low (L. A. Pagliaro & A. M. Pagliaro, 1995a; A. M. Pagliaro & L. A. Pagliaro, 1996; L. A. Pagliaro & A. M. Pagliaro, in press). More data are needed.

☐ Substance Use and Breast Feeding

Over half of all new mothers in North America breast feed their infants.[14] Although breast milk is generally considered to be the best form of infant nutrition for the first months of life and is important for psychological development, breast feeding can expose neonates and infants to many drugs and chemicals, including virtually all of the substances of abuse.[15] Various substances of abuse are excreted in breast milk because of their basic pharmacology. In order to cross the blood-brain barrier and elicit their primary psychotropic effects, the substances of abuse must be lipid soluble, a property that also assures that they are significantly excreted in human breast milk. In fact, for some substances of abuse (e.g., nicotine), concentrations in breast milk can be higher than in maternal serum (see Table 3-5). As identified in Table 3-5, chronic moderate to high maternal use of any of the substances of abuse places breast-fed neonates and infants at risk for direct pharmacologic effects, including addiction.

When mothers require pharmacotherapy with a drug that is a substance of abuse (e.g., opiate analgesic) for acute, short-term use (e.g., a few days), then the lowest effective dose should be prescribed for use as long before breast feeding as possible, and the breast fed neonate or infant should be carefully monitored for untoward effects. When mothers require pharmacotherapy (particularly at moderate or high dosages) for chronic, long-term use (e.g., a few weeks), then breast feeding probably should be discontinued indefinitely or at least until the pharmacotherapy is no longer needed (L. A. Pagliaro & A. M. Pagliaro, 1999b). For mothers who use various substances of abuse, particularly those who have patterns of abuse or compulsive use (see Chapter 1, An Overview of Substance Use Among Women, for a brief review), it is recommended that breast feeding be discontinued. Appropriate treatment or referral services should be implemented for these mothers and their neonates and infants, as needed (see Chapter 11, Preventing and Treating Substance Use Disorders Among Women).

☐ Conclusion

Teratogenesis is a complex process that is influenced by many factors including maternal, placental, fetal, environmental, and substance of abuse factors, particularly the pharmacology of a particular substance of abuse. To minimize the risk for and incidence of substance-induced teratogenesis, it is necessary to recognize that all substances of abuse have the potential to cause teratogenic effects under certain conditions. Thus, as a precaution, women who are pregnant, or women who are thinking about becoming pregnant, should be encouraged, whenever possible, to abstain from, or to minimize, their use of the various substances of abuse. In particular, they should be advised to avoid alcohol because of the strong evidence associating its use with significant teratogenic effects (i.e., FAS) (Pagliaro, 1991; L. A. Pagliaro & A. M. Pagliaro, 1995a; A. M. Pagliaro & L. A. Pagliaro, 1996; L. A. Pagliaro & A. M. Pagliaro, in press). It also is important to note that when substances of abuse are used during pregnancy, their respective withdrawal syndromes may be expected among neonates. In addition, most of the substances of abuse, when used by the mother near term, can cause expected pharmacologic effects and toxicities among neonates. Fortunately, associated withdrawal syndromes and other pharmacologically-related effects are generally reversible with proper recognition and treatment.

Health and social care professionals who are concerned about the health of women and their neonates, infants, and children should be aware of the teratogenic effects associated with the maternal use of the substances of abuse during pregnancy. Further research examining the relationship between substance use by pregnant women and its associated teratogenic effects is needed. There is extensive documentation relating maternal alcohol and tobacco use to serious risk for teratogenesis. However, a high percentage of pregnant women continue to unnecessarily expose themselves and their unborn babies to the harmful effects associated with these substances of abuse. In this regard, women should be advised regarding these possible harmful effects, including possible long-term effects on their infants and children (e.g., FAS). In addition, greater attention needs to be given to the development and implementation of effective psychotherapeutic interventions designed to prevent or minimize substance use among women of child bearing age (see Chapter 11, Preventing and Treating Substance Use Disorders Among Women). Attention to relapse prevention also is a major challenge.

(text continues on page 84)

TABLE 3-5. Substances of abuse excreted in human breast milk[a]

Substance of Abuse	Approximate Average Concentration in Breast Milk[b]	Effect Upon Breast-Fed Neonate/Infant
Alcohol (e.g., beer, wine, distilled liquor)	N/A	Not significant at low to moderate levels of maternal use.[c] May inhibit milk ejection and decrease neonatal milk consumption with higher levels of maternal use because of effects on taste and amount ingested.
Amphetamines (e.g., dextroamphetamine)	100 µg/ml	Amphetamines are secreted in human breast milk. However, there is a paucity of reported data regarding the effects on breast-fed neonates and infants. Thus, the effects upon nursing neonates and infants are unknown.
Barbiturates (e.g., pentobarbital, phenobarbital)	variable and depends upon specific barbiturate	May cause sedation among breast-fed neonates and infants. Breast feeding over extended periods of time by women who are using moderate to high doses of the barbiturates may result in addiction among their nursing neonates and infants. The barbiturate withdrawal syndrome may be observed among neonates and infants when breast feeding or maternal use is discontinued.
Benzodiazepines (e.g., alprazolam, clonazepam, diazepam)	variable and depends upon specific benzodiazepine; appears to be less significant with lorazepam or oxazepam use	Possible accumulation of benzodiazepine and its metabolites may occur among breast-fed neonates due to immature hepatic function (i.e., inability to metabolize the benzodiazepines) particularly during the first week of life. Infants of mothers who use moderate to high doses of the benzodiazepines may develop addiction and display the benzodiazepine withdrawal syndrome (e.g., crying, irritability) when breast feeding or maternal benzodiazepine use is discontinued.
Caffeine	5 µg/ml	Not significant at low to moderate levels of maternal use. May cause CNS excitation (e.g., irritability) among neonates and infants whose mothers have high levels of use. Effects may be more significant among premature neonates.
Chloral hydrate	100 µg/ml (i.e., ≥50% of maternal blood concentration)	Both chloral hydrate and its active metabolite are detectable in breast milk for up to 24 hours following last maternal use. May cause sedation among breast-fed neonates and infants.

Drug	Concentration	Effects
Cocaine	N/A	Cocaine is detectable in breast milk for up to 36 hours after maternal use. May cause CNS excitation (e.g., irritability) among neonates and infants whose mothers have high levels of use. Effects may be more significant among premature neonates.
Nicotine	50 ng/ml	Nicotine and cotinine (a metabolite) are found in higher concentrations in breast milk than in maternal serum. Symptoms of CNS excitation (e.g., increased heart rate, restlessness) may be noted among neonates and infants of mothers who use nicotine. A nicotine withdrawal syndrome may occur when breast feeding or maternal use of nicotine is discontinued.
Opiates (e.g., codeine, heroin, meperidine, morphine, oxycodone)	variable and depends upon specific opiate	All of the opiates are excreted in human breast milk. Accumulation can occur over several days and cause sedation and respiratory depression among neonates and infants of mothers who use opiates. In addition, an opiate withdrawal syndrome may occur when breast feeding or maternal opiate use is discontinued.
Tetrahydrocannabinol (THC) (e.g., hashish, hashish oil, marijuana)	200 ng/ml	Maternal THC use may cause drowsiness among breast-fed neonates and infants. However, because of the paucity of reported data, other effects upon neonates and infants are largely unknown.

[a]Adapted from: O'Mara, N.B., & Nahata, M.C. (1995). Drugs excreted in human breast milk. In L. A. Pagliaro & A. M. Pagliaro (Eds.), *Problems in pediatric drug therapy* (3rd ed., pp. 247–335). Hamilton, IL: Drug Intelligence

[b]Note that neonates who are exclusively fed breast milk, consume, on average, approximately 150 ml of breast milk per kg of body weight per day.

[c]However, as noted by Heil and Subramanian (1998): "Chronic alcohol consumption also may affect the quantity as well as quality of various milk constituents that are necessary to ensure optimal nourishment of the offspring" (p. 183).

Although not widely researched, clinical experience and the available data suggest that exposure to substances of abuse is significant among breast-fed neonates and infants. An awareness and recognition of this source of exposure will enable adults, including mothers and health and social care professionals, to: 1) decrease the exposure of neonates, infants, and children to substances of abuse; and, 2) recognize and appropriately deal with the consequences of maternal substance use when related behavior is observed among exposed neonates, infants, and children.

☐ Notes

1. Note that we have deliberately chosen the term *substance use* and not *substance abuse* because the use of substances of abuse (e.g., alcohol) during pregnancy at levels or in patterns that would not constitute abuse (i.e., harm) for the mother may result in devastating effects upon her fetus, neonate, or infant (see related discussion later in this chapter).
2. Thalidomide, although withdrawn from the market in North America, continued to be used in many other parts of the world (e.g., Africa and South America) (Teixeira et al., 1994). Amidst some degree of controversy, it was reapproved for use in North America in 1998 for the treatment of several medical disorders, including leprosy (Cutler, 1994).
3. Although not cited in the original article, the source for this research appears to be Gittler and McPherson (1990). A similar prevalence rate (i.e., 11.35%) also has been noted by Vega (1992) in a statewide study in California. Note that these figures apply to illicit substance use only and therefore do not include such substances as alcohol, caffeine, nicotine, prescription sedative-hypnotics, etc.
4. In this regard, it is important to note that: "the addictive properties of psychoactive drugs lead individuals to increase usage, both frequency and dose, which leads to varying degrees of toxicity to themselves and, if pregnant, their offspring" (Zimmerman, 1991, p. 541).
5. Other factors may also play a significant role. For example, among a large statewide sample of both pregnant and nonpregnant women from Alabama, positive urine screens for illicit substances of abuse varied according to obstetrical history. These data indicated a linear increase in the percentage of "positive urines" in direct correlation with the number of reported abortions and with the number of reported premature births (Pegues, Engelgau, & Woernle, 1994).
6. It should be noted that maternal substance use raises a potential plethora of legal and ethical issues (Brooks, Zuckerman, Bamforth, Cole, & Kaplan-Sanoff, 1994; Farr, 1995; Garcia, 1993; Garrity-Rokous, 1994; Goldsmith, 1990; Horowitz, 1990; Humphries, 1999; Madden, 1993; Millard, 1996; Murray, 1991; Shogren, 1996; Siegel, 1994; Smucker, 1996; Whitmire, 1994a; 1994b; Young, 1994). As noted by Garcia (1993), "some policies have pitted mothers against their fetuses and children . . . new paradigms [are required] to minimize conflict and to achieve just and therapeutic balances between the rights and needs of those involved" (p. 1311). We will not attempt to address or resolve these issues here. Our focus, however, will be on optimizing the health and well-being of pregnant women and their developing fetuses and neonates.
7. This information also is important in relation to perinatal health. For example,

   > For the period 1978–1984, the infant mortality rate for infants whose mothers were substance users (as indicated on birth certificates) was about three times higher than the citywide rate (46.7/1,000 vs 15.5/1,000 live births). The percentage of newborns of low birth weight (under 2,500 grams or less than 5½ lb) born to these women was more than three times the citywide rate (32.8/1,000 vs 9.6/1,000 live births). Recent information indicates that the infant mortality rate may be increasing in New York City, after more than a decade of decline, due to births to mothers who are abusing cocaine or who have AIDS. (Deren, Frank, & Schmeidler, 1990, p. 179)

In addition, it has been found that women who use substances of abuse while pregnant are significantly more likely to neglect, physically abuse, or sexually abuse their newborns and infants (see Chapter 7, Women as Perpetrators of Substance Use Related Violence). Unfortunately, it appears that "the incidence and prevalence of perinatal drug exposure is substantial and rising" (Cole, Jones, & Sadofsky, 1990, p. 5).

8. For information regarding effects among children and adolescents, the reader is referred to the text, *Substance use among children and adolescents: Its nature, extent, and effects from conception to adulthood* (A. M. Pagliaro & L. A. Pagliaro, 1996).

9. Michael Dorris, the author of *The broken cord: A family's ongoing struggle with fetal alcohol syndrome*, shared the following description of his adopted son, Adam, who suffers from FAS:

> Adam has a lot of chronic ailments—seizures, poor eyesight and hearing, curvature of the spine, and bad coordination to name a few. He also has borderline mental retardation. Even as an adult with years of special education behind him, he cannot make change for a dollar, tell time, understand the plot of a TV movie, or live independently.
>
> Adam was an innocent victim before he ever drew a breath. He will not get better, and his security will forever hinge upon the kindness and professional care of others. He will never understand precisely what he's missing and, so, is not consciously unhappy or dissatisfied, but he is often lonely and uncomfortable, always confused, rarely charming. He does not possess the drive and motivation of the mentally handicapped people romanticized on *L.A. Law* and *Life Goes On*. He is completely without malice or guile, but he also lacks foresight and common sense. (p. 238)

10. Our rationale for this approach is demonstrated in the numerous occasions in which we have been asked to consult on a particular case in which the patient may display several typical physical symptoms (e.g., altered palmar crease pattern, flat philtrum) and related psychological sequelae (e.g., A-D/HD; conduct or antisocial personality disorder; learning disability), but possesses an IQ in the normal range (e.g., 100). In the presence of sufficient symptoms to confirm a diagnosis of FAS, we do not allow a "normal" IQ to dissuade our diagnosis. Instead, we explain that the maternal alcohol consumption during pregnancy and resultant FAS most likely significantly reduced the individual's IQ. However, this is not readily apparent in the case under discussion because the reduction was not (as is generally expected by most clinicians—and parents) from the normal range to subnormal range, but from *above normal* range to normal range (i.e., if alcohol had not been consumed during pregnancy resulting in FAS, the patient's IQ would not have been 100, but would have been 120, or perhaps higher) (Pagliaro & Pagliaro, clinical patient file notes).

11. There are 454 grams in 1 pound.

12. In relation to smoking cessation, the use of nicotine gums, when combined with cognitive behavioral programs, has demonstrated an enhanced effect. Oncken et al. (1996) studied the short-term use of nicotine gum among pregnant smokers and found that: 1) it enhanced smoking cessation; 2) it delivered less nicotine to the pregnant women than did their usual cigarette smoking; and, 3) it was not associated with any significant differences in either fetal or maternal hemodynamic parameters (in comparison to those pregnant women who continued to smoke).

13. A systematic review of 40 different smoking cessation trials implemented with pregnant women from 1975 to 1997 found a small, but significant increase in smoking cessation and a corresponding small, but significant increase in mean birth weight (Lumley, Oliver, & Waters, 1998). This unimpressive finding tends to be consistent with findings from other substance use treatment studies (i.e., that the best form of treatment is *prevention*).

14. Note that this number can range from 20% to 60% depending upon custom and attitudes toward breast feeding in various reporting jurisdictions (Federal, 1996).

15. In addition, a European Collaborative Study, Newell et al. (1992) noted "that mothers with established infection can transmit HIV infection through breast milk" (p. 1007). They also reported in their analysis a two-fold increase in risk of HIV infection among breast-fed infants.

    Because intravenous drug use is a major route of transmission of HIV to women, women, who are (or were) intravenous drug users, should be advised to generally refrain from breast feeding their neonates and infants until their status as HIV-negative is confirmed. (See earlier discussion regarding intravenous drug use and risk for HIV infection).

CHAPTER 4

Effects of Maternal Substance Use on Mothering and Child Rearing

If, as noted by the authors of this text, substance abuse kills the heart and murders the soul, it is no more apparent than in the context of the effects of substance use upon mothering and child rearing. As noted in Chapter 2, Explaining Substance Use Among Women, citing the early classic study of female alcoholics by Wall (1937), "Their attitude toward their children was either one of indifference or neglect. In most instances the children were unwanted..." (p. 952).

Wall's observations are distressing, but not unexpected given the nature of substance abuse. As noted more recently by a group of researchers, "Addiction prevents a mother from responding to her infant's needs; her primary focus is on her drug of choice, not on her child" (Brooks, Zuckerman, Bamforth, Cole, & Kaplan-Sanoff, 1994, p. 204).

A similar theme is noted by Woodhouse (1992) in an excerpt from a life history that she conducted with Mary Ann, a 28-year-old black woman who was a crack cocaine user:

> As she got more addicted to crack, she developed an attitude about her kids that she describes as "hey, get the fuck out of here." She wanted them away from her. She said, "Drugs keep you from loving the people who you love, you only love the drugs...." When she wanted to "do" cocaine, she simply sent them away. (p. 276) (See also later discussion in this chapter concerning abandonment).

In the following pages of this chapter we will examine more closely the nature and consequences of maternal substance use on mothering and child rearing.

☐ Mother-Infant Dyads

Beginning at birth,[1] the mother-infant dyad (and the interactions that take place within this dyad) are significantly and adversely impacted by maternal substance use (Brooks et al., 1994; Fineman et al., 1997; Freier, 1994; Gottwald & Thurman, 1994; Jeremy & Bernstein, 1984; Kelley, 1992). As noted by Freier (1994):

Maternal characteristics [of substance users] are affected by high-stress environments [with few social supports] and life events [involving drug procurement and use]. Also, withdrawal or abstinence symptoms in the infant, and/or poor state regulation, further complicate the interaction. (p. 176)

The interaction is further complicated if, as is occurring with increased frequency, the mother has become HIV-positive as a consequence of her substance abuse[2] (e.g., from prostitution to support a crack cocaine habit or, as is becoming increasingly common among women intravenous drug users, from sharing contaminated needles and syringes) (Kelley, 1992; A. M. Pagliaro & L. A. Pagliaro, 1994; Pagliaro, Pagliaro, Thauberger, Hewitt, & Reddon, 1993; Smith, 1993). Several studies (e.g., Astori, Piazza, Maccabruni, Caselli, & Lanzi, 1997) have found a significantly high incidence of psychosomatic disorders among infants of HIV-positive mothers. These disorders have been attributed to "a distorted relationship with their mother" (p. 23).

☐ Issues of Separation, Loss, and Abandonment

Maternal drug use can, and frequently does, result in issues of separation, loss, and abandonment.[3] While the source of these problems clearly is maternal substance use, the root of these problems appears to begin in the immediate neonatal period with significant difficulties in establishing the normal process of maternal-infant attachment. As noted, for example, by Kelley (1992):

> Mothers who used drugs [during pregnancy] reported problems in attachment to their children, sense of competence as a parent, social isolation, depression, concerns regarding their own health, and perceived their children as very demanding. (p. 326)

The separation of infants and children from their substance using mothers may not always be of the mother's choosing, but is always directly related to her substance using lifestyle (e.g., when she is incarcerated for a substance-related offense). In this regard, it has been noted that over 50% of women inmates in the United States were living with dependent children prior to incarceration (Lynch, Smith, Graziadei, & Pittayathikhum, 1994).[4]

In a study on the effects of maternal alcoholism on separation of children from their incarcerated mothers it was found that:

> Two-thirds of these mothers reported significant periods of time, not due to incarceration, when minor children did not reside with them. Fewer than half of the placements were mandated by child-protective services. Having two or more children while actively alcoholic or residing with a substance abuser correlated strongly with separate residence. (Goldberg, Lex, Mello, Mendelson, & Bower, 1996, p. 228)

Maternal cocaine addiction also was found to be highly correlated with separation of children from their mothers and placement in foster care (Hawley, 1993).

Further evidence of the high risk (i.e., ~50% overall) for disruption in primary care giving that is routinely reported among infants of substance abusing mothers comes from a randomized longitudinal cohort study by Nair et al. (1997). Among this study's sample of substance abusing mothers, they noted particular risk for separation if the mothers: abused heroin; had two or more other children; had other children in foster care; and were depressed.

Abandonment

As noted in the definition of abandonment and related comments in Table 4-1, abandonment usually does not involve permanently giving up custody in a secretive manner (e.g., leaving the child at night on the doorstep of a church or an orphanage), but rather involves leaving a child (or children) for a period of several hours or several days without adequate supervision and care. Abedin, Young, and Beeram (1993), for example, described a cohort of neonates, born to substance abusing mothers, who were "abandoned" in the hospital (i.e., the neonates were medically suitable and ready for discharge, but remained hospitalized "because of lack of a suitable home or caretaker," p. 714).[5]

Most often, however, abandonment occurs in the context of a mother leaving her children alone in their residence without adequate care or supervision while she goes out to procure and use her desired substance of abuse. As noted by Lown, Winkler, Fullilove, & Fullilove (1993) in their study of women crack cocaine addicts:

> One woman, who repeatedly left her one-year-old son in his room alone while she went to get crack, described her reasoning: "Your son can wait, he's not going to starve to death, just a few more hours. Then you can accumulate the money, you can get the milk, you can get the Pampers, and you can get the food, but just wait. Let me take this hit. That's how it affects you."[6] (p. 97)

Maternal abandonment can, as has on regular occasion been reported in the popular press, have horrendous consequences for the abandoned child ranging from psychological trauma to death. Consider, for example, the following related excerpt from one of our clinical student's observation reports:[7]

> One of the men started sharing about his childhood and all of these feelings of hate and resentment toward his mother came out. His mother had left him when he was about three years of age together with his one and one-half year old brother stuck in a crib for 3 or 4 days while she went drinking. The baby died and he was left cold, wet, and hungry locked up with his dead baby brother. At this point in his story, the man began crying and sobbing uncontrollably and you could literally feel the pain and anger coming out of him. (Pagliaro & Pagliaro, Clinical Patient Teaching File Notes, 1995)

☐ Physical Abuse and Neglect

Children of substance abusing mothers are at significantly increased risk for experiencing physical abuse and neglect (Bays, 1990; Egami, Ford, Greenfield, & Crum, 1996; Famularo, Kinscherff, Bunshart, Spivak, & Fenton, 1989; Kelley, 1992; Leifer, Shapiro, & Kassem, 1993; Muller, Fitzberald, Sullivan, & Zucker, 1994; Murphy & Rosenbaum, 1999). For example, as noted by Kelley (1992):

> The strong association between maternal substance abuse and child maltreatment serious enough to necessitate removal of children from their parents found in this study is consistent with findings from other studies. (p. 326)

Several factors associated with high risk for child abuse or neglect have been identified and are presented in Table 4-2. Physical and psychological indicators of child neglect are identified in Tables 4-3 and 4-4, respectively.

(text continues on page 92)

TABLE 4-1. Mental and physical disorders associated with the abuse or neglect of children by their mothers*

Disorder	Definition	Comments
Battered Child Syndrome	Physical abuse of a child by an adult.	The perpetrator of the abuse is usually a parent and the abuse is often deliberately made to look accidental. The condition is usually distinguished by noted variations in the stages of bone and soft tissue healing (i.e., the pattern of healing indicates that injuries have been sustained by the child over a protracted period of time).
Child Abandonment	Parental conduct that demonstrates a conscious rejection of the obligations of parents to their children. These obligations are an integral part of parenthood and cannot be abrogated for the convenience of the parent.	Usually involves leaving the child for a specific period of time (e.g., a few hours to a few days) without proper supervision or care.
Child Abuse	Actions that result in emotional, physical, or sexual harm to a child.	Child abuse, which subsumes the concept of child neglect (see definition in this table), can be caused by acts of either commission or omission on the part of those responsible for the care of the child. Child abuse is an indictable criminal offense and when detected (and in many jurisdictions—when suspected) by a health or social care professional *must* be reported to the appropriate authorities. "Children born to mothers who used illicit drugs during pregnancy . . . had a higher than expected risk of subsequent abuse." (Jaudes et al., 1995, p. 1065) ". . . the Acting Director of the Substance Abuse and Mental Health Services Administration reported that . . . approximately 90% of the individuals reported to authorities for neglect and/or abuse of children were currently drug abusers." (Metsch et al., 1995, p. 74)

Child Neglect	Failure of those who are responsible for the care of the child to provide for the child's basic emotional, nutritional, and physical needs in circumstances that may likely result in harm or threatened harm to the child's health and welfare.	"Physical neglect was also reported by 60% of the [cocaine] addicted mothers." (Hawley, 1993, p. 1)
Emotional Neglect	A type of child neglect in which the behavior(s) of the caregivers are deemed (by both community standards and professional opinion) to cause psychological harm to the child.	This term is often used to differentiate psychological child neglect from physical forms of child neglect. "Emotional neglect or abuse of the children was reported by 60% of the cocaine-addicted mothers." (Hawley, 1993, p. 1)
Failure to Thrive (FTT) (nonorganic origin)	A condition in which a neonate, an infant, or a young child fails to maintain his or her body weight and height (length) above the 5th percentile norms (note that at least one time since birth the weight and height are required to be above this criterion).	FTT of an organic origin may be associated with virtually any severe, chronic medical condition. Nonorganic FTT is associated with a lack of adequate nutrition (i.e., calories). However, nonorganic FTT generally has its origins in a poor maternal-child relationship (i.e., lack of bonding). Lack of appropriate intervention may result in the death of the child by starvation.
Shaken Baby Syndrome	A syndrome in which a neonate, infant, or young child is subjected to violent, whiplash-type shaking by an adult perpetrator.	In most cases, the perpetrator is a parent or caregiver, although it may (rarely) be an older sibling. The resultant injuries may include coma, convulsions, and increased intracranial pressure due to hemorrhaging within the CNS. Death is not uncommon and it is often not until an autopsy is performed that the syndrome is detected. Retinal hemorrhages and bruising on the arms, legs, or trunk of the body (by which the victim was forcibly held during the assault) are usually present.

*These mental and physical disorders are interrelated, both definitionally and operationally (for example, it is not uncommon for substance abusing mothers to engage in several of these abusive and negligent behaviors). Thus, health and social care professionals should be familiar with these various related disorders in order to appropriately assess possible co-occurrence in the same child victim, as well as his or her siblings.

TABLE 4-2. High risk factors for child abuse and neglect

- Aggressive tendencies (mother and/or spouse[a])
- Alcohol or other substance abuse (mother and/or spouse)
- Depression (mother and/or spouse)
- Mental disorders (mother and/or spouse)
- Parenting stress (e.g., financial problems, legal problems, other children in the home)[b] (mother and/or spouse)
- Personality (child, mother, and/or spouse)
- Prenatal history of substance exposure[c] (child)
- Substance-induced cognitive impairment (e.g., being stoned, drunk, or high; mother and/or spouse)
- Unwanted pregnancy (mother and/or spouse)
- Young age (mother)

[a]Spouse is used here to denote a significant other (e.g., boyfriend, girlfriend, husband) who resides with the mother and shares in parenting responsibilities.

[b]Parenting stress is defined as the total amount of stress experienced that is directly related to the social role and responsibility of being a parent. The amount, degree, and impact of the parental stress experienced is moderated by child characteristics (e.g., "demandingness"), parental characteristics (e.g., mood), and situational characteristics (e.g., relationship with spouse) (Abidin, 1990).

[c]Prenatal history of substance exposure serves as a risk factor in two distinct ways. First, it is highly correlated with continuing maternal substance use postnatally. Second, substance exposed neonates often suffer from substance withdrawal symptoms, including (depending upon the substance[s] involved): apathy, irritability, feeding difficulties, and abnormal sleep patterns. These withdrawal symptoms tend to make the infant appear "less lovable" to the mother and, therefore, they function to adversely impact on the maternal-child bonding process. (See related discussion in body of the Chapter).

Murder

Approximately 10% of incarcerated men and 9% of incarcerated women in the United States have committed murder (Lynch et al., 1994). Substance abuse was involved in a majority of the cases of women who had committed murder (Finnegan, 1991) (See Chapter 7, Women as Perpetrators of Substance Use Related Violence). Of these cases, a significant number were perpetrated against their own children. The following are presented as horrific examples of the very worst effects that substance abuse can have in this context upon mothering and child rearing:

> Fairy-tale princesses are born humble. Elisa fit that bill: she was conceived in a homeless shelter in the Fort Greene section of Brooklyn, New York, and born addicted to crack. . . .
> Fairy-tale princesses, however, are not bludgeoned to death by their mothers. They are not violated with a toothbrush and a hairbrush, and the neighbors do not hear them moaning and pleading at night. Last week, two months before her seventh birthday, Elisa Izquierdo lay in her casket, wearing a crown of flowers. The casket was open, which was an anguished protest on someone's part; no exertion of the undertaker's art could conceal all Elisa's wounds. Before she smashed her daughter's head against a cement wall, Awilda Lopez told police, she had made her eat her own feces and used her head to mop the floor. All this over a period of weeks, or maybe months. The fairy tale was ended.[8] (van Biema, 1995, p. 39)

TABLE 4-3. Physical indicators of child neglect*

- Lack of supervision, particularly for long periods of time or in potentially dangerous situations
- Poor growth and development, in comparison to established norms
- Poor hygiene, including body odors and lice infestations
- Unaddressed physical health care needs, such as gross dental problems and severe uncorrected hearing or vision impairment

*Obviously, these indicators, both individually and collectively, can be symptomatic of other social (e.g., poverty) and mental (e.g., severe mental retardation) conditions. They are meant to provide the health or social care provider with an indication that child neglect should be considered and actively confirmed or ruled-out.

Unfortunately, the tragic scenario is played out repeatedly on a daily basis across North America as reported by Metsch et al. (1995):

> ... the Acting Director of the Substance Abuse and Mental Health Services Administration reported that 59% of the child abuse and neglect *fatalities* involving children previously known to the authorities were drug-exposed children ... (p. 74)

☐ Concerns for the School-Aged Child

Children raised by substance abusing mothers are adversely affected, not only emotionally (e.g., in relation to psychological sequelae associated with issues such as poor maternal-child bonding [attachment] and abandonment) and physically (e.g., in relation to neglect and physical abuse), but also cognitively (e.g., in relation to academic performance) (Deren, 1986).

Starting from infancy, Cregler and Mark (1986) noted that, maternal substance use can adversely impact (as has been demonstrated in this chapter) the care-giving environment, which, in turn, can have long-term negative effects on childhood cognitive development. In addition, the conflict and stress in a dysfunctional substance abusing

TABLE 4-4. Psychological indicators of child neglect*

- Assumption of adult roles and decision making responsibilities by the child who may act accordingly in a pseudo-mature or precocious manner
- Begging for or stealing food
- Delinquent behavior, including substance use, stealing, and vandalism
- Depression
- School problems, including frequent, unexplained absences and academic performance that is significantly below measured academic abilities

*See comments made in footnote, Table 4-3.

family, coupled with a general lack of child supervision, further adversely impact childhood academic performance (Krutilla, 1993).[9]

As summarized by Smith (1993): "Children and youth exposed in utero to drugs and alcohol and/or who are growing up in a family in which these substances are misused are vulnerable for [school] failure . . ." (p. 1435).

☐ Consequences for the Next Generation of Mothers

As noted previously, the pain and suffering inflicted upon children by their substance abusing mothers does not end or resolve itself in childhood. If these children survive, it follows them, particularly if they are girls, into their own adulthood. For example, many of these girls will, themselves, resort to substance abuse in adulthood (Regan, Ehrlich, & Finnegan, 1987)[10] (See Chapter 2, Explaining Substance Use Among Women, for further discussion). Many of these girls also will suffer, as adults, from depression, and attempt to take their own lives. In this regard, Bryant and Range (1995), who studied suicidality among college women, found that:

> Women who reported sexual maltreatment [during childhood] in combination with other types of maltreatment [by their parents] were significantly more suicidal than those not maltreated or who reported other types of maltreatment. (p. 87)

As noted earlier in this chapter, the inter-generational cycle of: maternal substance use; adverse impact on mothering; and consequent pain and suffering of the affected children; is self-perpetuating and, without appropriate professional intervention, never ending. Consider, in this regard, the findings of Regan, Ehrlich, and Finnegan (1987):

> Results reveal that a history of violence or abuse was related to drug abuse and also to the placement of one's own child(ren) in foster care. Data suggest that failure to resolve the conflicts and feelings resulting from childhood sexual trauma and/or use of illicit drugs to cope with these feelings appears to disrupt the ability of women to parent their own children. (p. 315)

Concern for a crisis among black women and their children in relation to substance abuse was voiced a decade ago by Staples (1990):

> Young addicted black women are incarcerated, babies are born with congenital addiction, and black motherhood is destroyed as the maternal instinct is subordinated to the pursuit of addiction. (p. 196)

Given the benefit of retrospective analysis of related data over the past decade, we would echo Staple's concern expanding it to all substance abusing women.

☐ Conclusion

Substance abuse among women has had, and is continuing to have, devastating effects on mothering and child rearing, from birth through adolescence. Inter-generational effects also are being observed with a loss of support and care among generations of mothers (i.e., mother–grandmother–great grandmother), all of whom have directly experienced the adverse effects of substance use on mothering and child rearing.

Issues addressed in this chapter include: separation, loss, and abandonment; physical abuse and neglect; concerns for school-aged children; and consequences for the next generation of mothers. It is only with sufficient knowledge and understanding of these issues that the dedicated efforts made by health and social care professionals may be able to assuage the associated pain and suffering that exists today and help break the cycle before future generations are also affected.

☐ Notes

1. See Chapter 3, Substance Use During Pregnancy and Lactation: Effects on the Developing Fetus, Neonate, and Infant, for a review and discussion of substance use related prenatal concerns and effects.
2. See Chapter 8, Women, Substance Use, HIV Infection, and AIDS.
3. These factors, which are discussed in this chapter in terms of effects upon the child, can in later years contribute to the continuing cycle of substance abuse (See Chapter 2, Explaining Substance Use Among Women, for further information).
4. Sixty-six percent of these women inmates report that their dependent children were being cared for by a relative (e.g., sister or mother) other than their current or former spouse (Lynch, 1994). Kelley (1992) found comparable results: "Over 40% of the drug-exposed children were in foster care, most often with the maternal grandmothers" (p. 317).
5. The authors subsequently made comment on both the difficulty in finding family support (e.g., mothers or grandmothers of the new mothers) to assist in caring for these newborns and the speculated reason for this difficulty: "We believe that the lack of family support is the consequence of the cycle of generational drug abuse that these young women became part of" (Abedin, Young, & Beeram, 1993, p. 438).

    Note the implications that this lack of family support has on the future potential for physical abuse and neglect of the infants and children involved (See Table 4–2).
6. Lown et al. (1993) go on to comment:

    > In response to having her children taken away by the local child welfare agency, this same woman said: "It hurts, it really hurts because you really want to do it. You really want to take care of your kids and everything, but the drug is—just constantly—it's like a monkey on your back. I want it, I want it, I want it, I want it." (pp. 97–98)

7. The clinical context of this observation was in a mixed-gender group therapy session for Native American Indians.
8. But why did this mother murder her daughter and in such a horrendous fashion?

    > "Drugs, drugs, drugs—that's all she was interested in," says neighbor Doris Sepulveda, who watched the Lopezes trying to sell a child's tricycle outside their building. Another neighbor, Eric Latorre, recalls seeing the whole family out at 2 a.m. as Awilda sought crack. Awilda had reportedly come to believe that Elisa, whom she called a mongoloid and filthy little whore, had been put under a spell by her father—a spell that had to be beaten out of the child. Neighbors, some of whom say they called the authorities, later told the press of muffled moaning and Elisa's voice pleading, "Mommy, Mommy, please stop! No more! No more! I'm sorry!" (Epperson & Rivera, 1995, p. 42)

9. These adverse academic effects are obviously significantly compounded by deficits in IQ or the presence of learning disorders—as occurs, for example, in the FAS (See Chapter 3, Substance Use During Pregnancy and Lactation: Effects on the Developing Fetus, Neonate, and Infant, for further examples and related discussion).
10. Perhaps as might intuitively be expected, the results from several studies have indicated that mothers who use substances of abuse, both licit (e.g., alcohol, tobacco) and illicit (e.g., cocaine, heroin, marijuana), were less likely than nonusing mothers to be concerned about their child(ren) using substances of abuse. As noted by Hahn (1993), "Compared to nonusers, illicit drug users were . . . less likely to view alcohol or other drug use by their children as serious" (p. 237). The same was found to be true for parents who smoked tobacco.

CHAPTER 5

Substance Use Among Elderly Women: Effects on Healthy Aging

Several of the substances of abuse are commonly used by elderly women, including alcohol and other sedative-hypnotics, opiate analgesics, and nicotine, in the form of tobacco cigarettes. Generally, these substances of abuse are used without interfering with an elderly woman's general health and safety. However, when patterns of use are associated with personal (e.g., mental distress; physical injury; death) and social (e.g., social isolation; abuse of a spouse) harm, they must be seriously considered and dealt with effectively. Currently, there is an increasing number of elderly women who display problematic patterns of substance use. Unfortunately, this situation is expected to continue into the next century and worsen significantly (L. A. Pagliaro & A. M. Pagliaro, 1992; Szwabo, 1993; Westemeyer, 1992).

Traditionally, problematic patterns of substance use among elderly women remained largely unrecognized because of a low level of suspicion, misdiagnosis of symptomatology, and concealment. Health and social care professionals concerned about healthy aging among women must respond more adequately to the increasing number of elderly women who use substances of abuse in harmful ways. They also must recognize that elderly women are at particular risk for developing problematic patterns of substance use. In addition, because elderly women comprise a diverse population of ethnically, socioeconomically, and culturally diverse women, they require individualized prevention and treatment approaches tailored to their specific needs. The purpose of this chapter is to place in perspective the phenomenon of substance use among elderly women in North America and to offer some new insights into dealing with problematic patterns of use in this age group. Particular attention is given to problematic patterns of alcohol and benzodiazepine use.

☐ Identifying Problematic Patterns of Substance Use Among Elderly Women

For too many years, society has looked at elderly people through rose-colored glasses. Even health and social care professionals who are most actively involved in promoting healthy aging may fail to see that the ageism prevalent in North American society works two ways. Negative ageism, that stereotypes all elderly women as "senile," is only one side of the coin. The other side of the coin imbues all elderly women with only the most positive human qualities, including wisdom and virtue. This "reverse stereotype" gives rise to the common misconception that elderly women couldn't possibly have problematic patterns of substance use (Pagliaro & Pagliaro, 1990).

People who are 65 years of age and older constitute the "fastest growing segment of the American population" (National Institute on Alcohol Abuse and Alcoholism, 1998, p. 1). Thus, it is expected that approximately 25% of North Americans will be elderly by the year 2011 (Abrams, Berkow, & Fletcher, 1990; Lawson, 1989; Marshall, 1987; McDonald & Abrahams, 1990; Pagliaro, 1994). Problematic patterns of substance use will continue to increase among this age group regardless of race, ethnicity, or socioeconomic level unless serious efforts are made to understand and deal with this complex phenomenon.

Several studies provide evidence that over 20% of elderly people have been or are suffering from alcoholism and that a significant number of elderly people, particularly women, display problematic patterns of benzodiazepine and other prescription sedative-hypnotic use (Adams, Magruder-Habib, Trued, & Broome, 1992; Bell, 1988; Curtis, Geller, Stokes, Levine, & Moore, 1989; Lee, 1984, 1985). In addition, elderly people have been increasingly involved in supply and trafficking of such abusable psychotropics as cocaine and heroin. They also may supply their children or grandchildren with their prescriptions in order to "keep them off the streets," or sell their prescriptions to supplement their incomes (Baker & Gonzalez, 1988; Bell, 1988; Dowsett, 1989; McConnell, 1983; Rodell, 1994). Arrests of elderly people for acting as couriers of illicit substances of abuse (e.g., cocaine, heroin), sometimes internationally, also are increasing. Of this population of elderly people, most are women.

Commonly asked questions are: What factors contribute to problematic patterns of substance use among elderly women?; How can these problematic patterns of substance use be prevented?; and What treatment approaches are best for elderly women who display problematic patterns of substance use? Answering these questions is difficult because the causes of substance use among elderly women are so varied and, thus, prevention and treatment are complex. For example, consider the following case:

> Mary, the 63-year-old daughter of a wealthy Chicago businessman, had a history of numerous hospital admissions for gastritis, anemia, fatigue, and minor accidents. "I just have a bad stomach and I'm a bit accident-prone," she used to explain. No one ever considered alcohol as a possible common cause of all her problems until it was an obvious factor in one hospital admission. Then, finally questioned about her alcohol use, she admitted to a drinking problem that she said started when her son committed suicide several years earlier. Careful history taking, however, revealed that her alcohol use had been out of control for nearly 30 years. (Fletcher, 1984, p. 18)

Despite their common occurrence, problematic patterns of substance use are *not* usually identified among elderly women by health and social care professionals (Jinks & Raschko, 1990; Pagliaro, 1994). Health and social care professionals also may prescribe or administer substances of abuse without adequate attention to the possibility for the development of problematic patterns of use, drug interactions, or cross-tolerance (e.g., between alcohol and the benzodiazepines). As noted by Graham, Parran, & Jaen (1992), "In none of the records was there evidence that the physician had sufficient knowledge of the patient's alcohol use to safely prescribe a benzodiazepine" (p. 179).

Low Level of Suspicion

Generally, drug addicts are visualized as emaciated young men living on the streets, with tattoos, long-hair, and dirty and shabby clothes. A well-dressed silver-haired great-grandmother is not often visualized (L. A. Pagliaro & A. M. Pagliaro, 1992). Yet, statistics indicate that a significant number of elderly women have, or are at a significant risk for developing, serious problems associated with their substance use (Brown, 1982; Chenitz, Salisbury, & Takano-Stone, 1990; Szwabo, 1993). The same data also indicate that the incidence of problematic patterns of use may be as high for elderly women as it is for younger women.

Problematic patterns of substance use among elderly women is not limited to elderly women who are residing in their own homes in a middle-class community. Zimering and Domeischel (1982) estimated that 20% of some nursing home residents suffered from alcoholism. Baker (1982) reported that over 30% of veteran administration domiciliary residents suffered from alcoholism and Whitcup and Miller (1987) reported that over 20% of their survey of elderly psychiatric inpatients were chemically dependent. Acute care settings also are affected. Brosnahan (1988) reported that at least 40% of elderly hospital admissions had some problem with alcohol or other substance of abuse. In addition, an estimated 30% of elderly emergency room admissions require further assessment for problematic patterns of substance use and up to 20% of elderly admissions to medical services have screened positive for alcoholism (Curtis, Geller, Stokes, Levine, & Moore, 1989; Jacyk, Tabisz, Badger, & Fuchs, 1991).

Sometimes it appears that health and social care professionals deliberately overlook alcoholism or other problematic patterns of substance use among their elderly patients. Consider the experience of one elderly woman: "I would visit my doctor stinking of booze and when he asked me if I drank alcohol, I would simply reply no. Nothing further would be said" (Lasker, 1983, p. 16). This low level of suspicion could be related to: 1) a hesitancy of health and social care professionals to get involved because of the required time commitment; 2) a reluctance to diagnose alcoholism or other problematic patterns of substance use because of a perceived lack of professional training and an inability to assess and deal with the problem; 3) a lack of knowledge about appropriate treatment services to refer elderly women to and an uncertainty as to the success of known treatment approaches; and 4) a feeling that it is best to leave well enough alone (i.e., why take away these "pleasures" from elderly women and subject them to embarrassment and, perhaps, expensive and ineffective treatment) (see Table 5-1). As noted by Watts (1984) and others (e.g., Haldeman & Gafner, 1990; Parette, Hourcade, & Parette, 1990): "many alcoholism counselors have shared many of the same biases and prejudices toward the elderly as that of society as a whole ... [and, because of these biases and prejudices,] many older problem drinkers are overlooked or ignored" (p. 6).

Misdiagnosis

The misdiagnosis of problematic patterns of substance use among elderly women is a serious problem (D'Archangelo, 1993; Marcus, 1993; McMahon, 1993; Miller, Belkin, & Gold, 1991; Ziring & Adler, 1991). For example, Curtis, Geller, Stokes, Levine, & Moore (1989) reported that only 37% of elderly patients who had a positive screen for alcoholism were identified ($p < .05$). In addition, the elderly patients who had alcoholism were significantly less likely to be diagnosed by their physician if they were

TABLE 5-1. Reasons why geriatric clinicians avoid or are resistant to diagnosing and treating elderly women who have problematic patterns of substance use

- Confusion regarding inconsistent terminology associated with the phenomena of substance use;
- Discomfort associated with confronting elderly women who display problematic patterns of substance use and denial behaviors;
- Impatience with required long-term treatment approaches;
- Inadequate knowledge of and experience using assessment instruments (normed instruments, interview techniques) aimed at identifying elderly women who have problematic patterns of substance use;
- Inadequate knowledge of the etiology of substance use, patterns of substance use, and multimodal treatment approaches;
- Inadequate use of multidisciplinary pluralism in approaching elderly women who display problematic patterns of substance use;
- Legal implications associated with misdiagnosis of substance use;
- Negative attitudes toward elderly women who have problematic patterns of substance use;
- Recognition of own problematic patterns of substance use; and
- Unfamiliarity with available resources for referral.

(Hoffman & Henemann, 1986; Pagliaro & Pagliaro, 1990; Parette, Hourcade, & Parette, 1990).

white, female, or had completed high school (p < .01). As reported by Adams, Magruder-Habib, Trued, & Broome (1992), alcohol abuse is a prevalent and important problem among elderly emergency department patients. However, physicians detected only 21% of elderly patients who abused alcohol. In another study by McInnes and Powell (1994), "Medical staff did not recognize substance misuse in older hospital patients . . ." (p. 444).

Common signs and symptoms associated with problematic patterns of substance use, including confusion and other cognitive deficits and increased incidence of accidents, are frequently and inappropriately ascribed to old age (Freund, 1984; Watts, 1984). Whitcup and Miller (1987) reported that ". . . unrecognized drug withdrawal in the psychiatrically hospitalized elderly patient is [often] confused initially with myocardial infarction, hypertensive emergencies, encephalopathy, and infection . . ." (p. 297). Of course, the major tragedy of such misdiagnoses is that appropriate and possibly effective treatment is delayed or not implemented. This situation can have a significant negative affect on the quantity and quality of an elderly woman's life. Health and social care professionals must be increasingly alert to the signs and symptoms associated with problematic patterns of substance use among elderly women (Thibault & Maly, 1993; Willenbring, Christensen, Spring, & Ramussen, 1987; Zimberg, 1985).

Concealment

Almost two decades ago, Glantz (1985) argued that elderly people are less willing to admit to substance abuse than are younger people. Many elderly women remain unidentified as having problematic patterns of substance use, and, hence, remain untreated because of their abilities to conceal their substance use. The concealment occurs both actively and passively and often involves help from enablers who may be caring health and social care professionals, loving family members and friends, and concerned employers (Bienenfeld, 1987). Related to the notion of concealment is the following situation that was shared as part of official testimony by a physician during a Congressional hearing on alcohol and drugs (Shelowitz, 1987):

> Doctors are emotionally unwilling to tab [elderly people] with a primary diagnosis of alcoholism, [or] drug abuse, and so they are very willing to put down some of the other things that are the specific things that get them to the hospital such as a fracture, [or] automobile accident that occurred when they were drunk or overusing drugs; so that [the other thing] becomes the primary diagnosis. (p. 245)

Perhaps because they may be more inclined to think of substance abuse as sinful or as a sign of moral weakness, elderly women are particularly prone to: 1) using extensive denial mechanisms; and 2) avoiding treatment programs (Lawson, 1989; Malcolm, 1992). Because elderly women are generally widowed, retired, or living away from adult children, disruptions in daily routines, changes in usual grooming, absenteeism from work, work related accidents, motor vehicle crashes while driving to and from work, and being drunk or hung-over on the job no longer serve as deterrents or avenues for referral to treatment (e.g., employee assistance programs [EAP]). For this reason, it is frequently not only the health or social care professionals in the clinic, general hospital unit, or emergency room, but those in the community home health and social care settings (e.g., community health nurses, nursing home staff, social workers) who are most apt to detect significant problematic patterns of substance use among elderly women. Thus, all health and social care professionals must become more aware of the problem of concealment. They must know what to look for and know what appropriate questions to ask their patients who are elderly women so that problematic patterns of substance use can be identified and dealt with (Gulino & Kadin, 1986; Kofoed, 1985; Saunders, 1985; Senior Citizens Bureau, 1983; Substance abuse in the elderly, 1986).

Elderly women who live with or near their children or other family members also may be affected by concealment. Families often play a significant role in the concealment of problematic patterns of substance use among their elderly relatives. Commonly, family members, including children and grandchildren, function as enablers and supply their elderly aunt or grandmother with substances of abuse in order to: 1) make the disruptive or bothersome elderly relative easier to deal with; 2) provide one of the final "pleasures" left to her in her old age; 3) relieve the pain associated with a particular chronic medical disorder (e.g., severe rheumatoid arthritis); 4) resolve feelings of guilt regarding an inability to help the elderly relative in other ways (e.g., visiting more often); and 5) keep the disruptive elderly relative hidden from public view and, therefore, prevent or decrease family embarrassment associated with her difficult behavior (Anderson, 1990; Bienenfeld, 1987; Champlin, 1983; Haugland, 1989; Older alcoholics, 1987; Rosenblum, 1989).

In all three areas, low level of suspicion, misdiagnosis, and concealment, ageism is a contributing factor (Gulino & Kadin, 1986; Haugland, 1989). As emphasized by Haldeman and Gafner (1990), nurses, physicians, social workers, and other health and social care professionals continue to lack positive attitudes toward the elderly.

Problematic Patterns of Substance Use Among Elderly Women

The substances of abuse most widely used in problematic ways by elderly women are the CNS depressants, particularly, the sedative-hypnotics (Brosnahan, 1988; Caroselli-Karinja, 1985; Dolphin & Driver, 1988; Saunders, 1985; Whitcup & Miller, 1987). Sedative-hypnotics produce a depression of the central nervous system resulting in sedation and, at higher doses, hypnosis (i.e., sleep). Of the various substances of abuse classified as sedative-hypnotics, principally two groups are most frequently problematic for elderly women: 1) alcohol (e.g., beer, wine, distilled liquor); and 2) benzodiazepines (e.g., alprazolam; diazepam [Valium®]; flurazepam; lorazepam; triazolam) (Bernstein, Folkman, & Lazarus, 1989; Closser, 1991; Haugland, 1989; Jinks & Raschko, 1990; L. A. Pagliaro, 1988e; L. A. Pagliaro & A. M. Pagliaro, 1992b; Pizzi & Mion, 1993; Smart & Adlaf, 1988). Because of the significant nature and growing recognition of problematic patterns of alcohol and benzodiazepine use among elderly women, separate sections on each of these sedative-hypnotics are presented in this chapter.

Alcohol[1]

Problematic patterns of alcohol use generally are associated with alcoholism and its related sequelae. Alcoholism may be defined as the sporadic or continuous inappropriate use of alcohol that harms or interferes with a person's physical or mental health, work, family, and/or social life. The nature of alcoholism includes the characteristics of being: 1) progressive (i.e., the condition slowly becomes more serious over time); 2) chronic (i.e., whether problematic patterns of alcohol use are sporadic or continuous, the pattern of use recurs for long periods of time and, in some cases, over a lifetime); and 3) insidious (i.e., even though most relatives, friends, or coworkers may be aware of an elderly women's problematic pattern of alcohol use, she is, herself, usually unable to recognize the problem without some external assistance) (Jacobson, 1983; Seixas, 1982a).

The number of elderly people in North America who meet criteria for alcoholism has been generally estimated to be between 2 and 3 million (Bloom, 1983; Lamy, 1984; Lasker, 1983; Price & Andrews, 1982; Williams, 1982). Although alcohol use generally decreases with age (Bercsi, Brickner, & Saha, 1993; Lisansky Gomberg, 1995), these estimates appear much too conservative. A more realistic estimate seems closer to 5 million (Adrian, 1986; Senior Citizens Bureau, 1983; Williams, 1984). Demographic trends and addiction profile studies increasingly make clear that alcohol use among Americans will be a major health concern over the next several decades (Gupta, 1993; Liberto, Oslin, & Ruskin, 1992; L. A. Pagliaro, 1994) and requires attention in regard to its assessment in the elderly population (Atkinson, 1990).

An awareness of the typical signs and symptoms associated with alcoholism among the elderly is required because: 1) a diagnosis of alcoholism is frequently overlooked in the elderly population (Lamy, 1984); and 2) the presentation and symptom patterns of alcoholism are often different from those displayed by younger people (Willenbring, Christensen, Spring, & Ramussen, 1987). In addition to the classic signs and symptoms of alcoholism (i.e., starting the day with a drink; drinking alone; gulping down drinks; developing an increased tolerance to alcohol; experiencing blackouts; and displaying personality changes) (Segal & Sisson, 1985; Seixas, 1982b), elderly

TABLE 5-2. Nonpathognomonic symptoms of problematic patterns of substance use that are commonly misdiagnosed

accidents, increased	malnutrition
amnesia	memory loss
anxiety	mental status change
cognitive function, impaired	multiple chronic medical disorders
confusion	panic attack
dementia	seizures, unrelated to a convulsive disorder
depression	self-neglect
diarrhea	sexual performance, decreased
disorientation	sleep disturbances
dysrhythmias, transient	slurred speech
falls, repeated	social isolation
fevers of unknown origin	unsteady gait
gastritis	unusual behavior
incontinence	

(Adams et al., 1992; Atkinson & Kofoed, 1982; Curtis et al., 1989; Freund, 1984; Miller, Whitcup, Sacks, & Lynch, 1985; Pagliaro & Pagliaro, 1990; Rains & Ditzler, 1993; Whitcup & Miller, 1987; Willenbring, Christensen, Spring, & Ramussen, 1987; Zimberg, 1985).

women who suffer from alcoholism frequently have an increased incidence of accidents (e.g., falls, burns), depression, periods of self-neglect, tendencies toward social isolation, and memory impairment and other cognitive deficits (Bienenfeld, 1987; Freund, 1986; Nolan & Blass, 1992; Pagliaro & Pagliaro, 1990; Senior Citizens Bureau, 1983; Zwerling et al., 1996). However, because many of these signs and symptoms can be ascribed to several medical and psychological disorders typically associated with old age, the diagnosis of alcoholism is often missed (Adams, Magruder-Habib, Trued, & Broome, 1992; Hartford & Samorajski, 1982; Wattis, 1981) (see Table 5-2).

An adequate clinical assessment of elderly women for problematic patterns of alcohol use should include an in-depth interview and a psychometric screening with an instrument such as the CAGE (i.e., Have you felt a need to cut down on your drinking? Have people annoyed you by criticizing your drinking? Have you felt bad or guilty about your drinking? Have you had a drink first thing in the morning to steady your nerves or to get rid of a hangover [eye opener]?), the Michigan Alcoholism Screening Test (MAST), or other appropriate screening test. Although the validity and reliability of these psychometric instruments (i.e., CAGE, MAST) have been found to be lower in the elderly when compared to the young (Blankfield & Maritz, 1990; Moran, Naughton, & Hughes, 1990; National Institute on Alcohol Abuse and Alcoholism, 1998), they can be of value for differentiating those elderly women who may have problematic patterns of alcohol use from those who do not (Adams, Magruder-Habib, Trued, & Broome, 1992; Horn, Paccaud, Niquille, Koehn, Magnenat, & Yersin, 1992; Buchsbaum, Buchanan, Welsh, Centor, & Schnoll, 1992; Luckie, White, Miller, Icenogle, & Lasoski, 1995; Mulford & Fitzgerald, 1992; Thibault & Maly, 1993) (see Chapter 9, Assessing and Diagnosing Substance Use Disorders Among Women, for a comprehensive discussion of the psychometric screening instruments used to assist in the diagnosis of alcoholism and other substance use disorders).

Among the major hazards associated with problematic patterns of alcohol use among elderly women is the interaction of alcohol with other substances of abuse that also cause central nervous system depression (e.g., prescription and nonprescription sedative-hypnotics) (Dufour, Archer, & Gordis, 1992; Hartford & Samorajski, 1982; Lamy, 1988; Morse, 1988; L. A. Pagliaro & A. M. Pagliaro, 1999b; Richelson, 1984; Szwabo, 1993). When alcohol and other sedative-hypnotics are used concurrently, central nervous system depression can be significantly potentiated and may, as commonly occurs with the combination of alcohol and the benzodiazepines, result in death (Chan, 1984; L. A. Pagliaro, 1988e; Schuckit & Pastor, 1978). Elderly women are particularly vulnerable to these synergistic effects because of several age-related changes, including: 1) a diminished lean body mass ratio and decreased volume of distribution that result in a higher peak blood alcohol concentration than is observed in younger women when equivalent amounts of alcohol (based on body surface area) are consumed; 2) subclinical malnutrition; and 3) decreased reserve capacity of the vital organs (i.e., heart, liver, kidney), which place elderly women at particular risk for a heightened susceptibility to the adverse effects of alcohol (Bienenfeld, 1987; Dufour, Archer, & Gordis, 1992; Laforge & Mignon, 1993; Lamy, 1988; Morse, 1988; L. A. Pagliaro & A. M. Pagliaro, 1999b; Ticehurst, 1990).

Whereas some elderly women may develop problematic patterns of alcohol use during their younger years which continue into their old age, others (i.e., those who abstained from alcohol use or drank socially during their younger years) never experienced any severe alcohol-related problems until their old age (Abrams & Alexopoulos, 1987; Atkinson, 1990; Finlayson, Hurt, Davis, & Morse, 1988; Finney & Moos, 1984; Fitzgerald & Mulford, 1992; Mulford & Fitzgerald, 1992). The former group, those elderly women with *early-onset alcoholism,* comprises approximately one-half of elderly women diagnosed with alcoholism. The latter group, those elderly women with *late-onset alcoholism,* comprises the remaining one-third of elderly women diagnosed with alcoholism (Haugland, 1989). Elderly women diagnosed with either early-onset or late-onset alcoholism can be further divided into: 1) bender or binge drinkers (i.e., those elderly women who drink heavily for short periods of time, such as on weekends or on the anniversary of the death of a loved one); and 2) daily or chronic drinkers (i.e., those elderly women who drink heavily every day or whenever alcohol is available to them) (Lawson, 1989; Wallace, 1982).

Early-onset alcoholism Elderly women who have early-onset alcoholism seem to display alcohol related personality characteristics (e.g., neurosis, self-indulgence) (Atkinson, 1990) similar to those characteristics observed among younger women who are diagnosed with alcoholism. Elderly women within this group tend to follow a typical pattern of progression in relation to the use of alcohol. They also are more likely to discharge themselves from alcohol treatment programs (Liberto, Oslin, & Ruskin, 1992; Schonfeld & Dupree, 1991).

Elderly women who have early-onset alcoholism usually have a positive family history for alcoholism (Bienenfeld, 1987; Tobias, Lippman, Pary, Oropilla, & Embry, 1989) and generally began drinking alcohol during their mid-teens or early-twenties. The major problems they experienced related to their alcohol use (e.g., being arrested for impaired driving, divorce related to alcoholism and its stressful effects on family relationships, being fired from a job or passed over for promotion) usually occurred during their early thirties. However, they did not seek help or treatment for their alcohol related problems until they were approximately forty years of age. They also may have sought treatment once again during their early fifties.

The prognosis for these elderly long-term alcoholic women is generally poor. A significant number of these women die before they reach 65 years of age (Hollobon, 1986b; Lemonick, 1987). However, approximately one out of six of these women cure themselves (i.e., undergo untreated or spontaneous remission) (Lawson, 1989; Sullivan, 1990). Unfortunately, these women appear to have a significantly greater risk for developing anxiety disorders, depressive disorders, and dementia as they grow older, even if they modify their drinking behavior (Schonfeld & Dupree, 1991). It is quite likely that these mental disorders are the residual result of not adequately addressing—through appropriate treatment—the underlying psychopathology that was associated with their early drinking behavior, a phenomenon identified as the dry drunk syndrome (A. M. Pagliaro & L. A. Pagliaro, 1995b).

Late-onset alcoholism Late-onset alcoholism among elderly women is characterized by a pattern of alcohol use that began later in life. For these elderly women, their alcohol use was usually associated with a stressful life event or change in lifestyle (e.g., the death of a spouse or loved one; divorce; medical disorders; retirement; terminal cancer) (Bruera, Moyano, Seifert, Fainsinger, Hanson, & Suarex-Almazor, 1995; Busby, Campbell, Borrie, & Spears, 1988; Finney & Moos, 1984; Liberto, Oslin, & Ruskin, 1992; Lisansky Gomberg, 1995) (see Table 5-3). Elderly women generally suffer from this form of alcoholism (Brody, 1982; Counte, Salloway, & Christman, 1982; Edwards, 1985; Haldeman & Gafner, 1990; McDonald & Abrahams, 1990; Mishara, 1982; Olsen-Noll & Bosworth, 1989; Parker, 1982). This form of alcoholism also appears to be more prominent among elderly women from middle and upper middle class socioeconomic groups (Atkinson, 1988). Elderly women who have late-onset alcoholism also are characterized as having a higher incidence of both psychological (e.g., anxiety, depression, insomnia) and medical (e.g., cancer, rheumatoid arthritis) disorders (Bruera, Moyano, Seifert, Fainsinger, Hanson, & Suarex-Almazor, 1995; Porcino, 1985; Tobias, Lippman, Pary, Oropilla, & Embry, 1989). However, the most distinguishing characteristic of this group of elderly women is that severe problems related to their alcohol use were not experienced until they were fifty years of age or older.

As noted earlier, it is commonly believed that the reason that these seemingly well-adjusted elderly women became problem drinkers during their old age is related to

TABLE 5-3. Life events and lifestyle changes associated with aging

- Age-related changes in cognitive functioning and memory;
- Declining physical health, including significant increases in both chronic pain and chronic illnesses;
- Fear of personal injury associated with living alone and the inability to physically defend oneself or one's property;
- Institutionalization and associated effects;
- Psychological stress and depression associated with thoughts regarding the nearness of death and other mentioned factors;
- Retirement, with associated loss of financial flexibility and self-esteem; and
- Social isolation associated with decreased physical mobility and loss of friends/spouse/children due to death or relocation.

their inability to adequately cope with painful or unwelcome changes in their lives (Brody, 1982; Edwards, 1985; Mishara, 1982; Porcino, 1985).[2] As described by an elderly woman recovering from her alcoholism (Lasker, 1983):

> I thought alcohol was my only friend. It helped me to not feel and to cope with the desperation inside. Alcohol went from being my best friend to a powerful and controlling enemy, but it kept me company. There were no more excuses for drinking. I didn't know there was any other way [to live]. (p. 18)

For elderly people suffering from early- and late-onset alcoholism, the leading cause of death is cardiovascular disease (i.e., coronary heart disease and strokes) (Day, James, Butler, & Campbell, 1993; Goldstein, 1983; Klatsky, Armstrong, & Friedman, 1990; Segal & Sisson, 1985; Sullivan, 1990). The next leading cause of death is cancer, particularly cancer of the breast (Lemonick, 1987), lung, and rectum. Following these leading causes of death, in order of decreasing incidence of mortality, are: accidents, including burns, falls, and motor vehicle crashes (Bienenfeld, 1987; Haugland, 1989); and suicide, which is the ninth leading cause of death among elderly people (Boxwell, 1988; Frances, Franklin, & Flavin, 1986; Tobias, Lippmann, Pary, Oropilla, & Embry, 1989). As noted by Richardson, Lowenstein, & Weissberg (1989), one fourth of suicides in the United States are carried out by people who are 60 years of age or older. Other causes of death include hepatic disease, such as cirrhosis, hepatitis, and hepatic failure (Hollobon, 1986b; Skog, 1984); and esophageal varices and hemorrhage, aggravated by both alcohol-induced increased gastric acid production and vomiting (Segal & Sisson, 1985; Sullivan, 1990). Not unexpectedly, alcohol-related hospitalizations are a common occurrence among elderly women (Adams, Yuan, Baboriak, & Broome, 1993)[3] (see Table 5-4 for a list of the major adverse effects related to the chronic abuse of alcohol).

Benzodiazepines

Of the prescribed sedative-hypnotics, the benzodiazepines (see Table 5-5) have been most clearly associated with problematic patterns of substance use among elderly women (Closser, 1991; Grantham, 1987; McInnes & Powell, 1994). However, elderly women themselves are *not* solely responsible for this situation. Credit also must be given to society and, more specifically: 1) nursing home directors and administrators; 2) adult children of elderly parents; and 3) physicians, pharmacists, nurses, and other health and social care professionals, who inappropriately prescribe, dispense, and administer benzodiazepines to elderly women and fail to monitor the use of these prescription drugs by these women and their individual responses. Women generally receive more multiple and repeat prescriptions for benzodiazepines and are more likely to be prescribed excessive dosages than are men (Matteo, 1988). Unfortunately, elderly women are at the greatest risk for physician-perpetuated problematic patterns of benzodiazepine and other abusable psychotropic (e.g., opiate analgesics) use (Busby, Campbell, Borrie, & Spears, 1988; Glantz & Backenheimer, 1988; Grantham, 1987).

Elderly women residing in nursing homes likewise have been reported to be at significant risk for physician-perpetuated benzodiazepine and other psychotropic use.[4] It has been noted by several authors that over 50% of the elderly residents of nursing homes receive benzodiazepines, often unnecessarily (Beardsley, Larson, Burns, Thompson, & Kamerow, 1989; Lyndon & Russell, 1990; Riesenberg, 1988; Waxman,

(text continues on page 108)

TABLE 5-4. Adverse effects related to chronic alcohol abuse among elderly women[a]

accidents, general (e.g., burns, falls)	hypoglycemia
addiction (physical dependence)	Korsakoff's psychosis
anemia	malnutrition
ascites	memory dysfunction
brain damage, including loss of gray and white matter	motor vehicle crashes
	nutritional deficiencies
cancers (e.g., breast cancer)	osteoporosis (alcoholic bone disease)
cardiac dysrhythmias	pancreatitis
cardiomyopathy	peripheral neuropathy
child abuse, physical and psychological (e.g., of grandchildren)	polyneuropathy
	positional asphyxiation
cirrhosis of the liver	psychomotor impairment
cognitive dysfunction	psychosis
dementia	self-neglect
depression	sleep apnea
endocrine changes	social problems (e.g., divorce, poverty, job loss, legal problems, spousal abuse)
esophageal varices	
falls (and associated fractures and trauma)	
	sudden cardiac death
gastritis (i.e., antral, hemorrhagic)	suicide
hangovers	tardive dyskinesia[b]
heart disease	violent behavior
hip fractures	vitamin deficiencies (e.g., thiamine)
hyperlipidemia (hypertriglyceridemia)	Wernicke-Korsakoff Syndrome

[a]It should be noted that moderate alcohol consumption, defined as one drink per day, has been reportedly associated with some potential health benefits. For example, moderate alcohol consumption among post-menopausal women has been associated with increased estrogen (estradiol) levels. These increased estrogen levels have been correlated with a significantly reduced risk for cardiovascular disease among these women (Klatsky, 1990; National Institute on Alcohol Abuse and Alcoholism, 1998; Gavaler, Deal, Van Thiel, Arria, & Allan, 1993). Note that not all authors (e.g., Longnecker & Tseng, 1998) agree that this risk reduction is mediated by effects on estrogens. In addition, increased estrogen levels may exacerbate estrogen dependent cancers, such as uterine cancer (Gavaler, 1995).

[b]Jeste et al. (1995) noted a cumulative incidence of tardive dyskinesia of 26%, 52%, and 60% after 1, 2, or 3 years exposure, respectively, to high potency antipsychotics among elderly patients. This risk was most significant for elderly patients with a history of "alcohol abuse/dependence."

(Alcohol and the Liver, 1993; Bell et al., 1992; Bienenfeld, 1987; Blendis, 1987; Day, James, Butler, & Campbell, 1993; Freund, 1984; Harper & Kril, 1990; Iber, 1990; Klein & Iber, 1991; Korsten & Lieber, 1985; Kosberg, 1988; Lindberg & Oyler, 1990; Longnecker & Tseng, 1998; Mello, Mendelson, & Teoh, 1993; National Institute on Alcohol Abuse and Alcoholism, 1998; Pagliaro & Pagliaro, 1990; Sampson, 1998; Schapira, 1990; Stepka, Rogala, & Czyzyk, 1993; Stinson & DeBakey, 1992; Tobias et al., 1989; Van Natta, Malin, Bertolucci, & Kaelber, 1985).

TABLE 5-5. Factors specifically associated with problematic patterns of benzodiazepine use among elderly nursing home residents

- Attitude of ageism by staff;
- Attitude of sexism, particularly toward elderly women by staff;
- Inadequate number of direct physician visits to elderly residents;
- Excessive use of underqualified personnel (e.g., inadequately supervised nursing aides) in performance of patient care needs;
- Inappropriate management of life crises (e.g., death of spouse);
- Lack of initial individual patient assessment and periodic reassessment;
- Large resident to staff ratio;
- Misuse of order forms and procedures for prescription renewals; and
- Overuse/inappropriate use of PRN (as needed) orders.

(McInnes & Powell, 1994; Pagliaro & Pagliaro, 1990; Riesenberg, 1988; Waxman, Klein, & Carner, 1985).

Klein, & Carner, 1985; Willard, 1989). Baker and Oleen (1988) reported that up to 53% of prescriptions for benzodiazepines were written for use on an as needed basis. They also reported that the proportion of people who received such prescriptions increased with age. Of these people, 57% were using a sedative-hypnotic every day, and this regular use increased with advancing age.

Although benzodiazepines have been excessively prescribed for people in all age groups (Hohmann, Larson, Thompson, & Beardsley, 1991; Miller & Gold, 1991), an inordinately large percentage of prescriptions have been made for elderly women. Several reasons have been given for this observation: "Drugs make managing patients easier—and far less expensive" (Drew, 1989, p. 56); "Patients who are drowsy, asleep, or slowed down are simply less of a management problem" (Waxman et al., 1985, p. 886); and ". . . this pattern of use is compatible with the concept of sedation as 'chemical restraint' " (Beers, Avorn, & Soumerai, 1988, p. 3016). As further illustrated by Shelowitz (1987) citing testimony presented to a Congressional Committee on Aging:

> There is heavy use of tranquilizers on our floor. . . . There are times when they (the nurses) wake the patients in order to give them tranquilizers so that the patients would stay out of their hair. By keeping the patients drugged up, they are being turned into vegetables. Many of these patients are having psychological problems that are not being treated. They are being medicated so that we don't have to deal with them. (p. 243)

Noted also were comments from a nursing home investigator who testified that: ". . . for the beleaguered nurse's aid, tranquilizers are a happy solution. If patients are sedated, they cause the staff few problems. The administrator is happy too, because bed bound patients bring the highest rate of reimbursement" (Shelowitz, 1987, p. 243).

Despite the legal implementation of regulations such as the Nursing Home Reform Law (Public Law 100–203, 1987) that specifies the right of elderly residents within skilled nursing care facilities to be free from physical or mental abuse, corporal punishment, involuntary seclusion, and any physical or chemical restraints imposed for the purpose of discipline or convenience, which are not required to treat the resident's medical disorders, in practice, a significant percentage of elderly nursing home residents routinely have this right violated (see Table 5-5 for a list of factors specifically associated with inappropriate benzodiazepine use among elderly nursing home residents).

In addition to their well recognized adverse effects affecting the central nervous system, including ataxia (incoordination), blurred vision, confusion, drowsiness, and emotional blunting (Closser, 1991; Grantham, 1987; L. A. Pagliaro & A. M. Pagliaro, 1998, 1999b), the use of the benzodiazepines has been demonstrated in several published studies and reports (e.g., Hollobon, 1986a; Lauritzen, McNair, & Lund, 1993; Sorock & Shimkin, 1988) to be significantly correlated with an increased risk of falls among elderly people. One report (Risk of falling, 1989) encouraged prescribers and other health and social care professionals to apply the American Psychiatric Association's recommendation to review all benzodiazepine pharmacotherapy prescribed for longer than 3 months because the risk of falls is so significant among elderly women who use benzodiazepines and because of the potential associated harm (e.g., fractured hip), particularly to frail elderly women.

In an attempt to deal with the increasing inappropriate prescription of the benzodiazepines, the council of the Royal Pharmaceutical Society first issued the following guidelines over a decade ago in 1989 (Council statement, 1989). These guidelines have since become part of the official British National Formulary:

1. Benzodiazepines are indicated for the short-term relief (two to four weeks only) of anxiety that is severe, disabling, or subjecting the individual to unacceptable distress, occurring alone or in combination with insomnia or short-term psychosomatic, organic, or psychotic illness.
2. The use of benzodiazepines to treat short-term mild anxiety is inappropriate and unsuitable.
3. Benzodiazepines should be used to treat insomnia only when it is severe, disabling, or subjecting the individual to extreme distress.

Although issued over a decade ago, these guidelines have not yet received serious consideration nor have they been widely implemented in North America.[5]

☐ Treating Problematic Patterns of Substance Use Among Elderly Women

Providing appropriate and effective treatment for elderly women who display problematic patterns of substance use often appears to be a Catch-22 situation. For example, Gulino and Kadin (1986) noted that "elderly alcoholics are excluded from alcoholism services because of age, and from geriatric services because of alcoholism" (p. 151). Even when alcoholism is diagnosed, elderly women are less likely to have treatment recommended. When treatment is recommended, it is less likely to be initiated. And, if it is initiated, it is less likely to be as aggressive as for the young (Curtis, Geller, Stokes, Levine, & Moore, 1989). There are several reasons for the reluctance of health and social care professionals to recommend and be involved with the treatment of substance use among elderly women (see Table 5-1). Regardless of the validity of these reasons in a particular situation, the distressing fact is that less than one in five elderly women who display problematic patterns of substance use receive adequate treatment (Olsen-Noll & Bosworth, 1989). This situation is particularly tragic because appropriate treatment has been found to be effective with successful outcomes (Closser, 1991; Kashner, Rodell, Ogden, Guggenheim, & Karson, 1992; Leclair &

Rosenthal, 1980; Rosenblum, 1989; Williams, 1984) (see Chapter 11, Preventing and Treating Substance Use Disorders Among Women).

In order to achieve optimal substance abuse treatment for elderly women who have substance use disorders, treatment *must* be tailored to each elderly woman's individual needs and abilities. In an effort to help health and social care professionals to meet this challenge, the remainder of this chapter describes The Mega Interactive Model of Substance Use Among Elderly Women (MIMSUAEW).[6] This model was modified from a model developed by A. M. Pagliaro and L. A. Pagliaro (1992), and is presented to assist health and social care professionals to assess problematic patterns of substance use among elderly women and devise, deliver, and evaluate individualized treatment programs for these women.

☐ The Mega Interactive Model of Substance Use Among Elderly Women

The Mega Interactive Model of Substance Use Among Elderly Women (Figure 5-1) depicts the phenomenon of substance use among elderly women in North America as being comprised of four major interrelated and interacting dimensions:

1. the *Substance of Abuse Dimension,* including substance of abuse variables and pattern of use variables;
2. the *Elderly Woman Dimension,* including the physical, psychological, and social variables that may be related to a particular elderly woman's pattern of substance use;
3. the *Societal Dimension,* which includes the societal variables that may affect an elderly woman's substance use or treatment (e.g., ageism, social programs for elderly people); and
4. the *Time Dimension,* including the length of time that a substance of abuse has been used by a particular elderly woman and the historical period during which the use occurred.

Applying MIMSUAEW

The multidimensional aspects of MIMSUAEW: the Substance of Abuse Dimension (Abusable Psychotropic Dimension); the Elderly Woman Dimension; the Societal Dimension; and the Time Dimension are briefly described in order to assist health and social care professionals to better understand the potential applications of this model in their clinical practice settings.

The Substance of Abuse Dimension The pharmacology, pharmacokinetics, toxicology, abuse liability, addiction potential, and related parameters of a particular substance of abuse are critical factors that have received the preponderance of attention in relation to disentangling the antecedents and consequences of substance use. The importance of these Substance, or Abusable Psychotropic, Variables is not to be denied and, as such, comprise an important component of MIMSUAEW. However, all substance use is not problematic and, thus, quantitative behavioral measures and qualitative descriptions of substance use behavior are needed. A particularly useful way to approach this task is to consider the Pattern of Use Variables.

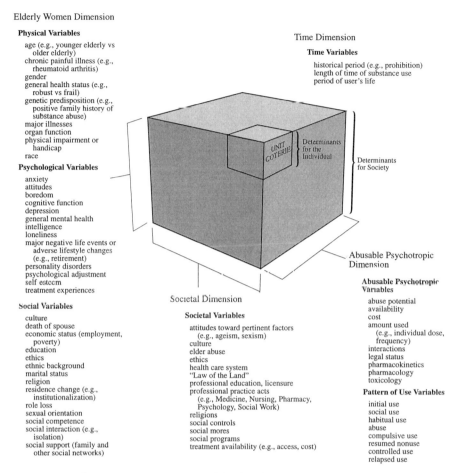

FIGURE 5-1. The Mega Interactive Model of Substance Use Among Elderly Women (MIMSUAEW).

The Pattern of Use Variables presents the use of one or more substances of abuse as becoming increasingly more compulsive and harmful as an elderly woman progresses through a series of well-defined patterns of use:

1. nonuse;
2. initial use;
3. social use (including medical and religious or ceremonial use);
4. habitual use;
5. abuse;
6. compulsive use;
7. resumed nonuse;
8. controlled use; and
9. relapsed use (see Figure 5-2)

Although evidence has not been presented that supports the notion that initial or social use patterns progress to abuse or compulsive use patterns among all elderly

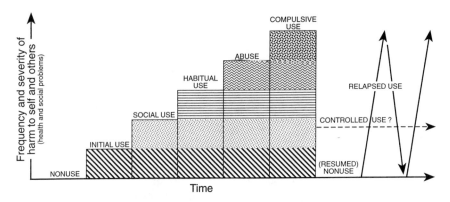

FIGURE 5-2. Patterns of substance use.

women and for all substances of abuse, the approach presented offers a means for identifying actual or potential problematic patterns of use that may require different treatment approaches for different elderly women. Each of these patterns of use is described.

Nonuse. Many elderly women are nonusers. They may never have used any substance of abuse or may not have used them for years and, thus, consider themselves nonusers. However, for example, an elderly woman who has a history of alcohol or other substance use as a means for coping with stressful life situations or to increase perceived social skills, may be at risk for problematic patterns of use when confronted with situations such as the death of her spouse or a move to a senior's lodge.

Initial Use. The initial or first-time use of a particular substance of abuse, generally involves some degree of curiosity and does *not* usually develop into a pattern of abuse or compulsive use. An elderly woman, curious about the effects of a substance of abuse, may use it only once when the opportunity presents itself. The scenario associated with this pattern of substance use is often associated with experimentation by youth or young adults. Elderly women, too, may not have previously used a particular substance of abuse, but tried it when it was offered to them in a certain circumstance. For example, an elderly woman may try a substance of abuse at the encouragement of her children or grandchildren. One elderly professor shared with the authors that she had never used marijuana. However, when her college-aged granddaughter offered her some, she tried it, just to see what it was like. Another example was related during a dinner party conversation when a retired owner of a large construction company shared that she had recently tried cocaine when it was offered to her by her son (A. M. Pagliaro & L. A. Pagliaro, unpublished data, 1992). It is not uncommon for a recently widowed elderly woman to be offered "something for her nerves" or to "help her sleep" by a well-meaning friend, relative, or physician and, thus, use a benzodiazepine, or other substance of abuse, for the first time.

Social Use. The second pattern of substance use is that of Social Use. Characteristically, although an elderly woman may actively seek the substance of abuse, there are no major harmful effects associated with its use. An example of this pattern of use is drinking an alcoholic beverage during a luncheon with friends at a restaurant. In this situation, the point is that the elderly woman went to the restaurant not primarily for the alcohol, but once there sought the alcohol, and used it. The use of alcohol is a common part of adult socializing in North America that usually continues into old age. Dinner parties, holiday celebrations, golf tournaments, fishing trips, bridge parties, and other get togethers provide the opportunity for the social consumption of alcohol. When this pattern of substance use has been developed through the earlier adult years, it generally continues into old age.

Habitual Use. The next pattern of substance use is that of Habitual Use. Habitual use involves the establishment of substance use. For example, drinking a cup of coffee every morning to wake-up and get going, or going for a drink every Wednesday evening after volunteering at the homeless shelter to unwind. The major characteristics of this pattern of substance use include the absence of major harmful effects associated with the habitual use of the particular substance and the absence of physical dependence (i.e., addiction). However, psychological dependence (i.e., habituation) is a prominent feature of this pattern of substance use.

With age, it is not unusual that certain substances of abuse (e.g., caffeine), which had been habitually used through the earlier adult years, may affect elderly women differently because of age related physiological changes. These changes may result in a change in the established pattern of their use. Often a pattern of habitual use of another substance of abuse develops. For example, some elderly women who previously consumed coffee daily over their adult years may complain of a sensitivity to caffeine, explaining that they cannot drink coffee after 5 p.m., or they will be up all night. These elderly women may now "prefer a cognac or brandy after dinner each night" to help them "relax and sleep better" (authors' personal files). It should be noted here that the focus is on the pattern of substance use (i.e., the broader picture of substance use) as opposed to only the specific substance used. The next two patterns of use (i.e., Abuse and Compulsive Use) involve more intensive patterns of substance use and more serious harmful effects.

Abuse. The fourth pattern of substance use is that of Abuse. In this pattern of use, the substance of abuse is actively sought out by the elderly woman. For example, a homebound elderly woman, who has consumed her available supply of alcohol or tobacco products, may order groceries from a local market for delivery to her home for the sole purpose of obtaining a supply of alcoholic beverages or cigarettes. Another elderly woman may secure a supply of benzodiazepines, opiate analgesics, or other prescription drugs by means of "physician shopping."

The pattern of Abuse also is characterized by the phenomenon that the substance of abuse continues to be used despite related harmful effects. For example, a pattern of Abuse would be identified for an elderly woman who has chronic obstructive pulmonary disease and who continues to smoke a pack of cigarettes daily despite her need to use continuous oxygen and her limited ability to perform her usual activities of daily living without assistance. Another example of this pattern of use would be an elderly woman who has severe cardiovascular disease and who continues to moderately consume alcohol against the advice of her cardiologist who has warned her that continued use may significantly decrease her life-expectancy. In this pattern of use, the harm associated with the substance use generally is recognized by the elderly woman (i.e., worsening of pulmonary function, increased heart disease), but, regardless, she cannot stop using the substance of abuse and continues to actively seek and use the particular substance (or substances) of abuse.

Compulsive Use. The most serious and harmful pattern of substance use among elderly women is that of Compulsive Use. This pattern of substance use is characterized by a total lack of control over the substance used. Elderly women who use a substance of abuse generally acknowledge that they just cannot help themselves. In addition to feelings of loss of control over their use of the substance of abuse, be it alcohol, diazepam [Valium®], or nicotine, it becomes their major focus of life and, subsequently, most of their time is spent thinking about, obtaining, and using the substance despite its expected and predictable harmful consequences (e.g., cardiovascular disease; death).

Resumed Nonuse, Controlled Use, and Relapsed Use. Traditionally, once the pattern of compulsive use was reached, an elderly woman's return to previous and less serious patterns of use was thought to be virtually impossible. Although this issue continues to be argued among researchers (e.g., Levy, 1992), it seems that until further research evidence to the contrary is accumulated, once this pattern of use occurs, the only way substance use can be effectively controlled with any degree of confidence is by total abstinence. Currently, this general therapeutic guideline appears to apply to all substances of abuse, and to all people who use them compulsively.

With a better understanding of these patterns of substance use, health and social care professionals can better assess elderly women for both potential and active problems related to their substance use. They also will be better able to devise prevention and treatment strategies that more appropriately reflect the needs of elderly women who have, or who are developing, serious substance use problems (e.g., patterns of Abuse and Compulsive Use). They also will be better able to assist elderly women directly or through appropriate referrals to maintain resumed nonuse patterns when needed and devise effective relapse prevention strategies.

The Elderly Woman Dimension As noted earlier in this chapter, the elderly population in North America is expected to increase to the extent that approximately 1 in 4 people will be elderly by the end of the first decade of the twenty-first century. Other data indicate that these elderly people will be mostly women comprising a multitude of ethnic, socioeconomic, and cultural backgrounds. As health care resources are continually being used by this aging group of North Americans and monies become increasingly limited to assist them, efforts are being increasingly directed at promoting healthier lifestyles and abilities in self-care and care by family in an attempt to conserve these limited resources.

While it is expected that most elderly women will be residing in their own homes and will be directly involved in their own health promotion, many other elderly women will be in need of health and other social care services. These elderly women will likewise face many of the same challenges that elderly women face today (see Table 5-3) and they also will face the challenges of the new century. Thus, substance use, particularly patterns of Abuse and Compulsive Use, as influenced by individual physical, psychological, and social variables, is expected to remain an important and significant area of concern to health and social care professionals as they plan services for future generations of elderly women.

The influence of various specific sets of variables, that are encountered when the physical, psychological, and social aspects of the Elderly Woman Dimension are considered for a specific elderly woman, is significant and must be fully addressed when planning and implementing her treatment program. For example, effective plans and approaches for an elderly alcoholic woman would differ significantly if the elderly woman in question was: 1) a 55-year-old, middle class woman, who was divorced, suffering from loneliness, and had no immediate family available for social support; 2) a 65-year-old, married woman, who was recently retired, financially secure, and living in her own residence with her husband, who also is an alcoholic; 3) a 70-year-old woman with severe hypertension, living in a publicly supported senior citizens residence, who is active in her community church; 4) a 68-year-old woman living by herself in a rented apartment, who is suffering from reactive depression related to the recent loss of her life partner to cirrhosis of the liver; or 5) a 62-year-old woman, a recent immigrant, who is married, does not speak English, and is the principle source of financial support for her family, including her three grandchildren. Clearly all elderly women alcoholics are *not* alike and consideration of the variables associated with the Elderly Woman Dimension can greatly assist in differentiating the unique aspects of each individual elderly woman that are amenable to intervention. It is through this differentiation that treatment plans can be individualized and therapeutic outcomes maximized by means of the use of appropriate multidisciplinary intervention (see Chapter 11, Preventing and Treating Substance Use Disorders Among Women).

The Societal Dimension The Societal Dimension is often given less attention than the other dimensions of MIMSUAEW. Reflecting "the laws of the land," professional ethics, realms of professional practice, attitudes toward substance use, and a myriad of other variables, this dimension has significant impact on the services that are available for and provided to elderly women and should not be ignored. For example, the availability of treatment programs for elderly women who display problematic patterns of substance use in terms of access and cost needs to be considered when planning or recommending intervention at the local, state and province, or national levels. Other societal variables, such as culture, can likewise have a significant effect upon treatment outcome. It is less likely, for example, that an elderly woman will seek, enter, or complete treatment if her substance use is characterized as a sign of moral weakness within her family or cultural group. While the variables found in the Societal Dimension of MIMSUAEW are generally not amenable to immediate change, they significantly affect availability of services and must, therefore, be realistically addressed and dealt with in an appropriate manner.

Time Dimension The last dimension of MIMSUAEW is the Time Dimension. This dimension, likewise, is often given insufficient attention. The Time Dimension includes such variables as the historical period during which a substance of abuse is used, the length of time a substance of abuse is used in relation to its pattern of use, and also the specific period of the elderly woman's life when it is used. The Time Dimension plays a significant role in terms of the context of substance use in relation to each of the other three variable dimensions and, subsequently, the harmful effects. For example, the harmful effects associated with the use of nicotine in the form of chronic cigarette smoking for an elderly woman in Ancient China were significantly different than today. During this historical period, the penalty prescribed by the emperor for tobacco smoking was death by beheading. Similarly, heroin addiction was not a problem prior to the end of the 19th century because heroin had not as yet been synthesized as a cure for morphine addiction. In a more recent context, the crack form of cocaine, now widely used by people across the life-span, was virtually unknown a decade ago. In addition, the chronic use of marijuana and other psychedelics, largely unobserved among today's elderly, may become more prominent as the "Hippie" or "baby boomer" moves into old age.

Applications of MIMSUAEW

The phenomenon of substance use is actually one of the many phenomena of human existence. As such, it is a complex multidimensional entity that requires a complex multifactorial approach so that it can be understood and effectively dealt with. MIMSUAEW is a conceptual model that can be used to explore the multifactorial phenomenon of substance use among elderly women and to diagnose and treat patterns of use that are potentially or actually harmful or problematic.

Diagnosis The diagnosis of potential or problematic patterns of substance use among elderly women is generally far more difficult than for younger women because elderly women often present with atypical signs and symptoms as they do for other medical and psychological disorders. Diagnosis also may be difficult when an elderly woman is confused (i.e., suffering from cognitive impairment that is organic [e.g., Alzheimer's disease] or drug induced [e.g., adverse drug reaction]), have communication problems (e.g., lack of fluency in English; hearing deficits), are easily fatigued, or have other disorders (e.g., severe chronic obstructive pulmonary disease) that make assessment difficult. In addition, whereas several screening instruments (e.g., CAGE; MAST) and diagnostic tests have been developed for use with younger adults, their use may be significantly limited because they have not as yet been normed or validated for the elderly (Blankfield & Maritz, 1990). To facilitate the rapid initial screening of elderly people for substance use disorders, the MIMSUAEW Flowchart (see Figure 5-3) has been formulated as a means for determining the need to further assess elderly women with the more comprehensive MIMSUAEW. The flow chart also can be used to assess family member involvement as enablers, facilitators, and contributors to problematic patterns of substance use among elderly women.

When MIMSUAEW is used, instead of focusing solely on the substance of abuse (e.g., alcohol versus diazepam versus tobacco versus cocaine), focus is on the *interaction* among the particular substance of abuse and its pattern of use variables; the physical, psychological, and social variables noted for a particular elderly woman or relative; and the broader societal context in which this woman and her family live. An examination of these dimensions in relation to the Time Dimension can enable health and social care professionals to identify the factors that are indicative of a potential or actual problematic pattern of substance use, its severity, and its related prognosis (e.g., early-onset versus late-onset alcoholism).

The Substance of Abuse Dimension, which delineates the substance of abuse and the pattern of use variables, will indicate whether or not a significant potential exists for compulsive use and toxicity for a particular substance of abuse (e.g., alcohol versus caffeine). An examination of the two sets of variables for a particular elderly woman can reveal whether the substance of abuse has a narrow or wide therapeutic index (e.g., alphamethylfentanyl versus methadone) or whether it has a high or a low addiction potential (e.g., cocaine versus LSD). By considering the legal status and the availability of a particular substance of abuse (e.g., legal tobacco versus illegal marijuana), it also can be ascertained whether or not the elderly woman is likely to be involved with the judicial system and the associated likelihood of incarceration.

The Substance of Abuse Variables and the Time Dimension further address the frequency of use of a particular substance (e.g., 2 packages of cigarettes per day for the last 30 years versus 1 package per day for the last 3 years). When combined with information regarding the Pattern of Use Variables, the Substance of Abuse Dimension provides a measure of the potential severity of a particular elderly woman's pattern of

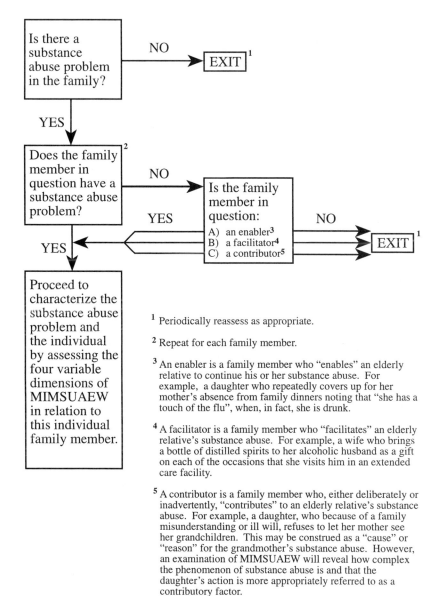

FIGURE 5-3. The MIMSUAEW flowchart.

use (e.g., social use versus compulsive use). This situation can be further delineated by identifying any concomitant high risk factors under the Elderly Woman Dimension, Physical Variables (e.g., heart disease, kidney dysfunction).

A review of the Psychological Variables (e.g., cognitive function, self-esteem, general mental health) can assist in planning treatment strategies aimed at significant factors related to an elderly woman's pattern of substance use, which are related to her cognitive abilities and readiness for various forms of treatment. Under the Societal Dimension, health and social care workers are reminded of their roles as health and social care professionals and members of a society that is concerned about the promotion of health among elderly women. Thus, an examination of the variables obtained for a specific elderly woman can provide them with a diagnosis of problematic patterns of substance use, an indication of prognosis in terms of morbidity, mortality, and recidivism, and guidelines for planning intervention strategies (i.e., self-help, residential treatment, Alcoholics or Narcotics Anonymous, multimodal therapy).

By identifying and listing the variables under each of the dimensions, health and social care professionals can generate a comprehensive description of an elderly woman in relation to her substance use. If this is done for a group, or if the variables are gathered from a large sample of elderly women comprising a particular population and subjected to factor analysis, then a typology can be generated. Hypotheses describing relationships among variables also can be developed and tested (e.g., by means of path analysis techniques) in an effort to promote knowledge development in this important area of women's health.

Treatment Once the various dimensions of MIMSUAEW have been considered for an elderly woman, MIMSUAEW can help to direct treatment planning by identifying those variables in each dimension that are amenable to change or modification. For example, if under the Substance of Abuse Dimension, the substance used is identified as being particularly harmful, then a less harmful substance from the same pharmacologic classification might be substituted (e.g., methadone for heroin) or if the method of administration is identified as being particularly harmful, then a less harmful method of use might be used as part of a treatment plan (e.g., replacing heroin injections with heroin cigarettes in order to lower the risk of HIV infection from sharing contaminated needles).

Likewise under the Elderly Woman Dimension: Psychological Variables, if specific stresses and maladaptive coping mechanisms are identified, then techniques of stress reduction targeted at these specific stresses and the development of better coping abilities would be an integral component of the prescriptive treatment plan. If, under the Elderly Woman Dimension: Social Variables, a lack of family support has been identified as a major contributing factor to the problematic pattern of substance use, then intervention might include attempts to increase family or other support (e.g., family counseling).

As with the other dimensions, if, for example, under the Societal Dimension, a lack of adequate health care resources (e.g., senior programs, geriatric specialists) has been identified as a major factor contributing to problematic patterns of substance use, then intervention might include attempts to increase social assistance (e.g., develop specific social programs for the elderly) or increase focus on attracting geriatric specialists to the particular community.

Treatment Evaluation Evaluation of treatment is one of the most crucial, yet perhaps most frequently overlooked steps in helping people to confront and manage their problematic patterns of substance use. It is useless for health and social care professionals to prescribe treatment or for an elderly woman to follow a plan of treatment if that treatment is ineffective. Using MIMSUAEW, evaluation can be readily performed by comparing the variables obtained for an individual elderly woman before treatment (i.e., base-line assessment), during treatment (i.e., formative evaluation), and at a specified planned interval after treatment is completed (i.e., summative evaluation).

For example, under the Elderly Woman Dimension: Social Variables, if employment status (e.g., retirement) has been previously identified as a major contributing factor in the elderly person's history of problematic patterns of substance use, and if sufficient attention has not been given to the development of appropriate activities for leisure time, then a positive prognosis is less likely despite other treatment interventions. While program evaluators and researchers may be particularly interested in the summative evaluation in terms of program success and recidivism rates, the health and social care professional will be as interested in the formative evaluation because if it is determined that a treatment plan is ineffective, then it can be modified in-stream in an attempt to optimize therapy for a particular elderly woman.

MIMSUAEW also is useful in that it can reveal factors that may, for a particular elderly woman, contribute to relapsed use if not addressed (e.g., an elderly woman may resume the use of a particular substance of abuse which was used previously to bolster inadequate coping abilities when she is faced with another significant stress, such as the recent death of a loved one, diagnosis of cancer, or loss of financial support). In addition, MIMSUAEW can be useful as a framework for helping elderly women understand the factors affecting their patterns of substance use and for enabling them to become better consumers and participants in their own health care planning and treatment.

☐ Conclusion

Problematic patterns of substance use among elderly women is not only increasing, but is expected to worsen during the first decade of the twenty-first century. Health and social care professionals must be better prepared to recognize and effectively deal with this important area of women's health. Problematic patterns of substance use among elderly women remains largely unrecognized because of: 1) a low level of suspicion; 2) misdiagnosis; and 3) concealment. It is axiomatic that problems cannot be solved unless they are first recognized. Health and social care professionals must recognize that elderly women, as a group, are at a high risk for developing problematic patterns of substance use. Thus, every effort must be made to properly assess and diagnose these patterns of substance use, prescribe appropriate treatment, evaluate treatment, and revise treatment approaches as necessary in order to promote healthy aging.

The Mega Interactive Model of Substance Use among Elderly Women (MIMSUAEW) has been presented as a conceptual model to assist health and social care professionals to understand and better deal with the complex phenomenon of substance use among elderly women. By focusing attention on all four major variable dimensions (i.e., substance of abuse, elderly woman, societal, and time), instead of solely on the specific substance used, MIMSUAEW provides health and social care professionals with a unique, comprehensive, and usable tool for promoting healthy aging within the contexts of their clinical practice.

☐ Notes

1. See also related discussion in Chapter 1, An Overview of Substance Use Among Women.
2. It should be noted that not all reported research is supportive of this conclusion. For example, Welte and Mirand (1995) found that chronic stress, not acute stress—such as bereavement or

retirement, was positively correlated with alcohol abuse among a general sample of elderly adults.
3. For example, alcohol use can aggravate serious chronic health conditions (e.g., diabetes), which commonly occur among elderly women, resulting in increased morbidity and mortality. As noted by Emanuele, Swade, & Emanuele (1998):

> Alcohol consumption by diabetics can worsen blood sugar control in those patients. For example, long-term alcohol use in well-nourished diabetics can result in excessive blood sugar levels. Conversely, long-term alcohol ingestion in diabetics who are not adequately nourished can lead to dangerously low blood sugar levels. Heavy drinking, particularly in diabetics, also can cause the accumulation of certain acids in the blood that may result in severe health consequences [i.e., diabetic ketoacidosis]. Finally, alcohol consumption can worsen diabetes-related medical complications such as disturbances in fat metabolism [e.g., hypertriglyceridemia], nerve damage [i.e., peripheral neuropathy], and eye disease [i.e., diabetic retinopathy]. (p. 211)

4. It has also been noted that: "The prevalence of problem drinking in nursing homes is as high as 49 percent in some studies . . ." (National Institute on Alcohol Abuse and Alcoholism, 1998, p. 1).
5. The authors recommend that a drug and chart review be performed for all elderly women who have been prescribed benzodiazepines for more than 1 month.

    Care also must be exercised so that one form of inappropriate and unsafe drug therapy is not simply replaced with another. As noted by Zullich, Grasela, Fiedler-Kelly, & Gengo (1992) in their study of a triplicate benzodiazepine program, "although 22 percent of the patients (in long-term care facilities) previously receiving BZDs (benzodiazepines) were discontinued from these drugs, more than half of these patients were switched to alternative therapy, including tricyclic antidepressants and antipsychotic drugs" (p. 539).
6. Note that this model is derived as a specific application of The Mega Interactive Model of Substance Use Among Women (see Chapter 1, An Overview of Substance Use Among Women, for additional details and discussion).

PART III

SOCIAL CONSIDERATIONS

CHAPTER 6

Women as Victims of Substance Use Related Violence

Accidents and acts of violence associated with substance use result in significant morbidity and mortality (Roth & Moore, 1995; Travis, 1996; L. A. Pagliaro, 1993b)[1] (see Chapter 1, An Overview of Substance Use Among Women). In this context women suffer significantly more victimization than do men.

This chapter examines the increasing number of substance use related accidents among and acts of violence against women and their associated significant mortality and morbidity. Attention is given to accidental falls and motor vehicle crashes, and acts of violence, particularly assaults, homicides, and suicides (see Table 6-1). The focus of the chapter is women as *victims*. For information regarding women as *perpetrators*, see Chapter 7, Women as Perpetrators of Substance Use Related Violence.

☐ Accidents and Acts of Violence

Accidents

The most common substance use-related accidents involving women are falls and motor vehicle crashes. Substance use related accidents, which are a major source of morbidity and mortality among women, also include industrial or worksite accidents associated with alcohol and marijuana use. Women also are often included among the unfortunate victims of fatal public transportation (e.g., airplane, bus, train) accidents, which have been related to pilots and drivers operating their airplanes, buses, taxis, or trains while intoxicated.

Falls Substance use can contribute to a variety of accidents involving falls (see also Chapter 5, Substance Use Among Elderly Women: Effects on Healthy Aging). These falls range from falling down a set of stairs while intoxicated with alcohol, to jumping from a condominium balcony in an effort to fly after a hit of LSD. Significant alcohol

TABLE 6-1. Substance use related violent physical injuries among women

Accidents	Homicides
• falls	• intentional (e.g., spousal violence)
• motor vehicle crashes	• unintentional (e.g., fatal motor vehicle crashes)
Assaults	**Suicides**
• battery during pregnancy	• attempted
• dating violence	• completed
• physical abuse/assault	
• sexual abuse/assault	

consumption before a fall has been reported for 28% of adult patients (Hussain, Wijetunge, Brubnic, & Jackson, 1994).[2]

Motor Vehicle Crashes Women comprise a significant group of victims of motor vehicle crashes as passengers in cars and trucks, bicycle riders, and pedestrians. Substance use appears to contribute to motor vehicle crashes as a consequence of its direct pharmacologic effects on the central nervous system. Although various substances of abuse, alone and in combination, have been implicated in "driving under the influence" (Poklis, Maginn, & Barr, 1987, p. 57), most motor vehicle crashes involving women are directly correlated with alcohol consumption (Greenfeld, 1998; Hussain et al., 1994; Lex, Goldberg, Mendelson, Lawler, & Bower, 1994; Simpson, Mayhew, & Warren, 1982).[3,4] (See Figure 6-1).

The use of marijuana also has been associated with motor vehicle crashes involving women. In fact, it has been found in the systems of many victims involved in fatal motor vehicle crashes (see Chapter 1, An Overview of Substance Use Among Women). Marijuana decreases performance on a variety of driving tasks (e.g., emergency response; lane position variability) (Smiley, Moskowitz, & Ziedman, 1985) and is often used in combination with alcohol. However, precisely for this reason, it is difficult to implicate the exact role of marijuana in motor vehicle crashes because "the increased accident risk of THC-positive drivers may be largely explained by alcohol use" (Gieringer, 1988, p. 99).

Assaults

An assault can be defined as a violent physical or verbal personal attack on another person.[5] Although women can be perpetrators, more commonly they are victims of an assault. In fact 2 to 4 million women are battered each year in North America and lifetime risk for being battered is approximately 30% (American Medical Association, 1995; McCauley et al., 1995).[6] In most of these cases, the woman's male partner[7] is the perpetrator and, in a significant number of these cases, the assault results in serious physical injury. Psychologic sequelae (e.g., posttraumatic stress disorder), which may be significant and long-lasting, are only recently being addressed.

Alcohol and other substances of abuse, used alone or in combination, dramatically increase the risk for violent behavior (Lee & Weinstein, 1997). In fact, alcohol use has consistently emerged as a significant predictor of marital violence.[8] The direct pharmacologic effects of alcohol and other substances of abuse (e.g., decreased social inhibitions and impaired judgement caused by the use of sedative-hypnotics, including

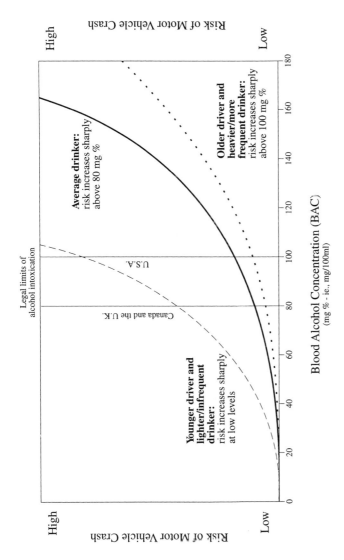

* modified from Shanks, 1990, p. 239

FIGURE 6-1. Risk of motor vehicle crash: Relationship to BAC, age, driving experience, and drinking experience.*

alcohol; increased aggressiveness caused by alcohol or amphetamine use, particularly among males; paranoia caused by amphetamine or cocaine use) account for the significant correlation between substance use and assaults (Miller & Potter-Efron, 1990; L. A. Pagliaro, 1995b; A. M. & L. A. Pagliaro, 1996; L. A. Pagliaro & A. M. Pagliaro, 1992a; A. M. Pagliaro, 1998; A. M. Pagliaro, R. A. Lang, & L. A. Pagliaro, 1998). In addition, certain personality types (e.g., antisocial personality) and mental disorders (e.g., conduct disorder) commonly are noted among male perpetrators. These men also are often diagnosed with substance use disorders and include among their symptomatology, "aggression to people and animals" and "repeated physical fights or assaults" (American Psychiatric Association, 1994, pp. 90, 650)[9] (see Chapter 10, Dual Diagnoses Among Women).

Substance use related assaults involving women have been placed into the following nonexclusive categories for discussion: battery during pregnancy; dating violence; physical abuse/assault; and sexual abuse/assault. The published literature pertaining to each of these categories will be briefly reviewed and discussed.

Battery During Pregnancy

> The beating of pregnant women may be the deepest secret in the dark world of domestic violence. It is hard to reconcile society's traditional response to a pregnant woman—pampering and praising her—with the image of a woman cowering in her own home, shielding her protruding abdomen from punches and kicks. (Roan, 1995, E1)

The image described is at the same time horrendous and relatively common with up to 20% to 40% of pregnant women reportedly being physically or sexually assaulted at some time during their pregnancies (Roan, 1995; Wallace, 1996).[10] Battery during pregnancy has been established as an important risk to the health of both pregnant women and their unborn babies and has been correlated with ". . . anxiety, depression, housing problems, inadequate prenatal care, and drug and alcohol use" (Campbell, Poland, Waller, & Ager, 1992, p. 219). Battery during pregnancy may exacerbate or trigger smoking, drinking, or other substance use by the mother as a maladaptive coping mechanism. (See Chapter 3, Substance Use During Pregnancy and Lactation: Effects on the Developing Fetus, Neonate, and Infant for a discussion of the possible teratogenic effects associated with substance use by pregnant women). In addition, violence during pregnancy has been associated with adverse effects for the fetus or neonate including miscarriages, preterm labor, still-births, and low birth weight (Murphy & Rosenbaum, 1999).[11]

Dating Violence Dating violence, also referred to as courtship violence or premarital abuse, is relatively common among young women. As occurs in other types of assaults, substance use has been implicated as a contributory factor in approximately half of the reported cases of dating violence (Bogal-Allbritten & Allbritten, 1985; Laner, 1983). This contribution can occur in several ways, such as increasing aggressive behavior in the user and also increasing high risk behaviors for victimization (e.g., hitchhiking, going on a blind date) (Windle, 1994).[12] In addition, the coincidence of substance use and prior consensual sexual intercourse also confound interpretation (Wallace, 1996).

Some authors (e.g., Gelles & Pedrick-Cornell, 1985) have argued that substance use is more of an excuse for, rather than a cause of, dating violence. In this regard, substance use among women involved in dating violence can be considered as a maladaptive coping mechanism aimed at both diminishing personal responsibility for the aggressor and allowing the victim to justify her date's behavior. As noted by Aramburu and Leigh (1991), "Research on attributions about drunken violence has suggested that intoxication serves to decrease responsibility attributed to aggressors while increasing responsibility attributed to victims" (p. 31). This theory helps to explain how the victim can remain in the abusive relationship. For example, one of our adult patients shared that he hit his girlfriend "only gently" and only when she needed "a therapy slap." His girlfriend concurred that he only hit her when she was "out of line" and "deserved it." However, when he drank alcohol or cranked amphetamines, the "therapy slaps" would become more severe and result in bruising and black eyes. When confronted, the girlfriend would simply respond, "He really didn't mean it; he was drunk" or "He was high and I shouldn't have bothered him" or "I should have stayed out of his way" (Pagliaro & Pagliaro, 1992, clinical patient file notes). Dating violence also includes sexual abuse/assault such as date rape (Christoffel, 1990; Erickson & Rapkin, 1991) (see the discussion of Sexual Abuse/Assault later in this chapter).

Physical Abuse/Assault   As noted previously, substance use, particularly alcohol use (Quigley & Leonard, 1999), is integrally related to violent behavior.

> Currently abused [female] patients were much more likely than patients not currently being abused to report that their partner drank too much alcohol or used street drugs. They were also more likely to report a substance abuse problem themselves. (McCauley et al., 1995, p. 741)

A majority of people who present to emergency rooms with serious craniofacial trauma, and their assailants, were intoxicated at the time of the assault (Dannenberg, Parver, & Fowler, 1992; Hall & Ofodile, 1991; Hussain, Wijetunge, Brubnic, & Jackson, 1994; Ord & Benian, 1995). As noted by Hall & Ofodile (1991):

> The rising incidence of drug addiction and the violence associated with it has led in recent years to a changing pattern of facial fractures in the inner cities of the United States. Trauma from fists, kicks, and blunt objects, such as baseball bats, are now the primary cause of mandibular fractures. (pp. 422–423)

As noted earlier in this chapter (see section, Assaults) the use of substances of abuse, such as alcohol and cocaine, have been directly correlated with aggressive and violent behavior. Substance use was found to be significantly correlated with both frequency of fighting and frequency of victimization. In addition, Choi and Pope (1994), among others, have noted that androgenic-anabolic steroid (AAS) use (for example, among body-builders and athletes) also is directly correlated with aggressive behavior and frequently with assaults against women:

> These findings support the anecdotal evidence that wives and girlfriends of AAS users may be at risk of serious injury from users while they are on-drug. Thus, AAS use may impose risks not only to the user, but also to the women close to them. (p. 21)

Sexual Abuse/Assault   Sexual abuse/assault of women can occur at any age and accounts for ~10% of all violent crimes (Plouffe, 1995/1996). In over 90% of all cases of sexual abuse/assault women are the victims (Pintea-Reed, 1998). Ninety percent of all reported rapes are intra-racial and black North American women are at significantly greater risk of being raped than are white North American women (Marsh, 1993). Only approximately one-third of rapes are reported to the police (Perkins & Klaus, 1996).

Substance use, particularly alcohol use, appears to play a significant role in these sexual offenses by: disinhibiting social taboos against rape[13]; and, in males, also increasing testosterone levels and, consequently, sexual aggressiveness (L. A. Pagliaro, 1993b). Substance use also has played an even more direct and calculating role in sexual abuse/assault in relation to drug-assisted rape. Over 20 different substances of abuse have been implicated in this activity in which the victim is generally administered the drug unknowingly in order to render her defenseless against the rapist. The drugs most commonly used have been the sedative-hypnotics (i.e., alcohol, the barbiturates, the benzodiazepines) and gamma hydroxybutyrate (GBH)—the so-called date rape drug. The victim often is left with total amnesia or incomplete recollection of the rape and of the events leading up to it (Seymour & Smith, 1999a, 1999b).[14]

Homicide

Homicide can be defined as the unlawful taking of another person's life. Homicide can be intentional (e.g., shooting as part of a domestic dispute) or unintentional (e.g., driving while under the influence of alcohol and running over a mother and her child in a cross-walk). Approximately 1500 women are killed each year in North America by current or past intimate male partners (American Medical Association, 1995; Violence between intimates, 1994).[15] Husbands account for ~60% of the assailants in spouse killings (Dawson & Langan, 1994). In a majority of cases, both intentional and unintentional homicides are related to substance use (Lindenbaum, Carroll, Daskal, & Kapusnick, 1989; Pagliaro & Pagliaro, 1993; Royce, 1989; Violence between intimates, 1994).[16] This scenario has been repeated to us countless times by patients during our forensic psychological assessments.

In relation to unintentional homicide, the following is a typical case that illustrates the effects of substance use and the tragic consequences that occur all too frequently.

> I worked hard all day on several large orders until 7 p.m. when I got paid by my boss and headed home. On the way home I thought it might be nice to have a taste of cocaine . . . went to the dealer's home and bought a gram. Got a box of new rigs from the dealer and fixed half. Wrapped the remaining one-half gram and put it in my pocket. Got into my GMC half-ton and started driving away. By this point I'm paranoid and think someone is in the box of my truck and they're waiting until I slow down to get [i.e., arrest] me . . . so I start running over curbs and drive around corners fast so that I can shake the guy out of the back of my truck . . . Police cruiser started to follow me. I had to get away at any cost. I was running for my life . . . I remember hitting hard a couple of times [running into other vehicles], but I don't remember the third hit at all . . . don't remember all the details . . . when they caught me, one cop said "two people died there because of you . . ." (Pagliaro & Pagliaro, 1991, clinical patient file notes)[17]

☐ Suicide

Suicide occurs more commonly among men, whereas attempted suicide, which is commonly interpreted as a desperate cry for attention or help, occurs more commonly among women.[18] Indeed, women reportedly attempt suicide several times more frequently than do men. However, they generally utilize less lethal means (e.g., drug

TABLE 6-2. Major risk factors associated with suicide ideation and attempts by women*

- Alcoholic family
- Battering (victimization)
- Depression
- Dissatisfaction with family relationships
- External locus of control
- Gender identity crisis
- HIV infection/AIDS
- Hopelessness
- Lack of reasons for living
- Lack of social support
- Lesbian or bisexual sexual orientation
- Loneliness
- Low self-esteem
- Physical or sexual abuse
- Previous psychiatric inpatient treatment
- Previous suicide attempt
- Serious early childhood losses
- Substance use

*Modified from Coté, Biggar, & Dannenberg, 1992; McCauley et al., 1995; L. A. Pagliaro, 1995a; A. M. Pagliaro & L. A. Pagliaro, 1996; Stark & Flitcraft, 1995.

overdosage versus firearm) and, consequently, have a significantly higher rate of survival (Bagley et al., 1990; Pronovost et al., 1990; Rich et al., 1992). "Women who abuse alcohol and other substances appear to be at increased risk for attempting suicide" (Lex, 1994, p. 218). Indeed, as noted by Kreek (1992):

> Drug abuse in the setting of suicide attempts are far more common in women than in men; 43% of emergency room visits of females were drug abuse related suicide attempts or gestures. (p. 107)

A comprehensive search of the computerized Medline, CINAHL, and PsyINFO databases was conducted to identify those factors reported in the literature as being associated with suicides and suicide attempts. Eighteen major risk factors were identified. These risk factors are presented in alphabetical order in Table 6-2.

Depression was found to be the most frequently reported factor associated with suicide or suicide attempts. An examination of this factor and its relationship to the other identified risk factors revealed that it was significantly correlated with suicide ideation and attempts and most of the other identified risk factors. This finding supports the notion that depression should probably be considered as a general factor. Although, retrospectively, depression is strongly correlated with suicide ideation and attempts (i.e., most women who attempt suicide are depressed), prospective correlations are much lower (i.e., most depressed women do not attempt suicide). Thus, the predictive power of depression in identifying women who may be at significant risk for suicide is limited. This becomes even more apparent when one considers that "women are twice as likely as men to experience major depression, yet women are one-fourth as likely as men to take their own lives" (Murphy, 1998, p. 165).

Use of the sedative-hypnotics (e.g., alcohol, diazepam [Valium®]) decreases social inhibitions that might otherwise dissuade an individual from committing suicide (Gomberg, 1989).[19,20] In addition, the substances of abuse are often used, more often by women than by men, as the actual means of a suicide attempt (i.e., overdose) (Coleridge, Cameron, Drummer, & McNeil, 1992; Lex, 1994; Pagliaro, 1990).

Although anyone can attempt suicide, knowledge of the reported risk factors can increase the ability of contacts (e.g., spouses, relatives, friends, counselors, psychologists, or other health and social care professionals) to appropriately identify those women who appear to be at particular risk. Once identified, a program of effective intervention can be developed and implemented. Appropriate clinical intervention is always predicated upon careful and comprehensive assessment. Specific psychometric instruments (e.g., various suicide scales) have been developed and used to assess suicidal tendencies; however, most such measures (e.g., the Beck Depression Inventory) are limited by their focus on depression as the major underlying construct (Morgan, 1994; Wozencraft & Ellegrin, 1991).

The literature and the authors' clinical experiences indicate that a good clinical interview provides the best available method for assessment. In this regard, counselors, psychologists, and other health and social care professionals might begin by: 1) identifying women who are at risk (i.e., those who possess several of the risk factors noted in Table 6–2); 2) looking for clues (e.g., begins giving away prized possessions); 3) conducting a complete evaluation for additional suicide risk factors; and 4) asking specifically about suicide (e.g., ideation, previous attempts, specific suicide plan). Once the suicidal risk has been identified and characterized, appropriate intervention strategies must be implemented.

> There are said to be occasions when a wise man chooses suicide—but generally speaking, it is not in an excess of reasonableness that people kill themselves. Most men and women die defeated . . . (Voltaire, 1694–1778)

☐ Conclusion

Substance use is integrally related to the occurrence of accidents among and acts of violence against women. Accidental injuries among women are most commonly associated with falls and motor vehicles crashes. Serious morbidity and mortality among women also are associated with assaults, including: battery during pregnancy; dating violence; physical abuse/assault; and sexual abuse/assault. Women are commonly the victims of substance use related homicide and suicide. Knowledge of the factors that place women at particular risk for substance use related violence is necessary in order to appropriately prevent or reduce its occurrence. Knowledge of these factors also is required to enable health and social care professionals to provide appropriate therapeutic intervention for women who have been victimized.

☐ Notes

1. For example, Klatsky and Armstrong (1993) noted that: "Among persons reporting 6 or more drinks/day, women and persons below 50 years of age were at especially high risk [for all unnatural deaths]" (p. 1156).

2. We evaluated a rather interesting related forensic case involving a young woman in her mid-twenties. She was in attendance with her boyfriend at a Rolling Stones concert. When she went to buy some beers at the concession stand, a person in line offered her a hit of LSD for five dollars. She purchased the LSD and consumed it with some beer on the way back to her seat, next to her boyfriend, in the stadium. Once back in her seat she began to ruminate about her relationship with her boyfriend and began a "telepathic dialogue" with him. After a while she felt that she would "show him" and got up from her seat, ran about 6 paces down the aisle stairs, did a "perfect" handstand on the rail of the second floor stadium balcony and then propelled herself off into the air. She subsequently landed on a woman who was attending the concert on the main floor level causing some bodily harm (and, hence, the reason for her being arrested and charged with aggravated bodily assault and our forensic psychological evaluation of her) (Pagliaro & Pagliaro, 1997, clinical patient file notes).
3. The corollary of this finding is not that one should drink less and drive, but that one should not drink at all and drive. As noted by Royce (1989), "One need not be legally drunk to kill somebody with an automobile. Nor must one be an alcoholic" (p. 325).
4. . . . it appears that alcohol may have differential effects on women compared with men. Women appear to be more vulnerable to physiological damage from prolonged alcohol use. They may also be more vulnerable to impairment of performance from low doses of alcohol. Such differential effects of alcohol may affect both drinking performance and injury resulting from motor vehicle crashes. (Waller & Blow, 1995, p. 120)
5. A term increasingly used in this context is "wife abuse." Wife abuse is defined as the deliberate attempt by a male partner in an intimate relationship to control or intimidate his female partner. The couple may or may not be married and the abuse may take many forms including physical abuse, psychological abuse, and sexual abuse.
6. This number can be as high as 60% in some reporting jurisdictions (Federal, 1996).
7. Several studies have noted that nonspousal partners are significantly more likely to resort to physical assault. As noted by Roberts (1987), "More than twice as many women in cohabitating relationships filed charges against the batterers than did women in marital relationships" (p. 81).

    The reported data may be confounded by other factors, such as possible reluctance of a wife to file charges against her husband. However, the consistency of this finding over the last decade would tend to indicate that there is substance to this observed relationship.
8. Alcohol is associated with a substantial proportion of human violence, and perpetrators are often under the influence of alcohol (Secretary of Health and Human Services, 1993).
9. As noted by Marsh (1993, p. 150):

    In regard to the abuser, there is no normal profile and they may come from any socioeconomic class. In public the abuser may appear to be a good father, husband, and all-around law abiding citizen. However, when the abuser comes home he exhibits low self-esteem, abuses drugs and/or alcohol and often refuses to accept responsibility for his behavior. He usually feels he did the right thing by battering his mate in an attempt to control her.

10. Data suggest that men, who are abusive to the women that they are in a relationship with, often start their pattern of abuse when the woman becomes pregnant (Raftis & Reynolds, 1996). "Reasons" provided for this abusive behavior are varied, but tend to center on jealousy for the attention that the pregnant woman is receiving and in relation to the perception that "the baby" gets more care and attention than "the father." Other factors, such as the perception of increased familial responsibility and permanence of the commitment/relationship, also appear to play a significant role in this behavior that is further aggravated by substance use, particularly alcohol (Pagliaro & Pagliaro, 1990–1996, clinical patient file notes).
11. Postpartum abuse of the mother also can occur and is associated with: a history of previous abuse (e.g., during pregnancy); substance use by the mother (i.e., the victim); and substance use by her partner (i.e., the perpetrator) (Wilson et al., 1996).

132 Social Considerations

12. These findings are confounded by the occurrence of dual diagnoses (see Chapter 10, Dual Diagnoses Among Women).
13. This disinhibition phenomenon and related sense of lack of culpability appears to be particularly pervasive in cases of date rape and marital rape (i.e., when the perpetrator is an intimate of the victim) (Barnard, 1990).
14. Adult sexual victimization appears to be a predictive indicator of suicide risk. "One in four rape victims, in contrast to 1 in 20 nonvictimized women, had engaged in a suicidal act" (Stepakoff, 1998). (See discussion of Suicide).
15. In a study of the behavior of males, who had committed partner homicide-suicide, the most highly correlated factors were victim separation from the perpetrator and a previous history of domestic violence (Morton, Runyan, Morocco, & Butts, 1998).
16. In terms of alcohol *alone* ~50% of all homicide victims and ~65% of all homicide defendants were drinking at the time of the murder (Dawson & Langan, 1994).
17. The two people who died were a young couple who had just become engaged to be married. The adult male driver was subsequently convicted of vehicular manslaughter.
18. We generally consider this view to be a simplistic overgeneralization for a behavior that has decidedly complex etiology. See related discussion and Table 6–2 "Major Risk Factors Associated with Suicide Ideation and Attempts by Women" for additional details.
19. The sedative-hypnotics can also cause depression, which as previously noted, is associated with suicide attempts (Madianos, Gefou-Madianou, & Stefanis, 1994; L. A. Pagliaro & A. M. Pagliaro, 1993).
20. An interesting corollary is that CNS stimulant use might prevent or treat depression. Support for this hypothesis comes from reports of self-medicating for depression with CNS stimulants, such as cocaine, by depressed patients (Pagliaro, Jaglalsingh, & Pagliaro, 1992). In addition, Kawachi, Willet, Colditz, Stampfer, & Speizer (1996), in a long-term prospective study, found a significant inverse relationship between coffee intake (i.e., consumption of the CNS stimulant caffeine) and risk for suicide among women.

Women as Perpetrators of Substance Use Related Violence

A number of research studies support a relationship between crimes perpetrated by women and substance use (e.g., Abram, 1989; Modestin & Ammann, 1995; Moon, Thompson, & Bennett, 1993; Russell, 1993). However, the nature of this complex relationship is incompletely understood (see Figure 7-1) and gives rise to several rudimentary questions (Abram, 1989; Bradford, Greenberg, & Motayne, 1992). For example, in regard to women: Does substance use contribute to crime?; Does crime contribute to substance use?; What part do other variables (e.g., antisocial personality) play in the relationship between substance use and crime?; Are certain types of crime more strongly related to substance use (e.g., violent versus nonviolent crime)?; Is the use of certain substances of abuse more strongly related to crime? This chapter attempts to address these and other related questions. The general nature of the relationship between substance use by women and violent and nonviolent crime is considered first. This overview is followed by a discussion of pharmacopsychologic-related crime and concludes with a brief discussion of domestic violence perpetrated by women.

☐ Substance Use and Crime

It is commonly thought that substance use, particularly the hustling and other activities required to maintain a particular pattern of use, is a major contributor to crime (i.e., that crack heads, pot heads, and heroin addicts commonly commit serious physical or sexual assaults, robberies, and other crimes in order to maintain their habits). However, this notion, although often popularized in the media, has not been clearly substantiated by the available research data (Bradford, Greenberg, & Motayne, 1992; Collins, 1981; Spunt, Goldstein, Brownstein, & Fendrich, 1994). These data indicate that, while women commonly commit crimes to maintain their substance use, they are not involved in more serious crimes than other groups (e.g., men, youth) and they do not, as a group, pose a significant risk for engaging in violent crimes (Drugs, 1994; Miller & Gold, 1994; Nurco, Cisin, & Ball, 1985). As a rule, when women are involved in crimes, their crimes, more often than not, involve drug dealing, prostitution, and

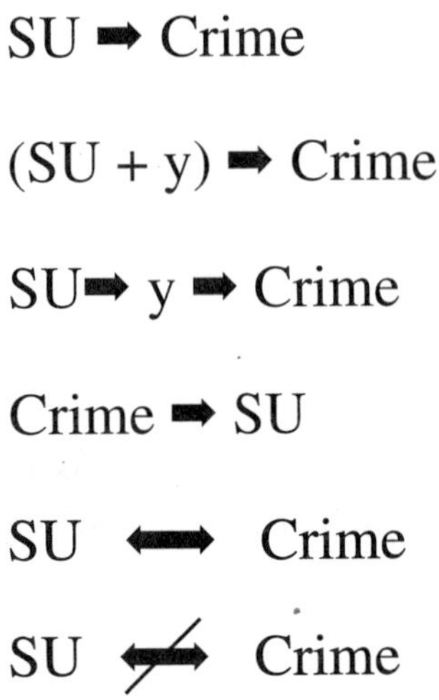

SU ➡ Crime

(SU + y) ➡ Crime

SU ➡ y ➡ Crime

Crime ➡ SU

SU ⬌ Crime

SU ⇎ Crime

FIGURE 7-1. Substance use (SU) and crime: Proposed relationships.

theft rather than violent crimes (see later discussion in the section, Examples of Substance Use Related Violence Perpetrated by Women, for notable exceptions to this rule).

Although violent (e.g., homicide, rape) and nonviolent (e.g., prostitution, shoplifting) crimes are committed by women who use various substances of abuse, several researchers (e.g., Taylor & Albright, 1981) concur with Weisz, Martin, Walter, & Fernandez (1991) that "the distinction between perpetrators of personal and property crimes is rarely definitive" (p. 791). As concluded by Abram (1989):

> There is substantial evidence that drug users tend to engage in income-generating crime.... The relationship between drug use and violent crime, however, has been inconsistently reported and is less well documented.... Although drug users commit violent offenses, they engage in fewer violent offenses than nondrug using counterparts. (p. 135)

This finding has been corroborated by a summary report from the Office of National Drug Control Policy, which found that:

> Inmates incarcerated for robbery, burglary, larceny, and drug trafficking most often committed their crime to obtain money for drugs. Inmates who committed homicide, sexual assault, assault, and public-order offenses were least likely to commit their offense to obtain money for drugs. (Chaiken, 1995, p. 8)

However, the use of one substance of abuse, alcohol, has been consistently associated with aggressive behavior and violent crime (Bradford, Greenberg, & Motayne, 1992; Greenfeld, 1998; Lau & Pihl, 1994; Weisman & Taylor, 1994; Yarvis, 1994). As noted by Collins (1981), "The consistency and strength of the alcohol-crime empirical association is sufficient to justify the inference that alcohol is sometimes causally implicated in the occurrence of serious crime" (p. 289).

TABLE 7-1. Alcohol use and criminal behavior: Methodologic limitations*

- Biased sampling (e.g., incarcerated inmates, students)
- Failure to control relevant variables (e.g., gender, race)
- Lack of interactional studies
- Lack of longitudinal studies
- Lack of prospective studies
- Lack of sufficient attention to the nature of the targets (victims) of the crime
- Lack of uniformity in the definitions of alcohol use
- Lack of uniformity in the definitions of crime
- Poorly described context within which drinking and crime co-occurred
- Unclear distinction between subgroups of alcohol users and perpetrators
- Use of law enforcement statistics (which by their nature are biased toward reporting only the most extreme cases)

*Modified from: Bradford, Greenberg, and Motayne (1992, p. 607); Volavka, Martell, and Convit (1992, pp. 246–247); and Westermeyer (1990, p. 53).

Alcohol Use and Violent Crime

A consistent and positive relationship between the use of alcohol and violent crime involving aggressive behavior has been identified (Lisansky Gomberg, 1991; Greenfeld, 1998; Milner & Chilamkurti, 1991; L. A. Pagliaro & A. M. Pagliaro, 1992a). As noted by Holcomb and Anderson (1983), "A relationship between violence and alcohol intoxication has been recognized for centuries" (p. 159). Unfortunately, although much empirical data exist,[1] research examining this relationship has been plagued by several methodologic limitations (see Table 7-1). These limitations serve to confound the interpretation of results and limit their generalization. For example, some researchers have suggested that an aggressive personality is an antecedent of alcohol use and alcohol-related aggression (i.e., aggressive personality → alcohol use → alcohol-related aggression). Others (e.g., Roman, 1981) suggest that situational factors (see Table 7-2) influence the relationship between alcohol use and crime in various ways. However, the commonly associated relationship between alcohol use and violent crime, including aggravated sexual assault and homicide, can be explained, for the most part, by two pharmacologic mechanisms (i.e., direct effects of alcohol and cofactor effects) and one social mechanism (i.e., cognitive social learning) (Graham, 1980; Pernanen, 1981).[2]

Pharmacologic Mechanisms[3]   The first pharmacologic mechanism involves the direct effect of alcohol as a sedative-hypnotic (see Chapter 1, An Overview of Substance Use Among Women). As a sedative-hypnotic, alcohol depresses the CNS, which decreases social inhibitions (i.e., alcohol functions as a disinhibitor) and impairs cognitive processing (i.e., problem solving and, hence, the ability to develop strategies to effectively deal with frustrating or threatening situations). For example, aggressive and sexual behavior, or thoughts about such behavior, that have been suppressed because of acquiescence to social norms (e.g., being a "good" mother or wife)

TABLE 7-2. Situational factors that may significantly affect the relationship between alcohol use and crime*

Drinker
- drinking alone
- drinking with others
  - relatives
  - acquaintances
  - strangers
- drinking in the presence of other drinkers
  - relatives
  - acquaintances
  - strangers
- drinking in the presence of nondrinkers
  - relatives
  - acquaintances
  - strangers

Role relationships vis-à-vis expected aggressive behavior
- dominant relationships in which aggression is or is not expected from the drinker
- submissive relationships in which aggression is or is not expected from the drinker
- equal-power relationships in which aggression may be directed from or received by the drinker

Mobility
- drinker remains in drinking environment
- drinker moves from drinking environment to another environment

Definition of drinking situation
- drinking for "escape" or other desired effects
- recreational/"time-out" drinking
- religious/ceremonial drinking

Drinking environment
- drinking in the home
- drinking in a private nonhome setting
- drinking in a tavern/bar
- drinking in an open space (e.g., park)

Weapons
- absence of aggression-related weaponry (e.g., gun; knife)
- drinker's or other's possession of aggression-related weaponry (e.g., gun; knife)
- copresence of aggression-related weaponry (e.g., gun; knife)

Social control
- absence of labeling/social control factors
- presence of labeling/social control factors

*Modified from: Roman (1981, p. 150).

or concern for associated consequences (e.g., adverse publicity, harm to self or others, incarceration), are released from conscious control, making them more likely to be acted on (Pihl, Peterson, & Lau, 1993; Sayette, Wilson, & Elias, 1993; Zeichner, Allen, Giancola, & Lating, 1994). As noted by Blum (1981):

> Alcohol may alter perceptions, cognitive performance, moods/emotions, and response capabilities and preferences. Less adaptive solutions, such as violence, can occur with

decrements in judgment. Violence may also be adaptive, or perceived as such. Meanings imposed on the environment may change. Violence variability may be a function of cues that are subliminal to the observer but are notably altered perceptions within the person. (pp. 115–116)

Obviously, this pharmacologic mechanism would be expected to significantly interact with the personality of the user (i.e., assuming that two women drank alcohol to the same level of intoxication, the disinhibitory effects would most likely result in an increased risk for violent behavior in the woman who had such a predisposition [e.g., a woman with antisocial personality disorder] in comparison to the woman who did not) (Abram, 1989; Fishbein et al., 1993; Irwin, Schukin, & Smith, 1990).

In addition, available data suggest that the effect of social inhibition is more pronounced for women who have lower IQ scores. This observation is consistent with the conclusion of Lau and Pihl (1994) "that acute alcohol intoxication interferes with the ability to integrate previously acquired knowledge in the formulation of behavioral strategies" (p. 701). This observation also is consistent with the more general notion that state-like psychometric variables (e.g., mood) are more readily influenced by substance use than are trait-like variables (e.g., IQ; personality) (Blum, 1981, see discussion in section, Substance Use-Induced Automatism, for a noted exception to this general notion).

The second suggested pharmacologic mechanism involves an interaction between alcohol use and another variable that also is related to violent behavior. For example, assuming that level of frustration is positively related to violent behavior, there may be situations in which the level of frustration in a particular situation is insufficient to lead to violent behavior (i.e., the critical threshold has not been exceeded). Similarly, a situation could exist in which the level of alcohol use was insufficient to lead to violent behavior. However, if these two risk factors (i.e., level of frustration and alcohol use) are combined, then violent behavior is likely to occur because the threshold for such behavior is much more likely to be exceeded as a result of the interaction of these two variables.

Social Mechanism The third mechanism, the social mechanism, involves intervening psychological and sociological variables, including cognitive social learning variables (e.g., expectations). When drinking alcohol, women expect certain effects from the alcohol and behave in a manner that they have learned is expected of them (George & Dermen, 1988; Lindman & Lang, 1994). For example, if women drink to feel more attractive, and if the social role expectation of being attractive is to be more sexually active, then they will be more likely, when drinking, to behave (i.e., act) in accordance with this expectation (Aramburu & Leigh, 1991; Dermen & George, 1989). This relationship was described by MacAndrew and Edgerton (1969) in their cross-cultural ethnographic study of drinking behavior that rejected the disinhibition theory of drunken comportment and advanced the "time-out hypothesis."

As noted by Labouvie and McGee (1986): "Alcohol and drug use may be adopted because it facilitates the overt expression of otherwise latent or covert needs" (p. 292). In this context, the associated drunkenness may be an excuse for sexual promiscuity or aggressive behavior. "Alcohol/drugs seem to set the stage for aggressive sexual behavior by reducing the perpetrator's inhibitions and providing an excuse for the abuse" (Milgram, 1993, p. 58). Accordingly, as noted by the Roman philosopher, Senecca (5 BC–65 AD), "drunkenness is nothing but a form of insanity deliberately assumed." It is clear that, at least for some women, alcohol use is a significant antecedent for involvement in violent crime, including physical assault, sexual assault, and homicide (Collins, 1981). This relationship between alcohol use and violent crime appears to be particularly significant for women who have a positive past history for violent behavior (Pincus & Lewis, 1991).

Alcohol Use, Violent Crime, and Antisocial Personality Disorder

> It is worse to be sick in soul than in body, for those afflicted in body only suffer, but those afflicted in soul both suffer and do ill. (Pluttarch, 95 AD, *Afflictions of Soul and Body*)

Diagnostic criteria for antisocial personality disorder include aggressiveness, deceitfulness, impulsivity, irresponsibility, lack of remorse, repeated arrests, and repeated physical fights. As noted in the DSM-IV (American Psychiatric Association, 1994), "The essential feature of Antisocial Personality Disorder is a pervasive pattern of disregard for, and violation of, the rights of others that begins in childhood or early adolescence and continues into adulthood" (p. 645). Given the nature of antisocial personality disorder, it is not surprising that researchers have identified strong positive relationships among this disorder, alcohol use, and violent crime (Abram, 1989; Irwin, Schuckit, & Smith, 1990; Penick et al., 1984; Ross, Glaser, & Germanson, 1988). As reported by Abram (1989):

> This study suggests that pure alcoholics have a lower likelihood of criminal recidivism than alcoholics with an accompanying drug or antisocial disorder. Moreover, pure drug users, or even alcoholic drug users have a lower likelihood of committing a violent crime than their antisocial counterparts. (p. 144)

Such violent crime also may be perpetrated against family members: "Particularly high rates of violence are found in those [families] where alcoholism is combined with antisocial personality disorder" (Bland & Orne, 1986, p. 129).[4]

☐ Substance Use and Commerce- and Pharmacopsychologic-Related Crime

Crimes related to substance use can be broadly divided into two groups: those related to commerce; and those related to the pharmacopsychologic effect(s) of the substance of abuse involved in the crime (see Table 7-3). Except for those crimes related to the pharmacopsychologic effects of specific substances of abuse, which are predominantly of a violent nature, most substance use related crime is nonviolent (Hoffman & Goldfrank, 1990)[5].

Commerce-Related Crime

Most commerce-related crime is accounted for by drug trafficking. Drug trafficking includes the various activities associated with the production, distribution, sale, purchase, and possession of illicit substances of abuse. "Nationally, female involvement with drugs has dramatically increased in both personal consumption (abuse) and distribution and sales" (Moon, Thompson, & Bennett, 1993, p. 48). Other crimes that are commonly related to maintaining particular patterns of substance use among women include prostitution and robbery (or theft).

Prostitution Prostitution has long been a readily available means for women to support their drug habits (Pagliaro et al., 1993). Most of these prostitutes work from

TABLE 7-3. Types of substance use related crime*

Commerce-related crime
- crimes related to drug trafficking
  - production, distribution, sale, purchase, and possession
  - corruption of law enforcement and political officials
- crimes related to maintaining substance use
  - possession and use
  - drug trafficking, prostitution, and robbery to obtain money to purchase substances of abuse

Pharmacopsychologic-related crime
- crimes related to intoxication with a substance of abuse
  - driving while intoxicated (DWI), homicide, physical assault, sexual assault, and vehicular and other manslaughter
- substance use-induced automatism
  - homicide, physical assault, sexual assault, and manslaughter

*Note that there is some overlap between categories dependent upon who is committing the crime and her reason for doing so.

---

street corners or parks.[6] However, an increasing trend, concurrent with the increasing spread of crack cocaine, has been the direct exchange of sex for crack cocaine (Ratner, 1993; Rolfs, Goldberg, & Sharrar, 1990). As noted by Goldsmith (1988): "Organized prostitution is no longer necessary; the exchange is more direct" (p. 2009). This exchange occurs more formally in crack houses, many of which have special rooms or areas set aside specifically for these exchanges and their own live-in crack whores (Inciardi, 1993).

Exchanging sex-for-crack occurs much more frequently in a less formal manner. In these cases women typically choose their dates, not because of good looks, a fancy car, love, or other characteristic reasons, but because the date, who could be of the same or opposite gender, has cocaine and is willing to share it. In most of these cases, the terms of the barter are not formally stated, but are socially understood.

Robbery Robbery, including theft from place of employment, is another common method used by women to obtain the funds necessary to support their illicit substance use (Mott, 1986).

Pharmacopsychologic-Related Crime

Pharmacopsychologic-related crime is that crime which is directly related to the effects of substance use on those parts of the brain (i.e., amygdala, hippocampus, and related structures of the limbic system) associated with human cognition, learning and memory, and emotion. The pharmacopsychologic-related crimes are crimes related, directly or indirectly, to intoxication with the various substances of abuse. As noted earlier in this chapter, the use of some substances of abuse (e.g., alcohol) has been demonstrated to be closely associated with criminal behavior, particularly violent crimes, such as, homicide (Spunt, Goldstein, Brownstein, & Fendrich, 1994), physical assault, sexual assault, and vehicular manslaughter. This section will briefly discuss some possible mechanisms underlying these phenomena, particularly substance use-induced automatism.

Substance Use-Induced Automatism The relationship between automatism and violent crime was popularly characterized in Robert Louis Stevenson's (1903) *The Strange Case of Dr. Jekyll and Mr. Hyde:*

> It was the curse of mankind that these incongruous fagots were thus bound together—that in the agonized womb of consciousness, these polar twins would be continuously struggling. How, then, were they dissociated? . . . I declare, at least, before God, no man morally sane could have been guilty of that crime upon so pitiful a provocation, and that I struck in no more reasonable spirit than that in which a sick child may break a plaything.

Several closely related definitions can be found for the term automatism (Beran, 1992; D'Orban, 1989; Fenwick, 1990). The one that we find to be the most useful and clear is the definition provided by *Taber's Cyclopedic Medical Dictionary* (Thomas, 1993):

> Automatic actions or behavior without conscious volition or knowledge. The subject, though (generally) amnesic, appears normal to an observer, but the real personality is latent during a secondary state or period of automatism . . . Such patients are not responsible for their acts and must not be left alone. They may carry out complicated acts without remembering having done so . . . (p. 180)

Automatism has been associated with several physical (e.g., diabetes mellitus, epilepsy) and psychological (e.g., posttraumatic stress disorder, severe psychological blow) conditions (Bisson, 1993; Febbo, Hardy, & Finlay-Jones, 1993–94; Hindler, 1989; Treiman, 1986; van Rensburg, Gagiano, & Verschoor, 1994). Somnambulism, or sleep walking, may be considered to be one of the most common and well known forms of automatism (Beran, 1992; Fenwick, 1987). However, the characterization of automatism and explanations of its possible mechanism of action in relation to the commission of violent crimes have been most studied in the context of epilepsy. As noted by van Rensburg et al. (1994):

> Ictal aspects include the specific part of the brain from which the seizure originates, the loss of integration of incoming sensorial stimuli with motor-emotional output, the loss of higher control associated with a reversion to primitive automatic behaviour and the emergence of repressed feelings and aggressive instincts. Post-ictal violent behaviour may stem from the epileptic's misinterpretation of well-meant attempts by bystanders to protect him or her against the consequences of his or her confused conduct—and is usually characterized by a clouded consciousness, paranoid ideas and hallucinations. (p. 373)

Drug-induced automatism is, as the name implies, a condition of automatism that occurs as a direct result of the pharmacologic action of a drug. Several types and classifications of drugs can cause drug-induced automatism. These include the various substances of abuse (e.g., alcohol; amphetamines; barbiturates; benzodiazepines; cocaine); antidepressant drugs (e.g., clomipramine [Anafranil®]; fluoxetine [Prozac®]); and several other diverse groups of drugs, for example anabolic steroids (e.g., oxandrolone), several antineoplastics (e.g., chlorambucil [Leukeran®]), cimetidine (Tagamet®), and the corticosteroids (e.g., prednisone) (Pagliaro & Foster, 1990). The likelihood of occurrence and the potential severity of drug-induced automatism generally increases directly in relation to both the dosage and the number of drugs used that are capable of producing automatism (L. A. Pagliaro & A. M. Pagliaro, 1991; A. M. Pagliaro, 1998; A. M. Pagliaro, R. A. Lang, & L. A. Pagliaro, 1998).

Although probably occurring fairly commonly, drug-induced automatism is frequently overlooked by health and social care professionals, who are generally neither aware of, nor alert to, this real drug-induced psychological effect. Further contributing to overlooked diagnoses of drug-induced automatism are the facts that the affected person may engage in complicated acts and appear, for all practical intents and purposes, to be "normal" to the observer.

One classic case of drug-induced automatism described by Grinspoon and Hedblom (1975) illustrates the effects of repeated amphetamine use by a woman over several hours with accompanying sleep deprivation:

> During an argument with her paramour, this 32-year-old woman pulled a pistol out of her waistband, stuck it in his stomach, and calmly fired. When the victim got out of the car, she followed him and stated, "You wanted to die, I showed you." She then shot the victim twice more.... After interrogation at police headquarters, Mrs. C got up saying, "Well, I've got to go; I've got a hair appointment."
>
> Originally, amphetamines were prescribed for Mrs. C to help her lose weight. However, she soon discovered that they relieved her loneliness and depression; gradually, over a period of 18 months, she increased the dose to 400–600 mg. per day. Hallucinations were not infrequent. She became suspicious. "Even the people who were helping me were against me." Six months before the shooting, she bought a pistol to protect herself and her children at night....
>
> Mrs. C became very involved with another man while her husband was away in Viet Nam. As the time for her husband's return drew near, she became panic-stricken over how to end their affair. "Yet I was fantastically jealous if he even mentioned another woman...."
>
> "I hadn't slept for four days, was constantly active, and was taking pills like a chicken with its head cut off." (She was taking 600–1200 mg. per day.) Just before the incident, she told her paramour that she was going to leave for good. Teasingly, he said that he would bring his new girl friend by. "I was wild inside like a caged animal, but calmly told him that he never would. He asked how I would stop him and I told him I'd kill him and I did." (pp. 1171–1172).

In other cases of drug-induced automatism, paranoid psychosis frequently is involved in the commission of a violent crime (Manschreck, Schneyer, Weisstein, Laughery, Rosenthal, Celada, & Berner, 1990; Osran & Weinberger, 1994). The paranoia appears to be a central feature in these cases. Even among subjects who do not have a history of violent behavior, the paranoia seems to elicit violent behavior, behavior thought to be "self-defensive" by the perpetrator. As noted by Pincus and Lewis (1991), "The specific causes of psychoses or organic brain syndromes are probably not relevant variables in determining violence. It seems to be the *paranoia* with which these conditions are associated that is the crucial ingredient" (p. 150).

Clinical features that should alert astute clinicians to the potential for drug-induced automatism, include: 1) lack of apparent motive for a particular behavior in an otherwise "normal" person (i.e., nonpsychotic, nonsociopathic person, with normal intelligence); 2) total or partial amnesia of the event; and 3) consumption of a sufficient amount of one, or more, drugs that are capable of causing automatism. In addition, a higher incidence of drug-induced automatism may be noted among people who have a past history of epilepsy, personality disorders, posttraumatic stress disorder, psychoses, sleep disorders, or severe head trauma (A. M. Pagliaro, 1998; L. A. Pagliaro & A. M. Pagliaro, 1991).[7]

☐ Examples of Substance Use Related Violence Perpetrated by Women

Having reviewed the mechanisms associated with substance use related violence, the most frequently encountered types will now be examined. When women are involved in substance use related violent behavior, it is generally in a domestic context.[8] As noted by Wallace (1996, p. 5): "Violence is not only as American as apple pie, it is often as homemade." The violence is generally directed toward either the woman's adult male cohabitant or toward the children in the home. These patterns of violence will be briefly discussed under the headings of Physical Abuse/Assault and Sexual Abuse/Assault.

Physical Abuse/Assault[9]

> The U.S. Advisory Board on Child Abuse and Neglect declared in a recent report that the overwhelming increase in cases of child maltreatment has created a national emergency and that the national system for responding to child maltreatment is failing. (Child Abuse, 1991, p. 101)

Approximately two-thirds of parents use violence against their children and the use of alcohol or other substances of abuse contribute to this violent behavior (Lujan, DuBruyn, May, & Bird, 1989; Miller, 1990; Suh & Abel, 1990; Wolfner & Gelles, 1993). Estimates suggest that over 1.5 million children in North America are abused each year by family members or other intimates (Aday, 1994). This form of abuse, generally a combination of both physical and verbal abuse, is typified in "Sharon's" story of when she was seven-years-old:

> "You can't do anything right, you stupid bitch," my mother would holler at me while smacking me across the head with her open hand. "Stupid bitch" and "bad girl" were practically the only words she ever said to me.
> From age six, I did all the housework. Nothing I did, from peeling potatoes to scrubbing floors, was ever good enough. I got no thanks, just beatings and threats that she'd kill me if I complained to my father. . . . Our lives went down the toilet faster than the booze went down her throat . . .
> She needed more than his earnings and the welfare for necessities—booze, cigarettes, and the odd loaf of bread. So, she got domestic jobs in rich Rosedale homes. She got the wages; I did the labour. She'd keep me out of school, where I was in trouble anyway, to go with her to houses she had keys for, where the lady wasn't home. She'd watch the soaps and help herself at the overstocked bars, spiking the half-empty bottles with water, while I cleaned. When she'd inspect my work, she'd complain that it wasn't good enough, smack me, and curse me out. (Webber, 1991, pp. 65–67)

However, the full nature and extent of the relationship between parental violence aimed at children and substance use by parents (and other caregivers) has not been adequately studied and remains inconclusive. As noted by Miller (1990), "Our data on the importance of parental alcohol and drug problems to the willingness to use parental violence toward children was less clear [than the effect of this violence in subsequently contributing to substance use among the children as they get older]" (p. 195).

Although alcohol and drug use among perpetrators are commonly associated with their physical abuses of children (Famularo, Kinscherff, & Fenton, 1992; Kelley, 1992; Muller, Fitzgerald, Sullivan, & Zucker, 1994), "no physical child abuse perpetrator typology has been adequately validated" (Milner & Chilamkurti, 1991, p. 345) in the general population. Additional factors, such as poverty, stress, and lack of social support, also appear to contribute significantly to this form of violent behavior (Christoffel, 1990). However, in alcoholic families, "for both fathers and mothers, lifetime alcohol problems predicted extent of child maltreatment" (Muller et al., 1994, p. 438). In addition, in high risk multiproblem families (e.g., American Indian families living in poverty on reservations) "alcohol abuse is present in virtually all families that abuse/neglect children" (DeBruyn, Lujan, & May, 1992, p. 305). Although this association may not be unique or causal, it is significant and requires appropriate consideration, particularly in regard to the increasing incidence of serious cases of physical abuse during childhood (Donnelly, 1991).

Increasing numbers of women are being arrested for the physical assault of their partners and reports would indicate that these women engage in rates of violence comparable to those reported for men. Some of these women exhibit primary perpetrator characteristics and batter their male partners. In some cases the actions appear to be in response to a previous history, often during childhood and adolescence, of severe physical and/or sexual abuse.[10] However, the majority reportedly engaged in the violent physical assaults in either self-defense or retaliation for previous battering by their partner (Hamberger & Potente, 1994).[11] Whatever the reason for the violent physical assault by these women, the results tend to be more lethal. For example, female inmates who had been convicted of harming intimate victims were twice as likely as their male counterparts to have killed their victim. In addition, "about a third of female prisoners incarcerated for homicide killed their husband, ex-husband, or boyfriend" (Violence between intimates, 1994, p. 7). They also have killed their lesbian lovers, as well (Pagliaro & Pagliaro, 1996, clinical patient file notes).

Sexual Abuse/Assault

Sexual abuse/assault of children and adolescents can occur at any age, including the neonatal period,[12] and perpetrators can be family members, acquaintances, or total strangers. The reported incidence of sexual abuse/assault during childhood or adolescence, which has been generally based upon recollected self-reports by adults, has increased 10-fold from 6% to 60%. The actual incidence is probably closer to 12% (Feldman, Feldman, Goodman, McGrath, Pless, Corsini, & Bennett, 1991; Finkelhor & Dziuba-Leatherman, 1994).

Substance use, particularly alcohol, appears to play a significant role in these sexual offenses by: disinhibiting social taboos against child molestation, particularly those involving incest; and also increasing testosterone levels and, consequently, sexual aggressiveness (L. A. Pagliaro, 1993b). Sociological variables, such as social class, do not appear to be significantly related to childhood sexual abuse (Finkelhor, Hotaling, Lewis, & Smith, 1990; Wyatt, 1985). However, other sociologic factors, such as ethnicity, do appear to be related with lower risk reported for Jews and a higher risk reported for Hispanics (Christoffel, 1990). Age also has been found to be a significant factor.

Adults, who perpetrate child molestation or rape, vary considerably in relation to psychological and social variables, but most display problematic patterns of alcohol use (Green & Kaplan, 1994; Hillbrand, Foster, & Hirt, 1990; Ritter, 1989; Stiffman,

1989). In addition, a number of studies have purported a "cycle of alcohol abuse in men leading to domestic violence and sexual abuse in women and children" (Yellowlees & Kaushik, 1992, p. 197). Although these studies have, almost exclusively, focused upon men as the perpetrators of sexual abuse, a similar parallel scenario can occur involving women (Green & Kaplan, 1994) as illustrated by the following excerpt from the diary of one of our patients:

> A dresser was next to the window, with a woman's hand mirror, tissues, and lipstick littered on top. One small cut glass tumbler was always there, it seemed, half-filled with the clear yellow liquid visible through the flying ducks etched in the side of the glass.
> The young boy tentatively was in one bed, pretending to sleep. His black hair and deep set eyes, visible above the covers, accentuated his sad, perpetually unsmiling, face. The woman sat on the side of the other bed, her housecoat open with only a bra underneath. Her disheveled hair and sagging facial muscles framed the wild, uncaring look in her eyes. The bottles were on the floor beside her.
> "C . . .", she said, "come and sleep with me". The older boy tentatively entered the room, not knowing what to expect.
> "Come and sleep with me, you can sleep next to the wall." The boy looked at his mother, looked at her eyes, with their crazy, unloving gaze. He was lonely, his father on one of his interminable "business trips," no friends in this new neighborhood, the cleaning lady gone home.
> He looked at his mother's open housecoat, with her naked body showing. She looked so different than she did in the mornings, fully clothed and acting "normally." Then he knew she loved him. Now he wasn't sure, but he knew he couldn't trust her.
> The boy was afraid. Why was she acting so crazy? Why did she not seem to love him now? Why did no one else seem to notice? Why did no one else say anything about this craziness?
> "Come on, you've got your pajamas on, just climb into bed here."
> He walked over towards her, she grabbed him when he got close, and held him close to her breasts. He struggled away and, climbing over her, lay down on the other side of the bed next to the wall.
> "Don't you love me, C . . .? Don't you want me to hold you?"
> The tears started to well up inside, as the numbness set in on the outside. He wanted her love, but hated her craziness, hated her like this.
> "Yeh," he said.
> He lay facing the wall, legs curled up, in a position that was to become etched in his memory, an image that would come blazing back years later.
> She snuggled up close to him, her breasts touching his back, her arm around him. Her sickening menstrual breath, saturated with alcohol, enveloped him. He felt paralyzed, too numb and afraid to move.
> The feelings came flooding in. What if he left her bed? What would she do to his little brother in the next bed? Would she smother him like she did with little E . . . ? He mustn't leave his brother alone here with her. What was she doing? Why was she touching him when she didn't love him now?
> He felt the security of her touch, but the fear and hatred of her craziness. Afraid to move, afraid to tell her he hated her, he felt her hand move down his body. Wanting her touch, but paralyzed with fear, he lay there, staring at the wall, screaming with despair and loneliness inside. (Pagliaro & Pagliaro, 1992, clinical patient file notes)

As noted by O'Hagan (1993) in her discussion of "Tony, aged 7 years" and his alcoholic mother, these children repeatedly experience their mother's "drunken anger, drunken threats, and drunken physical affection and protestations of love," which, in turn, causes anger, embarrassment, humiliation, shame, stress, and the "pervasive apprehension that mother will be drunk again" (pp. 67–68). It is then perhaps not surprising that childhood victims of sexual abuse are at increased risk of developing subsequent problematic patterns of substance use (Famularo, Kinscherff, & Fenton, 1992; Van Hasselt, Ammerman, Glancy, & Bukstein, 1992).[13]

☐ Conclusion

Substance use, particularly alcohol use, has long been associated with violent crime, particularly when antisocial personality disorder is present. Proposed mechanisms for this association include direct pharmacologic mechanisms resulting in disinhibition (i.e., decreased impulse control) and resultant increased aggressiveness. Social mechanisms also have been postulated. Commerce-related crime, including drug trafficking, prostitution, and robbery, have been perpetrated by women, generally in order to maintain their own use of various substances of abuse. Pharmacopsychologic-related crime associated with drug-induced automatism involving women also appears to provide an important explanation for much of the violence related to substance use and has been largely overlooked.

This chapter has reviewed substance use related crime perpetrated by women. As noted by several respondents to the National Institute of Justice's 1994 survey (McEwen, 1995), the relationship between substance use and violent crime remains a serious, and apparently escalating, social problem:

> Drug activity is the one factor most affecting our court. (judge)
>
> Most crime is related to drug use. (judge)
>
> Domestic violence, child abuse, larceny, and robbery cases are increasing due to drug abuse . . . (police chief)
>
> Our workload problems are a result of the overwhelming number of cases that are a direct or indirect result of drugs. (sheriff)
>
> (pp. 1–2)

For the women involved as perpetrators of substance use related violence, particularly that directed against their own children, substance use can truly be said to kill the heart and murder the soul (Pagliaro & Pagliaro, unpublished treatise).

☐ Notes

1. For example, the analysis of emergency room and coroner data consistently suggests a significant positive relationship between alcohol consumption and violent crime related morbidity and mortality. As noted by Cherpitel in 1993:

    . . . those with violence-related injuries were more likely than those with other injuries to have positive breathalyzer readings and to report drinking prior to the event, frequent heavy drinking, consequences of drinking, experiences associated with alcohol dependence and loss of control, and prior treatment for an alcohol problem. (p. 79) and again in 1994:

> Violence-related fatalities were more likely to involve alcohol (47%) than non-fatal injuries (19%) . . . (p. 211)

As noted by Klatsky and Armstrong (1993):

> In adjusted analyses, persons reporting intake of 6 or more drinks daily were at greatly increased risk of death from suicide (6 times) and homicide (7 times), and at moderately increased risk of death from MVAs [motor vehicle accidents] (2 times). Lighter and ex-drinkers were not at significantly increased risk for all unnatural deaths or any of its subsets. (p. 1156)

2. These explanations provide assistance in regard to better understanding the phenomenon. However, it is quite likely that various mechanisms may account for the relationship between alcohol use and violent crime and that, in specific instances, one mechanism may account for more of the data than another.
3. See also the related discussion later in the "Substance Use-Induced Automatism" section.
4. Lex, Goldberg, Mendelson, Lawler, & Bower (1994) reported that for their sample of women who had been convicted for drunken driving, a significant number displayed only adult symptoms of antisocial personality disorder (i.e., the criteria for conduct disorder during childhood or adolescence were not met). They suggested, accordingly, that antisocial personality disorder may present differently among women than men and that for a significant number of women who have antisocial personality disorder, it occurs "largely consequent to substance abuse" (p. 56).
5. Although a comprehensive discussion of drug legalization is beyond the scope of this chapter, a general perusal of Table 7-3 would suggest that, while most substance use-related crime could be eliminated by drug legalization, violent crime, which is related to the intrinsic pharmacopsychologic effects of selected substances of abuse would likely increase (see this chapter, Alcohol Use and Violent Crime).

   Before proceeding, we would like to note that the entire issue of drug legalization is obviously quite complex and involves many factors (e.g., the potential generation of considerable additional tax revenues for governments in desperate need of such revenues). However, with an appreciation of the complexity of this issue and having carefully considered the arguments in favor and against, we do *not* currently favor drug legalization (i.e., drug legalization would cause more harm than good).
6. Rich Connell, a *Los Angeles Times* staff writer, noted the following rather typical arrest history for a recovering female crack cocaine addict:

   > Late 1983: Collecting welfare and doing occasional work at beauty salons, lives in the Crenshaw area with a daughter when she first tries a marijuana cigarette sprinkled with crack cocaine. She sinks quickly into addiction, and begins selling possessions to buy more drugs.
   >
   > 1984: Turns to street prostitution to fund her habit.
   >
   > January, 1986: Living in a Western Avenue motel, is arrested for prostitution and spends seven days in jail.
   >
   > October, 1987: Arrested on petty theft charge. Two days in jail.
   >
   > November, 1987: County Department of Children's Services takes two children, including one born in 1986, after a neighbor complains about neglect. The two children remain in protective placement, one with a relative, seven years later.

February, 1988: Arrested on prostitution charge. One day in jail.

April, 1988: Arrested for prostitution. Spends 62 days in jail.

April, 1989: Cited for prostitution, fails to appear in court and an arrest warrant is issued.

April, 1989: She gives birth prematurely to a crack baby during an emergency Cesarean at County-USC Medical Center. The baby is found to have cocaine in its system and water on the brain. Child welfare officials take custody. The infant spends about three months in the hospital and three years in foster care before being adopted.

October, 1989: Arrested on warrant and serves about seven weeks in jail.

November, 1990: Arrested for violating probation. Spends 78 days in jail.

June, 1991: Arrested for crack sales near MacArthur Park. Charge reduced to possession of narcotics. Serves 80 days in county jail and is placed on three years probation.

November, 1991: Arrested for probation violation. Serves 18 days.

October, 1992: Arrested for violation of probation on narcotics charge. Serves 32 days in jail and nine months in state prison.

June, 1993: Cited for prostitution.

September, 1993: Arrested for prostitution. Serves 12 days in jail.

November, 1993: Arrested for prostitution. Serves four days in jail.

March, 1994: Pregnant again and living on the streets near MacArthur Park, enters a county funded live-in drug treatment program.

December, 1994: She remains in the treatment program, where her young child is also allowed.

(1994, p. A1)

7. Alcohol-related automatism also has been referred to legally as "extreme drunkenness" (L. A. Pagliaro, 1995b) or "pathologic intoxication" (Lange, 1987). As noted by Pincus and Lewis (1991):

> Pathologic intoxication is not associated with slurred speech or incoordination and may last for only a few minutes. It usually occurs when alcohol is imbibed under circumstances "conducive" to violence, that is, at a bar or a party, and it has been difficult to reproduce this state of intoxication by administering alcohol in a laboratory setting. Those who become pathologically intoxicated are usually heavy drinkers. The condition may be more common in criminals. In a sense, it is an alcoholic "blackout" during which violence is committed. (p. 148)

8. In this context women are usually the victims of violence (see Chapter 6, Women as Victims of Substance Use Related Violence).
9. Although not discussed in this chapter, attention also should be given to the abuse that children and adolescents suffer as a result of parental neglect directly related to their parents'

substance use (Ney, Fung, & Wickett, 1992). This form of abuse, although difficult to specifically define in terms of its nature and extent, is believed to be widespread and a significant contributor to morbidity and mortality among children and adolescents of all ages. Consider, for example, the following:

> Last year, in an article on the youngest victims of the crack epidemic, the *Oakland Tribune* reported that police, making a routine drug bust, "found a crack mother passed out on her bed, with her seven-month-old baby sitting in a pool of vomit, chewing on cigarettes. A glass crack pipe was nestled between mother and child." Readers of almost every major urban newspaper have read similar stories about preschool children forced to beg food from neighbors, premature infants born addicted to crack, and babies who remain in hospitals for months because their mothers have abandoned them. (DeBettencourt, 1990, p. 17)

The abuse and neglect found in families with chronic compulsive patterns of substance use, particularly alcohol use, continue past infancy and throughout childhood. As noted by one of our patients "I was born and raised in the "sticks" . . . we had no heat in the house, no food, but we always had two gallons of St. George's wine to get up and have at breakfast . . . my brother and I would have to go and beg for food from our neighbors . . . I was big for my age and started drinking heavy with the best of them around 11 years . . . my parents encourage drinking" (Pagliaro & Pagliaro, 1994, clinical patient file notes).

10. P. is a 29-year-old single woman charged with stabbing her boyfriend. She reported a history of extended and intrusive sexual abuse by her stepfather from the ages of 9 to 29 and a series of date rapes by different men. P.'s interpersonal relationships were characterized by physical violence, alcohol abuse, and sexual exploitation. (Pollock & Kear-Colwell, 1994, p. 17)

    Note the similarities here with those noted in the Battered Woman Syndrome (see next endnote).
11. The Battered Woman Syndrome refers to a constellation of psychological symptoms that develop in a woman as a result of having lived in an intimate relationship in which she has been the repeated victim of physical, sexual, or psychological abuse. In several well-noted legal cases, women, who had a history of having been battered by their husbands, killed their husbands while the husband was asleep in a drunken stupor, utilized the Battered Woman Syndrome as a defense, and were acquitted (Wallace, 1996).
12. For example, Chasnoff et al. (1986) described several cases of "mother-child incest initiated during the neonatal period . . . the mothers all were estranged from their sexual partners, had demonstrated some confusion regarding sexual identity, and had sought assistance with chemical dependency during pregnancy" (p. 577).
13. El-Bassel et al. (1995) also noted the latter association (i.e., the association between childhood sexual abuse and substance abuse as an adult), ". . . childhood sexual abuse was significantly associated with [a history of] problem drinking [among jailed women] (p. 365).

    It has been suggested by Fleming, Mullen, Sibthorpe, Attewell, & Bammer (1998) that the nature of the relationship between childhood sexual abuse and alcohol abuse is complex and may involve cofactors, such as "having a mother who was perceived as cold and uncaring" (p. 1787). Thus, the tragedy comes full circle and begins anew when, for example, an alcoholic mother sexually abuses her own daughter.

CHAPTER 8

Women, Substance Use, HIV Infection, and AIDS

AIDS, the acquired immunodeficiency syndrome, is a communicable, uniformly fatal disease caused by infection with the human immunodeficiency virus (HIV). HIV is a retrovirus, which also has been referred to as the Human T-Lymphotrophic Virus type III (HTLV-III) or the Lymphadenopathy-Associated Virus (LAV), and exists in several forms (e.g., HIV-1, HIV-2) (Pagliaro, Pagliaro, Thauberger, Hewitt, & Reddon, 1993; A. M. Pagliaro & L. A. Pagliaro, 1992a, 1994). Worldwide, the number of individuals infected with HIV is currently estimated by the WHO to be approximately 40 million (Mertens & Low-Beer, 1996).[1]

Since the first case of AIDS was reported in North America in the early 1980s, the number of cases has risen geometrically, as has occurred in other parts of the world, so that currently over 200,000 North Americans have been diagnosed with AIDS and over 6,000 new HIV-positive cases are reported each month (Interventions, 1997). In addition, it is estimated that well over one million people in North America are currently infected with the HIV (Ahluwalia, DeVellis, & Thomas, 1998; Cases of Acquired Immunodeficiency Syndrome, 1992; Centers for Disease Control, 1991) and will eventually develop AIDS (Chin & Mann, 1990; A. M. Pagliaro & L. A. Pagliaro, 1992a). Virtually all of these people, and untold numbers of their contacts to whom the HIV has been spread, are probably unaware that they have been infected, a situation that was noted, almost two decades ago, by Macdonald (1986) and likely has not changed.

Important progress has been made in prolonging the life of people who have contracted the HIV (Fife, 1991; Matthews, Cersosimo, & Spivack, 1991; Moore, Hidalgo, Sugland, & Chaisson, 1991; Morse, Lechner, Santora, & Rozek, 1990; Pagliaro, Pagliaro, Thauberger, Hewitt, & Reddon, 1990). However, of increasing distress to public health professionals is the continuing spread of this disease worldwide at an alarming rate among people of all ages, socioeconomic backgrounds, and sexual orientations, particularly those people in urban populations in which the frequency of associated high risk behaviors (e.g., unprotected sexual intercourse with multiple partners) is believed to be relatively common (Champion & Shain, 1998; Chin & Mann, 1990; Interventions, 1997). As noted by Fordyce and Shum (1997):

150   Social Considerations

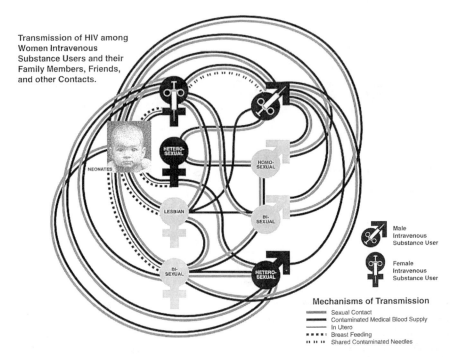

FIGURE 8-1. Transmission of HIV among intravenous substance users and their family members, friends, and other contacts.

> As the AIDS epidemic has matured in the United States, the characteristics of affected populations has shifted from a predominantly white homosexual/bisexual population to one now including increasingly more minorities, injecting drug users, and women. (p. 2)

While the preponderance of significant work continues to be aimed primarily at the prevention of HIV infection and AIDS among homosexual men (e.g., Coates, Stall, & Hoff, 1990; Getty & Stern, 1990),[2] of equal concern worldwide is the spread of HIV infection and AIDS among heterosexual women of whom a significant percentage have been infected as a result of unsafe behaviors associated with: 1) intravenous drug use; and 2) sexual contact with intravenous drug users (IVDUs) (AIDS Cases Doubling, 1987; AIDS risk increases, 1990; Erickson, 1997; Lee, 1988; Ostrow, 1987; Piot, Plummer, Mhalu, Lamboray, Chin, & Mann, 1988; Tortu, Beardsley, Deren, & Davis, 1994).[3]

As noted by Reyes (1998) in relation to both Latino heterosexual women and Latina lesbian women:

> The transmission of the HIV+ virus by sharing needles and involvement in the sex trade industry with male customers, or unprotected sex with men as means for payment of drugs, pose major risk factors for this population. (p. 187)

Figure 8-1 illustrates the lines and mechanisms of HIV transmission within groups of intravenous drug users as well as between and among other groups in society.[4]

☐ HIV/AIDS Incidence Among Women

Women are now considered, by many (e.g., A. M. Pagliaro & L. A. Pagliaro, 1994) to be the fastest growing group of new HIV/AIDS cases and it has been forecast by the WHO that the male:female ratio of new HIV infection cases will soon be close to 1:1.[5] The significant increase among women in the incidence of HIV infection and AIDS during the past decade of the 1990s came at a time when the opposite trend (i.e., reduction in incidence) was being noted among men (Havrekos, 1998).

> Although the projected number of cases decreased steadily during this period for homosexual and bisexual men, the projected number of cases for injection drug users, women, and persons with other risks increased between 1993 and 1998. (Lemp et al., 1997, p. 182)

> Notably, in men aged 20 and 25 years, HIV prevalence declined about 50% in white men. . . . In contrast, HIV prevalence in women aged 20 and 25 years rose by 36% and 45%, respectively because of increasing heterosexual transmission. (Rosenberg & Biggar, 1998, p. 1894)

> Although the rate of new HIV infections is falling in the general population, the incidence among African-American women jumped from 30.1 cases per 100,000 in 1991, to 50.1 cases per 100,000 women in 1995. (Stevens, 1998, p. 21)

This alarming trend has made AIDS the "leading cause of death among women [in the United States] between the ages of 25 and 44 [years]" (Interventions, 1997, p. 3)[6] and it shows no sign of abatement (Hoover, Doherty, Vlahov, & Miotti, 1996; Ward & Duchin, 1997–98; Wortley & Fleming, 1997).

A concomitant increase in perinatal transmission of HIV from mother to infant has been noted and accounts for virtually all new HIV infections among infants and children (Update: Perinatal, 1997). "Through 1993, an estimated 15,000 HIV-infected children were born to HIV-positive women in the United States" (Update: Perinatal, 1997, p. 1120). Most of these HIV-infected children developed AIDS within the first year of life (Bamji et al., 1996). Currently, treatment of HIV-pregnant women and their newborns with zidovudine pharmacotherapy has been associated with a two-thirds reduction in the risk for perinatal HIV transmission (Simonds et al., 1998; Update: Perinatal, 1997). Even with this "good news" it is evident that AIDS has evolved into a disease of women and their children (Ahluwalia, DeVellis, & Thomas, 1998; Havens, Mellins, & Pilowski, 1996). Alarmingly, seventy percent of all new [HIV] infections in women are among 15 to 24-year-olds (Madsen, 1996, p. 1).

☐ Intravenous Drug Use and AIDS

Currently, in North America, IVDUs[7] are the primary source of transmission of the HIV infection to:

1. **women** by shared contaminated needles and syringes (AIDS Risk Increases, 1990; Beery, 1990a; Campbell, 1990; Guinan & Hardy, 1987) and unprotected sexual contact with IVDUs (Cohen & Wofsy, 1989; Erickson, 1997; Health Care Providers, 1989; Wermuth et al., 1991);
2. **heterosexuals** by unprotected sexual contact (Cohen & Wofsy, 1989; Lee, 1988); and
3. **neonates** by in utero transmission (Berkelman & Curran, 1989; Institute of Medicine, 1988; Turner, Miller, & Moses, 1989; Update: Perinatal, 1997), infection during delivery (M. Jackson, 1990), or breast feeding (American Academy, 1988; Curran et

al., 1988; Thiry et al., 1985; Ziegler, Cooper, Johnson, & Gold, 1985). In addition, infants and children also may be infected as a result of sexual abuse, a mode of transmission that has been reported with other sexually transmitted diseases and suggested by the reported data (Fischl et al., 1987; Martin, Katz, & Miller, 1987; Scott, Buck, Letterman, Bloom, & Parks, 1984; STD testing, 1988).

In order to better understand the patterns of HIV infection among IVDUs, and between these IVDUs and their families, friends, and contacts, it is essential to identify the behaviors by which the virus is transmitted in this population group (e.g., sharing infected needles; unprotected sexual intercourse with multiple partners) (Coleman & Curtis, 1988; Magura, Shapiro, Siddiqi, & Lipton, 1990; Piot, Plummer, Mhalu, Lamboray, Chin, & Mann, 1988; Power, Hartnoll, & Daviaud, 1988; Robinson, Thorton, Rout, & MacKenzie, 1987; Schoenbaum et al., 1989). It also is necessary to determine the relationship between these behaviors and the amount of knowledge IVDUs have about HIV infection and AIDS, as well as their perceptions of self-risk, before effective intervention strategies can be planned and implemented (Bourne, 1988; A. M. Pagliaro & L. A. Pagliaro, 1992a, 1994a, 1994b). Attention to demographics also is required so that interventions can be tailored to the specific needs of the various subgroups that comprise the intravenous drug using population (e.g., inner city youth, prostitutes, health care professionals) (Friedland, 1989). As recommended by Leukefeld, Battjes, and Amsel (1990):

> Research should focus on risk behaviors. What are these behaviors? What is the prevalence and incidence of these behaviors? What is their meaning? What factors support the maintenance of risk behaviors? How are behaviors changing in response to the AIDS epidemic? (p. 285)

Knowledge and Behavior

Public health professionals frequently engage in activities (e.g., health education) aimed at promoting healthy lifestyles in an effort to ameliorate negative health conditions (e.g., obesity, stress, high serum cholesterol). Selected educational approaches are generally predicated upon an implicit association between knowledge and behavior. Unfortunately, the implementation of educational approaches has been called into question because several intervening variables (e.g., attitudes, values, beliefs, age, motivation, risk perception) purportedly affect the relationship between knowledge and behavior (Adeokun, Weeramunda, Carballo, & Tawil, 1989; Agrafiotis, Ioannidi, Konstantinidis, & Stylianou, 1989; Leukefeld, Battjes, & Amsel, 1990; Nelkin, 1987; Orenstein, 1989).

Results from the PIARG Projects[8]

The PIARG projects were undertaken in order to determine the knowledge, attitudes, and behaviors of IVDUs in relation to HIV infection and AIDS. Complete data sets were obtained from 1,054 subjects who were categorized as hard-core IVDUs. Women comprised approximately one-quarter of the sample (i.e., n = 261) and the data presented are derived from this subset of subjects. The women IVDUs who participated in the PIARG Projects were characterized according to several demographic variables (see Table 8-1) and substance use history (see Table 8-2). In relation to knowledge, behaviors, and perceived risks for HIV infection and AIDS, the statistical and content analyses of the data revealed that the majority of subjects:

TABLE 8-1. Demographics of women intravenous drug users (n = 261)

Q-6. What is your current age?
  mean: 29.69 years ± 6.98 sd
  range: 15 to 43 years of age
Q-8A. Please specify your racial group.
  caucasian: 30%
  Native American Indian[a]: 62%
Q-13. How many years of full-time education have you completed?
  mean: 11.78 years ± 9.49 sd
Q-15. What is your usual occupation?[b]
  35% prostitution
  11% selling drugs
Q-16. What is your current marital status?
  37% married
  37% single
  11% separated
  15% other (e.g., widowed)

[a]The category of Native American Indian was comprised of participants who identified themselves as either Treaty Indians or Metis (i.e., possessing both Native American Indian and nonNative American Indian heritage).
[b]A wide range of divergent occupations were reported. Only those occupations that were reported at a rate of 10% or greater are included in this table.

1. possessed a high level of accurate knowledge in relation to HIV infection and AIDS, although some specific knowledge deficits were noted (see Table 8-3);
2. practiced intravenous drug use behaviors that were unsafe in relation to HIV infection (e.g., used shared needles; shared needles with others[9]) (see Table 8-4);
3. practiced sexual behaviors that were unsafe in relation to risk for HIV infection (e.g., unprotected sexual intercourse with multiple partners)[10]; and
4. reported self-perception of low risk for HIV infection (see Table 8-5 and discussion below).

In relation to these findings, it also was noted that emergency needle exchange or give away programs, which have been widely and commonly implemented throughout Europe and Canada by public health agencies (Stimson, 1988; van den Hoek, Coutinho, Zadelhoff, van Haastrecht, & Goudsmit, 1987), and largely by "underground" groups in the United States (Des Jarlais & Friedman, 1988; O'Brien, 1989; Selwyn, 1988), as emergency measures in an attempt to prevent the spread of HIV infection and AIDS among IVDUs, would not seem to be particulary beneficial to a significant proportion of the IVDUs who voluntarily participated in this study (i.e., chronic or "hard core" IVDUs). It appears that such strategies would be generally ineffective because of one or more of five major reported behaviors (see Table 8-6).

The reported low level of self-perceived risk for acquiring the HIV infection among the intravenous drug using subjects is a factor that may contribute significantly to the continuation of the high risk behavior of needle sharing. Among the women who par-

TABLE 8-2. Drug use history for women (n = 261)[a]

Q-19. How old were you when you first injected a drug?
    range: 11 to 33 years of age
    mean: 16 years of age
    mode: 16 years of age
    median: 16 years of age

Q-20. What drug was used this first time?
    methamphetamine ("speed") — 28%
    pentazocine (Talwin)[b] — 28%
    3-methoxy-4,5-methylenedioxyamphetamine ("MDA") — 14%
    cocaine — 13%[c]
    heroin — 10%
    miscellaneous[d] — 7%

Q-21. In how many of the last 6 months did you inject drugs?
    range: 1 to 6 months
    mean: 6 months
    mode: 6 months (65% of subjects injected 6/6 months)
    median: 6 months

Q-22. In an average month when you injected, how many days did you inject?
    mean: 24 days

Q-23. On an average day when you injected, how many times per day did you inject?
    mean: 11.05 ± 8.25 sd

[a]All results presented in this table have been rounded to the nearest whole number to facilitate presentation.
[b]Alone or in combination with methylphenidate (Ritalin®) ("Ts & Rs").
[c]It should be noted that cocaine use, when compared with heroin use, has been associated with a higher risk for HIV infection among IVDUs (Chaisson et al., 1989). This association is related to: 1) the frequency of injection; and 2) increase in sexual activity associated with the use of cocaine, including the frequent barter of sexual favors for the drug (Goldsmith, 1988). (See related discussion on Sex for Drugs later in this Chapter).
[d]Miscellaneous included several different drugs (e.g., hydromorphone [Dilaudid®], pyribenzamine [PBZ®]).

ticipated as subjects, 69% stated that their "chances of getting the AIDS virus" were either "somewhat unlikely" or "very unlikely" (see Table 8-5), even though, as previously noted, over one-third of these subjects reported prostitution as their "usual occupation" and commonly engaged in high risk sexual behaviors and needle sharing. These observations may help account for the apparent inconsistency noted between the subjects' measured level of knowledge, which was generally high (see Table 8-3), and behavior, which was generally high risk in relation to infection with HIV (see Table 8-4).[11] This low perception of risk, or what has been described as an "illusion of unique invulnerability" (p. 173) (Gerrad, Gibbons, & Warner, 1991; Momas, Helal, Pretet, Marsal, & Poinsard, 1997), is identified as an important factor that should be addressed in both future research and in planning and developing effective intervention programs.

TABLE 8-3. Knowledge of HIV infection and AIDS among women IVDUs

Q-99 through Q-110. (HIV Infection and AIDS Knowledge Questions)*
  18.98 ± 4.46 sd (range 7 to 24)
Sample Responses in Relation to AIDS Knowledge Deficit.
Q-103. AIDS leads to death.
  "maybe there will be a cure"
  "sometimes people can just be carriers, I think"
  "there's the odd one who probably makes it"
  "not all people who are carriers die"
Q-110. There is a cure for AIDS at present.
  "They want to make a profit before they disclose it . . ."
  "They say they have one in China"
  "The doctor who discovered polio vaccine just discovered something"
  "They claim there is . . ."

*The correct answer given to all of these knowledge questions would result in a maximum possible score of 24.

☐ Sex for Drugs

The current cocaine epidemic in North America, which started in the mid-1970s, is said to be routinely associated with the most degrading and dehumanizing sexist behaviors toward women. This section will briefly explore that contention and demonstrate the causal association of cocaine use, HIV infection, and AIDS among women.

> . . . there is some evidence that addiction supported by trading sex for money or drugs places the woman at greater risk [for becoming HIV-positive] than either drug use alone or working within the sex industry alone . . . (Watson, Kail, & Ray, 1993, p. 211)

TABLE 8-4. Findings in relation to unsafe injection drug use[a]

Q-33. When you injected in the last 6 months, how often was it with a needle and syringe that was already used by someone else?[b]
  always: 5%
  mostly: 7%
  about half the time: 13%
  occasionally: 40%
  never: 36%[c]

[a]n = 140.
[b]Response totals add to over 100% due to rounding error.
[c]Other studies have found similar percentages of IVDUs who report never sharing needles. For example, Black et al. (1986), 32%, and Rezza et al. (1989), 33%.

TABLE 8-5. Self-perception of risk for HIV infection among women IVDUs (n = 261)*

Q-121. How likely are your chances of getting the AIDS virus?
   32% very unlikely
   37% somewhat unlikely
   21% somewhat likely
   10% very likely
   0% don't know

*The underestimation of risk for HIV infection among IVDUs also has been reported by other researchers (e.g., Feingold, Ziegler, Laufer, & Mayer, 1990). For our sample of women IVDUs comments in the "very unlikely" category were content analyzed to reveal the following three major factors: 1.) "I'm Quitting IV Drugs" (e.g., "Because I intend to quit"); 2.) "I Do Safer Sex" (e.g., "I am never sleeping with someone without a condom"); and 3.) "I'm Being More Careful" (e.g., "I'm very careful now").

Prostitution can be simply defined as the direct exchange of physical sexual services for money or items of monetary value (e.g., substances of abuse). While there have always been prostitutes (given that it truly is the world's oldest profession), there has never been a higher incidence of prostitution among North American women than since the beginning of the crack cocaine epidemic in the early 1980s. Because obtainment of the next high becomes the primary (and sole) focus for all women who use crack cocaine compulsively, all such women risk having to trade physical sexual services (i.e., prostitution) for their next rock (i.e., piece of crack cocaine) or hit (i.e., inhaling smoke from a crack pipe), particularly if they do not have sufficient money to purchase their desired substance of abuse. As noted by Lown, Winkler, Fullilove, and Fullilove (1993):

> The crack high is an intense experience of euphoria that users are desperate to recapture once the high abates. Addicts will use whatever they have to obtain more crack. When money and possessions are depleted, they may be forced to barter sexual favours for a "hit on the pipe." (p. 91)

In inner city neighborhoods where crack cocaine use is epidemic, men, particularly those who both desire sexual gratification and require a sense of dominance over women (i.e., those men who have no respect for women and, most likely, harbor deep feelings of hostility and resentment toward women), routinely literally take advantage of women who have compulsive patterns of crack cocaine use.[12] As noted by French (1993) in his study of black crack cocaine smokers:

> Of greater importance than the actual sensation of physical sex was the feeling of power and control many customers experience when they are in sexual contact with skeezers. The issue of control was a theme throughout the sexual interactions between our subjects . . .
>
> **Interviewer:** When you're in the crack house and some girl is giving you a blow job, what's the difference between that feeling and any other time that you have sex?
> **Mack:** I feel like I have something on this girl right now, she can't really say anything. I have the ups on her and she's the one down, I'm the one up.

> **Interviewer:** Why is that?
> **Mack:** 'Cause I have what she wants, which is cocaine. If I didn't have the cocaine I'd probably have to wait on her, I probably couldn't command. She'd be saying, "Look I have to go, could you please hurry up here." I would probably have to wait on her. This way she has to chase me. (p. 225)

Examples of degradation abound, as noted by Lown et al. (1993) in their study of crack cocaine use in a variety of urban black communities:

> I sucked his dick, right, and he came in my mouth and I was spitting out—and he gave me $4. I was crying and shit because I knew how bad I [had] gotten. I was like, oh my God, $4 and I was out there beggin for a fucking dollar. Before, I would never do that shit [fellatio], and I was doing it for nothing. (p. 95)

> ... and I heard this young girl, and I swear to God I'm not lying, this young girl said—she walked up and down the hall [of the apartment house], and she said, "I need 75 cents, anybody down?" And this dude said, "Here, need one in the bathroom." I'm not going to go into explicits, okay ... She went to the bathroom and she said, "I want to give somebody some. Anybody I got. I'm going to give somebody some head. Just 75 cents. I need 75 cents to get a tray" [a $3 vial of crack]. (p. 95)

Or as noted by Koester & Swartz (1993) in their study of black inner city crack cocaine users and dealers from Denver:

> It is degrading to think about some of the things I have done for drugs that I wouldn't even do with my man, but I did them with the dealer because that is what he wanted and that was the only way I was going to get it, if I did the sex his way. It might have been painful like anal sex they call it, but I did them and it is degrading because it just is. (p. 196)

> I might do like I did in Kansas City ... This chick wanted a hundred dollars' worth of dope. I had her fuck everybody in the house. There were about eight drunk motherfuckers. They tore her ass up. Then I turned around and didn't give her exactly what I told her I was going to give her. (p. 197)

Or as noted by Ouellet, Wiebel, Jimenez, and Johnson (1993) in their study of inner city black, brown, and white cocaine users in Chicago:

> I saw her date every man in the place for some coke ... She was giving one head, the other was fucking her from the back ... If it's ten niggers in there it doesn't make a difference. (p. 80)

☐ Conclusion

Acquired Immune Deficiency Syndrome (AIDS) remains a uniformly fatal disease with no demonstrated effective cure. Although important progress has been made in relation to prolonging the life of people who have been infected with HIV, the control of the spread of this devastating disease among people of all ages remains one of prevention through public education and emergency intervention strategies. While important work and progress continues in relation to HIV infection and AIDS among homosexuals, including bisexuals, of concern is the apparently unrestrained spread of this ravaging disease among heterosexual women, which appears to be generally associated, particularly in North America, with intravenous drug use or sexual contact with intravenous drug users.

(text continues on page 160)

TABLE 8-6. Behaviors of hard-core IVDUs that contravene the intended efficacy of needle-exchange programs

Behavior	Sample Related Quotes from Women IVDUs	Comments
Exchanging supplied new needles and syringes for substances of abuse	—	As noted in the Sex for Drugs section of this chapter, everything that compulsive substance abusers have (or can do) is up for barter in order to try to obtain more of their favorite substance of abuse.
Sharing needles and syringes communally	"If I was with a very good friend, and it would be about ½ the time, because it is a bonding, as part of a ritual (lesbian relationship)" "Didn't have fresh ones and it was an honor of sorts if someone would let you use their [out]fit . . . to say 'no' would be like kicking them in the teeth . . . although I did say no to someone who was yellow . . ." "Me and my old man could do it separately, but we do it together because it's a thrill . . . it's like a part of a sexual fantasy, I sit on his lap and I do his arm as if it's my own" "With my old man . . . getting high together is like getting off together" "The buddy system, if you're in with someone really tight, it's an honor to share your needle . . . most of the time it was with my girlfriend (lesbian relationship)—either she got them or I got them, then we shared . . ."	The sharing was done as part of the sexual ritual of "fixing." The relationship between injection drug use and sex has been long recognized from a psychoanalytic perspective as well as in terms of the social context of needle sharing. For example, Turner, Miller, and Moses (1989) noted that "sharing injection equipment among friends and injecting each other appears to have strong sexual connotations" (p. 192).
Need for immediate gratification	"I wanted to crank right away. I was feeling sick and didn't care . . ." "Couldn't wait to get a new rig . . . needed that fix" "When you want a crank, you want it now not later" "I didn't have one and I wanted to fix right now" "Like I said, I was desperate for a fix . . ." "Because I needed to do the stuff"	This need was generally in relation to either a.) euphoric drug effect(s); or b.) amelioration of drug withdrawal symptoms (i.e., subjects reported that they would not wait for a new or clean needle and syringe when not immediately available).

Category	Quotes	Commentary
	"after 15 or 20 hits the rigs become plugged and you can't wait for it to be cleaned" "Just desperate for that fix . . . couldn't wait to get a new rig" "Just wanted that fix and didn't want to wait" "It gets pretty crazy when you're doing cocaine, you just want that next hit" "Because once you start cranking, you don't care. If a rig plugs or is too barbed to use again, you're not going to wait . . ."	Reyes (1998) reports similar risk behavior for Latina women: In tandem to the issue of contracting the HIV+ virus through high risk behaviors such as sharing needles and engaging in unsafe sex, the use of alcohol and other drugs has been identified as a significant co-factor which may lower inhibitions, and impair judgement and the ability to adopt protective measures, and thus contribute to risk behavior. (p. 187)
Being in a state of intoxication or drug-induced cognitive impairment	"Mainly when you get confused and don't remember whose rig is whose . . . then you say, 'Who gives a fuck, let's just crank it'" "Maybe a few times I didn't [use clean needles] because I was too stoned" "I fucked-up once in a while when I was too stoned to be careful . . . it happens" "I looked too stoned to go to the pharmacy . . . after your first injection, you can't make it anywhere" "can't remember whose is whose" "Too high at the time . . ." "I was too high . . ." "I was high and just didn't care"	
Laziness	"We sometimes use each others, especially when you feel lazy" "Sometimes you just get lazy . . ." "I was too lazy to get another one, or was too impatient. When you want to fix you just grab your dope and the closest needle" "Too lazy to clean them" "A clean one was not available and I was too lazy to clean one"	Although several psychologic constructs may be used to denote laziness (e.g., amotivation), the term lazy was used by the respondents and has been left in its uninterpreted form in order that further study and differentiation of this construct may be performed.

Much in the way of effective intervention remains to be done in order to: 1) maintain and further increase knowledge concerning HIV infection and AIDS; and 2) decrease associated high risk drug use and sexual behaviors among female IVDUs. Specifically, attention must be directed at factors identified as supporting needle sharing behavior, such as exchanging new needles and syringes for drugs; the ritual of "fixing"; the need for immediate gratification; dislike of bleach for needle cleaning; the state of intoxication or drug induced cognitive impairment while "fixing"; and laziness. Additional attention to risk perception for HIV infection and AIDS and its relationship to knowledge and behaviors also is required.

Further research studies, directed at both prevention and treatment, must include representative samples of women subjects (Cotton, Finkelstein, He, & Feinberg, 1993). In addition, focus must be directed to the unique behaviors, characteristics, and needs of women as they relate to prevention of HIV infection and the treatment of AIDS.[13]

☐ Notes

1. Estimates, however, are difficult to make and are subject to considerable error because of: 1) Generally poor reporting practices in many countries, particularly the developing countries; 2) The difficulty associated with obtaining an accurate diagnosis; and 3) Lack of uniform mandatory testing and reporting requirements (Johnston, 1991; Pagliaro et al., 1993; Singleton, Tabnak, Kuan, & Rutherford, 1996).
2. For example, even in current clinical trials of newer anti-AIDS drugs, such as the protease inhibitors, women are significantly under represented as subjects (i.e., often less than 20%) (Summary sheets, 1997).
3. Other vectors for HIV transmission to women include: contaminated blood transfusions; needle-stick injuries; prostitution (see discussion later in this chapter); and sexual intercourse with bisexual men (Chu et al., 1992; Pagliaro & Pagliaro, 1992a, 1993, 1994) (See Figure 8–1).
4. Although emergency intervention strategies, such as needle-exchange programs (Bardsley, Turvey, & Blatherwick, 1990; Stimson, 1989; Temple, 1990) were implemented in many major cities in an effort to halt the spread of HIV among people who used drugs intravenously and have been recommended for further implementation (Interventions, 1997), we believe that this simplistic approach has not and will not yield significant long-term reductions in the spread of HIV infection by means of contaminated needles and syringes. (See related discussion later in this chapter).
5. This epidemiologic trend is both alarming for women because of its consequences and tragic because it could have been prevented. When the first cases of AIDS were diagnosed around 1980 in the United States and throughout much of the early part of the AIDS epidemic (i.e., until the late 1980s), AIDS was primarily a male disease limited, for the most part, to gay men. The epidemiology of spread of this fatal disease to women, both heterosexual and lesbian, is discussed in the remainder of this chapter.
6. A compounding risk factor in terms of mortality for HIV-positive women is substance abuse, which is reportedly responsible "for most pre-AIDS deaths" (Mylonakis et al., 1998).
7. It is now estimated that well over one million Americans are intravenous drug users (Macdonald, 1986; Schuster, 1988) and that between one-quarter and one-third of these people are already HIV positive (Booth, 1988; Hahn, Onorato, Jones, & Dougherty, 1989). HIV infection rates also have significantly increased among intravenous drug users in Europe during the late 1980s and early 1990s (e.g., Bourne, 1988; Brettle & Nelles, 1988; Corkum, 1989; Harms, Laukamm-Josten, Bienzle, & Guggenmoos-Holzmann, 1987).
8. PIARG is an acronym for the Pagliaro Interdisciplinary-Interagency AIDS Research Group, which functioned under the auspice of the Substance Abusology Research Unit (SARU) at the University of Alberta. The PIARG research team was formally comprised of members

from several Departments at the University of Alberta, the Alberta Solicitor General's Department (ASG), and the Alberta Alcohol and Drug Abuse Commission (AADAC).

9. The significant degree of needle sharing, which has been found in this study, is consistent with that found in other studies (e.g., Chaisson et al., 1989; Dolan et al., 1987; Friedland et al., 1985; Seligman, Campbell, Keeler, & Halpin, 1989) of intravenous drug users.

10. In this regard it is noteworthy that the most frequently reported "usual occupation" for females was prostitution (35%—see Table 8–1). However, anal intercourse, a high risk sexual behavior in relation to the transmission of HIV, was rarely reported by any of the subjects who participated in this study and a content analysis of the comments made by the female subjects (e.g., "I still have a virgin ass!"; "don't do that"; "I'm not going to let some trick fuck me up the ass"; "Greek style? I'm not into pain"; "I'm not that type of girl"; "Couldn't pay me enough. It fucking hurts too much.") suggest a significant bias against this form of sexual behavior among this group of IVDUs.

11. This observed lack of congruence between knowledge and behavior among intravenous drug users is consistent with that reported by Brabant et al. (1990). Similarly, MacDonald et al. (1990), noted a lack of congruence between knowledge and high risk sexual behavior among young adults who do not consider themselves to be at high risk for HIV infection.

12. The advantage taken of and degradation bestowed upon these women have become routinized, and to a large extent socially accepted, in many inner city black neighborhoods in North America. This acceptance is reflected in the vernacular nomenclature (i.e., "crack ho [whore]"; "Cambodian", "Skeezer"; "Strawberry"; and "Toss" [or "Toss-Up"]) used, by children and adults alike, to describe and refer to crack using women who trade sex for drugs. The derogatory terms used to refer to these women are used, consciously or not, to dehumanize and objectify them. Thus, allowing the subjection of these women to profoundly degrading behavior without the need for human compunction, compassion, or, at a later time, remorse.

> Randy, a 22-year-old crack smoker, did not conceal his disrespect for the skeezer:
>
> "A skeezer will do anything. You give her anything, she'll give you some sex. You can give her money. Two dollars. A dollar. Or you can give her a pack of cigarettes. You can give her a little piece of crack. Anything, man. You can get it for nothing. They give it up so cheap now." (French, 1993, p. 222)
>
> There were times where men . . . would feel like . . . "she's just a strawberry . . . I'll take her anyway." And when I tell them pay me, "Pay you? Who the fuck you think you are?" (excerpt from an interview with a black homeless prostitute) (Boyle & Anglin, 1993, p. 177)

Once these concepts become entrenched, as they already have, in these communities, it is difficult not to have them become generalized (i.e., overgeneralized). As noted by Lown et al. (1993):

> The existence of sex-for-drugs exchange in the crack culture affects the status of all women living in crack-affected communities, the status of those who do not use the drug as well as those who do. (p. 92)

13. For example, although relatively rare among men, with a few noted exceptions periodically reported in the lay press, "HIV disclosure-related violence" is relatively common and a real concern among newly diagnosed HIV-positive women (Gielen, O'Campo, Faden, & Eke, 1997). Other examples of unique areas of concern to women include issues related to pregnancy and breastfeeding (Cohen & Alfonso, 1994).

PART IV

CLINICAL CONSIDERATIONS

Assessing and Diagnosing Substance Use Disorders Among Women

The cornerstone of appropriate therapeutic intervention is appropriate assessment and diagnosis. The best designed treatment program in the world[1] will have *zero* efficacy if, for example, either a woman with a substance use disorder is not appropriately diagnosed (and hence not entered into treatment) or if a woman without a substance use disorder is incorrectly diagnosed as having a substance use disorder (and hence erroneously entered into treatment).

Statistically, we can conceptualize the two types of misdiagnoses just described as Type I and Type II diagnostic errors (see Figure 9-1). Type I diagnostic error represents false positive diagnoses (i.e., diagnosing a woman as having a particular substance use disorder when, in fact, she does not). Type II diagnostic error represents false negative diagnoses (i.e., not diagnosing a woman as having a particular substance use disorder when, in fact, she does).[2]

Unfortunately, in clinical practice health and social care professionals will always be faced with the spectre of Type I and Type II diagnostic errors. This situation occurs because the science of substance abusology[3] is an inexact science and because of the nature of human error (i.e., try as we may, we are not perfect and can make mistakes). However, we can determine and set selection criterion values to selectively adjust the probability of encountering either Type I or Type II error.[4,5] Making the correct diagnosis in relation to substance use disorders (i.e., minimizing Type I and Type II errors) involves careful clinical judgement and decision making. In general, when using standardized psychometric instruments to determine alcohol or substance use and related disorders we can elect to increase the cut-off score in order to provide better discrimination (i.e., fewer false positives or Type I errors), but at the cost of reduced sensitivity (i.e., more false negatives or Type II errors).

Psychometric instruments have been commonly used to assess individuals for possible Substance Use Disorders (SUDs) (including alcoholism). These instruments include: Alcohol Use Disorders Identification Test (AUDIT); Brief Michigan Alcoholism Screening Test (Brief MAST; B-MAST); CAGE; Drug Abuse Screening Test (DAST); Index of Alcohol Involvement (IAI); MacAndrew Alcoholism Scale (MAC); Malmö Modified Michigan Alcoholism Screening Test (Mm-MAST); Maternal Short-MAST

WOMAN'S ACTUAL CONDITION

		No SUD	SUD
Diagnosis Made by Health or Social Care Provider	SUD	Type I Error "false positive"	Correct Diagnosis
	No SUD	Correct Diagnosis	Type II Error "false negative"

FIGURE 9-1. Type I and Type II diagnostic errors.

(M-SMAST); Maternal Substance Use Screening Questionnaire; Michigan Alcoholism Screening Test (MAST); Rapid Alcohol Problems Screen (RAPS); Short Michigan Alcoholism Screening Test (SMAST); and the TWEAK.[6] Each of these psychometric instruments is briefly discussed. However, before proceeding, the concepts of validity and reliability as they relate to the selection and use of psychometric instruments are reviewed in order that the scoring procedures and interpretation of results can be appropriately understood.

Validity In terms of psychometric instruments, validity is simply an indicator that the instrument actually measures what it purports to measure (e.g., an IQ test measures IQ; a screening test for alcoholism screens for alcoholism). There are several types of validity. The three types of validity that are most relevant in this context are content validity, criterion-related validity, and face validity.

Content Validity. Content validity refers to how well the items included in the instrument measure (or reflect) the entire domain that is the subject of measurement. For example, in relation to alcoholism, there are several different types of alcoholics (e.g., binge drinkers, early onset) and if the items only relate to one type, the others would be missed.

Criterion-Related Validity. Criterion-related validity is a measure of the extent to which the results of the psychometric test agree with an independent indicator of the same attribute. For example, the agreement between a diagnosis of alcohol abuse based on the results of psychometric testing and a diagnosis of alcohol abuse based on a clinical interview and DSM-IV criteria.

Face Validity. Face validity is simply an indicator that the items on a psychometric instrument "appear" to be appropriate. For example, if measuring alcoholism, then the items would be expected to involve drinking behaviors.[7]

Reliability In terms of psychometric instruments, reliability is simply an indicator that the instrument consistently provides the same results. Statistical synonyms for reliability in this context are consistency, repeatability, replicability, and stability.[8]

The value and usefulness of a psychometric test depends not only on the test's validity and reliability, but also on the truthfulness[9] of the woman who is being tested (i.e., the test-taker). In this regard, the following questions require careful consideration by health and social care professionals who are involved, directly or indirectly, in assessing women for SUDs, using selected psychometric tests. This consideration is required in order to help assure that truthful responses are obtained so as not to invalidate the interpretations based upon the analysis of the provided responses:

- has the woman been referred for psychometric testing primarily because of: a driving while impaired (DWI) charge; parole sentencing; threat of job loss; or child custody proceedings?
- is the woman aware that self-report data will be corroborated with a clinical interview and other assessment procedures?
- does the woman display psychopathic or antisocial personality disorder characteristics?
- does the woman demonstrate inadequate test taking behavior (e.g., leaves numerous items blank; answers true to all items).

☐ Psychometric Instruments

Alcohol Use Disorders Identification Test (AUDIT)

The AUDIT is a 10-item psychometric instrument (see Table 9-1) developed from a six-country WHO collaborative project to detect alcohol use disorders (Saunders,

TABLE 9-1. Alcohol Use Disorders Identification Test (AUDIT)

1. How often did you have a drink containing alcohol in the past year?
2. How many drinks containing alcohol did you have on a typical day when you were drinking in the past year?
3. How often did you have 6 or more drinks on one occasion in the past year?
4. How often during the last year have you found that you were not able to stop drinking once you had started?
5. How often during the last year have you failed to do what was normally expected from you because of drinking?
6. How often during the last year have you needed a first drink in the morning to get yourself going after a heavy drinking session?
7. How often during the last year have you had a feeling of guilt or remorse after drinking?
8. How often during the last year have you been unable to remember what happened the night before because you had been drinking?
9. Have you or someone else been injured as a result of your drinking?
10. Has a relative or friend or doctor or other health care worker been concerned about your drinking or suggested you cut down?

Source: Saunders, Aasland, Babor, de la Fuente, & Grant, 1993.

TABLE 9-2. Brief MAST (B-MAST)

1. Do you feel you are a normal drinker?	(2)
2. Do friends or relatives think you are a normal drinker?	(2)
3. Have you ever attended a meeting of Alcoholics Anonymous (AA)?	(5)
4. Have you ever lost friends or girlfriends/boyfriends because of drinking?	(2)
5. Have you ever gotten into trouble at work because of drinking?	(2)
6. Have you ever neglected your obligations, your family, or your work for two or more days in a row because you were drinking?	(2)
7. Have you had delirium tremens (DTs), severe shaking, heard voices, or seen things that weren't there after heavy drinking?	(5)
8. Have you ever gone to anyone for help about your drinking?	(5)
9. Have you ever been in a hospital because of drinking?	(5)
10. Have you ever been arrested for drunk driving after drinking?	(2)

Source: Pokorny, Miller, & Kaplan, 1972.

Aasland, Babor, de la Fuente, & Grant, 1993).[10] The 10-item core instrument appears to be particularly useful for the early detection of individuals displaying hazardous or harmful drinking while the 8-item clinical instrument is better suited for the identification of individuals with alcohol dependence (Bohn, Babor, & Kranzler, 1995). The AUDIT was normed on a large representative sample of subjects in attendance at several primary health care facilities.

Scoring Responses to each item are scored from 0 to 4, giving a maximum possible score of 40. A cut-off (discriminating) score of 8 is recommended (Mackenzie, Langa, & Brown, 1996; Saunders, Aasland, Babor, de la Fuente, & Grant, 1993). Higher cut-off scores (e.g., 12) provide better discrimination in the prediction of alcohol-related social problems, but at the cost of reduced sensitivity (Conigrave, Hall, & Saunders, 1995).

Validity and Reliability The AUDIT has good construct validity. It has good internal consistency (reliability) with reported Cronbach's alpha coefficients in the 0.80s range (Allen, Litten, Fertig, & Babor, 1997).

The AUDIT is reportedly as or more sensitive than the B-MAST, the CAGE, the Mm-MAST, and the RAPS (Bradley, Boyd-Wickizer, Powell, & Buman, 1998; Cherpitel, 1997, 1998; Mackenzie, Langa, & Brown, 1996; Seppa, Makela, & Sillanaukee, 1995). The reported accuracy of AUDIT in detecting suspected heavy drinkers in the early phases was reportedly particularly significant for women (Seppa, Makela, & Sillanaukee, 1995). In addition, the AUDIT does not appear to be affected by age, gender, or ethnic biases (Clay, 1997; Steinbauer, Cantor, Holzer, & Volk, 1998).

Brief MAST (B-MAST)

The B-MAST is a 10-item psychometric instrument (see Table 9-2) developed by Pokorny, Miller, and Kaplan (1972) to detect alcoholism.

Scoring Each item (question) in the B-MAST is assigned a weight (listed in the right hand column of the instrument) of 0 to 5. Items 1 and 2 are scored negatively. An overall score of six or greater provides presumptive evidence of alcoholism.

Validity and Reliability The Brief MAST is reportedly significantly less sensitive than the AUDIT, CAGE, or RAPS (Cherpitel, 1997, 1998; Mackenzie, Langa, & Brown, 1996). The sensitivity of the B-MAST to detect moderate alcohol problems in the general population is low (~30%), presumably because the items deal primarily with severe alcohol problems (Chan, Pristach, & Welte, 1994; Lockhart et al., 1986). It also has been found to be less sensitive and less specific when used to screen for alcoholism among the elderly (Willenbring et al., 1987).

CAGE

The CAGE is a 4-item psychometric instrument (see Table 9-3) developed by Mayfield, McLeod, and Hall (1974) to detect alcoholism.

Scoring Each affirmative answer is given a score of one. A total score equal to or greater than two is indicative of alcoholism.

Validity and Reliability Face (content) validity is excellent. However, its strong face validity makes faking quite easy. The CAGE has demonstrated high sensitivity (~80%) and specificity (~85%) for alcoholism (Maly, 1993). However, sensitivity is apparently reduced when used in populations of white women (Bradley, Boyd-Wickizer, Powell, & Burman, 1998; Osterling, Berguland, Nilsson, & Kristenson, 1993; Seppae, Koivula, & Sillanaukee, 1992). Sensitivity of the CAGE is also reportedly low when used with elderly men and women (Adams, Barry, & Fleming, 1996; Fulop et al., 1993; Jones et al., 1993). In terms of performance, the CAGE has been found to be comparable to the S-MAST (Maisto, Connors, & Allen, 1995). It is quicker to administer than the S-MAST or AUDIT (i.e., 1 versus 3 minutes). However, its internal consistency (reliability) is lower and its standard error of measurement is larger (Hays, Hill, Gillogly, Lewis, et al., 1993; Hays, Merz, & Nicholas, 1995).

Drug Abuse Screening Test (DAST)

The DAST is a 28-item psychometric assessment instrument (see Table 9-4) developed by Skinner (1982) to detect substance abuse (excluding alcohol). A 20-item short version (DAST-20) also is in use.

Scoring Each yes-no response is assigned zero or one point and summed. Items 4, 5, and 7 are scored negatively. Scores on the DAST of 12 or greater are indicative of a substance use problem.

Validity and Reliability The DAST has very good concurrent and discriminant validity and is able to attain 85% overall accuracy in classifying patients according to DSM criteria (Gavin, Ross, & Skinner, 1989). The DAST has been reported to have high internal consistency (reliability) (Staley & el-Guebaly, 1990) and test-retest reliability (El Bassel, Schilling, Schinke, Orlandi, et al., 1997). Skinner (1982) reported a Cronbach alpha coefficient of 0.92 for the DAST and 0.95 for the DAST-20. Both versions of the DAST also demonstrated adequate internal consistency (reliability) when used with a sample of male and female psychiatric outpatients (Cocco & Carey, 1998). No validity data are available for the DAST-20.

TABLE 9-3. CAGE: An alcoholism screening test

- Have you ever felt you should CUT down on your drinking?
- Have people ANNOYED you by criticizing your drinking?
- Have you ever felt bad or GUILTY about your drinking?
- Have you ever had a drink first thing in the morning to steady your nerves or to get rid of a hangover (i.e., as an EYE-OPENER)?

Source: Mayfield, McLeod, & Hall, 1974.

TABLE 9-4. Drug Abuse Screening Test (DAST)

1. Have you used drugs other than those required for medical reasons?
2. Have you abused prescription drugs?
3. Do you abuse more than one drug at a time?
4. Can you get through the week without using drugs (other than those required for medical reasons)?
5. Are you always able to stop using drugs when you want to?
6. Do you abuse drugs on a continuous basis?
7. Do you try to limit your drug use to certain situations?
8. Have you had "blackouts" or "flashbacks" as a result of drug use?
9. Do you ever feel bad about your drug abuse?
10. Does your spouse (or parents) ever complain about your involvement with drugs?
11. Do your friends or relatives know or suspect you abuse drugs?
12. Has drug abuse ever created problems between you and your spouse?
13. Has any family member ever sought help for problems related to your drug use?
14. Have you ever lost friends because of your use of drugs?
15. Have you ever neglected your family or missed work because of your use of drugs?
16. Have you ever been in trouble at work because of drug abuse?
17. Have you ever lost a job because of drug abuse?
18. Have you gotten into fights when under the influence of drugs?
19. Have you ever been arrested because of unusual behaviour while under the influence of drugs?
20. Have you ever been arrested for driving while under the influence of drugs?
21. Have you engaged in illegal activities in order to obtain drugs?
22. Have you ever been arrested for possession of illegal drugs?
23. Have you ever experienced withdrawal symptoms as a result of heavy drug intake?
24. Have you had medical problems as a result of your drug use (e.g., memory loss, hepatitis, convulsions, bleeding, etc.)?
25. Have you ever gone to anyone for help for a drug problem?
26. Have you ever been in hospital for medical problems related to your drug use?
27. Have you ever been involved in a treatment program specifically related to drug use?
28. Have you been treated as an out-patient for problems related to drug abuse?

Source: Skinner, 1982.

Index of Alcohol Involvement (IAI)

The IAI is a 25-item psychometric assessment instrument (see Table 9-5) designed by MacNeil (1991) to detect alcohol abuse. The IAI was normed with a sample of university undergraduate students in the Western U.S. Subjects were primarily female (60%) and white (87%), and had a mean age of 24 years.

TABLE 9-5. Index of Alcohol Involvement (IAI)

Index of Alcohol Involvement (IAI)

Name: _____ Today's Date: _____

This questionnaire is designed to measure your use of alcohol. It is not a test, so there are no right or wrong answers. Answer each item as carefully and as accurately as you can by placing a number beside each one as follows:

1 = Never
2 = Very rarely
3 = A little of the time
4 = Some of the time
5 = A good part of the time
6 = Most of the time
7 = Always

1. ____ When I have a drink with friends, I usually drink more than they do.
2. ____ My family or friends tell me I drink too much.
3. ____ I feel that I drink too much alcohol.
4. ____ After I've had one or two drinks, it is difficult for me to stop drinking.
5. ____ When I am drinking, I have three or fewer drinks.
6. ____ I feel guilty about what happened when I have been drinking.
7. ____ When I go drinking, I get into fights.
8. ____ My drinking causes problems with my family or friends.
9. ____ My drinking causes problems with my work.
10. ____ After I have been drinking, I cannot remember things that happened when I think about them the next day.
11. ____ After I have been drinking, I get the shakes.
12. ____ My friends think I have a drinking problem.
13. ____ I drink to calm my nerves or make me feel better.
14. ____ I drink when I am alone.
15. ____ I drink until I go to sleep or pass out.
16. ____ My drinking interferes with obligations to my family or friends.
17. ____ I have one or more drinks when things are not going well for me.
18. ____ It is hard for me to stop drinking when I want to.
19. ____ I have one or more drinks before noon.
20. ____ My friends think my level of drinking is acceptable.
21. ____ I get mean and angry when I drink.
22. ____ My friends avoid me when I am drinking.
23. ____ I avoid drinking to excess.
24. ____ My personal life gets very troublesome when I drink.
25. ____ I drink 3 to 4 times a week.

Source: MacNeil, 1991.

(text continues on page 174)

TABLE 9-6. MacAndrew Alcoholism Scale (MAC)

1. I like to read newspaper articles on crime.
2. Evil spirits possess me at times.
3. I have a cough most of the time.
4. I am a very sociable person.
5. I have not lived the right kind of life.
6. I think I would like the kind of work a forest ranger does.
7. My soul sometimes leaves my body.
8. I am certainly lacking in self-confidence.
9. I do many things which I regret afterwards (I regret things more than others seem to).
10. I was suspended from school one or more times for bad behavior.
11. I enjoy a race or game more when I bet on it.
12. In school I was sometimes sent to the principal for bad behavior.
13. My table manners are not quite as good at home as when I am out in company.
14. I know who is responsible for most of my troubles.
15. The sight of blood doesn't frighten me or make me sick.
16. I have never vomited blood or coughed up blood.
17. I like to cook.
18. I used to keep a diary.
19. I liked school.
20. I am worried about sex.
21. I have had periods in which I carried on activities without knowing later what I had been doing.
22. I frequently notice my hand shakes when I try to do something.
23. My parents often objected to the kind of people I went around with.
24. I have been quite independent and free from family rule.

25. I have few or no pains.
26. I have had blank spells in which my activities were interrupted and I did not know what was going on around me.
27. I sweat very easily even on cool days.
28. I have often felt that strangers were looking at me critically.
29. If I were a reporter I would very much like to report sporting news.
30. I have never been in trouble with the law.
31. I seem to make friends about as quickly as others do.
32. Many of my dreams are about sex.
33. I cannot keep my mind on one thing.
34. I have more trouble concentrating than others seem to have.
35. While in trains, busses, etc., I often talk to strangers.
36. I enjoy gambling for small stakes.
37. I can express my true feelings only when I drink.
38. I deserve severe punishment for my sins.
39. When I was young I often did not go to school even when I should have gone.
40. I have, at times, had to be rough with people who were rude or annoying.
41. I was fond of excitement when I was young.
42. If I was in trouble with several friends who were as guilty as I was, I would rather take the whole blame than give them away.
43. I readily become one hundred percent sold on a good idea.
44. I have frequently worked under people who seem to have things arranged so that they get credit for good work but are able to pass off mistakes onto those under them.
45. I like to wear expensive clothes.
46. The one to whom I was most attached and whom I most admired as a child was a woman (mother, sister, aunt, or other woman).
47. I have some habits that are really harmful.
48. I have recently considered killing myself.
49. In everything I do lately I feel that I am being tested.

Source: MacAndrew (1965).

TABLE 9-7. Malmö Modified Michigan Alcoholism Test (Mm-MAST)

1. Do you take a drink before going to a party?
2. Do you usually drink half a bottle of wine or corresponding amounts of alcohol over the weekend?
3. Do you drink a couple of drinks (or beers) a day to relax?
4. Do you tolerate more alcohol now than you did 10 years ago?
5. Do you have difficulties not drinking more than your friends?
6. Do you fall asleep after moderate drinking without knowing how you got to bed?
7. Do you have a bad conscience after drinking?
8. Do you take a drink (a beer) the day after a party?
9. Do you try to avoid alcoholic beverages for a determined period of time, e.g., a week?

Source: Kristenson & Trell, 1982.

Scoring Items 5, 20, and 23 are reversed and then summed with the remaining items. Scores can range from 25 to 175. Scores over 75 indicate alcohol abuse with higher scores indicating increasing severity.

Validity and Reliability The IAI has good construct and factorial validity. It has excellent internal consistency (reliability) with a reported Cronbach's alpha coefficient of 0.90.

MacAndrew Alcoholism Scale (MAC)

The MAC is a 49-item psychometric assessment instrument (see Table 9-6) designed by MacAndrew (1965) to detect alcoholism and other SUDs. It is a content scale that was empirically derived from the Minnesota Multiphasic Personality Inventory (MMPI). It was revised (MAC-R) with the development of the MMPI-2 (i.e., four religious items were dropped and replaced with four items that differentiate alcoholics from nonalcoholics). It is reportedly difficult to fake, unless the subject can also fake the MMPI-2. The MAC was normed with samples of men, but has been since utilized with diverse samples. However, some score adjustment is recommended before interpretation with certain specific groups (see Scoring).

Scoring Each item of the MAC is unit scored (i.e., zero or one) and summed. Items 8, 13, 16, 18, 19, 20, 28, 30, 32, 33, 34, 37 are scored false. The remaining items are scored true. Scores of 26 to 28 are indicative of abuse;[11] 29 to 31 are indicative of addiction, with certainty and/or severity of problem increasing as the score increases above 31. Due to the limitations of the norming sample utilized, some score adjustments have been recommended. Black men and men who are obese tend to score higher as groups than white, nonobese norms. Their total raw scores can be adjusted by subtracting two points. For women, who tend to score lower than male norms as a group, adjust their total raw scores by adding three points.

Validity and Reliability The MAC is less sensitive (valid) in terms of identifying other substance use disorders, particularly among women (Cernovsky, 1987). It

TABLE 9-8. Maternal Short-MAST (M-SMAST)

Do you think your mother is/was an alcoholic?
1. Do you feel your mother has been a normal drinker?
2. Did your mother/father, grandparent, or other near relative ever complain about your mother's drinking?
3. Did your mother ever feel guilty about her drinking?
4. Did friends and relatives think your mother was a normal drinker?
5. Was your mother able to stop drinking when she wanted to?
6. Has your mother ever attended a meeting of Alcoholics Anonymous?
7. Has your mother's drinking ever created problems between her and your father (or step-parent) or another near relative?
8. Has your mother ever gotten into trouble at work because of drinking?
9. Has your mother ever neglected her obligations, family, or work for two or more days in a row because she was drinking?
10. Has your mother ever gone to anyone for help about her drinking?
11. Has your mother ever been in a hospital because of drinking?
12. Has your mother ever been arrested for drunken driving, driving while intoxicated, or driving under the influence of alcoholic beverages?
13. Has your mother ever been arrested, even for a few hours, because of other drunken behavior?

Source: Crews & Sher, 1992; Selzer, Vinokur, & Van Rooijen, 1976.

also is less sensitive in terms of differentiating alcoholic and nonalcoholic groups of patients with schizophrenia or other major mental disorders (Gripshover & Dacey, 1994; Miller & Streiner, 1990; Preng & Clopton, 1986; Searles, Alterman, & Purtill, 1990).

Malmö Modified Michigan Alcoholism Screening Test (Mm-MAST)

The Mm-MAST is a 9-item psychometric assessment instrument (see Table 9-7) designed by Kristenson & Trell (1982) to detect alcoholism.

Scoring A cut-off (discriminating) score of 4 is recommended (Seppae, Koivula, & Sillanaukee, 1992).

Validity and Reliability Validity data are not available. The Mm-MAST has displayed relatively poor internal consistency (reliability) when used for women with a reported Cronbach's alpha coefficient of 0.58 in a female population (Osterling et al., 1993).

Maternal Short-MAST (M-SMAST)

The M-SMAST is a 13-item psychometric assessment instrument (see Table 9-8) designed by Crews and Sher (1992) to detect alcoholism among the mothers of the respondents.[12] The M-SMAST was normed with samples of college freshmen who were at least 18 years of age, equally distributed for gender, and predominantly white (85%).

TABLE 9-9. Maternal substance use screening questions

Drinking Questions:
In the past year,
1. Have you ever had a drinking problem?   Yes   No
2. Have you tried to cut down on your drinking?   Yes   No
3. Do you ever have five or more drinks at a time? Yes   No
4. How many drinks does it take for you to feel
   high or get a buzz?   0 (don't drink)
        1   2   3   4   5   6   7   or more

Drug Questions:
In the past year,
1. Have you ever had a drug problem?   Yes   No
2. Have you used any drugs in the past 24 hours?   Yes   No

Circle which ones: marijuana, cocaine, heroin, LSD, methadone,

Other: _____

Source: Kemper, Greteman, Bennett, & Babonis, 1993.

Scoring See MAST and SMAST.

Validity and Reliability Validity, based upon agreement of results with other measures, appears to be good. The M-SMAST has acceptable internal consistency (reliability) with a reported Cronbach's alpha coefficient of 0.74. Both validity and reliability may be enhanced by the elimination of items 1, 3, 4, and 5 (Crews & Sher, 1992).

Maternal Substance Use Screening Questionnaire

Maternal Substance Use Screening Questionnaire is a 6-item psychometric assessment instrument (see Table 9-9) designed by Kemper, Greteman, Bennett, and Babonis (1993) to detect both alcohol and other substance use among mothers.

Scoring An affirmative response to any of the four drinking questions is deemed to constitute a positive screen for alcohol use. Similarly, an affirmative response to either of the two substance use questions is deemed to constitute a positive screen for substance use.

Validity and Reliability The questions or items comprising the Maternal Substance Use Screening Questionnaire have not been formally assessed in terms of their validity and reliability. However, they appear to have face validity. In addition, in a clinical comparison to both the DAST and the MAST, the questions were found to be significantly more sensitive and valid in determining maternal substance abuse (Kemper et al., 1993).

Michigan Alcoholism Screening Test (MAST)

The MAST is a 24-item psychometric assessment instrument (see Table 9-10) designed by Selzer (1971) to detect alcoholism among adults. It was designed to accommodate

TABLE 9-10. Michigan Alcoholism Screening Test (MAST)

PLEASE CIRCLE EITHER YES OR NO FOR EACH ITEM AS IT APPLIES TO YOU.

Yes	No	(2)	50.	Do you feel you are a normal drinker?
Yes	No	(2)	51.	Have you ever awakened the morning after some drinking the night before and found that you could not remember a part of the evening before?
Yes	No	(1)	52.	Does your wife, husband, a parent, or other near relative ever worry or complain about your drinking?
Yes	No	(2)	53.	Can you stop drinking without a struggle after one or two drinks?
Yes	No	(1)	54.	Do you ever feel guilty about your drinking?
Yes	No	(2)	55.	Do friends or relatives think you are a normal drinker?
Yes	No	(2)	56.	Are you able to stop drinking when you want to?
Yes	No	(5)	57.	Have you ever attended a meeting of Alcoholics Anonymous (AA)?
Yes	No	(1)	58.	Have you ever gotten into physical fights when drinking?
Yes	No	(2)	59.	Has drinking ever created problems between you and your wife, husband, a parent, or other near relative?
Yes	No	(2)	60.	Has your wife, husband, a parent, or other near relative ever gone to anyone for help about your drinking?
Yes	No	(2)	61.	Have you ever lost friends or girlfriends/boyfriends because of your drinking?
Yes	No	(2)	62.	Have you ever gotten into trouble at work because of drinking?
Yes	No	(2)	63.	Have you ever lost a job because of drinking?
Yes	No	(2)	64.	Have you ever neglected your obligations, your family, or your work for two or more days in a row because you were drinking?
Yes	No	(1)	65.	Do you drink before noon fairly often?
Yes	No	(2)	66.	Have you ever been told you have liver trouble? Cirrhosis?
Yes	No	(5)	67.	After heavy drinking, have you ever had delirium tremens (DTs) or severe shaking, or heard voices, or seen things that weren't really there?
Yes	No	(5)	68.	Have you ever gone to anyone for help about your drinking?
Yes	No	(5)	69.	Have you ever been in a hospital because of drinking?
Yes	No	(2)	70.	Have you ever been a patient in a psychiatric hospital or on a psychiatric ward of a general hospital where drinking was part of the problem that resulted in hospitalization?
Yes	No	(2)	71.	Have you ever been seen at a psychiatric or mental health clinic, or gone to a doctor, social worker, or clergyman for help with any emotional problem where drinking was part of the problem?
Yes	No	(2)	72.	Have you ever been arrested for drunken driving while intoxicated or driving under the influence of alcoholic beverages?
Yes	No	(2)	73.	Have you ever been arrested, even for a few hours, because of other drunken behavior?

Source: Selzer, 1971.

TABLE 9-11. Rapid Alcohol Problems Screen (RAPS)

Rapid Alcohol Problems Screen (RAPS)
- Do you sometimes take a drink in the morning when you first get up?
- During the past year, has a friend or family member ever told you about things you said or did while you were drinking that you could not remember?
- During the past year, have you had a feeling of guilt or remorse after drinking?
- During the past year, have you failed to do what was normally expected of you because of drinking?
- During the past year, have you lost friends or girlfriends or boyfriends because of drinking?

Source: Cherpital, 1995.

---

lack of candor from respondents. The MAST was normed with samples that were primarily comprised of white men between 25 and 44 years of age. It was originally designed to be administered orally to subjects by health and social care professionals, but has been frequently self-administered by the respondent.

Scoring Each item in the MAST is assigned a weight (listed in the left hand column of the instrument) of zero to five. Items 1, 4, 6, and 7 are scored negatively. An overall score of 3 points or less is considered to indicate nonalcoholism; 4 points is suggestive of alcoholism; and 5 points or more indicates alcoholism.

Validity and Reliability The MAST has excellent validity, having been found to correctly identify over 90% of men who have alcoholism. It has excellent internal consistency (reliability) with a reported Cronbach's alpha coefficient of 0.93. Data were normed predominantly from samples of men in their mid-twenties to mid-forties and the MAST, therefore, may not be as specific or sensitive in relation to detecting alcoholism among women (Blankfield & Maritz, 1990; Kemper et al., 1993; Selzer, Gomberg, & Nordhoff, 1979) or among the elderly (Fulop et al., 1993; Jones, Lindsey, Yount, Soltys, & Farani-Enayat, 1993).

Rapid Alcohol Problems Screen (RAPS)

The RAPS is a 5-item psychometric assessment instrument (see Table 9-11) developed by Cherpitel (1995) to detect alcoholism.

Scoring A positive response to one of the questions is considered a positive test.

Validity and Reliability The RAPS reportedly performs better in terms of sensitivity and specificity across gender and racial groups than most similar short psychometric instruments (Cherpitel, 1997, 1998).[13]

Short Michigan Alcoholism Screening Test (SMAST)

The SMAST is a 13-item psychometric assessment instrument (see Table 9-12) developed by Selzer, Vinokur, and Van Rooijen (1976) to detect alcoholism.

TABLE 9-12. Short Michigan Alcoholism Screening Test (SMAST)

PLEASE CIRCLE EITHER YES OR NO FOR EACH ITEM AS IT APPLIES TO YOU.

Yes	No	(2)	1.	Do you feel you are a normal drinker?
Yes	No	(1)	2.	Does your wife, husband, a parent, or other near relative ever worry or complain about your drinking?
Yes	No	(1)	3.	Do you ever feel guilty about your drinking?
Yes	No	(2)	4.	Do friends or relatives think you are a normal drinker?
Yes	No	(2)	5.	Are you able to stop drinking when you want to?
Yes	No	(5)	6.	Have you ever attended a meeting of Alcoholics Anonymous (AA)?
Yes	No	(2)	7.	Has drinking ever created problems between you and your wife, husband, a parent, or other near relative?
Yes	No	(2)	8.	Have you ever gotten into trouble at work because of drinking?
Yes	No	(2)	9.	Have you ever neglected your obligations, your family, or your work for two or more days in a row because you were drinking?
Yes	No	(5)	10.	Have you ever gone to anyone for help about your drinking?
Yes	No	(5)	11.	Have you ever been in a hospital because of drinking?
Yes	No	(2)	12.	Have you ever been arrested for drunken driving while intoxicated or driving under the influence of alcoholic beverages?
Yes	No	(2)	13.	Have you ever been arrested, even for a few hours, because of other drunken behavior?

Source: Selzer, Vinokur, & Van Rooijen, 1976.

Scoring Each item is unit scored (i.e., zero or one) and summed. Items 1 and 4 are scored negatively. The recommended interpretation of the total score is as follows: 0 or 1, nonalcoholic; 2, possible alcoholic; and 3 or greater, alcoholic.

Validity and Reliability The SMAST has been found to be an appropriate screening test for women (Hays & Revetto, 1992) and comparable to the CAGE in regard to performance (Maisto, Connors, & Allen, 1995). However, the SMAST is less specific than the MAST when used to screen for alcoholism among elderly men and women (Willenbring, Christensen, Spring, & Ramussen, 1987).

TWEAK

The TWEAK is a 5-item psychometric assessment instrument (see Table 9-13) designed by Russell et al. (1994) to detect alcoholism among women, particularly during pregnancy.

TABLE 9-13. TWEAK: An alcoholism screening test developed for women

TWEAK: An Alcoholism Screening Test Developed for Women
- TOLERANCE: How many drinks can you hold?*
- Have close friends or relatives WORRIED or complained about your drinking in the past year?
- EYE OPENER: Do you sometimes take a drink in the morning when you first get up?
- AMNESIA: Has a friend or family member ever told you about things you said or did while you were drinking that you could not remember?
- Do you sometimes feel the need to CUT DOWN on your drinking?

Source: Russell et al., 1994.
*In version 2 of the TWEAK, this item question is replaced with "How many drinks does it take you to get high?" (Chan, Pristach, Welte, & Russell, 1993).

Scoring The TWEAK test is scored based on a seven-point scale, two points each for a positive response to either one of the first two questions and one point for each of the last three questions. A total score of two or more points indicates that the woman is likely to have an alcohol problem.

Validity and Reliability The TWEAK reportedly has a higher sensitivity and specificity than the CAGE or B-MAST in detecting alcoholism or heavy drinking (Chan, Pristache, Welte, & Russell, 1993) and performs adequately for both black and white women (Bradley, Boyd-Wickizer, Powell, & Burman, 1998). Among black women who are pregnant, the TWEAK was found to be as sensitive as the MAST (Russell, 1994; Russell et al., 1994).

☐ Conclusion

This chapter has reviewed the assessment and diagnosis of SUDs, particularly alcoholism, among women. While the clinical interview remains the cornerstone of diagnosis, the use of various psychometric instruments can be of tremendous assistance, particularly in relation to screening (i.e, rapidly and accurately identifying those women who likely are suffering from a SUD).

In order to make proper use of the available psychometric instruments, health and social care professionals must be familiar with the inherent strengths and weaknesses of each instrument. They also must be familiar with the basic assumptions, concepts, and principles that govern the use of these instruments. Accordingly, a brief review and discussion of types of error related to interpretation of test results and the concepts of validity and reliability also have been presented.

☐ Notes

1. See Chapter 11, Preventing and Treating Substance Use Disorders Among Women, for an overview of various treatment approaches and a discussion of related issues.

2. The concept and application of selectively adjusting criterion values in order to get (manipulate) the incidence (probability) of Type I or II diagnostic errors is not only utilized in the clinical setting, but in other contexts as well. If we think of convicting a woman of a crime when she is, in fact, innocent of that crime or not convicting a woman of a crime when she is, in fact, guilty of that crime as examples of Type I and Type II error, then we can appreciate that this philosophical and scientific approach is the basis of our Western Judeo-Christian system of jurisprudence. In that system we adjust the criterion values (in this case in relation to the required amount of evidence) to favor Type II error (i.e., as only requiring reasonable doubt) because we (i.e., society) have decided that it is better to let a guilty woman go free than to falsely imprison (or execute) an innocent woman.
3. The science of substance abusology (A. M. Pagliaro, 1991; 1992; 1994) has been identified as a transdisciplinary science concerned with understanding human abusable psychotropic use. Produced by scientists who embrace many different philosophies of science, it is based on the assumption that no one philosophy of science (e.g., positivism, post-positivism, postmodernism) is privileged in regard to its scientific aims, methodologies, or claims to fact.
4. Note that the probabilities of Type I and Type II diagnostic errors are inversely related (i.e., as the probability of one type of error increases, the probability of the other decreases).
5. Note that the statistics under discussion are population statistics (i.e., they are meant to represent the "true state of affairs" in a population (e.g., all women with SUDs) and they utilize "samples" from the population (e.g., the women subjects with SUDs in a particular study) to test various assumptions or premises). The results presented by these statistics are then generalizable to the population (e.g., all of the women with SUDs), but may not always be applicable to the individual woman that a health or social care professional may be assessing (e.g., she may be the "exception to the rule"—because, in this statistical context, she is an "outlier" in the population [i.e., she is one of those members of the population that "resides" at one extreme or the other of the normal distribution (bell-shaped) population curve]). Therefore, health and social care providers should recognize the limitations of these tests and interpret the results they obtain with due clinical caution and only use them in conjunction with other data sources (e.g., clinical interview) when establishing a diagnosis.
6. Other related psychometric instruments have been developed and used (e.g., Alcohol Beliefs Scale; Spouse Sobriety Influence Inventory), but their focus of attention and clinical utility is toward the identification of factors among *already diagnosed* alcoholics that may be of assistance in treatment. Therefore, these instruments are not addressed in this chapter. In addition, instruments (e.g., Adolescent Drug Involvement Scale) that are specifically developed for and limited to use with children, adolescents, or men are likewise not addressed in this chapter.
7. Note that face validity and content validity are not always equivalent and that the content validity is the most important of the two. For example, many of the questions on the MacAndrew Alcoholism Scale do not appear to have face validity, but do have content validity.
8. Internal consistency, reliability, or inter-item consistency, is typically indicated by Cronbach's alpha coefficient or the Kuder-Richardson coefficient.
9. Deliberate conscious deviation from truthful responses in order to meet a personal agenda, such as avoidance of incarceration (i.e., responding as if no problem exists, when, in fact, it does) or continuance of unwarranted disability payments (i.e., responding as if a problem exists when, in fact, it does not), is referred to as "faking good" and "faking bad," respectively.
10. The AUDIT also consists of an 8-item clinical instrument.
11. A score of 24 generally is considered to be the standard MAC cut-off score, but improved results (i.e., fewer false-positives) are obtained by increasing this criterion value as indicated to 26.
12. By corollary the M-SMAST also detects adult child of an alcoholic (ACOA) status among those who complete the instrument.
13. The AUDIT reportedly provides similar results across both gender and racial groups (Cherpital, 1997, 1998).

10
CHAPTER

Dual Diagnoses Among Women

Dual diagnosis is a term that refers quite simply and literally to the occurrence of two mental disorders within the same person at the same time (L. A. Pagliaro, 1990b). Other closely related terms, such as dual addiction, which has been used to refer to concomitant alcoholism and drug abuse (Kreek & Stimmel, 1984),[1] comorbidity, which has been used to refer to cases of two diagnosable entities in the realm of substance abuse and mental illness (Belfer, 1993), and dual disorder, which has been used to refer to concurrent diagnoses of alcoholism plus a psychiatric diagnosis (Daley, Moss, & Campbell, 1987, p. 3), also are in common use. This diversity in terms has contributed to semantic confusion in the published literature and in clinical settings (Fields, 1995).

As used in the context of this text, dual diagnosis is defined as the occurrence in a woman of one, or more, anxiety, mood (e.g., major depressive), psychotic, posttraumatic stress, or other mental disorder, in addition to a substance use disorder (SUD).[2] These disorders may or may not be directly related. In cases in which concurrent disorders are directly related, the SUD(s) may be either an antecedent or a consequence of the mental disorder(s) (see Table 10-1) (Lehman, Myers, Corty, & Thompson, 1994; Pagliaro, 1995b).

A significant percentage of adults who present with a *primary* diagnosis of a SUD *or* a mental disorder can be expected to have a dual diagnosis.[3] As noted by Barry, Fleming, Greenley, Widlak, Kropp, & McKee (1995), "The use of nonprescribed mood altering substances is a major problem among adults with serious mental illnesses" (p. 313), and, as noted by Ross, Glaser, & Germanson, (1998), alcohol-dependent women are "more likely to present with comorbid drug abuse, particularly use of amphetamines, tranquilizers, and sedatives" (p. 313). Several studies and reports have suggested that a dual diagnosis can be expected in approximately 10% to 20% of patients who have mental disorders. The authors' clinical experiences and the literature (e.g., Davidson, 1995; Miller, Belkin, & Gibbons, 1994) also have suggested that the incidence of dual diagnosis is significantly *higher* when only those patients whose primary disorder is a significant SUD (e.g., compulsive patterns of substance use; polysubstance use) are considered. In this situation, greater than 50% (and often close to 100%) of patients can be expected to have a dual diagnosis.

Women who have a dual diagnosis present major and significant health care requirements (Galanter, Egelko, Edwards, & Vergaray, 1994). Women who present with a SUD and another mental disorder (e.g., major depressive disorder) have a significantly

TABLE 10-1. Mental disorders, in addition to addiction and habituation, that are commonly associated with abusable psychotropic use*

Abusable Psychotropic	Amnesic Disorder	Anxiety Disorders	Delirium	Mood Disorders	Psychotic Disorders	Sexual Dysfunction	Sleep Disorders
CNS Depressants							
Opiates				✓		✓	✓
Sedative-Hypnotics	✓	✓	✓	✓		✓	✓
Solvents and Inhalants	✓	✓	✓	✓			
CNS Stimulants							
Amphetamines		✓	✓	✓	✓	✓	✓
Caffeine		✓					✓
Cocaine		✓	✓	✓	✓	✓	✓
Nicotine							✓
Psychedelics	✓	✓	✓	✓			

*Modified from the American Psychiatric Association, 1994, p. 177.

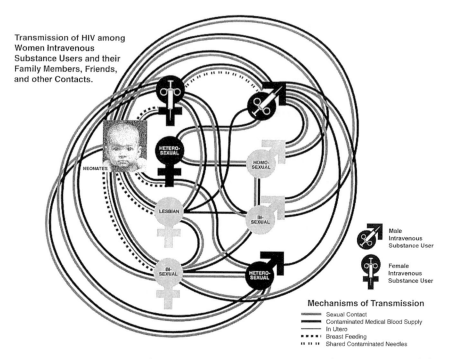

FIGURE 10-1. Transmission of HIV among women intravenous substance users and their family members, friends, and other contacts.

poorer prognosis than those who present with only a SUD or another mental disorder. However, as expected, even those women who have a dual diagnosis respond better to treatment when their multiple problems are adequately addressed with treatment appropriately tailored to their particular needs. As noted by Frances and Allen (1986), it would be better to cut the shoes to fit the feet rather than the other way around.

Indeed, dual diagnosis is commonly reported among women who have problematic patterns of substance use (Goldbloom, 1993; Ross, Glaser, & Germanson, 1998). Increasingly, tri-diagnosis (i.e., dual diagnosis plus a diagnosis of HIV infection) (L. A. Pagliaro, 1990b) also is being recognized increasingly (Fisher, 1991; Irwin et al., 1995; Silberstein et al., 1994) (see Chapter 8, Women, Substance Use, HIV Infection, and AIDS). The nature of the relationship between substance use and HIV infection is clear, but can be indirect (see Figure 10-1). Several studies and reports (e.g., Pagliaro et al., 1993) have noted that substance use functions as an antecedent risk factor placing women at significant risk for HIV infection in several specific ways including: 1) "sharing unclean needles and other drug paraphernalia with infected persons"; and 2) "loosening inhibitions and increasing the likelihood that women will engage in unprotected sex or trade sex for drugs or money" (p. 6) (See Chapter 8, Women, Substance Use, HIV Infection, and AIDS).

Although the availability of appropriate treatment services for women who have dual diagnoses has increased significantly during the 1990s, it remains all too common for them to be refused admission to a drug abuse treatment center because of their other mental disorder (e.g., clinical depression, schizophrenia) or to be refused admission to a mental health facility because of their problematic substance use (e.g., compulsive use of alcohol or cocaine) (Ponce & Jo, 1990). This Catch-22 situation reflects a general lack of appropriate education and training for health and social care professionals (Belfer, 1993), particularly in the fields of mental health and substance abuse. A survey by Adger, McDonald, and DeAngelis (1990) found that:

> At the medical student and residency training levels, only 44% and 40% of programs, respectively, required any formal instruction, and only 27% and 34%, respectively, offered an elective for medical students or residents. Although most respondents endorsed the inclusion of both required and elective alcohol and drug education in the curriculum, few programs that did not include it already had a future plan for it. (p. 555)

It also reflects the widespread and common use of people who have histories of a SUD (e.g., recovering alcoholics) as drug counselors for the treatment of women who have dual diagnoses. Although these people have an important role to play in the complex treatment of dual diagnosis, they are not qualified academically or clinically as primary therapists. For example, as noted by Penick et al. (1990):

> Many of the traditional caregivers in the substance abuse field are, themselves, recovering from chemical dependency; [these individuals, generally,] tend to know and use only one approach to treatment. If they are recovering themselves, the approach taken is usually the one that "worked" for them. When confronted with failure, substance abuse workers typically have no "fall back" position to draw upon, continuing instead to do "more of the same" rather than shift to a different treatment strategy. (pp. 7–8)

Women can present with any of a number of possible dual diagnoses (i.e., there is a seemingly unending number of combinations and permutations of mental disorders and SUDs). In fact, "dual diagnosis patients are [generally] heterogeneous as to their psychiatric diagnoses, as well as the various substances they abuse" (Stowell, 1991, p. 98). However, a review of the published literature suggests that the majority of cases of dual diagnosis among women involve problematic patterns of alcohol, amphetamine, cocaine, marijuana, and nicotine use concurrent with a mental disorder from one or more of the following five categories: 1) mood disorders (e.g., major depressive disorder); 2) anxiety disorders (e.g., panic disorder, posttraumatic stress disorder); 3) personality disorders (e.g., borderline personality disorder); 4) psychotic disorders (e.g., schizophrenia); and 5) sexual or gender identity disorders (e.g., sexual dysfunction) (Clark & Zweben, 1994; Fields, 1995; Gold & Slaby, 1991; Najavits, Weiss, & Shaw, 1997; Nixon & Glen, 1995; Westreich, Guedj, Galanter, & Baird, 1997). Each of these mental disorders and related patterns of substance use are discussed briefly.

☐ Dual Diagnosis: Substance Use and Mood Disorders

Major depressive disorders are likely the most common mental disorders that concurrently occur with substance use disorders (Coryell, 1991). This combination of mental disorders is particularly common among adolescent girls and women (Bukstein, Glancy, & Kaminer, 1992; Kendler, Heath, Neale, Kessler, & Eaves, 1993; Westreich, Guedj, Galanter, & Baird, 1997). Unfortunately, because of the nature of the present health care system which tends to compartmentalize disorders (e.g., substance use disorder versus other mental disorders—see earlier introductory discussion of dual diagnosis) and, consequently, their treatment, all too often the concurrent depressive disorders are "miss"-diagnosed.

Clinical depression can exist as either an antecedent or consequence of substance use, particularly the use of any of the CNS depressants. Of these substances of abuse, alcohol and the other sedative-hypnotics (e.g., benzodiazepines) are the most prominent in this regard.

Suggested reasons for a consequential association between a SUD and another mental disorder (e.g., depression) include: "physiological symptoms of withdrawal, the apathy of the alcoholic personality, the state of chronic intoxication, and concomitant drug use" (Slaby, 1991, p. 3). In this regard, it is important to note that the direct pharmacologic effect of alcohol and the other sedative-hypnotics is depression (L. A. Pagliaro, 1995a; Pagliaro & Pagliaro, 1998).

Several reasons also have been suggested for an antecedent association. Girls whose parents have problematic patterns of substance use (e.g., alcoholism) have been identified as having a proclivity for developing symptoms of depression. As noted by Perez-Bouchard, Johnson, and Ahrens (1993), "the dysfunctional family environment that often results from alcoholism or other substance abuse fosters a depressogenic attributional style ... that can be a risk factor for future depression" (p. 476). In addition, among women who have not yet been diagnosed as being depressed, a tendency to self-medicate with either cocaine (Pagliaro, Jaglalsingh, & Pagliaro, 1992; Weiss, Griffin, & Mirin, 1992) or alcohol is commonly observed as an attempt to temporarily diminish the distressing features of depression (Slaby, 1991). However, as noted by Breslau, Kilbey, and Andreski (1993), other underlying variables may be involved: "Neuroticism and the correlated psychologic vulnerabilities may commonly predispose to nicotine dependence *and* major depression or anxiety disorders" (p. 941). In addition, some personality disorders, such as antisocial personality, are highly correlated with both substance use and depression (Coryell, 1991). Genetic factors also have been cited as a major contributing factor to the comorbidity between major depressive disorder and alcoholism among women (Kendler et al., 1993).

Of particular concern is the fact that regardless of the nature of the association (i.e., as antecedent or consequence), it is all too frequently accompanied by suicide attempts and completed suicide. As noted by Berman and Schwartz (1990), "It is generally agreed that there is a progressive increase in depressive mood from abstainer to substance user and a corresponding increase in suicide attempts among adolescents with depression, substance abuse, or both" (p. 310). This observation also is supported by Runeson & Rich (1992) who note that "Depressive and substance use disorders predominate in the psychopathological backgrounds of suicides of all ages. In five published studies of consecutive suicides by adolescents and young adults, the average reported rates are 41% for major depression and 48% for substance abuse" (p. 197).[4] As noted by Quinnett (1995): "The most dangerous combination of risk factors [for suicide] for people of any age is untreated depression combined with substance abuse and addiction" (p. 65). (See Chapter 6, Women as Victims of Substance Use Related Violence, for additional discussion of depression and suicide among women.)

☐ Dual Diagnosis: Substance Use and Anxiety Disorders

Many dually diagnosed women have been the victims of mental, physical, or sexual abuse. This abuse is often perpetrated by the victim's sexual partners (i.e., spouse or significant other) (Westreich, Guedj, Galanter, & Baird, 1997) or is associated with a "history of repetitive childhood physical and/or sexual assault" (Najavits, Weiss, & Shaw, 1997). The long-term, traumatic nature of this pattern of abuse gives rise to several types of anxiety disorders among women, including panic disorder and posttraumatic stress disorder. Particular sensitivity must be used for these women in selecting therapeutic interventions (i.e., initial gender specific treatment options may significantly decrease these women's anxiety and, therefore, facilitate group participation and the therapeutic process of recovery).

☐ Dual Diagnosis: Substance Use and Psychotic Disorders

Substance use related disorders have been commonly noted in several studies among a significant proportion of cohorts of schizophrenics. In addition, several substances of abuse have the direct ability to pharmacologically cause or mimic psychotic disorders. Although usually of a transitory nature, these effects are characteristically associated with acute intoxication (see Table 10-1). For example, the stimulants (i.e., amphetamines; cocaine) and the psychedelics (i.e., lysergic acid diethylamide [LSD], phencyclidine [PCP]) may cause symptoms of psychosis (i.e., delusions, hallucinations, disorganized speech, grossly disorganized or catatonic behavior) that are virtually indistinguishable from those associated with acute schizophrenia (American Psychiatric Association, 1994). In fact, the psychedelics have been commonly referred to pharmacologically as psychotomimetics or psychotogens (i.e., drugs that mimic or cause psychosis).

☐ Dual Diagnosis: Substance Use and Personality Disorders

People who have antisocial or borderline personality disorders appear to be at a greater risk for dual diagnosis (Coryell, 1991; Fields, 1995; Norris & Extein, 1991; Slaby, 1991). Both of these personality disorders have their onset during adolescence and include a proclivity for potentially self-damaging impulsive behavior, including the binge use of the various substances of abuse.[5]

A gender difference in relation to substance use and borderline personality disorder has been noted:

> The borderline female is often on a spectrum of affective disorders, whereas the borderline male more often overlaps with severe conduct disorders, sociopathy, drug addiction and alcoholism, the episodic dyscontrol syndrome, or the attention deficit hyperactivity disorder with learning disabilities. (Andrulonis, 1991, p. 23)

☐ Dual Diagnosis: Substance Use and Sexual or Gender Identity Disorders

Women who have been victims of severe sexual abuse as children or who have gender identity disorders are at risk for substance use disorders (Bayatpour, Wells, & Holford, 1992; Gardner & Cabral, 1990). In addition, substance use and sexual behavior/performance can be related in several different ways (see Table 10-2) as noted in the following quotations by Ogden Nash (1902–1971), "Candy is dandy, but liquor is

TABLE 10-2. Substance use and sexual behavior*

1. Sexual dysfunction may be directly related to the pharmacologic effect(s) of the substance of abuse.
2. Stress may lead independently to both sexual dysfunction and substance use.
3. Substances of abuse may be used to facilitate sexual behavior or performance.
4. Substances of abuse may be used to cope or deal with inadequate or undesirable sexual behavior or performance (e.g., to self-medicate sexual and gender identity disorders or feelings related to childhood or adult sexual victimization).
5. Cognitive impairment, including reasoning impairment associated with mental disorders (e.g., schizophrenia), may lead independently to substance use and sexual disorders.
6. The use of substances of abuse may result from the pattern of socialization required to meet sexual partners (e.g., women seeking homosexual sex at lesbian bars or inner city women seeking sex in a crack house in order to obtain crack [i.e., "crack whore" or "skeezer"]).

*Modified from L. A. Pagliaro, 1995d; Slaby, 1991.

quicker", and William Shakespeare (1564–1616), "It [alcohol] provoketh the desire, but taketh away the performance."

☐ Treatment[6]

Effective treatment begins with proper attention to the potential for dual diagnosis and its subsequent appropriate diagnosis. It can then be managed either by an appropriately qualified health or social care provider (e.g., clinical psychologist, family therapist, psychiatrist) or can be cotreated by qualified professionals specializing in the treatment of substance use disorders and the other mental disorders (e.g., major depression), respectively (O'Connell, 1990).

The following list, developed by Meyer (1986) and cited by Weiss (1992), summarizes the possible combinations of relationships between the disorders comprising a dual diagnosis. Consideration of these relationships may be of assistance in the development and delivery of effective treatment:

1. Mental disorders may serve as risk factors for substance use disorders.
2. Mental disorders may modify the course of a substance use disorder.
3. The signs and symptoms of mental disorders may occur during the course of chronic intoxication with a substance of abuse.
4. Mental disorders may develop as a result of substance use and persist despite the discontinuation of the substance use.
5. Substance use and the signs and symptoms of mental disorders may become linked meaningfully to each other over time.
6. A mental disorder and a substance use disorder may occur in the same person, but may be unrelated.

In addition, dual diagnosis treatment programs need to address the unique life experiences and special therapeutic needs of ethnically and culturally diverse groups of women. As noted by Clark and Zweben (1994):

The [woman] patient who has a dual diagnosis is particularly vulnerable to violence, if not from generic mental illness, from a drug-using culture that is conducive to violence. Ethnic dual diagnosis patients may reside in communities where drug-related violence is common. Furthermore, both males and females may have been victims of childhood sexual abuse and violence. Female patients, of course, are at greater risk for violence. . . . Naturally, a victim of violence with eroded coping skills, a substance abuse problem, and psychiatric problems may not present as an ideal patient. . . . [They may] either resign themselves to a passive-aggressive demeanor or assume a highly charged aggressive stance. It is critical for the clinician to recognize that a victim of violence, even if presenting as a perpetrator, will be adversely affected by that violence. The African American, Native American, and Hispanic American dual diagnosis patient may be particularly at risk for the violence associated with racial discrimination, including harassment by police, social agencies, and treatment providers. (pp. 115–116)

In order to address the unique life experiences and special therapeutic needs of these and all women suffering from dual diagnoses, the following guidelines, developed from our clinical experience in the treatment of dually diagnosed women, are presented:

1. Therapy should be sensitive and empathetic.
2. Therapy should be active and purposeful.
3. Therapy should promote abstinence from substance use.
4. Therapy should provide insight and resolution of psychological conflicts.
5. Therapy should build self-confidence and self-esteem.
6. Therapy should develop and promote healthy defense mechanisms and coping styles.
7. Therapy should empower patients with a sense of control over their lives and responsibility for their actions (behaviors).
8. Therapy should be provided in a safe and trusting environment.
9. Therapy should be guided by the needs of the patient.
10. Therapy should be multimodal and utilize appropriate referrals to other health and social care providers as required by the patient.
11. Therapy should encourage participation in peer self-help programs (as deemed appropriate for the individual patient).
12. Therapy should provide for follow-up or aftercare (relapse prevention) services.

☐ Conclusion

Dual diagnosis is defined as the concurrent presentation within a person of one or more substance use disorders and one or more other mental disorders (e.g., anxiety disorder, major depressive disorder). Dual diagnosis is frequently encountered among women who are seeking treatment for a substance use disorder or another significant mental disorder. Thus, all women seeking treatment for substance use disorders should be assessed for other concurrent mental disorders so that appropriate treatment can be planned and implemented. Although women can present with any number of combinations of substance use disorders and other mental disorders, they most frequently present with problematic patterns of alcohol, cocaine, marijuana, or nicotine use in the context of a mood disorder, personality disorder, psychotic disorder, or gender identity disorder. Proper diagnosis of dual diagnoses among women is essential in regard to planning and providing appropriate treatment (see Chapter 11, Preventing and Treating Substance Use Disorders Among Women).

☐ Notes

1. In this regard, we prefer the use of the term polysubstance use, which is more accurate and less confusing (see Chapter 1, An Overview of Substance Use Among Women).
2. Although DSM-IV diagnostic categories have generally been used in this definition, dual diagnosis is not dependent upon adherence to the DSM-IV taxonomy. Indeed, the term dual diagnosis is not even officially used in DSM-IV (American Psychiatric Association, 1994).
3. In the authors' clinical practice, which specializes in the treatment of dual diagnosis patients, it has been noted that the vast majority of the patients themselves are generally unaware that they have a dual diagnosis. The dual diagnosis has not been previously diagnosed and they are consciously aware only that they are depressed or that they have a drinking problem (i.e., the reason for their referral). They are not aware that they have two, and generally more, mental disorders and that these mental disorders are generally highly interrelated.
4. A similar observation was made by Blixen, McDougall, and Suen (1997) concerning their sample of dually diagnosed elderly patients:

    > The leading psychiatric disorder diagnosis for our sample of hospitalized psychiatric elders was depression. Over one-third (37.6%) had a substance abuse disorder in addition to a psychiatric disorder, and almost three-fourths (71%) of this dual diagnosis group abused alcohol and 29% abused both alcohol and other substances. In addition, significantly more elders in the dual diagnosis group (17.7%) than in the group with only a mental disorder diagnosis (3.3%) made a suicide attempt prior to admission to hospital. (p. 307)

5. See Chapter 7, "Women as Perpetrators of Substance Use Related Violence," for additional discussion of co-morbidity of antisocial personality disorder among women.
6. See also Chapter 11, Preventing and Treating Substance Use Disorders Among Women.

Preventing and Treating Substance Use Disorders Among Women

The use of various substances of abuse is related to significant harm among women, as demonstrated in the previous chapters of this text. Therefore, it is obvious that the use of substances of abuse should be prevented, or, at least, minimized whenever possible. Real benefit may be achieved with appropriate intervention. For example, a national meta-analytic study of treatment techniques indicated a significant decrease in substance use, which was maintained for five years following treatment. In addition, and of particular significance for women, the study also found that treatment for substance use disorders resulted in: 1) 30% decrease in loss of child custody; 2) 40% decrease in time spent living on the street; and 3) 43% decrease in suicide attempts (National, 1998).[1]

This chapter describes primary, secondary, and tertiary prevention (treatment) strategies[2] that are aimed at: 1) preventing women from beginning substance use; 2) minimizing the harmful effects associated with substance use once it has begun and, perhaps, also achieving patterns of resumed nonuse; and 3) helping women who have developed patterns of abuse or compulsive use to achieve abstinence with attention to minimizing the associated harmful effects of their substance use (Figure 11-1). As noted in Chapter 1, An Overview of Substance Use Among Women, and Chapter 2, Explaining Substance Use Among Women, substance use among women is a long-standing, complex, and pervasive human concern. Therefore, it is illogical and naive to expect that a singular, and often simplistic prevention approach (e.g., increasing a woman's knowledge concerning the dangers associated with substance use or increasing her self-esteem or decision making abilities) will ultimately be effective. As Botvin and Botvin (1992) noted in their review of this issue:

> Traditional approaches to substance abuse prevention relying on the provision of factual information about the adverse consequences of substance use/abuse or attempting to foster the development of self-esteem and responsible decision making have produced disappointing results. These approaches are ineffective because they are based on faulty assumptions about the causes of substance abuse. The existing literature suggests that substance abuse is the result of the complex interaction of a number of etiologic determinants [as illustrated by the Mega Interactive Model of Substance Use Among Women]. Knowledge concerning the dangers of substance use appears to play a much less promi-

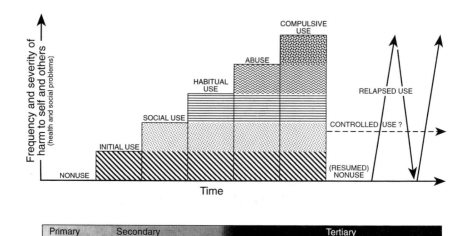

FIGURE 11-1. Prevention in relation to patterns of substance use.

nent role than previously believed. Considerably more important are the social influences that promote substance use and the psychological factors that help determine susceptibility to these influences. (p. 299)

Thus, in order to meet the needs of women in regard to primary, secondary, and tertiary prevention treatment needs, a wide range of services are required. As illustrated in the above quote, a preponderance of substance use prevention efforts are misguided because they do not adequately address the underlying psychological and social factors. The amenability of these factors to primary, secondary, or tertiary prevention techniques are identified in Table 11-1. In fact, a quick perusal of this table indicates that virtually all of the factors associated with substance use among women are amenable to primary, secondary, and tertiary prevention.

☐ Primary Prevention

Primary prevention (i.e., prevention of substance use before it begins) appears to be the ideal goal. In regard to women, most efforts must be directed at young girls and adolescent girls. However, attention to primary prevention also is needed during adulthood to reflect the various patterns of substance use that are observed among women during the various periods of their lives. For example, a middle-age woman may be at risk for developing problematic patterns of substance use because of her association with her colleagues at a new law firm where she is articling after finishing her legal degree following the divorce of her husband of 23 years.

The goals for the primary prevention of substance use should include: 1) reducing the number of antecedent risk factors; 2) reducing the acquisition of vulnerabilities; and 3) increasing the number of protective factors. A review of Table 11-1 indicates that some trait-like variables associated with substance use (e.g., antisocial personality disorder, genetic predisposition) are not amenable to primary prevention (i.e., they cannot be predicted or controlled prior to their occurrence and, once they have oc-

TABLE 11-1. Variables associated with substance use and amenability to primary, secondary, or tertiary prevention techniques

Woman Dimension	Prevention Techniques*		
	Primary	Secondary	Tertiary
Psychological Variables			
• Antisocial personality disorder	n/a		√
• Depression	√	√	√
• External locus of control	n/a	√	√
• Gender identity crisis	√	√	√
• Low self-esteem	√	√	√
• Previous substance use	√	√	√
• Serious early childhood losses	(√)	√	√
Social Variables			
• Dissatisfaction with family relationships	√	√	√
• Family alcohol and other substance use	(√)	√	√
• Physical or sexual abuse	(√)	√	√
• Previous inpatient treatment for mental disorders	(√)	√	√
Societal Dimension			
Societal Variables			
• Social programs and services (treatment availability and accessibility)	√	√	√
• Media messages	√	√	√

*Key: √ = amenable; (√) = partially amenable; n/a = not amenable.

curred, it is too late for primary prevention) and, thus, require secondary prevention techniques). Other variables (e.g., serious early childhood losses; physical or sexual abuse; previous psychiatric inpatient treatment) are only partially amenable to primary prevention techniques.

Unfortunately, most of the attempts aimed at achieving the goals of primary prevention, particularly in relation to women, have ended in failure (Shore, 1994). Several reasons for this failure have been suggested, including: 1) the lack of appropriate focus and goals (Burman, 1993; Gleason, 1994; Reyes, 1993); 2) the lack of appropriate research-based theory to develop and guide prevention strategies (Abbott, 1994; Paone, 1992); and 3) the lack of political commitment or social resolve (Hands, Banwell, & Hamilton, 1995; Waterson & Ettore, 1989).[3]

☐ Secondary Prevention

Secondary prevention is concerned with early intervention among women who have already begun to use one or more substances of abuse, but for whom the serious related harmful effects have not yet occurred. For example, secondary prevention strategies may include programs aimed at helping pregnant women, most of whom drink alcohol, not drink while pregnant; or providing women who are intravenous drug users (IVDUs) with sterile injection equipment or with bleach kits to clean their used needles to avoid or decrease the risk for being infected with or spreading the HIV.

Secondary prevention techniques could be used with all of the variable risk factors identified in Table 11-1. For example, if it was noted that a woman was depressed and was using alcohol to self-medicate her depression, perhaps in relation to a gender identity crisis, then the provision of, or a referral for, appropriate counseling, psychotherapy, and other necessary therapy should be made to help her manage her depression and decrease or cease her alcohol use (e.g., gender specific program for lesbian women who have alcoholism). This intervention may help the woman to resolve her gender identity crisis, resolve the accompanying depression, and, consequently prevent the development of problematic patterns of substance use often seen among lesbian women who are depressed.

Similarly, a young woman living on her own because of family discord associated with her teenage drug using lifestyle and promiscuity, whose mother has recently died in a motor vehicle crash (MVC) and is now living back at home with her alcoholic father ("in order to look after him"), should be recognized as being at risk for the resumption of her alcohol and other substance use and the development of problematic patterns of substance use (e.g., abuse or compulsive use). This woman should be regularly assessed for normal grieving and referred to, for example, a bereavement group of women who have lost loved ones as a result of MVC, monitored for grief resolution and provided with, along with her father, appropriate counseling, psychotherapy, and other appropriate treatment services (e.g., AA), as needed.

☐ Tertiary Prevention

Tertiary prevention involves minimizing the harm related to a history of problematic patterns of substance use among women who usually have developed patterns of abuse or compulsive use (see Chapter 1, An Overview of Substance Use Among Women, Figure 1-4). Aspects of tertiary prevention typically involve active medical or psychological treatment, including residential treatment and rehabilitation involving the achievement of abstinence and relapse prevention.

Primary, Secondary, and Tertiary Treatment Approaches

This section provides an overview of the various approaches used for the treatment of women who have problematic patterns of substance use with attention to their reported success or failure.[4]

Although many programs exist to treat women who have problematic patterns of substance use, the methods used can be conveniently grouped into eight major categories:

1. pharmacotherapy;
2. psychotherapy;
3. family therapy;
4. social skills training;
5. Alcoholics Anonymous and other 12-step programs;
6. therapeutic communities;
7. short-term residential treatment programs; and
8. feminist treatment approaches.

Each of these treatment approaches will be briefly discussed.[5] (See also Table 11-2)

Pharmacotherapy Pharmacotherapy, involving a variety of drugs, has been and continues to be, the mainstay of the medical treatment of both acute overdoses involving the various substances of abuse and their respective withdrawal syndromes. Pharmacotherapy also has been shown to be a useful adjunct to cessation (i.e., drug-assisted abstinence), maintenance (i.e., drug substitution), and relapse prevention programs. In addition, pharmacotherapy is often a necessary and integral component of the treatment of women who have dual diagnoses, particularly for the symptomatic management of depression (see Chapter 10, Dual Diagnoses Among Women).

Past advances in regard to the pharmacologic treatment of substance use disorders are quite diverse. In regard to the opiates, the use of methadone (Dolophine®), for opiate addiction maintenance (i.e., methadone maintenance); naltrexone (Trexan®) for the treatment of opiate addiction; clonidine as an aid for opiate detoxification; and naloxone (Narcan®) for the treatment of opiate overdose show this diversity. Other examples of pharmacologic intervention include the use of flumazenil (Anexate®) for the treatment of benzodiazepine overdose and disulfiram (Antabuse®) for the treatment of problematic patterns of alcohol use. Attention also has been given to the pharmacologic management of the withdrawal syndromes associated with the use of cocaine and nicotine (e.g., bromocriptine-aided cocaine withdrawal and buspirone-aided nicotine withdrawal, respectively).

Another area of attention has been the active development of dosage forms and drug delivery systems that can help to prevent or to reduce illicit patterns of substance use. For example, a highly successful approach has been the development of combination pentazocine/naloxone tablets (Talwin-Nx®) to prevent the illicit intravenous use of pentazocine (Talwin®). As a result of this pharmacologic strategy, the illicit intravenous use of pentazocine has all but been eliminated in the United States. In the United States, the oral pentazocine tablets have been formulated with 0.5 mg of

(text continues on page 198)

TABLE 11-2. An example of a comprehensive alternatives model*

Level of experience	Corresponding motives [examples]	Possible alternatives [examples]
Physical	Desire for physical satisfaction; physical relaxation; relief from sickness; desire for more energy; maintenance of physical dependency.	Athletics; dance; exercise; hiking; diet; health training; carpentry; gardening or other outdoor work.
Sensory	Desire to stimulate sight, sound, touch, taste; need for sensual-sexual stimulation; desire to magnify sensorium.	Sensory awareness training; sky diving; experiencing sensory beauty of nature (e.g., bird watching, hiking, mountain climbing, sailing).
Emotional	Relief from psychological pain; attempt to solve personal perplexities; relief from bad mood; escape from anxiety; desire for emotional insight; liberation of feeling; emotional relaxation.	Competent individual counseling; well-run group therapy; instruction in psychology of personal development.
Interpersonal	To gain peer acceptance; to break through interpersonal barriers; to communicate, especially nonverbally; defiance of authority figures; cement two-person relationships; relaxation of interpersonal inhibition; solve interpersonal hangups.	Expertly managed sensitivity and encounter groups; well-run group therapy; instruction in social customs; confidence training; social-interpersonal counseling; emphasis on assisting others in distress via education; marriage.
Social [including Socio-Cultural & Environmental]	To promote social change; to find identifiable subculture; to tune out intolerable environmental conditions (e.g., poverty); changing awareness of the masses.	Social service; community action in positive social change; helping the poor, aged, infirmed, young; tutoring handicapped; ecology action.
Political	To promote political change; to identify with anti-establishment subgroup; to change drug legislation; out of desperation with the social-political order; to gain wealth or affluence or power.	Political service; political action; nonpartisan projects such as ecological lobbying; field work with politicians and public officials; running for office.

Intellectual	To escape mental boredom; out of intellectual curiosity; to solve cognitive problems; to gain new understanding in the world of ideas; to study better; to research one's own awareness; for science.	Intellectual excitement through reading, discussion; creative games and puzzles; self-hypnosis; training in concentration; synectics—training in intellectual breakthroughs; memory training.
Creative-Aesthetic	To improve creativity in the arts; to enhance enjoyment of art already produced (e.g., music); to enjoy imaginative mental productions.	Nongraded instruction in producing and/or appreciating art, music, drama, crafts, handiwork, cooking, sewing, gardening, writing, singing, etc.
Philosophical	To discover meaningful values; to grasp the nature of the universe; to find meaning in life; to help establish personal identity; to organize a belief structure.	Discussions, seminars, courses in the meaning of life; study of ethics, morality, the nature of reality; relevant philosophical literature; guided exploration of value systems.
Spiritual-Mystical	To transcend orthodox religion; to develop spiritual insights; to reach higher levels of consciousness; to have Divine Visions; to communicate with God; to augment yogic practices; to get a spiritual shortcut; to attain enlightenment; to attain spiritual powers.	Exposure to nonchemical methods of spiritual development; study of world religions; introduction to applied mysticism, meditation; yogic techniques.
Miscellaneous	Adventure, risk, drama, "kicks," unexpressed motives; prodrug general attitudes, etc.	"Outward Bound" survival training; combinations of alternatives above; pronaturalness attitudes; brain-wave training; meaningful employment, etc.

*From: Cohen (1974, pp. 6–7).

naloxone (Narcan®), an opiate analgesic antagonist. The addition of naloxone to the pentazocine tablet formulation prevents illicit intravenous pentazocine use. The naloxone is poorly absorbed from the gastrointestinal tract following oral ingestion and, thus, has virtually no effect on the analgesic action of pentazocine. However, if the Talwin Nx® tablet is illicitly crushed, dissolved, and injected intravenously, the naloxone is immediately absorbed, blocking the desired action of the pentazocine. Unfortunately, the Talwin Nx® tablet formulation is not available in Canada where the illicit intravenous use of pentazocine continues often with significant adverse effects (e.g., overdosage, pulmonary fibrosis), particularly among young Native American Indian women living in the inner cities.

Likewise, the transdermal nicotine delivery systems (e.g., Habitrol®, Nicoderm®) and nicotine nasal sprays (Nicotrol NS®) have become important adjuncts to smoking cessation programs and have demonstrated positive effects in relation to decreasing tobacco smoking. On the horizon are a number of promising developments in pharmacology, including several aimed at the pharmacologic prevention and treatment of cocaine addiction. As polysubstance use becomes even more prominent in North America, clinically significant interactions involving the substances of abuse and their methods of use also will need to be increasingly addressed.

Although pharmacologists have been successful in developing useful knowledge of the pharmacology, toxicology, abuse potential, and addiction liability of the substances of abuse among men, increased attention must be directed toward the prevention and treatment of substance use disorders among women, whose use of the various substances of abuse is increasingly significant. In this regard, clinical pharmacologists, and other health and social care providers, must recognize that:

1. Certain substances of abuse (e.g., prescription sedative-hypnotics) hold particular attraction for women and are selected and used preferentially by women for a variety of reasons.
2. Women are at particular risk for social problems (e.g., domestic violence, sexual assaults) associated with substance use.
3. Women have unique issues and needs such as child care responsibilities that must be adequately addressed in order to optimize treatment success and minimize risk of recidivism.
4. Women require individualized and diverse prevention and treatment approaches (e.g., gender, age, and culture-specific therapy groups) because of their heterogeneity.

In relation to the prevention and treatment of substance use among women, the major applications of drug therapy involve:

1. the treatment or acute overdoses;
2. the management of withdrawal syndromes;
3. the maintenance of abstinence;
4. substituting or replacing a particular substance of abuse with a less harmful one; and
5. the symptomatic management of dual diagnoses.

Each of these applications is presented and briefly discussed.

Acute Overdoses. Specific pharmacologic antagonists are available for two groups of the substances of abuse classified as CNS depressants (i.e., opiate analgesics and benzodiazepine sedative-hypnotics). These antagonists are, respectively, naloxone [Narcan®] and flumazenil [Anexate®, Romazicon®] and reverse the toxic and other pharmacologic effects associated with these substances of abuse.

Naloxone (Narcan®) is an essentially pure opiate antagonist that has virtually no direct observable effects other than its antagonistic effects. These effects are elicited within the CNS by competitive inhibition (i.e., it selectively competes with opiate analgesics for binding sites on endogenous endorphin receptors). By displacing the opiate from its binding sites, naloxone immediately inhibits the pharmacologic activity of the opiates, including, in cases of severe overdose, life-threatening respiratory depression. However, when administered to a person who is physiologically dependent on (i.e., addicted to) the opiates, naloxone can precipitate an acute opiate withdrawal syndrome with the usual associated signs and symptoms (e.g., increased blood pressure, nausea, tachycardia, and vomiting). The onset of action for naloxone is generally within two minutes of administration. Effects last for approximately one to two hours. In this regard, naloxone may need to be periodically readministered in cases of overdoses involving the long-acting opiates (e.g., methadone) (L. A. Pagliaro & A. M. Pagliaro, 1998, 1999b).

Flumazenil (Anexate®) is an essentially pure benzodiazepine receptor antagonist. Flumazenil elicits its antagonistic effects within the CNS by means of competitive inhibition. The onset of action for flumazenil is generally within two minutes of intravenous injection with effects lasting for approximately one hour. Although flumazenil effectively antagonizes the sedative and hypnotic effects (i.e., conscious sedation or general anesthesia) produced by the benzodiazepines, it is less effective in regard to reversing their respiratory depressive effects. The use of flumazenil for a person who is physiologically dependent on (i.e., addicted to) the benzodiazepines may sometimes precipitate convulsions and caution is indicated (Flumazenil, 1992; Kararokiros & Tsipis, 1990; L. A. Pagliaro & A. M. Pagliaro, 1998, 1999b).

Withdrawal Syndromes. Several drugs have been used, with varying degrees of success, to reduce the unpleasant physiological and psychological signs and symptoms associated with the withdrawal of various substances of abuse, including alcohol, opiates, and cocaine (Taylor & Slaby, 1992).[6] Alcohol withdrawal often is treated quite successfully with a long-acting benzodiazepine, usually chlordiazepoxide (Librium®), the dosage of which is gradually reduced over a one to two week period. When appropriately used, chlordiazepoxide can make the alcohol withdrawal syndrome virtually symptomless (L. A. Pagliaro & A. M. Pagliaro, 1999b). Although less efficacious, clonidine (Catapres®), an alpha-adrenergic agonist also used clinically for its antihypertensive effects, has been used to manage opiate (e.g., heroin, methadone) withdrawal syndromes (Gold & Dackis, 1984; Mirin, 1995; Washton, Gold, & Pottash, 1985). The signs and symptoms of withdrawal are effectively managed by gradually decreasing the clonidine dosage over a one- to two-week period.[7]

Amantadine (Symmetrel®), bromocriptine (Parlodel®), carbidopa/levodopa (Sinemet®), pergolide mesylate (Permax®), and other drugs that possess dopaminergic activity have been used to treat the psychological craving associated with the cocaine withdrawal syndrome (Holloway, 1991; Jonas & Gold, 1992; Tutton & Crayton, 1993). However, results have been varied and further research is required before the wide-spread clinical use of these drugs for the treatment of cocaine craving can be generally recommended.

A relatively recent development for the treatment of nicotine withdrawal (i.e., in association with the cessation of tobacco smoking) was the approval of bupropion

(Wellbutrin®, Zyban®), an antidepressant. Buproprion pharmacotherapy is continued for two to three months while monitoring patient response and progress in terms of smoking cessation (L. A. Pagliaro & A. M. Pagliaro, 1999b).

Abstinence Maintenance. Several drugs have been developed to encourage the maintenance of abstinence among people who have ceased the abuse or compulsive use of alcohol.[8] These drugs generally exert unpleasant effects (or block the desired effects) when the substance of abuse is used. Thus, the ability of these drugs to promote abstinence is by means of their association with aversive stimuli. The prototype drug with the longest history of use in this regard is disulfiram (Antabuse®) for the maintenance of abstinence in regard to alcohol use.

Disulfiram blocks the metabolism of alcohol at the acetaldehyde stage by means of inhibition of the enzyme, acetaldehyde dehydrogenase. Consequently, when alcohol is consumed, even in small quantities, acetaldehyde accumulates in the blood stream and elicits a number of unpleasant effects, including: blurred vision, chest pain, confusion, copious vomiting, dyspnea (shortness of breath), flushing, hyperventilation (rapid breathing), hypotension (low blood pressure), nausea, respiratory difficulty, syncope (fainting), tachycardia (rapid heart beat), throbbing headache, vertigo (dizziness), and weakness. The intensity of this reaction, which is known as the disulfiram-alcohol-reaction (or more commonly as the Antabuse® reaction or disulfiram flush), is generally proportional to the amount of disulfiram used as a component of the alcohol abstinence maintenance program and the amount of alcohol consumed at a particular drinking session (L. A. Pagliaro & A. M. Pagliaro, 1999b).

Therapy is begun following at least one day of abstinence from alcohol use in order to avoid precipitating the disulfiram reaction. Subsequently, disulfiram is orally ingested on a daily basis each morning for a period of months to years until abstinence can be maintained without the aid of the drug.[9]

A more recent pharmacologic approach for promoting abstinence in regard to alcohol use is naltrexone (ReVia®) pharmacotherapy. Naltrexone, a long-acting oral opiate antagonist, was originally developed and marketed under the brand name Trexan® for the treatment of abuse and compulsive use patterns of opiate use (i.e., physical dependence or addiction) (Greenstein, Arndt, McLellan, O'Brien, & Evans, 1984; Holloway, 1991; Kirchmayer, Davoli, & Verster, 1998; Mirin, 1995). However, it was discovered by serendipity that it also blocked the euphorogenic effect of alcohol.[10]

When used as an adjunct to effective psychotherapy, naltrexone has been found to demonstrate significant clinical utility with reports of less craving for alcohol, a lower rate of relapse, and, when drinking, the consumption of fewer drinks per occasion (Volpicelli, Watson, King, Sherman, & O'Brien, 1994). However, long-term safety and efficacy have not yet been clearly established. In addition, because it is a potent opiate antagonist, caution must be exercised when naltrexone is used for women who have alcoholism and who are also addicted to the opiates because naltrexone can precipitate an acute opiate withdrawal syndrome among these women. Likewise, women who require opiate analgesics for the symptomatic management of chronic cancer or other malignant pain would require alternative pain relief measures until the effects of naltrexone dissipated (Naltrexone, 1995; Volpicelli, Watson, King, Sherman, & O'Brien, 1995).

Several selective serotonin reuptake inhibitors (e.g., fluoxetine [Prozac®], sertraline [Zoloft®]) also have been investigated in relation to their possible effects on alcohol euphoria and craving. Results have been mixed with a tendency toward being weakly efficacious for this indication (Anton, 1994).

Drug Substitution. Drug substitution is based on the principle of harm reduction, which is an integral component of tertiary prevention (see earlier discussion). As such, drug substitution does not attempt to stop the use of substances of abuse, rather, it attempts to change the level of harm associated with the use of a particular substance of abuse, including its method of use. The two major examples of drug substitution in North America are: 1) the substitution of methadone for heroin; and 2) the substitution of alternative methods of nicotine use for tobacco smokers.

Methadone (Dolophine®), a long-acting opiate, has been used for over 30 years in North America as a legal form of opiate addiction maintenance for people who are addicted to heroin and who have been unsuccessful at opiate detoxification. The goal of methadone pharmacotherapy for the maintenance of opiate addiction is to prevent the occurrence of the signs and symptoms of the opiate withdrawal syndrome. Thus, it allows heroin addicts to discontinue their illicit heroin use because the methadone will ward off the withdrawal syndrome that would otherwise occur. Opiate addiction maintenance also prevents hustling and other behaviors (e.g., breaks and entries) often used by heroin addicts to support their heroin habits.

While prescribed in dosages not associated with euphoric and other desirable effects, methadone maintenance keeps the edge off for women who are addicted to heroin and, thus, allows them to maintain parenting, therapy, work, and other social functions. Although continuing a woman's opiate addiction, methadone offers several benefits in that it: is effective orally and, thus avoids the hazards associated with the intravenous injection of heroin, such as HIV infection; decreases heroin craving; produces neither euphoria nor excessive sedation; is relatively inexpensive; and is legal. L-alpha-acetyl-methadol (LAAM®, ORLAAM®), a long-acting (i.e., three days) methadone derivative, also is in current clinical use (Holloway, 1991; LAAM, 1994; Mirin, 1995). Unfortunately, the withdrawal syndrome associated with methadone actually is more severe than that associated with heroin. Thus, many women who select to enrol in opiate (methadone) maintenance programs, remain on the programs for long periods of time (i.e., several years). Women who do not remain on them, usually resort back to their original heroin use.

The widest use of drug substitution in North America involves the use of nicotine in the form of chewing gums, nasal sprays, and transdermal drug delivery systems, or "patches," to manage the nicotine withdrawal syndrome associated with the cessation of tobacco smoking. Whereas methadone maintenance is just that, maintenance, it is generally expected that nicotine substitutes be used only for short periods of time (e.g., up to 12 weeks) as a means to help women to cease their nicotine use. While potentially beneficial, studies have repeatedly demonstrated that the use of nicotine substitutes is only effective when combined with effective counseling or psychotherapy programs (Wetter, Fiore, Gritz, Lando, Stitzer, & Hasselblad, 1998). For example, as noted by Covey and Glassman (1991):

> Evidence of the addictive nature of chronic tobacco use suggests that pharmacologic interventions, in conjunction with behaviorally oriented therapy, may present the best hope for achieving smoking cessation in refractory smokers. (p. 69)

Or, as noted by Generali (1992):

> Smoking cessation rates associated with nicotine transdermal patch therapy have varied in clinical trials. However, appropriate patient instruction and an extensive behavioral modification program ensure optimal response to transdermal nicotine therapy. (p. 34)

TABLE 11-3. Intrapersonal and interpersonal skills training elements*

Intrapersonal Skills	Interpersonal Skills
• Becoming aware of anger	• Assertiveness training
• Becoming aware of negative thinking	• Communicating emotions
• Coping with persistent problems	• Communicating in intimate relationships
• Decision-making	• Enhancing social support networks
• Increasing pleasant activities	• Giving and receiving compliments
• Managing anger	• Giving criticism
• Managing negative thinking	• Initiating conversations
• Managing thoughts about alcohol or other substance use	• Receiving criticism
	• Receiving criticism about substance use
• Planning for emergencies	• Refusing offers to use substances of abuse
• Problem-solving	• Refusing requests
• Relaxation training	• Using body language

*Modified from: Kadden (1994, p. 281).

The use of nicotine substitutes is meant as a temporary adjunct to smoking cessation. These drug substitutes should be used only when tobacco smoking has been discontinued and gradually terminated with dosage reductions over a 2 to 3 month period (L. A. Pagliaro & A. M. Pagliaro, 1999b).

Dual Diagnoses. Appropriate pharmacotherapy for mental disorders is a common and integral component of the treatment of problematic patterns of substance use among people who have a dual diagnosis (see Chapter 10, Dual Diagnoses among Women). The two most commonly treated categories of mental disorders, in this regard, are anxiety disorders and depression (Anton, 1994; Ryan & Puig-Antich, 1987). Many of the following treatment modalities can be used, in addition to pharmacotherapy, for treating women who have dual diagnoses.

Psychotherapy Cognitive therapy is probably the most commonly used form of psychotherapy for the treatment of problematic patterns of substance use among women. Cognitive therapy, in this context, is based on the assumption that problematic patterns of substance use are reflective of maladaptive coping (i.e., the woman has not learned other ways to cope with her problems or meet certain individual needs). Psychotherapy is, therefore, directed at the correction or modification of irrational belief systems, maladaptive or deficient coping skills, and faulty thinking patterns or styles.

Training in self-observation, the sharing of thoughts and emotions with the therapist, the systematic analysis of the validity of negative and irrational self-statements, and the gradual substitution of positive logical thinking patterns based on rational belief systems are attempted as part of the cognitive therapy process. Through this process, women are gradually made more aware of their problems, which may have been denied or avoided, and helped to develop the strategies, skills, and abilities they need to effectively deal with them.

The development, or strengthening, of specific intrapersonal and interpersonal skills, including anger control, leisure time management, problem solving, and resistance training (see Table 11-3 for a more comprehensive list), is an integral component of cognitive therapy. Cognitive therapy is often applied in the context of relapse prevention in order to help to assure that the positive gains achieved during early abstinence are maintained. A central component to the achievement of this goal involves teaching women how to identify high-risk situations that may lead to patterns of relapsed use and apply previously learned and rehearsed techniques to effectively avoid or deal with them.

As noted by Turner (1995):

> A treatment approach that uses a combination of cognitive and feminist therapy could be most effective. Therapists can serve as powerful role models as can other women who are also in treatment.... Enhancing the self-esteem and resiliency of adolescent young women by teaching them positive coping skills in environments where they feel valued, might have positive effects on the prevention of the depression as well as alcoholic drinking. (pp. 113–115)

Group psychotherapy for women also can be extremely effective. Additional details of group therapy will be discussed within the contexts of the following sections: Family Therapy; Social Skills Training; Alcoholics Anonymous; Therapeutic Communities; and Short-Term Residential Treatment Programs. Some other general guidelines that can assist family therapists, regardless of their specific theoretical orientations, are presented in Table 11-4.

Family Therapy   The family often plays a significant role in the etiology and maintenance of problematic patterns of substance use among women as has been identified throughout the various chapters of this text. Family therapy[11] (see Table 11-5) attempts to correct the dysfunctional behavior of family members, both individually and as a group (Kosten et al., 1986). Behavioral and strategic-structural family therapies are the most commonly used, excluding mixed therapies. These systemic approaches will be briefly discussed in the context of their application to the treatment of problematic patterns of substance use among women.

Strategic-Structural Family Therapy.   Strategic-structural, or simply structural, family therapy attempts to restructure maladaptive family boundaries that separate women from the members of the family. For example, a mother and daughter may form a close, protective alliance that excludes the daughter's husband from the knowledge that the daughter has had an abortion because she is "just not ready to have a baby." In reaction to this exclusion, the husband may feel alienated from his family and become increasingly indifferent to his wife and unsupportive of, or antagonistic toward, his mother-in-law. Such engagement may result in the partner withdrawing from the family by working all the time or seeking comfort and support from another woman. In another example, a woman may be involved in a constant, bitter conflict with her partner and engage one or more of their children or adolescents in this conflict by asking them to take sides. In this situation, the mother also may use another of her children to displace her anger, frustration, and blame (i.e., use the child as a scapegoat or physically or verbally abuse the child).

The general approaches used with the strategic-structural model of family therapy include reframing, validation, facilitated communication, and paradoxical directives.

TABLE 11-4. General guidelines for the family therapist*

- Respect the hierarchal structure of the family, if appropriate. If not, try to help the family reestablish a functional hierarchy.
- Listen to what is being said and not said, asking relevant questions for both.
- Don't interrupt a family member while he or she is speaking to ask for clarification. Wait until they have finished.
- Observe nonverbal behavior closely, as a basis for understanding family relationships and for possible intervention.
- Give equal attention to each family member.
- Do not attempt to minimize problems to the family. Be honest and open.
- Empathize with the stated family issues.
- Be nonjudgmental so that the family feels free to discuss problems without fear of censure.
- Establish open communication patterns early in therapy.
- Be aware of your own biases (and countertransference tendencies).
- Be flexible enough to shift your approach if you find that it is not working.
- Do not give advice, only suggestions as they fit the therapeutic plan.
- Do not allow yourself to be triangled or manipulated. *You* are the therapist.
- Evaluate each individual in terms of depression, guilt, self-esteem, etc.
- When you sense the family feels it has failed, attempt to bring up past successful experiences as reinforcement.
- Become a role model to the family.
- Allow the family to see you as a person who makes mistakes and owns up to these mistakes. Allow them to see you as a person with feelings.
- Try to have a purpose and reason for all of your actions or lack of action.
- Do not copy another therapist's style. Be yourself. Act in a manner that is comfortable for you and fits your personality.
- Your role is to provide options for the family to select and pursue. You plant a seed for positive growth that will enable the therapeutic process to bring about a change.

*Modified from: Frankel (1990, p. 263).

Reframing, which also is used as a method with cognitive psychotherapy, simply refers to the process of conceptualizing a problem in a new and different way. The purpose of reframing is generally to: 1) put a problem in proper (generally smaller) perspective; and 2) lessen the negative views that the family members have regarding their perceived notion of the cause of the problem. For example, a husband may identify his wife's alcohol use as an act of defiance. Whereas, the therapist may reframe a woman's alcohol use as an expression of insecurity and low self-esteem. This reframing of the reasons related to the woman's alcohol use may then shift the treatment approach from one of punishment to one of understanding and support.

Validation refers to the process by which the therapist, in acting as a role model for the family members, acknowledges and expresses understanding for each individual family members' feelings and desires. This process encourages the "hearing out" of individual family members' concerns before they are reacted to or judged.

Social Skills Training

Social skills training attempts to help women deal more effectively with their families, friends, or employers. Social skills training is accom-

TABLE 11-5. Types of family therapy and their major components or focus*

Behavioral
- Assertion training
- Contingency contracting
- Parent management training
- Problem-solving skills training

Contextual (Functional)
- Integration of behavioral, cognitive, emotional, and spiritual aspects of family

Strategic-Structural
- Restructure maladaptive patterns

Systemic
- Address behavioral limit-setting and intergenerational conflicts

Mixed
- A combination of various family therapy components

*While this categorization has been selected to facilitate organization and discussion, it is recognized that other, perhaps more comprehensive or detailed, categorizations of types of family therapy also are available.

plished by detailed, focused training sessions. These training sessions typically deal with common problems related to the woman's lack of sufficiently developed social skills and may include: nonverbal expression; refusing unreasonable requests; making difficult requests; expressing and receiving positive emotions; replying appropriately to criticism; and initiating social conversations (Oei & Jackson, 1980).

Alcoholics Anonymous Alcoholics Anonymous (AA) was started in 1935 in Akron, Ohio by Bill W. (a stockbroker) and Bob S. (a physician), who were its first two members. Alcoholics Anonymous has since spread across North America and now holds meetings worldwide. As noted by Trice (1983), AA has become, particularly in North America, the most frequently used form of alcohol treatment. According to several other researchers and therapists (e.g., Room & Greenfield, 1993; Weisner, Greenfield, & Room, 1995), the popularity of AA is due in large part to its American themes of individualism, equality, and spirituality, which are embodied in the Twelve Steps (see Table 11-6). As noted by Kurtz (1988; 1993), the organizational structure of AA also supports these themes in that there is no central authority or hierarchy, the only officer in AA groups is a secretary, and members avoid the use of last names.

Alcoholics Anonymous is regarded as neither a medical nor psychological approach to treatment. As such the organization maintains that alcoholism is a disease without cure and that treatment is social.[12] Alcoholics Anonymous relies on a rather informal form of group therapy and social support (i.e., frequent meetings comprised of recovering members) and a buddy system (i.e., the use of sponsors who have remained sober for a period of time by working the twelve steps and who can, thus, show newcomers the way to sobriety). As part of the group therapy, members hear from other members that they are not alone and that they share common, painful experiences in relation to their alcohol use. In addition, in conjunction with Step 1, members learn to overcome their strong denial of their own drinking problem. The confrontation of denial is clearly reflected in the members' introduc-

TABLE 11-6. The 12 steps of Alcoholics Anonymous*

1. We admitted that we were powerless over alcohol, that our lives had become unmanageable.
2. We came to believe that a Power greater than ourselves could restore us to sanity.
3. We made a decision to turn our will and our lives over to the care of God as we understood Him.
4. We made a searching and fearless moral inventory of ourselves.
5. We admitted to God, to ourselves, and to another human being the exact nature of our wrongs.
6. We were entirely ready to have God remove all these defects of character.
7. We humbly asked Him to remove our shortcomings.
8. We made a list of all persons we had harmed, and became willing to make amends to them all.
9. We made direct amends to such people wherever possible, except when to do so would injure them or others.
10. We continued to take personal inventory and when we were wrong promptly admitted it.
11. We sought through prayer and meditation to improve our conscious contact with God as we understood Him, praying only for knowledge of His will for us and the power to carry that out.
12. Having had a spiritual awakening as a result of these steps, we tried to carry this message to alcoholics and to practice these principles in all our affairs.

*From: *The Little Red Book*, 1986.

tions of themselves at AA group meetings, "Hello, my name is _____ and I'm an alcoholic."

Members are encouraged to work through and practice the twelve steps daily and, because the AA model purports that there is no cure for alcoholism,[13] maintain a lifelong abstinence by continued membership in the fellowship (i.e., AA). For many alcoholics, AA provides both the social support necessary to maintain abstinence and an effective surrogate for their previously patterned drinking time or familiar bar scene (i.e., AA meetings serve as a place to go on evenings, weekends, and holidays for socialization with friends who, in addition to other benefits, provide understanding and help to alleviate social isolation and loneliness).[14]

Some feminists (e.g., Beckman, 1993) have noted that the style and approach utilized by AA can be of significant benefit to women: "AA, a fellowship originally designed by and composed primarily of men, appears to be equally or more effective for women than for men" (p. 246). However, some women, particularly marginalized women, such as black women and lesbians (Swallow, 1983) reportedly find traditional AA programs to be less effective than programs that have been redesigned specifically for women (e.g., with the adoption of a feminist 12-step approach). "Many participants were uncomfortable with AA's tendency to individualize problems, clothe recovery in the language of Christian spirituality, and encourage 'surrender' and 'powerlessness'" (Hall, 1994, p. 572).[15] In response to the perceived deficiencies in the AA program, several different specific women's programs have been developed (e.g., Women for Sobriety [WFS], see Table 11-7).

TABLE 11-7. The 13 affirmations of Women for Sobriety*

1. I have a drinking problem that once had me.
2. Negative emotions will destroy only myself.
3. Happiness is a habit I will develop.
4. Problems bother me only to the degree I permit them to.
5. I am what I think.
6. Life can be ordinary or it can be great.
7. Love can change the course of my world.
8. The fundamental object of life is emotional and spiritual growth.
9. The past is gone forever.
10. All love given returns two-fold.
11. Enthusiasm is my daily exercise.
12. I am a competent woman and have much to give life.
13. I am responsible for myself and my actions.

*From Kaskutas, 1994, p. 188.

The overall effectiveness of AA is difficult to ascertain because AA maintains no formal records; research is not an AA mandate; the amount of time that members remain active in AA is extremely variable; and drop-out rates are high (Alford, Koehler, & Leonard, 1991; Fingarette, 1988; Miller & McCrady, 1993).[16]

Therapeutic Communities Therapeutic communities (TCs) are based on the assumption that problematic patterns of substance use are primarily symptomatic of psycho-social maladaptation to society, often as a result of incompetence in dealing with stress or social privation and alienation. As noted by O'Brien and Biase (1984), the goals of TC programs are:

1. to eliminate the user's drug-taking behavior,
2. to assist the user in learning to respond to distress (personal and environmental) in a more healthy manner, and
3. to assist users to readjust and return to the outside community as a functioning, independent person. (p. 16)

These goals are achieved by providing residential care for women who have problematic patterns of substance use. The residential care is usually provided for 9 to 18 months and gives women the opportunity to live with others who have similar problems in a highly structured home-like environment. As such, the TC provides a setting where everyone shares in the work and responsibility to see that community problems are minimized. Ideally, during their residential treatment, women will be able to increasingly assume skills and responsibilities, which they can transfer to the larger community upon their completion of the program. Regular meetings are held throughout the day in informal settings (e.g., sitting around the kitchen table). These meetings serve to facilitate the running of the TC (e.g., division of work, provision of feedback on the quality of residents' work performance) and provide a format for decision making processes. A significant amount of therapy also occurs informally throughout the day during which residents learn to take responsibility for and per-

TABLE 11-8. Characteristics of a women-oriented substance use treatment program

- Academic assistance
- Alcohol/substance use education
- Child care
- Components to build self-esteem
- Dual diagnosis treatment
- Employment/vocational counseling
- Financial counseling
- Follow-up (aftercare)
- Group therapy
- HIV counseling and testing
- Housing assistance (transitional housing)
- Individual therapy
- Legal services
- Life-skills programs
- Medical care
- Mothering courses
- Nutritional counseling
- Outreach and in-home services
- Relapse prevention programs
- Stress management programs
- Transportation
- Violence and sexual abuse services
- Women's support groups

form their tasks while interacting with the other residents. Recreational and leisure activities also provide a means for socializing and learning to interact more positively with others.

Most TCs practice a form of egalitarianism. For example, in regard to deciding how to handle a resident who is having difficulty getting on the program or in dealing with setting a program policy, all residents have an equal opportunity to share input and have an equal vote with the staff members.[17] All TCs require total abstinence from the use of alcohol, cocaine, heroin, LSD, and marijuana, but many still allow caffeine (i.e., coffee) and nicotine (i.e., tobacco) use.

The TCs have served as a model for many halfway house programs, which have been designed to facilitate a woman's return to the community (i.e., ease the transition process) after being released from a locked residential treatment facility or correctional facility. Such women often require more assistance with the transition back to the community as well as more supervision and monitoring than can be provided by usual outpatient treatment services.

Women who complete TC programs have been found to "show a success rate of more than 75%" (Rosenthal, 1984, p. 55). However, most patients (i.e., ~75%) do not complete the entire course of treatment provided by a TC (Cohen, 1982). For these patients "outcome results indicate that reduction of illicit drug use, crime, and unemployment is commensurate to the length of time an addict participates in a therapeutic community" (Coombs, 1981, p. 199). In an effort to increase women's participation and attendance in TCs, several authors (e.g., Beckman, 1994; Brown, Sanchez, Zweben, & Aly, 1996; Laken & Hutchins, 1995; Mora, 1998; Penniman & Agnew, 1989; Uziel-Miller, Lyons, Kissiel, & Love, 1998) have suggested specific changes to make the TCs more responsive to women's needs. These changes include reducing the waiting time between initial contact with the program and entry into the program; the employment of more staff members who are women; the development and use of gender specific therapy groups and culturally specific therapy groups; inclusion of mothering issues (such as dealing with children's problems); and incorporation of childcare programs.[18] See Table 11-8 for a list of components for an optimal women-oriented substance use treatment program.

Short-Term Residential Treatment Programs Short-term (in comparison to TCs) residential treatment programs (e.g., Hazelden) began to develop during the

TABLE 11-9. Overview of the program objectives and elements in a typical short-term residential treatment program*

Program Objectives
   Maintain "sobriety"
   Learn about substance abuse and the process of recovery
   Recognize the effects of substance abuse on self and others (i.e., family, friends, coworkers)
   Develop strategies to maintain sobriety
   Share thoughts and feelings with others (i.e., in group therapy sessions)
   Utilize the basics of the AA program
Program Key Elements
   Personal inventory and plan
   Daily schedule of program activities
   Educational component
   Group therapy sessions
   Provision of safe and supportive environment

*Modified from Laundergan & Williams (1993, p. 148)

early 1970s (Laundergan & Williams, 1993) in response to several identified needs. These needs included: 1) a growing need for services, particularly for women who had problems related to cocaine use; 2) a desire among patients for treatment services other than those where they may be institutionalized for months; and 3) limitations placed by third party insurance carriers for the reimbursement of fees paid for provided treatment services. See Table 11-9 for an overview of the program objectives and elements comprising a typical short-term residential treatment program.

Feminist Treatment Approaches Exploring the issue of the need for treatment approaches to better meet the needs of women, Woodhouse (1992) used a life history method to further the understanding of women accessing treatment for problematic patterns of substance use so that the realities of their lives could be identified and better understood. Violence (e.g., rape, incest), male dominance, loss, guilt, dependence, motherhood issues, and depression emerged as themes in their lives. As emphasized by Woodhouse (1992):

> The life histories related by the participants in this study clearly validate the need for treatment centers to make gender issues and life experiences paramount in treatment. . . . Additional research should also concentrate on creating positive environments for the children of substance-abusing mothers, as the chaotic lives they lead clearly make them vulnerable for future addiction, regardless of potential genetic involvement. (pp. 278–280)

Another treatment approach, the Wellesley College program—Project WAIT, or the Theatre Model, was proposed by Gleason (1994). This treatment approach was directed at primary prevention of alcohol use among college women. In developing the model,

> The expert-helper model is rejected, and replaced by a model in which program participants are empowered to deal with problems of living and provided with opportunities for growth without continued reliance on professional help. . . . The goals of the program include: choosing when, where, and how much to drink, maintaining control of what they

consume and under what circumstances they consume it, avoiding situations and events that can be damaging to themselves or others, and creating a climate that encourages others to do likewise. (p. 17)

More specifically, the theatre model provides 6 to 10 skits that reflect substance use and other situations that audience members may have encountered or may encounter in the future (e.g., peer pressure to drink, vulnerability to sexual abuse, drunk driving, loss of judgment in high-risk situations that may lead to unwanted consequences, family drinking, how to assess one's own alcohol and other substance use). The format engages the audience and thus reflects the use of women's skills and needs in developing relationships. It also values empathetic and intuitive learning styles, and takes advantage of the positive effects of peer pressure.

Central to many feminist treatment approaches are the ideals of fostering self-concept and empowerment among women (Burman, 1994; Hagan, Finnegan, & Nelson-Zlupko, 1994; Hamilton, 1993). We have observed in our clinical practices that these goals, as well as positive therapeutic effect, can be accomplished by giving voice to women by means of encouraging storytelling. Through the telling of their stories[19] women come to know themselves more fully, develop their self-esteem, obtain a sense of relief, and begin or proceed with the therapeutic healing process. As noted by McGovern (1994):

> Our stories give life and meaning to the facts and events of our lives. When stories are broken, as happens in the disjointed lives of those suffering from the effects of addiction and mental illness, the re-storying or restoration of such lives is an essential element of a healing process. (p. 165)

☐ Relapse

The rate of relapse, or recidivism, following successful treatment of problematic patterns of substance use among women is quite high (see Figure 11-2). Although much research has examined treatment factors, such as, the involvement of family in treatment, provision of special services, staff characteristics, and time in treatment, these factors have not been able to account for the majority of variance in posttreatment return to problematic patterns of substance use (Saunders, Bailey, Phillips, & Allsop, 1993). Obviously, much more research is required in this area.

Our own clinical experience and the currently available research data would suggest that the use of the following three recommendations would at least minimize the potential for relapsed use:

1. individualize treatment to the needs and characteristics of the woman (i.e., cut the shoe to fit the foot);[20]
2. use specific indicators or performance goals to objectively evaluate the success of treatment outcomes and, subsequently, the degree of relapse or efficacy of relapse prevention (see Table 11-10); and
3. periodically, as individually indicated, prophylactically re-assess patients and proactively intervene to prevent relapse.[21]

☐ Conclusion

Much effort has been directed toward finding effective programs and techniques to prevent or treat problematic patterns of substance use among women. However, to

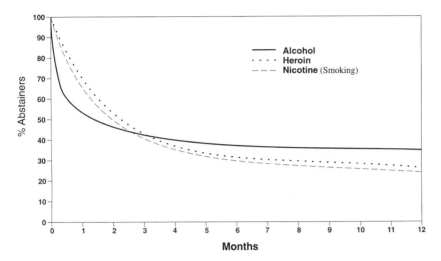

FIGURE 11-2. Typical relapse rates following treatment for problematic patterns of substance use.

date, only marginal success has been achieved in these areas, as demonstrated by: 1) the increasing numbers of women who engage in problematic patterns of substance use; and 2) the extremely high recidivism rates that accompany virtually all current treatment programs.

An overview of the major available prevention and treatment programs has been presented together with general guidelines to assist practitioners (see Table 11-11). The theme that is consistently and repeatedly found in the research literature is that different women who have problematic patterns of substance use respond differently to different treatment approaches (i.e., what works best for one woman may not work best, or in some cases, at all, for another woman). Thus, instead of attempting to find

---

TABLE 11-10. Performance goals/criterion in relation to evaluation of treatment success and relapse prevention*

---

1. Interviewer's clinical evaluation of improvement
2. Job/home and social adjustment
3. Self-reported reduction in substance use
4. Reduction in sociopathy
5. Intrapersonal adjustment (e.g., with family, friends, and co-workers)
6. Social involvement
7. Abstinence

---

*From: Foster, Horn, & Wanberg (1972, p. 1079).

TABLE 11-11. General guidelines for the treatment of women who have a substance use disorder (SUD)

- Conduct a comprehensive assessment prior to planning and initiating treatment.
- Remember that reasons for substance use may differ from one woman to another and even for the same woman over time.
- Be nonjudgmental in approaching treatment.
- Individualize treatment approaches.
- Recognize that different types of treatment may be required (i.e., the type of treatment that works best for one woman may not necessarily work best for another).
- Remember that success or failure ultimately is the woman's responsibility (i.e., do not become codependent or over-responsible).
- Assess for, treat, or appropriately refer for treatment, any accompanying mental disorders (i.e., dual diagnoses).
- Break the denial of problems associated with substance use.
- Respect women who have SUDs; do not treat them in a condescending manner.
- Provide education in a straightforward, nonbiased way that is appropriately tailored to cognitive abilities and to developmental, learning, and social needs of the woman.
- Work toward realistic and achievable goals that have been mutually agreed upon.
- Appropriately address underlying problems (e.g., lack of self-esteem; poor coping skills; previous sexual abuse).
- Involve family, friends, and others as appropriate in confrontation, treatment planning, and program implementation.
- Use gender specific groups (i.e., group women together according to age, culture, race, and SES).
- Use community social agencies designed for women.
- Make referrals to other appropriate health and social care professionals and agencies.
- Provide appropriate follow-up or aftercare services.
- Provide appropriate childcare services (both domestic and therapeutic).

and use the single "best" program, it is recommended that health and social care professionals become familiar with the various types and approaches to prevention and treatment and then select the one(s) that is (are) best suited to the specific needs of their patients. In this regard, the Mega Interactive Model of Substance Use Among Women (MIMSUAW) can serve as a particularly useful heuristic device.

☐ **Notes**

1. At the end of the five-year period, the overall decrease in illicit substance use among treated adults remained at 21%.
2. There are generally three levels of prevention: primary, secondary, and tertiary prevention. In regard to substance use, *primary prevention* is aimed at preventing the initial use of the substances of abuse in a potentially susceptible population, for example, drug education programs in primary schools. Interdisciplinary action at this level includes prevention of substance use in schools, public places, and the workplace by way of specialized programs, municipal legislation (smoke-free restaurants), programs to decrease incidence of drinking and driving, and avoiding substance use related accidents in the workplace. *Secondary pre-*

vention involves the early diagnosis and provision of immediate therapeutic efforts aimed at discontinuing substance use; reducing the possibility of others in contact with the user from using; and limiting any harm associated with use. It also involves teaching people to identify early signs of harmful effects so that appropriate treatment can be sought early. *Tertiary prevention* is aimed at limiting the degree of associated harm and promoting optimal health and social function when harmful effects of substance use are irreversible (e.g., cirrhosis of the liver, emphysema or lung cancer, heart disease, Wernicke-Korsakoff's syndrome). Interventions include instruction concerning how to manage irreversible harmful effects with the goal to maintain remaining function and prevent further deterioration of function.

3. Because the major focus of primary prevention programs is on children and adolescents, the reader is referred to the text, *Substance use among children and adolescents: Its nature, consequences, and effects from conception to adulthood* (A. M. Pagliaro & L. A. Pagliaro, 1996), for additional discussion.

4. Several researchers (e.g., Blum, 1987; Tarter, 1990; Wodarski, 1990) have noted the need for multiple therapeutic approaches to effectively deal with the varied nature of substance use problems encountered among women. In this regard, as previously noted in Chapter 1, we recommend that the individual approaches to treatment noted in this chapter be considered and applied in the context of the Mega Interactive Model of Substance Use Among Women (MIMSUAW) (see Chapter 1, An Overview of Substance Use Among Women).

5. Other therapeutic modalities exist, but either lack empirical evidence of efficacy or are deemed generally to be inappropriate for use with women. For example, an Alternatives Model has been developed (see Table 11-2) and has demonstrated some therapeutic efficacy. However, it was originally developed and continues to be utilized primary with adolescents. The activities noted in Table 11–2 may, however, be beneficial for some women as an adjunct to their principle form of therapeutic intervention.

Another example is the use of contingency management approaches to drug abuse treatment. "Contingency management approaches to drug abuse derive from the operant behavioral psychology of B. F. Skinner. . . . The essence of this perspective is the belief that behavior is learned and reinforced by interaction with environmental contingencies" (Bigelow & Sullivan, 1999, p. 16).

As noted by Higgins (1999):

> Contingency management interventions almost always involve one or more of the following generic contingencies to motivate increases and decreases in the frequency of therapeutically desirable and undesirable behavior: (a) *positive reinforcement* involves delivery of a desired consequence (e.g., a voucher exchangeable for retail items), contingent on the individual meeting a therapeutic goal (e.g., negative [drug] urinalysis test results); (b) *negative reinforcement* involves removing an aversive or confining circumstance (e.g., intense criminal justice supervision), contingent on meeting a target therapeutic goal (e.g., attending counseling sessions); (c) *positive punishment* involves delivery of a punishing consequence (e.g., a professional reprimand), contingent on evidence of undesirable behavior (e.g., positive [drug] urinalysis test results); and (d) *negative punishment* involves removal of a positive condition (e.g., the monetary value of a voucher to be earned is reduced), contingent on evidence of the occurrence of an undesirable behavior (e.g., missing a scheduled counseling session). (p. 5)

Although these techniques have been used with reported success among a sample of cocaine-dependent pregnant women (Elk, 1999), we are not inclined to use, or recommend the use of, these techniques for the following reasons. First, the basic behavioristic paradigm that underlies this therapeutic technique is philosophically incompatible with our humanistic approach to health care. Second, manipulation, particularly of women, with money to achieve an end that they are not prepared to voluntarily achieve is, in our opinion, both paternalistic and sexist (i.e., it presumes: that we know what is best; that women cannot be voluntarily educated or convinced to engage in the desired behavior; that women have no right to "free choice" regarding their lifestyle; and that the ends justify the means). Third, it shifts the primary focus of attention from health outcomes to economic outcomes. As explained by Elk (1999):

> These findings have important implications for cost-effective treatment of drug abuse.... In addition to the obvious health benefits for the patient, there are obvious health and economic benefits to the community. (p. 140)

6. Generally, the signs and symptoms associated with the various withdrawal syndromes are simply the opposite of those normally expected as the desired pharmacologic effects. For example, the desired effects for the sedative-hypnotics are calmness, muscle relaxation, and sleep; the signs and symptoms associated with sedative-hypnotic withdrawal syndromes include, conversely, such effects as anxiety, muscle tremor (or convulsion), and insomnia.
7. We generally would not recommend pharmacological adjuncts for the management of the heroin withdrawal syndrome because it is generally relatively mild and can usually be handled cold turkey (i.e., signs and symptoms of the withdrawal syndrome resemble those of a bad case of influenza). However, the methadone withdrawal syndrome may be quite severe with convulsions and other physiological effects that require appropriate treatment under medical supervision. Even when not required medically, we strongly recommend that patients undergo withdrawal in an inpatient setting, particularly patients with histories of long-standing or high-dose use of alcohol or another substance of abuse, in order to provide appropriate psychological support and significantly improve compliance (i.e., ensure that the patient successfully completes the withdrawal process). The average stay for people in detoxification units or centers in these situations is typically approximately three days (Rush & Ekdahl, 1990).
8. Abstinence, in this context, is actually a form of relapse prevention (see later discussion in this chapter, Relapse Prevention).
9. Although controlled studies have not demonstrated significant efficacy when disulfiram is used alone (Mirin, 1995), we have found disulfiram to be effective in highly motivated compliant patients as an initial adjunct to Alcoholics Anonymous, or another 12-step program, and weekly psychotherapy. The youngest women for whom we have successfully used disulfiram have been in their early twenties.
10. The CNS depressant effects, including alcohol-related effects on cognition, do not appear to be significantly affected by naltrexone (Naltrexone, 1995). Thus, it is *not* a sobriety pill.
11. When the concept of circular or reciprocal causality is applied, this approach also is commonly referred to as a systemic (i.e., family systems oriented) approach or model (Lewis, Piercy, Sprenkle, & Trepper, 1990). This approach or model should not be confused with systemic family therapy, a particular model of family therapy that uses a cybernetic process. Systemic intervention or treatment differs from psychologic and pharmacologic approaches because of the inherent focus of these intervention strategies. Whereas the focus of the latter is on the woman as an individual, the focus of the former is on the entire family as a group that includes a member(s) (i.e., the woman) who displays problematic patterns of substance use. In this regard, the substance using member is often identified as the "thermostat" of family health and functioning. Recognizing that a change in the behavior of one family member can affect all family members, therapists attempt (optimally) to assess and treat all the members of the family, including nuclear and extended family members, as a group.
12. In this regard, AA has often been labeled as a social form of treatment.
13. This AA belief would be consonant with what we describe as compulsive use in the Patterns of Substance Use (see Figure 11–1 and Chapter 1, An Overview of Substance Use Among Women, for additional details). In this regard, we would concur with the AA philosophy that treatment, to be successful, must include a lifetime of total abstinence.
14. The number of AA meetings that a current member attends generally ranges from one daily to one weekly. The number of meetings attended on a regular basis is dictated, in large part,

by factors such as: the amount of time that a member has been sober (e.g., one day versus one year); the personality of the member (e.g., avoidant, dependent, or compulsive); and accessibility (e.g., is the scheduled meeting nearby; does the member require and have available transportation; is the style of the meeting compatible with the member's needs?). However, in some cases an individual member will develop a cult-like relationship with AA (i.e., will become obsessive and compulsive regarding AA doctrine; will limit social interaction to AA meetings and members; will increasingly become estranged from other social groups such as family and colleagues) (Pagliaro & Pagliaro, 1992, 1995, clinical patient file notes). These situations, although relatively infrequently encountered, should be appropriately monitored for and dealt with as part of the patient's program of counseling or psychotherapy.

15. The characteristics of AA referenced by Hall (1994) and others refer not only to the wording in the 12-Steps, but also to the generally accepted motto "Let go and let God" and the Serenity Prayer, which is often used to conclude group meetings:

> God grant me the serenity to accept the things I cannot change, the courage to change the things I can, and the wisdom to know the difference. –Reinhold Niebuhr (1892–1971)

Our clinical experience with women who have substance use problems indicates that regardless of culture, race, or sexual orientation, women generally do not have any significant problems with this approach and most actually derive significant benefit from it. However, we have noted in the last decade that younger women (i.e., in their twenties), who are agnostic, generally find the approach utilized in AA philosophically incompatible with their own views and, therefore, therapeutically ineffectual (Pagliaro & Pagliaro, 1990–1999, clinical patient file notes).

16. Obviously, the approach used by AA will not be suitable for all women and we would *not* recommend it as the sole approach to therapy. However, for patients who are willing to attend the AA meetings, we have found it to be an effective and useful adjunct to individual psychotherapy and family therapy and can highly recommend it in this regard. In addition, the efficacy of AA programs appears to be substantiated de facto by the large number of members who speak positively about it and the use of the AA approach by similar groups (e.g., Cocaine Anonymous [CA], Gamblers Anonymous [GA], and Narcotics Anonymous [NA]). It also has been extended to other 12-step self-help groups for families who have members who display problematic patterns of substance use (e.g., Al-ATEEN; Al-ANON; Families of Alcoholics [FA]). In addition, AA has consistently been rated highly by health and social care professionals (e.g., Chang, Astrachan, & Bryant, 1994).

17. Primary clinical and custodial staff employed by TCs are generally paraprofessionals who have successfully rehabilitated themselves from previous substance use with the assistance of a TC program. Ancillary staff include professionals from various disciplines (e.g., law, medicine, psychology) who are generally used on a contractual basis (De Leon, 1985). Although this staffing pattern is beginning to change with the use of more certified counselors and social workers, the utilization of clinical psychologists and other university educated social and health care professionals remains low in these programs.

18. The last noted suggested change (i.e., "childcare programs") is considerably far more important than just a convenience. As noted by Finkelstein (1993):

> Barriers to treatment access for women have primarily revolved around their children.... Too often mothers are faced with a choice between treatment or caring for their children. (p. 1285)

19. We encourage story telling among our patients through the use of many approaches (e.g., orally in individual and group therapy sessions; written in the form of diaries, articles to be submitted for publication, and even autobiographical books; and other modes of expression, such as poems or songs).

20. The use of patient-treatment matching has significantly increased in recent years (e.g., Kaminer & Frances, 1991; Mattson, 1994; Project MATCH, 1993).

21. Some of this periodic monitoring is addressed, for example, in aftercare programs and in continued attendance at AA meetings, both of which have been positively correlated with significant posttreatment abstinence (Johnsen & Herringer, 1993; Kennedy & Minami, 1993; McBride, 1991). We would suggest, particularly for women who have engaged in compulsive patterns of substance use, that (as per the AA model discussed earlier in this chapter and our previous discussion of patterns of use in Chapter 1, An Overview of Substance Use Among Women) the propensity for substance use be considered a life-long problem. Whenever possible, once women are abstinent, we gradually decrease the frequency and length of their psychotherapy sessions (e.g., from bi-weekly, to weekly, to every other week, to monthly, to every other month, to telephone contact every six months). This strategy helps to maintain a communication linkage and life-line (help-line) for each patient that demonstrates continued concern and provides an opportunity for the early detection of problems by the therapist and for patients to request needed assistance *before* problems get out of control. In our practice, this strategy has resulted in a long-term (i.e., as long as we can maintain patient contact, generally in excess of five years) relapse rate of less than 20% (Pagliaro & Pagliaro, unpublished research data).

PART V

RESOURCES AND REFERENCES

APPENDIX I

Abbreviations and Symbols Used in the Text

Abbreviation/Symbol	Meaning
AA	Alcoholics Anonymous
AAS	androgenic-anabolic steroid
ADD	attention deficit disorder
A-D/HD	attention-deficit/hyperactivity disorder
AIDS	acquired immunodeficiency syndrome
am	morning
ARBD	alcohol-related birth defects
ARND	alcohol-related neurodevelopmental disorder
AUDIT	Alcohol Use Disorders Identification Test
BAC	blood alcohol concentration
B-MAST	Brief Michigan Alcoholism Screening Test
BZDs	benzodiazepines
CD	conduct disorder
CDC	Center for Disease Control
CNS	central nervous system
DAST	Drug Abuse Screening Test
DSM-IV	*Diagnostic and Statistical Manual of Mental Disorders*, 4th edition
DUI	driving under the influence
DWI	driving while intoxicated; driving while impaired
EAP	employee assistance program
e.g.	for example
et al.	and others
FAS	fetal alcohol syndrome
GABA	gamma-amino butyric acid
GBH	gamma hydroxybutyrate
HIV	human immunodeficiency virus
HPA	hypothalamus-pituitary-adrenal

IAI	Index of Alcohol Involvement
i.e.	that is
IQ	intelligence quotient
IVDU	intravenous drug user
kg	kilogram(s); one-thousand grams
LSD	lysergic acid diethylamide
MAC	MacAndrew Alcoholism Scale
MAST	Michigan Alcoholism Screening Test
MDMA	3,4-methylenedioxymethamphetamine
mg	milligram(s); one-thousandth of a gram
MIMSUAW	Mega Interactive Model of Substance Use Among Women
MIMSUAEW	Mega Interactive Model of Substance Use Among Elderly Women
ml	milliliter(s); one-thousandth of a liter
Mm-MAST	Malmö Modified Michigan Alcoholism Screening Test
mo	month(s)
M-SMAST	Maternal Short-Michigan Alcoholism Screening Test
MVA	motor vehicle accident
N/A	data are not available
ng	nanogram(s); one-billionth of a gram
NIAAA	National Institute on Alcohol Abuse and Alcoholism
NIDA	National Institute on Drug Abuse
PCP	phencyclidine
pH	hydrogen ion concentration
pKa	hydrogen ion concentration at which 50% of a solution is in an ionized form
p.	page
pm	evening
pp.	pages
PRN	as required; as needed
RAPS	Rapid Alcohol Problems Screen
SIDS	sudden infant death syndrome
SMAST	Short Michigan Alcoholism Screening Test
STD	sexually transmitted disease
SUD	substance use disorder
TC	therapeutic community
TGIF	thank goodness it's Friday
THC	tetrahydrocannabinol
UC	unit coterie
U.S.	United States
U.S.A.	United States of America
vs	versus
y.o.	years old

Appendix I: Abbreviations and Symbols

®	registered trademark symbol
%	percent
~	approximately
:	ratio
μg	microgram(s); one-millionth of a gram
♂	male
♀	female
5-HT	serotonin (5-hydroxytryptamine)
<	less than
≤	less than or equal to
>	greater than
≥	greater than or equal to
=	equals

Substances of Abuse: Generic, Trade, and Common Names

Generic Name	Trade Name	Classification	Subclassification	Common Street Names
Alcohol (ethanol; ethyl alcohol)	Various brand names of beer, wine, and distilled liquor	CNS Depressant: Sedative-Hypnotic	Alcohol	alleviator, angel's food, apple fritter, Bacchus, bamboo juice, barley-bree, barley broth, barleycorn, beggar boy's, beggar boy's ass, belsh, belt, berpwater, bit of blink, bitters, blue ribbon, blue ruin, blue stone, blue tape, bob, boilermaker, booze, bracer, brew, brewer's fizzle, Brian O'Flinn, Brian O'Linn, Brian O'Lynn, bush girlfriend, cat's water, cheerer, cheerer-upper, chit-chat, clap of thunder, cocktail, cocky's joy, cold one, cooler, corker, courage in a bottle, cream of the valley, cream of the wilderness, cup of cheer, cup of comfort, dago red, daily mail, day and night, deadeye, demon vino, drink, drinkypoo, eye-opener, eyewash, eyewater, flash of lightning, frog's wine, Geneva, Geneva courage, giggle and titter, golden cream, Gordon, Gordon water, grape, grapes of wrath, grapes, grappo, Gunga Din, gunpowder, hair of the dog, hair of the dog that bit one, happy sale, heart's ease, hi-ball, highball, Holland tape, hops, Huckleberry Finn, hum, hum cap, humming October, in-jay, jackey, jacky, Jersey lightning, jigger, jinny, johnnie, joy-juice, juice, jolt, jump-steady, juniper, juniper-juice, just what the doctor ordered, kick in the guts, kill-cobbler, kill-priest, knock down, knock-me-down, leg-opener, light blue, lunatic broth, lunatic soup, lush, mad dog, madman's broth, merry-go-down, mother's milk, mother's ruin, mouthwash, nap, nappy, nightcap, nip, nipper, old boy, old red goofy, old Tom, one for the road, paint, panther piss,

Generic Name	Trade Name	Classification	Subclassification	Common Street Names
Alfentanil	Alfenta®	CNS Depressant: Analgesic	Opiate	pharoah, pharo, pink-eye, pinkie, pissticide, pistol shot, porter, porter's ale, quencher, rag water, ribbon, right sort, rosy, rouge, royal poverty, ruby, ruin, satin, short one, short snort, shot, sky blue, tall one, the grape, the grapes, the vine, Tom, tonic, twankay, water of life
Alprazolam	Apo-Alpraz®, Novo-Alprazol®, Nu-Alpraz®, Xanax®	CNS Depressant: Sedative-Hypnotic	Benzodiazepine	
Amobarbital	Amytal®	CNS Depressant: Sedative-Hypnotic	Barbiturate	amies, blue, blue angel, blue birds, blue clouds, blue devils, blue dolls, blue dots, blue heavens, blue jackets, blues, blue tips, blue velvet, double blue, jack-ups
Amphetamine	Benzedrine®, Biphetamine®	CNS Stimulant	Amphetamine	amps, B, B-Bomb, beans, benj, bennies, benny, benz, benzadrina, benzies, brother Ben, bomber pilot, cartwheels, copilot, crasses, drin, greenies, hearts, minibennie, peaches, roses, whites
Anileridine	Leritine®	CNS Depressant: Analgesic	Opiate	
Aprobarbital	Alurate®	CNS Depressant: Sedative-Hypnotic	Barbiturate	aprobarbs, barbs
Benzphetamine	Didrex®	CNS Stimulant	Amphetamine	
Bromazepam	Lectopam®	CNS Depressant: Sedative-Hypnotic	Benzodiazepine	

Butabarbital	Barbased®, Busodium®, Buta-Barb®, Butalan®, Butatran®, Buticaps®, Butisol®, Mebutal®	CNS Depressant: Sedative-Hypnotic	Barbiturate
Butorphanol	Stadol-NS®	CNS Depressant: Analgesic	Opiate
Cannabis (marijuana, hashish)	Not commercially available	Psychedelic	Acapulco, Acapulco gold, Acapulco red, African black, African bush, Angola black, Aunt Mary, baby buds, bad green, bale, bhang, bhang ganjah, black, black Columbus, black ganja, black gold, black gungeon, black gungi, black gunion, black gunnion, black gunny, black hash, black mo, black moat, black mold, black mole, black monte, black mota, black mote, black Russian, block, blond, blond hash, blond hashish, blond Lebanese, blue cheese, blue sage, bo-bo, bo-bo bush, brick, broccoli, brown, brown weed, bud, bull jive, bullet Thai, bush, cam, cam red, cam trip, Cambodian red, Cambodian trip weed, Canadian black, candy bar, charas, chocolate, chunkies, Colombian, Colombian gold, Colombian green, Columbian gold, Columbian pink, Columbian red, Congo brown, Congo dirt, Congo mataby, cube, dagga, dagha, ditch dope, dreamstick, ganga, ganja, ganjah, gold, gold bud, gold Colombian, gold Columbian, golden leaf, grass, green bud, green goddess, green moroccan, hash, Hawaiian, hemp, herb, herbs, Indian hay, Indian hemp, Indian rope, Indian weed, Jamaica ganga,

Generic Name	Trade Name	Classification	Subclassification	Common Street Names
				Jamaica gold, Jamaican, Jamaican red, Jane, Jane, Jary Jane, jay, keef, kef, keff, keif, khif, kief, kif, killer weed, Kona gold, leaf, leaves, Lebanese hash, Lebanese red, Lebanon red, Lipton's Tea, Mary J., Mary Jane, Maryjane, Maui Waui, Maui wowee, Maui wowie, Mex, Mexican, monster weed, murder weed, Panama, Panama gold, Panamanian gold, Panama red, Panamanian red, pukalolo, puna butter, red leb, red Lebanese, reefer, righteous bush, rope, sense, sinse, sinsemilla, smoke, stash, supergrass, superweed, sweet Mary, T., Texas tea, Thai pot, Thai-weed, Thaistick, the herb, the weed, trip weed, turnip greens, weed
Chlordiazepoxide	Apo-chlordiaz-epoxide®, Libritabs®, Librium®, Limbitrol®, Limbitrol DS®, Lipoxide®, Medilium®, Menrium®, Novo-Poxide®, Reposans-10®, Solium®	CNS Depressant: Sedative-Hypnotic	Benzodiazepine	
Chlorphentermine	Pre-sate®	CNS Stimulant		
Clobazam	Frisium®	CNS Depressant: Sedative-Hypnotic	Benzodiazepine	

Clonazepam	Klonopin®, PMS-Clonazepam®, Rivotril®	CNS Depressant: Sedative-Hypnotic	Benzodiazepine
Clorazepate	Apo-chlorazepate®, Gen-Xene®, Novo Clorazepate®, Novo-Clopate®, Tranexene®, Tranexene-SD Half Strength Tablets®, Tranexene T-TAB®, Tranxene®	CNS Depressant: Sedative-Hypnotic	Benzodiazepine
Cocaine	Cocaine Topical Solution®	CNS Stimulant	angel, angie, baking soda base, base, bernese, Bernice, Bernies, Bernies flake, big bloke, big-C, bloke, blow, C., Cadillac, California cornflakes, Cecil, cee, C-game, chalk, coca, cocaina, cocanuts, cocunut, coka, Coke, cola, cookie, Corine, Corinne, Corrine, crack, flake, free base, frisky, frisky powder, girl, girlfriend, girli, girly, glad stuff, gold dust, golden girl, Inca message, incentive, initiative, joy dust, joy flakes, joy powder, lady, Lady Snow, Lady White, leaf, line, magic flake, Mama coca, nose candy, nose powder, nose stuff, number three, old lady White, paradise, perico, Peruvian flake, pimp dust, pogo pogo, rock, rock candy, rocks, sleighride, sniff, snow, snow stuff, snow-caine, snowball, snowflakes, sophisticated lady, star stuff, stardust, superblow, sweet stuff, talc, the leaf, the ultimate drug, toot, tootonium, tootuncommon, uptown, W.C., whiff, white,
Note:	Forms commonly used illicitly, e.g., crack, are not commercially available		

Generic Name	Trade Name	Classification	Subclassification	Common Street Names
Codeine	Various combination products (e.g., acetaminophen with codeine, aspirin with codeine)	CNS Depressant: Analgesic	Opiate	white cross, white nurse, white stuff, white tornado cement, cod, cods, codys, deens, deines, denes, fours, schoolboy
Dextro-amphetamine	Biphetamine®, Dexedrine®, Ferndex®, Osydess II®, Spancap No. 1®	CNS Stimulant	Amphetamine	beans, benn, bennies, black beauties, blues, brown, brown & clears, brownies, browns, Christmas tree, copilots, crank, crystal meth, dexie, dexo, dexies, dex, green & clears, hearts, horse hearts, ice, jolly beans, orange, oranges, peaches, pep pills, pink football, purple hearts, purple passion, truck-drivers
Diazepam	Apo-diazepam®, Diazemuls®, E-pam®, Meval®, Novo-Dipam®, PMS-Diazepam®, T-Quil®, Valium®, Valrelease®, Vazepam®, Vivrol®, Zetran®	CNS Depressant: Sedative-Hypnotic	Benzodiazepine	B.B., blue, blue bombers, blues, dies, dis, dyes, ums, V., vals, vees, Vs
Diethylpropion	M-Orexic®, Nobesine-75®, Nu-Dispoz®, Regebon®	CNS Stimulant		

Estazolam	Ro-Diet®, Tenuate®, Tepanil® Prosom®	CNS Depressant: Sedative-Hypnotic	Benzodiazepine
Fenfluramine	Ponderal®, Pondimin®	CNS Stimulant	
Fentanyl	Duragesic®, Innovar®, Sublimaze®	CNS Depressant: Analgesic	Opiate	fen
Flurazepam	Apo-flurazepam®, Dalmane®, Durapam®, Novo-Flupam®, Novoflurazepam®, PMS-Flurazepam®, Som-Pam®, Somnol®	CNS Depressant: Sedative-Hypnotic	Benzodiazepine
Halazepam	Pax pam®	CNS Depressant: Sedative-Hypnotic	Benzodiazepine
Heroin (Diacetylmorphine)		CNS Depressant: Analgesic	Opiate	8, A-bomb, antifreeze, Aunt Hazel, balloon, balot, big boy, big daddy, big Harry, big time, big-H, black stuff, black tar, blanca, blanco, bomb, boy, bozo, brother, brown, brown dope, brown rock, brown sugar, caballo, caca, capital H., China white, Chinese red, Chinese white, deck, dope, downtown, eight, gato, girl, H, Harry, Hazel, hero, heroina, horse, jack, jazz, junk, kabayo, kaka, lady, Mexican brown, Mexican horse, mojo, Perisan dust, Perisan brown, poison, poppy, red chicken, red rock, scag,

Generic Name	Trade Name	Classification	Subclassification	Common Street Names
Hydrocodone	Codone®, Dicodid®, Hycodan®, Robidone®, Vicodin®	CNS Depressant: Analgesic (antitussive)	Opiate	scat, schmack, shit, shmack, skag, skid, smack, smak, stuff, yen-shee
Hydromorphone	Dilaudid®, PMS-Hydromorphone®	CNS Depressant: Analgesic	Opiate	big-D, D, Ds, dees, dids, dilies, dillies, dilly, drugstore stuff, footballs, hospital heroin, juice, junk, little-D, lords, shit, white stuff
Ketazolam	Loftram®	CNS Depressant: Sedative-Hypnotic	Benzodiazepine	
Levorphanol	Levo Dromoran®	CNS Depressant: Analgesic	Opiate	
Lorazepam	Alzapam®, Apo-lorazepam®, Ativan®, Loraz®, Novo-Lorazem®, Novolorazepam®, Nu-Loraz®, PMS-Lorazepam®, Pro-Lorazepam®	CNS Depressant: Sedative-Hypnotic	Benzodiazepine	
Lysergic Acid Diethylamide	Not commercially available	Psychedelic		A., acid, acid cube, barrel, barrels, black acid, black tabs, blotter, blotter acid, blue, blue acid, blue angelfish, blue barrel, blue cheer, blue dot, blue doubledomes, brown acid, brown caps, brown dots, California sunshine, candy, cap, contact lens, crackers, cube, dome, domes, dots, Hoffmann's bicycle, L.B.J., L.D.J., L.S.D.,

Mazindol	Mazanor®, Sanorex®	CNS Stimulant	Lucy in the Sky with Diamonds, mickey mouse, microdot, mind-detergent, mind-tripper, orange, orange crystal, orange cube, orange micro, orange Owsley, orange sunshine, orange wafers, orange wedges, osley, Owsley, Owsley acid, ozzy, paisley caps, paper acid, pink swirl, pink wafers, pink wedges, pink witches, purple, purple barrels, purple dot, purple dragon, purple flats, purple haze, purple microdots, purple Owsley, Raggedy Ann, red dot, red dragon, strawberries, strawberry fields, sugar, sugar cube, sunshine pill, the chief, the cube, trips, wedge, wedges, wedgies, white domes, white double domes, white lightning, white Owsley, windowpane
Meperidine (Pethidine)	Demerol®, Merpergan®	CNS Depressant: Analgesic	Opiate demis, demies, dems, junk, meps, morals
Mephobarbital	Mesara®, Mephoral®	CNS Depressant: Sedative-Hypnotic	Barbiturate
Mescaline	Not commerically available	Psychedelic	beans, big chief, biscuits, button, cactus, cactus buttons, chief, chocolate mesc, dog biscuits, dry whiskey, footballs, full moons, half moons, hikori, hikuli, magic pumpkin, mesc, mescal, mescal bean, mescal button, mescalina, mescalito, moon, P., peyote, peyote button, peyotl
Metharbital	Gemonil®	CNS Depressant: Sedative-Hypnotic	Barbiturate
Methadone	Dolophine®, Methadose®	CNS Depressant: Analgesic	Opiate biscuits, chalk, dollies, dollys, dolo, done, medicine, meth, phy, water

Generic Name	Trade Name	Classification	Subclassification	Common Street Names
Methamphet-amine	Desoxyn®, Desoxyn Gradumets®, Methedrine®	CNS Stimulant	Amphetamine	crystal, meth, speed
Methaqualone	Qualude® (not commercially available in North America)	CNS Depressant: Sedative-Hypnotic		ludes
Methohexital	Brevimytal®, Brevital®, Brietal®	CNS Depressant: Sedative-Hypnotic	Barbiturate	
Methylphenidate	PMS-Methyl-phenidate®, Ritalin®, Ritalin-SR®	CNS Stimulant		rits, Rs
Midazolam	Versed®	CNS Depressant: Sedative-Hypnotic	Benzodiazepine	
Morphine	Astramorph®, Duramorph®, Epimorph®, Infumorph®, M-Eslon®, Morphine HP®, Morphitec®, MS Contin®, MS.IR®, Oramorph SR®, Rescudose®, RMS Uniserts®, Roxanol®, Statex®	CNS Depressant: Analgesic	Opiate	Aunt Emma, big-M, dreamer, eli lilly, em, emm, emsel, G.O.M., good old M., junk, M, M.S., M. sul, Mary, medicine, Miss Emma, Miss Morph, mojo, monkey, monkey morf, monkey-medicine, morfina, morph, morphema, morphi, morphia, morphie, morphina, morphinum, morpho, morphy, morshtop, mort, old Steve, pins and needles, racehorse Charley, red cross, red cross M., sister, slumber medicine, slumber party, snow, snowball, stuff, sweet Jesus, sweet Morpheus, white merchandise, white nurse, white silk, witch

Drug	Trade Names	Classification	Type	Street Names
Nalbuphine	Nubain®	CNS Depressant: Analgesic	Opiate	
Nitrazepam	Mogadon®	CNS Depressant: Sedative-Hypnotic	Benzodiazepine	
Oxazepam	Apo-oxazepam®, Novoxapam®, Oxpam®, PMS-Oxazepam®, Serax®, Zapex®	CNS Depressant: Sedative-Hypnotic	Benzodiazepine	
Oxycodone	Percodan®, Roxicodone®, Supeudol®	CNS Depressant: Analgesic	Opiate	percs, perks
Oxymorphone	Numorphan®	CNS Depressant: Analgesic	Opiate	
Pemoline	Cylert®	CNS Stimulant		
Pentazocine	Talacen®, Talwin®	CNS Depressant: Analgesic	Opiate	big T, tea, tee, Ts
Pentobarbital	Nembutal®, Nova Rectal®, Novo-Pentobarb®	CNS Depressant: Sedative-Hypnotic	Barbiturate	abbot, amarilla, blockbuster, canary, jacket, neb, nem, nemb, nembies, nemishes, nemmies, nimbles, nimbies, nimby, yellow angels, yellow bams, yellow birds, yellow bullets, yellow dolls, yellow jackets
Phencyclidine	Not commercially available	Psychedelic		angel death, angel dust, angel hair, angel mist, angel puke, animal tranquilizer, aurora borealis, bad grass, black whack, busy bee, buzz, C.J., cannabinol, ciclon, ciclon de cristal, cosmos, cozmos, crystal, crystal flake, crystal joint, crystal weed, cyclone, D.O.A., death wish, devil dust, dipper, double dipper, dummy dust, dust joint, dust of angels, elefante, elephant, elephant tranquilizer, fairy dust, heaven dust, hercules, hog, hog tranquilizer, horse trank, horse tranquilizer, P.C.P., pig killer, pig tranquilizer, whack, yerba mala, zombie buzz

Generic Name	Trade Name	Classification	Subclassification	Common Street Names
Phendimetrazine	Adipost®, Anorex®, Appecon®, Bacarate®, Bontril PDM®, Dital®, Nolahist®, Nolanine Timed-Release®, Obalan®, Obezine®, Panrexin®, Parazine®, Phendiet®, Phenzine®, Prelu-Z®, Sprx-1®, Sprx-2®, Sprx-3®, Statobex®, Timecelles®, Trimtabs®, Wehless-105®	CNS Stimulant		
Phenmetrazine	Preludin Endurets®	CNS Stimulant		
Phenobarbital	Barbita®, Gardenal®, Luminal®, Solfoton®	CNS Depressant: Sedative-Hypnotic	Barbiturate	barbs, goofballs, pheno, phennies

Phentermine	Adipex®, Adipex-P®, Anoxine-AM®, Dapex®, Dapex-37.5®, Fastin®, Ionamin®, Obe-Nix®, Obephen®, Obermine®, Obestin®, Obestin-30®, Panshape®, Parmine®, Pby-Trim®, Phentercot®, Phentrol 4®, Phentrol 5®, Phentride®, Phentrol Z®, T-Diet®, Teramin®, Wilpowr®, Zantryl®	CNS Stimulant	
Prazepam	Centrax®	CNS Depressant: Sedative-Hypnotic	Benzodiazepine
Primidone (metabolized to phenobarbital)	Apo-Primidone®, Myidone®, Mysoline®, Primoline®, Sertan®	CNS Depressant: Sedative-Hypnotic	Barbiturate
Propoxyphine	642®, Darvocet-N®, Darvon-N®, Darvon®,	CNS Depressant: Analgesic	Opiate	football, yellow, vons

Generic Name	Trade Name	Classification	Subclassification	Common Street Names
	Dolene®, Doraphen®, Doxaphene®, Novo-Propoxyn®, Profene®, Propoxycon®, ProPox®			
Psilocybin	Not commercially available	Psychedelic		God's flesh, hombrecitos, las mujercitas, los ninos, magic mushrooms, Mexican mushrooms, mushrooms, sacred mushrooms, schrocms, spores
Quazepam	Doral®	CNS Depressant: Sedative-Hypnotic	Benzodiazepine	
Secobarbital	Barbasec®, Novosecobarb®, Seconal®	CNS Depressant: Sedative-Hypnotic	Barbiturate	40s, apple, bala, billys, blunt, border, border red, bullet, bullet head, Canadian bouncer, cardinales, colorado, devil, diablo rojas, dolls, F-forties, forties, gumdrop, hors d'oeurves, ju-ju, juju, lillys, M & Ms, marshmallow reds, Mexican jumping beans, Mexican red, perla, pink ladies, pink marshmallow reds, pinks, prescription reds, R.D., red, red birds, red bullets, red dolls, red jackets, red lillies, reds, rojas, rojita, roll of reds, round head, sec, seccies, seccy, secs, seggies, seggy, sex, sickey, suckonal
Sufentanil	Sufenta®	CNS Depressant: Analgesic	Opiate	
Temazepam	Razepam®, Restoril®, Temaz®	CNS Depressant: Sedative-Hypnotic	Benzodiazepine	

Thiopental	Pentothal®	CNS Depressant: Sedative-Hypnotic	Barbiturate
Triazolam	Apo-Triazo®, Gen-Triazo-lam®, Halcion®, Novo-Triolam®, Nu-Triazo®	CNS Depressant: Sedative-Hypnotic	Benzodiazepine

APPENDIX III

Directory of Major North American Substance Use Treatment Centers, Referral Agencies, and Related Information Sources for Women

In order to facilitate access to the data contained in this directory, it has been arranged in three parts. **Part I** provides a directory of substance use treatment centers, referral agencies, and related information sources for women arranged in *alphabetical order by organizational name*. **Part II** provides a directory of substance use treatment centers, referral agencies, and related information sources for women arranged in *alphabetical order by the state or province* in which they are located. **Part III** provides a separate directory of major North American AIDS hotlines *listed in alphabetical order by state or province*.

While it is recognized that this directory is apt to be incomplete and subject to change, it is hoped that the names and telephone numbers provided may at least serve as an initial source of contact for the interested health or social care professional.[1]

Note: Most major active treatment hospitals have poison control/treatment facilities that are able to appropriately deal with cases of substance overdosage. For telephone numbers not listed in this appendix, readers should consult their local telephone directory or operator for assistance.

Appendix III: Directory   **239**

☐ PART I. Directory of Substance Use Treatment Centers, Referral Agencies, and Related Information Sources for Women Listed in Alphabetical Order by Organizational Name

ACTION Drug Prevention Program
806 Connecticut Avenue NW, Suite M513
Washington, DC 20525
202–634–9380

Addiction Research Foundation (ARF)
33 Russell Street
Toronto, ON M58 2S1, Canada
416–595–6059
416–595–6072
416–595–6000
800–463–6273

Addiction Services, Department of
Barbosa Avenue, Avenue 414
Rio Piedras, PR 00928
809–763–3133

Addiction Services, Division of, Department of Mental Health
117 East Washington Street
Indianapolis, IN 46204
317–232–7816

Adult Children of Alcoholics (ACOA)
PO Box 3216
Torrance, CA 90505
213–534–1815

Adult Children of Alcoholics, Interim World Service Organization
PO Box 3216
2522 West Sepulveda Boulevard
Torrance, CA 90505
213–534–1815

Alabama Coalition Against Domestic Violence
334–832–4842

Alabama Coalition Against Rape
(through the Light House)
PO Box 4091
Montgomery, AL 36102-4091

Alabama Poison Control System, Inc.
Tuscaloosa, AL
800–462–0800 (Alabama only)
205–345–0600

Al-Anon Family Groups
PO Box 862 Midtown Station
New York, NY 10018
212–302–7240

Alaska Network on Domestic Violence and Sexual Assault
130 Seward Street, Suite 501
Juneau, AK 99801
907–586–3650
Hotlines:
800–487–1090 (Juneau)
800–478–8999 (Anchorage)

Alberta Alcohol and Drug Abuse Commission (AADAC) Counselling Services
1177 11 Avenue SW
2nd Floor, Stephenson Building
Calgary, AB T2R 0G5, Canada
403–297–3071   (FAX 403–297–3036)

Alberta Alcohol and Drug Abuse Commission (AADAC) Downtown Treatment Centre
10010 102A Avenue
Edmonton, AB T5J 3G2, Canada
780–427–2736   (FAX 780–427–4180)

Alberta Alcohol and Drug Abuse Commission (AADAC) Library
10909 Jasper Avenue, Suite 200
Edmonton, AB T5J 3M9, Canada
780–427–7303

Alberta Alcohol and Drug Abuse Commission (AADAC) Northern Addictions Centre
11333 106 Street
Grande Prairie, AB T8V 6T7, Canada

Alberta Alcohol and Drug Abuse Commission (AADAC) Poundmaker's Lodge
Box 34007 Kingsway Mall Post Office
Edmonton, AB T5G 3G4, Canada
780–458–1884   (FAX 780–458–1883)

Alberta Alcohol and Drug Abuse Commission (AADAC) Poundmaker's Lodge
Outpatient and Adolescent
10010 102A Avenue 2nd Floor
Edmonton, AB T5J 3G2, Canada
780-420-0356 (FAX 780-427-2736)

Alberta Alcohol and Drug Abuse Commission (AADAC) Recovery Centre
10302 107 Street
Edmonton, AB T5J 1K2, Canada
780-427-4291 (FAX 780-422-2881)

Alberta Alcohol and Drug Abuse Commission (AADAC) Training and Professional Development
10909 Jasper Avenue, 7th Floor
Edmonton, AB T5J 3M9, Canada
780-427-7305

Affiliated Chemical Dependency Services
489 State Street
Bangor, ME 04401
201-945-7267

Akron Regional Poison Control Center
Akron, OH
800-362-9922 (Ohio only)
216-379-8562
216-379-8446 (TTY)

Alabama Department of Mental Health/Mental Retardation
Montgomery, AL
205-270-4640

Alabama Poison Control Systems, Inc.
Tuscaloosa, AL
800-462-0800 (Alabama only)
205-345-0600

Alaska Council on Prevention of Alcohol and Drug Abuse, Inc.
Anchorage, AK
907-258-6021

Alaska Department of Education
Division of Education Program Support
801 West 10th Street, Suite 200
Juneau, AK 99801-1894
907-465-8730/2843

Alcohol Abuse and Recovery Bureau, Ohio Department of Health
170 North High Street, 3rd Floor
Columbus, OH 43266-0586
614-466-3445

Alcohol and Drug Abuse Administration Department of Health and Mental Hygiene
Baltimore, MD
410-225-6914

Alcohol and Drug Abuse Association, Inc. Florida
Tallahassee, FL
904-878-2196

Alcohol and Drug Abuse Bureau Department of Human Resources
505 East King Street
Carson City, NV 89710
702-885-4790

Alcohol and Drug Abuse, Bureau of
Carson City, NV
702-687-6239

Alcohol and Drug Abuse Division Department of Health
4210 East 11th Avenue
Denver, CO 80220
303-331-8201

Alcohol and Drug Abuse Division Department of Health
PO Box 3378
Honolulu, HI 96801
808-548-4280

Alcohol and Drug Abuse Division Department of Institutions
Helena, MT 59601
406-444-2827

Alcohol and Drug Abuse, Division of
Joe Foss Building, 523 East Capitol
Pierre, SD 57501
605-773-3123

Alcohol and Drug Abuse, Division of
State Capitol
1800 Washington Street East, Room 451
Charleston, WV 25305
304-348-2276

Alcohol and Drug Abuse, Division of Department of Mental Health
Robert E. Lee State Office Building
11th Floor
Jackson, MS 39201
601-359-1288

Alcohol and Drug Abuse, Division of Department of Mental Health
PO Box 687
1915 South Ridge Drive
Jefferson City, MO 65102
314-751-4942

Appendix III: Directory   **241**

Alcohol and Drug Abuse, Division of, Office of Human Services
PO Box 3868
1201 Capitol Access Road
Baton Rouge, LA 70821-3868
504–342–9354
504–342–9352

Alcohol and Drug Abuse Institute Library
University of Washington
Seattle, WA
206–543–0937

Alcohol and Drug Abuse Prevention, Bureau of
Freeway Medical Center
Little Rock, AR
501–280–4506

Alcohol and Drug Abuse Prevention, Office of
Health and Welfare Building
Hazen Drive
Concord, NH 03301
603–271–4627
603–271–6100

Alcohol and Drug Abuse Program
Department of Health and Rehabilitative Services
1317 Winewood Boulevard
Tallahassee, FL 32301
904–488–0900

Alcohol and Drug Abuse Programs, Office of, Oregon Prevention Resource Center
1178 Chemeketa Street NE, Suite 102
Salem, OR 97310
503–378–2163
503–945–5763

Alcohol and Drug Abuse Programs, Office of
103 South Maine Street
Waterbury, VT 05676
802–241–2170/2175
802–241–2178

Alcohol and Drug Abuse Programs
Hathaway Building
Cheyenne, WY 82002
307–777–7115 Extension 7118

Alcohol and Drug Abuse Resource Center, Texas Commission on
Austin, TX
512–867–8821

Alcohol and Drug Abuse Section
Division of Mental Health and Mental Retardation Services
325 North Salisbury Street
Raleigh, NC 27611
919–733–4670

Alcohol and Drug Abuse Services
Department of Social and Rehabilitation Services
Biddle Building, 300 SW Oakley
Topeka, KS 66606-1861
913–296–3925

Alcohol and Drug Abuse Services Administration, Office of Information, Prevention and Education
Washington, DC
202–576–7315

Alcohol and Drug Abuse Services
Department of Mental Health and Mental Retardation
706 Church Street, 4th Floor
Nashville, TN 37219
615–741–1921

Alcohol and Drug Abuse, South Dakota Division of
Joe Foss Building, 523 East Capitol
Pierre, SD 57501
605–773–3123

Alcohol and Drug Addiction Services, Ohio Department of
Columbus, OH
614–466–6379

Alcohol and Drug Association, Tennessee
Statewide Clearinghouse
Nashville, TN
615–244–7066

Alcohol and Drug Problems Association of North America
444 North Capitol Street NW, Suite 706
Washington, DC 20001
202–737–4340

Alcohol and Drug Program, Human Services Program
LBJ Tropical Medical Center
Pago Pago, AS 05799
011–684–633–1212

Alcohol and Drug Programs, Department of, State of California
Sacramento, CA
916–327–8447

Alcohol and Drugs Program, Social Services Division, Government of American Samoa
Pago Pago, AS 96799
684-633-4485

Alcohol and Drug Programs, Department of
111 Capitol Mall, Suite 450
Sacramento, CA 95814
916-445-0834

Alcohol and Drug Resource Center, North Carolina
Durham, NC
919-493-2881

Alcohol and Drug Services
878 Peachtree Street NE, Suite 318
Atlanta, GA 30309
404-894-6352

Alcohol and Other Drug Abuse, Office of
PO Box 7851
1 West Wilson Street
Madison, WI 53707
608-266-3442

Alcohol, Drug Abuse, and Mental Health Administration
5600 Fishers Lane, Room 12-105
Rockville, MD 20857
301-443-4797

Alcohol, Drugs, & Pregnancy Helpline
312-541-1272
800-638-BABY (2229)

Alcohol Hotline
800-ALCOHOL (252-6465)

Alcohol Research Group
Epidemiology and Behavioral Medicine
Institute of Medical Research
San Francisco, CA
510-642-5208

Alcoholics Anonymous (AA)
15 E 26th Street, Room 1810
New York, NY 10010
212-683-3900

Alcoholics Anonymous (AA)
General Services Office
Box 459 Grand Central Station
New York, NY 10163
212-686-1100

Alcoholism and Alcohol Abuse
194 Washington Avenue
Albany, NY 12210
518-474-5417

Alcoholism and Drug Abuse, Council of Nebraska
Lincoln, NE
402-474-1992

Alcoholism and Drug Abuse, Division of, Department of Human Services
State Capitol Judicial Wing
Bismarck, ND 58505
701-224-2769

Alcoholism and Drug Abuse, Division of, Department of Public Institutions
PO Box 94728
Lincoln, NE 68509
402-471-2851 Extension 5583

Alcoholism and Drug Abuse, Division of, Mississippi Department of Mental Health
Jackson, MS
601-359-1288

Alcoholism and Drug Abuse, Division of, New Jersey State Department of Health
Trenton, NJ
609-984-6961

Alcoholism and Drug Abuse, Office of Comm. Behav. Health, Department of Health Services
411 N 24th Street
Phoenix, AZ 85008
602-220-6455

Alcoholism and Drug Abuse, Office of, Department of Health & Social Services
Pouch H-05-F
Juneau, AK 99811
907-586-6201

Alcoholism and Drug Abuse Prevention Office of, Bureau of Rehabilitation
State House Station 11
Augusta, ME 04333
207-289-2781

Alcoholism and Drug Dependency
Department of Health
Division of Mental Health
PO Box 520
Christiansted, St. Croix, VI 00820
809-773-5150

Alcoholism and Substance Abuse, Bureau of, Washington Department of Social and Health Services
Mail Stop OB-44W
Olympia, WA 98504
206-753-5866

Alcoholism and Substance Abuse, Department of
100 West Randolph Street, Suite 5–600
Chicago, IL 60601
312–814–3840

Alcoholism and Substance Abuse Services, New York State Office of
Albany, NY
518–473–3460

Alexian Brothers Medical Center
800 Biesterfield Road
Elk Grove, IL 60007
800–431–5005

American Academy of Health Care Providers in the Addictive Disorders
260 Beacon Street
Somerville, MA 02143
617–661–6248

American Academy of Psychiatrists in Alcoholism and Addictions (AAPAA)
PO Box 376
Greenbelt, MD 20768
301–220–0951

American College Health Association (ACHA) Task Force on Alcohol and Other Drugs
1300 Piccard Drive, Suite 200
Rockville, MD 20850
301–963–1100

American Council for Drug Education
204 Monroe Street, Suite 110
Rockville, MD 20850
301–294–0600
800–488–3784

American Council on Alcoholism
800–527–5344

American Medical Association (AMA), Department of Mental Health, Division of Substance Abuse
535 North Dearborn Street
Chicago, IL 60610
312–645–5000

American Nurses' Association (ANA)
2420 Pershing Road
Kansas City, MO 64108
816–474–5720   (FAX 816–471–4903)

American Public Health Association (APHA), Section on Alcohol and Drugs
1015 Fifteenth Street NW
Washington, DC 20005
202–789–5600

American Society of Addiction Medicine (ASAM)
5225 Wisconsin Avenue NW, Suite 409
Washington, DC 20016
212–206–6770
or
12 West 21st Street
New York, NY 10010
202–244–8948

Anchorage Poison Center
Anchorage, AK
800–478–3193 (Alaska only)
907–261–3193

Anesthetists in Recovery (AIR)
5626 Preston Oaks Road, Unit 40D
Dallas, TX 75240
214–960–7296
913–383–2878

Anti-Addiction Services, Department of
Box 21414 Rio Piedras Station
Rio Piedras, PR 00928-1414
809–764–3795

Arizona Center Against Sexual Assault
2333 North Central, Suite 100
Phoenix, AZ 85004
602–254–6400 Extension 121

Arizona Department of Health Services
Office of Community Behavioral Health
1740 West Adams, Room 001
Phoenix, AZ 85007
602–255–1152

Arizona Poison and Drug Information Center
University of Arizona
Arizona Health Sciences Center
Tucson, AZ
800–362–0101 (Arizona only)
602–626–6016

Arizona Prevention Resource Center
Arizona State University
Tempe, AZ
602–965–9666

Arkansas Coalition Against Domestic Violence
501–399–9486

Arkansas Coalition Against Violence to Women and Children
523 South Louisiana, Suite 230
Little Rock, AR 72201
800–269–4668 (in state)
501–399–9486

Arkansas Poison and Drug Information Center
Little Rock, AR
800–482–8948 (MDs/hospitals, Arkansas only)
501–666–5532 (MDs/hospitals)
501–661–6161

Arthur Center/Audrain Medical Center
100 Nifong, Building 5, Suite 120
Columbia, MO 65203-5661
314–875–7995 (Local)
314–581–1785 (Mexico)
800–530–5465 (USA Statewide)

Aspen Health Services
7711 Center Avenue, #300
Huntington Beach, CA 92647
800–283–8334

Assaulted Women's Help Line (Canada)
416–863–0511

Assistant Secretary of Defense—Health Affairs, Office of the
Pentagon Room 3D-360
Washington, DC 20301-1200
202–695–4964

Association of Labor, Management Administrators, and Consultants on Alcoholism (ALMACA)
1800 North Kent Street, Suite 907
Arlington, VA 22209
703–522–6272

Association for Medical Education and Research in Substance Abuse (AMERSA)
Center for Alcohol and Addiction Services
Box G, Brown University
Providence, RI 02912
401–863–3173

Bathurst Poison Control
Bathurst, NB, Canada
506–546–4666

Battered Women Fighting Back!, Inc.
617–482–9497

Battered Women's Bilingual Hotline
800–548–2722

B.C. Drug and Poison Information Centre
Vancouver, BC, Canada
604–682–5050

Be Sober Referral Line
800-BE-SOBER (237–6237)

Betty Ford Center Referral Line
800–854–9211

Billings Rape Task Force
1245 N 29th Street
Billings, MT 59101
406–245–6721 (Office)
(serves Eastern Montana)

Black Children of Alcoholic and Drug Addicted Persons (BCOADAP)
c/o National Black Alcoholism Council
417 Dearborn Street
Chicago, IL 60605
312–663–5780

Blodgett Regional Poison Center
Grand Rapids, MI
800–632–2727 (517/616/906 area codes only)
800-356-3232 (TTY)
616–774–2963

Blue Ridge Poison Center
Charlottesville, VA
800-451-1428 (Virginia, West Virginia, North Carolina, District of Columbia, Tennessee, and Maryland)
804–924–5543

Brown University Center for Alcohol and Addiction Studies
Brown University, Butler Hospital, Box G
Providence, RI 02912
401–863–3173

California Alliance Against Domestic Violence
415–457–2464

California Coalition Against Sexual Assault
Cal CASA c/o LACAAW
6043 Hollywood Blvd, Suite 200
Los Angeles, CA 90028
213–462–1281

Calgary Poison and Drug Information Services
Calgary, AB, Canada
800–332–1414 (Alberta only)
403–670–1414

California Smokers Helpline
800–7-NOBUTTS (800–766–2887)

Canadian Association for Children of Alcoholics
PO Box 159, Station H
Toronto, ON M4C 5H9, Canada
416–601–0091

Canadian Centre on Substance Abuse
Ottawa, ON, Canada
613-235-4048
800-559-4514

CARE Program Wyoming
University of Wyoming
Laramie, WY
307-766-4119

CDC's Sexually Transmitted Diseases Hotline
Rockville, MD
800-227-8922

CDC's National AIDS Information Clearinghouse
Rockville, MD
800-458-5231

Center for Education in Maternal and Child Health
38th and R Streets NW
Washington, DC 20057
202-625-8400

Center for Health Promotion
George Mason University
Fairfax, VA
703-993-3697

Center for Health Promotion and Education
Centers for Disease Control
1600 Clifton Road
Building 1 South, Room SSB249
Atlanta, GA 30333
404-320-3492

Center for Substance Abuse Treatment, Drug Abuse Information and Treatment
Referral hotline
800-662-HELP (4357)

Center of Alcohol Studies
Rutgers, The State University
Smithers Hall Busch Campus
Pascataway, NJ 08854
201-932-2190

Central and Southern Illinois Regional Poison Resource Center
Springfield, IL
800-252-2022 (Illinois only)
217-753-3330

Central New York Poison Control Center
Syracuse, NY
800-252-5655 (New York only)
315-476-4766

Central Ohio Poison Center
Columbus, OH
800-682-7625 (Ohio only)
614-228-1323
614-228-2272 (TTY)

Central Pennsylvania Poison Center
Hershey, PA
800-521-6110
717-531-6111
717-531-6039

Chemical Dependency Bureau, Department of Institutions
Helena, MT
406-444-2878

Chemical Dependency Program Division, Department of Human Services
444 Lafayette Road
St. Paul, MN 55155-3823
612-296-4610

Chemical People/WQED, The
4802 Fifth Avenue
Pittsburgh, PA 15213
412-622-1491

Chicago & Northeastern Illinois Regional Poison Control Center
Chicago, IL
800-942-5969 (northeastern Illinois only)
312-942-5969

Children of Alcoholics Foundation, Inc.
200 Park Avenue, 31st Floor
New York, NY 10166
212-351-2680
800-359-2623

Choiceline
800-824-6423

Clinical Drug Consultants and Associates
c/o Substance Abusology Research Unit
Suite #500, University Extension Center
8303-112 Street, University of Alberta
Edmonton, AB T6G 2T4, Canada
780-492-2856
780-389-4141

Coalition of Hispanic Health and Human Services Organizations (COSSMHO)
1030 15th Street NW, Suite 1053
Washington, DC 20005
202-371-2100

Coalition for Drug Free Hawaii Prevention Resource Center
Honolulu, HI
808-593-2221

Coalition on Alcohol and Drug Dependent Women and Their Children
202–737–8122

CoAnon Family Groups
PO Box 64742 66
Los Angeles, CA 90064
213–859–2206

Cocaine Anonymous (CA)
3740 Overland Avenue, Suite G
Los Angeles CA 90034
213–559–5833
800–347–8998

Cocaine Helpline
800-COCAINE (262–2463)

Colorado Coalition Against Sexual Assault (CCASA)
PO Box 18663
Denver, CO 80218
303–861–7033

Colorado Department of Human Services
Denver, CO
303–692–2930

Community Intervention
529 S 7th Street, #907
Minneapolis, MN 55415

CompCare Publications
PO Box 27777, 2415 Annapolis Lane
Minneapolis, MN 55441

Comprehensive Health
Oklahoma Department of Education
2500 North Lincoln Boulevard
Oklahoma City, OK 73105-4599
405–521–2106

Connecticut Alcohol and Drug Abuse Commission
999 Asylum Avenue, 3rd Floor
Hartford, CT 06105
203–566–4145

Connecticut Clearinghouse
334 Farmington Avenue
Plainville, CT 06062
302–793–7971
800–232–4424
800–793–9791

Connecticut Coalition Against Domestic Violence
203–524–5890

Connecticut Poison Control Center
Farmington, CT
800–343–2722 (Connecticut only)
203–679–3473 (administration)
203–679–4346 (TDD)

Connecticut Sexual Assault Crisis Services, Inc.
110 Connecticut Boulevard
East Hartford, CT 06108
203–282–9881
860–522–4636 (Information Line)

Crisis Call Center
PO Box 8016
Reno, NV 89507
702–323–4533
702–323–6111 (Hotline)
800–992–5757 (in state)

CSAP's National Resource for the Prevention of Alcohol, Tobacco, Other Drug Abuse and Mental Illness in Women
Alexandria, VA
800–354–8824

DC Rape Crisis Center
PO Box 34125
Washington, DC 20043
202–232–0789
202–333–7273 (hotline)

Delaware Division of Alcoholism, Drug Abuse and Mental Health
1901 N DuPont Highway
Newcastle, DE 19720
302–421–6101

Delaware Valley Mental Health Foundation
1833 Butler Avenue
Doyestown, PA 18901
215–345–0444

Department of Health
CN 360
Trenton, NJ 08625
609–292–3147

Department of Health and Human Services (HHS)
Council on Sexual Violence
202–690–8157

Department of Health/BHSD-DSA
Santa Fe, NM
505–827–2601

Department of Public Instruction
Alcohol & Drug Defense Section
301 North Wilmington Street
Raleigh, NC 27601–2825
919–715–1676

Domestic Violence & Sexual Assault Program
454 Hathaway Building
Cheyenne, WY 82002–0480
307–777–6086

Drug Abuse Bureau
Ohio Department of Health
170 N Hight Street, 3rd Floor
Columbus, OH 43266-0586
614–466–7893

Drug Abuse Prevention Program
Texas Education Agency
Division of Accelerated Instruction
1701 North Congress Avenue
Austin, TX 78701-1494

Drug Abuse Program
State Department of Education
Learner Support Systems
994 Capitol Square Building
St. Paul, MN 55101
612–296–3925

Drug and Alcohol Nursing Association, Inc. (DANA)
113 West Franklin Street
Baltimore, MD 21201
301–752–3318   (FAX 301–752–8295)

Drug and Alcohol Programs
PA Department of Health
PO Box 90
Harrisburg, PA 17108
717–787–9857

Drug and Alcohol Registry of Treatment (DART)
ON, Canada
800–565–8603

Drug-Free Workplace Helpline
800–967–5752

Drug Information Services for Kentucky, Division of Substance Abuse
Frankfort, KY
502–564–2880

Drug Policy Office
The White House
Washington, DC 20500
202–456–6554

Drugs and Crime Data Center and Clearinghouse
Rockville, MD
800–666–3332

Drug Store Information Clearinghouse, The
South Carolina Commission on Alcohol and Drug Abuse
Columbia, SC
803–734–9559

Duke University Regional Poison Control Center
Durham, NC
800–672–1697 (North Carolina only)
919–684–8111

Duluth Domestic Abuse Intervention Project
(some batterers' treatment information too)
218–722–2781

El Paso Poison Control Center
El Paso, TX
915–533–1244 (southwestern Texas and southern New Mexico only)

Employee Assistance Professionals Association (EAPA)
4601 North Fairfax Drive, Suite 1001
Arlington, VA 22203
703–522–6272

Fairbanks Hospital/The Turning Point
8102 Clearvista Parkway
Indianapolis, IN 46256
317–849–8222
800–225–HOPE (Indianapolis residents)

Families Anonymous, Inc.
PO Box 548
Van Nuys, CA 91408
818–989–7841

Family Violence Prevention Fund
Health Resource on Domestic Violence
800–313–1310

FAS/FAE Prevention Program
Vermont Department of Health
1193 North Avenue, PO Box 70
Burlington, VT 05401
802–863–7330

Florida Council of Sexual Abuse Services, Inc.
850 6th Avenue, North
Naples, FL 33940
941–649–1404
941–649–5660

Florida Poison Information Center at Tampa General Hospital
Tampa, FL
800-282-3171 (Florida only)
813-253-4444

Food and Drug Administration, Legislative, Professional, and Consumer Affairs Branch (HFD-365)
5600 Fishers Lane
Rockville, MD 20857
301-295-8012

Fresno Regional Poison Control Center
Fresno, CA
800-346-5922 (Fresno, Kern, Kings, Madera, Mariposa, Merced, and Tulare counties only)
209-445-1222

Georgia Network to End Sexual Assault
c/o Houston Drug Action Council (HODAC)
2762 Watson Boulevard
Warner Robins, GA 31093
912-953-5674
800-338-6745 (in state)

Georgia Regional Poison Control Center
Atlanta, GA
800-282-5846 (Georgia only)
404-589-4400
404-525-3323 (TTY)

Georgia State Crime Lab
Division of Forensic Science/Crime Lab
Decatur, GA
404-244-2666

Governor's Alliance Against Drugs
John W. McCormack State Office Building
One Ashburton Place, Room 611
Boston, MA 02108
617-727-0786

Halfway House Alcoholism Programs of North America Association of (AHHAP)
786 E 7th Street
St. Paul, MN 55106

Hawaii Poison Center
Honolulu, HI
800-362-3585 (outer islands of Hawaii only)
800-362-3586
808-941-4411

Hawaii State Coalition Against Sexual Assault
1164 Bishop Street, Suite 124
Honolulu, HI 96813
(Mail is forwarded)
808-242-4335
808-973-8337

Fenway Community Health Center's Victim Recovery Program
617-267-0900

Hazelden Center for Youth & Families
11505 36th Avenue North
Plymouth, MN 55441
619-559-2022

Hazelden Foundation
Box 11
Center City, MN 55012
800-822-0800 (training and education)
800-328-9000 (educational materials)

Health and Social Welfare La Fotraleza
Advisor to the Governor
San Juan, PR
809-722-1917

Health and Welfare, Department of
450 West State Street
Boise, ID 83720
208-334-5935

Health Communications, Inc.
3201 SW 15th Street
Deerfield Beach, FL 33442

HEALTH EDCO, Inc. (formerly Spenco)
PO Box 21207
Waco, TX 76702-1207

Health Planning and Development
1660 L Street NW
Washington, DC 20036
202-673-7481

Health Promotion Resource Center
Stanford Center for Research in Disease Prevention
1000 Welch Road
Palo Alto, CA 94304-1885
415-723-0003

Health Related Services
Mississippi Department of Education
550 High Street
Jackson, MS 39205
601-359-2459

Healthy Nations National Program Office
UCHSC University, North Pavilion
Denver, CO
303-372-3272

Hennepin Regional Poison Center
Minneapolis, MN
612-347-3141

Hudson Valley Regional Poison Center
Nyack, NY
800–336–6997 (New York only)
914–353–1000

Idaho Coalition Against Sexual and Domestic Violence
200 North Fourth Street, Suite 10
Boise, ID 83702
208–384–0419

Idaho Poison Center
Boise, ID
800–632–8000 (Idaho only)
208–378–2707

Idaho RADAR Network Center
Boise State University
Boise, ID
208–385–3471

Illinois Coalition Against Sexual Assault (ICASA)
123 S. 7th Street, Suite 500
Springfield, IL 62701-1302
217–753–4117

Indian Health Service
Colorado River Service
Route 1, Box 12
Parker, AZ 85344
602–669–2137

Indiana Coalition Against Sexual Assault (INCASA)
2511 E. 46th Street, Suite N3
Indianapolis, IN 46205
317–568–4001
800–656-HOPE (4673)

Indiana Poison Center
Indianapolis, IN
800–382–9097 (Indiana only)
317–929–2323
317–929–2336 (TTY)

Indiana Prevention Resource Center
Indiana University
Bloomington, IN
812–855–1237

Institute on Black Chemical Abuse (IBCA) Resource Center
2614 Nicollet Avenue
Minneapolis, MN 55408
612–871–7878

Inter-American Drug Information System
OAS/CICAD
Washington, DC
202–458–3809

Intermountain Regional Poison Control Center
Salt Lake City, UT
800–456–7707 (Utah only)
801–581–2151

International Doctors in Alcoholics Anonymous (IDAA)
7250 France Avenue South, Suite 400C
Minneapolis, MN 55435
612–835–4421

International Institute on Inhalant Abuse
Englewood, CO
303–788–1951

International Lawyers in Alcoholics Anonymous (ILAA)
1092 Elm Street, Suite 201
Rocky Hill, CT 06067
203–529–7474

International Nurses Anonymous (INA)
1020 Sunset Drive
Lawrence, KS 66044
913–842–3893

Iowa Coalition Against Domestic Violence
515–244–8028

Iowa Coalition Against Sexual Assault Iowa (CASA)
1540 High Street, Suite 102
Lucas State Office Building
Des Moines, IA 50309
515–244–7424

Iowa Substance Abuse Information Center
Cedar Rapids Public Library
Cedar Rapids, IA
319–398–5133

Johnson Institute
7151 Metro Boulevard
Minneapolis, MN 55435
800–231–5165
800–247–0484
800–447–6660 (in Canada)

Join Together—A National Resource for Communities Fighting Substance Abuse
Boston, MA
617–437–1500

Kansas Coalition Against Sexual and Domestic Violence (KCSDV)
820 SE Quincy, Suite 416
Topeka, KS 66612
913–232–9784

Knoxville Poison Control Center
Interstate Centers, KY
615–544–9400 (southern Kentucky only)

Knoxville Poison Control Center
Knoxville, TN
615–544–9400 (eastern Tennessee and southern Kentucky only)

Lake County Council Against Sexual Assault (LaCASA)
1 South Greenleaf Street
Gurnee, IL 60031
708–244–1187

Lehigh Valley Poison Center
Allentown, PA
215–433–2311

Libertas Treatment Center
1701 Dousman Street
Green Bay, WI 54303
414–498–8600

Life Line/Finger Lakes Regional Poison Control Center
Rochester, NY
800–333–0542 (Ontario and Wayne counties only)
716–275–5151
716–275–2700 (TTY)

London Poison Control
London, ON, Canada
519–667–6565

Long Island Regional Poison Control Center
East Meadow, NY
516–542–2323/2324/2325
516–542–3813
516–747–3323 (TTY)

Los Angeles County Regional Poison Control Center
Los Angeles, CA
800–777–6476 (Los Angeles, Santa Barbara, and Ventura counties only)
213–484–5151
213–664–2121 (MDs and hospitals)

Louisiana Foundation Against Sexual Assault (LaFASA)
PO Box 1450
Independence, LA 70443
504–878–3849

Mahoning Valley Poison Center
St. Elizabeth Hospital Medical Center
Youngstown, OH
800–426–2348 (Ohio, and Mercer and Lawrence counties in Pennsylvania only)
216–746–2222
216–746–5510 (TTY)

Maine Coalition Against Sexual Assault
PO Box 5326
Augusta, ME 04332
207–784–5272
207–759–9985

Maine Poison Control Center at Maine Medical Center
Portland, ME
800–442–6305 (Maine only)
207–871–2382 (Emergency Room)

Marijuana Anonymous World Service Office
800–766–6779

Marin Institute Resource Center for the Prevention of Alcohol and Other Drug Problems, The
24 Belvedere Street
San Rafael, CA 94901
415–456–5692

Mary Bridge Poison Center
Tacoma, WA
800–542–6319 (Washington only)
206–594–1414

Maryland Coalition Against Sexual Assault (MCASA)
c/o Howard County Sexual Assault Center
Suite G-118, 10015 Old Columbia Road
Columbia, MD 21046
410–290–6432

Maryland Poison Center
Baltimore, MD
800–492–2414 (Maryland only)
410–528–7701

Maryland State Alcohol and Drug Abuse Administration
201 West Preston Street
Baltimore, MD 21201
301–225–6925

Massachusetts Coalition Against Sexual Assault
1 Salem Square
Worcester, MA 01608
508–754–1019

Massachusetts Poison Control System
Boston, MA
800-682-9211 (Massachusetts only)
617-232-2120

Mental Health, Alcoholism and Drug Dependency Services, Division of
PO Box 520
St. Croix, VI 00820
809-773-1992

Mental Health and Substance Abuse, Department of
PO Box 8896
Tamuning, GU 96911
011-671-477-9704/5

Mental Health and Substance Abuse Services, Oklahoma State Department of
PO Box 53277 Capitol Station
Oklahoma City, OK 73152
405-271-7474
405-271-8755

Mental Health Prevention Unit, Division of
Richmond
St. Croix, VI
809-774-7700

Mental Health, Virginia Department of
Office of Prevention
Richmond, VA
804-371-7564

Mental Illness and Substance Abuse Division of Community Programs Department of Mental Health
PO Box 3710
200 Interstate Park Drive
Montgomery, AL 36193
205-271-9250

Mercy Hospital Chemical Dependency Services
800 Mercy Drive
Council Bluffs, IA 51503
712-328-5113
402-398-6866
800-432-9211 (Iowa)
800-831-4140 (Nebraska)

Mercy Hospital Poison Control Center
Charlotte, NC
704-379-5827

Metropolitan Organization to Counter Sexual Assault (MOCSA)
3217 Broadway, Suite 500
Kansas City, MO 64111
816-931-4527
816-531-0233 (Hotline)
816-561-1222 (Survivor)

Mid-America Poison Control Center
University of Kansas Medical Center
Kansas City, KS
800-332-6633 (Kansas only)
913-588-6633

Middle Tennessee Regional Poison/Clinical Toxicology Center
Nashville, TN
800-288-9999 (mid-Tennessee only)
615-322-6435 (Nashville and adjacent counties only)

Minnesota Coalition Against Sexual Assault (MCASA)
2344 Nicollet Avenue South, #170A
Minneapolis, MN 55404-3342
612-872-7734
800-964-8847 (in state)

Minnesota Regional Poison Center
St. Paul, MN
800-222-1222 (Minnesota only)
612-221-2113

Mississippi Coalition Against Sexual Assault
Mississippi State Department of Health
PO Box 1700
Jackson, MS 39215-1700
601-960-7470

Mississippi Regional Poison Control Center
Jackson, MS
601-354-7660

Moncton Poison Control
Moncton, NB, Canada
506-857-5555

Motherisk
Hospital for Sick Children
Toronto, ON M5G 1X8, Canada
416-813-6780

Mothers Against Drunk Driving (MADD)
511 E John Carpenter Freeway Suite 700
Irving, TX 75062
214-744-6233
800-GET-MADD
800-992-6233

Mulberry Center/Parkside
420 Mulberry Street
Evansville, IN 47710
812–426–8201
800–788–6541

Nar-Anon Family Groups
PO Box 2562
Palos Verdes Peninsula, CA 90274
213–547–5800

Narcotics Anonymous (NA)
PO Box 9999
Van Nuys, CA 91409
818–780–3951

National Asian Pacific American Families Against Drug Abuse
6303 Friendship Court
Bethesda, MD 20817
301–530–0945

National Asian Pacific American Families Against Substance Abuse, Inc.
420 E. Third Street, Suite 909
Los Angeles, CA 90013-1647
213–617–8277

National Association for Children of Alcoholics, Inc. (NACOA)
31582 Coast Highway, Suite B
South Laguna, CA 92677
714–499–3889
or
Rockville, MD
301–468–0985

National Association for the Dually Diagnosed
800–331–5362

National Association for Native American Children of Alcoholics (NANACOA)
PO Box 18736
Seattle, WA 98114
206–322–5601
800–322–5601

National Association for Perinatal Addiction Research and Education (NAPARE)
11 E. Hubbard Street, Suite 200
Chicago, IL 60611
312–329–2512

National Association of Alcoholism and Drug Abuse Counselors (NAADC)
3717 Columbia Pike, Suite 300
Arlington, VA 22204
703–920–4644

National Association of Lesbian and Gay Alcoholism Professionals
1147 South Alvarado
Los Angeles, CA 90006
213–381–8524

National Association of Social Workers (NASW)
7981 Eastern Avenue
Silver Spring, MD 20910
301–565–0333

National Association of State Alcohol and Drug Abuse Directors (NASADAD)
444 N Capitol Street NW, Suite 642
Washington, DC 20001
202–783–6868

National Black Alcoholism Council (NBAC)
1629 K Street NW, Suite 802
Washington, DC 20006
202–296–2696

National Black Women's Health Project
202–835–0117

National Capital Poison Center
Washington, DC
202–625–3333
202–784–4660 (TTY)

National Catholic Council on Alcoholism
1200 Varnum Street, NE
Washington, DC 20017-2796

National Center for Education in Maternal and Child Health
3520 Prospect Street NW, Suite 1
Washington, DC 20057
202–625–8410

National Center on Women and Family Law, Inc.
212–674–8200

National Certification Reciprocity Consortium/Alcohol and Other Drug Abuse (NCRC)
PO Box 157
Atkinson, NH 03811
603–898–1516

National Clearinghouse for Alcohol and Drug Information (NCADI)
PO Box 2345
Rockville, MD 20847-2345
301–468–2600
800–729–6686

National Clearinghouse for Family
Planning Information
PO Box 2225
Rockville, MD 20852
301–251–5153

National Clearinghouse for Primary Care
Information
8201 Greensboro Drive, Suite 600
McLean, VA 22102
703–821–8955

National Clearinghouse for the Defense of
Battered Women
215–351–0010

National Clearinghouse on Family
Violence
800–267–1291

National Clearinghouse on Marital and
Date Rape
510–524–1582

National Coalition Against Domestic
Violence
202–638–6388
303–839–1852

National Coalition Against Sexual Assault
202–483–7165

National Coalition of Hispanic Health
Services Organization
1501 16th Street, NW
Washington, DC 20036
202–387–5000

National Coalition on Sexual Assault
(NCASA)
912 N. 2nd Street
Harrisburg, PA 17102
717–232–7460

National Cocaine Hotline
800-COCAINE (262–2463)

National Consortium of Chemical
Dependency Nurses, Inc. (NCCDN)
975 Oak, Suite 675
Eugene, OR 97401
800–87-NCCDN
503–485–4421

National Council on Alcoholism and Drug
Dependence (NCADD)
12 West 21st Street
New York, NY 10010
212–206–6770
212–777–8923
800-NCA-CALL (622–2255)

National Criminal Justice Reference
Service (NCJRS)
Box 6000
Rockville, MD 20850
301–251–5500

National Drug and Alcohol Treatment
Information Line
800–662-HELP (4357)
800–662–9832 (Spanish)
800–228–0427 (TDD)

National Families in Action
2296 Henderson Mill Road, Suite 204
Atlanta, GA 30345
404–934–6364

National Health Information
Clearinghouse
PO Box 1133
Washington, DC 20013-1133
703–522–2590 (Virginia)
800–336–4797

National Institute on Alcohol Abuse and
Alcoholism (NIAAA)
5600 Fishers Lane, Room 14C-17
Rockville, MD 20857
301–443–2954

National Institute on Drug Abuse (NIDA)
5600 Fishers Lane, Room 10–04
Rockville, MD 20857
301–443–4577
800–662-HELP

National Mental Health Association
Information
800–969–6642
800–433–5959

National Nurses' Society on Addictions
(NNSA)
5700 Old Orchard Road, 1st Floor
Skokie, IL 60077-1024
708–966–5010   (FAX 708–966–9418)

National Organization of Victim Assistance
(NOVA)
1757 Park Road NW
Washington, DC 20010
800–879–6682
202–232–6682

National Prevention Network
444 North Capitol Street, NW, Suite 642
Washington, DC 20001
202–783–6868

National Resource Center on Domestic Violence
800–537–2238

National Safety Council
444 North Michigan
Chicago, IL 60611
312–527–4800

National Self-Help Clearinghouse
25 West 43rd Street
New York, NY 10036
212–642–2944

National Victims Center
800-FYI-CALL
703–276–2880

National Women's Resource Center for the Prevention of Perinatal Abuse of Alcohol and Other Drugs
800–354–8824

Nebraska Domestic Violence and Sexual Assault Coalition
315 S. 9th Street, Suite 18
Lincoln, NE 68508-2252
402–476–6256
402–475–7273 (hotline)
800–876–6238 (hotline)
(Physicians may call to reach the sexual assault program in their local area)

New Hampshire Coalition Against Domestic and Sexual Violence
PO Box 353
Concord, NH 03302-0353
603–224–8893
800–852–3388 (hotline)
800–735–2964 (TDD/VOICE)

New Hampshire Poison Information Center
Lebanon, NH
800–562–8236 (New Hampshire only)
603–650–5000

New Jersey Coalition Against Sexual Assault (NJCASA)
5 Elm Row, Suite 306
New Brunswick, NJ 08901-2103
908–418–1354

New Jersey Poison Information and Education System
Newark, NJ
800–962–1253 (New Jersey only)
201–923–0764
201–926–8008 (TTY)

New Mexico Coalition of Sexual Assault Programs, Inc
4004 Carlisle, NE, Suite P
Albuquerque, NM 87107
505–883–8020

New Mexico Poison and Drug Information Center
Albuquerque, NM
800–432–6866 (New Mexico only)
505–843–2551

New York City Poison Control Center
New York, NY
212–340–4494
212–764–7667

New York State Coalition Against Sexual Assault (NYSCASA)
The Women's Building
79 Central Avenue
Albany, NY 12206
518–434–1580

North Carolina Coalition Against Sexual Assault (NCCASA)
582B Farringdom Street
Lunberton, NC 28358
910–739–6278

North Dakota Council on Abused Women's Service
Coalition Against Sexual Assault in North Dakota
418 E. Rosser, #320
Bismarck, ND 58501
701–293–7273
701–251–2300
701–255–6240 (Office)
800–472–2911 (hotline [in state])

North Texas Poison Center
Dallas, TX
800–441–0040 (Texas only)
214–590–5000

Northwest Regional Poison Center
Erie, PA
800–822–3232 (northwestern Pennsylvania, northeastern Ohio, and southwestern New York)
814–452–3232

Office for Substance Abuse Prevention (OSAP)
5600 Fishers Lane, Room 9A-54
Rockville, MD 20857
301–443–0365

Office of Smoking and Health
Centers for Disease Control and Prevention
800-CDC-1311

Office on Alcohol and Drug Abuse Prevention
PO Box 1437
Donaghey Plaza North, Suite 400,
Little Rock, AR 72203-1437
501-682-6650

Office on Smoking and Health
3005 Rhodes Building
Chamblee, GA 30341
404-488-5705

Ohio Coalition on Sexual Assault (OCOSA)
4041 N. High Street, Suite 408
Columbus, OH 43214
614-268-3322

Oklahoma Coalition Against Domestic Violence and Sexual Assault
220 Classen Boulevard, Suite 1300
Oklahoma City, OK 73106
405-557-1210

Oklahoma Department of Mental Health and Substance Abuse Services
PO Box 53277 Capitol Station
Oklahoma City, OK 73152
405-271-7474

Ontario Association of Interval and Transition Houses (OAITH)
229 College Street
Toronto, ON M5T 1R4, Canada
416-977-6619

Oregon Coalition Against Domestic and Sexual Violence (OCADSV)
520 NW Davis Street, #310
Portland, OR 97204
503-223-7411
800-OCADSV-2 (hotline [in state])

Oregon Poison Center
Portland, OR
800-452-7165 (Oregon only)
503-494-8968

Parkview Hospital of Topeka
3707 SW 6th Avenue
Topeka, KS 66606
913-235-3000

Pathways Inc.
Rape Crisis Program
201 22nd Street
Ashland, KY 41105-0790
606-324-1141

Pennsylvania Coalition Against Rape (PCAR)
910 N. Second Street
Harrisburg, PA 17102-3119
717-232-6745
800-692-7445 (hotline [in state])

Pittsburgh Poison Center
Pittsburgh, PA
412-681-6669

Poison Center
Omaha, NE
800-955-9119 (Nebraska, Iowa, Missouri, South Dakota, and Wyoming)
402-390-5555

Poison Control Center
Children's Hospital of Michigan
Detroit, MI
313-745-5711

Poison Control Centre
Halifax, NS, Canada
902-428-8161

Poison Control Center
Iowa City, IA
800-272-6477 (Iowa only)
319-356-2922

Poison Control Centre
Regina, SK, Canada
306-359-4545

Poison Control Centre
Saskatoon, SK, Canada
306-653-1010
306-966-1010
306-966-1012

Poison Control Center, The
Interstate Centers, WY
800-955-9119 (Wyoming and Nebraska)
402-390-5555

Poison Control Center, The
Philadelphia, PA
215-386-2100
215-590-2003

Poison Control Line
Centre de Toxicologie de Québec
Quebec City, PQ, Canada
800–463–5060
418–656–8090

Poison Information Center of Northwest Ohio
Interstate Centers, MI
800–589–3897 (southeastern Michigan only)

Poison Information Center of Northwest Ohio
Medical College of Ohio Hospital
Toledo, OH
800–589–3897 (northwestern Ohio and southeastern Michigan only)
419–381–3897

Prevention and Recovery from Alcohol and Drug Abuse, Office of
2744-B Woodale Boulevard
Baton Rouge, LA 70892
504–922–0725

Prevention Center
Florida Department of Education
325 West Gaines Street, Suite 414
Tallahassee, FL 32399-0400
904–488–6304

Prevention of Alcohol, Tobacco, Other Drug Abuse and Mental Illness in Women, CSAP's National Resource for the
Alexandria, VA
1–800–354–8824

Prevention Resource Center Library
Springfield, IL
217–525–3456

Prevention Resource Center Minnesota
St. Paul, MN
612–224–5121

Prevention Resource Center North Dakota
Bismarck, ND
701–224–3603

Prevention Support Services
The Medical Foundation
Boston, MA
617–451–0049

Project Connect
Lesbian and Gay Community Services Center
New York, NY
212–620–7310

Project Cork Institute
Dartmouth Medical School
Hanover, NH
603–646–3935

Prostitutes Anonymous World Service Office and Referral Center
402–393–0828

Provincial Poison Control Centre
St. John's, NF, Canada
709–722–1110

Provincial Poison Information Centre
Winnipeg, MB, Canada
204–787–2591

Psychologists Helping Psychologists (PHP)
23439 Michigan Avenue
Dearborn, MI 48124
313–565–3821

Public Health Services
LBJ Tropical Medical Center
Pago Pago, AS 96799

Quest International
PO Box 566
537 Jones Road
Grandville, OH 43023
614–587–2800

RADAR Network Clearinghouse
West Virginia Library Commission
Charleston, WV
304–558–2044

Rape, Abuse & Incest National Network (RAINN)
252 Tenth Street, NE
Washington, DC 2002
202–544–1034
800–656-HOPE (4673)

Rape Crisis CONTACT
PO Box 9525
Wilmington, DE 19809
302–761–9800 (Office)
302–761–9100 (Hotline)
302–761–9700 (TDD/TTY [New Castle County])
800–262–9800 (Kent & Sussex Counties)

Rapid City Regional Hospital Addiction Recovery Center
915 Mountain View Road
Rapid City, SD 57702
605–399–7200

Recovered Alcoholic Clergy Association (RACA)
5615 Midnight Pass Road, Siesta Key
Sarasota, FL 54242

Regional Poison Control System and Drug & Poison Information Center
Cincinnati, OH
800–872–5111 (Ohio only)
513–558–5111

Residents Initiatives Drug Information and Strategy Clearinghouse
Rockville, MD
301–251–5546

Resource Center on Substance Abuse Prevention and Disability
1331 F Street, NW, Suite 800
Washington, DC 20004
202–783–2900

Rhode Island Poison Center
Rhode Island Hospital
Providence, RI
401–277–5727

Rhode Island Rape Crisis Center
300 Richmond Street, Suite 205
Providence, RI 02903
401–421–4100

Rocky Mountain Poison and Drug Center
Denver, CO
800–332–3073 (Colorado only)
800–525–5042 (Montana only)
800–446–6179 (Las Vegas, Nevada only)
303–629–1123

Rutgers Center of Alcohol Studies
Piscataway, NJ
908–932–4442

Saint John Poison Control
Saint John, NB, Canada
506–648–6222

Saint Luke's Medical Center
11311 Shaker Boulevard
Cleveland, OH 44104
216–368–7970

Salt Lake City Rape Crisis Center
2035 S 1300 E
Salt Lake City, UT 84105
801–467–7279 (Office)
801–463–7273

Salud Mental y Contra la Addicion, Administracion de Servicios de
San Juan, PR
809–767–5990

Samaritan Regional Poison Center
Good Samaritan Medical Center
Phoenix, AZ
602–253–3334

San Diego Regional Poison Center
San Diego, CA
800–876–4766 (Imperial and San Diego counties only)
619–543–6000

San Francisco Bay Area Regional Poison Control Center
San Francisco, CA
800–523–2222 (Alameda, Contra Costa, Del Norte, Humboldt, Marin, Mendocino, Napa, San Francisco, San Mateo, and Sonoma counties only)
415–476–6600

San Francisco Women Against Rape
3543 18th Street
San Francisco, CA 94110
415–861–2024 (Office)
415–647–7273 (hotline)

Santa Clara Valley Medical Center, Regional Poison Control Center
San Jose, CA
800–662–9886 (Monterey, San Benito, San Luis Obispo, Santa Clara, and Santa Cruz counties only)
408–299–5112

Seattle Poison Center
Seattle, WA
800–732–6985 (Washington only)
206–526–2121
206–526–2223 (TTY)

Secular Organizations for Sobriety (SOS)
PO Box 5
Buffalo, NY 14215
716–834–2922

Sexual Assault, Rape, Domestic Violence Crisis Hotline
800–656–4673

Smokers Anonymous (SA) World Services
2118 Greenwich Street
San Francisco, CA 94123
415–922–8575

Social Workers Helping Social Workers
Route 63
Goshen, CT 06756
203–489–3808

Society of Teachers of Family Medicine (STFM)
PO Box 8729
Kansas City, MO 64114
800–274–2237

SOS
University of Delaware
209 Laurel Hall
Newark, DE 19716
302–831–8992 (Office)
302–831–2226 (hotline)
(serves University of Delaware, Newark)

South Carolina Coalition Against Domestic Violence & Sexual Assault
PO Box 7776
Columbia, SC 29210
803–254–3699

South Carolina Commission on Alcohol and Drug Abuse
3700 Forest Drive
Columbia, SC 29204
803–734–9520

South Dakota Coalition Against Domestic Violence and Sexual Assault
PO Box 141
Pierre, SD 57501
605–945–0869

Southern Poison Center, Inc.
Memphis, TN
901–528–6048
901–522–5985 (administration)

Spokane Poison Center
Spokane, WA
800–572–5842 (eastern Washington, northern Idaho, western Montana, and northwestern Oregon only)
509–747–1077

St. Anthony Poison Control
St. Anthony, NF, Canada
709–454–3333 Extension 149

St. Joseph Medical Center
3600 East Harry
Wichita, KS 67218
316–689–4850

St. Peter Chemical Dependency Center
4800 College Street
Lacey, WA 98503
800–332–0465

Substance Abuse and Health Promotion, Division of
Department of Public Health
Lucas State Office Building, 4th Floor
Des Moines, IA 50319
515–281–3641

Substance Abuse and Traffic Safety Michigan, Information Center
Lansing, MI
517–482–9902

Substance Abuse Bureau
190 St. Francis Drive, Room 3350 North
Sante Fe, NM 87503
505–827–2589

Substance Abuse Coalition Washington State
Bellevue, WA
206–637–7011

Substance Abuse, Division of
Department for Mental Health and Mental Retardation Services
275 East Main Street
Frankfort, KY 40621
502–564–2880

Substance Abuse, Division of
Department of Mental Health, Retardation and Hospitals
PO Box 20363
Cranston, RI 02920
401–464–2091

Substance Abuse, Division of
Department of Social Services
PO Box 45500
120 N 200 West, 4th Floor
Salt Lake City, UT 84145-0500
801–538–3939

Substance Abuse Information Resource Center, Office of
Augusta, ME
207–624–6528

Substance Abuse Librarians and Information Specialists (SALIS)
Alcohol Research Group
1816 Scenic Avenue
Berkeley, CA 94702

Substance Abuse Prevention and Disability Resource, Center on
Washington, DC
202-783-2900

Substance Abuse Prevention, Office for
5600 Fishers Lane, Room 9A-54
Rockville, MD 20857
301-443-0365

Substance Abuse Rhode Island, Department of
Cranston, RI
401-464-2380

Substance Abuse Services, Division of
150 Tremont Street
Boston, MA 02111
617-727-8614

Substance Abuse Services, Division of
Executive Park S, Box 8200
Albany, NY 12203
518-457-7629

Substance Abuse Services, Georgia Prevention Resource Center
Atlanta, GA
404-657-2296

Substance Abuse Services, Office of Department of Mental Health, Mental Retardation and Substance Services
PO Box 1797
109 Governor Street
Richmond, VA 23214
804-786-3906

Substance Abuse Services, Office of Department of Public Health
PO Box 30206
2150 Apollo Drive
Lansing, MI 48909
517-335-8809

Substance Abuse Services, Office of, Public Information Office
3500 N. Logan Street, PO Box 30035
Lansing, MI 48909
519-373-8345

Substance Abuse, Utah State Division of
Department of Social Services
PO Box 45500
120 North 200 West, 4th Floor
Salt Lake City, UT 84145-0500
801-538-3939

Substance Abusology Research Unit
Faculty of Nursing, University of Alberta
500 University Extension Centre
8303 112 Street
Edmonton, AB T6G 2T4, Canada
780-492-2856
780-492-9954 FAX

Susquehanna Poison Center
Danville, PA
800-352-7001 (Pennsylvania only)

TARGET
National Federation TARGET Program
Kansas City, MO
816-464-5400

Tennessee Coalition Against Sexual Assault
56 Lindsley Avenue
Nashville, TN 37210
615-259-9055

Texas Association Against Sexual Assault
TAASA at the Montgomery County Women's Center
PO Box 8666
Woodlands, TX 77387
713-367-8003 Extension 229
512-440-7273
512-445-1049 (Voice Mail)

Texas Commission on Alcohol and Drug Abuse
1705 Guadalupe Street
Austin, TX 78701
512-463-5510

Texas State Poison Control Center
Galveston, TX
800-392-8548 (MDs and ambulance personnel, Texas only)
713-654-1701 (Houston only)
409-772-1420
409-765-1420
409-539-7700

Triad Poison Center
Greensboro, NC
800-722-2222 (Alamance, Forsyth, Guilford, Rockingham, and Randolph counties only)
919-379-4105

Tulsa Regional Medical Center/Behavioral Health Services
744 W 9th Street
Tulsa, OK 94127
918-599-5880

UC Davis Medical Center Regional Poison Control Center
Sacramento, CA
800–342–9293 (northern California only)
916–734–3692

UC Irvine Regional Poison Center
Orange, CA
800–544–4404 (Inyo, Mono, Orange, Riverside, and San Bernardino counties only)
714–634–5988

University of Wisconsin Hospital Regional Poison Control Center
Madison, WI
608–262–3702

U.S. Congress, House Select Committee on Narcotics Abuse and Control
H2–234 House, Annex 2
Washington, DC 20515
202–226–3040

U.S. Department of Health and Human Services
200 Independence Avenue, SW
Washington, DC 20201
202–245–6296

U.S. Department of Justice Drug Enforcement Administration, Office of Public Affairs, Prevention Program Coordinator
1405 I Street, NW, Room 1209
Washington, DC 20537
202–633–1469
202–633–1230

U.S. Department of Transportation, National Highway Traffic Safety Administration
400 7th Street, SW
Washington, DC 20590
202–426–9550

U.S. Mexico Border Health Association
El Paso, TX
915–581–6645

Utah Alcoholism Foundation
2880 S Main Street, Suite 210
Salt Lake City, UT 84115

Vermont Network Against Domestic Violence & Sexual Assault
PO Box 405
Montpelier, VT 05601
800–489–7273
802–233–1302 (Office)

Vermont Poison Center
Burlington, VT
802–658–3456 (Vermont and bordering New York counties only)
802–656–2721 (education programs)

Victoria Poison Control
Vancouver, BC, Canada
800–567–8911 (BC only)
250–595–9211 (Victoria only)
250–682–5050 (lower mainland)

Virginia Poison Center
Richmond, VA
800–552–6337 (Virginia only)
804–786–9123

Virginians Aligned Against Sexual Assault (VAASA)
508 Dale Avenue, Suite B
Charlottesville, VA 22903-4547
804–979–9002

Washington Coalition of Sexual Assault Programs (WCSAP)
110 East Fifth, Suite 214
Olympia, WA 98501
360–754–7583

West Virginia Foundation for Rape Information & Services
112 Braddock Street
Fairmont, WV 26554
304–366–8126

Western N.C. Poison Control Center
Asheville, NC
800–542–4225 (North Carolina only)
704–255–4490

West Virginia Poison Center
Charleston, WV
800–642–3625 (West Virginia only)
304–348–4211

Wilderness Treatment Center
200 Hubbart Dam Road
Marion, MT 59925
406–854–2832

Wisconsin Coalition Against Sexual Assault (WCASA)
1400 East Washington Avenue, Suite 148
Madison, WI 53703
608–257–1516

Wisconsin Clearinghouse
Madison, WI
608–263–2797

Women for Sobriety
PO Box 618
Quakertown, PA 18951
215-536-8026
800-333-1606

Women's Health Network
1325 G Street, NW
Washington, DC 20005
202-347-1140

YWCA
1130 W Broadway
Missoula, MT 59802
406-543-6691 (Office)
406-542-1994 (hotline)
(serves Missoula, Granite Lake, Sanders, and Revalli)

YWCA
322 E 300 S
Salt Lake City, UT 84111
801-355-2804

☐ PART II. Directory of Substance Use Treatment Centers, Referral Agencies, and Related Information Sources for Women Listed in Alphabetical Order by State or Province

Alabama (AL)
Alabama Coalition Against Domestic Violence
334-832-4842

Alabama Coalition Against Rape
(through the Light House)
PO Box 4091
Montgomery, AL 36102-4091
334-286-5980

Alabama Department of Mental Health/Mental Retardation
Montgomery, AL
205-270-4640

Alabama Poison Control System, Inc.
Tuscaloosa, AL
800-462-0800 (Alabama only)
205-345-0600

Children's Hospital of Alabama Regional Poison Control Center
Birmingham, AL
800-292-6678 (Alabama only)
205-933-4050
205-939-9201
205-939-9202

Domestic Violence Coalition
334-793-5214

Division of Mental Illness and Substance Abuse Community Programs, Department of Mental Health
PO Box 3710
200 Interstate Park Drive
Montgomery, AL 36193
205-271-9250

Alaska (AK)
Alaska Council on Prevention of Alcohol and Drug Abuse, Inc.
Anchorage, AK
907-258-6021

Alaska Network on Domestic Violence and Sexual Assault
130 Seward Street, Suite 501
Juneau, AK 99801
907-586-3650
Hotlines:
800-487-1090 (Juneau)
800-478-8999 (Anchorage)

Alcoholism and Drug Abuse Office, Department of Health & Social Services
Pouch H-05-F
Juneau, AK 99811
907-586-6201

Anchorage Poison Center
Providence Hospital
Anchorage, AK
800-478-3193 (Alaska only)
907-261-3193

Domestic Violence Coalition
907-586-3650

Alberta (AB)
Alberta Alcohol and Drug Abuse Commission (AADAC) Counseling Services
Stephenson Building, 2nd Floor
1177 11 Avenue SW
Calgary, AB T2R 0G5, Canada
403-297-3071 (FAX 403-297-3036)

Alberta Alcohol and Drug Abuse
Commission (AADAC)
Downtown Treatment Centre
10010 102A Avenue
Edmonton, AB T5J 3G2, Canada
780–427–2736 (FAX 780–427–4180)

Alberta Alcohol and Drug Abuse
Commission (AADAC) Library
10909 Jasper Avenue, Room 200
Edmonton, AB T5J 3M9, Canada
780–427–7303

Alberta Alcohol and Drug Abuse
Commission (AADAC)
Northern Addictions Centre
11333 106 Street
Grande Prairie, AB T8V 6T7, Canada

Alberta Alcohol and Drug Abuse
Commission (AADAC)
Poundmaker's Lodge
Box 34007 Kingsway Mall Post Office
Edmonton, AB T5G 3G4, Canada
780–458–1884 (FAX 780–458–1883)

Alberta Alcohol and Drug Abuse
Commission (AADAC)
Poundmaker's Lodge
Outpatient and Adolescent
10010 102A Avenue, 2nd Floor
Edmonton, AB T5J 3G2, Canada
780–420–0356 (FAX 780–427–2736)

Alberta Alcohol and Drug Abuse
Commission (AADAC) Recovery Centre
10302 107 Street
Edmonton, AB T5J 1K2, Canada
780–427–4291 (FAX 780–422–2881)

Alberta Alcohol and Drug Abuse
Commission (AADAC) Training and
Professional Development
10909 Jasper Avenue, 7th Floor
Edmonton, AB T5J 3M9, Canada
780–427–7305

Calgary Poison and Drug Information
Services
Calgary, AB, Canada
800–332–1414 (Alberta only)
403–670–1414

Clinical Drug Consultants and Associates
c/o Substance Abusology Research Unit
Suite #500, University Extension Centre
8303 112 Street, University of Alberta
Edmonton, AB T6G 2T4, Canada
780–492–2856
or
Mulhurst Bay, AB T0C 2C0, Canada
780–389–4141
or
Maple Bay, BC V9L 5X6, Canada
250-701-0597

Substance Abusology Research Unit
Faculty of Nursing, University of Alberta
#500 University Extension Centre
8303 112 Street
Edmonton, AB T6G 2T4, Canada
780–492–2856 (FAX 780–492–9954)

American Samoa (AS)
Alcohol and Drug Program, Human Services
Program
LBJ Tropical Medical Center
Pago Pago, AS 05799
011–684–633–1212

Alcohol and Drug Program
Social Services Division
Government of American Samoa
Pago Pago, AS 96799
684–633–4485

Public Health Services
LBJ Tropical Medical Center
Pago Pago, AS 96799

Arizona (AZ)
Alcoholism and Drug Abuse
Office of Comm. Behav. Health
Department of Health Services
411 N 24th Street
Phoenix, AZ 85008
602–220–6455

Arizona Center Against Sexual Assault
2333 North Central, Suite 100
Phoenix, AZ 85004
602–254–6400 Extension 121

Arizona Department of Health Services
Office of Community Behavioral Health
1740 West Adams, Room 001
Phoenix, AZ 85007
602–255–1152

Appendix III: Directory

Arizona Poison and Drug Information
Center
University of Arizona
Arizona Health Sciences Center
Tucson, AZ
800–362–0101 (Arizona only)
602–626–6016

Arizona Prevention Resource Center
Arizona State University
Tempe, AZ
602–965–9666

Domestic Violence Coalition
602–279–2900
800–782–6400

Indian Health Service
Colorado River Service
Route 1, Box 12
Parker, AZ 85344
602–669–2137

Samaritan Regional Poison Center
Good Samaritan Medical Center
Phoenix, AZ
602–253–3334

Arkansas (AR)
Alcohol and Drug Abuse Prevention,
Bureau of
Freeway Medical Center
Little Rock, AR
501–280–4506

Arkansas Coalition Against Violence to
Women and Children
523 South Louisiana, Suite 230
Little Rock, AR 72201
800–269–4668 (in state)
501–399–9486

Arkansas Poison and Drug Information
Center
Little Rock, AR
800–482–8948 (MDs and hospitals, Arkansas only)
501–661–6161
501–666–5532 (MDs and hospitals)

Domestic Violence Coalition
501–663–1668

Office on Alcohol and Drug Abuse
Prevention
Donaghey Plaza North, Suite 400
PO Box 1437
Little Rock, AR 72203-1437
501–682–6650

British Columbia (BC)
BC Drug and Poison Information Centre
Vancouver, BC, Canada
604–682–5050

Clinical Drug and Psychological
Consultants
Maple Bay, BC V9L 5X6
250–701–0597 (FAX 250-701-0598)

Poison Control
Victoria, BC
800–567–8911 (BC only)
250–595–9211 (Victoria only)
250–682–5050 (lower mainland)

California (CA)
Adult Children of Alcoholics
Interim World Service Organization
PO Box 3216
2522 West Sepulveda Boulevard
Torrance, CA 90505
213–534–1815

Alcohol and Drug Programs, Department of
111 Capitol Mall, Suite 450
Sacramento, CA 95814
916–445–0834

Alcohol and Drug Programs, Department of
State of California
Sacramento, CA
916–327–8447

Alcohol Research Group
Epidemiology and Behavioral Medicine
Institute of Medical Research
San Francisco, CA
510–642–5208

Aspen Health Services
7711 Center Avenue, #300
Huntington Beach, CA 92647
800–283–8334

California Smokers Helpline
800–7-NOBUTTS (766–2887)

CoAnon Family Groups
PO Box 64742-66
Los Angeles, CA 90064
213–859–2206

Cocaine Anonymous (CA)
3740 Overland Avenue, Suite G
Los Angeles, CA 90034
213–559–5833
800–347–8998

California Alliance Against Domestic
Violence
415–457–2464

California Coalition Against Sexual Assault
Cal CASA c/o LACAAW
6043 Hollywood Boulevard, Suite 200
Los Angeles, CA 90028
213–462–1281

Domestic Violence Coalition
209–524–1888 (Central)
310–655–6098 (Southern)

Families Anonymous, Inc.
PO Box 548
Van Nuys, CA 91408
818–989–7841

Fresno Regional Poison Control Center
Fresno, CA
800–346–5922 (Fresno, Kern, Kings, Madera, Mariposa, Merced, and Tulare counties only)
209–445–1222

Health Promotion Resource Center
Stanford Center for Research in Disease Prevention
1000 Welch Road
Palo Alto, CA 94304-1885
415–723–0003

Los Angeles County Regional Poison
Control Center
Los Angeles, CA
800–777–6476 (Los Angeles, Santa Barbara, and Ventura counties only)
800–825–2722 (MDs and hospitals, California only)
213–484–5151
213–664–2121 (MDs and hospitals)

Marin Institute Resource Center for the Prevention of Alcohol and Other Drug Problems, The
San Rafael, CA
415–456–5692

Nar-Anon Family Groups
PO Box 2562
Palo Verdes Peninsula, CA 90274
213–547–5800

Narcotics Anonymous (NA)
PO Box 9999
Van Nuys, CA 91409
818–780–3951

National Asian Pacific American Families Against Substance Abuse, Inc.
Los Angeles, CA
213–617–8277

National Association for Children of Alcoholics, Inc. (NACOA)
31582 Coast Highway, Suite B
South Laguna, CA 92677
714–499–3889

National Association of Lesbian and Gay Alcoholism Professionals
1147 South Alvarado
Los Angeles, CA 90006
213–381–8524

San Diego Regional Poison Center
San Diego, CA
800–876–4766 (Imperial and San Diego counties only)
619–543–6000

San Francisco Bay Area Regional Poison Control Center
San Francisco, CA
800–523–2222 (Alameda, Contra Costa, Del Norte, Humboldt, Marin, Mendocino, Napa, San Francisco, San Mateo, and Sonoma counties only)
415–476–6600

San Francisco Women Against Rape
3543 18th Street
San Francisco, CA 94110
415–861–2024 (Office)
415–647–7273 (hotline)

Santa Clara Valley Medical Center
Regional Poison Control Center
San Jose, CA
800–662–9886 (Monterey, San Benito, San Luis Obispo, Santa Clara, and Santa Cruz counties only)
408–299–5112

Smokers Anonymous (SA) World Services
2118 Greenwich Street
San Francisco, CA 94123
415–922–8575

Substance Abuse Librarians and Information Specialists (SALIS)
Alcohol Research Group
1816 Scenic Avenue
Berkeley, CA 94702

UC Davis Medical Center Regional Poison
Control Center
Sacramento, CA
800–342–9293 (northern California only)
916–734–3692

UC Irvine Regional Poison Center
Orange, CA
800–544–4404 (Inyo, Mono, Orange,
Riverside, and San Bernardino counties
only)
714–634–5988

Colorado (CO)
Alcohol and Drug Abuse Division
Department of Health
4210 East 11th Avenue
Denver, CO 80220
303–331–8201

Colorado Coalition Against Sexual Assault
(CCASA)
PO Box 18663
Denver, CO 80218
303–861–7033

Colorado Department of Human Services
Denver, CO
303–692–2930

Domestic Violence Coalition
303–573–9018

Healthy Nations National Program Office
UCHSC University, North Pavilion
Denver, CO
303–372–3272

International Institute on Inhalant Abuse
Englewood, CO
303–788–1951

Rocky Mountain Poison and Drug Center
Denver, CO
800–332–3073 (Colorado only)
800–525–5042 (Montana only)
800–446–6179 (Las Vegas, Nevada only)
303–629–1123

Connecticut (CT)
Connecticut Alcohol and Drug Abuse
Commission
999 Asylum Avenue, 3rd Floor
Hartford, CT 06105
203–566–4145

Connecticut Clearinghouse
Plainville, CT
302–793–7971

Connecticut Coalition Against Domestic
Violence
203–524–5890

Connecticut Poison Control Center
Farmington, CT
800–343–2722 (Connecticut only)
203–679–3473 (administration)
203–679–4346 (TDD)

Connecticut Sexual Assault Crisis Services,
Inc.
110 Connecticut Boulevard
East Hartford, CT 06108
203–282–9881
860–522–4636 (Information Line)

International Lawyers in Alcoholics
Anonymous (ILAA)
1092 Elm Street, Suite 201
Rocky Hill, CT 06067
203–529–7474

Social Workers Helping Social Workers
Route 63
Goshen, CT 06756
203–489–3808

Delaware (DE)
Alcoholism, Drug Abuse and Mental Health,
Delaware Division of
1901 N DuPont Highway
Newcastle, DE 19720
302–421–6101

Domestic Violence Coalition
800–701–0456

Rape Crisis CONTACT
PO Box 9525
Wilmington, DE 19809
302–761–9800 (Office)
302–761–9100 (hotline)
302–761–9700 (TDD/TTY [New Castle
County])
800–262–9800 (Kent & Sussex Counties)

SOS
University of Delaware
209 Laurel Hall
Newark, DE 19716
302–831–8992 (Office)
302–831–2226 (hotline)
(serves University of Delaware, Newark)

District of Columbia (Washington, DC)
ACTION Drug Prevention Program
806 Connecticut Avenue, NW M513
Washington, DC 20525
202–634–9380

Alcohol and Drug Abuse Services
Administration
Office of Information, Prevention and
Education
Washington, DC
202-576-7315

Alcohol and Drug Problems Association of
North America
444 North Capitol Street, NW, Suite 706
Washington, DC 20001
202-737-4340

American Public Health Association (APHA)
Section on Alcohol and Drugs
1015 Fifteenth Street, NW
Washington, DC 20005
202-789-5600

American Society of Addiction Medicine
(ASAM)
5225 Wisconsin Avenue, NW, Suite 409
Washington, DC 20016
212-206-6770

Center for Education in Maternal and Child
Health
38th and R Streets, NW
Washington, DC 20057
202-625-8400

Coalition of Hispanic Health and Human
Services Organizations (COSSMHO)
1030 15th Street, NW, Suite 1053
Washington, DC 20005
202-371-2100

DC Rape Crisis Center
PO Box 34125
Washington, DC 20043
202-232-0789
202-333-7273 (hotline)

Domestic Violence Coalition
202-783-5332

Drug Policy Office
The White House
Washington, DC 20500
202-456-6554

Health Planning and Development
1660 L Street, NW
Washington, DC 20036
202-673-7481

Inter-American Drug Information System
OAS/CICAD
Washington, DC
202-458-3809

National Association of State Alcohol and
Drug Abuse Directors (NASADAD)
444 N Capitol Street, NW, Suite 642
Washington, DC 20001
202-783-6868

National Black Alcoholism Council (NBAC)
1629 K Street, NW, Suite 802
Washington, DC 20006
202-296-2696

National Capital Poison Center
Washington, DC
202-625-3333
202-784-4660 (TTY)

National Catholic Council on Alcoholism
1200 Varnum Street, NE
Washington, DC 20017-2796

National Center for Education in Maternal
and Child Health
3520 Prospect Street, NW, Suite 1
Washington, DC 20057
202-625-8410

National Coalition of Hispanic Health
Services Organization
Washington, DC
202-387-5000

National Health Information Clearinghouse
PO Box 1133
Washington, DC 20013-1133
703-522-2590 (Virginia)
800-336-4797

National Prevention Network
444 North Capitol Street, NW, Suite 642
Washington, DC 20001
202-783-6868

Resource Center on Substance Abuse
Prevention and Disability
1331 F Street, NW, Suite 800
Washington, DC 20004
202-783-2900

U.S. Congress
House Select Committee on Narcotics Abuse
and Control
H2-234 House Annex 2
Washington, DC 20515
202-226-3040

U.S. Department of Health and Human
Services
200 Independence Avenue, SW
Washington, DC 20201
202-245-6296

Women's Health Network
1325 G Street, NW
Washington, DC 20005
202-347-1140

Florida (FL)
Alcohol and Drug Abuse Association, Inc.
Tallahassee, FL
904-878-2196

Alcohol and Drug Abuse Program,
Department of Health and Rehabilitative Services
1317 Winewood Boulevard
Tallahassee, FL 32301
904-488-0900

Domestic Violence Coalition
904-668-6862

Florida Council of Sexual Abuse Services, Inc.
850 6th Avenue, North
Naples, FL 33940
941-649-1404
941-649-5660

Florida Poison Information Center at Tampa General Hospital
Tampa, FL
800-282-3171 (Florida only)
813-253-4444

Health Communications, Inc.
3201 SW 15th Street
Deerfield Beach, FL 33442

Recovered Alcoholic Clergy Association (RACA)
5615 Midnight Pass Road, Siesta Key
Sarasota, FL 54242

Georgia (GA)
Alcohol and Drug Services
878 Peachtree Street NE, Suite 318
Atlanta, GA 30309
404-894-6352

Center for Health Promotion and Education
Centers for Disease Control
1600 Clifton Road
Building 1 South, Room SSB249
Atlanta, GA 30333
404-320-3492

Domestic Violence Coalition
800-643-1212

Georgia Network to End Sexual Assault
c/o Houston Drug Action Council (HODAC)
2762 Watson Boulevard
Warner Robins, GA 31093
912-953-5674
800-338-6745 (in state)

Georgia Regional Poison Control Center
Atlanta, GA
800-282-5846 (Georgia only)
404-589-4400
404-525-3323 (TTY)

National Families in Action
2296 Henderson Mill Road, Suite 204
Atlanta, GA 30345
404-934-6364

Office on Smoking and Health
3005 Rhodes Building
Chamblee, GA 30341
404-488-5705

Substance Abuse Services
Georgia Prevention Resource Center
Atlanta, GA
404-657-2296

Guam (GU)
Mental Health and Substance Abuse, Department of
PO Box 8896
Tamuning, GU 96911
011-671-477-9704/5

Hawaii (HI)
Alcohol and Drug Abuse Division
Department of Health
PO Box 3378
Honolulu, HI 96801
808-548-4280

Coalition for Drug Free Hawaii
Prevention Resource Center
Honolulu, HI
808-593-2221

Domestic Violence Coalition
808-486-5072

Hawaii Poison Center
Honolulu, HI
800-362-3585 (outer islands of Hawaii only)
800-362-3586
808-941-4411

Hawaii State Coalition Against Sexual
Assault
1164 Bishop Street, Suite 124
Honolulu, HI 96813
(Mail is forwarded)
808–242–4335
808–973–8337

Idaho (ID)
Health and Welfare, Department of
450 West State Street
Boise, ID 83720
208–334–5935

Idaho Coalition Against Sexual and
Domestic Violence
200 North Fourth Street, Suite 10
Boise, ID 83702
208–384–0419

Idaho Poison Center
Boise, ID
800–632–8000 (Idaho only)
208–378–2707

Domestic Violence Coalition
208–384–0419

Idaho RADAR Network Center
Boise State University
Boise, ID
208–385–3471

Spokane Poison Center
Interstate Centers, ID
800–572–5842 (northern Idaho only)

Illinois (IL)
Alcoholism and Substance Abuse,
Department of
100 West Randolph Street, Suite 5-600
Chicago, IL 60601
312–814–3840

Alexian Brothers Medical Center
800 Biesterfield Road
Elk Grove, IL 60007
800–431–5005

American Medical Association (AMA)
Department of Mental Health, Division of
Substance Abuse
535 North Dearborn Street
Chicago, IL 60610
312–645–5000

Black Children of Alcoholic and Drug
Addicted Persons (BCOADAP)
c/o National Black Alcoholism Council
417 Dearborn Street
Chicago, IL 60605
312–663–5780

Central and Southern Illinois Regional
Poison Resource Center
Springfield, IL
800–252–2022 (Illinois only)
217–753–3330

Chicago & Northeastern Illinois Regional
Poison Control Center
Chicago, IL
800–942–5969 (northeastern Illinois only)
312–942–5969

Domestic Violence Coalition
800–241–8456

Illinois Coalition Against Sexual Assault
(ICASA)
123 S. 7th Street, Suite 500
Springfield, IL 62701-1302
217–753–4117

Lake County Council Against Sexual Assault
(LaCASA)
1 South Greenleaf Street
Gurnee, IL 60031
708–244–1187

National Association for Perinatal Addiction
Research and Education (NAPARE)
11 E Hubbard Street, Suite 200
Chicago, IL 60611
312–329–2512

National Nurses' Society on Addictions
(NNSA)
5700 Old Orchard Road, 1st Floor
Skokie, IL 60077-1024
708–966–5010 (FAX 708–966–9418)

Indiana (IN)
Addiction Services, Division of
Department of Mental Health
117 East Washington Street
Indianapolis, IN 46204
317–232–7816

Domestic Violence Coalition
800–332–7385

Indiana Coalition Against Sexual Assault
(INCASA)
2511 E. 46th Street, Suite N3
Indianapolis, IN 46205
317–568–4001
800–656–HOPE (4673)

Indiana Poison Center
Indianapolis, IN
800–382–9097 (Indiana only)
317–929–2323
317–929–2336 (TTY)

Indiana Prevention Resource Center
Indiana University
Bloomington, IN
812–855–1237

Iowa (IA)
Domestic Violence Coalition
800–942–0333

Iowa Coalition Against Domestic Violence
515–244–8028

Iowa Coalition Against Sexual Assault
(CASA)
1540 High Street, Suite 102
Lucas State Office Building
Des Moines, IA 50309
515–244–7424

Iowa Substance Abuse Information Center
Cedar Rapids Public Library
Cedar Rapids, IA
319–398–5133

Mercy Hospital Chemical Dependency
Services
800 Mercy Drive
Council Bluffs, IA 51503
712–328–5113
402–398–6866
800–432–9211 (Iowa)
800–831–4140 (Nebraska)

Poison Control Center
Iowa City, IA
800–272–6477 (Iowa only)
319–356–2922

Poison Control Center, The
Interstate Centers, IA
800–955–9119

Substance Abuse and Health Promotion,
Division of
Department of Public Health
Lucas State Office Building, 4th Floor
Des Moines, IA 50319
515–281–3641

Kansas (KS)
Alcohol and Drug Abuse Services
Department of Social and Rehabilitation
Services
300 SW Oakley Biddle Building
Topeka, KS 66606-1861
913–296–3925

Domestic Violence Coalition
913–232–9784

International Nurses Anonymous (INA)
1020 Sunset Drive
Lawrence, KS 66044
913–842–3893

Kansas Coalition Against Sexual and
Domestic Violence (KCSDV)
820 SE Quincy, Suite 416
Topeka, KS 66612
913–232–9784

Mid-America Poison Control Center
University of Kansas Medical Center
Kansas City, KS
800–332–6633 (Kansas only)
913–588–6633

Parkview Hospital of Topeka
3707 SW 6th Avenue
Topeka, KS 66606
913–235–3000

St. Joseph Medical Center
3600 East Harry
Wichita, KS 67218
316–689–4850

Kentucky (KY)
Domestic Violence Coalition
502–875–4132

Drug Information Services for Kentucky
(DISK)
Division of Substance Abuse
Frankfort, KY
502–564–2880

Kentucky Regional Poison Center of Kosair
Children's Hospital
Interstate Centers, IN
502–589–8222

Knoxville Poison Control Center
Interstate Centers, KY
615–544–9400 (southern Kentucky only)

Pathways, Inc.
Rape Crisis Program
201 22nd Street
Ashland, KY 41105-0790
606–324–1141

Substance Abuse, Division of
Department for Mental Health and Mental Retardation Services
275 East Main Street
Frankfort, KY 40621
502–564–2800

Louisiana (LA)
Alcohol and Drug Abuse, Division of
Office of Human Services
PO Box 3868
1201 Capitol Access Road
Baton Rouge, LA 70821-3868
504–342–9354
504–342–9352

Domestic Violence Coalition
800–837–5400

Louisiana Foundation Against Sexual Assault (LaFASA)
PO Box 1450
Independence, LA 70443
504–878–3849

Prevention and Recovery from Alcohol and Drug Abuse, Office of
2744-B Woodale Boulevard
Baton Rouge, LA 70892
504–922–0725

Maine (ME)
Affiliated Chemical Dependency Services
489 State Street
Bangor, ME 04401
207–945–7267

Alcoholism and Drug Abuse Prevention, Office of
Bureau of Rehabilitation
State House Station 11
Augusta, ME 04333
207–289–2781

Domestic Violence Coalition
207–941–1194

Maine Coalition Against Sexual Assault
PO Box 5326
Augusta, ME 04332
207–784–5272
207–759–9985

Maine Poison Control Center at Maine Medical Center
Portland, ME
800–442–6305 (Maine only)
207–871–2381 (Emergency Room)

Substance Abuse Information Resource Center, Office of
Augusta, ME
207–624–6528

Manitoba (MB)
Provincial Poison Information Centre
Winnipeg, MB, Canada
204–787–2591

Maryland (MD)
Alcohol and Drug Abuse Administration
Department of Health and Mental Hygiene
Baltimore, MD
410–225–6914

Alcohol and Drug Abuse Administration
Maryland State
201 West Preston Street
Baltimore, MD 21201
301–225–6925

Alcohol, Drug Abuse, and Mental Health Administration
5600 Fishers Lane, Room 12-105
Rockville, MD 20857
301–443–4797

American Academy of Psychiatrists in Alcoholism and Addictions (AAPAA)
PO Box 376
Greenbelt, MD 20768
301–220–0951

American College Health Association (ACHA)
Task Force on Alcohol and Other Drugs
1300 Piccard Drive, Suite 200
Rockville, MD 20850
301–963–1100

CDC's National AIDS Information Clearinghouse
Rockville, MD
800–458–5231

CDC's Sexually Transmitted Diseases
Hotline
Rockville, MD
800–227–8922

Domestic Violence Coalition
800–634–3577

Drug and Alcohol Nursing Association, Inc.
(DANA)
113 West Franklin Street
Baltimore, MD 21201
301–752–3318 (FAX 301–752–8295)

Drugs and Crime Data Center and
Clearinghouse
Rockville, MD
800–666–3332

Maryland Coalition Against Sexual Assault
(MCASA)
c/o Howard County Sexual Assault Center
Suite G-118, 10015 Old Columbia Road
Columbia, MD 21046
410–290–6432

Maryland Poison Center
Baltimore, MD
800–492–2414 (Maryland only)
410–528–7701

National Asian Pacific American Families
Against Drug Abuse
6303 Friendship Court
Bethesda, MD 20817
301–530–0945

National Association for Children of
Alcoholics
Rockville, MD
301–468–0985

National Association of Social Workers
(NASW)
7981 Eastern Avenue
Silver Spring, MD 20910
301–565–0333

National Clearinghouse for Alcohol and
Drug Information (NCADI)
PO Box 2345
Rockville, MD 20852
301–468–2600

National Clearinghouse for Family Planning
Information
PO Box 2225
Rockville, MD 20852
301–251–5153

National Institute on Alcohol Abuse and
Alcoholism (NIAAA)
5600 Fishers Lane, Room 14C-17
Rockville, MD 20857
301–443–3885

National Institute on Drug Abuse (NIDA)
5600 Fishers Lane, Room 10-04
Rockville, MD 20857
301–443–4577
800–662–HELP

Office for Substance Abuse Prevention
(OSAP)
5600 Fishers Lane, Room 9A54
Rockville, MD 20857
301–443–0365

Residents Initiatives Drug Information and
Strategy Clearinghouse
Rockville, MD
301–251–5546

Massachusetts (MA)
American Academy of Health Care
Providers in the Addictive Disorders
260 Beacon Street
Somerville, MA 02143
617–661–6248

Domestic Violence Coalition
617–248–0922

Governor's Alliance Against Drugs
John W. McCormack State Office Building
One Ashburton Place, Room 611
Boston, MA 02108
617–727–0786

Join Together—A National Resource for
Communities Fighting Substance Abuse
Boston, MA
617–437–1500

Massachusetts Coalition Against Sexual
Assault
1 Salem Square
Worcester, MA 01608
508–754–1019

Massachusetts Poison Control System
Boston, MA
800–682–9211 (Massachusetts only)
617–232–2120

Prevention Support Services
The Medical Foundation
Boston, MA
617–451–0049

Substance Abuse Services, Division of
150 Tremont Street
Boston, MA 02111
617-727-8614

Michigan (MI)
Blodgett Regional Poison Center
Grand Rapids, MI
800-632-2727 (517, 616, and 906 area codes only)
800-356-3232 (TTY)
616-774-2963

Domestic Violence Coalition
517-484-2924

Poison Control Center
Children's Hospital of Michigan
Detroit, MI
313-745-5711

Poison Information Center of Northwest Ohio
Interstate Centers, MI
800-589-3897 (southeastern Michigan only)

Psychologists Helping Psychologists (PHP)
23439 Michigan Avenue
Dearborn, MI 48124
313-565-3821

Substance Abuse and Traffic Safety
Michigan Information Center
Lansing, MI
517-482-9902

Substance Abuse Services, Office of
Department of Public Health
PO Box 30206
2150 Apollo Drive
Lansing, MI 48909
517-335-8809

Substance Abuse Services, Office of
Public Information Office
3500 N. Logan Street, PO Box 30035
Lansing, MI 48909
519-373-8345

Minnesota (MN)
Chemical Dependency Program Division
Department of Human Services
444 Lafayette Road
St. Paul, MN 55155-3823
612-296-4610

Community Interventions
529 S 7th Street, #907
Minneapolis, MN 55415

CompCare Publications
PO Box 27777, 2415 Annapolis Lane
Minneapolis, MN 55441

Domestic Violence Coalition
800-646-0994

Drug Abuse Program
State Department of Education
Learner Support Systems
994 Capitol Square Building
St. Paul, MN 55101
612-296-3925

Halfway House Alcoholism Programs of N. America, Association of (AHHAP)
786 E. 7th Street
St. Paul, MN 55106

Hazelden Center for Youth & Families
11505 36th Avenue North
Plymouth, MN 55441
619-559-2022

Hazelden Foundation
Box 11
Center City, MN 55012
800-822-0800 (training and education)
800-328-9000 (educational materials)

Hennepin Regional Poison Center
Minneapolis, MN
612-347-3141

Institute on Black Chemical Abuse (IBCA)
2614 Nicollet Avenue
Minneapolis, MN 55408
612-871-7878

International Doctors in Alcoholics Anonymous (IDAA)
7250 France Avenue South, Suite 400C
Minneapolis, MN 55435
612-835-4421

Johnson Institute
7151 Metro Boulevard
Minneapolis, MN 55435
800-231-5165
800-247-0484
800-447-6660 (in Canada)

Minnesota Coalition Against Sexual Assault (MCASA)
2344 Nicollet Avenue South, #170A
Minneapolis, MN 55404-3342
612-872-7734
800-964-8847 (in state)

Minnesota Regional Poison Center
St. Paul, MN
800-222-1222 (Minnesota only)
612-221-2113

Prevention Resource Center Minnesota
St. Paul, MN
612-224-5121

Mississippi (MS)
Alcoholism and Drug Abuse, Division of
Mississippi Department of Mental Health
Robert E. Lee State Office Building
11th Floor
Jackson, MS 39201
601-359-1288

Domestic Violence Coalition
601-981-9196

Health Related Services
Mississippi Department of Education
550 High Street
Jackson, MS 39205
601-359-2459

Mississippi Coalition Against Sexual Assault
Mississippi State Department of Health
PO Box 1700
Jackson, MS 39215-1700
601-960-7470

Mississippi Regional Poison Control Center
Jackson, MS
601-354-7660

Missouri (MO)
Alcohol and Drug Abuse, Division of
Department of Mental Health
PO Box 687
1915 South Ridge Drive
Jefferson City, MO 65102
314-751-4942

American Nurses' Association (ANA)
2420 Pershing Road
Kansas City, MO 64108
816-474-5720
(FAX 816-471-4903)

Arthur Center/Audrain Medical Center
100 Nifong, Building 5, Suite 120
Columbia, MO 65203-5661
314-875-7995 (Local)
314-581-1785 (Mexico)
800-530-5465 (USA Statewide)

Domestic Violence Coalition
314-634-4161

Metropolitan Organization to Counter
Sexual Assault (MOCSA)
3217 Broadway, Suite 500
Kansas City, MO 64111
816-931-4527
816-531-0233 (hotline)
816-561-1222 (Survivor)

Poison Control Center, The
Interstate Centers, MO
800-955-9119

Society of Teachers of Family Medicine
(STFM)
PO Box 8729
Kansas City, MO 64114
800-274-2237

TARGET
National Federation TARGET Program
Kansas City, MO
816-464-5400

Montana (MT)
Alcohol and Drug Abuse Division
Department of Institutions
Helena, MT 59601
406-444-2827

Billings Rape Task Force
1245 N 29th Street
Billings, MT 59101
406-245-6721 (Office)
(serves Eastern Montana)

Chemical Dependency Bureau
Department of Institutions
Helena, MT
406-444-2878

Domestic Violence Coalition
406-256-6334

Rocky Mountain Poison and Drug Center
Interstate Centers, MT
800-525-5842

Spokane Poison Center
Interstate Centers, MT
800-572-5842 (western Montana only)

YWCA
1130 W Broadway
Missoula, MT 59802
406-543-6691 (Office)
406-542-1994 (hotline)
(serves Missoula, Granite Lake, Sanders, and Revalli)

Nebraska (NE)
Alcoholism and Drug Abuse Council of
Nebraska
Lincoln, NE
402–474–1992

Alcoholism and Drug Abuse, Division of
Department of Public Institutions
PO Box 94728
Lincoln, NE 68509
402–471–2851 Extension 5583

Nebraska Domestic Violence and Sexual
Assault Coalition
315 S. 9th Street, Suite 18
Lincoln, NE 68508-2252
402–476–6256
402–475–7273 (hotline)
800–876–6238 (hotline)
(Physicians may call to reach the sexual
assault program in their local area)

Poison Center, The
Omaha, NE
800–955–9119 (Nebraska, Iowa, Missouri,
South Dakota, and Wyoming)
402–390–5555

Nevada (NV)
Alcohol and Drug Abuse Bureau
Department of Human Resources
505 East King Street
Carson City, NV 89710
702–885–4790
702–687–6239

Crisis Call Center
PO Box 8016
Reno, NV 89507
702–323–4533
702–323–6111 (hotline)
800–992–5757 (in state)

Domestic Violence Coalition
800–500–1556

Rocky Mountain Poison and Drug Center
Interstate Centers, NV
800–446–6179 (Las Vegas only)

New Brunswick (NB)
Bathurst Poison Control
Bathurst, NB, Canada
506–546–4666

Moncton Poison Control
Moncton, NB, Canada
506–857–5555

Saint John Poison Control
Saint John, NB, Canada
506–648–6222

Newfoundland (NF)
Provincial Poison Control Centre
St. John's, NF, Canada
709–722–1110

St. Anthony Poison Control
St. Anthony, NF, Canada
709–454–3333 Extension 149

New Hampshire (NH)
Alcohol and Drug Abuse Prevention, Office
of
Health and Welfare Building
Hazen Drive
Concord, NH 03301
603–271–4627
603–271–6100

National Certification Reciprocity
Consortium/Alcohol and Other Drug Abuse
(NCRC)
PO Box 157
Atkinson, NH 03811
603–898–1516

New Hampshire Coalition Against Domestic
and Sexual Violence
PO Box 353
Concord, NH 03302-0353
603–224–8893
800–852–3388 (hotline)
800–735–2964 (TDD/VOICE)

New Hampshire Poison Information Center
Lebanon, NH
800–562–8236 (New Hampshire only)
603–650–5000

Project Cork Institute
Dartmouth Medical School
Hanover, NH
603–646–3935

New Jersey (NJ)
Alcoholism and Drug Abuse, Division of
New Jersey State Department of Health
Trenton, NJ
609–984–6961

Center of Alcohol Studies
Rutgers, the State University of New Jersey
Smithers Hall, Busch Campus
Pascataway, NJ 08854
201–932–2190

Department of Health
CN 360
Trenton, NJ 08625
609–292–3147

New Jersey Coalition Against Sexual Assault (NJCASA)
5 Elm Row, Suite 306
New Brunswick, NJ 08901-2103
908–418–1354

New Jersey Poison Information and Education System
Newark, NJ
800–962–1253 (New Jersey only)
201–923–0764
201–926–8008 (TTY)

Rutgers Center of Alcohol Studies
Piscataway, NJ
908–932–4442

New Mexico (NM)
Department of Health/BHSD-DSA
Santa Fe, NM
505–827–2601

New Mexico Coalition of Sexual Assault Programs, Inc.
4004 Carlisle, NE, Suite P
Albuquerque, NM 87107
505–883–8020

New Mexico Poison and Drug Information Center
Albuquerque, NM
800–432–6866 (New Mexico only)
505–843–2551

Substance Abuse Bureau
190 St. Francis Drive, Room 3350 North
Sante Fe, NM 87503
505–827–2589

New York (NY)
Al-Anon Family Groups
PO Box 862 Midtown Station
New York, NY 10018
212–302–7240

Alcoholics Anonymous (AA)
15 East 26th Street, Room 1810
New York, NY 10010
212–683–3900

Alcoholics Anonymous (AA)
General Services Office
Box 459 Grand Central Station
New York, NY 10163
212–686–1100

Alcoholism and Alcohol Abuse, Division of
194 Washington Avenue
Albany, NY 12210
518–474–5417

Alcoholism and Substance Abuse Services, New York State Office of
Albany, NY
518–473–3460

American Society of Addiction Medicine (ASAM)
12 West 21st Street
New York, NY 10010
202–244–8948

Central New York Poison Control Center
Syracuse, NY
800–252–5655 (New York only)
315–476–4766

Children of Alcoholics Foundation, Inc.
200 Park Avenue, 31st Floor
New York, NY 10166
212–351–2680

Domestic Violence Coalition
800–942–6906 (English)
800–942–6908 (Spanish)

Hudson Valley Regional Poison Center
Nyack, NY
800–336–6997 (New York only)
914–353–1000

Life Line/Finger Lakes Regional Poison Control Center
Rochester, NY
800–333–0542 (Ontario and Wayne counties only)
716–275–5151
716–275–2700 (TTY)

Long Island Regional Poison Control Center
East Meadow, NY
516–542–2323/2324/2325
516–542–3813
516–747–3323 (TTY)

National Council on Alcoholism and Drug Dependence (NCADD)
12 West 21st Street
New York, NY 10010
212–206–6770/800–NCA–CALL
212–777–8923

National Self-Help Clearinghouse
25 West 43rd Street
New York, NY 10036
212–642–2944

New York City Poison Control Center
New York, NY
212-340-4494
212-764-7667

New York State Coalition Against Sexual
Assault (NYSCASA)
The Women's Building
79 Central Avenue
Albany, NY 12206
518-434-1580

Project Connect
Lesbian and Gay Community Services
Center
New York, NY
212-620-7310

Secular Organizations for Sobriety (SOS)
PO Box 5
Buffalo, NY 14215
716-834-2922

Substance Abuse Services, Division of
Executive Park S, Box 8200
Albany, NY 12203
518-457-7629

North Carolina (NC)
Alcohol and Drug Abuse Section, Division of
Mental Health and Mental Retardation
Services
325 North Salisbury Street
Raleigh, NC 27611
919-733-4670

Alcohol and Drug Resource Center, North
Carolina
Durham, NC
919-493-2881

Domestic Violence Coalition
919-956-9124

Duke University Regional Poison Control
Center
Durham, NC
800-672-1697 (North Carolina only)
919-684-8111

Mercy Hospital Poison Control Center
Charlotte, NC
704-379-5827

North Carolina Coalition Against Sexual
Assault (NCCASA)
582B Farringdom Street
Lumberton, NC 28358
910-739-6278

Triad Poison Center
Greensboro, NC
800-722-2222 (Alamance, Forsyth, Guilford,
Rockingham, and Randolph counties only)
919-379-4105

Western NC Poison Control Center
Asheville, NC
800-542-4225 (North Carolina only)
704-255-4490

North Dakota (ND)
Alcoholism and Drug Abuse, Division of
Department of Human Services
State Capitol/Judicial Wing
Bismarck, ND 58505
701-224-2769

North Dakota Council on Abused Women's
Service
Coalition Against Sexual Assault in North
Dakota
418 E. Rosser, #320
Bismarck, ND 58501
701-293-7273
701-251-2300
701-255-6240 (Office)
800-472-2911 (hotline [in state])

Prevention Resource Center, North Dakota
Bismarck, ND
701-224-3603

Nova Scotia (NS)
Poison Control Center
Halifax, NS
902-428-8161

Ohio (OH)
Akron Regional Poison Control Center
Akron, OH
800-362-9922 (Ohio only)
216-379-8562
216-379-8446 (TTY)

Alcohol Abuse and Recovery Bureau
Ohio Department of Health
170 North High Street, 3rd Floor
Columbus, OH 43266-0586
614-466-3445

Alcohol and Drug Addiction Services, Ohio
Department of
Columbus, OH
614-466-6379

Central Ohio Poison Center
Columbus, OH
800-682-7625 (Ohio only)
614-228-1323
614-228-2272 (TTY)

Domestic Violence Coalition
800-934-9840

Drug Abuse Bureau
Ohio Department of Health
170 North High Street, 3rd Floor
Columbus, OH 43266-0586
614-466-7893

Mahoning Valley Poison Center
St. Elizabeth Hospital Medical Center
Youngstown, OH
800-426-2348 (Ohio, Mercer, and
Lawrence counties in Pennsylvania only)
216-746-2222
216-746-5510 (TTY)

Northwest Regional Poison Center
Interstate Centers, OH
800-822-3232 (northeastern Ohio only)

Ohio Coalition on Sexual Assault (OCOSA)
4041 N. High Street, Suite 408
Columbus, OH 43214
614-268-3322

Poison Information Center of Northwest
Ohio
Medical College of Ohio Hospital
Toledo, OH
800-589-3897 (northwestern Ohio and
southeastern Michigan only)
419-381-3897

Quest International
PO Box 566
537 Jones Road
Grandville, OH 43023
614-587-2800

Regional Poison Control System and Drug
& Poison Information Center
Cincinnati, OH
800-872-5111 (Ohio only)
513-558-5111

Saint Luke's Medical Center
11311 Shaker Boulevard
Cleveland, OH 44104
216-368-7970

Oklahoma (OK)
Domestic Violence Coalition
800-522-9054

Mental Health and Substance Abuse
Services, Oklahoma State Department of
PO Box 53277 Capitol Station
Oklahoma City, OK 73152
405-271-7474
405-271-8755

Oklahoma Coalition Against Domestic
Violence and Sexual Assault
220 Classen Boulevard, Suite 1300
Oklahoma City, OK 73106
405-557-1210

Tulsa Regional Medical Center/Behavioral
Health Services
744 W 9th Street
Tulsa, OK 94127
918-599-5880

Ontario (ON)
Addiction Research Foundation (ARF)
33 Russell Street
Toronto, ON M5S 2S1, Canada
416-595-6059
416-595-6072
416-595-6000
800-463-6273

Canadian Association for Children of
Alcoholics
PO Box 159, Station II
Toronto, ON M4C 5H9, Canada
416-601-0091

Canadian Centre on Substance Abuse
Ottawa, ON
613-235-4048

Drug and Alcohol Registry of Treatment
(DART)
800-565-8603

London Poison Control
London, ON, Canada
519-667-6565

Motherisk
Hospital for Sick Children
Toronto, ON M5G 1X8, Canada
416-813-6780

Ontario AIDS Hotline
800-668-2437

Ontario Association of Interval and
Transition Houses (OAITH)
229 College Street
Toronto, ON M5T 1R4, Canada
416-977-6619

Oregon (OR)
Alcohol and Drug Abuse Programs, Office of
Oregon Prevention Resource Center
1178 Chemeketa Street NE, Suite 102
Salem, OR 97310
503-378-2163
503-945-5763

National Consortium of Chemical
Dependency Nurses Inc. (NCCDN)
975 Oak, Suite 675
Eugene, OR 97401
800–87–NCCDN
503–485–4421

Oregon Coalition Against Domestic and
Sexual Violence (OCADSV)
520 NW Davis Street, #310
Portland, OR 97204
503–223–7411
800–OCADSV-2 (hotline [in state])

Oregon Poison Center
Portland, OR
800–452–7165 (Oregon only)
503–494–8968
Prevention Resource Center Oregon

Spokane Poison Center
Interstate Centers, OR
800–572–5842 (northwestern Oregon only)

Pennsylvania (PA)
Central Pennsylvania Poison Center
Hershey, PA
800–521–6110
717–531–6111
717–531–6039

Delaware Valley Mental Health Foundation
1833 Butler Avenue
Doylestown, PA 18901
215–345–0444

Domestic Violence Coalition
800–932–4631

Drug and Alcohol Programs
PA Department of Health
PO Box 90
Harrisburg, PA 17108
717–787–9857

Lehigh Valley Poison Center
Allentown, PA
215–433–2311

Mahoning Valley Poison Center
Interstate Centers, PA
800–426–2348 (Lawrence and Mercer
counties only)

Northwest Regional Poison Center
Erie, PA
800–822–3232 (northwestern Pennsylvania,
northeastern Ohio, and southwestern New
York)
814–452–3232

PENNSAIC
Erie, PA
814–459–0245

Pennsylvania Coalition Against Rape
(PCAR)
910 N. Second Street
Harrisburg, PA 17102-3119
717–232–6745
800–692–7445 (hotline [in state])

Pittsburgh Poison Center
Pittsburgh, PA
412–681–6669

Poison Control Center, The
Philadelphia, PA
215–386–2100
215–590–2003

Susquehanna Poison Center
Danville, PA
800–352–7001 (Pennsylvania only)

The Chemical People/WQED
4802 Fifth Avenue
Pittsburgh, PA 15213
412–622–1491

Women for Sobriety
PO Box 618
Quakertown, PA 18951
215–536–8026

Puerto Rico (PR)
Addiction Services, Department of
Barbosa Avenue, Avenue 414
Rio Piedras, PR 00928
809–763–3133

Anti-Addiction Services, Department of
Box 21414 Rio Piedras Station
Rio Piedras, PR 00928-1414
809–764–3795

Domestic Violence Coalition
809–722–2907

Health and Social Welfare La Fotraleza
Advisor to the Governor
San Juan, PR
809–722–1917

Salud Mental y Contra la Addicion,
Administracion de Servicios de
San Juan, PR
809–767–5990

Quebec (PQ)
Poison Control Line
Centre de Toxicologie de Québec
Québec City, PQ, Canada
800-463-5060
418-656-8090

Rhode Island (RI)
Brown University Center for Alcohol and Addiction Studies
Box G, Brown University, Butler Hospital
Providence, RI 02912
401-863-3173

Domestic Violence Coalition
800-494-8100

Rhode Island Poison Center
Rhode Island Hospital
Providence, RI
401-277-5727

Rhode Island Rape Crisis Center
300 Richmond Street, Suite 205
Providence, RI 02903
401-421-4100

Substance Abuse, Division of
Department of Mental Health, Retardation, and Hospitals
PO Box 20363
Cranston, RI 02920
401-464-2091

Substance Abuse, Rhode Island Department of
Cranston, RI
401-464-2380

Saskatchewan (SK)
Poison Control Centre
Regina, SK
306-359-4545

Poison Control Centre
Saskatoon, SK
306-653-1010
306-966-1010
306-966-1012

South Carolina (SC)
Alcohol and Drug Abuse, South Carolina Commission on
3700 Forest Drive
Columbia, SC 29204
803-734-9520

Domestic Violence Coalition
800-260-9293

Drug Store Information Clearinghouse
South Carolina Commission on Alcohol and Drug Abuse
Columbia, SC
803-734-9559

South Carolina Coalition Against Domestic Violence & Sexual Assault
PO Box 7776
Columbia, SC 29210
803-254-3699

South Dakota (SD)
Alcohol and Drug Abuse, South Dakota Division of
Joe Foss Building
523 East Capitol
Pierre, SD 57501
605-773-3123

Domestic Violence Coalition
605-225-5122

Rapid City Regional Hospital Addiction Recovery Center
915 Mountain View Road
Rapid City, SD 57702
605-399-7200

South Dakota Coalition Against Domestic Violence and Sexual Assault
PO Box 141
Pierre, SD 57501
605-945-0869

Tennessee (TN)
Alcohol and Drug Abuse Services
Department of Mental Health and Mental Retardation
706 Church Street, 4th Floor
Nashville, TN 37219
615-741-1921

Alcohol and Drug Association
Tennessee Statewide Clearinghouse
Nashville, TN
615-244-7066

Domestic Violence Coalition
800-356-6767

Knoxville Poison Control Center
Knoxville, TN
615-544-9400 (eastern Tennessee and southern Kentucky only)

Middle Tennessee Regional Poison/Clinical Toxicology Center
Nashville, TN
800–288–9999 (mid-Tennessee only)
615–322–6435 (Nashville and adjacent counties only)

Southern Poison Center, Inc.
Memphis, TN
901–528–6048
901–522–5985 (administration)

Tennessee Coalition Against Sexual Assault
56 Lindsley Avenue
Nashville, TN 37210
615–259–9055

Texas (TX)
Alcohol and Drug Abuse Resource Center, Texas Commission on
Austin, TX
512–867–8821

Alcohol and Drug Abuse, Texas Commission on
1705 Guadalupe Street
Austin, TX 78701
512–463–5510

Anesthetists in Recovery (AIR)
5626 Preston Oaks Road, Unit 40D
Dallas, TX 75240
214–960–7296
913–383–2878

Domestic Violence Coalition
800–252–5400

El Paso Poison Control Center
El Paso, TX
915–533–1244 (southwestern Texas and southern New Mexico only)

Mothers Against Drunk Driving
511 East John Carpenter Freeway, Suite 700
Irving, TX 75062
214–744–6233

North Texas Poison Center
Dallas, TX
800–441–0040 (Texas only)
214–590–5000

Texas Association Against Sexual Assault
TAASA at the Montgomery County Women's Center
PO Box 8666
Woodlands, TX 77387
713–367–8003 Extension 229
512–440–7273
512–445–1049 (Voice Mail)

Texas State Poison Control Center
Galveston, TX
800–392–8548 (MDs and ambulance personnel, Texas only)
409–772–1420
713–654–1701 (Houston only)
409–765–1420
409–539–7700

U.S./Mexico Border Health Association
El Paso, TX
915–581–6645

Utah (UT)
Domestic Violence Coalition
801–538–4100

Intermountain Regional Poison Control Center
Salt Lake City, UT
800–456–7707 (Utah only)
801–581–2151

Salt Lake City Rape Crisis Center
2035 S 1300 E
Salt Lake City, UT 84105
801–467–7279 (Office)
801–463–7273

Substance Abuse, Utah State Division of
Department of Social Services
PO Box 45500
120 North 200 West, 4th Floor
Salt Lake City, UT 84145-0500
801–538–3939

Utah Alcoholism Foundation
2880 S Main Street, Suite 210
Salt Lake City, UT 84115

YWCA
322 E 300 S
Salt Lake City, UT 84111
801–355–2804

Vermont (VT)
Alcohol and Drug Abuse Programs, Office of
103 South Maine Street
Waterbury, VT 05676
802–241–2170/2175
802–241–2178

FAS/FAE Prevention Program
Vermont Department of Health
1193 North Avenue, PO Box 70
Burlington, VT 05401
802–863–7330

Vermont Network Against Domestic
Violence & Sexual Assault
PO Box 405
Montpelier, VT 05601
800–489–7273
802–233–1302 (Office)

Vermont Poison Center
Burlington, VT
802–658–3456 (Vermont and bordering New
York counties only)
802–656–2721 (education programs)

Virgin Islands (VI)
Alcoholism and Drug Dependency
Department of Health
Division of Mental Health
PO Box 520
Christiansted,
St. Croix, VI 00820
809–773–5150

Domestic Violence Coalition
800–838–8238

Mental Health, Alcoholism, and Drug
Dependency Services, Division of
PO Box 520
St. Croix, VI 00820
809–773–1992

Mental Health Prevention Unit, Division of
Richmond,
St. Croix, VI
809–774–7700

Virginia (VA)
Association of Labor, Management
Administrators and Consultants on
Alcoholism (ALMACA)
1800 North Kent Street, Suite 907
Arlington, VA 22209
703–522–6272

Blue Ridge Poison Center
Charlottesville, VA
800–451–1428 (Virginia, West Virginia, North
Carolina, District of Columbia, Tennessee,
and Maryland)
804–924–5543

Center for Health Promotion
George Mason University
Fairfax, VA
703–993–3697

CSAP's National Resource for the
Prevention of Alcohol, Tobacco, Other Drug
Abuse, and Mental Illness in Women
Alexandria, VA
1–800–354–8824

Employee Assistance Professionals
Association (EAPA)
4601 North Fairfax Drive, Suite 1001
Arlington, VA 22203
703–522–6272

Mental Health, Virginia Department of
Office of Prevention
Richmond, VA
804–371–7564

National Association of Alcoholism and
Drug Abuse Counselors (NAADC)
3717 Columbia Pike, Suite 300
Arlington, VA 22204
703–920–4644

National Clearinghouse for Primary Care
Information
8201 Greensboro Drive, Suite 600
McLean, VA 22102
703–821–8955

Substance Abuse Services, Office of
Department of Mental Health
Mental Retardation and Substance Services
PO Box 1797, 109 Governor Street
Richmond, VA 23214
804–786–3906

Virginia Poison Center
Richmond, VA
800–552–6337 (Virginia only)
804–786–9123

Virginians Aligned Against Sexual Assault
(VAASA)
508 Dale Avenue, Suite B
Charlottesville, VA 22903-4547
804–979–9002

Washington (WA)
Alcohol and Drug Abuse Institute Library
University of Washington
Seattle, WA
206–543–0937

Alcoholism and Substance Abuse, Bureau of
Washington Department of Social and
Health Services
Mail Stop OB 44W
Olympia, WA 98504
206–753–5866

Domestic Violence Coalition
800–562–6025

Mary Bridge Poison Center
Tacoma, WA
800–542–6319 (Washington only)
206–594–1414

National Association for Native American Children of Alcoholics (NANACoA)
PO Box 18736
Seattle, WA 98114
206-322-5601

Seattle Poison Center
Seattle, WA
800-732-6985 (Washington only)
206-526-2121
206-526-2223 (TTY)

Spokane Poison Center
Spokane, WA
800-572-5842 (eastern Washington, northern Idaho, western Montana, and northwestern Oregon only)
509-747-1077

St. Peter Chemical Dependency Center
4800 College Street
Lacey, WA 98503
800-332-0465

Substance Abuse Coalition Washington State
Bellevue, WA
206-637-7011

Washington Coalition of Sexual Assault Programs (WCSAP)
110 East Fifth, Suite 214
Olympia, WA 98501
360-754-7583

West Virginia (WV)
Alcohol and Drug Abuse, Division of
State Capitol
1800 Washington Street East, Room 451
Charleston, WV 25305
304-348-2276

Domestic Violence Coalition
304-765-2250

RADAR Network Clearinghouse
West Virginia Library Commission
Charleston, WV
304-558-2044

West Virginia Foundation for Rape Information & Services
112 Braddock Street
Fairmont, WV 26554
304-366-8126

West Virginia Poison Center
Charleston, WV
800-642-3625 (West Virginia only)
304-348-4211

Wisconsin (WI)
Alcohol and Other Drug Abuse, Office of
PO Box 7851
1 West Wilson Street
Madison, WI 53707
608-266-3442

Domestic Violence Coalition
608-255-0539

Libertas Treatment Center
1701 Dousman Street
Green Bay, WI 54303
414-498-8600

National Rural Institute on Alcohol and Drug Abuse
Eau Claire, WI
715-836-2031

University of Wisconsin Hospital Regional Poison Control Center
Madison, WI
608-262-3702

Wisconsin Clearinghouse
Madison, WI
608-263-2797

Wisconsin Coalition Against Sexual Assault (WCASA)
1400 East Washington Avenue, Suite 148
Madison, WI 53703
608-257-1516

Wyoming (WY)
Alcohol and Drug Abuse Programs
Hathaway Building
Cheyenne, WY 82002
307-777-7115 Extension 7118

CARE Program Wyoming
University of Wyoming
Laramie, WY
307-766-4119

Domestic Violence & Sexual Assault Program
454 Hathaway Building
Cheyenne, WY 82002-0480
307-777-6086

Domestic Violence Coalition
800-990-3877

Poison Control Center, The Interstate Centers, WY
800-955-9119 (Wyoming and Nebraska)
402-390-5555

PART III. Directory of Major North American AIDS Hotlines Listed in Alphabetical Order by State or Province

CDC National AIDS Hotline
800–342–AIDS (2437) [English]
800–344–SIDA (7432) [Spanish]
800–283–2437 [Native American]
800–553–AIDS (7432) [Hearing Impaired]
800–922–2438 [Multilingual/Asian Pacific]

Alabama
Alabama AIDS Hotline
Montgomery
800–228–0469

Alaska
Alaska AIDS Hotline
Juneau
800–478–2437

Alberta
Alberta Health—STD Control
403–427–2830 (Edmonton)
800–772–AIDS (throughout Alberta)

Arizona
Arizona AIDS Hotline
Phoenix
800–334–1540

British Columbia
British Columbia Ministry of Health
604–872–6652 (Vancouver)
800–972–2437 (throughout BC)

California
Southern California AIDS Hotline
Los Angeles
800–922–2437
800–553–2437 (TTY)

Northern California AIDS Hotline
San Francisco
800–FOR–AIDS
415–864–6606 (TTY)

Colorado
Colorado Department of Health
Denver
800–252–2437

Connecticut
Connecticut AIDS Hotline
Hartford
203–566–1157

Delaware
Delaware AIDS Hotline
Wilmington
800–422–0429

District of Columbia
District of Columbia AIDS Hotline
Washington
202–332–2437

Florida
Florida AIDS Hotline
Tallahassee
800–545–SIDA
800–352–2437 (English Hotline)
800–AID–S101 (Haitian Creole Hotline)

Georgia
Georgia AIDS Hotline
800–551–2728
404–876–9944
404–876–9950 (TTY)

Hawaii
Hawaii AIDS Hotline
Honolulu
808–922–1313

Idaho
Idaho AIDS Hotline
Boise
800–677–2437

Illinois
Illinois AIDS Hotline
Chicago
800–243–2437
800–782–0423 (TTY)

Indiana
Indiana AIDS Hotline
Indianapolis
800–848–2437

Iowa
Iowa AIDS Hotline
Des Moines
800–445–2437

Kentucky
Kentucky AIDS Information Service
Frankfort
800–654–2437

Louisiana
Louisiana AIDS Hotline
New Orleans
800-992-4379

Maine
Maine AIDS Hotline
Portland
800-851-2437

Manitoba
AIDS Infoline
Manitoba Department of Health
204-945-AIDS (Winnipeg)
800-782-AIDS (throughout Manitoba)

Maryland
Maryland AIDS Hotline
Baltimore
800-638-6252
800-553-3140 (TTY)

Massachusetts
Massachusetts AIDS Hotline
Boston
800-235-2331
800-235-2331 (TTY)
617-262-7248 (Spanish Hotline)

Michigan
Michigan AIDS Hotline
Royal Oak
800-872-2437
800-332-0849 (TTY)

Minnesota
Minnesota AIDSline
Minneapolis
800-248-2437

Mississippi
Mississippi AIDS Hotline
Jackson
800-537-0851

Missouri
Missouri AIDS Hotline
Jefferson City
800-533-2437

Montana
Montana AIDS Hotline
Helena
800-233-6668

Nebraska
Nebraska AIDS Hotline
Omaha
800-782-2437

Nevada
Nevada AIDS Hotline
Carson City
800-842-2437

New Brunswick
New Brunswick Department of Health
506-453-2536

AIDS New Brunswick
506-459-7518
800-561-4009 (throughout NB)

Newfoundland
Newfoundland Department of Health
Disease Control
709-576-3430

New Hampshire
Domestic Violence Coalition
800-852-3388

New Hampshire AIDS Information Line
Concord
800-872-8909

New Jersey
Domestic Violence Coalition
800-572-7233

New Jersey AIDS Hotline
Trenton
800-624-2377

New Mexico
AIDS Hotline
Santa Fe
800-545-2437

Domestic Violence Coalition
800-773-3645

New York
New York AIDS Hotline
Buffalo
800-541-2437
800-233-SIDA

North Dakota
Domestic Violence Coalition
800-472-2911

North Dakota AIDS Hotline
Bismarck
800-472-2180

Northwest Territories
AIDS Information Line
403-873-7017
800-661-0795 (throughout NT)

Nova Scotia
Nova Scotia Department of Health
Epidemiology Division
902–424–8698

Ohio
Ohio AIDS Hotline
Columbus
800–332–2437
800–DEA–FTTY (TTY)

Oklahoma
Oklahoma AIDS Hotline
Oklahoma City
800–522–9054
800–522–9054 (TTY)

Ontario
Ontario Ministry of Health
AIDS Section
416–668–6066
Throughout Ontario: 800–668–2437 (English and other languages)
800–267–7432 (French)

Oregon
Oregon AIDS Hotline
Portland
800–777–2437

Pennsylvania
Pennsylvania AIDS Hotline
Harrisburg
800–445–7720

Prince Edward Island
PEI Department of Health
902–368–4530

Puerto Rico
Linea de Auxilio SIDA y Enfermedades de Transmission Sexual
Rio Piedras
809–765–1010

Quebec
Quebec Department of Health
418–643–9395
800–463–5656 (throughout Quebec)

Rhode Island
Rhode Island AIDS Hotline
Providence
800–726–3010

Saskatchewan
Saskatchewan Health Education Line
306–787–3148
800–667–7766 (throughout Saskatchewan)

South Carolina
South Carolina AIDS Hotline
Columbia
800–322–2437

South Dakota
South Dakota AIDS Hotline
Sioux Falls
800–592–1861

Tennessee
Tennessee AIDS Hotline
Nashville
800–525–2437

Texas
Texas AIDSLINE
Austin
800–299–2437
800–252–8012 (TTY)

Utah
Utah AIDS Hotline
Salt Lake City
801–538–6094

Vermont
Vermont AIDS Hotline
Burlington
800–882–AIDS

Virginia
Virginia AIDS Hotline
Richmond
800–533–4148
800–533–4148 (TTY)

Virgin Islands
Virgin Islands AIDS Hotline
Christiansted
809–773–1311

Washington
Washington AIDS Hotline
Olympia
800–272–AIDS

West Virginia
West Virginia AIDS Hotline
Charleston
800–642–8244

Wisconsin
Wisconsin AIDSline
Milwaukee
800–334–2437

Wyoming
Wyoming AIDS Hotline
Cheyenne
800–327–3577

Yukon
Yukon Ministry of Health
403–668–9444 (Whitehorse)
800–661–0507 (throughout Yukon)

☐ Note

1. In an effort to keep this list as complete and up-to-date as possible, we encourage, and appreciate, readers informing us of noted additions or corrections.

References

Aaro, H. K., & Fuelli, P. (1992). Smoking habits in early pregnancy and attitudes towards smoking cessation among pregnant women and their partners. *Family Process, 9*(4), 494–499.
Abbott, A. A. (1994). A feminist approach to substance abuse treatment and service delivery. Special Issue: Women's health and social work: Feminist perspectives. *Social Work in Health Care, 19*(3–4), 67–83.
Abedin, M., Young, M., & Beeram, M. R. (1993). Infant abandonment: Prevalence, risk factors, and cost analysis. *American Journal of Diseases of Children, 147,* 714–716.
Abel, E. L. (1995). An update on incidence of FAS: FAS is not an equal opportunity birth defect [Review]. *Neurotoxicology & Teratology, 17*(4), 437–443.
Abel, E. L., Martier, S., Kruger, M., Ager, J., & Sokol, R. J. (1993). Ratings of fetal alcohol syndrome facial features by medical providers and biomedical scientists. *Alcoholism: Clinical and Experimental Research, 17,* 717–721.
Abel, E. L., & Sokol, R. J. (1987). Incidence of fetal alcohol syndrome and economic impact of FAS-related anomalies. *Drug and Alcohol Dependence, 19,* 51–70.
Abel, E. L., & Sokol, R. J. (1991). A revised conservative estimate of the incidence of FAS and economic impact. *Alcoholism: Clinical and Experimental Research, 15,* 514–524.
Abidin, R. R. (1990). *Parenting stress index* (3rd ed.). Charlottesville, VA: Pediatric Psychology.
Abma, J. C., & Mott, F. L. (1991). Substance use and prenatal care during pregnancy among young women. *Family Planning Perspectives, 23*(3), 117–122.
Abram, K. M. (1989). The effect of co-occurring disorders on criminal careers: Interaction of antisocial personality, alcoholism, and drug disorders. *International Journal of Law and Psychiatry, 12,* 133–148.
Abrams, R. C., & Alexopoulos, G. S. (1987). Substance abuse in the elderly: Alcohol and prescription drugs. *Hospital and Community Psychiatry, 8,* 1285–1287.
Adams, W. L., Barry, K. L., & Fleming, M. F. (1996). Screening for problem drinking in older primary care patients. *JAMA: Journal of the American Medical Association, 276*(24), 1964–1967.
Abrams, W. B., Berkow, R., & Fletcher, A. J. (1990). *The Merck manual of geriatrics.* Rahway, NJ: Merck Sharp & Dohme Research Laboratories.
Adams, W. L., Magruder-Habib, K., Trued, S., & Broome, H. L. (1992). Alcohol abuse in elderly emergency department patients. *Journal of the American Geriatrics Society, 40*(12), 1236–1240.
Adams, W. L., Yuan, Z., Barboriak, J. J., & Broome, H. L. (1993). Alcohol-related hospitalizations of elderly people. *Journal of the American Medical Association, 270,* 1222–1225.
Aday, L. A. (1994). Health status of vulnerable populations. *Annual Review of Public Health, 15,* 487–509.

Adeokun, L. A., Weeramunda, J., Carballo, M., & Tawil, O. (1989). Knowledge of HIV/AIDS and sexual practices in Sri Lanka. *International Conference on AIDS Abstracts, 5,* 973.
Adger, H., Jr., McDonald, E. M., & DeAngelis, C. (1990). Substance abuse education in pediatrics. *Pediatrics, 88,* 555–560.
Adler, T. (1992). Prenatal cocaine exposure has subtle, serious effects. *The American Psychological Association Monitor, 23*(11), 17.
Adrian, M. (1986). Older Canadians: Alcohol and other drug use. *The Addiction Research Foundation Journal, 15,* 9.
Adrian, M., Din, C. M., MacGregor, L. J., & Stoduto, G. (1995). Substance use as a measure of social integration for women of different ethnocultural groups into mainstream culture in a pluralist society: The example of Canada. *International Journal of the Addictions, 30*(6), 699–734.
Agrafiotis, D., Ioannidi, E., Konstantinidis R., & Stylianou, J. (1989). Knowledge, attitudes and beliefs of Greek people on AIDS. *International Conference on AIDS Abstracts, 5,* 911.
Agurell, S., Halldin, M., Lindgren, J., Ohlsson, A., Widman, M., Gillespie, M., & Hollister, L. (1986). Pharmacokinetics and metabolism of delta-1-tetrahydrocannabinol and other cannabinoids with emphasis on man. *Pharmacological Review, 38,* 21–43.
Ahijevych, K. L. M. (1993). Cigarette smoking behavior among African American women and the feasibility of a low-intensity smoking cessation intervention. *Dissertation Abstracts International, 53*(9).
Ahluwalia, I. B., DeVellis, R. F., & Thomas, J. C. (1998). Reproductive decisions of women at risk for acquiring HIV infection. *AIDS Education and Prevention, 10*(1), 90–97.
AIDS cases doubling every 12 months (1987). *Canadian Clinical Laboratory, 11,* 10.
AIDS risk increases for some, national research council finds in ten-year review of epidemic (1990). *Hospital and Community Psychiatry, 41,* 937–938.
Alberta Family and Social Services. (1990, November-a). Child abuse: What is it? What to do about it. *Office for the Prevention of Family Violence.*
Alberta Family and Social Services. (1990, November-b). Wife abuse: What is it? What to do about it. *Office for the Prevention of Family Violence.*
Alberta Family and Social Services. (1997, April). Elder abuse: What is it? What to do about it. *Office for the Prevention of Family Violence.*
Alcohol and the liver. (1993, January). *Alcohol Alert, 1–4.*
Alcohol-related traffic fatalities among youth and young adults—United States, 1982–1989. (1991). *Morbidity and Mortality Weekly Report, 40,* 178–179, 185–187.
Alford, G. S., Koehler, R. A., & Leonard, J. (1991). Alcoholics Anonymous-Narcotics Anonymous: Model in patient treatment of chemically dependent adolescents: A 2-year outcome study. *Journal of Studies on Alcohol, 52,* 118–126.
Allan, C. A., & Cooke, D. (1984). Stressful life events and alcohol abuse in women: A critical review. *Journal of Studies on Alcoholism, 79,* 425–432.
Allan, C. A., & Cooke, D. (1986). Women, life events and drinking problems. *British Journal of Psychiatry, 148,* 462.
Allen, D. N., Sprenkel, D. G., & Vitale, P. A. (1994). Reactance theory and alcohol consumption laws: Further confirmation among collegiate alcohol consumers. *Journal of Studies on Alcoholism, 55,* 34–40.
Allen, J. P., Litten, R. Z., Fertig, J. B., & Babor, T. (1997). A review of research on the Alcohol Use Disorders Identification Test (AUDIT) [Review]. *Alcoholism, Clinical and Experimental Research, 21*(4), 613–619.
Altshuler, L. L., Burt, V. K., & Hendrick, V. (1996). Psychotropic guidelines for breastfeeding mothers. *American Journal of Psychiatry, 153*(9), 1236–1247.
Altshuler, L. L., Cohen, L., Szuba, M. P., Burt, V. K., Gitlin, M., & Mintz, J. (1996). Pharmacologic management of psychiatric illness during pregnancy: Dilemmas and guidelines. *American Journal of Psychiatry, 153*(5), 592–606.
American Academy of Pediatrics, Committee on Drugs. (1989). Transfer of drugs and other chemicals into human milk. *Pediatrics, 84,* 924–936.

American Academy of Pediatrics, Committee on Substance Abuse and Committee on Children with Disabilities. (1993). Fetal alcohol syndrome and fetal alcohol effects. *Pediatrics, 91,* 1004–1006.
American Academy of Pediatrics, Task Force on Pediatric AIDS. (1988). Perinatal human immunodeficiency virus infection. *Pediatrics, 82,* 941–944.
American Medical Association. (1995). *Diagnostic and treatment guidelines on mental health effects of family violence.* Chicago: Author.
American Nurse's Association Organization. (January 1 / 1999). Position statements: Abuse of prescription drugs. *ANA Organization* [On-line] Available: http://www.ana.org/
American Psychiatric Association. (1994). *Diagnostic and statistical manual of mental disorders* (4th ed.). Washington, DC: Author.
Anderson, E. G. (1990). Keeping an eye on older patients and their drugs. *Geriatrics, 45,* 81–82.
Anderson, P. O. (1991). Drug use during breast feeding. *Clinical Pharmacy, 10,* 594–624.
Andrulonis, P. A. (1991). Disruptive behavior disorders in boys and the borderline personality disorder in men. *Annals of Clinical Psychiatry, 3,* 23–26.
Anton, R. F. (1994). Medications for treating alcoholism. *Alcohol Health & Research World, 18,* 265–271.
Aramburu, B., & Leigh, B. C. (1991). For better or worse: Attributions about drunken aggression toward male and female victims. *Violence & Victims, 6,* 31–41.
Araya, R. (1994). Women's drinking and society. *Addiction, 89,* 954–956.
Arnold, G. L., Kirby, R. S., Langendoerfer, S., & Wilkins-Haug, L. (1994). Toluene embryopathy: Clinical delineation and developmental follow-up. *Pediatrics, 93,* 216–220.
Asante, K., & Nelms-Matzke, J. (1985). Survey of children with chronic handicaps and fetal alcohol syndrome in the Yukon and Northwest B. C. Ottawa: National Native Advisory Council on Alcohol and Drug Abuse, Health and Welfare Canada. Unpublished report.
Ashley, M. J., Olin, J. S., & le Riche, W. H. (1977). Morbidity in alcoholics: Evidence for accelerated development of physical disease in women. *Archives of Internal Medicine, 137,* 883–887.
Astley, S. J., & Little, R. E. (1990). Maternal marijuana use during lactation and infant development at one year. *Neurotoxicology and Teratology, 12,* 161–168.
Astori, M. G., Piazza, F., Maccabruni, A., Caselli, D., & Lanzi, G. (1997). Course of mother-child relations in cases of maternal HIV infection. *Pediatria Medica e Chirurgica, 19*(1), 23–25.
Atkinson, R. M. (1988). Editorial: Alcoholism in the elderly population. *Mayo Clinic Proceedings, 63,* 825–829.
Atkinson, R. M. (1990). Aging and alcohol use disorders: Diagnostic issues in the elderly. *International Psychogeriatrics, 2,* 55–72.
Atkinson, R. M., & Kofoed, L. L. (1982). Alcohol and drug abuse in old age: A clinical perspective. *Substance and Alcohol Actions/Misuse, 3,* 353–368.
Autti-Rämö, I., & Granström, M.-L. (1991). The psychomotor development during the first year of life of infants exposed to intrauterine alcohol of various duration: Fetal alcohol exposure and development. *Neuropediatrics, 22,* 59–64.
Autti-Rämö, I., Korkman, M., Hilakivi-Clarke, L., Lehtonen, M., Halmesmäki, E., & Granström, M.-L. (1992). Mental development of 2-year-old children exposed to alcohol in utero. *The Journal of Pediatrics, 120,* 740–746.
Bagley, C., Durie, D., Hall, R., Harrington, G., Hunter, W., Kiddey, K., & Tanney, B. (1990). *Facing the Facts: Suicide in Canada* [Brochure]. Ottawa: Suicide Information & Education Centre.
Baird, D., Galanter, M., Guedj, P., & Westreich, L. (1997). Differences between men and women in dual-diagnosis treatment. *The American Journal on Addictions, 6*(4), 311–317.
Baker, F. M. (1982). Ethnic & cultural variations in the care of the aged. *Journal of Geriatric Psychiatry, 15,* 225–237.
Baker, J. N., & Gonzalez, D. (1988, October 17). Is Grandma in a drug ring? Seniors front a pill scam. *Newsweek,* 36.
Baker, M. I., & Oleen, M. A. (1988). The use of benzodiazepine hypnotics in the elderly. *Pharmacotherapy, 8*(4), 241–247.

Baker, S. (1992). As a woman I wasn't going to feel comfortable. *Alcohol Concern Magazine, 7*(4), 12–13.
Baker, T. B., Fiore, M. C., Gritz, E. R., Hasselblad, V., Lando, H. A., Stitzer, M. L., & Wetter, D. W. (1998). The agency for health care policy and research: Smoking cessation clinical practice guideline: Findings and implications for psychologists. *The American Psychological Association, 53*(6), 657–669.
Balshem, M., Oxman, G., van Rooyen, D., & Girod, K. (1992). Syphilis, sex and crack cocaine: Images of risk and mortality. *Social Science and Medicine, 35,* 147–160.
Bamji, M., Thea, D. M., Weedon, J., Krasinski, K., Matheson, P. B., Thomas, P., Lambert, G., Abrams, E. J., Steketee, R., & Heagarty, M. (1996). Prospective study of human immunodeficiency virus 1-related disease among 512 infants born to infected women in New York City. The New York City Perinatal HIV Transmission Collaborative Study Group. *Pediatric Infectious Disease Journal, 15*(10), 891–898.
Bandura, A. (1977). *Social Learning Theory.* Englewood Cliffs, NJ: Prentice Hall.
Bandstra, E. S., & Burkett, G. (1991). Maternal-fetal and neonatal effects of in utero cocaine exposure. *Seminars in Perinatology, 15*(4), 288–301.
Bardsley, J., Turvey, J., & Blatherwick, J. (1990). Vancouver's needle exchange program. *Canadian Journal of Public Health, 81,* 39–45.
Barnard, C. P. (1990). Alcohol and sex abuse in the family: Incest and marital rape. *Aggression, Family Violence and Chemical Dependency, 131*–144.
Barry, K. L., Fleming, M. F., Greenley, J., Widlak, P., Kropp, S., & McKee, D. (1995). Assessment of alcohol and other drug disorders in the seriously mentally ill. *Schizophrenia Bulletin: National Institute of Mental Health, 21*(2), 313–321.
Barry Robe, L. (1986). *Co-starring famous women and alcohol: The dramatic truth behind the tragedies and triumphs of 200 celebrities.* Minneapolis, MN: Compcare.
Bayatpour, M., Wells, R. D., & Holford, S. (1992). Physical and sexual abuse as predictors of substance use and suicide among pregnant teenagers. *Journal of Adolescent Health, 13,* 128–132.
Bays, J. (1990). Substance abuse and child abuse: Impact of addiction on the child. *Pediatric Clinics of North America, 37,* 881–904.
Bays, J. (1992). The care of alcohol- and drug-affected infants. *Pediatric Annals, 21*(8), 485–495.
Beardsley, R. S., Larson, D. B., Burns, B. J., Thompson, J. W., & Kamerow, D. B. (1989). Prescribing of psychotropics in elderly nursing home patients. *Journal of the American Geriatrics Society, 37*(4), 327–330.
Beattie, M. (1987). *Codependent.* Center City, MN: Hazelden.
Beattie, M. (1990). *Codependents' guide to the Twelve Steps.* New York: Prentice Hall.
Beckman, L. J. (1975). Women alcoholics: A review of social and psychological studies. *Journal of Studies on Alcohol, 36*(7), 797–824.
Beckman, L. J. (1993). Alcoholics Anonymous and gender issues. *Research on Alcoholics Anonymous: Opportunities and Alternatives,* 233–247.
Beckman, L. J. (1994a). Entry of women of diverse backgrounds into alcoholism treatment. *Addictions: Concepts and Strategies for Treatment,* 365–374.
Beckman, L. J. (1994b). Treatment needs of women with alcohol problems. *Alcohol Health and Research World, 18,* 206.
Beckman, L. J., & Ackerman, K. T. (1995). Women, alcohol, and sexuality. *Recent Developments in Alcoholism, 12,* 267–285.
Beers, M., Avorn, J., & Sourmerai, S. B. (1988). Psychoactive medication use in intermediate-care facility residents. *Journal of the American Medical Association, 260,* 3016–3020.
Beery, M. (1990). Women and HIV/AIDS. *The Washington Nurse, 20*(8), 27.
Belfer, M. L. (1993). Substance abuse with psychiatric illness in children and adolescents: Definitions and terminology. *American Journal of Orthopsychiatry, 63*(1), 70–79.
Bell, K. (1988, June 7). Many elderly abuse drugs. *The Canadian Press,* (Document 1211299).
Bell, M. D., Rao, V. J., Wetli, C. V., & Rodriguez, R. N. (1988). Positional asphyxiation in adults. A series of 30 cases from the Dade and Broward County Florida Medical Examiner Offices from 1982 to 1990. *American Journal of Forensic Medicine & Pathology, 13*(2), 101–107.

Benowitz, N. L. (1988). Pharmacologic aspects of cigarette smoking and nicotine addiction. *New England Journal of Medicine, 319,* 1318–1330.

Bepko, C. (1989/1991). Disorders of power: Women and addiction in the family. In M. McGoldrick, C. M. Anderson, & F. Walsh (Eds.), *Women in families: A framework for family therapy* (pp. 406–426). New York: W. W. Norton.

Beran, R. G. (1992). Automatisms—The current legal position related to clinical practice and medicolegal interpretation. *Clinical & Experimental Neurology, 29,* 81–91.

Bercsi, S. J., Brickner, P. W., & Saha, D. C. (1993). Alcohol use and abuse in the frail, homebound elderly: A clinical analysis of 103 persons. *Drug and Alcohol Dependence, 33,* 139–149.

Berenson, A. B., San Miguel, V. V., & Wilkinson, G. S. (1992). Violence and its relationship to substance use in adolescent pregnancy. *Journal of Adolescent Health, 13,* 470–474.

Bergman, U., Rosa, F. W., Baum, C., Wiholm, B.-E., & Faich, G. A. (1992). Effects of exposure to benzodiazepine during fetal life. *The Lancet, 340,* 694–696.

Berkelman, R. L., & Curran, J. W. (1989). Epidemiology of HIV infection and AIDS. *Epidemiologic Reviews, 11,* 222–228.

Berman, A. L., & Schwartz, R. H. (1990). Suicide attempts among adolescent drug users. *American Journal of Diseases of Children, 144,* 310–314.

Berman, B. A., & Gritz, E. R. (1991). Women and smoking: Current trends and issues for the 1990s. *Journal of Substance Abuse, 3*(2), 67–73.

Berenson, D. (1991). Powerlessness—Liberating or enslaving? Responding to the feminist critique of the Twelve Steps. In C. Bepko (Ed.), *Feminism and addiction* (pp. 67–84). Binghamton, NY: Haworth.

Bernstein, L. R., Folkman, S. M., & Lazarus, R. S. (1989). Characterization of the use and misuse of medications by an elderly, ambulatory population. *Medical Care, 27,* 654–663.

Bernstine, J. B. (1956). Maternal blood and breast milk estimation following the administration of chloral hydrate during the puerperium. *Journal of Obstetrics and Gynaecology of the British Empire, 63,* 228–231.

Bertucci, V., & Krafchik, B. R. (1994). Diagnosis: Fetal alcohol syndrome. *Pediatric Dermatology, 11,* 180.

Bienenfeld, D. (1987). Alcoholism in the elderly. *American Family Physician, 36,* 163–169.

Bigelow, G. E., & Silverman, K. (1999). Theoretical and empirical foundations of contingency management treatments for drug abuse. *Motivating Behavior Change Among Illicit-Drug Abusers: Research on Contingency Management Interventions, 15*–31.

Billingham, R., & Sack, A. (1986). Courtship violence and the interactive status of the relationship. *Journal of Adolescent Research, 1,* 315–325.

Bissell, L., & Haberman, P. W. (1984). *Alcoholism in the Professions.* Oxford University.

Bisson, J. I. (1993). Automatism and post-traumatic stress disorder. *British Journal of Psychiatry, 163,* 830–832.

Black, J. L., Dolan, M. P., DeFord, H. A., Rubenstein, J. A., Penk, W. E., Robinowitz, R., & Skinner, J. R. (1986). Sharing of needles among users of intravenous drugs. *New England Journal of Medicine, 314,* 446–447.

Bland, R., & Orn, H. (1986). Family violence and psychiatric disorder. *Canadian Journal of Psychiatry, 31,* 129–137.

Blankfield, A., & Maritz, J. S. (1990). Female alcoholics: III. Some clinical associations of the Michigan Alcoholism Screening Test and diagnostic implications. *Actas Psychiatrica Scandinavica, 81,* 483–487.

Blendis, L. M. (1987). Nutrition in alcoholism. *Medicine North America, 16,* 3085–3092.

Blixen, C. E., McDougall, G. J., & Suen, L. J. (1997). Dual diagnosis in elders discharged from a psychiatric hospital. *International Journal of Geriatric Psychiatry, 12*(3), 307–313.

Bloom, P. J. (1983). Alcoholism after sixty. *American Family Physician, 28,* 111–113.

Blum, R. H. (1981). Violence, alcohol, and setting: An unexplored nexus. In J. J. Collins, Jr. & M. E. Wolfgang (Eds.), *Drinking and crime: Perspectives on the relationships between alcohol consumption and criminal behavior* (pp. 110–142). New York: Guilford.

Blum, R. W. (1987). Adolescent substance abuse: Diagnostic and treatment issues. *Pediatric Clinics of North America, 34,* 523–537.
Bogal-Allbritten, R. B., & Allbritten, W. L. (1985). The hidden victims: Courtship violence among college students. *Journal of College Student Personnel, 26,* 201–204.
Bohn, M. J., Babor, T. F., & Kranzler, H. R. (1995). The Alcohol Use Disorders Identification Test (AUDIT): Validation of a screening instrument for use in medical settings. *Journal of Studies on Alcohol, 56*(4), 423–432.
Booth, B. M., Fortney, J., Lancaster, B., & Ross, R. (1998, May). Age, ethnicity, and comorbidity in a national sample of hospitalized alcohol-dependent women veterans. *Psychiatric Services, 49*(5), 663–668.
Booth, R. E., Watters, J. K., & Chitwood, D. D. (1993). HIV risk-related sex behaviors among injection drug users, crack smokers, and injection drug users who smoke crack. *American Journal of Public Health, 83*(8), 1144–1148.
Booth, W. (1988). CDC paints a picture of HIV infection in U.S. *Science, 239,* 253.
Bost, J., Jacob, T., Seilhamer, R. A., & Windle, M. (1999). Adult children of alcoholics: Drinking, psychiatric, and psychosocial status. *Psychology of Addictive Behaviors, 13*(1), 3–21.
Botvin, G. J., Baker, E., Botvin, E. M., Filazzola, A. D., & Millman, R. B. (1984). Prevention of alcohol misuse through the development of personal and social competence: A pilot study. *Journal of Studies on Alcohol, 45,* 550–552.
Botvin, G. J., Baker, E., Renick, N., Filazzola, A., & Botvin, E. M. (1984). A cognitive-behavioral approach to substance abuse prevention. *Addictive Behavior, 9,* 137–147.
Botvin, G. J., & Botvin, E. M. (1992). Adolescent tobacco, alcohol, and drug abuse: Prevention strategies, empirical findings, and assessment issues. *Developmental and Behavioral Pediatrics, 13,* 290–301.
Botvin, G. J., Renick, N. L., & Baker, E. (1983). The effect of scheduling format and booster sessions on a broad spectrum psychosocial approach to smoking prevention. *Journal of Behavioral Medicine, 6,* 359–379.
Bourne, P. G. (1988). AIDS and drug use: An international perspective. *Journal of Psychoactive Drugs, 20,* 153–157.
Bourque, L. B., Tashkin, D. P., Clark, V. A., & Schuler, R. (1991). Demographic and health characteristics of heavy marijuana smokers in Los Angeles county. *The International Journal of the Addictions, 26*(7), 739–755.
Bowes, W. A., Jr. (1980). The effect of medications on the lactating mother and her infant. *Clinical Obstetrics and Gynecology, 23,* 1073–1080.
Bowlby, J. (1973a). *Attachment and loss. Vol. 1: Attachment.* New York: Basic.
Bowlby, J. (1973b). *Attachment and loss. Vol. 2: Separation-anxiety and anger.* New York: Basic.
Boxwell, A. O. (1988). Geriatric suicide: The preventable death. *Nurse Practitioner, 13,* 10–11, 15, 18–19.
Boyle, K., & Anglin, M. D. (1993). "To the curb": Sex bartering and drug use among homeless crack users in Los Angeles. In M. S. Ratner (Ed.). *Crack pipe as pimp: An ethnographic investigation of sex-for-crack exchanges,* (pp. 159–186). New York: Lexington Books.
Brabant, M., Bruneau, J., Lamothe, F., Soto, J., Arshinoff, R., Coates, R., Vinceletee, J., Rankin, J., & Fauvel, M. (1990). Knowledge of HIV and risk behaviors among injection drug users in Montreal and Toronto. *International Conference on AIDS Abstracts, 6,* 227.
Bradford, J. M. W., Greenberg, D. M., & Motayne, G. G. (1992). Substance abuse and criminal behavior. *Psychiatric Clinics of North America, 15,* 605–622.
Bradley, K. A., Boyd-Wickizer, J., Powell, S. H., & Burman, M. L. (1998). Alcohol screening questionnaires in women: A critical review. *JAMA, 280*(2), 166–171.
Brady, K. T., Grice, D. E., Dustan, L., & Randall, C. (1993). Gender differences in substance use disorders. *American Journal of Psychiatry, 150,* 1707–1711.
Breslau, N., Kilbey, M. M., & Andreski, P. (1993). Vulnerability to psychopathology in nicotine-dependent smokers: An epidemiologic study of young adults. *American Journal of Psychiatry, 150,* 941–946.

Brettle, R. P., & Nelles, B. (1988). Special problems of injecting drug-misusers. *British Medical Bulletin, 44*, 149–160.
Brody, J. A. (1982). Aging and alcohol abuse. *Journal of the American Geriatrics Society, 30*, 123–126.
Bronell, D. J. (1993). An outcome study of a prevention/treatment program addressing the effects of familial alcoholism on adult daughters of alcoholics. *Dissertation Abstracts International, 53*(9-B).
Brook, J. S., Cohen, P., & Jaeger, L. (1998). Development variations in factors related to initial and increased levels of adolescent drug involvement. *Journal of Genetic Psychology, 159*(2), 179–194.
Brooks, C. S., Zuckerman, B., Bamforth, A., Cole, J., & Kaplan-Sanoff, M. (1994). Clinical issues related to substance-involved mothers and their infants. *Infant Mental Health Journal, 15*(2), 202–217.
Brosnahan, M. (1988). Hospital detects seniors' addictions. *The Addiction Research Foundation Journal, 17*, 3.
Brouhard, B. H. (1994). Cocaine ingestion and abnormalities of the urinary tract. *Clinical Pediatrics: The Peer-Reviewed Journal for the Clinician, 33*(3), 157–158.
Brown, B. B. (1982). Professionals' perceptions of drug and alcohol abuse among the elderly. *The Gerontologist, 22*, 519–525.
Brown, B. B., & Chiang, C. (1983–1984). Drug and alcohol abuse among the elderly: Is being alone the key? *International Journal of Aging and Human Development, 18*(1), 1–12.
Brown, L. S. (1994). *Subversive dialogues: Theory in feminist therapy*. New York: Basic Books.
Brown, S., & Lewis, V. (1995). The alcoholic family: A developmental model of recovery. In S. Brown & I. D. Yalom (Eds.), *Treating Alcoholism*, (pp. 279–315) San Francisco, CA: Jossey-Bass.
Brown, V. B., Melchior, L. A., Reback, C., & Huba, G. J. (1994). Psychological functioning and substance abuse before and after the 1992 Los Angeles riot in a community sample of women. *Journal of Psychoactive Drugs, 26*(4), 431–437.
Brown, V. B., Sanchez, S., Zweben, J. E., & Aly, T. (1996). Challenges in moving from a traditional therapeutic community to a women and children's TC model. *Journal of Psychoactive Drugs, 28*(1), 39–46.
Bruera, E., Moyano, J., Seifert, L., Fainsinger, R. L., Hanson, J., & Suarex-Almazor, M. (1995). The frequency of alcoholism among patients with pain due to terminal cancer. *Journal of Pain and Symptom Management, 10*(8), 599–603.
Bryant, S. L., & Range, L. M. (1995). Suicidality in college women who report multiple versus single types of maltreatment by parents: A brief report. *Journal of Child Sexual Abuse, 4*(3), 87–94.
Buchi, K. F. (1998). The drug-exposed infant in the well-baby nursery [Review]. *Clinics in Perinatology, 25*(2), 335–350.
Buchsbaum, D. G., Buchanan, R. G., Welsh, J., Centor, R. M., & Schnoll, S. H. (1992). Screening for drinking disorders in the elderly using the CAGE questionnaire. *Journal of the American Geriatrics Society, 40*, 662–665.
Bukstein, O. G., Glancy, L. J., & Kaminer, Y. (1992). Patterns of affective comorbidity in a clinical population of dually diagnosed adolescent substance abusers. *Journal of the American Academy of Child and Adolescent Psychiatry, 31*, 1041–1045.
Bullows, J., & Penfold, A. (1993). Tackling dependency. *Nursing Times, 89*(2), 27–29.
Burd, L., & Moffatt, M. E. K. (1994). Epidemiology of fetal alcohol syndrome in American Indians, Alaskan Natives, and Canadian Aboriginal peoples: A review of the literature. *Public Health Reports, 109*, 688–693.
Burman, S. (1993). Chemically-dependent women in treatment: A study of the experiences in and responses to different treatment models. *Dissertation Abstracts International, 54*(5-A), 1973.
Burman, S. (1994). The disease concept of alcoholism: Its impact on women's treatment. *Journal of Substance Abuse Treatment, 11*(2), 121–126.

Burns, K. A., Chethik, L., Burns, W. J., & Clark, R. (1997). The early relationship of drug abusing mothers and their infants: An assessment at eight to twelve months of age. *Journal of Clinical Psychology, 53*(3), 279–287.

Burns, M. M. (1980). Alcohol abuse among women as indirect self-destructive behavior. In N. L. Farberow (Ed.), *The many faces of suicide: Indirect self-destructive behavior* (pp. 220–231). San Francisco, CA: McGraw-Hill.

Busby, W. J., Campbell, A. J., Borrie, M. J., & Spears, G. F. (1988). Alcohol use in a community-based sample of subjects aged 70 years and older. *Journal of the American Geriatrics Society, 36*, 301–305.

Buydens-Branchey, L., & Branchey, M. H. (1992). Cortisol in alcoholics with a disordered aggression control. *Psychoneuroendocrinology, 17*, 45–54.

Caetano, R. (1994). Drinking and alcohol-related problems among minority women. *Alcohol Health & Research World, 18*(3), 233–241.

Calhoun, B. C., & Watson, P. T. (1991). The cost of maternal cocaine abuse: I. Perinatal cost. *Obstetrics and Gynecology, 78*(5), 731–734.

Campbell, C. A. (1990). Women and AIDS. *Social Science and Medicine, 30*, 407–415.

Campbell, J. D., Poland, M. L., Waller, J. B., & Ager, J. (1992). Correlates of battering during pregnancy. *Research in Nursing & Health, 15*, 219–226.

Canino, G. (1994). Alcohol use and misuse among Hispanic women: Selected factors, processes, and studies. *The International Journal of Addictions, 29*(9), 1083–1100.

Carlson, R. G., & Siegal, H. A. (1991). The crack life: An ethnographic overview of crack use and sexual behavior among African-Americans in a Midwest metropolitan city. *Journal of Psychoactive Drugs, 23*, 11–20.

Caroselli-Karinja, M. (1985). Drug abuse and the elderly. *Journal of Psychosocial Nursing, 23*, 25–30.

Caruso, K., & Bensel, R. (1993). Fetal alcohol syndrome and fetal alcohol effects: The University of Minnesota experience. *Minnesota Medicine, 76*, 25–29.

Cases of acquired immunodeficiency syndrome—US, June 1981–December 1991. (1992). *The Annals of Pharmacotherapy, 26*, 445–446.

Casey, J. C., Griffin, M. L., & Googins, B. K. (1993). The role of work for wives of alcoholics. *American Journal of Drug & Alcohol Abuse, 19*(1), 119–131.

Castro, L. C., Azen, C., Hobel, C. J., & Platt, L. D. (1993). Maternal tobacco use and substance abuse: Reported prevalence rates and associations with the delivery of small for gestational age neonates. *Obstetrics & Gynecology, 81*(3), 396–401.

Centers for Disease Control. (1991). Mortality attributable to HIV infection/AIDS. *Morbidity and Mortality Weekly Report, 40*, 41–44.

Cernovsky, Z. Z. (1987). A failure to detect MAC's false negatives in female alcohol and drug addicts. *Addictive Behaviors, 12*(4), 367–369.

Chaiken, J. M. (1995). *Drugs and crime facts, 1994* (NCJ-154043). Washington, DC: U.S. Department of Justice.

Chaisson, R. E., Bacchetti, P., Osmond, D., Brodie, B., Sande, M. A., & Moss, A. R. (1989). Cocaine use and HIV infection in intravenous drug users in San Francisco. *Journal of the American Medical Association, 261*, 561–565.

Champion, J. D., & Shain, R. N. (1998). The context of sexually transmitted disease: Life histories of woman abuse. *Issues in Mental Health Nursing, 19*(5), 463–479.

Champlin, L. (1983). The aging alcoholic: Silent, often invisible—in need of care. *Geriatrics, 38*, 31, 34, 39–40, 44.

Chan, A. W. (1984). Effects of combined alcohol and benzodiazepine: A review. *Drug and Alcohol Dependence, 13*, 315–344.

Chan, A. W., Pristach, E. A., & Welte, J. W. (1994). Detection of alcoholism in three populations by the brief-MAST. *Alcoholism, Clinical and Experimental Research, 18*(3), 695–701.

Chan, A. W., Pristach, E. A., Welte, J. W., & Russell, M. (1993). Use of the TWEAK test in screening for alcoholism/heavy drinking in three populations. *Alcoholism, Clinical and Experimental Research, 17*(6), 1188–1192.

Chang, G., Astrachan, B. M., & Bryant, K. J. (1994). Emergency physicians' ratings of alcoholism treaters. *Journal of Substance Abuse Treatment, 11,* 131–135.

Chasnoff, I. J. (1992). Cocaine, pregnancy, and the growing child. *Current Problems in Pediatrics, 22,* 302–321.

Chasnoff, I. J., Burns, W. J., Schnoll, S. H., Burns, K., Chisum, G., & Kyle-Spore, L. (1986). Maternal-neonatal incest. *American Journal of Orthopsychiatry, 56,* 577–580.

Chenitz, W. C., Salisbury, S., & Takano-Stone, J. (1990). Drug misuse and abuse in the elderly. *Issues in Mental Health Nursing, 11,* 1–16.

Cherpitel, C. J. (1993). Alcohol and violence-related injuries: An emergency room study. *Addiction, 88,* 79–88.

Cherpitel, C. J. (1994). Alcohol and casualties: A comparison of emergency room and coroner data. *Alcohol & Alcoholism, 29,* 211–218.

Cherpitel, C. J. (1995). Screening for alcohol problems in the emergency room: A rapid alcohol problems screen. *Drug and Alcohol Dependence, 40*(2), 133–137.

Cherpitel, C. J. (1997). Comparison of screening instruments for alcohol problems between black and white emergency room patients from two regions of the country. *Alcoholism, Clinical and Experimental Research, 21*(8), 1391–1397.

Cherpitel, C. J. (1998). Differences in performance of screening instruments for problem drinking among blacks, whites and Hispanics in an emergency room population. *Journal of Studies on Alcohol, 59*(4), 420–426.

Chesley, S., Lumpkin, M., Schatzki, A., Galpern, W. R., Greenblatt, D. J., Shader, R. I., & Miller, R. G. (1991). Prenatal exposure to benzodiazepine—I. *Neuropharmacology, 30*(1), 53–58.

Chick, J., Gough, K., Falkowski, W., Kershaw, P., Hore, B., Mehta, B., Ritson, B., Ropner, R., & Torley, D. (1992). Disulfiram treatment of alcoholism. *British Journal of Psychiatry, 161,* 84–89.

Child abuse and neglect a national emergency, U.S. advisory board declares in first report. (1991). *Hospital and Community Psychiatry, 42,* 101–102.

Chin, J., & Mann, J. M. (1990). HIV infections and AIDS in the 1990s. *Annual Review of Public Health, 11,* 127–142.

Chirgwin, K., DeHovitz, J. A., Dillon, S., & McCormack, W. M. (1991). HIV infection, genital ulcer disease, and crack cocaine use among patients attending a clinic for sexually transmitted disease. *American Journal of Public Health, 81,* 1576–1579.

Chisholm, P. (1994). Sobering questions: An Alberta case raises new debate over the so-called drunk defence. *Maclean's, 107,* 100–102.

Choi, P. Y. L., & Pope, H. G., Jr. (1994). Violence toward women and illicit androgenic-anabolic steroid use. *Annals of Clinical Psychiatry, 6*(1), 21–25.

Christoffel, K. K. (1990). Violent death and injury in U.S. children and adolescents. *American Journal of Diseases of Children, 144,* 697–706.

Chu, S. Y., Peterman, T. A., Doll, L. S., Beuhler, J. W., & Curran, J. W. (1992). AIDS in bisexual men in the United States: Epidemiology and transmission to women. *American Journal of Public Health, 82*(2), 220–224.

Church, M. W. (1993). Does cocaine cause birth defects? *Neurotoxicology and Teratology, 15,* 289.

Church, M. W., Crossland, W. J., Holmes, P. A., Overbeck, G. W., & Tilak, J. P. (1998). The drug-exposed infant in the well-baby nursery. [Review]. *Clinics in Perinatology, 25*(2), 335–350.

Clark, H. W., & Zweben, J. E. (1994). Dual diagnosis, minority populations, and women. In M. S. Miller (Ed.), *Treating coexisting psychiatric and addictive disorders* (pp. 111–126). Center City, MN: Hazelden.

Clarren, S. K., & Smith, D. W. (1978). Medical progress: The fetal alcohol syndrome. *New England Journal of Medicine, 298,* 1063–1067.

Clay, S. W. (1997). Comparison of AUDIT and CAGE questionnaires in screening for alcohol use disorders in elderly primary care. *Journal of the American Osteopathic Association, 97*(10), 588–592.

Clemenger, M. (1993). Under the influence. *Nursing Times, 89*(2), 24–26.

Closser, M. H. (1991). Benzodiazepines and the elderly: A review of potential problems. *Journal of Substance Abuse Treatment, 8*, 35–41.
Coates, T. J., Stall, R. D., & Hoff, C. C. (1990). Changes in sexual behavior among gay and bisexual men since the beginning of the AIDS epidemic. In L. Temoshok & A. Baum (Eds.), *Psychosocial perspectives on AIDS*. Hillsdale, NJ: Lawrence Erlbaum Associates.
Cocco, K. M., & Carey, K. B. (1998). Psychometric properties of the Drug Abuse Screening Test in psychiatric outpatients. *Psychological Assessment, 10*(4), 408–414.
Cohen, A. Y. (1974). *The journey beyond trips: Alternatives to drugs*. Edmonton, AB: AADAC.
Cohen, J. B., & Wofsy, C. B. (1989). Heterosexual transmission of HIV. In J. A. Levy (Ed.), *AIDS—pathogenesis and treatment* (pp. 135–157). New York: Marcel Dekker.
Cohen, M. A. A., & Alfonso, C. A. (1994). Dissemination of HIV: How serious is it for women, medically and psychologically? *Forging a Women's Health Research Agenda: Policy Issues for the 1990s, 736*, 114–121.
Cohen, M. A. A., Palacios, A., Aladjem, A., Hernandez, I., Horton, A., Lefer, J., Lima, J., & Mehta, P. (1991). How can we combat excess mortality in Harlem: A one day survey of substance abuse in adult general care. *International Journal of Psychiatry in Medicine, 21*, 369–378.
Cohen, S. (1982). Therapeutic communities for substance abusers. *Drug Abuse & Alcoholism Newsletter, 11*(2), 1–4.
Coke emergencies up, DAWN report. (1992). *The Journal, 21*, 3.
Cole, C. K., Jones, M., & Sadofsky, G. (1990). Working with children at risk due to prenatal substance abuse. *PRISE Reporter, 21*, 5.
Coleman, R. M., & Curtis, D. (1988). Distribution of risk behaviors for HIV infection amongst intravenous drug users. *British Journal of Addiction, 83*, 1331–1334.
Coleridge, J., Cameron, P. A., Drummer, O. H., & McNeil, J. J. (1992). Survey of drug-related deaths in Victoria. *Medical Journal of Australia, 157*, 459–462.
Coles, C. D. (1993). Saying "goodbye" to the "crack baby." *Neurotoxicology and Teratology, 15*, 290–292.
Collins, J. J., Jr. (1981). Alcohol use and criminal behavior: An empirical, theoretical and methodological overview. In J. J. Collins, Jr. (Ed.), *Drinking and crime* (pp. 288–316). New York: Guilford.
Collishaw, N., & Leahy, K. (1991). Mortality attributable to tobacco use in Canada. *Chronic Diseases in Canada, 12*, 46.
Conigrave, K. M., Hall, W. D., & Saunders, J. B. (1995). The AUDIT questionnaire: Choosing a cut-off score. Alcohol Use Disorder Identification Test. *Addiction, 90*(10), 1349–1356.
Connell, R. (1994). Column one: The hidden devastation of crack; The epidemic is eating away everyone's quality of life. Violent crime, overtaxed social services and drug-addicted babies are having an impact as great as. *Los Angeles Times*, pp. A-1.
Consensus report. Drug concentration and driving impairment. (1985). *Journal of the American Medical Association, 254*, 2618–2621.
Coombs, R. H. (1981). Back on the streets: Therapeutic communities' impact upon drug users. *American Journal on Drug and Alcohol Abuse, 8*, 185–201.
Cordier, S., Ha, M.-C., Ayme, S., & Goujard, J. (1992). Maternal occupational exposure and congenital malformations. *Scandinavian Journal of Work Environment Health, 18*, 11–17.
Corkum, S. (1989). Stai con me eti daro l'AIDS. *VitaSana*, Maggio, 34–40.
Cornelius, M. D., Richardson, G. A., Day, N. L., Cornelius, J. R., Geva, D., & Taylor, P. M. (1994). A comparison of prenatal drinking in two recent samples of adolescents and adults. *Journal of Studies on Alcohol, 55*, 412–419.
Coryell, W. (1991). Genetics and dual diagnosis. In M. S. Gold & A. E. Slaby (Eds.), *Dual diagnosis in substance abuse* (pp. 29–41). New York: Marcel Dekker.
Coté, T. R., Biggar, R. J., & Dannenberg, A. L. (1992). Risk of suicide among persons with AIDS: A national assessment. *Journal of the American Medical Association, 268*, 2066–2068.
Cotton, D. J., Finkelstein, D. M., He, W., & Feinberg, J. (1993). Determinants of accrual of women to a large, multicenter clinical trials program of human immunodeficiency virus infection. *Journal of Acquired Immune Deficiency Syndromes, 6*, 1322–1328.

Council statement: Benzodiazepines. (1989). *The Pharmaceutical Journal, 243,* 200.
Counte, M. A., Salloway, J. C., & Christman, L. (1982). Age and sex related drinking patterns in alcoholics. In I. Wood, W. Gibson, & M. F. Elias (Eds.), *Alcoholism and aging* (pp. 17–27). New York: Research Institute on Alcoholism.
Covey, L. S., & Glassman, A. H. (1991). New approaches to smoking cessation. *Physician Assistant, 15,* 69–70, 73–74, 77.
Crabtree, B. L. (1984). Review of naltrexone, a long-acting opiate antagonist. *Clinical Pharmacy, 3,* 273–280.
Cregler, L. L., & Mark, H. (1986). Medical complications of cocaine abuse. *New England Journal of Medicine, 315,* 1495–1500.
Crews, T. M., & Sher, K. J. (1992). Using adapted short MASTs for assessing parental alcoholism: Reliability and validity. *Alcoholism: Clinical and Experimental Research, 16*(3), 576–584.
Cullen, J. W. (1982). Behavioral, psychological, and social influences on risk factors, prevention, and early detection. *Cancer, 50,* 1946–1953.
Cunningham, J. A., Sobell, L. C., & Chow, V. M. C. (1993). What's in a label? The effects of substance types and labels on treatment considerations and stigma. *Journal of Studies on Alcohol, 54,* 693–699.
Cunningham, L. (1996). Women strive to overcome barriers to treatment. *Alcoholism and Drug Abuse Weekly, 8,* 3.
Curran, J. W., Jaffe, H. W., Hardy, A. M., Morgan, W., Selik, R. M., & Dondero, T. J. (1988). Epidemiology of HIV infection and AIDS in the United States. *Science, 239,* 610–616.
Curtis, J. R., Geller, G., Stokes, E. J., Levine, D. M., & Moore, R. D. (1989). Characteristics, diagnosis, and treatment of alcoholism in elderly patients. *Journal of the American Geriatrics Society, 37,* 310–316.
Curtis, P. A., & McCullough, C. (1993). The impact of alcohol and other drugs on the child welfare system. *Child Welfare, 72,* 533–542.
Cutler, J. (1994). Thalidomide revisited [Letter to the editor]. *The Lancet, 343,* 795–796.
Cyr, M. G., & Moulton, A. W. (1993). The physician's role in prevention, detection, and treatment of alcohol abuse in women. *Psychiatric Annals, 23*(8), 454–462.
Daley, D. C., Moss, H., & Campbell, F. (1987). *Dual disorders: Counseling clients with chemical dependency and mental illness.* Center City, MN: Hazelden.
Dannenberg, A. L., Parver, L. M., & Fowler, C. J. (1992). Penetrating eye injuries related to assault. *Archives of Ophthalmology, 110,* 849–852.
D'Archangelo, E. (1993). Substance abuse in later life. *Canadian Family Physician, 39,* 1986–1988, 1991–1993.
Das, G. (1994). Cocaine abuse and reproduction. *International Journal of Clinical Pharmacology and Therapeutics, 32*(1), 7–11.
Dawson, G. W., & Vestal, R. E. (1982). Smoking and drug metabolism. *Pharmacology and Therapeutics, 15,* 207–221.
Dawson, J. M., & Langan, P. A. (1994). Murder in families. *Bureau of Justice Statistics Special Report.* Washington, DC: U.S. Department of Justice.
Day, C. P., James, O. F. W., Butler, T. J., & Campbell, R. W. (1993). QT prolongation and sudden cardiac death in patients with alcoholic liver disease. *Lancet, 341,* 1423–1428.
Day, N. L., & Richardson, G. A. (1991). Prenatal alcohol exposure: A continuum of effects. *Seminars in Perinatology, 15,* 271–279.
Day, N. L., Richardson, G. A., Geva, D., & Robles, N. (1994). Alcohol, marijuana, and tobacco: Effects of prenatal exposure on offspring growth and morphology at age six. *Alcoholism: Clinical and Experimental Research, 18,* 786–794.
Day, N., Sambamoorthi, U., Taylor, P., Richardson, G., Robles, N., Jhon, Y., Scher, M., Stoffer, D., Cornelius, M., & Jasperse, D. (1991). Prenatal marijuana use and neonatal outcome. *Neurotoxicology and Teratology, 13*(3), 329–334.
Deal, J. E., & Wampler, K. (1986). Dating violence: The primacy of previous experience. *Journal of Social and Personal Relationships, 3,* 457–471.

DeBettencourt, K. B. (1990). The wisdom of Solomon: Cutting the cord that harms. *Children Today, 19,* 17–20.

DeBruyn, L. M., Lujan, C. C., & May, P. A. (1992). A comparative study of abused and neglected American Indian children in the Southwest. *Social and Scientific Medicine, 35,* 305–315.

Deen, T. (1995). Health: Women are more severely affected by smoking. *Inter Press Service English News Wire,* July 26.

DeFronzo, J., & Pawlak, R. (1993a). Being female and less deviant: The direct and indirect effects of gender on alcohol abuse and tobacco smoking. *Journal of Psychology, 127*(6), 639–647.

DeFronzo, J., & Pawlak, R. (1993b, October). Effects of social bonds and childhood experiences on alcohol abuse and smoking. *Journal of Social Psychology, 133*(5), 635–642.

Del Boca, F. K. (1994). Sex, gender, and alcoholic typologies. *Annals of the New York Academy of Sciences, 708,* 34–48.

De Leon, G. (1985). The therapeutic community: Status and evolution. *The International Journal of the Addictions, 20,* 823–844.

Deren, S. (1986). Children of substance abusers: A review of the literature. *Journal of Substance Abuse Treatment, 3,* 77–94.

Deren, S., Beardsley, M., Davis, R., & Tortu, S. (1993). HIV risk factors among pregnant and nonpregnant high-risk women in New York City. *Journal of Drug Education, 23*(1), 57–66.

Deren, S., Frank, B., & Schmeidler, J. (1990, April). Children of substance abusers in New York State. *New York State Journal of Medicine, 90,* 179–184.

Dermen, K. H., & George, W. H. (1989). Alcohol expectancy and the relationship between drinking and physical aggression. *Journal of Psychology, 123,* 153–161.

Deshpande, S. N., & Nagpal, R. S. (1993). Benzodiazepine abuse among female outpatients in India. *Addictive Behaviors, 18,* 595–596.

Des Jarlais, D. C., & Friedman, S. R. (1988). Transmission of human immunodeficiency virus among intravenous drug users. In V. T. DeVita, S. Hellman, & S. Rosenberg (Eds.), *AIDS: Etiology, diagnosis, treatment, and prevention* (2nd ed.). Philadelphia: J. B. Lippincott.

Des Jarlais, D. C., Friedman, S. R., & Strug, D. (1986). AIDS and needle sharing within the IV-drug use subculture. In D. A. Feldman & T. M. Johnson (Eds.), *The social dimension of AIDS: Method and theory.* New York: Praeger.

Dewey, W. L. (1986). Cannabinoid pharmacology. *Pharmacological Reviews, 38,* 151–178.

DeWitt, C. B. (1991, June). Drug use forecasting. *Research in Action.* Washington, DC: U.S. Department of Justice, 1–8.

DeWitt, C. B., O'Neil, J. A., & Baldau, V. (1991, August). Drug use forecasting: Drugs & crime 1990 annual report. *Research in Action.* Washington, DC: U.S. Department of Justice, 1–24.

DiFranza, J. R., & Lew, R. A. (1995). Effect of maternal cigarette smoking on pregnancy complications and sudden infant death syndrome. *Journal of Family Practice, 40,* 385–394.

Dolan, M. P., Black, J. L., Deford, H. A., Skinner, J. R., & Robinowitz, R. (1987). Characteristics of drug abusers that discriminate needle-sharers. *Public Health Reports, 102,* 395–398.

Dole, V. P. (1971). Methadone maintenance treatment for 25,000 heroin addicts. *Journal of the American Medical Association, 215,* 1131–1134.

Dole, V. P., & Nyswander, M. E. (1980). Methadone maintenance: A theoretical perspective. In D. J. Lettieri, M. Sayers, & H. Walenstein Pearson (Eds.), *Theories on drug abuse: Selected contemporary perspectives. National Institute on Drug Abuse Research Monograph, 30,* 256–261.

Dolphin, R., & Driver, D. (1988). Hidden addictions: The increasing abuse of prescription drugs. *Maclean's, 101,* N2–N4.

Donnelly, A. H. C. (1991). What we have learned about prevention: What we should do about it. *Child Abuse & Neglect, 15,* 99–106.

D'Orban, P. T. (1989). Automatism: A medico-legal conundrum. *Irish Journal of Psychological Medicine, 6,* 71–80.

Dorris, M. (1989). *The broken cord.* New York: Harper Collins.

Dorris, M. (1990, November). Fetal alcohol syndrome: The sobering facts about the nation's number one preventable birth defect. *Parents, 238,* 240, 243, 245.

Dow-Edwards, D. L. (1991). Cocaine effects on fetal development: A comparison of clinical and animal research findings. *Neurotoxicology and Teratology, 13*(3), 347–352.
Dow-Edwards, D. (1993). The puzzle of cocaine's effects following maternal use during pregnancy: Still unsolved. *Neurotoxicology and Teratology, 15,* 295–296.
Dowsett, B. (1989, June 12). There's no age restriction on drug dealing. *The London Free Press,* C1.
Dreher, M. (1984). Marijuana use among women—An anthropological view. *Advances in Alcohol and Substance Abuse, 3*(3), 51–64.
Drew, L. R. H. (1989, February 6). A poor rest home remedy: Drugs in place of care. *Newsweek,* 56.
Drugs and crime facts, 1993 (NCJ No. 146246). (1994). Washington, DC: U.S. Department of Justice.
Dufour, M. C., Archer, L., & Gordis, E. (1992). Alcohol and the elderly. *Clinical Geriatric Medicine, 8,* 127–141.
Duimstra, C., Johnson, D., Kutsch, C., Wang, B., Zentner, M., Kellerman, S., & Welty, T. (1993). A fetal alcohol syndrome surveillance pilot project in American Indian communities in the Northern Plains. *Public Health Reports, 108,* 225–229.
DuPont, R. L., & Saylor, K. E. (1992). Depressant substances in adolescent medicine. *Pediatrics in Review, 13*(10), 381–386.
Dusenbury, L., & Botvin, G. J. (1992). Substance abuse prevention: Competence enhancement and the development of positive life options. *Journal of Addictive Diseases, 11,* 29–45.
Edwards, D. W. (1985). An investigation of the use and abuse of alcohol and other drugs among 50 aged male alcoholics and 50 aged female alcoholics. *Journal of Alcohol and Drug Education, 30,* 24–30.
Egami, Y., Ford, D. E., Greenfield, S. F., & Crum, R. M. (1996). Psychiatric profile and sociodemographic characteristics of adults who report physically abusing or neglecting children. *American Journal of Psychiatry, 153*(7), 921–928.
El-Bassel, N., Ivanoff, A., Schilling, R. F., Gilbert, L., & Chen, D.-R. (1995). Correlates of problem drinking among drug-using incarcerated women. *Addictive Behaviors, 20*(3), 359–369.
El-Bassel, N., Schilling, R. F., Schinke, S., Orlandi, M., et al. (1997). Assessing the utility of the Drug Abuse Screening Test in the workplace. *Research on Social Work Practice, 7*(1), 99–114.
Electric Library. (July 30/1996). A portrait of addicted Jews: JACS aids those seeking a way out [On-line]. Available: http://www.elibrary.com/
Electric Library. (July 30/1996). Alcohol and other drug abuse among women [On-line]. Available: http://www.elibrary.com/
Electric Library. (July 30/1996). Collaboration seen as key for dually diagnosed women [On-line]. Available: http://www.elibrary.com/
Electric Library. (July 30/1996). College women and alcohol: A relational perspective [On-line]. Available: http://www.elibrary.com/
Electric Library. (July 30/1996). Drug studies raise question: What's happening to American women? [On-line]. Available: http://www.elibrary.com/
Electric Library. (July 30/1996). Health: Women are more severely affected by smoking [On-line]. Available: http://www.elibrary.com/
Electric Library. (July 30/1996). How women drink [On-line]. Available: http://www.elibrary.com/
Electric Library. (July 30/1996). NIDA Conference on women and drug abuse [On-line]. Available: http://www.elibrary.com/
Electric Library. (July 30/1996). Oprah admits to smoking cocaine [On-line]. Available: http://www.elibrary.com/
Electric Library. (July 30/1996). Risk factors for drinking over a woman's life span [On-line]. Available: http://www.elibrary.com/
Electric Library. (July 30/1996). The war on drugs is lost [On-line]. Available: http://www.elibrary.com/
Electric Library. (July 30/1996). The impact of family violence on the use of alcohol by women [On-line]. Available: http://www.elibrary.com/

Electric Library. (July 30/1996). Women at greater risk than men from alcohol abuse, studies show; men drink more, and more men drink. But biological factors force women to pay a higher toll for tippling; Home edition [On-line]. Available: http://www.elibrary.com/

Eliason, M. J., & Williams, J. K. (1990). Fetal alcohol syndrome and the neonate. *The Journal of Perinatal and Neonatal Nursing, 3*(4), 64–72.

Elk, R. (1999). Pregnant women and tuberculosis-exposed drug abusers: Reducing drug use and increasing treatment compliance. *Motivating Behavior Change Among Illicit-Drug Abusers: Research on Contingency Management Interventions,* 123–144.

Elmer, G. I., Miner, L. L., & Pickens, R. W. (1998). The contribution of genetic factors in cocaine and other drug abuse. In S. T. Higgins & J. L. Katz (Eds.), *Cocaine abuse: Behavior, pharmacology, and clinical applications* (pp. 289–311). San Diego: Academic.

Emanuele, N. V., Swade, T. F., & Emanuele, M. A. (1998). Alcohol's harmful effects on bone. *Alcohol World Health and Research, 22*(3), 211–219.

Epperson, S. E., & Rivera, E. (1995). Abandoned to her fate. *Time, 146*(24), 38–42.

Ericksen, K. P., & Trocki, K. F. Behavioral risk factors for sexually transmitted disease in American households. *Social Science of Medicine, 34,* 843–853.

Erickson, J. R. (1997). Human immunodeficiency virus infection risk among female sex partners of intravenous drug users in southern Arizona. *Holistic Nursing Practice, 11*(2), 9–17.

Erickson, P. G., & Murray, G. F. (1989). Sex differences in cocaine use and experiences: A double standard revived? *American Journal of Drug & Alcohol Abuse, 15*(4), 135–152.

Erickson, P. I., & Rapkin, A. J. (1991). Unwanted sexual experiences among middle and high school youth. *Journal of Adolescent Health, 12*(4), 319–325.

Ewing, J. A. (1984). Detecting alcoholism. The CAGE questionnaire. *Journal of the American Medical Association, 252,* 1905–1907.

Famularo, R., Kinscherff, R., Bunshart, D., Spivak, T., & Fenton, L. (1989). Parental compliance to court-ordered treatment interventions in cases of child maltreatment. *Child Abuse and Neglect, 13,* 507.

Famularo, R., Kinscherff, R., & Fenton, T. (1992). Parental substance abuse and the nature of child maltreatment. *Child Abuse & Neglect, 16,* 475–483.

Farley, T. A., Hadler, J. L., & Gunn, R. A. (1990). The syphilis epidemic in Connecticut: Relationship to drug use and prostitution. *Sexually Transmitted Diseases, 17,* 163–168.

Farr, K. A. (1995). Fetal abuse and the criminalization of behavior during pregnancy. *Crime and Delinquency, 41*(2), 235–245.

Febbo, S., Hardy, F., & Finlay-Jones, R. (1993–94). Dissociation and psychological blow automatism in Australia. *International Journal of Mental Health, 22,* 39–59.

Federal, Provincial and Territorial Advisory Committee on Population Health. (1996, September 10 and 11). Report on the health of Canadians. Toronto: *Meeting of Ministers of Health.*

Feingold, L., Ziegler, S., Laufer, D., & Mayer, K. (1990). The New England behavioral health study. *International Conference on AIDS Abstracts, 6,* 268.

Feldman, W., Feldman, E., Goodman, J. T., McGrath, P. J., Pless, R. P., Corsini, L., & Bennett, S. (1991). Is childhood sexual abuse really increasing in prevalence? An analysis of the evidence. *Pediatrics, 88,* 29–33.

Fenwick, P. (1987). Somnambulism and the law: A review. *Behavioral Sciences & the Law, 5,* 343–357.

Fenwick, P. (1990). Automatism, medicine and the law. *Psychological Medicine, 17,* 1–27.

Fetal alcohol syndrome. (1991). *Alcohol Alert, National Institute on Alcohol Abuse and Alcoholism,* PH297(13), 1–4.

Fields, R. (1995). Dual diagnosis: Definition, population, treatment. *Professional Counselor, 10*(2), 16.

Fife, K. H. (1991). Pharmacotherapeutics for the AIDS patient. *American Journal of Pharmaceutical Education, 55,* 394–397.

Fineman, N. R., Beckwith, L., Howard, J., & Espinosa, M. (1997). Maternal ego development and mother-infant interaction in drug-abusing women. *Journal of Substance Abuse Treatment, 14*(4), 307–317.

Fingarette, H. (1988). *Heaving drinking: The myth of alcoholism as a disease.* San Francisco, CA: University of California.

Finkelhor, D., & Dzuiba-Leatherman, J. (1994). Victimization of children. *American Psychologist, 49,* 173–183.

Finkelhor, D., Hotaling, G., Lewis, I. A., & Smith, C. (1990). Sexual abuse in a national survey of adult men and women: Prevalence, characteristics, and risk factors. *Child Abuse & Neglect, 14,* 19–28.

Finkelstein, N. (1993). Treatment programming for alcohol and drug-dependent pregnant women. *The International Journal of the Addictions, 28*(13), 1275–1309.

Finlayson, R. E., Hurt, R. D., Davis, L. J., Jr., & Morse, R. M. (1988). Alcoholism in elderly persons. A study of the psychiatric and psychosocial features of 216 in-patients. *Mayo Clinic Proceedings, 63,* 761–768.

Finnegan, L. P. (1991). Perinatal substance abuse: Comments and perspectives. *Seminars in Perinatology, 15*(4), 331–339.

Finney, J. W., & Moos, R. H. (1984). Life stressors and problem drinking among older adults. In M. Galanter (Ed.), *Recent developments in alcoholism* (Vol. 2, pp. 267–288). New York: Plenum.

Firearms and crimes of violence (NCJ-146844). (1994). Washington, DC: U.S. Department of Justice.

Fischl, M. A., Dickinson, G. M., Scott, G. B., Klimas, N., Fletcher, M. A., & Parks, W. (1987). Evaluation of heterosexual partners, children, and household contacts of adults with AIDS. *Journal of the American Medical Association, 257,* 640–644.

Fishbein, D. H., Jaffe, J. H., Snyder, F. R., Haertzen, C. A., & Hickey, J. E. (1993). Drug users' self-reports of behaviors and affective states under the influence of alcohol. *International Journal of the Addictions, 28,* 1565–1585.

Fisher, D. G. (Ed.). (1991). *AIDS and alcohol/drug abuse: Psychosocial research.* New York: Harrington Park.

Fitzgerald, J. L., & Mulford, H. A. (1992). Elderly vs. younger problem drinker "treatment" and recovery experiences. *British Journal of Addiction, 87,* 1281–1291.

Fleming, J., Mullen, P. E., Sibthorpe, B., Attewell, R., & Bammer, G. (1998). The relationship between childhood sexual abuse and alcohol. *Addiction, 93*(12), 1787–1798.

Fligiel, S. E., Venkat, H., Gong, H., & Tashkin, D. P. (1988). Bronchial pathology in chronic marijuana smokers: A light and electron microscopic study. *Journal of Psychoactive Drugs, 20,* 33–42.

Flumazenil. (1992). *The Medical Letter on Drugs and Therapeutics, 34,* 66–68.

Fordyce, E. J., Thomas, P., & Shum, R. (1997). Evidence of an increasing AIDS burden in rural America. *Statistical Bulletin—Metropolitan Insurance Companies, 78*(2), 2–9.

Forman, R., Klein, J., Meta, D., Barks, J., Greenwald, M., & Koren, G. (1993). Maternal and neonatal characteristics following exposure to cocaine in Toronto. *Reproductive Toxicology, 7,* 619–622.

Forth-Finegan, J. L. (1991). Sugar and spice and everything nice: Gender socialization and women's addiction—A literature review. In C. Bepko (Ed.), *Feminism and addiction* (pp. 19–48). Binghamton, NY: Haworth.

Foster, F. M., Horn, J. L., & Wanberg, K. W. (1972). Dimensions of treatment outcome. *Quarterly Journal of Studies on Alcohol, 33,* 1079–1098.

Frances, R. J., & Allen, M. H. (1986). The interaction of substance-use disorders with nonpsychotic psychiatric disorders. In R. Michels & J. O. Cavenar, Jr. (Eds.), *Psychiatry* (Vol. I). New York: Basic Books.

Frank, D. A., & Zuckerman, B. S. (1993). Children exposed to cocaine prenatally: Pieces of the puzzle. *Neurotoxicology and Teratology, 15,* 298–300.

Frankel, L. (1990). Structural family therapy for adolescent substance abusers and their families. In A. S. Friedman & S. Granick (Eds.), *Family therapy for adolescent drug abuse* (pp. 47–61). New York: Lexington.

Freiberg, P. (1998, February). We know how to stop the spread of AIDS: So why can't we? *Monitor: American Psychological Association,* 32.

Freier, K. (1994). In utero drug exposure and maternal-infant interaction: The complexities of the dyad and their environment. *Infant Mental Health Journal, 5*(2), 176–188.

French, J. F. (1993). Pipe dreams: Crack and the life in Philadelphia and Newark. In R. S. Ratner (Ed.), *Crack Pipe as Pimp: An Ethnographic Investigation of Sex-For-Crack Exchanges* (pp. 205–232). New York: Lexington Books.

Freund, G. (1984). Current research directions on alcohol problems and aging. *Alcohol Health & Research World, 8*(3), 11–15.

Freund, G. (1986). The interaction of chronic alcohol consumption and aging on brain structure and function. *Alcoholism: Clinical and Experimental Research, 6,* 13–21.

Fried, P. A., & Watkinson, B. (1990). 36- and 48-month neurobehavioral follow-up of children prenatally exposed to marijuana, cigarettes, and alcohol. *Developmental and Behavioral Pediatrics, 11*(2), 49–58.

Friedland, G. (1989). Parenteral drug users. In R. A. Kaslow & D. P. Francis (Eds.), *The epidemiology of AIDS: Expression, occurrence, and control of human immunodeficiency virus type 1 infection* (pp. 153–178). New York: Oxford University.

Friedland, G. H., Harris, C., Butkus-Small, C., Shine, D., Moll, B., Darrow, W., & Klein, R. S. (1985). Intravenous drug abusers and the acquired immunodeficiency syndrome (AIDS). *Archives of Internal Medicine, 145,* 1413–1417.

Fulop, G., Reinhardt, J., Strain, J. J., Paris, B., Miller, M., & Fillit, H. (1993). Identification of alcoholism and depression in a geriatric medicine outpatient clinic. *Journal of the American Geriatrics Society, 41*(7), 737–741.

Gabiano, C., Tovo, P.-A., de Martino, M., Galli, L., Giaquinto, C., Loy, A., Schoeller, M. C., Giovannini, M., Ferranti, G., Rancilio, L., Caselli, D., Segni, G., Livadiotti, S., Conte, A., Rizzi, M., Viggiano, D., Mazza, A., Ferrazzin, A., Tozzi, A. E., & Cappello, N. (1992). Mother-to-child transmission of human immunodeficiency virus type 1: Risk of infection and correlates of transmission. *Pediatrics, 90*(3), 369–374.

Gable, S., & Shindledecker, R. (1992). Behavior problems in sons and daughters of substance abusing parents. *Child Psychiatry and Human Development, 23,* 99–115.

Gabriel, K., Hofmann, C., Glavas, M., & Weinberg, J. (1998). The hormonal effects of alcohol use on the mother and fetus. *Alcohol Health & Research World, 23*(3), 170–177.

Galanter, M., Egelko, S., Edwards, H., & Vergaray, M. (1994). A treatment system for combined psychiatric and addictive illness. *Addiction, 89,* 1227–1235.

Garcia, S. A. (1993). Maternal drug abuse: Laws and ethics as agents of just balances and therapeutic interventions. *International Journal of the Addictions, 28,* 1311–1339.

Gardner, D. K. (1987). Drug passage into breast milk: Principles and concerns. *Journal of Pediatric and Perinatal Nutrition, 1,* 27–37.

Gardner, J. J., & Cabral, D. A. (1990). Sexually abused adolescents: A distinct group among sexually abused children presenting to a children's hospital. *Journal of Paediatrics and Child Health, 26,* 22–24.

Garriott, J. C. (1993). Drug use among homicide victims: Changing patterns. *American Journal of Forensic Medicine & Pathology, 14,* 234–237.

Garrity-Rokous, F. E. (1994). Punitive legal approaches to the problem of prenatal drug exposure. *Infant Mental Health Journal, 15*(2), 218–237.

Gaudin, J. M., Jr. (1993). Child neglect: A guide for intervention. *U.S. Department of Health and Human Services.*

Gavaler, J. S. (1982). Sex-related differences in ethanol-induced liver disease: Artifactual or real? *Alcoholism: Clinical Experimental Research, 6,* 186–196.

Gavaler, J. S. (1995). Alcohol effects on hormone levels in normal postmenopausal women and in postmenopausal women with alcohol-induced cirrhosis. In M. Galanter (Ed.), *Recent Developments in Alcoholism, Volume 12: Women and Alcoholism* (pp. 199–208). New York: Plenum.

Gavaler, J. S., Deal, S. R., Van Thiel, D. H., Arria, A., & Allan, M. J. (1993). Alcohol and estrogen levels in postmenopausal women: The spectrum of effect. *Alcoholism: Clinical & Experimental Research, 17*(4), 786–790.

Gavaler, J. S., Rizzo, A., Rossaro, L., Van Thiel, D. H., Brezza, E., & Deal, S. R. (1993). Sexuality of alcoholic women with menstrual cycle function: Effects of duration of alcohol abstinence. *Alcoholism: Clinical and Experimental Research, 17*(3), 778–781.

Gearhart, J. G., Beebe, D. K., Milhorn, H. T., & Meeks, R. (1991). Alcoholism in women. *American Family Physician, 44*(3), 907–913.
Gelles, R., & Pedrick-Cornell, C. (1985). *Intimate violence in families.* Beverly Hills, CA: Sage.
Generali, J. A. (1992). Nicotine transdermal patches. *Facts and Comparisons Drug Newsletter, 11,* 33–34.
George, W. H., & Dermen, K. H. (1988). Self-reported alcohol expectancies for self and others as a function of behavior type and dosage set. *Journal of Substance Abuse, 1,* 71–78.
George, W. H., La Marr, J., Barrett, K., & McKinnon, T. (1999). Alcoholic parentage, self-labeling, and endorsement of ACOA-codependent traits. *Psychology of Addictive Behaviors, 13*(1), 39–48.
Gerrard, M., Gibbons, F. X., & Warner, T. D. (1991). Effects of reviewing risk-relevant behavior on perceived vulnerability among women marines. *Health Psychology, 10*(3), 173–179.
Gettman, J. (1994). Heroin returning to center stage. *High Times, 23.*
Gettman, J. (1995). Marijuana and the human brain. *Highwitness News, 3*(235), 26–29.
Getty, G., & Stern, P. (1990). Gay men's perceptions and responses to AIDS. *Journal of Advanced Nursing, 15,* 895–905.
Gibb, B. (1987). Sex, drugs, and alcohol: A losing combination. *Listen, 40,* 11–14.
Gielen, A. C., O'Campo, P., Faden, R. R., & Eke, A. (1997). Women's disclosure of HIV status: Experiences of mistreatment and violence in an urban setting. *Women and Health, 25*(3), 19–31.
Gieringer, D. H. (1988). Marijuana, driving, and accident safety. *Journal of Psychoactive Drugs, 20*(1), 93–101.
Gieron-Korthals, M. A., Helal, A., & Martinez, C. R. (1994). Expanding spectrum of cocaine induced central nervous system malformations. *Brain & Development, 16,* 253–256.
Gilbody, J. S. (1991). Effects of maternal drug addiction on the fetus. *Adverse Drug Reactions and Acute Toxicology Reviews, 10,* 77–88.
Gilchrist, L. D., Gillmore, M. R., & Lohr, M. J. (1990). Drug use among pregnant adolescents. *Journal of Consulting and Clinical Psychology, 58,* 402–407.
Ginsberg, K. A., Blacker, C. M., Abel, E. L., & Sokol, R. J. (1991). Fetal alcohol exposure and adverse pregnancy outcomes. *Contributions to Gynecology and Obstetrics, 18,* 115–129.
Gittler, J., & McPherson, M. (1990). Prenatal substance abuse. *Children Today, 14*(4), 3–7.
Glantz, M. D. (1985). The detection, identification and differentiation of elderly drug misuse and abuse in a research survey. In E. Gottheil, K. A. Druley, T. E. Skoloda, et al. (Eds.), *The combined problems of alcoholism, drug addiction and aging* (pp. 113–129). Springfield, IL: Charles C. Thomas.
Glantz, M. D., & Backenheimer, M. S. (1988). Substance abuse among elderly women. *Clinical Gerontologist, 8*(1), 3–25.
Gleason, N. A. (1994). Preventing alcohol abuse by college women: A relational perspective. *Journal of American College Health, 43*(1), 15–24.
Gold, M. S., & Dackis, C. A. (1984). New insights and treatments: Opiate withdrawal and cocaine addiction. *Clinical Therapeutics, 7,* 6–21.
Gold, M. S., & Slaby, A. E. (1991). *Dual diagnosis in substance abuse.* New York: Marcel Dekker.
Goldberg, M. E., Lex, B. W., Mello, N. K., Mendelson, J. H., & Bower, T. A. (1996). Impact of maternal alcoholism on separation of children from their mothers: Finding from a sample of incarcerated women. *American Journal of Orthopsychiatry, 66*(2), 228–238.
Goldbloom, D. S. (1993). Alcohol misuse and eating disorders: Aspects of an association [Review]. *Alcohol & Alcoholism, 28*(4), 375–381.
Goldsmith, S. (1990). Prosecution to enhance treatment. *Children Today, 19,* 13–16.
Goldstein, D. B. (1983). *Pharmacology of alcohol.* New York: Oxford University.
Goldstein, M. B., & Engwall, D. B. (1992). The politics of prevention: Changing definitions of substance use/abuse. *Journal of Health & Social Policy, 3,* 69–83.
Gomberg, E. L. (1986). Women: Alcohol and other drugs. *Drugs & Society, 1*(1), 75–109.
Gomberg, E. S. (1986). Women and alcoholism: Psychosocial issues. *Women and Alcohol: Health-Related Issues.* Washington, DC: US Department of Health and Human Services.
Gomberg, E. S. L. (1989). Suicide risk among women with alcohol problems. *Addictions Nursing Network, 1*(4), 3–7.

Gomberg, E. S. L. (1995). Older women and alcohol: Use and abuse. *Recent Developments in Alcoholism, 12,* 61–79.

Gordis, E., & Alexander, D. (1992). From the National Institutes of Health: Progress toward preventing and understanding alcohol-related fetal injury. *Journal of the American Medical Association, 268,* 3183.

Gore, T. (1991). A portrait of at-risk children. *Journal of Health Care for the Poor and Underserved, 2*(1), 95–105.

Gore Gearhart, J., Beebe, D. K., Milhorn, H. T., & Meeks, G. R. (1991). Alcoholism in women. *American Family Physician, 44*(3), 907–911.

Gori, G. B., Benowitz, N. L., & Lynch, C. J. (1986). Mouth versus deep airways absorption of nicotine in cigarette smokers. *Pharmacology, Biochemistry and Behavior, 25,* 1181–1184.

Gotoh, M. (1994). Alcohol dependence of women in Japan. *Addiction, 89,* 953–954.

Gottwald, S. R., & Thurman, S. K. (1994). The effects of prenatal cocaine exposure on mother-infant interaction and infant arousal in the newborn period. *Topics in Early Childhood Special Education, 14*(2), 217–231.

Graham, A. V., Parran, T. V., Jr., & Jaen, C. R. (1992). Physician failure to record alcohol use history when prescribing benzodiazepines. *Journal of Substance Abuse, 4,* 179–185.

Graham, K. (1980). Theories of intoxicated aggression. *Canadian Journal of the Behavioural Sciences, 12,* 141–158.

Grantham, P. (1987). Benzodiazepine abuse. *British Journal of Hospital Medicine, 37,* 292–300.

Green, A. H., & Kaplan, M. S. (1994). Psychiatric impairment and childhood victimization experiences in female child molesters. *Journal of the American Academy of Child & Adolescent Psychiatry, 33*(7), 954–961.

Greenfeld, L. A. (1998, April). Alcohol and crime: An analysis of national data on the prevalence of alcohol involvement in crime. *U.S. Department of Justice* (NCJ 168632). Washington, DC.

Greenstein, R. A., Arndt, I. S. C., McLellan, A. T., O'Brien, C. P., & Evans, B. (1984). Naltrexone: A clinical perspective. *Journal of Clinical Psychiatry, 45,* 25–28.

Griffith, D. R., Azuma, S. D., & Chasnoff, I. J. (1994). Three-year outcome of children exposed prenatally to drugs. *Journal of American Child and Adolescent Psychiatry, 33,* 20–27.

Grinspoon, L., & Hedblom, P. (1975). *The speed culture: Amphetamine use and abuse in America.* Cambridge, MA: Harvard University.

Gripshover, D. L., & Dacey, C. M. (1994). Discriminative validity of the MacAndrew Scale in settings with a high base rate of substance abuse. *Journal of Studies on Alcohol, 55*(3), 303–308.

Gritz, E. R., & Crane, L. A. (1991). Use of diet pills and amphetamines to lose weight among smoking and nonsmoking high school seniors. *Health Psychology, 10,* 330–335.

Grover, S. M., & Thomas, S. P. (1993). Substance use and anger in mid-life women. *Issues in Mental Health Nursing, 14,* 19–29.

Guinan, M. E., & Hardy, A. (1987). Epidemiology of AIDS in women in the United States. *Journal of the American Medical Association, 257,* 2039–2042.

Gulino, C., & Kadin, M. (1986). Aging and reactive alcoholism. *Geriatric Nursing, 7,* 148–151.

Gupta, K. L. (1993). Alcoholism in the elderly. Uncovering a hidden problem. *Postgraduate Medicine, 93,* 203–206.

Gupton, A., Thompson, L., Arnason, R. C., Dalke, S., & Ashcroft, T. (1995, August). Pregnant women and smoking. *The Canadian Nurse, 91*(8), 26–30.

Haddad, J., & Messer, J. (1994). Fetal alcohol syndrome: Report of three siblings. *Neopediatrics, 25,* 109–111.

Hagan, T. A., Finnegan, L. P., Nelson-Zlupko, L. (1994). Impediments to comprehensive treatment models for substance-dependent women: Treatment and research questions. *Journal of Psychoactive Drugs, 26*(2), 163–171.

Hahn, E. J. (1993). Parental alcohol and other drug (AOD) use and health beliefs about parent involvement in AOD prevention. *Issues in Mental Health Nursing, 14*(3), 237–247.

Hahn, R. A., Onorato, I. M., Jones, T. S., & Dougherty, J. (1989). Prevalence of HIV infection among intravenous drug users in the United States. *Journal of the American Medical Association, 261,* 2677–2684.

Haldeman, K., & Gafner, G. (1990). Are elderly alcoholics discriminated against? *Journal of Psychosocial Nursing, 28,* 6–8, 10–11.
Hall, J. M. (1990). Alcoholism recovery in lesbian women: A theory in development. *Scholarly Inquiry for Nursing Practice: An International Journal, 4*(2), 109–122.
Hall, J. M. (1994). The experiences of lesbians in Alcoholics Anonymous. *Western Journal of Nursing Research, 16*(5), 556–576.
Hall, S. C., & Ofodile, F. A. (1991). Mandibular fractures in an American inner city: The Harlem Hospital Center experience. *Journal of the National Medical Association, 83,* 421–423.
Hamberger, L. K., & Potente, T. (1994). Counseling heterosexual women arrested for domestic violence: Implications for theory and practice. *Violence and Victims, 9*(2), 125–137.
Hamilton, G. J. (1993). Further labeling within the category of disability due to chemical dependency: Borderline personality disorder. In M. E. Willmuth & L. Holcomb (Ed.), *Women with disabilities: Found voices* (pp. 153–157). Binghamton, NY: Haworth.
Handal, K. A., Schauben, J. L., & Salamone, F. R. (1983). Naloxone. *Annals of Emergency Medicine, 12,* 438–445.
Handler, A. S., Mason, E. D., Rosenberg, D. L., & Davis, F. G. (1994). The relationship between exposure during pregnancy to cigarette smoking and cocaine use and placenta previa. *American Journal of Obstetrics and Gynecology, 170*(3), 884–889.
Hands, M. A., Banwell, C. L., & Hamilton, M. A. (1995). Women and alcohol: Current Australian research. *Drug and Alcohol Review, 14,* 17–25.
Hanna, E., Dufour, M. C., Elliott, S., Stinson, F., & Harford, T. C. (1992). Dying to be equal: Women, alcohol, and cardiovascular disease. *British Journal of Addiction, 87*(11), 1593–1597.
Hannig, V. L., & Phillips, J. A. (1991). Maternal cocaine abuse and fetal anomalies: Evidence for teratogenic effects of cocaine. *Southern Medical Journal, 84,* 498–499.
Hanson, B., Beschner, G., Walters, J. M., & Bovelle, E. (1985). *Life with heroin.* Lexington, MA: Lexington.
Harmin, M., Kirschenbaum, H., & Simon, S. B. (1973). *Clarifying values through subject matter: Applications for the classroom* (pp. 32–34). Minneapolis, MN: Winston.
Harms, G., Laukamm-Josten, U., Bienzle, U., & Guggenmoos-Holzmann, I. (1987). Risk factors for HIV infection in German I.V. drug abusers: Clinical, serological and epidemiological features. *Klinische Wochenschrift, 65,* 376–379.
Harper, C. G., & Kril, J. J. (1990). Neuropathology of alcoholism. *Alcohol and Alcoholism, 25,* 207–216.
Harris, S. R., Osborn, J. A., Weinberg, J., Loock, C., & Junaid, K. (1993). Effects of prenatal alcohol exposure on neuromotor and cognitive development during early childhood: A series of case reports. *Physical Therapy, 73,* 608–617.
Harrison, L. D. (1992). Trends in illicit drug use in the United States: Conflicting results from national surveys. *International Journal of the Addictions, 27*(7), 817–847.
Hartford, J. T., & Samorajski, T. (1982). Alcoholism in the geriatric population. *Journal of the American Geriatrics Society, 30,* 18–23.
Haug, K., Aaro, L. E., & Fugelli, P. (1992). Smoking habits in early pregnancy and attitudes towards smoking cessation among pregnant women and their partners. *Family Practice, 9*(4), 494–499.
Haugland, S. (1989). Alcoholism and other drug dependencies. *Primary Care, 16,* 411–429.
Hauschildt, E. (1992, October/November). Massive U.S. drug "war" a failure: Policy group. *The Journal, 21,* 5.
Havens, J. F., Mellins, C. A., & Pilowski, D. (1996). Mental health issues in HIV-affected women and children. *International Review of Psychiatry, 8*(2–3), 217–225.
Haverkos, H. W. (1998). HIV/AIDS and drug abuse: Epidemiology and prevention. *Journal of Addictive Diseases, 17*(4), 91–103.
Hawley, T. L. (1993). Maternal cocaine addiction: Correlates and consequences. *EDRS Availability.*
Hays, R. D., Hill, L., Gillogly, J. J., Lewis, M. W., et al. (1993). Response times for the CAGE, short-MAST, AUDIT, and JELLINEK alcohol scales. *Behavior Research Methods, Instruments, & Computers, 25*(2), 304–307.

Hays, R. D., Merz, J. F., & Nicholas, R. (1995). Response burden, reliability, and validity of the CAGE, short MAST, and AUDIT alcohol screening measures. *Behavior Research Methods, Instruments, and Computers, 27*(2), 277–280.

Hays, R. D., & Revetto, J. P. (1992). Old and new MMPI-derived scales and the short-MAST as screening tools for alcohol disorder. *Alcohol and Alcoholism, 27*(6), 685–695.

Health care providers shun drug addicts with AIDS (1989). *AIDS Alert, 4,* 93–97.

Heil, S. H., & Subramanian, M. G. (1998). Alcohol and the hormonal control of lactation. *Alcohol Health & Research World, 22*(3), 178–184.

Heller, M. C., Sobel, M., & Tanaka-Matsumi, J. (1996). A functional analysis of verbal interactions of drug-exposed children and their mothers: The utility of sequential analysis. *Journal of Clinical Psychology, 52*(6), 687–697.

Hemminki, K., & Vineis, P. (1985). Extrapolation of the evidence on teratogenicity of chemicals between humans and experimental animals: Chemicals other than drugs. *Teratogenesis, Carcinogenesis, and Mutagenesis, 5,* 251–318.

Herr, B. M., & Pettinati, H. M. (1984). Long term outcome in working and homemaking alcoholic women. *Alcoholism: Clinical and Experimental Research, 8*(6), 576–579.

Herridge, P., & Gold, M. S. (1988). Pharmacological adjuncts in the treatment of opioid and cocaine addicts. *Journal of Psychoactive Drugs, 20,* 233–242.

Hibbs, J. R., & Gunn, R. A. (1991). Public health intervention in a cocaine-related syphilis outbreak. *American Journal of Public Health, 81,* 1259–1262.

Hickl-Szabo, R. (1987, January 24). Crying infants sedated with gasoline fumes, Manitoba official says. *The Globe and Mail, 143*(42, 787), pp. A1-A2.

Higgins, P. G., Clough, D. H., Frank, B., & Wallerstedt, C. (1995). Changes in health behaviors made by pregnant substance users. *The International Journal of the Addictions, 30*(10), 1323–1333.

Higgins, S. T. (1999). Introduction. *Motivating behavior change among illicit-drug abusers: Research on continency management interventions,* 3–13.

Hill, R. M., Hegemier, S., & Tennyson, L. M. (1989). The fetal alcohol syndrome: A multihandicapped child. *Neurotoxicology, 10,* 585–596.

Hill, S. Y. (1993). Personality characteristics of sisters and spouses of male alcoholics. *Alcoholism: Clinical and Experimental Research, 17*(4), 733–739.

Hill, S. Y. (1995a). Mental and physical health consequences of alcohol use in women. *Recent Developments in Alcoholism: Women and Alcoholism, 12,* 181–197. New York: Plenum.

Hill, S. Y. (1995b). Neurobiological and clinical markers for a severe form of alcoholism in women. *Alcohol Health & Research World, 10*(3), 249–256.

Hill, S. Y., & Steinhauer, S. R. (1993). Event-related potentials in women at risk for alcoholism. *Alcohol, 10,* 349–354.

Hillbrand, M., Foster, H., Jr., & Hirt, M. (1990). Rapists and child molesters: Psychometric comparisons. *Archives of Sexual Behavior, 19*(1), 65–71.

Hilleman, D. E., Mohiuddin, S. M., Del Core, M. G., & Sketch, M. H., Sr. (1992). Effect of buspirone on withdrawal symptoms associated with smoking cessation. *Archives of Internal Medicine, 152,* 350–352.

Hindler, C. G. (1989). Epilepsy and violence. *British Journal of Psychiatry, 155,* 246–249.

Hinkin, C. H., & Kahn, M. W. (1995). Psychological symptomatology in spouses and adult children of alcoholics: An examination of the hypothesized personality characteristics of codependency. *The International Journal of the Addictions, 30*(7), 843–861.

Hoegerman, G., Wilson, C. A., Thurmond, E., & Schnoll, S. H. (1990). Drug-exposed neonates. *Western Journal of Medicine, 152,* 559–564.

Hoff, R. A., Mitchell, M., Moffett, C., Reynolds, H., Rosenheck, R., & Steiner, J. L. (1998). Preventive health care for mentally ill women. *Psychiatric Services, 49*(5), 696–698.

Hoffman, A. L., & Henemann, M. E. (1986). Alcoholism: Development, consequences, and interventions. In N. J. Ester & M. E. Heinemann (Eds.), *Alcohol problems in elderly persons* (pp. 257–272). St. Louis: CV Mosby.

Hoffman, R. S., & Goldfrank, L. R. (1990). The impact of drug abuse and addiction on society. *Emergency Medicine Clinics of North America, 8*, 467–480.
Hoffmann, D., & Wynder, E. L. (1986). Chemical constituents and bioactivity of tobacco smoke. *JARC Scientific Publications, 74*, 145–165.
Hohmann, A. A., Larson, D. B., Thompson, J. W., & Beardsley, R. S. (1991). Psychotropic medication prescription in U.S. ambulatory medical care. *DICP, The Annals of Pharmacotherapy, 25*, 85–89.
Holcomb, W. R., & Anderson, W. P. (1983). Alcohol and multiple drug abuse in accused murderers. *Psychological Reports, 52*, 159–164.
Hollister, L. E. (1986). Health aspects of cannabis. *Pharmacological Reviews, 38*, 1–20.
Hollister, L. E. (1988). Cannabis—1988. *Acta Psychiatrica Scandinavica, 345* (Suppl), 108–118.
Hollobon, J. (1986a). Adverse drug reactions tied to falls by elderly. *The Addiction Research Foundation Journal, 15*(6), 7.
Hollobon, J. (1986b). By drinking half as much women get cirrhosis twice as fast as men. *The Addiction Research Journal, 15*, 1–2.
Holloway, M. (1991). Prescription for addiction. *Scientific American*, 94–103.
Holmstrom, C. (1990). Women and substance abuse. *Canadian Journal of Psychiatric Nursing, 31*(2), 6–10.
Hoover, D. R., Doherty, M. C., Vlahov, D., & Miotti, P. (1996). Incidence and risk factors for HIV-1 infection—a summary of what is known and the psychiatric relevance. *International Review of Psychiatry, 8*(2–3), 137–148.
Horn, T., Paccaud, F., Niquille, M., Koehn, V., Magnenat, P., & Yersin, B. (1992). Drinking patterns among medical in-patients with reference to MAST categories: A comparative study. *Alcohol and Alcoholism, 27*, 439–447.
Horowitz, R. (1990). Perinatal substance abuse. *Children Today, 19*, 8.
Hoyme, H. E. (1990). Teratogenically induced fetal anomalies. *Clinics in Perinatology, 17*(3), 547–567.
Hughes, J. R., Oliveto, A. H., Helzer, J. E., Higgins, S. T., & Bickel, W. K. (1992). Should caffeine abuse, dependence, or withdrawal be added to DSM-IV and ICD-10? *American Journal of Psychiatry, 149*(1), 33–40.
Hume, R. F., Jr., Gingras, J. L., Martin, L. S., Hertzberg, B. S., O'Donnell, K., & Killam, A. P. (1994). Ultrasound diagnosis of fetal anomalies associated with in utero cocaine exposure: Further support for cocaine-induced vascular disruption teratogenesis. *Fetal Diagnosis and Therapy, 9*(4), 239–245.
Humphries, D. (1999). *Women's Health/Criminology, 232*, pp. 6–9, CIP. LC98–46648.
Hussain, K., Wijetunge, D. B., Brubnic, S., & Jackson, I. T. (1994). A comprehensive analysis of craniofacial trauma. *The Journal of Trauma, 36*, 34–47.
Iancu, I., Dolberg, O., & Zohar, J. (1994). Caffeine—The most commonly used psychoactive drug, worldwide. [Editorial]. *Harefuah, 126*(3), 166–168.
Iber, F. L. (1990). Alcoholism and associated malnutrition in the elderly. *Progress in Clinical and Biological Research, 326*, 157–173.
Ikuesan, B. A. (1994). Drinking problems and the position of women in Nigeria. *Addiction, 89*, 941–944.
Inciardi, J. A. (1993). Kingrats, chicken heads, slow necks, freaks, and blood suckers: A glimpse at the Miami sex-for-crack market. In M. S. Ratner (Ed.), *Crack pipe as pimp: An ethnographic investigation of sex-for-crack exchanges* (pp. 37–67). New York: Lexington.
Infante-Rivard, C., Fernandez, A., Gauthier, R., David, M., & Rivard, G. E. (1993). Fetal loss associated with caffeine intake before and during pregnancy. *Journal of the American Medical Association, 270*, 2940–2943.
Interventions to Prevent HIV Risk Behaviors [Review]. (1997). *NIH Consensus Statement, 15*(2), 1–41.
Irwin, K. L., Edlin, B. R., Wong, L., Faruque, S., McCoy, H. V., Word, C., Schilling, R., McCoy, C. B., Evans, P. E., & Holmberg, S. D. (1995). Urban rape survivors: Characteristics and prevalence of human immunodeficiency virus and other sexually transmitted infections. *Obstetrics & Gynecology, 85*, 330–336.
Irwin, M., Schuckit, M., & Smith, T. L. (1990). Clinical importance of age at onset in Type 1 and Type 2 primary alcoholics. *Archives of General Psychiatry, 47*, 320–324.

Jackson, G. G. (1980a). Is women's liberation enough?: Substance abuse among Afro-American women. In R. Faulkinberry (Ed.), *Drug problems of the 70's: Solutions for the 80's* (pp. 98–104). Lafayette, LA: Endac Enterprises/Print Media.

Jackson, G. G. (1980b). Overlooked cultural factors in the substance abuse literature on females—The case of the Afro-American female. In R. Faulkinberry (Ed.), *Drug problems of the 70's: Solutions for the 80's* (pp. 81–87). Lafayette, LA: Endac Enterprises/Print Media.

Jackson, M. M. (1990). Infection prevention and control for HIV and other infectious agents in obstetric, gynecologic and neonatal settings. *NAACOGS Clinical Issues in Perinatal and Women's Health Nursing, 1*(1), 115–122.

Jacob, T., Windle, M., Seilhamer, R. A., & Bost, J. (1999). Adult children of alcoholics: Drinking, psychiatric, and psychosocial status. *Psychology of Addictive Behaviors, 13*(1), 3–21.

Jacobson, G. R. (1983). Detection, assessment, and diagnosis of alcoholism: Current techniques. In M. Galanter (Ed.), *Recent developments in alcoholism* (Vol. 1, pp. 377–413). New York: Plenum.

Jacobson, J. L., Jacobson, S. W., Sokol, R. J., Martier, S. S., Ager, J. W., & Kaplan-Estrin, M. G. (1993). Teratogenic effects of alcohol on infant development. *Alcoholism: Clinical and Experimental Research, 17,* 174–183.

Jacyk, W. R., Tabisz, E., Badger, M., & Fuchs, S. (1991). Chemical dependency in the elderly: Identification phase. *Canadian Journal of Aging, 10,* 10–17.

Jaudes, P. K., Ekwo, E., & Van Vooris, J. (1995). Association of drug abuse and child abuse. *Child Abuse and Neglect: The International Journal, 19*(9), 1065–1075.

Jeremy, R. J., & Bernstein, V. J. (1984). Dyads at risk: Methadone-maintained women and their four-month-old infants. *Child Development, 55*(4), 1141–1154.

Jeste, D. V., Caligiuri, M. P., Paulsen, J. S., Heaton, R. K., Lacro, J. P., Harris, M. J., Bailey, A., Fell, R. L., & McAdams, L. A. (1995). Risk of tardive dyskinesia in older patients. *Archives of General Psychiatry, 52,* 756–765.

Jinks, M. J., & Raschko, R. R. (1990). A profile of alcohol and prescription drug abuse in a high-risk community-based elderly population. *DICP, The Annals of Pharmacotherapy, 24,* 971–975.

Johnson, E., & Herringer, L. G. (1993). A note on the utilization of common support activities and relapse following substance abuse treatment. *Journal of Psychology, 127,* 73–77.

Johnson, E. M. (1990). Chemical dependency and black America: The government responds. *Journal of the National Black Nurses Association, 4*(2), 47–56.

Johnston, C. (1991). Statistician and physicians at odds over Canada's AIDS statistics. *Canadian Medical Association Journal, 144,* 483–484.

Jonas, J. M., & Gold, M. S. (1992). The pharmacologic treatment of alcohol and cocaine abuse: Integration of recent findings into clinical practice. *Pediatric Psychopharmacology, 15,* 179–190.

Jones, K. L., Smith, D. W., Ulleland, C. N., & Streissguth, P. (1973). Patterns of malformation of offspring of chronic alcoholic mothers. *Lancet, 1,* 1267–1271.

Jones, M. B., & Jones, M. K. (1976). Women and alcohol: Intoxication, metabolism, and the menstrual cycle. *New York Academy of Sciences, 273,* 576–587.

Jones, K. L. (1991). Developmental pathogenesis of defects associated with prenatal cocaine exposure: Fetal vascular disruption. *Clinics in Perinatology, 18*(1), 139–146.

Jones, K. L., & Smith, D. W. (1973). Recognition of the fetal alcohol syndrome in early infancy. *Lancet, 1,* 1267–1271.

Jones, T. V., Lindsey, B. A., Yount, P., Soltys, R., & Farani-Enayat, B. (1993). Alcoholism screening questionnaires: Are they valid in elderly medical outpatients? *Journal of General Internal Medicine, 8*(12), 674–678.

Jorgensen, K. M. (1992). The drug-exposed infant. *Critical Care Nursing Clinics of North America, 4,* 481–485.

Kadden, R. M. (1994). Cognitive-behavioral approaches to alcoholism treatment. *Alcohol Health & Research World, 18,* 279–286.

Kalant, O. J., Fehr, K. O., Arras, D., & Anglin, L. (1983). *Cannabis health risks: A comprehensive annotated bibliography (1844–1982).* Toronto: Addiction Research Foundation.

Kaminer, Y., & Frances, R. J. (1991). Inpatient treatment of adolescents with psychiatric and substance abuse disorders. *Hospital and Community Psychiatry, 42,* 894–896.

Kapur, R. P., Cheng, M. S., & Shephard, T. H. (1991). Brain hemorrhages in cocaine-exposed human fetuses. *Teratology, 44*, 11–18.
Karavokiros, K. A. T., & Tsipis, G. B. (1990). Flumazenil: A benzodiazepine antagonist. *Drug Intelligence and Clinical Pharmacy Annals of Pharmacotherapy, 24*, 976–981.
Karp, R. J., Qazi, Q., Hittleman, J., & Chabrier, L. (1993). Fetal alcohol syndrome. In R. J. Karp (Ed.), *Malnourished children in the United States: Caught in the cycle of poverty* (pp. 101–108). New York: Springer.
Kashner, T. M., Rodell, D. E., Ogden, S. R., Guggenheim, F. G., & Karson, C. N. (1992). Outcomes and costs of two VA inpatient treatment programs for older alcoholic patients. *Hospital and Community Psychiatry, 43*, 985–989.
Kaskutas, L. A. (1994). What do women get out of self-help? Their reasons for attending Women for Sobriety and Alcoholics Anonymous. *Journal of Substance Abuse Treatment, 11*(3), 185–195.
Kawachi, I., Willett, W. C., Colditz, G. A., Stampfer, M. J., & Speizer, F. E. (1996). Coffee intake was inversely associated with suicide in women. A prospective study of coffee drinking and suicide in women. *Archives of Internal Medicine, 11*(156), 521–525.
Kelley, S. J. (1992). Parenting stress and child maltreatment in drug-exposed children. *Child Abuse & Neglect, 16*, 317–328.
Kemper, K. J., Greteman, A., Bennett, E., & Babonis, T. R. (1993). Screening mothers of young children for substance abuse. *Developmental and Behavioral Pediatrics, 14*(5), 308–312.
Kendler, K. S., Heath, A. C., Neale, M. C., Kessler, R. C., & Eaves, L. J. (1993). Alcoholism and major depression in women: A twin study of the causes of comorbidity. *Archives of General Psychiatry, 50*, 690–698.
Kendler, K. S., Neale, M. C., Heath, A. C., Kessler, R. C., & Eaves, L. J. (1994). A twin-family study of alcoholism in women. *American Journal of Psychiatry, 151*(5), 707–715.
Kennedy, B. P., & Minami, M. (1993). The Beech Hill Hospital/Outward Bound Adolescent Chemical Dependency Treatment Program. *Journal of Substance Abuse Treatment, 10*, 395–406.
Kirchmayer, U., Davoli, M., & Verster, A. (1998, August 26). Naltrexone maintenance treatment in opioid dependence. *Cochrane Database of Systematic Reviews*, Issue 4.
Klatsky, A. L. (1990). Alcohol and coronary artery disease. *Alcohol Health & Research World, 14*(4), 289–300.
Klatsky, A. L., & Armstrong, M. A. (1993). Alcohol use, other traits, and risk of unnatural death: A prospective study. *Alcoholism, Clinical & Experimental Research, 17*(6), 1156–1162.
Klatsky, A. L., Armstrong, M. A., & Friedman, G. D. (1990). Risk of cardiovascular mortality in alcohol drinkers, ex-drinkers and nondrinkers. *The American Journal of Cardiology, 66*, 1237–1242.
Klein, S., & Iber, F. L. (1991). Alcoholism and associated malnutrition in the elderly. *Nutrition, 7*(2), 75–79.
Knupfer, G. (1991). Abstaining for foetal health: The fiction that even light drinking is dangerous. *British Journal of Addiction, 86*, 1063–1073.
Koester, S., & Schwart, J. (1993). Crack, gangs, sex, and powerlessness: A view from Denver. In R. S. Ratner (Ed.), *Crack pipe as pimp: An ethnographic investigation of sex-for-crack exchanges* (pp. 187–203). New York: Lexington Books.
Kofoed, L. L. (1985). OTC drug overuse in the elderly: What to watch for. *Geriatrics, 40*(10), 55–60.
Kofoed, L. L., Tolson, R. L., Atkinson, R. M., Toth, R. L., & Turner, J. A. (1987). Treatment compliance of older alcoholics: An elder-specific approach is superior to mainstreaming. *Journal of Studies on Alcohol, 48*, 47–51.
Kokotailo, P. K., Adger, H., Jr., Duggan, A. K., Repke, J., & Joffe, A. (1992). Cigarette, alcohol, and other drug use by school-age pregnant adolescents: Prevalence, detection, and associated risk factors. *Pediatrics, 90*, 328–334.
Konkol, R. J. (1994). Is there a cocaine baby syndrome? *Journal of Child Neurology, 9*, 225–226.
Koren, G. (1991). Drinking and pregnancy. *Canadian Medical Association Journal, 145*(12), 1552–1554.
Koren, G. (1993). Cocaine and the human fetus: The concept of teratophilia. *Neurotoxicology and Teratology, 15*, 301–304.

Koren, G., Gladstone, D., Robeson, C., & Robieux, I. (1992). The perception of teratogenic risk of cocaine. *Teratology, 46,* 567–571.

Korsten, M. A., & Lieber, C. S. (1985). Medical complications of alcoholism. In J. H. Mendelson & N. K. Mello (Eds.), *The diagnosis and treatment of alcoholism* (2nd ed., pp. 21–64). New York: McGraw-Hill.

Kosberg, J. I. (1988). Preventing elder abuse: Identification of high risk factors prior to placement decisions. *The Gerontologist, 28,* 43–50.

Kosten, T. R., Hogan, I., Jalali, B., Steidl, J., & Kleber, H. D. (1986). The effect of multiple family therapy on addict family functioning: A pilot study. *Alcohol and Substance Abuse in Women and Children, 5*(3), 51–62.

Koval, J. E. (1989). Violence in dating relationships. *Journal of Pediatric Health Care, 3,* 298–304.

Kraft, J. M., Blum, T. C., Martin, J. K., & Roman, P. M. (1993). Drinking patterns and the gender mix of occupations: Evidence from a national survey of American workers. *Journal of Substance Abuse, 5*(2), 157–174.

Kreek, M. J. (1992). Effects of drugs of abuse and treatment agents in women. *NIDA Monograph, 119,* 106–110.

Kreek, M. J., & Stimmel, B. (Eds.). (1984). *Dual addiction: Pharmacological issues in the treatment of concomitant alcoholism and drug abuse.* New York: Haworth.

Kreek, M. M., Schecter, A., Gutjahr, C. L., Bowen, D., Field, F., Queenan, J., & Merkatz, I. (1974). Analyses of methadone and other drugs in maternal and neonatal body fluids: Use in evaluation of symptoms in a neonate of a mother maintained on methadone. *American Journal of Drug and Alcohol Abuse, 1,* 409–419.

Krestan, J., & Bepko, C. (1991). Codependency: The social reconstruction of female experience. In C. Bepko (Ed.), *Feminism and addition* (pp. 49–66). Binghamton, NY: Haworth.

Kristenson, H., & Trell, E. (1982). Indicators of alcohol consumption: Comparison between a questionnaire (Mm-MAST), interviews and serum gammaglutamyltransferase (GGT) in a health survey of middle-aged males. *British Journal of Addiction, 77,* 297–334.

Krutilla, J. O. (1993, February 27). School expectations from the drug using family: Assisting and understanding the child and the home. *EDRS Availability.*

Kua, E. H. (1994). Chinese women who drink. *Addiction, 89,* 956–958.

Kurtz, E. (1988). *AA: The story.* San Francisco, CA: Harper & Row.

Kurtz, E. (1993). Research on Alcoholics Anonymous: The historical context. In B. S. McCrady & W. R. Miller (Eds.), *Research on Alcoholics Anonymous* (pp. 13–26). New Brunswick, NJ: Rutgers Center of Alcohol Studies.

Kwit, N. T., & Hatcher, R. A. (1935). Excretion of drugs in milk. *American Journal of Diseases in Children, 49,* 900–904.

LAAM—A long-acting methadone for treatment of heroin addiction. (1994). *The Medical Letter, 36,* 52.

Labouvie, E. W., & McGee, C. R. (1986). Relation of personality to alcohol and drug use in adolescence. *Journal of Contemporary Clinical Psychology, 4,* 289–293.

Lacombe, S., Stanislav, S. W., & Marken, P. A. (1991). Pharmacologic treatment of cocaine abuse. *Annals of Pharmacotherapy, 25,* 818–823.

Laforge, R. G., & Mignon, S. I. (1993). Alcohol use and alcohol problems among the elderly. *Rhode Island Medicine, 76*(1), 21–26.

Laken, M. P., & Hutchins, E. (1995). Recruitment and retention of substance-using pregnant and parenting women: Lessons learned. *Health Resources and Services Administration* (DHHS/PHS), Washington, DC. Maternal and Child Health Bureau, National Center for Education in Maternal and Child Health, Arlington, VA [BBB31142, BBB32080].

Lambert, G. A. (1991). Gender roles and psychological functioning of women married to chemically dependent men. *Dissertation Abstracts International, 53*(8-a), 2692.

Lammers, S. M. M., Schippers, G. M., & van der Staak, C. P. F. (1995). Submission and rebellion: Excessive drinking of women in problematic heterosexual partner relationships. *The International Journal of the Addictions, 30*(7), 901–917.

Lamy, P. P. (1984). Alcohol misuse and abuse among the elderly. *Drug Intelligence and Clinical Pharmacy, 18,* 649–651.

Lamy, P. P. (1988). Actions of alcohol and drugs in older people. *Generations, 12*(4), 9–13.
Laner, M. R. (1983). Courtship abuse and aggression: Contextual aspects. *Sociological Spectrum, 3*, 69–83.
Lange, E. (1987). The "semiconscious" form of pathologic alcoholic intoxication, its characteristics and differences from "classical" forms of pathologic intoxication. *Psychiatrie, Neurologie un Medizinische Psychologie, 39*, 193–201.
Langeland, W., & Hartgers, C. (1998). Child sexual and physical abuse and alcoholism: A review. [Review] *Journal of Studies on Alcohol, 59*(3), 336–348.
Larroque, B. (1992). Alcohol and the fetus. *International Journal of Epidemiology, 21*(Suppl. 1), S8–S16.
Lasker, M. N. (1983). Aging alcoholics need nursing help. *Journal of Gerontological Nursing, 12*(1), 16–19.
Lau, M. A., & Pihl, R. O. (1994). Alcohol and the Taylor aggression paradigm: A repeated measures study. *Journal of Studies on Alcohol, 55*, 701–706.
Laundergan, J. C., & Williams, T. (1993). The Hazelden residential family program: A combined systems and disease model approach. In T. J. O'Farrell (Ed.), *Treating alcohol problems: Marital and family interventions* (pp. 145–169). New York: Guilford.
Lauritzen, J. B., McNair, P. A., & Lund, B. (1993). Risk factors for hip fractures. A Review. *Danish Medical Bulletin, 40*, 479–485.
Lawson, A. W. (1989). Substance abuse problems of the elderly: Considerations for treatment and prevention. In G. W. Lawson & A. W. Lawson (Eds.), *Alcoholism and substance abuse in special populations* (pp. 95–113). Rockville, MD: Aspen.
Leclair, S., & Rosenthal, D. (1980). Counseling the elderly substance user/abuser. *Counseling and Values, 24*, 166–174.
Lee, B. L. (1984). MDs warned of sleep-aid dangers for aged. *The Addiction Research Foundation Journal, 13*, 7.
Lee, B. L. (1985). Older women in Canada hit by tranquillizer script shift. *The Addiction Research Foundation Journal, 14*, 4.
Lee, B. L. (1988). IV drug users will be major vector: AIDS set to hit general public. *The Addiction Research Foundation Journal, 17*, 1.
Lee, R. (1995). NIDA Conference on women and drug abuse. *Public Health Reports, 110*, 517.
Lee, W. V., & Weinstein, S. P. (1997). How far have we come? A critical review of the research on men who batter. *Recent Developments in Alcoholism, 13*, 337–356.
Lehman, A. F., Myers, C. P., Corty, E., & Thompson, J. W. (1994). Prevalence and patterns of "dual diagnosis" among psychiatric inpatients. *Comprehensive Psychiatry, 35*, 106–112.
Leifer, M., Shapiro, J. P., & Kassem, L. (1993). The impact of maternal history and behavior upon foster placement and adjustment in sexually abused girls. *Child Abuse and Neglect, 17*, 755–766.
Leigh, B. C., & Stall, R. (1993). Substance use and risky sexual behavior for exposure to HIV: Issues in methodology, interpretation, and prevention. *American Psychology, 48*, 11023–11034.
Lelo, A., Miners, J. O., Robson, R., & Birkett, D. J. (1986). Assessment of caffeine exposure: Caffeine content of beverages, caffeine intake, and plasma concentrations of methylxanthines. *Clinical Pharmacology and Therapeutics, 39*, 54–59.
Lemoine, P., Harousseau, H., & Borteyru, J. (1968). Children of alcoholic patients: Abnormalities observed in 127 cases. *Quest Medical, 21*, 476–482.
Lemonick, M. D. (1987, May 18). Should women drink less? *Time*, 46.
Lemp, G. F., Porco, T. C., Hirozawa, A. M., Lingo, M., Woelffer, G., Hsu, L. C., & Katz, M. H. (1997). Projected incidence of AIDS in San Francisco: The peak and decline of the epidemic. *Journal of Acquired Immune Deficiency Syndromes and Human Retrovirology, 16*(3), 182–189.
Lenz, W. (1962). Thalidomide and congenital abnormalities. *Lancet, 1*, 271.
Lesar, S. (1992). Prenatal cocaine exposure: The challenge to education. *Infant-Toddler Intervention: The Transdisciplinary Journal, 2*(1), 37–52.
Lesmes, G. R., & Donofrio, D. K. (1992). Passive smoking: The medical and economic issues. *American Journal of Medicine, 93*(suppl. 1A), 38S–42S.
Leukefeld, C. G., Battjes, R. J., & Amsel, Z. (1990). *NIDA Research Monograph 93: AIDS and intravenous drug use: Future directions for community-based prevention research.* Rockville, MD: National Institute on Drug Abuse.

Levin, J. M., Holman, B. L., Mendelson, J. H., Teoh, S. K., Garada, B., Johnson, K. A., & Springer, S. (1994). Gender differences in cerebral perfusion in cocaine abuse: Technetium-99m-HMPAO SPECT study of drug-abusing women. *The Journal of Nuclear Medicine, 35*(12), 1902–1909.

Levy, M. (1992). Alcohol and addictions. [Letter.] *American Journal of Psychiatry, 149*(8), 1117–1118.

Lewis, R. A., Piercy, F. P., Sprenkle, D. H., & Trepper, T. S. (1990). Family-based interventions for helping drug-abusing adolescents. *Journal of Adolescent Research, 5*, 82–95.

Lex, B. W. (1994). Alcohol and other drug abuse among women. *Alcohol Health & Research World, 18*(3), 212–219.

Lex, B. W., Goldberg, M. E., Mendelson, J. H., Lawler, N. S., & Bower, T. (1994). Components of antisocial personality disorder among women convicted for drunken driving. *Annals of the New York Academy of Sciences, 708*, 49–58.

Liberto, J. G., Oslin, D. W., & Ruskin, P. E. (1992). Alcoholism in older persons: A review of the literature. *Hospital and Community Psychiatry, 43*, 975–984.

Lillie-Blanton, M., MacKenzie, E., & Anthony, J. C. (1991). Black-white differences in alcohol use by women: Baltimore survey findings. *Public Health Reports, 106*(2), 124–133.

Lindberg, M. C., & Oyler, R. A. (1990). Wernicke's encephalopathy. *American Family Physician, 41*, 1205–1209.

Lindenbaum, G. A., Carroll, S. F., Daskal, I., & Kapusnick, R. (1989). Patterns of alcohol and drug abuse in an urban trauma center: The increasing role of cocaine abuse. *Journal of Trauma, 29*, 1654–1658.

Lindenberg, C. S., Solorzano, R., Kelley, M., Darrow, V., Gendrop, S. C., & Strickland, O. (1998). Competence and drug use: Theoretical frameworks, empirical evidence and measurement. *Journal of Drug Education, 28*(2), 117–134.

Lindman, R. E., & Lang, A. R. (1994). The alcohol-aggression stereotype: A cross-cultural comparison of beliefs. *International Journal of the Addictions, 29*, 1–13.

Linnoila, V. M., & Virkkunen, M. (1992). Aggression, suicidality, and serotonin. *Journal of Clinical Psychiatry, 53*, 46–51.

Lisansky Gomberg, E. S. (1991). Women and alcohol: Psychosocial aspects. In D. J. Pittman & H. Raskin White (Eds.), *Society, culture, and drinking patterns reexamined* (pp. 263–284). New Brunswick, NJ: Alcohol Research Documentation, Rutgers Center of Alcohol Studies.

Lisansky Gomberg, E. S. (1993). Antecedents and consequences. In E. S. Lisansky Gomberg & T. D. Nirenberg (Eds.), *Women and substance abuse* (pp. 118–141), Norwood, NJ: Albex.

Lisansky Gomberg, E. S. (1994). Risk factors for drinking over a woman's life span. *Alcohol Health & Research World, 18*(3), 220–227.

Lisansky Gomberg, E. S. (1995). Older women and alcohol use and abuse. *Recent Developments in Alcoholism: Women and Alcoholism, 12*, 61–79.

Little, B. B., Snell, L. M., & Rosenfeld, C. R. (1990). Failure to recognize fetal alcohol syndrome in newborn infants. *American Journal of Diseases of Children, 144*, 1142–1146.

Littrell, J. (1991). *Understanding and treating alcoholism*. Hillsdale, NJ: Lawrence Erlbaum.

Lohr, M. J., Gillmore, M. R., Gilchrist, L. D., & Butler, S. S. (1992). Factors related to substance use by pregnant school-age adolescents. *Journal of Adolescent Health, 13*, 475–482.

Longnecker, M. P., & Tseng, M. (1998). Alcohol, hormones, and postmenopausal women. *Alcohol Health & Research World, 22*(3), 185–189.

Los Angeles Times. (1994). Survey says substance abuse among working women rises with income; home edition, pp. D-5.

Los Angeles Times. (1995). Winfrey admits cocaine use, 'Life's great big secret'; bulldog edition, pp. A-7.

Lown, E. A., Winkler, K., Fullilove, R. E., & Fullilove, M. T. (1993). Tossin' and tweakin': Women's consciousness in the crack culture. *Women and AIDS: Psychological Perspectives, 4*, 90–105.

Luckie, L. F., White, R. E., Miller, W. R., Icenogle, M. V., & Lasoski, M. C. (1995). Prevalence estimates of alcohol problems in a veterans administration outpatient population: Audit vs. Mast. *Journal of Clinical Psychology, 51*(3), 422–425.

Lujan, C., DeBruyn, L. M., May, P. A., & Bird, M. E. (1989). Profile of abused and neglected American Indian children in the southwest. *Child Abuse & Neglect, 13,* 449–461.

Lumley, J., Oliver, S., & Waters, E. (1998). Smoking cessation programs implemented during pregnancy. *Cochrane Database of Systematic Review, Issue 4.*

Lyman, W. D. (1993). Perinatal AIDS: Drugs of abuse and transplacental infection. In H. Friedman et al. (Eds.), *Drugs of abuse, immunity, and AIDS* (pp. 211–217). New York: Plenum.

Lynch, J. P., Smith, S. K., Graziadei, H. A., & Pittayathikhum, T. (1994). Profile of inmates in the United States and in England and Wales, 1991. *U.S. Department of Justice* (NCJ-145863).

Lyndon, R. W., & Russell, J. D. (1990). Can overuse of psychotropic drugs by the elderly be prevented? *Australian and New Zealand Journal of Psychiatry, 24,* 77–81.

MacAndrew, C. (1965). The differentiation of male alcoholic outpatients from nonalcoholic psychiatric patients by means of the MMPI. *Quarterly Journal of Studies on Alcohol, 26,* 238–246.

MacAndrew, C., & Edgerton, R. B. (1969). *Drunken comportment: A social explanation.* Chicago: Aldine.

Macdonald, D. I. (1986). Coolfont report: A PHS plan for prevention and control of AIDS and the AIDS virus. *Public Health Reports, 101*(4), 341–348.

MacDonald, N. E., Wells, G. A., Fisher, W. A., Warren, W. K., King, M. A., Doherty, J. A., & Bowie, W. R. (1990). High-risk STD/HIV behavior among college students. *Journal of the American Medical Association, 263,* 3155–3159.

MacKenzie, D., Langa, A., & Brown, T. M. (1996). Identifying hazardous or harmful alcohol use in medical admissions. A comparison of AUDIT, CAGE and brief MAST. *Alcohol and Alcoholism, 31*(6), 591–599.

MacNeil, G. (1991). A short-form scale to measure alcohol abuse. *Research on Social Work Practice, 1,* 68–75.

Madden, R. G. (1993). State actions to control fetal abuse: Ramifications for child welfare practice. *Child Welfare, 72,* 129–140.

Madianos, M. G., Gefou-Madianos, D., & Stefanis, C. N. (1994). Symptoms of depression, suicidal behaviour, and use of substances in Greece: A nationwide general population survey. *Acta Psychiatrica Scandinavica, 89,* 159–166.

Madsen, J. (1996). Double jeopardy: Women, violence and HIV. *Canadian Council on Social Developments: Vis-A-Vis. A National Newsletter on Family Violence, 13*(3), 1, 4.

Magura, S., Shapiro, J. L., Siddiqi, Q., & Lipton, D. S. (1990). Variables influencing condom use among intravenous drug users. *American Journal of Public Health, 80,* 82–84.

Maisto, S. A., Connors, G. J., & Allen, J. P. (1995). Contrasting self-report screens for alcohol problems: A review. [Review] *Alcoholism, Clinical and Experimental Research, 19*(6), 1510–1516.

Making the links: A book for young women about sexual violence, drugs, and alcohol. (1990). Kingston, ON: Action on Women's Addictions—Research and Evaluation (AWARE).

Malcolm, T. (1992). The demon drink. *Nursing the Elderly, 4*(4), 22–24.

Maly, R. C. (1993). Early recognition of chemical dependence [published erratum appears in Primary Care] [Review]. *Primary Care: Clinics in Office Practice, 20*(1), 33–50.

Manschreck, T. C., Schneyer, M. L., Weisstein, C. C., Laughery, J., Rosenthal, J., Celada, T., & Berner, J. (1990). Freebase cocaine and memory. *Comprehensive Psychiatry, 31*(4), 369–375.

Marcus, M. T. (1993). Alcohol and other drug abuse in elders. *Journal of Enterostomal Therapy Nursing, 20,* 106–110.

Marques, P. R., & McKnight, A. J. (1991). Drug abuse risk among pregnant adolescents attending public health clinics. *American Journal of Drug and Alcohol Abuse, 17,* 399–413.

Marsh, C. E. (1993). Sexual assault and domestic violence in the Africa American community. *The Western Journal of Black Studies, 17*(3), 149–155.

Marshall, V. W. (1987). *Aging in Canada: Social perspectives.* (2nd ed.). Markham: Fitzhenry & Whiteside.

Martin, M. L., & Khoury, M. J. (1992). Cocaine and single ventricle: A population study. *Teratology, 46,* 267–270.

Martin, M. L., Khoury, M. J., Cordero, J. F., & Waters, G. D. (1992). Trends in rates of multiple vascular disruption defects, Atlanta, 1969–1989: Is there evidence of a cocaine teratogenic epidemic? *Teratology, 45,* 647–653.

Marx, C. M., Pucino, F., Carlson, J. D., Driscoll, R. N., & Ruddock, V. (1986). Oxycodone excretion in human milk in the puerperium. *Drug Intelligence and Clinical Pharmacy, 20,* 474.

Marzuk, P. M., Tardiff, K., Leon, A. C., Stajic, M., Morgan, E. B., & Mann, J. J. (1992). Prevalence of cocaine use among residents of New York City who committed suicide during a one-year period. *American Journal of Psychiatry, 149,* 371–375.

Masi, M. A., Hanley, J. A., Ernst, P., & Becklaki, M. R. (1988). Environmental exposure to tobacco smoke and lung function in young adults. *American Review of Respiratory Disease, 138,* 296–299.

Mathias, R. (1995, January/February). Survey provides first national data on drug use during pregnancy. *NIDA Notes,* 1–3.

Matin, K., Katz, B. Z., & Miller, G. (1987). AIDS and antibodies to human immunodeficiency virus (HIV) in children and their families. *Journal of Infectious Diseases, 155,* 54–63.

Matteo, S. (1988). The risk of multiple addictions—Guidelines for assessing a woman's alcohol and drug use. *Western Journal of Medicine, 149,* 741–745.

Matthews, S. J., Cersosimo, R. J., & Spivack, M. L. (1991). Zidovudine and other reverse transcriptase inhibitors in the management of human immunodeficiency virus-related disease. *Pharmacotherapy, 11,* 419–449.

Mattson, M. E. (1994). Patient-treatment matching: Rationale and results. *Alcohol Health & Research World, 18,* 287–295.

May, P. (1991). Fetal alcohol effects among North American Indians. *Alcohol Health & Research World, 15,* 239.

Mayfield, D., McLeod, G., & Hall, P. (1974). The CAGE questionnaire: Validation of a new alcoholism screening instrument. *American Journal of Psychiatry, 131*(10), 1121–1123.

Mayo, C. C., & Schlicke, C. P. (1942). Appearance of a barbiturate in human milk. *Proceedings of the Staff Meetings of the Mayo Clinic, 17,* 87–88.

McBride, W. G. (1961). Thalidomide and congenital abnormalities. *Lancet, 2,* 1358.

McBride, J. L. (1991). Abstinence among members of Alcoholics Anonymous. *Alcoholism Treatment Quarterly, 8,* 113–121.

McCauley, J., Kern, D. E., Kolodner, K., Dill, L., Schroeder, A. F., DeChant, H. K., Ryden, J., Bass, E. B., & Derogatis, L. R. (1995). The "battering syndrome": Prevalence and clinical characteristics of domestic violence in primary care internal medicine practices. *Annals of Internal Medicine, 123*(10), 737–746.

McConnell, H. (1983). US elderly reselling Rx drugs to live. *The Addiction Research Foundation Journal, 12,* 1–2.

McDonald, A. J., & Abrahams, S. T. (1990). Social emergencies in the elderly. *Emergency Medicine Clinics of North America, 8,* 443–459.

McEwen, T. (1995). *National assessment program: 1994 survey results* (NCJ 153517). Washington, DC: U.S. Department of Justice.

McGonigal, M. D., Cole, J., Schwab, C. W., Kauder, D. R., Rotondo, M. F., & Angood, P. B. (1993). Urban firearm deaths: A five-year perspective. *Journal of Trauma, 35,* 532–536.

McGovern, T. F. (1994). Therapy with the dually diagnosed person. *Treating Coexisting Psychiatric and Addictive Disorders* (pp. 161–176). Center City, MN: Hazelden.

McInnes, E. & Powell, J. (1994). Drug and alcohol referrals: Are elderly substance abuse diagnoses and referrals being missed? *British Medical Journal, 308*(6926), 444–446.

McMahon, A. L. (1993). Substance abuse among the elderly. *Nurse Practitioner Forum, 4*(4), 231–238.

Meade, L. (Author), Hirliman, G. (Producer), & Gasnier, L. (Director). (1937). *Reefer madness* [film]. Mt. Morris, IL: High Times Video.

Medina-Mora, E. (1994). Drinking and the oppression of women: The Mexican experience. *Addiction, 89,* 958–960.

Mello, N. K., Mendelson, J. H., & Teoh, S. K. (1993). An overview of the effects of alcohol on neuroendocrine function in women. In S. Zakhari (Ed.), *Alcohol and the endocrine system.* National Institute on Alcohol Abuse and Alcoholism Research Monograph No. 23, pp. 139–169. Bethesda, MD: the Institute.

Menninger, K. (1938). *Man against himself.* New York: Harcourt, Brace, and Company.

Merrick, J. C. (1993). Maternal substance abuse during pregnancy: Policy implications in the United States. *The Journal of Legal Medicine, 14,* 57–71.

Mertens, T. E., & Low-Beer, D. (1996). HIV and AIDS: Where is the epidemic going? *Bulletin of the World Health Organization, 74*(2), 121–129.

Metsch, L. R., Rivers, J. E., Miller, M., Bohs, R., McCoy, C. B., Morrow, C. J., Bandstra, E. S., Jackson, V., & Gissen, M. (1995). Implementation of a family-centered treatment program for substance-abusing women and their children: Barriers and resolutions. *Journal of Psychoactive Drugs, 27*(1), 73–83.

Meyer, R. E. (1986). How to understand the relationship between psychopathology and addictive disorders: Another example of the chicken and the egg. In R. E. Meyer (Ed.), *Psychopathology and addictive disorders* (pp. 3–16). New York: Guilford.

Milberger, S., Biederman, J., Faraone, S. V., Chen, L., & Jones, J. (1996). Is maternal smoking during pregnancy a risk factor for attention deficit hyperactivity disorder in children? *American Journal of Psychiatry, 153*(9), 1138–1142.

Milgram, G. G. (1993). Adolescents, alcohol and aggression. *Journal of Studies on Alcohol, 11,* 53–61.

Millard, D. D. (1996). Toxicology testing in neonates: Is it ethical, and what does it mean? [Review]. *Clinics in Perinatology, 23*(3), 491–507.

Miller, B. A. (1990). The interrelationships between alcohol and drugs and family violence. In M. De La Rosa, E. Y. Lambert, & B. Gropper (Eds.), *NIDA research monograph: Drugs and violence: Causes, correlates, and consequences* (pp. 177–207). Rockville, MD: Department of Health and Human Services.

Miller, B. A., & Downs, W. R. (1993). The impact of family violence on the use of alcohol by women. *Alcohol Health & Research World, 17*(2), 137–142.

Miller, B. A., & Downs, W. R. (1995). Violent victimization among women with alcohol problems [Review]. *Recent Developments in Alcoholism, 12,* 81–101.

Miller, B. A., Downs, W. R., & Testa, M. (1993). Interrelationships between victimization experiences and women's alcohol use. *Journal of Studies on Alcohol,* Supplement No. 11, 109–117.

Miller, B. A., Maguin, E., & Downs, W. R. (1997). Alcohol, drugs, and violence in children's lives. *Recent Developments in Alcoholism, 13,* 357–385.

Miller, F., Whitcup, S., Sacks, M., & Lynch, P. E. (1985). Unrecognized drug dependence and withdrawal in the elderly. *Drug and Alcohol Dependence, 15,* 177–179.

Miller, H. (1997). Prenatal cocaine exposure and mother-infant interaction: Implications for occupational therapy intervention [Review]. *American Journal of Occupational Therapy, 51*(2), 119–131.

Miller, H. R., & Streiner, D. L. (1990). Using the Millon Clinical Multiaxial Inventory's Scale B and the MacAndrew Alcoholism Scale to identify alcoholics with concurrent psychiatric diagnoses. *Journal of Personality Assessment, 54*(3–4), 736–746.

Miller, M. M., & Potter-Efron, R. T. (1990). Aggression and violence associated with substance abuse. In R. T. Potter-Efron & S. Potter-Efron (Eds.), *Aggression, Family Violence and Chemical Dependency,* (pp. 1–36). Binghamton, NY: Haworth.

Miller, N. S., Belkin, B. M., & Gibbons, R. (1994). Clinical diagnosis of substance use disorders in private psychiatric populations. *Journal of Substance Abuse Treatment, 11,* 387–392.

Miller, N. S., Belkin, B. M., & Gold, M. S. (1991). Alcohol and drug dependence among the elderly: Epidemiology, diagnosis, and treatment. *Comprehensive Psychiatry, 32,* 153–165.

Miller, N. S., & Gold, M. S. (1991). Benzodiazepines: A major problem. *Journal of Substance Abuse Treatment, 8,* 3–7.

Miller, N. S., & Gold, M. S. (1994). Criminal activity and crack addiction. *International Journal of the Addictions, 29,* 1069–1078.

Miller, W. R., & McCrady, B. S. (1993). The importance of research on Alcoholics Anonymous. In B. S. McCrady & W. R. Miller (Eds.), *Research on Alcoholics Anonymous* (pp. 3–11). New Brunswick, NJ: Rutgers Center of Alcohol Studies.

Miller-Tutzauer, C., Leonard, K. E., & Windle, M. (1991). Marriage and alcohol use: A longitudinal study of "maturing out". *Journal of Studies on Alcohol, 52*, 434–440.

Milner, J. S., & Chilamkurti, C. (1991). Physical child abuse perpetrator characteristics: A review of the literature. *Journal of Interpersonal Violence, 6*, 345–366.

Mirin, S. M. (1995). Practice guideline for the treatment of patients with substance use disorders: Alcohol, cocaine, opioids. *Supplement to The American Journal of Psychiatry, 152*(11), 1–59.

Mishara, B. L. (1982, September). Wine unto those that be of heavy heart: Issues concerning problem drinking in old age. *Canada's Mental Health*, pp. 33–35.

Modestin, J., & Ammann, R. (1995). Mental disorders and criminal behavior. *British Journal of Psychiatry, 166*, 667–675.

Momas, I., Helal, H., Pretet, S., Marsal, L., & Poinsard, R. (1997). Demographic and behavioral predictors of knowledge and HIV seropositivity: Results of a survey conducted in three anonymous and free counselling and testing centers. *European Journal of Epidemiology, 13*(3), 255–260.

Moon, D. G., Thompson, R. J., & Bennett, R. (1993). Patterns of substance use among women in prison. In B. Fletcher and R. Beverly (Eds.), *Women prisoners: A forgotten population*, (pp. 45–54). Westport, CT: Praeger.

Moore, R. D., Hidalgo, J., Sugland, B. W., & Chaisson, R. E. (1991). Zidovudine and the natural history of the acquired immunodeficiency syndrome. *New England Journal of Medicine, 324*, 1412–1416.

Moore, R. H. (1994). Underage female DUI offenders: Personality characteristics, psychosocial stressors, alcohol and other drug use, and driving-risk. *Psychological Reports, 74*, 435–445.

Mora, J. (1998). The treatment of alcohol dependency among Latinas: A feminist, cultural and community perspective. In M. Delgado (Ed.), *Alcohol use/abuse among Latinos: Issues and examples of culturally competent services* (pp. 164–177). Binghamton, NY: Haworth.

Moran, M. B., Naughton, B. J., & Hughes, S. L. (1990). Screening elderly veterans for alcoholism. *Journal of General Internal Medicine, 5*, 361–364.

Morgan, I. S. (1994). Recognizing depression in the adolescent. *American Journal of Maternal Child Nursing, 19*, 148–155.

Morra, L. G. (1992). *Drug education: Rural programs have many components and most rely heavily on federal funds* (GAO/HRD-92-34). Gaithersburg, MD: U.S. General Accounting Office.

Morse, G. D., Lechner, J. L., Santora, J. A., & Rozek, S. L. (1990). Zidovudine update: 1990. *DICP, The Annals of Pharmacotherapy, 24*, 754–760.

Morse, R. M. (1988). Substance abuse among the elderly. *Bulletin of the Menninger Clinic, 52*, 259–268.

Morton, E., Runyan, C. W., Moracco, K. E., & Butts, J. (1998). Partner homicide-suicide involving female homicide victims: A population-based study in North Carolina, 1988–1992. *Violence & Victims, 13*(2), 91–106.

Moser, R. P., & Jacob, T. (1997). Parent-child interactions and child outcomes as related to gender of alcoholic parent. *Journal of Substance Abuse, 9*, 189–208.

Mott, J. (1986). Opioid use and burglary. *British Journal of Addiction, 81*, 671–678.

Mphi, M. (1994). Female alcoholism problems in Lesotho. *Addiction, 89*, 945–949.

Mulford, H. A., & Fitzgerald, J. L. (1992). Elderly versus younger problem drinker profiles: Do they indicate a need for special programs for the elderly? *Journal of Studies on Alcohol, 53*, 601–610.

Muller, R. T., Fitzgerald, H. E., Sullivan, L. A., & Zucker, R. A. (1994). Social support and stress factors in child maltreatment among alcoholic families. *Canadian Journal of Behavioural Science, 26*(3), 438–461.

Murphy, G. E. (1998). Why women are less likely than men to commit suicide. *Comprehensive Psychiatry, 39*(4), 165–175.

Murphy, S., & Rosenbaum, M. (1999). *Pregnant women on drugs: Combining stereotypes and stigma.* New Brunswick, NJ: Rutgers University.

Murray, D. M., Pirie, P., Leupker, R. V., & Pallonen, U. (1989, April). Five- and six-year follow-up results from four seventh-grade smoking prevention strategies. *Journal of Behavioral Medicine, 12*(2), 207–218.

Murray, T. H. (1991). Prenatal drug exposure: Ethical issues. *Future of children, 1*(1), 105–112.

Mylonakis, E., Koutkia, P., Rich, J. D., Tashima, K. T., Fiore, T. C., Flanigan, T., & Carpenter, C. C. (1998). Substance abuse is responsible for most pre-AIDS deaths among women with HIV infection in Providence, Rhode Island, USA [letter]. *AIDS, 12*(8), 958–959.

Nace, E. P. (1995). *Achievement and addiction: A guide to the treatment of professionals.* New York: Brunner/Mazel.

Nair, P., Black, M. M., Schuler, M., Keane, V., Snow, L., Rigney, B. A., & Mager, L. (1997). Risk factors for disruption in primary caregiving among infants of substance abusing women. *Child Abuse and Neglect, 21*(11), 1039–1051.

Najavits, L. M., Weiss, R. D., & Shaw, S. R. (1997). The link between substance abuse and posttraumatic stress disorder in women: A research review. *The American Journal on Addictions, 6*(4), 273–283.

Naltrexone for alcohol dependence. (1995). *The Medical Letter, 37,* 64–66.

Nash, J. E., & Persaud, T. V. N. (1988). Embryopathic risks of cigarette smoking. *Experimental Pathology, 33,* 65–73.

National archive of criminal justice data (NACJD). (1994). Washington, DC: U.S. Department of Justice.

National five-year outcomes study confirms benefits of substance abuse treatment for adults, not adolescents. (1998). *Psychiatric Services, 49*(11), 1507–1508.

National Institute on Alcohol Abuse and Alcoholism. (1998, April). Alcohol and aging. *Alcohol Alert, 40.*

National Institute on Drug Abuse. (1984). *Drug abuse and drug abuse research, 43* (DHHS Publication No. ADM 85-1372). Washington, DC: U.S. Government Printing Office.

Nau, H., Kuhnz, W., Egger, H. J., Rating, D., & Helge, H. (1982). Anticonvulsants during pregnancy and lactation. Transplacental, maternal and neonatal pharmacokinetics. *Clinical Pharmacokinetics, 7,* 508–543.

Negative pulmonary effects of marijuana. (1987). *British Medical Journal, 295,* 1516–1518.

Nelkin, D. (1987). AIDS and the social sciences: Review of useful knowledge and research needs. *Reviews of Infectious Diseases, 9,* 980–986.

Neuspiel, D. R. (1992). Cocaine-associated abnormalities may not be causally related [Letter to the editor]. *American Journal of Diseases of Children, 146,* 278.

Neuspiel, D. R. (1993). Cocaine and the fetus: Mythology of severe risk. *Neurotoxicology and Teratology, 15,* 305–306.

Newell, M. L., Dunn, D., Peckham, C. S., Ades, A. E., Pardi, G., & Semprini, A. E. (1992). Risk factors for mother-to-child transmission of HIV-1: European collaborative study. *The Lancet, 339,* 1007–1012.

Newman, L. F., & Buka, S. L. (1991). Preventing the risk factors in childhood learning impairment. *Rhode Island Medical Journal, 74,* 251–262.

Ney, P. G., Fung, T., & Wickett, A. R. (1992). Causes of child abuse and neglect. *Canadian Journal of Psychiatry, 37,* 401–405.

Nicotine patches. (1992). *The Medical Letter on Drugs and Therapeutics, 34,* 37–38.

Nixon, S. J., & Glenn, S. W. (1995). Cognitive psychosocial performance and recovery in female alcoholics. *Behavior and Treatment Issues, 12,* 287–307.

Nolan, K. A., & Blass, J. P. (1992). Preventing cognitive decline. *Clinical Geriatric Medicine, 8*(1), 19–34.

Norris, C. R., Jr., & Extein, I. L. (1991). Diagnosing dual diagnosis patients. In M. S. Gold & A. E. Slaby (Eds.), *Dual diagnosis in substance abuse* (pp. 159–184). New York: Marcel Dekker.

Nucci, P., & Brancato, R. (1994). Ocular effects of prenatal cocaine exposure. *Ophthalmology, 101*(8), 1321.

Nurco, D. N., Cisin, I. H., & Ball, J. C. (1985). Crime as a source of income for narcotic addicts. *Journal of Substance Abuse Treatment, 2,* 113–115.

Nwanyanwu, O. C., Chu, S. Y., Green, T. A., Buehler, J. W., & Berkelman, R. L. (1993). Acquired immunodeficiency syndrome in the United States associated with injecting drug use, 1981–1991. *American Journal of Drug and Alcohol Abuse, 19,* 399–408.

O'Brien, M. (1989). Needle exchange programs: Ethical and policy issues. *AIDS and Public Policy Journal, 4*(2), 75–82.

O'Brien, W., & Biase, D. V. (1984). The therapeutic community: A current perspective. *Journal of Psychoactive Drugs, 16,* 9–21.

O'Connell, D. F. (1998). *Dual disorders: Essentials for assessment and treatment.* Binghamton, NY: Haworth.

O'Connell, D. F. (Ed.). (1990). *Managing the dually diagnosed patient: Current issues and clinical approaches.* Binghamton, NY: Haworth.

O'Doherty, F. (1991). Is drug use a response to stress? *Drug & Alcohol Dependence, 29*(1), 97–106.

Oei, T., & Jackson, P. (1980). Long-term effects of group and individual social skills training with alcoholics. *Addictive Behaviors, 5,* 129–136.

Oetting, E. R., & Beauvais, F. C. (1991). Critical incidents: Failure in prevention. *International Journal of the Addictions, 26,* 797–820.

Offidani, C., Pomini, F., Caruso, A., Ferrazzani, S., Chiarotti, M., & Fiori, A. (1995). Cocaine during pregnancy: A critical review of the literature [Review]. *Minerva Ginecologica, 47*(9), 381–390.

O'Hagan, K. (1993). *Emotional and psychological abuse of children.* Toronto: University of Toronto.

Older alcoholics are 'well hidden'. (1987). *The Addiction Research Foundation Journal, 16,* 2.

Olds, D. L., Henderson, C. R., Jr., & Tatelbaum, R. (1994). Intellectual impairment in children of women who smoke cigarettes during pregnancy. *Pediatrics, 93,* 221–226.

Olsen, J., Overvad, K., & Frische, G. (1991). Coffee consumption, birthweight, and reproductive failures. *Epidemiology, 2*(5), 370–374.

Olsen-Noll, C. G., & Bosworth, M. F. (1989). Alcohol abuse in the elderly. *American Family Physician, 39,* 173–179.

Olson, C. H. (1994). The effects of prenatal alcohol exposure on child development. *Infants and Young Children, 6*(3), 10–25.

Olson, H. C., Sampson, P. D., Barr, H., Streissguth, A. P., & Bookstein, F. L. (1992). Prenatal exposure to alcohol and school problems in late childhood: A longitudinal prospective study. *Development and Psychopathology, 4,* 341–359.

O'Malley, P. M., Johnston, L. D., & Bachman, J. G. (1991). Quantitative and qualitative changes in cocaine use among American high school seniors, college students, and young adults. *National Institute on Drug Abuse Research Monograph, 110,* 19–43.

O'Mara, N. B., & Nahata, M. C. (1995). Drugs excreted in human breast milk. In L. A. Pagliaro & A. M. Pagliaro (Eds.), *Problems in pediatric drug therapy* (3rd ed.). Hamilton, IL: Drug Intelligence.

Oncken, C. A., Hatsukami, D. K., Lupo, V. R., Lando, H. A., Gibeau, L. M., & Hansen, R. J. (1996). Effects of short-term use of nicotine gum in pregnant smokers. *Clinical Pharmacology & Therapeutics, 59*(6), 654–661.

Ord, R. A., & Benian, R. M. (1995). Baseball bat injuries to the maxillofacial region caused by assault. *Journal of Oral & Maxillofacial Surgery, 53,* 514–517.

Orenstein, M. (1989). *AIDS in Canada: Knowledge, behavior, and attitudes of adults.* Toronto: University of Toronto.

Osran, H. C., & Weinberger, L. E. (1994). Personality disorders and 'restoration to sanity'. *Bulletin of the American Academy of Psychiatry & the Law, 22,* 257–267.

Osterling, A., Berglund, M., Nilsson, L. H., & Kristenson, H. (1993). Sex differences in response style to two self-report screening tests on alcoholism. *Scandinavian Journal of Social Medicine, 21*(2), 83–89.

Ostrea, E. M., Chavez, C. J., & Stryker, J. C. (1978). In *The care of the drug dependent woman and her infant* (p. 18). Lansing, MI: Michigan Department of Public Health.

Ostrow, D. G. (1989). *Barriers to the recognition of links between drug alcohol and AIDS, in acquired immune deficiency syndrome and chemical dependency.* Rockville, MD: U.S. Department of Health and Human Services (DDH No. ADM 88-1513).

Ouellet, L. J., Wiebel, W. W., Jimenez, A. D., & Johnson, W. A. (1993). Crack cocaine and the transformation of prostitution in three Chicago neighborhoods. In M. S. Ratner (Ed.), *Crack pipe as pimp: An ethnographic investigation of sex-for-crack exchanges* (pp. 69–96). Lexington Books.

Pagliaro, A. M. (1990). Death of the medical model of addictions. *Proceedings of the Western Pharmacology Society, 33,* 286.

Pagliaro, A. M. (1991). The contributions of psychologic theories to the understanding of abusable psychotropic abuse phenomenon. *Canadian Psychology, 32,* 334.

Pagliaro, A. M. (1992). Producing knowledge of substance abusology: Assessment, choice, and evaluation of psychological theories of substance abuse (abstract). *Canadian Psychology, 33,* 398.

Pagliaro, A. M. (1994). The nature of scientific knowledge production. Evidence from the transdisciplinary science of substance abusology. *Canadian Psychology, 35*(2a), 40–43.

Pagliaro, A. M. (1997). Explaining substance use among women. *Canadian Psychology, 38*(2a), 34 (abstract).

Pagliaro, A. M. (1998). Drug-induced automatism: Theory and pharmacologic mechanisms. *Canadian Psychology, 39*(2a), 88 (abstract).

Pagliaro, A. M., Lang, R. A., & Pagliaro, L. A. (1998). Symposium: Drug-induced automatism: Implications for forensic psychologists. *Canadian Psychology, 39*(2a), 88 (abstract).

Pagliaro, A. M., & Pagliaro, L. A. (1999). The phenomenon of drug and substance abuse among the elderly—The Mega Interactive Model of Substance Abuse Among the Elderly (MIMSAE): Part II. *Journal of Pharmacy Technology, 10,* 22–33.

Pagliaro, A. M., & Pagliaro, L. A. (1992d). Sentenced to death? HIV infection and AIDS in prisons—current and future concerns. *Canadian Journal of Criminology, 34,* 201–214.

Pagliaro, A. M., & Pagliaro, L. A. (1994a). Just punishment? HIV and AIDS in correctional facilities. *Forum on Corrections Research, 6*(3), 40–43.

Pagliaro, A. M., & Pagliaro, L. A. (1994b, March 8). What do 261 "hard-core" intravenous drug using women know and do in relation to HIV infection and AIDS? A report from the PIARG major study. *Proceedings of the Eighth Annual Margaret Scott Wright Lectureship and Research Conference,* 27 (abstract).

Pagliaro, A. M., & Pagliaro, L. A. (1995a). Abusable psychotropic use among children and adolescents. In L. A. Pagliaro & A. M. Pagliaro (Eds.), *Problems in pediatric drug therapy* (3rd ed.) (pp. 507–540). Hamilton: Drug Intelligence Publications.

Pagliaro, A. M., & Pagliaro, L. A. (1995b, March 4). The Dry Drunk Syndrome and alcohol use disorders: Antecedent, consequence, or co-morbid condition. *Research Revelations '95:* Edmonton, Alberta: Research Exchange Forum, Heritage Medical Research Centre.

Pagliaro, A. M., & Pagliaro, L. A. (1996). *Substance use among children and adolescents: Its nature, extent, and effects from conception to adulthood.* New York: John Wiley & Sons.

Pagliaro, A. M., & Pagliaro, L. A. (1997). Teratogenic effects of in utero exposure to alcohol and other abusable psychotropics, Chapter 2 in M. Haack (Ed.), *Drug-dependent mothers and their children: Issues in public policy and public health* (pp. 31–63). New York: Springer.

Pagliaro, A. M., Pagliaro, L. A., Thauberger, P. C., Hewitt, D. S., & Reddon, J. R. (1990). AIDS and injection drug use: Changing dimensions of the epidemic. *Alberta Psychology, 19*(5), 5–7.

Pagliaro, A. M., Pagliaro, L. A., Thauberger, P. C., Hewitt, D., & Reddon, J. (1992, May 28). *Knowledge, behaviours, and risk perceptions of intravenous drug users in relation to HIV infection and AIDS.* (Poster presented at the Second Annual Conference of the Canadian Association for HIV Research, Vancouver, British Columbia).

Pagliaro, A. M., Pagliaro, L. A., Thauberger, P. C., Hewitt, D. S., & Reddon, J. R. (1993). Knowledge, behaviors, and risk perceptions of intravenous drug users in relation to HIV infection and AIDS: The PIARG projects. *Advances in Medical Psychotherapy, 6,* 1–28.

Pagliaro, L. A. (1983). Up in smoke? A brief overview of marijuana toxicity. *Kerygma, 41,* 1–4.

Pagliaro, L. A. (1985a, March). *Methadone maintenance: An appraisal.* (Unpublished report prepared for the Department of the Alberta Solicitor General), pp. 1–6.
Pagliaro, L. A. (1985b, August). *The Mega Interactive Model of Drug Abuse (MIMDA).* Paper presented at the 34th International Congress on Alcoholism and Drug Dependence, Calgary, Alberta, Canada.
Pagliaro, L. A. (1986). The phenomenon of addiction. *Alberta Psychology, 15*(4), 3–6.
Pagliaro, L. A. (1988a). The straight dope: "The 'Ice Man' cometh". *Alberta Psychology, 18*(6), 17.
Pagliaro, L. A. (1988b, April). Hooked on drugs: Overview of a growing problem. *Let's Talk, 13,* 4–5.
Pagliaro, L. A. (1988c, May). MIMDA: A new approach focuses on abuser's lifestyle. *Let's Talk, 13,* 10–11.
Pagliaro, L. A. (1988d, June). Marijuana and hashish: What are the risks? *Let's Talk, 13,* 12–14.
Pagliaro, L. A. (1988e, November 23 & 30). *Sedative-hypnotics: Toxicity and abuse.* Alberta and Ontario Hospital Associations Teleconference.
Pagliaro, L. A. (1988f, winter). Substance abuse in the elderly. *Centre for Gerontology Newsletter,* 4–60.
Pagliaro, L. A. (1990a). Overview of the problem of drug abuse in Canada [Abstract]. *Alberta Psychology, 19*(3), 11.
Pagliaro, L. A. (1990b). The straight dope: Dual diagnosis. *Alberta Psychology, 19*(5), 23–24.
Pagliaro, L. A. (1991a). The straight dope. *Psynopsis, 13*(2), 7.
Pagliaro, L. A. (1991b). The straight dope: Cannibalism, birth defects, homosexuality, and other myths associated with drug and substance abuse. *Psynopsis, 13*(4), 8.
Pagliaro, L. A. (1991c). The straight dope: Focus on prisons. *Psynopsis, 13*(3), 8.
Pagliaro, L. A. (1992a). Dr. Jekyll and Mr. Hyde . . . Drug-induced automatism. *Psynopsis, 14,* 11.
Pagliaro, L. A. (1992b). Focus on learning—Interpreting the interpretations. *Psynopsis, 14*(2), 7.
Pagliaro, L. A. (1992c). The straight dope: Predictions for 1992. *Psynopsis, 14*(1), 8.
Pagliaro, L. A. (1993a). Issues in substance abuse for Canadian teachers. In L. Stewin (Ed.), *Contemporary educational issues: The Canadian mosaic* (pp. 207–222). Toronto: Stewart.
Pagliaro, L. A. (1993b). The straight dope: Drug-induced violent behaviour: Questions and answers. *Psynopsis, 15*(3, Summer), 14.
Pagliaro, L. A. (1994, Winter). The problem of alcoholism among our elderly. *Psynopsis,* 10.
Pagliaro, L. A. (1995a). Adolescent depression and suicide—A review and analysis of the current literature. *Canadian Journal of School Psychology, 11,* 191–201.
Pagliaro, L. A. (1995b). Drug induced automatism: Fact or fiction? *Psymposium, 4,* 16–17.
Pagliaro, L. A. (1995c). Marijuana reconsidered. *Psymposium, 5,* 12–13.
Pagliaro, L. A. (1995d). Pharmacopsychology updates: Drugs and sexual (dys)function. *Psymposium, 4*(6), 20–21.
Pagliaro, L. A. (1995e). Pharmacopsychology updates: Psychotropic teratogens. *Psymposium, 5*(1), 18–19.
Pagliaro, L. A. (1995f). The straight dope: A consideration of substance-induced disorders. *Psynopsis, Spring,* 14.
Pagliaro, L. A. & Foster, R. (1990). Cancer chemotherapy and extortion. *The Medical Psychotherapist, 6,* 6–7.
Pagliaro, L. A., Jaglalsingh, L. H., & Pagliaro, A. M. (1992). Cocaine use and depression [letter]. *Canadian Medical Association Journal, 147,* 1636–1637.
Pagliaro, L. A., & Pagliaro, A. M. (1990, spring). Alcoholism in the elderly: Relationship to accidents and suicide. *Centre for Gerontology Newsletter,* 2–3.
Pagliaro, L. A., & Pagliaro, A. M. (1991). Drug induced automatism: Psychological aspects. *Canadian Psychology 32,* 204.
Pagliaro, L. A., & Pagliaro, A. M. (1992a). Drug induced aggression. *The Medical Psychotherapist, 8*(2–3), 9.
Pagliaro, L. A., & Pagliaro, A. M. (1992b). The phenomenon of drug and substance abuse among the elderly. Part I. An overview. *Journal of Pharmacy Technology, 8,* 65–73.

Pagliaro, L. A., & Pagliaro, A. M. (1993). The phenomenon of abusable psychotropic use among North American youth. *Journal of Clinical Pharmacology, 33*, 676–690.

Pagliaro, L. A., & Pagliaro, A. M. (1995a). Drugs as human teratogens. In L. A. Pagliaro & A. M. Pagliaro (Eds.), *Problems in pediatric drug therapy* (3rd ed., pp. 105–243). Hamilton, IL: Drug Intelligence Publications.

Pagliaro, L. A., & Pagliaro, A. M. (1995b). *Problems in pediatric drug therapy* (3rd edition). Hamilton, IL: Drug Intelligence Publications.

Pagliaro, L. A., & Pagliaro, A. M. (1998). *The pharmacologic basis of psychotherapeutics: An introduction for psychologists.* Washington, DC: Taylor & Francis.

Pagliaro, L. A., & Pagliaro, A. M. (1999a). *Psychologists' neuropsychotropic drug reference.* Philadelphia, PA: Brunner/Mazel.

Pagliaro, L. A., & Pagliaro, A. M. (1999b). *Psychologists' psychotropic drug reference.* Philadelphia, PA: Brunner/Mazel.

Pagliaro, L. A., & Pagliaro, A. M. (Eds.). (in press). *Problems in pediatric drug therapy* (4th ed.). Washington, DC: American Pharmaceutical Association.

Pajer, K. A. (1992). Psychotropic drugs and teratogenicity. In M. S. Keshavan & J. S. Kennedy (Eds.), *Drug-induced dysfunction in psychiatry* (pp. 49–74). New York: Hemisphere.

Paone, D. (1993). Guidelines for providing effective treatment for chemically dependent women of childbearing age. *Dissertation Abstracts International, 54*(1–A), 99.

Parette, H. P., Hourcade, J. J., & Parette, P. C. (1990). Nursing attitudes toward geriatric alcoholism. *Journal of Gerontological Nursing, 16*, 26–31.

Park, J. (1993). The culture of a public problem: Women and alcohol in New Zealand. *Community Mental Health in New Zealand, 8*(1), 42–49.

Parker, D. A. (1982). Commentary: The aging process and the misuse of alcohol. In I. Wood, W. Gibson, & M. F. Elias (Eds.), *Alcoholism and aging* (pp. 39–40). New York: Research Institute on Alcoholism.

Payne, P. A. (1990). Response to "Alcoholism recovery in lesbian women: A theory in development." *Scholarly Inquiry for Nursing Practice: An International Journal, 4*(2), 123–125.

Pearson, M. A., Hoyme, H. E., Seaver, L. H., & Rimsza, M. E. (1994). Toluene embryopathy: Delineation of the phenotype and comparison with fetal alcohol syndrome. *Pediatrics, 93*, 211–215.

Pegues, D. A., Engelgau, M. M., & Woernle, C. H. (1994). Prevalence of illicit drugs detected in the urine of women of childbearing age in Alabama public. *Public Health Reports, 109*, 530.

Penick, E. C., Nickel, E. J., Cantrell, P. F., Powell, B. M., Read, M. R., & Thomas, M. M. (1990). The emerging concept of dual diagnosis: An overview and implications. In D. F. O'Connell (Ed.), *Managing the dually diagnosed patient: Current issues and clinical approaches* (pp. 1–54). New York: Haworth.

Penick, E. C., Powell, B. J., Othmer, E., Bingham, S. F., Rice, A. S., & Liese, B. S. (1984). Subtyping alcoholics by coexisting psychiatric syndromes: Course, family history, outcome. In D. W. Goodwin, K. T. Van Dusen, and S. A. Mednick (Eds.), *Longitudinal research in alcoholism* (pp. 167–196). Boston, MA: Kluwer-Nijhoff.

Penninman, L. J., & Agnew, J. (1989). Women, work and alcohol. *Occupational Medicine: State of the Art Reviews, 4*(2), 263–273.

Perez-Bouchard, L., Johnson, J. L., & Ahrens, A. H. (1993). Attributional style in children of substance abusers. *American Journal of Drug and Alcohol Abuse, 19*, 475–489.

Perkins, C., & Klaus, P. (1996). National crime victimization survey: Criminal victimization 1994. *Bureau of Justice Statistics Bulletin*, U.S. Department of Justice, NCJ-158022.

Perlman, H. B. (1994, March 10). A portrait of addicted Jews: JACS aids those seeking a way out. *The Jewish Advocate*, PG.

Pernanen, K. (1981). Theoretical aspects of the relationship between alcohol use and crime. In J. J. Collins, Jr. (Ed.), *Drinking and crime* (pp. 1–61). New York: Guilford.

Pietrantoni, M., & Knuppel, R. A. (1991). Alcohol use in pregnancy. *Clinics in Perinatology, 18*, 93–111.

Pihl, R. O., Peterson, J. B., & Lau, M. A. (1993). A biosocial model of the alcohol-aggression relationship. *Journal of Studies on Alcohol, 11,* 128–139.
Pincus, J. H., & Lewis, D. O. (1991). Episodic violence. *Seminars in Neurology, 11,* 146–154.
Pintea-Reed, L. (1998). Women as victims of violent crimes. *Feminista!, 2*(5), 1–4.
Piot, P., Plummer, F. A., Mhalu, F. S., Lamboray, G., Chin, J., & Mann, J. M. (1988). AIDS: An international perspective. *Science, 239,* 573–579.
Pizzi, C. L., & Mion, L. C. (1993). Alcoholism in the elderly: Implications for hospital nurses. *Medical and Surgical Nursing, 2,* 453–458.
Plessinger, M. A., & Woods, J. R., Jr. (1991). The cardiovascular effects of cocaine use in pregnancy. *Reproductive Toxicology, 5,* 99–113.
Plessinger, M. A., & Woods, J. R., Jr. (1993). Maternal, placental, and fetal pathophysiology of cocaine exposure during pregnancy. *Clinical Obstetrics and Gynecology, 36*(2), 267–278.
Plouffe, J. M. (1995/1996). Statistics. *Let's Talk, 20*(4), 12.
Poklik, A. (1984). Decline in abuse of pentazocine/tripelennamine (Ts and blues) associated with the addiction of naloxone to pentazocine tablets. *Drug and Alcohol Dependence, 14,* 135–140.
Poklis, A., Maginn, D., & Barr, J. L. (1987). Drug findings in 'driving under the influence of drugs' cases: A problem of illicit drug use. *Drug and Alcohol Dependence, 20,* 57–62.
Pokorny, A. D., Miller, B. A., & Kaplan, H. B. (1972). The brief MAST; a shortened version of the Michigan Alcoholism Screening Test. *American Journal of Psychiatry, 129*(3), 342–348.
Pollock, P. H., & Kear-Colwell, J. J. (1994). Women who stab: A personal construct analysis of sexual victimization and offending behaviour. *British Journal of Medical Psychology, 67,* 13–22.
Ponce, D. E., & Jo, H. S. (1990). Substance abuse and psychiatric disorders: The dilemma of increasing incidence of dual diagnosis in residential treatment centers. *Residential Treatment for Children and Youth, 8*(2), 5–15.
Porcino, J. (1985). Psychological aspects of aging in women. *Women & Health: The Journal of Women's Health Care, 10*(2–3), 115–122.
Power, R., Hartnoll, R., & Daviaud, E. (1988). Drug injecting, AIDS, and risk behavior: Potential for change and intervention strategies. *British Journal of Addiction, 83,* 649–654.
Pratt, C. C., Schmall, V. L., Wilson, W., & Benthin, A. (1992). Alcohol problems in later life: Evaluation of a model community education program. *Community and Mental Health Journal, 28,* 327–335.
Preng, K. W., & Clopton, J. R. (1986). Application of the MacAndrew alcoholism scale to alcoholics with psychiatric diagnoses. *Journal of Personality Assessment, 50*(1), 113–122.
Prescriber's Letter. (1998, April). Smoking cessation products and programs (document #140422), 1–6.
Prevention plus II: Tools for creating and sustaining drug-free communities. (1989). Rockville, MD: Office for Substance Abuse Prevention (ADM89-1649).
Pribor, E. F., & Dinwiddie, S. H. (1992). Psychiatric correlates of incest in childhood. *American Journal of Psychiatry, 149,* 52–56.
Price, J. H., & Andrews, P. (1982). Alcohol abuse in the elderly. *Journal of Gerontological Nursing, 8,* 16–19.
Project MATCH (Matching Alcoholism Treatment to Client Heterogeneity): Rationale and methods for a multisite clinical trial matching patients to alcoholism treatment. (1993). *Alcoholism, Clinical and Experimental Research, 17,* 1130–1145.
Pronovost, J., Côté, L., & Ross, C. (1990, March). Epidemiological study of suicidal behaviour among secondary-school students. *Canada's Mental Health, 38*(1), 9–14.
Pruitt, A. W., Jacobs, E. A., Schydlower, M., Stands, B. O., & Sutton, J. M. (1990). Selection of substance abuse treatment programs. *Pediatrics, 86,* 139–140.
Public Law 100–203. (1987, December 22). 101 Stat., 1330–165.
Quigley, B. M., & Leonard, K. E. (1999). Husband alcohol expectancies, drinking, and marital-conflict styles as predictors of severe marital violence among newlywed couples. *Psychology of Addictive Behaviors, 13*(1), 49–59.
Quinnett, P. G. (1995, December). The 'S' question. *Professional Counselor,* 14–16, 64–66, 68.

Racine, A., Joyce, T., & Anderson, R. (1993). The association between prenatal care and birth weight among women exposed to cocaine in New York City. *Journal of the American Medical Association, 270*, 1581–1586.

Raftis, S., & Reynolds, W. (1996). *Give and take: A booklet for pregnant women about alcohol and other drugs.* AWARE Press Inc.

Rains, V. S., & Ditzler, T. F. (1993). Alcohol use disorders in cognitively impaired patients referred for geriatric assessment. *Journal of Addiction Disorders, 12*(1), 55–64.

Ratner, M. S. (Ed.). (1993). *Crack pipe as pimp: An ethnographic investigation of sex-for-crack exchanges.* New York: Lexington.

Regan, D. O., Ehrlick, S. M., & Finnegan, L. P. (1987). Infants of drug addicts: At risk for child abuse, neglect, and placement in foster care. *Neurotoxicology and Teratology, 9*(4), 315–319.

Rehm, J., Fichter, M. M., & Elton, M. (1993). Effects on mortality of alcohol consumption, smoking, physical activity, and close personal relationships. *Addiction, 88*(1), 101–112.

Remkes, T. (1993, June). Saying no—completely. *The Canadian Nurse, 89,* 25–28.

Reyes, A. A. (1993). A woman's place is in the home: A case study of the staff at a residential treatment program for substance abusing women. *Dissertation Abstracts International, 54*(1–A), 93.

Reyes, M. (1998). Latina lesbians and alcohol and other drugs: Social work implications. In M. Delgado (Ed.), *Alcohol use/abuse among Latinos: Issues and examples of culturally competent services* (pp. 179–192). Binghamton, NY: Haworth.

Rezza, G., Titti, F., Tempesta, E., di Giannantonia, M., Weisert, A., Rossi, G. B., & Verani, P. (1989). Needle sharing and other behaviors related to HIV spread among intravenous drug users. *AIDS, 3,* 247–248.

Rich, A. R., Kirkpatrick-Smith, J., Bonner, R. L., & Jans, F. (1992). Gender differences in the psychological correlates of suicidal ideation among adolescents. *Suicide and Listening Behavior, 22,* 364–373.

Richardson, R., Lowenstein, S., & Weissberg, M. (1989). Coping with the suicidal elderly: A physician's guide. *Geriatrics, 44*(9), 43–51.

Richelson, E. (1984). Psychotropics and the elderly: Interactions to watch for. *Geriatrics, 39*(12), 30–42.

Riesenberg, D. (1988). Drugs in the institutionalized elderly: Time to get it right? *Journal of the American Medical Association, 260,* 3054.

Risk of falling in elderly benzodiazepine users. (1989). *Facts and Comparisons Drug Newsletter, 8*(1), 5.

Ritter, B. (1989). Abuse of the adolescent. *New York State Journal of Medicine, 89,* 156–158.

Rivers, K. O., & Hedrick, D. L. (1992). Language and behavioral concerns for drug-exposed infants and toddlers. *The Transdisciplinary Journal, 2*(1), 63–73.

Rizk, B., Atterbury, J. L., & Groome, L. J. (1996). Reproductive risks of cocaine [Review]. *Human Reproduction Update, 2*(1), 43–55.

Roan, S. (1995). A dirty secret: Society would like to think that all expectant moms are cherished. But pregnancy may start—or increase—domestic violence. Home Edition, *Los Angeles Times,* pp. E-1.

Roberts, A. R. (1987). Psychosocial characteristics of batterers: A study of 234 men charged with domestic violence offenses. *Journal of Family Violence, 2*(1), 81–93.

Robins, L. N., & Price, R. K. (1991). Adult disorders predicted by childhood conduct problems: Results from the NIMH epidemiologic catchment area project. *Psychiatry, 54,* 116–132.

Robinson, G. M., Thornton, N. J., Rout, J., & MacKenzie, N. (1987). AIDS—risk behaviors and AIDS knowledge in intravenous drug users. *New Zealand Medical Journal, 100,* 209–211.

Rodell, C. (1994, March 15). 88-year-old granny is a heroin dealer. *National Enquirer,* 36.

Rolfs, R. T., Goldberg, M., & Sharrar, R. G. (1990). Risk factors for syphilis: Cocaine use and prostitution. *American Journal of Public Health, 80,* 853–857.

Roman, P. M. (1981). Situational factors in the relationship between alcohol and crime. In J. J. Collins, Jr. & M. E. Wolfgang (Eds.), *Drinking and crime: Perspectives on the relationships between alcohol consumption and criminal behavior* (pp. 143–151). New York: Guilford.

Room, R., & Greenfield, T. (1993). Alcoholics Anonymous, other 12-step movements and psychotherapy in the US population, 1990. *Addiction, 88,* 555–562.

Rose, S. M., Peabody, C. G., & Stratigeas, B. (1991). Undetected abuse among intensive case management clients. *Hospital and Community Psychiatry, 42,* 499–503.

Rosenberg, P. S., & Biggar, R. J. (1998). Trends in HIV incidence among young adults in the United States. *Journal of the American Medical Association, 279*(23), 1894–1899.

Rosenblum, G. (1989). A sobering story: Proof-positive that substance abusers—no matter what their age—can kick the habit. *New Choices, 29*(5), 62–69.

Rosenthal, M. S. (1984). Therapeutic communities: A treatment alternative for many but not all. *Journal of Substance Abuse Treatment, 1,* 55–58.

Ross, H. E., Glaser, F. B., & Germanson, T. (1988). The prevalence of psychiatric disorders in patients with alcohol and other drug problems. *Archives of General Psychiatry, 45,* 1023–1031.

Rosett, H. L., Weiner, L., Lee, A., Zuckerman, B., Dooling, E., & Oppenheimer, E. (1983). Patterns of alcohol consumption and fetal development. *Journal of the American College of Obstetricians and Gynecologists, 61,* 539–546.

Roth, J. A., & Moore, M. H. (1995). Reducing violent crimes and intentional injuries. *National Institute of Justice: Research in Action,* U.S. Department of Justice.

Royce, J. E. (1989). *Alcohol problems and alcoholism: A comprehensive survey.* New York: Free.

Runeson, B. S., & Rich, C. L. (1992). Diagnostic comorbidity of mental disorders among young suicides. *International Review of Psychiatry, 4,* 197–203.

Rush, B., & Ekdahl, A. (1990). Recent trends in the development of alcohol and drug treatment services in Ontario. *Journal of Studies on Alcohol, 51,* 514–522.

Russell, F. F., & Free, T. A. (1991). Early intervention for infants and toddlers with prenatal drug exposure. *Infants and Young Children, 3,* 78–85.

Russell, M. (1994). New assessment tools for risk drinking during pregnancy: T-ACE, TWEAK, and others. *Alcohol Health & Research World, 18*(1), 55–61.

Russell, M., Czarnecki, D. M., Cowan, R., McPherson, E., & Mudar, P. J. (1991). Measures of maternal alcohol use as predictors of development in early childhood. *Alcoholism: Clinical and Experimental Research, 15,* 991–1000.

Russell, M., Martier, S. S., Sokol, R. J., Mudar, P., Bottoms, S., Jacobson, S., & Jacobson, J. (1994). Screening for pregnancy risk-drinking. *Alcoholism, Clinical and Experimental Research, 18*(5), 1156–1161.

Russell, M. J., (1993). *Drug use forecasting quarterly report* (NCJ No. 142454). Washington, DC: U.S. Department of Justice.

Ryan, N. D., & Puig-Antich, J. (1987). Pharmacological treatment of adolescent psychiatric disorders. *Journal of Adolescent Health Care, 80,* 137–142.

Sampson, H. W. (1998). Alcohol's harmful effects on bone. *Alcohol Health & Research World, 22*(3), 190–194.

Sanchis, A., Rosique, D., & Catala, J. (1991). Adverse effects of maternal lorazepam on neonates. *DICP, The Annals of Pharmacotherapy, 25,* 1137–1138.

Sarvela, P. D., & Ford, T. D. (1992). Indicators of substance use among pregnant adolescents in the Mississippi delta. *Journal of School Health, 62,* 175–179.

Saunders, B., Baily, S., Phillips, M., & Allsop, S. (1993). Women with alcohol problems: Do they relapse for reasons different to their male counterparts? *Addiction, 88,* 1413–1422.

Saunders, J. B., Aasland, O. G., Babor, T. F., de la Fuente, J. R., & Grant, M. (1993). Development of the Alcohol Use Disorders Identification Test (AUDIT): WHO Collaborative Project on Early Detection of Persons with Harmful Alcohol Consumption—II. *Addiction, 88*(6), 791–804.

Saunders, S. J. (1985). *Alcohol and the elderly: Assessment and treatment approaches.* Toronto, ON: Addiction Research Foundation.

Sayette, M. A., Wilson, G. T., & Elias, M. J. (1993). Alcohol and aggression: A social information processing analysis. *Journal of Studies on Alcohol, 54,* 399–407.

Scanlon, J. W. (1991). The neuroteratology of cocaine: Background, theory, and clinical implications. *Reproductive Toxicology, 5,* 89–98.

Schapira, D. (1990). Alcohol abuse and osteoporosis. *Seminars in Arthritis and Rheumatism, 19,* 371–376.
Schenker, S., Becker, H. C., Randall, C. L., Phillips, D. K., Baskin, G. S., & Henderson, G. I. (1990). Fetal alcohol syndrome: Current status of pathogenesis. *Alcoholism: Clinical and Experimental Research, 14*(5), 635–647.
Schoenbaum, E. E., Hartel, D., Selwyn, P. A., Klein, R. S., Davenny, K., Rogers, M., Feiner, C., & Friedland, G. (1989). Risk factors for human immunodeficiency virus infection in intravenous drug users. *New England Journal of Medicine, 321,* 874–879.
Schonfeld, L., & Dupree, L. W. (1991). Antecedents of drinking for early- and late-onset elderly alcohol abusers. *Journal of Studies on Alcohol, 52,* 587–592.
Schuckit, M. A., Anthenelli, R. M., Bucholz, K. K., Hesselbrock, V. M., & Tipp, J. (1995). The time course of development of alcohol-related problems in men and women. *Journal of Studies on Alcohol, 56,* 218–225.
Schuckit, M. A., & Pastor, P. A. (1978). The elderly as a unique population: Alcoholism. *Alcoholism: Clinical and Experimental Research, 2*(1), 31–38.
Schuster, C. R. (1988). Intravenous drug use and AIDS prevention. *Public Health Reports, 103,* 261–266.
Schutte, K., Brennan, P., Hearst, J., & Moos, R. (1996, August). *Do depressive symptoms predict drinking behavior among women problem drinkers?* Presented at the 104th Annual Convention of the American Psychological Association at Toronto, Canada.
Schydlower, M., & Perrin, J. (1993). Prevention of fetal alcohol syndrome [Letter to the editor]. *Pediatrics, 92,* 739.
Science Daily News Release (November 13/1998). Why women are less likely than men to commit suicide [On-line]. Available: http://www.sciencedaily.com/
Scott, G. B., Buck, B. E., Letterman, J. G., Bloom, F. L., & Parks, W. P. (1984). Acquired immunodeficiency syndrome in infants. *New England Journal of Medicine, 310,* 76–81.
Searles, J. S., Alterman, A. I., & Purtill, J. J. (1990). The detection of alcoholism in hospitalized schizophrenics: A comparison of the MAST and the MAC. *Alcoholism, Clinical and Experimental Research, 14*(4), 557–560.
Secretary of Health and Human Services. (1993). NECASA: Violence and alcohol. *Eighth Special Report to the U.S. Congress on Alcohol and Health.*
Segal, R., & Sisson, B. V. (1985). Medical complications associated with alcohol use and the assessment of risk of physical damage. In T. E. Bratter & G. G. Forrest (Eds.), *Alcoholism and substance abuse: Strategies for clinical intervention* (pp. 137–175). New York: Free.
Seidman, D. S., Ever-Hadani, P., & Gale, R. (1990). Effect of maternal smoking and age on congenital anomalies. *Obstetrics and Gynecology, 76,* 1046–1050.
Seixas, F. A. (1982a). Criteria for the diagnosis of alcoholism. In N. J. Estes & M. E. Heinemann (Eds.), *Alcoholism: Development, consequences, and interventions* (2nd ed., pp. 49–67). St. Louis, MO: CV Mosby.
Seixas, F. A. (1982b). The course of alcoholism. In N. J. Estes & M. E. Heinemann (Eds.), *Alcoholism: Development, consequences, and interventions* (2nd ed., pp. 68–76). St. Louis, MO: CV Mosby.
Seligman, P. J., Campbell, R. J., Keeler, G. P., & Halpin, T. J. (1989). Human immunodeficiency virus seropositivity in intravenous drug users in Ohio. *Ohio Medicine, 85,* 56–59.
Selwyn, P. A. (1988). Sterile needles and the epidemic of acquired immunodeficiency syndrome: Issues for drug abuse treatment and public health. In L. Siegel (Ed.), *AIDS and substance abuse.* New York: Harrington Park.
Selzer, M. L. (1971). The Michigan Alcoholism Screening Test: The quest for a new diagnostic instrument. *American Journal of Psychiatry, 127,* 1653–1658.
Selzer, M. L., Gomberg, E. S., & Nordhoff, J. A. (1979). Men's and women's responses to the Michigan Alcoholism Screening Test. *Journal of Studies on Alcohol, 40,* 502–504.
Selzer, M. L., Vinokur, A., & Van Rooijen, L. (1976). A self-administered Short Michigan Alcoholism Screening Test (SMAST). *Journal of Studies on Alcohol, 36,* 117–126.
Senay, E. C., Kozel, N. J., & Gonzalez, J. P. (1991). Drug abuse and public health: A global perspective. *Drug Safety, 6*(Suppl. 1), 1–65.

Senior Citizens Bureau. (1983). Alcohol and the elderly. In *Proceedings from outreach conferences.* Edmonton, AB: Social Services and Community Health.

Seppä, K., Koivula, T., & Sillanaukee, P. (1992). Drinking habits and detection of heavy drinking among middle-aged women. *British Journal of Addiction, 87*(12), 1703–1709.

Seppä, K., Makela, R., & Sillanaukee, P. (1995). Effectiveness of the Alcohol Use Disorders Identification Test in occupational health screenings. *Alcoholism, Clinical and Experimental Research, 19*(4), 999–1003.

Sex tied to drugs = STD spread. (1988). *Journal of the American Medical Association, 260,* 2009.

Seymour, M. A., & Smith, D. E. (1999a, January). Street Drugs: Drug-assisted rape. *Psychopharmacology Update, 10*(1), 3.

Seymour, R. B., & Smith, D. E. (1999b, February). Street Drugs: Klonopin: The other "K." *Psychopharmacology, 10*(2), 5.

Shaw, G. (1996). Wrong way/women catching up to men—in drug abuse. *Newsday,* pp. A03.

Shaw, G., & Gray, K. (1996). Women, men equal—in drug abuse. *Newsday,* A04.

Sheinbaum, K. A., & Badell, A. (1992). Physiatric management of two neonates with limb deficiency and prenatal cocaine exposure. *Archives of Physical Medicine and Rehabilitation, 73,* 385–388.

Shelowitz, P. A. (1987). Drug use, misuse, and abuse among the elderly. *Medicine and Law, 6,* 235–250.

Shoemaker, F. W. (1993). Prevention of fetal alcohol syndrome [Letter to the editor]. *Pediatrics, 92,* 738–739.

Shogren, E. (1996). Drug-pregnancy case prosecutions OKd in S.C. Home Edition. *Los Angeles Times,* A12.

Shore, E. R. (1992). Drinking patterns and problems among women in paid employment. *Alcohol Health & Research World, 16*(2), 160–164.

Shore, E. R. (1994). Outcomes of a primary prevention project for business and professional women. *Journal of Studies on Alcohol, 55*(6), 657–659.

Shore, E. R., & Batt, S. (1991). Contextual factors related to the drinking behaviors of American business and professional women. *British Journal of Addiction, 86*(2), 171–176.

Siegel, B. (1994). In the name of the children; get treatment or go to jail, one South Carolina hospital tells drug-abusing pregnant women. Now it faces a lawsuit and a civil-rights investigation. Home edition. *Los Angeles Times,* p. 14.

Silberstein, C., Galanter, M., Marmor, M., Lifshutz, H., Krasinski, K., & Franco, H. (1994). HIV-1 among inner city dually diagnosed inpatients. *American Journal of Drug & Alcohol Abuse, 20,* 101–113.

Simonds, R. J., Stekette, R., Nesheim, S., Matheson, P., Palumbo, P., Alger, L., Abrams, E. J., Orloff, S., Lindsay, M., Bardeguez, A. D., Vink, P., Byers, R., & Rogers, M. (1998). Impact of zidovudine use on risk and risk factors for perinatal transmission of HIV. Perinatal AIDS collaborative transmission studies. *AIDS, 12*(3), 301–308.

Simpson, H. M., Mayhew, D. R., & Warren, R. A. (1982). Epidemiology of road accidents involving young adults: Alcohol, drugs and other factors. *Drug & Alcohol Dependence, 10*(1), 35–63.

Singer, L., Arendt, R., Song, L. Y., Warshawsky, E., & Kliegman, R. (1994). Direct and indirect interactions of cocaine with childbirth outcomes. *Archives of Pediatrics and Adolescent Medicine, 148*(9), 959–964.

Singleton, J. A., Tabnak, F., Kuan, J., & Rutherford, G. W. (1996). Human immunodeficiency virus disease in California. Effects of the 1993 expanded case definition of the acquired immunodeficiency syndrome. *Western Journal of Medicine, 164*(2), 122–129.

Skinner, H. A. (1982). The drug abuse screening test. *Addictive Behavior, 7,* 363–371.

Skog, O. (1984). The risk function for liver cirrhosis from lifetime alcohol consumption. *Journal of Studies on Alcohol, 45,* 199–208.

Slaby, A. E. (1991). Dual diagnosis: Fact or fiction? In M. S. Gold & A. E. Slaby (Eds.), *Dual diagnosis in substance abuse* (pp. 3–28). New York: Marcel Dekker.

Sloan, E. P., Zalenski, R. J., Smith, R. F., Sheaff, C. M., Chen, E. H., Keys, N. I., Crescenzo, M., Barrett, J. A., & Berman, E. (1989). Toxicology screening in urban trauma patients: Drug

prevalence and its relationship to trauma severity and management. *Journal of Trauma, 29*(12), 1647–1653.
Slutsker, L. (1992). Risks associated with cocaine use during pregnancy. *Obstetrics & Gynecology, 79*, 778–789.
Smart, R. G., & Adlaf, E. M. (1988). Alcohol and drug use among the elderly: Trends in use and characteristics of users. *Canadian Journal of Public Health, 79*, 236–242.
Smiley, A., Moskowitz, H. M., & Ziedman, K. (1985). Effects of drugs on driving: Driving simulator tests of secobarbital, diazepam, marijuana, and alcohol. *Clinical and Behavioral Pharmacology Research Report* (pp. 1–21) (DHHS No. ADM85-1386). U.S. Department of Health and Human Services.
Smith, E. M., Lewis, C. E., Kercher, C., & Spitznagel, E. (1994, October). Predictors of mortality in alcoholic women: A 20-year follow-up study. *Alcoholism, Clinical & Experimental Research, 18*(5), 1177–1186.
Smith, K. M. (1993). Families of recovering women alcoholics: A qualitative analysis of roles, rules, and rituals. *Dissertation Abstracts International, 54*(1), 325.
Smith, S. M. (1997). Alcohol-induced cell death in the embryo. *Alcohol Health & Research World, 21*(4), 287–297.
Smitherman, C. H. (1994). The lasting impact of fetal alcohol syndrome and fetal alcohol effect on children and adolescents. *Journal of Pediatric Health Care, 8*, 121–126.
Smoking-attributable mortality and years of potential life lost—United States, 1988. (1991). *Morbidity and Mortality Weekly Report, 40*, 62–63, 69–71.
Smoking control: Summary of the problem. (1983, September–October). *Public Health Reports, Suppl., 107* 116.
Smucker, P. (1996, July 17). S.C. court: Fetus abuse a crime/Mothers can be prosecuted. *Newsday*, p. A18.
Snodgrass, S. R. (1994). Cocaine babies: A result of multiple teratogenic influences. *Journal of Child Neurology, 9*(3), 227–233.
Sobell, M. B., & Sobell, L. C. (1972). Individualized behavior therapy for alcoholics: Rationale, procedures, preliminary results and appendix. In P. M. Baker (Ed.), *California Mental Health Research Monograph* [Research monograph No. 13]. State of California: Department of Mental Hygiene.
Soderman, P., Hartvig, P., & Fagerlund, C. (1984). Acetazolamide excretion into human breast milk. *British Journal of Clinical Pharmacology, 17*, 599–600.
Soderman, P., & Matheson, I. (1987). Clonazepam in breast milk. *European Journal of Pediatrics, 147*, 212–213.
Sorell, G. T., Silvia, L. Y., & Busch-Rossnagel, N. A. (1993). Sex-role orientation and self-esteem in alcoholic and nonalcoholic women. *Journal of Studies on Alcohol, 54*, 566–573.
Sorock, G. S., & Shimkin, E. E. (1988). Benzodiazepine sedatives and the risk of falling in a community-dwelling elderly cohort. *Archives of Internal Medicine, 148*, 2441–2444.
Spagnolo, A. (1993). Teratogenesis of alcohol. *Annali Dell Instituto Superiore Sanità, 29*(1), 89–96.
Spear, L. P. (1993). Missing pieces of the puzzle complicate conclusions about cocaine's neurobehavioral toxicity in clinical populations: Importance of animal models. *Neurotoxicology and Teratology, 15*, 307–309.
Spohr, H. L., Wilms, J., & Steinhausen, H. C. (1993). Prenatal alcohol exposure and long-term developmental consequences. *The Lancet, 341*(8850), 907–910.
Spunt, B., Goldstein, P., Brownstein, H., & Fendrich, M. (1994). The role of marijuana in homicide. *International Journal of the Addictions, 29*, 195–213.
Stafford, J. R., Jr., Rosen, T. S., Merrian, J. C., & Zaider, M. (1994). Ocular effects of prenatal cocaine exposure. *Ophthalmology, 101*(8), 1321.
Stafford, J. R., Jr., Rosen, T. S., Zaider, M., & Merriam, J. C. (1994). Prenatal cocaine exposure and the development of the human eye. *Ophthalmology, 101*, 301–308.
Staley, D., & el-Guebaly, N. (1990). Psychometric properties of the Drug Abuse Screening Test in a psychiatric patient population. *Addictive Behaviors, 15*(3), 247–264.
Staples, R. (1990). Substance abuse and the Black family crisis: An overview. *Western Journal of Black Studies, 14*(4), 196–204.

Stark, E., & Flitcraft, A. (1995). Killing the beast within: Woman battering and female suicidality [Review]. *International Journal of Health Services, 25*(1), 43–64.

STD testing of suspected sexually abused children at a pediatric hospital. (1988). *Canada Diseases Weekly Report, 14*–44, 201–203.

Steenman, H. F., Hermann, B. P., Wyler, A. R., & Richey, E. T. (1988). The MacAndrew Alcoholism Scale in epilepsy: A high false positive error rate. *Journal of Clinical Psychology, 44*(3), 457–460.

Steinbauer, J. R., Cantor, S. B., Holzer, C. E. 3rd, & Volk, R. J. (1998). Ethnic and sex bias in primary care screening tests for alcohol use disorders. *Annals of Internal Medicine, 129*(5), 353–362.

Stepakoff, S. (1998). Effects of sexual victimization on suicidal ideation and behavior in U.S. college women. *Suicide & Life-Threatening Behavior, 28*(1), 107–126.

Stepka, M., Rogala, H., & Czyzyk, A. (1993). Hypoglycemia: A major problem in the management of diabetes in the elderly. *Aging-Milano, 5,* 117–121.

Stevens, R. (1998). Understanding HIV-AIDS and the special needs of African-American women and adolescents. *Psychotherapy in Private Practice, 17*(3), 21–33.

Stiffman, A. R. (1989). Physical and sexual abuse in runaway youths. *Child Abuse & Neglect, 13,* 417–426.

Stimmel, B. (1986). Factors associated with alcohol and substance abuse in women and children. In B. Stimmel (Ed.), *Alcohol and substance abuse in women and children* (pp. 1–8). Binghamton, NY: Haworth.

Stimson, G. V. (1988). Injecting equipment exchange schemes in England and Scotland. In R. J. Battjes & R. W. Pickens (Eds.), *NIDA research monograph 80: Needle sharing among intravenous drug abusers: National and international perspectives.* Rockville, MD: National Institute on Drug Abuse.

Stimson, G. V. (1989). Syringe-exchange programmes for injecting drug users. *AIDS, 3,* 253–260.

Stinson, F. S., & DeBakey, S. F. (1992). Alcohol-related mortality in the United States, 1979–1988. *British Journal of Addiction, 87,* 777–783.

Stocker, S. (1998). Men and women in drug abuse treatment relapse at different rates and for different reasons. *NIDA Notes, 13*(4), 5–6.

Stone, R. (1992). Bad news on second-hand smoke. *Science, 257,* 607.

Stowell, R. J. A. (1991). Dual diagnosis issues. *Psychiatric Annals, 21,* 98–104.

Streissguth, A. P., Aase, J. M., Clarren, S. K., Randels, S. P., LaDue, R. H., & Smith, R. A. (1991). Fetal alcohol syndrome in adolescents and adults. *Journal of the American Medical Association, 265,* 1961–1967.

Streissguth, A. P., Barr, H. M., Olson, H. C., Sampson, P. D., Bookstein, F. L., & Burgess, D. M. (1994). Drinking during pregnancy decreases word attack and arithmetic scores on standardized tests: Adolescent data from a population-based prospective study. *Alcoholism: Clinical and Experimental Research, 18,* 248–254.

Streissguth, A. P., Randels, S. P., & Smith, D. F. (1992). Fetal alcohol syndrome [Reply to letter to the editor]. *Journal of the American Academy of Child and Adolescent Psychiatry, 31*(3), 563–564.

Streissguth, A. P., Sampson, P. D., Barr, H. M., Bookstein, F. L., & Olson, H. C. (1994). The effects of prenatal exposure to alcohol and tobacco: Contributions from the Seattle longitudinal prospective study and implications for public policy. In H. L. Needleman & D. Bellinger (Eds.), *Prenatal exposure to toxicants: Developmental consequences* (pp. 148–183). Baltimore: John Hopkins University.

Substance abuse: Frequent alcohol consumption among women of childbearing age. (1994). *Weekly Epidemiological Record, 69,* 180–182.

Substance abuse in the elderly: Gerontology association initiates research. (1986, April). *Hospital Alberta, 5.*

Suh, E. K., & Abel, E. M. (1990). The impact of spousal violence on the children of the abused. *Journal of Independent Social Work, 4,* 27–34.

Sullivan, L. W. (1990). *Seventh special report to the U.S. Congress on alcohol and health.* Rockville, MD: U.S. Department of Health and Human Services.

Survey finds increased adolescent drug use. (1995, Winter). *NIDA Invest*, pp. 1–2.
Svanum, S., & Ehrmann, L. C. (1992). Alcoholic subtypes and the MacAndrew Alcoholism Scale. *Journal of Personality Assessment, 58*(2), 411–422.
Swallow, J. E. (1983). *Out from under: Sober dykes and their friends*. San Francisco, CA: Spinsters, Ink.
Swan, N. (1995). NIDA refocuses its research on drug-related violence. (NIH Publication No. 95-3478). Rockville, MD: U.S. Department of Health and Human Services.
Swartz, J. (1991a). *Implications of the drug use forecasting data for TASC programs: Female arrestees* (pp. 1–32). Washington, DC: Bureau of Justice Assistance (NCJ 129671).
Swartz, J. (1991b). *Report III: Implications of the drug use forecasting data for TASC programs*. Washington, DC: Bureau of Justice Assistance.
Szwabo, P. A. (1993). Substance abuse in older women. *Clinical Geriatric Medicine, 9*(1), 197–208.
Tabor, B. L., Smith-Wallace, T., & Yonekura, M. L. (1990). Perinatal outcome associated with PCP versus cocaine use. *American Journal of Drug and Alcohol Abuse, 16*(3, 4), 337–348.
Tarter, R. E. (1990). Evaluation and treatment of adolescent substance abuse: A decision tree method. *American Journal of Drug & Alcohol Abuse, 16*(1–2), 1–46.
Tax, A. W. (1993, March). Wives of alcoholics: An analysis from a family systems/object relations theoretical perspective. *Dissertation Abstracts International, 53*(9–b), 4970.
Taylor, P. L., & Albright, W. J., Jr. (1981). Nondrug criminal behavior and heroin use. *The International Journal of the Addictions, 16*, 683–696.
Taylor, W. A., & Slaby, A. E. (1992). Acute treatment of alcohol and cocaine emergencies. In M. Galanter (Ed.), *Recent developments in alcoholism (Vol. 10). Alcohol and cocaine: similarities and differences* (pp. 179–191). New York: Plenum.
Teixeira, F., Hojyo, M. T., Arenas, R., Vega, M. E., Cortes, R., Ortiz, A., & Dominguez, L. (1994). Thalidomide: Can it continue to be used? [Letter to the editor]. *The Lancet, 344*, 196–197.
Temple, D. J. (1990). Update on AIDS epidemiology. *The Pharmaceutical Journal, 245*, 752–753.
The little red book. (1986). Center City, MN: Hazelden.
The Women and AIDS Program. (1993, October). *The risks! The rules! Latex*. ACT The AIDS Committee of Toronto. Toronto, ON: Author.
Thibault, J. M., & Maly, R. C. (1993). Recognition and treatment of substance abuse in the elderly. *Primary Care, 20*(1), 155–165.
Thiry, L., Sprechner-Goldberger, S., Jonckheer, T., Levy, J., Van de Perre, P., Henrivaux, P., Cogniaux-LeClerc, J., & Clumeck, N. (1985). Isolation of AIDS virus from cell-free breast milk of three healthy virus carriers [Letter]. *Lancet, 2*, 891–892.
Thomas, C. L. (Ed.). (1993). *Taber's cyclopedic medical dictionary*. Philadelphia: F.A. Davis.
Thomas, P. (1995). Planning the prevention of alcohol and other drug-related problems among women. *Drug and Alcohol Review, 14*, 7–15.
Ticehurst, S. (1990). Alcohol and the elderly. *Australian and New Zealand Journal of Psychiatry, 24*, 252–260.
Tobias, C. R., Lippmann, S., Pary, R., Oropilla, T., & Embry, C. K. (1989). Alcoholism in the elderly: How to spot and treat a problem the patient wants to hide. *Postgraduate Medicine, 86*, 67–70, 75–79.
Tonnesen, P., Norregaard, J., Simonsen, K., & Sawe, U. (1991). A double-blind trial of a 16-hour transdermal nicotine patch in smoking cessation. *New England Journal of Medicine, 325*, 311–315.
Tortu, S., Beardsley, M., Deren, S., & Davis, W. R. (1994). The risk of HIV infection in a national sample of women with injection drug-using partners. *American Journal of Public Health, 84*(8), 1243–1249.
Travis, J. (1996). The extent and costs of crime victimization: A new look. *National Institute of Justice: Research Preview*, U.S. Department of Justice.
Treiman, D. M. (1986). Epilepsy and violence: Medical and legal issues. *Epilepsia, 27*(Suppl. 2), S77–S104.
Trice, H. (1983). Alcoholics Anonymous. In D. A. Ward (Ed.), *Alcoholism: Introduction to theory and treatment* (2nd ed.). Dubuque, IA: Kendall/Hunt.

Tsai, E.-M., Lee, J.-N., Chao, M.-C., & Chai, C.-Y. (1993). Holoprosencephaly and trisomy 13 in a fetus with maternal early gestational amphetamine abuse—A case report. *Kao Hsiung Journal of Medical Science, 9,* 703–706.

Turner, C. F., Miller, H. G., & Moses, L. E. (1989). *Aids—sexual behavior and intravenous drug use.* Washington, DC: National Academy.

Turner, S. (1995). Alcoholic women's self-esteem. *Alcoholism Treatment Quarterly, 12*(4), 109–116.

Tutton, C. S., & Crayton, J. W. (1993). Current pharmacotherapies for cocaine abuse: A review. *Journal of Addictive Diseases, 12,* 109–127.

Twigg, B. (1995). Oprah admits to smoking cocaine. *Weekly Journal, PG.*

United States Department of Justice. (1991). *Uniform Crime Reports–1990.* Washington, DC: U.S. Government Printing Office.

United States Department of Justice. (1994). *Fact sheet: Drug use trends,* pp. 1–6. Washington, DC: Author.

Update: Perinatally acquired HIV/AIDS—United States. (1997). *MMWR - Morbidity and Mortality Weekly Report, 46*(46), 1086–1092.

Uziel-Miller, N. D., Lyons, J. S., Kissiel, C., & Love, S. (1998). Treatment needs and initial outcomes of a residential recovery program for African-American women and their children. *American Journal on Addictions, 7*(1), 43–50.

van Aalst, J. A., Shotts, S. D., Vitsky, J. L., Bass, S. M., Miller, R. S., Meador, K. G., & Morris, J. A., Jr. (1992). Long-term follow-up of unsuccessful violent suicide attempts: Risk factors for subsequent attempts. *The Journal of Trauma, 33,* 457–464.

Van Allen, M. I. (1992). Structural anomalies resulting from vascular disruption. *Pediatric Clinics of North America, 39,* 255–277.

van Biema, D. (1995). Abandoned to her fate. *Time,* 38–41.

van den Anker, J. N., & Sauer, P. J. J. (1992). Effect of cocaine use on the fetus [Letter to the editor]. *New England Journal of Medicine, 327*(9), 1393–1394.

Van Dyke, D. C., & Fox, A. A. (1990). Fetal drug exposure and its possible implications for learning in the preschool and school-age population. *Journal of Learning Disabilities, 23,* 160–163.

Van Dyke, R. B. (1991). Pediatric human immunodeficiency virus infection and the acquired immunodeficiency syndrome. *American Journal of Diseases of Children, 145,* 529–532.

Van Hasselt, V. B., Ammerman, R. T., Glancy, L. J., & Bukstein, O. G. (1992). Maltreatment in psychiatrically hospitalized dually diagnosed adolescent substance abusers. *Journal of the American Academy of Child and Adolescent Psychiatry, 31,* 868–874.

Van Natta, P., Malin, H., Bertolucci, D., & Kaelber, C. (1985). The influence of alcohol abuse as a contributor to mortality. *Alcohol, 2,* 535–539.

van Rensburg, P. H. J. J., Gagiano, C. A., & Verschoor, T. (1994). Possible reasons why certain epileptics commit unlawful acts during or directly after seizures. *Medicine & Law, 13,* 373–379.

Vega, W. A. (1992). *Profile of alcohol and drug abuse during pregnancy in California, 1992.* Berkeley, CA: University of California, School of Public Health.

Velleman, R., & Orford, J. (1993). The importance of family discord in explaining childhood problems in the children of problem drinkers. *Addiction Research, 1,* 39–57.

Violence between intimates. (1994). *Bureau of Justice Statistics: Selected Findings* (NCJ-149249).

Virkkunen, M., & Linnoila, M. (1993). Brain serotonin, type II alcoholism and impulsive violence. *Journal of Studies on Alcohol, 11,* 163–169.

Viscoli, C. M., Lachs, M. S., & Horwitz, R. I. (1993). Bladder cancer and coffee drinking: A summary of case-control research. *The Lancet, 341,* 1432–1437.

Volavka, J., Martell, D., & Convit, A. (1992). Psychobiology of the violent offender. *Journal of Forensic Sciences, 37*(1), 237–251.

Volkan, K. (1994). *Dancing among the Maenads. The psychology of compulsive drug use.* New York: Peter Lang.

Volpe, J. J. (1992). Effect of cocaine use on the fetus. *New England Journal of Medicine, 327*(6), 399–407.

Volpicelli, J. R., Clay, K. L., Watson, N. T., & Volpicelli, L. A. (1994). Naltrexone and the treatment of alcohol dependence. *Alcohol Health & Research World, 18,* 272–278.

Volpicelli, J. R., Watson, N. T., King, A. C., Sherman, C. E., & O'Brien, C. P. (1995). Effect of naltrexone on alcohol "high" in alcoholics. *American Journal of Psychiatry, 152,* 613–615.

Wall, J. H. (1937). A study of alcoholism in women. *American Journal of Psychiatry, 93,* 943–952.

Wallace, H. (1996). *Family violence: Legal, medical, and social perspectives.* Needham Heights, MA: Allyn and Bacon.

Wallace, J. (1982). Alcoholism from the inside out: A phenomenological analysis. In N. J. Estes & M. E. Heinemann (Eds.), *Alcoholism: Development, consequences, and interventions* (2nd ed., pp. 3–15). St. Louis, MO: CV Mosby.

Wallace, P (1991). Prevalence of fetal alcohol syndrome largely unknown. *Iowa Medicine, 81*(9), 381.

Waller, P. F., & Blow, F. C. (1995). Women, alcohol, and driving. *Recent Developments in Alcoholism, 12,* 103–123.

Walpole, I., Zubrick, S., Pontré, J., & Lawrence, C. (1991). Low to moderate maternal alcohol use before and during pregnancy, and neurobehavioural outcome in the newborn infant. *Developmental Medicine and Child Neurology, 33,* 875–883.

Ward, J. W., & Duchin, J. S. (1997–98). The epidemiology of HIV and AIDS in the United States [Review]. *AIDS Clinical Review,* 1–45.

Ward, R. E., Flynn, T. C., Miller, P. W., & Blaisdell, W. F. (1982). Effects of ethanol ingestion on the severity and outcome of trauma. *American Journal of Surgery, 144,* 153–157.

Washton, A. M., Gold, M. S., & Pottash, A. C. (1985). Opiate and cocaine dependencies. Techniques to help counter the rising tide. *Postgraduate Medicine, 77,* 293–300.

Waterson, J., & Ettorre, B. (1989). Providing services for women with difficulties with alcohol or other drugs: The current U.K. situation as seen by women practitioners, researchers and policy makers in the field. *Drug and Alcohol Dependence, 24,* 119–125.

Watson, D. D., Kail, B., & Ray, S. (1993). Sex for money and drugs. Handbook on risk of AIDS: Injection drug users and sexual partners, *National AIDS Research Consortium* (pp. 211–223).

Wattis, J. P. (1981). Alcohol problems in the elderly. *Journal of the American Geriatrics Society, 29,* 131–134.

Watts, T. D. (1984). Alcohol and the elderly: A review essay. *Journal of Alcohol and Drug Education, 29,* 6–8.

Waxman, H. M., Klein, M., & Carner, E. A. (1985). Drug misuse in nursing homes: An institutional addiction? *Hospital and Community Psychiatry, 36,* 886–887.

Webber, M. (1991). *Street kids: The tragedy of Canada's runaways.* Toronto: University of Toronto.

Weil, A. (1983). No bad drugs. *Newservice, 1,* 22–35.

Weisman, A. M., & Taylor, S. P. (1994). Effect of alcohol and risk of physical harm on human physical aggression. *Journal of General Psychology, 121,* 67–75.

Weisner, C., Greenfield, T., & Room, R. (1995). Trends in the treatment of alcohol problems in the US general population, 1979 through 1990. *American Journal of Public Health, 85,* 55–60.

Weisner, C., & Schmidt, L. (1992). Gender disparities in treatment for alcohol problems. *Journal of the American Medical Association, 268,* 1872–1876.

Weis, R. D. (1992). The role of psychopathology in the transition from drug use to abuse and dependence. In M. Glantz & R. Pickens (Eds.), *Vulnerability to abuse* (pp. 137–148). Washington, DC: American Psychological Association.

Weiss, R. D., Griffin, M. L., & Mirin, S. M. (1992). Drug abuse as self-medication for depression: An empirical study. *American Journal of Drug & Alcohol Abuse, 18,* 121–129.

Weisz, J. R., Martin, S. L., Walter, B. R., & Fernandez, G. A. (1991). Differential prediction of young adult arrests for property and personal crimes: Findings of a cohort follow-up study of violent boys from North Carolina's Willie M Program. *Journal of Child Psychology and Psychiatry, 32,* 783–792.

Weitzman, M., Gortmaker, S., Walker, D. K., & Sobol, A. (1990). Maternal smoking and childhood asthma. *Pediatrics, 85,* 505–511.

Welte, J. W., & Mirand, A. L. (1995). Drinking, problem drinking and life stressors in the elderly general population. *Journal of Studies on Alcohol, 56,* 67–73.

Wermuth, L. A., Robbins, R. L., Choi, K., & Eversley, R. (1991). Reaching and counselling women sexual partners. In J. L. Sorensen, L. A. Wermuth, D. R. Gibson, K. Choi, J. R. Guy-

dish, & S. L. Batki (Eds.), *Preventing AIDS in drug users and their sexual partners*. New York: Guilford.
Westermeyer, J. (1990). Methodological issues in the epidemiological study of alcohol-drug problems: Sources of confusion and misunderstanding. *American Journal of Drug and Alcohol Abuse, 16*, 47–55.
Westermeyer, J. (1992). Substance use disorders: Predictions for the 1990s. *American Journal on Drug and Alcohol Abuse, 18*, 1–11.
Westreich, L., Guedj, P., Galanter, M., & Baird, D. (1997). Differences between men and women in dual-diagnosis treatment. *American Journal on Addictions, 6*(4), 311–317.
Wetter, D. W., Fiore, M. C., Gritz, E. R., Lando, H. A., Stitzer, M. L., Hasselbad, V., & Baker, T. B. (1998). The agency for health care policy and research. Smoking cessation clinical practice guideline. Findings and implications for psychologists. *American Psychologist, 53*(6), 657–669.
Wheeler, S. F. (1993). Substance abuse during pregnancy. *Primary Care, 20*, 191–207.
Whitcup, S., & Miller, F. (1987). Addiction undiagnosed in elderly patients. *Journal of the American Geriatric Society, 35*, 297–301.
Whitlock, E. P., Ferry, L. H., Burchette, R. J., & Abbey, D. (1995). Smoking characteristics of female veterans. *Addictive Behaviors, 20*(4), 409–426.
Whitmire, R. (1994a). Addicted pregnant women get choice: Jail or treatment. *Gannett News Service*.
Whitmire, R. (1994b). Drug-using, pregnant women: Medical or criminal problem? *Gannett News Service*.
Wickens, B., & Wood, C. (1994, June 20). Grounds for debate. *MacLean's*, 48–49.
Wilens, T. E., Biederman, J., Spencer, T. J., & Frances, R. J. (1994). Comorbidity of attention-deficit hyperactivity and psychoactive substance use disorders. *Hospital and Community Psychiatry, 45*, 421.
Wilke, D. (1994). Women and alcoholism: How a male-as-norm bias affects research, assessment, and treatment. *Health & Social Work, 19*(1), 29–35.
Wilkins-Haug, L., & Gabow, P. A. (1991). Toluene abuse during pregnancy: Obstetric complications and perinatal outcomes. *Obstetrics & Gynecology, 77*, 504–509.
Willard, H. (1989, February 20). At 90, the zombie shuffle. *Newsweek*, 10.
Willenbring, M. L., Christensen, K. J., Spring, W. D., Jr., & Rasmussen, R. (1987). Alcoholism screening in the elderly. *Journal of the American Geriatrics Society, 35*, 864–869.
Williams, M. (1982, December). Alcohol problems in elderly compounded by many factors. NIAAA Information and Feature Service (IFS No. 103, p. 1).
Williams, M. (1984). Alcohol and the elderly: An overview. *Alcohol Health & Research World, 8*, 3–9.
Wilsnack, R. W., & Cheloha, R. (1987). Women's roles and problem drinking across the lifespan. *Social Problems, 34*(3), 231–248.
Wilsnack, R. W., Klassen, A. D., & Wilsnack, S. C. (1986). Retrospective analysis of lifetime changes in women's drinking behavior. In B. Stimmel (Ed.), *Alcohol and substance abuse in women and children* (pp. 9–28). Binghamton, NY: Haworth.
Wilsnack, R. W., & Wilsnack, S. C. (1992). Women, work, and alcohol: Failures of simple theories. *Alcoholism: Clinical and Experimental Research, 16*(2), 172–179.
Wilsnack, S. C., Wilsnack, R. W., & Hiller-Sturmhofel, S. (1994). How women drink. *Alcohol Health & Research World, 18*, 173.
Wilsnack, R. W., Wilsnack, S. C., & Klassen, A. D. (1984). Women's drinking and drinking problems: Patterns from a 1981 national survey. *American Journal of Public Health, 74*(11), 1231–1238.
Wilsnack, S. C., & Wilsnack, R. W. (1991). Epidemiology of women's drinking. *Journal of Substance abuse, 3*, 133–157.
Wilsnack, S. C., & Wilsnack, R. W. (1995). Drinking and problem drinking in US women: Patterns and recent trends. *Recent Developments in Alcoholism, 12*, 29–60.

Wilsnack, S. C., Wilsnack, R. W., & Klassen, A. D. (1986). Epidemiological research on women's drinking, 1978–1984. *Women and alcohol: Health-related issues.* Washington, DC: U.S. Department of Health and Human Services.

Wilson, L. A., Reid, A. J., Midmer, D. K., Biringer, A., Carroll, J. C., & Stewart, D. E. (1996). Antenatal psychosocial risk factors associated with adverse postpartum family outcomes. *CMAJ, 154*(6), 785–799.

Winchester-Vega, M. R. (1993, April). Women attorneys: Stress, job satisfaction, and their use of chemicals (DA9302760). *Dissertation Abstracts International, 53*(10), p. 3677A.

Wodarski, J. S. (1990). Adolescent substance abuse: Practice implications. *Adolescence, 25,* 667–668.

Wolfgang, L. A. (1997). Charting recent progress: Advances in alcohol research. *Alcohol Health & Research World, 21*(4), 277–286.

Wolfner, G. D., & Gelles, R. J. (1993). A profile of violence toward children: A national study. *Child Abuse & Neglect, 17,* 197–212.

Woodhouse, L. D. (1992). Women with jagged edges: Voices from a culture of substance abuse. *Qualitative Health Research, 2*(3), 262–281.

Wortley, P. M., & Fleming, P. L. (1997). AIDS in women in the United States. Recent trends. *Journal of the American Medical Association, 278*(11), 911–916.

Wozencraft, T., & Ellegrin, A. (1991). Depression and suicidal ideation in sexually abused children. *Child Abuse & Neglect, 15,* 505–511.

Wyatt, G. E. (1985). The sexual abuse of Afro-American and white-American women in childhood. *Child Abuse & Neglect, 9,* 507–519.

Yarvis, R. M. (1994). Patterns of substance abuse and intoxication among murderers. *Bulletin of the American Academy of Psychiatry & the Law, 22*(1), 133–144.

Yawn, B. P., Thompson, L. R., Lupo, V. R., Googins, M. K., & Yawn, R. A. Prenatal drug use in Minneapolis-St. Paul, Minnesota. A 4-year trend. *Archives of Family Medicine, 3*(6), 520–527.

Yellowlees, P. M., & Kaushik, A. V. (1992). The Broken Hill psychopathology project. *Australian & New Zealand Journal of Psychiatry, 26,* 197–207.

Young, I. (1994). Punishment, treatment, empowerment: Three approaches to policy for pregnant addicts. *Feminist Studies, 20,* 33.

Yudofsky, S. C., Stevens, L., Silver, J., Barsa, J., & Williams, D. (1984). Propranolol in the treatment of rage and violent behavior associated with Korsakoff's psychosis. *American Journal of Psychiatry, 141,* 114–115.

Zeichner, A., Allen, J. D., Giancola, P. R., & Lating, J. M. (1994). Alcohol and aggression: Effects of personal threat on human aggression and affective arousal. *Alcoholism, Clinical & Experimental Research, 18,* 657–663.

Ziegler, J. B., Cooper, D. A., Johnson, R. O., & Gold, J. (1985). Postnatal transmission of AIDS-associated retrovirus from mother to infant. *Lancet, 1,* 896–898.

Zimberg, S. (1983). Alcoholism in the elderly: A serious but solvable problem. *Postgraduate Medicine, 74,* 165–173.

Zimberg, S. (1985). Treating the older alcoholic. *Geriatric Medicine Today, 4,* 68–77.

Zimering, S., & Domeischel, J. R. (1982). Is alcoholism a problem in the elderly? *Journal of Drug Education, 12,* 103–111.

Zimmerman, E. F. (1991). Substance abuse in pregnancy: Teratogenesis. *Pediatric Annals, 20*(10), 541–544, 546–547.

Ziring, D. J., & Adler, A. G. (1991). Alcoholism. Are you missing the diagnosis? *Postgraduate Medicine, 89,* 139–141, 144–145.

Zullich, S. G., Grasela, T. H., Jr., Fiedler-Kelly, J. B., & Gengo, F. M. (1992). Impact of triplicate prescription program on psychotropic prescribing patterns in long-term care facilities. *The Annals of Pharmacotherapy, 26,* 539–546.

Zwerling, C., Sprince, N. L., Wallace, R. B., Davis, C. S., Whitten, P. S., & Heeringa, S. T. (1996). Alcohol and occupational injuries among older workers. *Accident Analysis and Prevention, 28*(3), 371–376.

Index

Abandonment, 88, 89. *See also* Child abandonment and Mothering
  fear of, 40–41
Abbreviations used in the text, 219–220
Abstinence maintenance, 200. *See also* Treatment
Abusable psychotropics, 4t, 5f. *See also* Substances of abuse
Abuse, 23, 113. *See also* Child abuse and Emotional abuse and Sexual abuse
Accidents, 123, 124t
  related to alcohol use, 13
Acculturation, 55, 61
Acknowledgments, vii
Acquired Immunodeficiency Syndrome, 149–161. *See also* Human Immunodeficiency Virus and PIARG Projects
  AIDS hotlines, 283–286
  cocaine use and, 17
  incidence among women, 151, 160
  intravenous drug users and, 151–152
  knowledge concerning, 155t
  leading cause of death among women, 151
  sources of information, 283–286
  transmission, 150f
Acts of violence, 123. *See also* Violence against children and Violent crime
Acute overdoses. *See* Overdoses
Addiction, 24
Adolescent drug involvement scale, 181
Adult children of alcoholics, 59, 181. *See also* Children of alcoholics
Affirmations of women for sobriety, 207. *See also* Feminist treatment approaches
African Americans. *See* Black women
Age, 50–52. *See also* Elderly women
Ageism, 98, 101, 108t, 111f
Aging, 105. *See also* Elderly women
AIDS. *See* Acquired Immunodeficiency Syndrome

AIDS Hotlines, 283–286
Alcohol, 11–13, 223–224. *See also* Alcoholism and Fetal alcohol syndrome
  abstinence maintenance, 200
  adverse effects, 13t, 107t, 120
  binge use, 12
  children of alcoholics, 31–32, 59
  chronic use, 12
  classification of use, 223
  common street names, 223–224
  crime related to use, 134–138, 145–146
  depression and, 13, 186, 190
  drinking age, 51–52
  drug-induced automatism and, 140
  effect of body fat, 13
  episodic use, 27
  extreme drunkenness, 147
  factors contributing to use, 11
  harm associated with use, 11–12
  in breast milk, 82t
  interaction with other drugs, 104
  marital violence and, 124
  motor vehicle crashes and, 124, 131
  pathological intoxication, 147
  physical abuse/assault and, 142–143
  potential beneficial effects of use, 107t, footnote
  related morbidity and mortality, 130, 145–146
  self-medication of depression, 186
  sexual abuse/assault and, 144–145, 148
  sexual performance and, 188
  suicide attempts and, 130
  teratogenic potential, 71–75
  treatment of problematic patterns of use, 195, 200, 209–210
  treatment of withdrawal syndrome, 199
  use by elderly women, 102–106
  use in nursing homes, 120
  violent behavior and, 124, 126, 127, 131, 142–145

335

Alcohol beliefs scale, 181
Alcohol-related birth defects, 74
Alcohol-related neurodevelopmental disorder, 74
Alcohol use disorders identification test (AUDIT), 167–168, 181
  clinical instrument, 181
  instrument, 167t
  scoring, 168
  use among women, 181
  validity and reliability, 168
Alcoholic husbands. *See* Husbands, Alcoholic
Alcoholics Anonymous, 205–207, 214–215
  as a social form of treatment, 214
  as adjunctive therapy, 215
  attendance at meetings, 214–215
  cult-like relationship, 215
  effectiveness for women, 206, 215
  Serenity Prayer, 215
  twelve steps, 206t
Alcoholism, 12–13, 104–106. *See also* Assessment of substance use disorders and Diagnosis of substance use disorders
  among elderly women, 99, 102–106, 114–115, 120
  bender drinkers, 12
  causes of death, 106
  characteristics, 102
  child maltreatment and, 143
  chronic drinkers, 12
  definition, 102
  depression and, 186
  dual diagnosis and, 182
  early onset, 104–105
  effects on mothering and child rearing, 88, 89
  incidence, 102
  late onset, 105–106
  lesbians and, 194
  signs and symptoms, 12, 102–103
  transmission from parents to offspring, 58
  Types I and II, 38
Alfentanil, 224. *See also* Opiates
Allen, Chaney, 52
Alprazolam, 224. *See also* Benzodiazepines
Alternatives model, 196–197t, 213
Amantadine, 199
Amnesic Disorder, 183
Amobarbital, 224. *See also* Barbiturates
Amphetamines, 14, 15–16, 224. *See also* Central nervous system stimulants
  closely related compounds, 15
  dextroamphetamine, 4, 14, 228
  drug-induced automatism and, 140, 141

  eating disorders and, 16
  effects, physical and psychological, 17f
  in breast milk, 82t
  mental disorders associated with use, 183t
  methamphetamine, 14, 16, 232
  pharmacologic action, 15
  psychosis related to use, 183t, 187
  use, 16
  violent behavior and, 126
Anal intercourse, 157, 161. *See also* Prostitution
Androgenic-anabolic steroids, 127, 140
Anexate®. *See* Flumazenil
Anger, 52, 60
Anileridine, 224. *See also* Opiates
Antabuse®. *See* Disulfiram
Antabuse®. Reaction, 200
Antisocial personality disorder, 38–39, 146
  alcohol use, violence, and, 137, 138
  depression and, 186
  dual diagnosis and, 187
Anxiety Disorders, 183t, 186
Aprobarbital, 224. *See also* Barbiturates
Asian women, 9
Assaults, 124t, 126, 142–143
Assessment of substance use disorders, 165–181. *See also* Diagnosis
Attachment and separation, 34, 41–42, 59, 88. *See also* Mothering
AUDIT. *See* Alcohol use disorders identification test
Automatism, 140. *See also* Drug-induced automatism
  definition, 140

Backlash theory of substance abuse, 52–53
Barbiturates, 75. *See also* Central nervous system depressants
  drug-induced automatism and, 140
  in breast milk, 82t
  teratogenic potential, 75
Battered child syndrome, 90t
Battered women syndrome, 148. *See also* Assaults and Automatism
Battery during pregnancy, 126, 131
Beer. *See* Alcohol
Bender drinkers, 12
Benzodiazepines, 106, 108–109. *See also* Central nervous system depressants
  depression and, 186
  drug-induced automatism and, 140
  falls and, 109
  guidelines for appropriate use, 109
  in breast milk, 82

nursing home residents and, 106, 108t, 108–109, 120
physician perpetuated use, 106, 108–109
prescription for elderly women, 98, 106, 108–109
teratogenic potential, 76
treatment of benzodiazepine overdose, 195, 199
use by elderly women, 102, 106, 108–109
use for treatment of alcohol withdrawal, 199
Benzphetamine, 224. *See also* Amphetamines
Bishop, Mrs. Jim, 32
Black women, 9, 52–55, 66, 87, 94, 127–128, 156–157, 161, 180, 189, 206. *See also* Women
B-MAST. *See* Brief MAST
Borderline personality disorder, 187
Breast feeding, 80–81
  average daily consumption, 83t
  HIV transmission and, 86
  incidence, 80, 85
  substances excreted in breast milk, 82–83t
Brief MAST (B-MAST), 168–169
  instrument, 168t
  scoring, 168
  use among elderly women, 169
  validity and reliability, 169
Bromazepam, 224. *See also* Benzodiazepines
Bromocriptine, 24, 199
Brown women, 9, 37, 44, 55, 56–58, 61, 66, 143, 189. *See also* Women
Bupropion, 199
Buspirone, 195
Butabarbital, 225. *See also* Barbiturates
Butorphanol, 225. *See also* Opiates

Caffeine, 4, 14, 16, 76. *See also* Central nervous system stimulants
  content of selected beverages, 18t
  effects of acute use, 18t
  in breast milk, 82t
  mental disorders associated with use, 183t
  teratogenic potential, 76–77
  use, 16
  use among White women, 169
  withdrawal syndrome, 16
CAGE, 169, 170
  instrument, 170
  scoring, 169
  use among elderly women, 103, 116, 169
  use among White women, 169
  validity and reliability, 169
Cambodian, 161. *See also* Sex-for-drugs-exchange

Canada, 56, 198
Cannabis, 20–21. *See also* Tetrahydrocannabinol
  adverse effects, 21t
  central nervous system toxicity, 21
  classification, 223
  common street names, 225–226
  formulations, 20
  motor vehicle crashes and, 124
  Reefer Madness, 20
  respiratory toxicity, 21
  teratogenic potential, 80
  theories of use, 60–61
  usage statistics, 20
Carbidopa/Levodopa, 199
Catapres®. *See* Clonidine
Caucasian women. *See* White women
Central nervous system (CNS) depressants, 4, 11–14. *See also* Substances of abuse
  alcohol, 11–13, 102–106, 107, 223–224
  barbiturates, 75
  benzodiazepines, 106, 108–109
  mental disorders associated with use, 183t
  opiates, 13–14
  teratogenic potential, 71–76
Central nervous system (CNS) stimulants, 4, 14–20. *See also* Substances of abuse
  amphetamines, 15–16, 224
  caffeine, 16, 18, 76–77
  cocaine, 16–18, 19, 77–79, 227–228
  dextroamphetamine, 4, 14, 79, 82, 228
  mental disorders associated with use, 183t
  methylphenidate, 79, 232
  nicotine, 18–20, 79–80
  self-medication for depression, 132
  teratogenic potential, 76–80
Central nervous system (CNS) toxicities, 21
Chasing the dragon, 10, 14. *See also* Heroin
Child abandonment, 89, 90t. *See also* Mothering
Child abuse, 3, 33, 35, 85, 89, 90t, 148
  alcohol use and, 142–143
  dual diagnosis and, 186–187
  high risk factors, 92t
  substance use during pregnancy and, 66
Child molestation, 34, 143–145
  alcohol use and, 143–145
Child neglect, 91t
  high risk factors, 92t
  physical indicators, 93t
  psychological indicators, 93t
Child Rearing, 4, 56, 87–96. *See also* Mothering
Childhood victimization, 33–35

Children of alcoholics, 31–32, 59. *See also* Adult children of alcoholics
Chlordiazepoxide, 199, 226. *See also* Benzodiazepines
Chloral hydrate. *See also* Sedative-hypnotics
  in breast milk, 82
Chlorphentermine, 226. *See also* Central nervous system stimulants
Chola lifestyles, 57
Christian, Meg, 39
Chronic drinkers, 12
Clayton, Jan, 40, 42–43
Clinical depression. *See* Depression
Clobazam, 226. *See also* Benzodiazepines
Clonazepam, 227. *See also* Benzodiazepines
Clorazepate, 227. *See also* Benzodiazepines
Clonidine, 195, 199
Coca Cola®, 10
Cocaine, 4, 10, 14, 16–18, 77, 154t, 154t footnote, 227–228. *See also* Central nervous system stimulants and Crack cocaine
  adverse effects, 19t
  AIDS and, 17–18
  classification, 227
  common street names, 227–228
  effects on mothering and child rearing, 87, 88, 89, 91, 92, 95
  in breast milk, 83t
  mental disorders associated with use, 183t
  obstetrical complications and, 78t
  psychosis related to use, 183t, 187
  self-medication of depression, 186
  sex-for-drugs and, 18
  teratogenic potential, 77–79
  treatment of withdrawal, 199
  usage statistics, 16–17
  violent behavior and, 126
Codeine, 4, 71, 228. *See also* Opiates
Codependency, 59
Coffee. *See* Caffeine
Cognitive dysfunction, 13, 93–94, 159t. *See also* Learning disorders and Memory impairment
Cognitive therapy, 202–203
Commerce-related crime, 138, 139t. *See also* Crime
Common street names list, 222–237
Compulsive use, 23–114
Concealment, 9, 100
Contents. *See* Table of contents
Content validity, 166
Contingency management approaches, 213–214
  sexism and, 213–214

Contributor, 117f
Controlled use, 23–24, 114
Coolie, 22
Courtship violence. *See* Dating violence
Crack cocaine, 16, 146–147. *See also* Cocaine and Sex-for-drugs exchange
  crack babies, 4, 147, 148
  crack whore, 161, 188t
Crawford, Joan, 32–33, 39
Crime. *See also* various specific crimes
  alcohol use and, 134–138
  commerce-related, 138–139
  extreme drunkenness, 147
  pathologic intoxication, 147
  perpetrated by women, 133–148
  pharmacopsychologic-related, 139–140
  relationship between substance use and, 134f
  substance use-induced automatism, 140–142
  violent crime, 135, 138
Criterion-related validity, 166. *See also* Validity
Crosby, Dixie Lee, 35
Crystal Meth. *See* Methamphetamine
Culture, 9, 52

DAST. *See* Drug abuse screening test
Date Rape. *See* Rape
Date rape drug. *See* Gamma hydroxybutyrate
Dating Violence, 126–127. *See also* Rape
Dedication of text, v
Delirium, 29, 183t
Demerol®. *See* Meperidine
Dependence on men, 10, 209
Depression, 34, 43, 49–50, 186, 209
  among adult children of alcoholics, 59
  among elderly dually diagnosed patients, 190
  dual diagnosis, 182, 185–186, 190
  dysfunctional family and, 186
  effects on mothering and child rearing, 88, 92
  incidence, 130
  related to alcohol use, 13
  self-medication of, 186
  suicide attempt and, 129–130, 186, 190
Developing fetus, 65
Dexedrine®. *See* Dextroamphetamine
Dextroamphetamine, 4, 14, 228. *See also* Central nervous system stimulants
  classification, 228
  common street names, 228

in breast milk, 82t
teratogenic potential, 76, 79
Diacetylmorphine. *See* Heroin
Diagnosis of substance use disorders, 98, 116–118, 165. *See also* Assessment and Diagnostic error and Dual diagnosis
  clinical interview, 180, 181
  concealment, 100–101
  low level of suspicion, 99
  misdiagnosis, 99–100
  of substance use among elderly women, 116–118
  psychometric instruments, 165–166, 167–180
Diagnostic error, 165
  adjustment of criterion values, 181
  definitions, 165
  probability, 181
  Type I, 165, 166f
  Type II, 165–166f
Diazepam, 228. *See also* Benzodiazepines
Diethylpropion, 228–229. *See also* Central nervous system stimulants
Dilaudid®. *See* Hydromorphone
Distilled spirits. *See* Alcohol
Disulfiram, 24, 195, 200, 214
  flush, 200
  reaction, 200
  use in combination with other therapeutic modalities, 214
Dolophine®. *See* Methadone
Dominant Culture. *See* Culture
Donlan, Joan, 50
Dorris, Michael, 85
Dr. Jekyll and Mr. Hyde, 140
Drinking Age, 51–52. *See also* Alcohol
Driving while impaired. *See* Impaired driving
Drug abuse screening test (DAST), 169, 170
  instrument, 170t
  scoring, 169
  use among psychiatric outpatients, 169
  validity and reliability, 169
Drug-induced automatism, 140–142. *See also* Automatism
Drug-induced disorders, 183t
Drug legalization, 146
Drug protective competence (DPC) instrument, 44
Drug substitution, 201–202
Drunk driving. *See* Impaired driving
Dry drunk syndrome, 105
DSM-IV, 6, 26–27, 166, 190
Dual addiction. *See* Dual diagnosis

Dual Diagnosis, 182–190, 202. *See also* Diagnosis of substance use disorders
  cultural diversity, 188–189
  definition, 182
  DSM-IV taxonomy and, 190
  elderly patients and, 190
  ethnic diversity, 188–189
  HIV risk and, 184
  incidence, 182
  relationships between the disorders comprising a dual diagnosis, 188
  sexual abuse and, 186–188
  substance use and amnesic disorders, 183t
  substance use and anxiety disorders, 183t, 186–187
  substance use and delirium, 183t
  substance use and gender identity disorders, 187–188
  substance use and mood disorders, 183t, 185–186
  substance use and personality disorders, 187
  substance use and psychotic disorders, 183t, 187
  substance use and sexual disorders, 183t, 187–188
  substance use and sleep disorders, 183t
  therapy guidelines, 189
  treatment, 184–185, 188–189, 195, 202
  types, 185
  use of drug counselors to provide treatment, 185
Dual disorder. *See* Dual diagnosis
Dutch women, 36. *See also* White women

Early-onset alcoholism, 104–105
Education, 34, 50, 54–55
Ego formation, 59–60
Elderly women, 29, 55, 97–120, 169, 178, 179. *See also* women
  ageism and, 98, 101, 108t, 111f
  alcoholism and, 99, 102–106, 114–115
  attitude toward substance abuse, 101
  bias, 97–100
  concealment, 100–101
  demographics, 114
  diagnosis of substance use disorders among, 116–118
  dual diagnosis and, 190
  identifying problematic patterns of substance use, 97–102
  life events and lifestyle changes, 105t
  low level of suspicion, 99
  misdiagnosis, 99–100
  most frequently abused drugs, 102

Elderly women *(continued)*
  nursing homes and substance use, 106, 108t, 108–109, 120
  percent of population, 98
  problematic patterns of substance use, 102–109
  treatment of substance abuse, 109–110, 118–119
Elderly woman dimension, 114–115
Emergency needle exchange, 153, 158–159t. *See also* PIARG projects
Emotional abuse, 32–35
Emotional neglect, 91t. *See also* Child neglect
Employment, 46–47
Empowerment, 209–210
Enablers, 101, 117
  flowchart, 117f
  rationale for, 101
Estazolam, 229. *See also* Benzodiazepines
Ethanol. *See* Alcohol
Ethnicity, 52
Ethyl alcohol. *See* Alcohol
Evaluation, 26
Event-related potentials, 31, 59
Explaining substance use, 28–61
Extreme drunkenness, 147. *See also* Alcoholism

Face validity, 166. *See also* Validity
Facilitator, 117f
Failure to thrive, 91t
Falls, 123–124
Familismo, 57. *See also* Latinas
Family therapy, 203–204
  guidelines for the family therapist, 204t
  strategic-structural, 203–204, 205t
  types, 205t
Fatal motor vehicle crashes, 5
Fear of abandonment, 40–41. *See also* Abandonment
Feminist orientation, 46, 48, 56, 206
Feminist treatment approaches, 209–210
  affirmations of women for sobriety, 207t
  combined with cognitive therapy, 203
  life history method, 209
  self-concept and empowerment, 210
  theatre model, 209–210
  use of story telling, 210, 215
  women-oriented program characteristics, 208t
Fenfluramine, 229. *See also* Central nervous system stimulants
Fentanyl, 229. *See also* Opiates
Fetal alcohol effects, 74

Fetal alcohol syndrome, 4, 72–75, 85. *See also* Alcohol
  associated abnormalities, 72t
  consensus case definition, 73
  craniofacial characteristics, 73f
  incidence, 74t
  IQ and, 85
  long-term sequelae, 75
Flumazenil, 24, 195, 199
Fluoxetine, 140, 200
Flurazepam, 229. *See also* Benzodiazepines
Ford, Betty, 44–45
Foster care, 95
FTT. *See* Failure to thrive

Gamma hydroxybutyrate, 128
Ganja, 53, 61
Garland, Judy, 35
Gasoline. *See* Volatile solvents and inhalants
GBH. *See* Gamma hydroxybutyrate
Gender Identity Disorders, 187. *See also* Sexual identity crisis
Gender mix of occupations, 48
Gender role, 37, 44–48
Generational Effects, 30–32, 58
Genetics, 30–32, 58
Glue. *See* Volatile solvents and inhalants
Gynecological problems, 43, 60. *See also* Reproductive problems

Habitrol®. *See* Nicotine
Habitual use, 23, 113
Habituation, 24
Haitian women, 9. *See also* Black women
Halazepam, 229. *See also* Benzodiazepines
Halfway houses, 208
Harm reduction, 201. *See also* Needle-exchange programs
Hashish. *See* Cannabis; *See also* Tetrahydrocannabinol
Hashish Oil. *See* Cannabis. *See also* Tetrahydrocannabinol
Hayward, Susan, 35
Hembrismo, 57. *See also* Latinas
Heroin, 4, 13, 154t, 154 footnote, 229–230. *See also* Opiates
  age of first use, 13
  chasing the dragon, 10, 14
  classification, 229
  common street names, 229–230
  overdosage, signs and symptoms, 14t
  purity, 14
  teratogenic potential, 71
  treatment of withdrawal syndrome, 214
  use, 14

Hispanic women, 9, 44, 55, 66, 143, 189. *See also* Latinas and Women
Historic period, 10
HIV. *See* Human immunodeficiency virus
Homeless women, 11, 34. *See also* Women
 effect of substance use treatment, 191
Homemakers, 47–48. *See also* Gender role
Homicides, 124t, 128, 143. *See also* Murder
 alcohol use and, 132
Human immunodeficiency virus, 17, 88, 149–161. *See also* Acquired immunodeficiency syndrome and PIARG projects
 cocaine use and, 17
 description, 149
 disclosure-related violence, 161
 dual diagnosis and, 184
 emergency needle exchange, 153, 158–159t
 incidence among women, 151, 160
 intravenous drug use and, 68, 70, 151, 160
 knowledge and behavior in relation to, 152–154, 155t, 161
 knowledge concerning, 155t
 mode of transmission, 184f
 perinatal transmission. *See* transmission during pregnancy
 self-perception of risk, 156t
 sex-for-drugs-exchange and, 155–157
 transmission, 150f, 151–152, 160
 transmission during pregnancy, 68, 151
 transmission in breast milk, 86
Human teratogenesis, 65. *See also* Teratogens
 determinants, 67f
 environmental factors, 68
 fetal factors, 68
 maternal factors, 68
 placental factors, 68
 substance of abuse factors, 68
 susceptibility, 69
 timing in relation to organogenesis, 68, 69f
Husbands, alcoholic, 35–37, 40–41, 128, 143, 148
Hydrocodone, 230. *See also* Opiates
Hydromorphone, 154t, f, 230. *See also* Opiates

IAI. *See* Index of alcohol involvement
Ice. *See* Methamphetamine
Impaired driving, 5, 51, 146
Incarcerated women, 34–35, 38–39, 88, 95, 134, 143, 148. *See also* Women
Incest. *See* Sexual abuse
Incidence of substance use, 3–4
Index of alcohol involvement (IAI), 171, 174
 instrument, 171t
 scoring, 174

 use among white women, 171
 validity and reliability, 174
Infant, 65
Information sources, 238–286
Initial use, 22–23, 112
Inmates. *See* Incarcerated women
Inner city women, 11. *See also* Women
Intelligence, 42–43, 96, 137
Interpersonal skills, 202t
Intervention, 45
Intrapersonal skills, 202t
Intravenous drug use, 13, 86. *See also* Substance use
 age of first use, 13
 breast feeding and, 86
 cognitive impairment and, 159t
 demographics, 153t
 drug use history, 154t
 incidence of HIV among, 160
 knowledge of HIV and AIDS, 155t
 laziness and, 159t
 mode of HIV transmission, 184f
 need for immediate gratification, 158–159t
 needle-exchange programs, 153, 158–159t, 160
 needle sharing, 155t, 158–159t, 161
 perception of HIV risk, 156
 risk of HIV transmission and, 68, 70, 149–150
 sexual connotations, 158t
 sharing needles and syringes, 158t
 unsafe injectable drug use, 155t
Intravenous drug users. *See* Intravenous drug use
IQ. *See* Intelligence
IVDUs *See* Intravenous drug users
Izquierdo, Elisa, 92, 95

Jamaican women, 9, 53–54. *See also* Black women and Women
Jews, 9, 143. *See also* Women
Jodedora, 57. *See also* Latinas
Jones, Marcia Mae, 30

Ketazolam, 230. *See also* Benzodiazepines
Korsakoff's psychosis, 29, 107t. *See also* Wernicke-Korsakoff Syndrome

LAAM®. *See* L-alpha-acetyl-methadol
Lactation, 65. *See also* Breast feeding
L-alpha-acetyl-methadol, 201
Late-onset alcoholism, 105. *See also* Alcoholism
Latinas, 37, 56–58, 61, 159t. *See also* Women
 chola lifestyles, 57–58

Latinas *(continued)*
  familismo, 57
  hembrismo, 57
  HIV risk among, 159t
  jodedora, 57–58
  lesbians, 37, 39–40, 56
  marianismo, 58
Law of the land, 9
Laziness, 159t
Learning disorders, 96. *See also* Cognitive dysfunction and Memory impairment
  indicator of child neglect, 93
Legal drinking age, 51
Legal restrictions, 9
Legalization. *See* Drug legalization
Lesbian women, 8, 37, 39–40, 56, 188t, 194, 206. *See also* Women
Levorphanol, 230. *See also* Opiates
Librium®. *See* Chlordiazepoxide
Lifespan, 50–51
List of figures, xiii
List of tables, xv–xvi
Loneliness, 37
Lopez, Awilda, 92, 95
Lorazepam, 230. *See also* Benzodiazepines
Loss, 41, 88, 209
Low level of suspicion, 99
LSD. *See* Lysergic acid diethylamide
Luminal®. *See* Phenobarbital
Lung cancer, 19, 21
Lysergic acid diethylamide, 4, 80, 131, 187, 230–231. *See also* Psychedelics
  classification, 230
  common street names, 230–231
  teratogenic potential, 80

MAC. *See* MacAndrew alcoholism scale
MacAndrew alcoholism scale (MAC), 172–173, 174–175
  instrument, 172–173t
  scoring, 174, 181
  use among patients with major mental disorders, 175
  use among women, 174
  validity and reliability, 174–175
Magic mushrooms. *See* Psilocybin
Major substances of abuse, Abusable psychotropics, 4t
Male dominance, 10, 156, 209
Malmö modified Michigan alcoholism screening test (Mm-MAST), 174, 175
  instrument, 174t
  scoring, 175
  use among women, 175
  validity and reliability, 175

Marianismo, 57. *See also* Latinas
Marijuana. *See* Cannabis. *See also* Tetrahydrocannabinol
Marriage, problematic, 29, 35–37
MAST. *See* Michigan alcoholism screening test
Maternal effects. *See* Mother-infant dyads and Mothering
Maternal short-MAST (M-SMAST), 175–176
  instrument, 175t
  scoring, 176
  use among adult children of alcoholics, 181
  use among White women, 175
  validity and reliability, 176
Maternal substance use, 66–68. *See also* Human teratogenesis and Mothering and Substance use
  attitude toward substance use by children and, 96
  extent of use, 66
  race and, 66
  types of substances, 67
Maternal substance use screening questionnaire, 176
Mazindol, 231. *See also* Central nervous system stimulants
MDA, 154t
Mebaral®. *See* Mephobarbital
Mega interactive model of substance use among elderly women (MIMSUAEW), 110–120
  application, 110, 116–119
  elderly woman dimension, 114–115
  flow chart, 117f
  interacting dimensions, 110
  model, 111f
  patterns of substance use, 110–114, 112f
  societal dimension, 115
  substance of abuse dimension, 110–114
  time dimension, 115
Mega interactive model of substance use among women (MIMSUAW), 6–26
  application, 6
  complexity, 7
  figure, 7
  heuristic use, 8
  interacting variable dimensions, 6
  unit coterie, 6
  variable dimensions, 8–21
    societal dimension, 9–10
    substance of abuse dimension, 10–21
    time dimension, 10
    women dimension, 8–9

Memory impairment. *See also* Learning disorders
  associated with alcohol use, 103
  associated with cannabis use, 21
Mental disorders associated with substance use, 183t
Meperidine, 4, 71, 231. *See also* Opiates
Mephobarbital, 231. *See also* Barbiturates
Mescaline, 4, 80, 231. *See also* Psychedelics
Methadone, 195, 201, 231. *See also* Opiates
  classification, 231
  common street names, 231
  teratogenic potential, 71
  treatment of overdose, 199
  use in opiate maintenance programs, 24, 195, 201
Methamphetamine, 14, 16, 154t, 232. *See also* Amphetamines
Methaqualone, 232. *See also* Central nervous system depressants
Metharbital, 231. *See also* Barbiturates
Methohexital, 232. *See also* Barbiturates
Methylphenidate, 154t, footnote, 232. *See also* Central nervous system stimulants
  classification, 232
  common street names, 232
  teratogenic potential, 76, 79
Michigan alcoholism screening test (MAST), 176–178, 181
  instrument, 177t
  scoring, 178
  use among elderly women, 103, 116, 178
  use among women, 178
  validity and reliability, 178
Midazolam, 232. *See also* Benzodiazepines
MIMSUAEW. *See* Mega interactive model of substance use among elderly women
MIMSUAW. *See* Mega interactive model of substance abuse among women
Misdiagnosis, 99–100
  reasons for misdiagnosis, 100t
Mm-MAST. *See* Malmö modified Michigan alcoholism screening test
M-MAST. *See* Maternal short-MAST
Monroe, Marilyn, 43
Mood disorders, 183t, 185
Morbidity, 3. *See also* Victims of substance use related crime
  alcohol related, 145–146
Morphine, 4, 13, 71, 232. *See also* Opiates
Mortality, 5. *See also* Victims of substance use related crime
  alcohol related, 130, 145–146
  tobacco smoking related, 19

Mother-infant attachment and separation, 41–42
Mother-infant dyads, 87–88
Mothering, 4, 85, 87–96, 209. *See also* Child abuse and Children of alcoholics
  as a potential obstacle to treatment, 215
  effect of substance use treatment, 191
  foster care, 95
  infant mortality rates, 84
  next generation, 94
  parental neglect, 148
  school-aged child, concerns for, 93–94
Motor vehicle crashes, 124
  alcohol and, 124, 131
  marijuana and, 124
  risk related to age and blood alcohol concentrations, 125f
Murder, 5, 92–93, 95. *See also* Homicide

Nalbuphine, 233. *See also* Opiates
Naloxone, 14, 24, 195, 198–199, 214
Naltrexone, 24, 195, 200
Narcan®. *See* Naloxone
Native-American women, 8, 11, 95, 143, 189, 198. *See also* Women
Nature-nurture controversy, 58
Need for immediate gratification, 158–159t
Needle-exchange programs, 153, 158–159t, 160, 194
Needle sharing, 155t, 158–159t, 161
Negative Stereotyping, 27
Neglect, 89–92
Nembutal®. *See* Pentobarbital
Neonatal urine tests, 70
Neonate, 65
Nicoderm®. *See* Nicotine
Nicotine, 4, 14, 18, 79. *See also* Central nervous system stimulants
  adjunct to tobacco smoking cessation, 85, 198
  in breast milk, 83t
  mental disorders associated with use, 183t
  teratogenic potential, 79–80
  transdermal drug delivery, 19, 24, 198, 201–202
  treatment of withdrawal, 195, 199–200
Nicotrol NS®. *See* Nicotine
Nitrazepam, 233. *See also* Benzodiazepines
Noctec®. *See* Chloral Hydrate
Noland, Mimi, 50
Nonabusable psychotropics, 5f
Nonuse, 112
North American women, 11. *See also* Women
Nurses, 43, 106, 108

Object relations, 40, 59–60
Obstetrical complications, 78
Opiates, 4, 13. *See also* Central nervous system depressants
　abstinence maintenance, 200
　addiction maintenance, 195, 201
　detoxification, 195, 199
　in breast milk, 83t
　mental disorders associated with use, 183t
　overdose, 14, 15
　overdose, sequence of events, 15f
　physiological effects, short-term, 14t
　teratogenic potential, 71
　treatment of addiction, 195, 200
　treatment of overdose, 195, 199
　treatment of withdrawal, 199
Organogenic variation, 69f. *See also* Human teratogenesis
ORLAAM®. *See* L-alpha-acetyl-methadol
Overdoses, 198–199
　benzodiazepines, 199
　flumazenil, 199
　naloxone, 199
　opiates, 199
Over-the-counter drug use, 52
Oxazepam, 233. *See also* Benzodiazepines
Oxycodone, 233. *See also* Opiates
Oxymorphone, 233. *See also* Opiates

Paranoia, 141
Paranoid psychosis, 141
Parental neglect, 148. *See also* Mothering
Parental violence, 142. *See also* Mothering
Parenting. *See* Mothering
Parlodel®. *See* Bromocryptine
Paternalism, 27, 213–214. *See also* Male dominance
Pathologic intoxication, 147. *See also* Alcoholism
Patient-treatment matching, 215
Patterns of substance use, 6f, 110–114, 112f
Patterns of use variable, 22–24, 110–114
　abuse, 23, 113
　compulsive use, 23, 114
　controlled use, 23–24, 114
　habitual use, 23, 113
　initial use, 22–23, 112
　nonuse, 112
　relapsed use, 23–24, 114
　resumed nonuse, 23–24, 114
　social use, 23, 112–113
PCP. *See* Phencydidine
Peer pressure
　positive effects, 210

Pemoline, 233. *See also* Central nervous system stimulants
Pentazocine, 4, 71, 154t, 195, 198, 233. *See also* Opiates
Pentazocine and naloxone, 4, 195, 198
Pentobarbital, 233. *See also* Barbiturates
Pergolide mesylate, 199
Permax®. *See* Pergolide Mesylate
Personality disorders, 37–39, 187. *See also* Antisocial personality disorder
Pethidine. *See* Meperidine
Peyote. *See* Mescaline
Pharmacologic antagonists, 198–199
　flumazenil, 199
　naloxone, 199
Pharmacopsychologic-related crime, 138, 139t. *See also* Crime
Pharmacotherapy, 195, 198. *See also* Treatment of substance use disorders
　abstinence maintenance, 200
　acute overdoses, 198–199
　drug substitution, 201–202
　withdrawal syndromes, 199–200
Phencyclidine, 4, 80, 187, 233. *See also* Psychedelics
Phendimetrazine, 234. *See also* Central nervous system stimulants
Phenmetrazine, 234. *See also* Central nervous system stimulants
Phentermine, 235. *See also* Central nervous system stimulants
Phenobarbital, 234. *See also* Barbiturates
Physical abuse, 32–35, 56, 66, 89–92, 127
　dual diagnosis and, 186–187
　incidence, 142
　perpetrated by women, 142–143
Physical assault, 127
　incidence, 142
　perpetrated by women, 142–143
Physical injuries, 124
PIARG projects, 152–155, 158–159, 160–161
Polysubstance use, 22, 50, 56, 190
Postpartum abuse, 131
Prazepam, 235. *See also* Benzodiazepines
Preface to text, xvii–xix
Pregnancy, 65–86
　battery during, 126, 131
　infant mortality rates, 84
　human teratogenesis, 65
　maternal substance use during, 66–68
　teratogens, 65
Premarital abuse. *See* Dating Violence
Prescription abuse, 49–50, 52, 60. *See also* Substance use

Prevention, 25, 191–195, 212–213. *See also* Treatment of substance use disorders
  alternatives model, 196–197t
  amenability of variables associated with substance use to, 193t
  primary prevention, 192, 194, 209, 212
  relationship to patterns of substance use, 192f
  secondary prevention, 194, 212–213
  tertiary prevention, 194–195, 201, 213
Primary prevention. *See* Prevention
Problematic marriages, 35–37. *See also* Husbands
Problems with object relations, 40
Propoxyphene, 235–236. *See also* Opiates
Prostitution, 133, 138–139, 146–147, 156, 161. *See also* Sex-for-drugs-exchange
  anal intercourse, 157, 161
  crack cocaine and, 156–157
  definition, 156
Prozac®. *See* Fluoxetine
Psilocybin, 4, 80, 236. *See also* Psychedelics
Psychedelics, 4, 20–21. *See also* Substances of Abuse
  mental disorders associated with use, 183t
  psychosis related to use, 183t, 187
  teratogenic potential, 80
Psychoanalytic theory, 59–60
Psychometric instruments, 165–181
  alcohol use disorders identification test (AUDIT), 167–168
  brief mast (B-MAST), 168–169
  CAGE, 169, 170
  drug abuse screening test (DAST), 169–170
  drug protective competency (DPC), 44
  faking good/bad, 181
  index of alcohol involvement (IAI), 171–174
  internal consistency, 181
  MacAndrew alcoholism Scale (MAC), 172–175
  Malmö modified Michigan alcoholism screening test (Mm-MAST), 174, 175
  maternal short-mast (M-MAST), 175–176
  maternal substance use screening questionnaire, 176
  Michigan alcoholism screening test (MAST), 176–178
  rapid alcohol problems screen (RAPS), 178
  reliability, 167
  short Michigan alcoholism screening test (SMAST), 178–179
  TWEAK, 179–180
  validity, 166

Psychotherapy, 202–203
  cognitive, 202–203
  group, 203
  interpersonal skills training, 202t
  intrapersonal skills training, 202t
Psychotic disorders, 183t, 187
Psychotogens. *See* Psychedelics
Psychotomimetics. *See* Psychedelics
Psychotropics, 5f

Quazepam, 236. *See also* Benzodiazepines

Race, 52. *See also* Asian, black, brown, native, and white
Rape, 127–128, 132, 143, 148, 209
Rapid alcohol problems screen (RAPS), 178
  instrument, 178t
  scoring, 178
  validity and reliability, 178
RAPS. *See* Rapid alcohol problems screen
Raspberries, 18. *See also* Sex-for-drugs-exchange
Reactance theory, 51–52
Recidivism. *See* Relapse
Reefer madness, 20
References, 287–333
Referral Agencies, 238–286
Relapse, 47, 210. *See also* Relapsed use
  performance goals/criterion, 211t
  prevention, 203, 210, 216
  rates, 211f
  recommendations to minimize, 210, 216
Relapsed use, 23–24, 114
Reliability of substance use assessment instruments, 167
Religious belief, 34, 60
Reproductive problems, 43–44. *See also* Gynecological problems
Resources, 217–286
Respiratory toxicities, 21
  associated with cannabis smoking, 21
  associated with tobacco smoking, 19–20
Resumed nonuse, 23–24, 114
ReVia®. *See* Naltrexone
Ritalin®. *See* Methylphenidate
Robbery, 139. *See also* Crime
Robe, Lucy Barry, 58
Romazicon®. *See* Flumazenil

School-aged child, 93–94
Science of substance abusology, 165, 181
Secobarbital, 236. *See also* Barbiturates
Seconal®. *See* Secobarbital
Secondary prevention. *See* Prevention

Second-hand smoke, 19
Sedative-hypnotics, 49–50. *See also* Central nervous system depressants
 depression and, 132
 mental disorders associated with use, 183t
 suicide attempts and, 130
 teratogenic potential, 71–76
 use among elderly women, 102–109
 withdrawal syndrome, 214
Self-concept, 60, 210
Self-esteem, 27, 33, 36, 49, 60
 among adult children of alcoholics, 59
Self-medication, 37
Separation, 41, 88. *See also* Attachment and separation
Serax®. *See* Oxazepam
Sertraline, 200
Sex-for-drugs-exchange, 18, 139, 154t, footnote, 155–157. *See also* Prostitution
 crack cocaine and, 156–157
 HIV infection and, 150
Sex-role conflicts, 45
Sex role theory, 34, 44–48
Sexism, 213–214
Sexual abuse, 32, 35, 56, 60, 66, 127–128, 148, 209. *See also* Child Abuse
 dual diagnosis and, 186–187
 effects on mothering, 94
 incidence, 143
 mother-child incest, 148
 perpetrated by women, 143–145, 148
Sexual assault, 32, 127–128. *See also* Child molestation
 incidence, 143
 perpetrated by women, 143–145, 148
Sexual behavior, 188
Sexual dysfunction, 60, 183
Sexual identity crisis, 39–40. *See also* Gender identity disorders
Sexual victimization, 127–128, 209. *See also* Rape and Sexual abuse
 as a predictor of suicide risk, 94, 132
Sexually transmitted diseases, 4. *See also* Acquired immunodeficiency syndrome
 cocaine use and, 17–18
Shaken baby syndrome, 91
Short Michigan alcoholism screening test (SMAST), 178–179, 181
 instrument, 179t
 scoring, 179
 use among elderly women, 179
 use among women, 179
 validity and reliability, 179

Short-term residential treatment programs, 208–209
 key program elements, 209t
 program objectives, 209t
Sinemet®, 199
Skeezer, 156, 161, 188t. *See also* Sex-for-drugs-exchange
Sleep deprivation, 141
Sleep disorders, 183
SMAST. *See* Short Michigan alcoholism screening test
Smoking. *See* Tobacco smoking
Social skills training, 204–205
Social stress, 52, 60
Social stress model of substance abuse, 60
Social support, 44, 46
Social use, 23, 112–113
Societal changes, 47
Societal dimension, 9, 115
Solvents and inhalants. *See* Volatile solvents and inhalants
Speed. *See* Methamphetamine
Spungen, Nancy, 37
Stereotyping, 27, 161
Story telling, 210, 215
Strategic-structural family therapy, 203–204
Strawberries, 18. *See also* Sex-for-drugs-exchange
Strawberry, 161. *See also* Sex-for-drugs-exchange
Stress, 119–120
Substance abusology, 165, 181
Substance of abuse dimension, 10
Substance use, 84. *See also* Alcoholism and Intravenous drug use and various individual substances
 abstinence maintenance, 200
 among elderly women, 97–102
 anxiety disorders and, 186–187
 assessment, 165–181
 associated variables amenable to prevention, 193t
 automatism and, 140–142
 commerce related crime, 138–139
 crime and, 133–148
 depressive disorders and, 185–186
 diagnosis, 98, 116–118, 165, 180
 drug substitution, 201–202
 dual diagnosis, 182–190
 gender identity disorders and, 187
 incidence among women, 3–4
 mood disorders and, 185–186
 morbidity among women, 3–4
 mortality among women, 5
 multifactorial etiology, 7

murder and, 92–93
nonpathognomonic symptoms of, 103t
overdoses, 198–199
personality disorders and, 187
prevention, 25, 191–195, 212–213
prostitution and, 138–139
psychotic disorders and, 187
relationship between crime and, 134f
robbery and, 139
sexual behavior and, 188
sexual disorders and, 187–188t
therapy guidelines, 189
treatment, 24–28, 118, 188, 191–216
withdrawal syndromes, 199–200, 214
Substance use disorders See Substance use
Substance use-induced automatism, 140. See also Automatism
Substance variables, 11
Substances of abuse. See also various individual substances
  classification, 223–237
  common street names, 223–237
  generic name, 223–237
  subclassification, 223–237
  trade name, 223–237
Sufentenil, 236. See also Opiates
Suicide, 5, 13, 49, 124t, 128–130, 129t, 186, 190
  attempts, 128, 129t
  depression and, 129–130, 186
  dual diagnosis and, 190
  effect of substance use treatment, 191
  related to alcohol use, 13, 107t
  risk factors, 94, 129t
  sexual victimization and, 132
Symbols used in the text, 221
Symmetrel®. See Amantadine
Systemic intervention, 214

Table of contents, ix
Talwin®. See Pentazocine
Talwin-Nx®. See Pentazocine and Naloxone
Tea. See Caffeine
Temazepam, 236. See also Benzodiazepines
Teratogenesis. See Human teratogenesis
Teratogens, 65. See also Human teratogenesis
  alcohol, 71–75
  barbiturates, 75
  benzodiazepines, 76
  caffeine, 76–77
  central nervous system stimulants, 76–80
  cocaine, 77–78
  determinants, 67f, 68
  dextroamphetamine, 79
  methylphenidate, 79
  nicotine, 79–80

opiates, 71
psychedelics, 80
sedative-hypnotics, 71–76
solvents and inhalants, 76
susceptibility, 69f
thalidomide, 66, 84
toluene, 76
Tertiary prevention. See Prevention
Tetrahydrocannabinol, 4. See also Cannabis
  in breast milk, 83t
  teratogenic potential, 80
Thalidomide tragedy, 66, 84. See also Human teratogenesis
THC. See Tetrahydrocannabinol
The 12 steps of Alcoholics Anonymous, 206
Theft. See Robbery
Theories of substance use, 28–61
  backlash theory of substance abuse, 52–53
  mega interactive model of substance use among elderly women, 110–120
  mega interactive model of substance use among women, 6–26
  psychoanalytic theory, 59–60
  reactance theory, 51–52
  social stress model of substance abuse, 60
Therapeutic communities, 207–208
  goals, 207
  limitations, 215
  specific orientation for women, 208t
Therapy. See Treatment of substance use disorders
Therapy guidelines, 189. See also Treatment of substance use disorders
Thiopental, 237. See also Barbiturates
Time dimension, 10, 115
Tobacco smoking, 4, 18–20, 79. See also Nicotine
  adjunct to smoking cessation, 198
  cancer deaths and, 19
  cessation programs, 198, 201–202
  constituents of tobacco smoke, 18
  lung-cancer deaths and, 19
  passive smoke, 19–20
  preventable illness and, 19
  second hand smoke, 19–20
  teratogenic potential, 79–80
Toluene. See also Volatile solvents and inhalants
  teratogenic potential, 76
Toss, 161. See also Sex-for-drugs-exchange
Toss-up, 161. See also Sex-for-drugs-exchange
Trade names list, 222–237
Tranquilizers, 49–50

Treatment of substance use disorders, 24–28, 118, 188, 191–216. *See also* Prevention
  abstinence maintenance, 200
  alternatives model, 196–197t, 213
  Alcoholics Anonymous, 205–207, 214–215
  cognitive therapy, 202–203
  combined cognitive and feminist therapies, 203
  contingency management approaches, 213–214
  drug substitution, 201–202
  dual diagnoses, 184–185, 188–189, 202
  effects of, 191
  evaluation, 26, 118–119
  family therapy, 203–204, 205t
  feminist approaches, 203, 209–210, 215
  gender specific, 187
  general guidelines, 212t
  group psychotherapy, 203
  issues for women, 24–25
  modalities, 195
  of acute overdoses, 198–199
  of elderly women, 109–110
  of withdrawal syndromes, 199–200
  patient-treatment matching, 215
  performance goals/criterion, 211t
  pharmacologic advances, 24–25
  pharmacotherapy, 195, 198–202
  psychotherapy, 202–203
  short-term residential treatment programs, 208–209
  social skills training, 204–205
  story telling, 210, 215
  therapeutic communities, 207–208, 215
  treatment centers, 238–286
  women-oriented program characteristics, 208t
Treatment centers, 238–286
Trexan®. *See* Naltrexone
Triazolam, 237. *See also* Benzodiazepines
TWEAK, 179–180
  instrument, 180t
  scoring, 180
  use among black women, 180
  use among white women, 180
  validity and reliability, 180
Type I diagnostic error, 165, 166f, 181
Type II diagnostic error, 165, 166f, 181

Validity of substance use assessment instruments, 166
  content validity, 166, 181
  criterion-related validity, 166
  face validity, 166, 181
Valium®. *See* Diazepam

Victims of substance use related violence, 33, 123–132, 209
  accidents, 123
  alcohol use and, 124, 126, 127, 131, 135–138
  amphetamine use and, 126, 127
  androgenic-anabolic steroid use and, 127
  assaults, 124, 126
  battery during pregnancy, 126, 131
  cocaine use and, 126
  dating violence, 126–127
  falls, 123–124
  homicide, 128
  motor vehicle crashes, 124
  physical abuse/assault, 127
  postpartum abuse, 131
  risk, 130
  role *See* gender role
  sexual abuse/assault, 127–128
  suicide, 128–130
  wife abuse, 131
Vin Mariani®, 10
Violence against children, 142–143. *See also* Child abuse and Child molestation
Violent crime, 135, 138. *See also* Victims of substance use related violence
Violent physical injuries. *See* Victims of substance use related violence
Volatile solvents and inhalants, 4t, 5f. *See also* Substances of abuse
  mental disorders associated with use, 183t
  teratogenic potential, 76

Wellbutrin®. *See* Bupropion
Wernicke-Korsakoff syndrome, 13, 107, 213
White women, 8–9, 31, 47, 50, 54, 55, 66, 100, 127–128, 157, 169, 171, 180. *See also* Women
Wife abuse, 131. *See also* Abuse
Wine. *See* Alcohol
Winfrey, Oprah, 27
Withdrawal syndromes, 51, 199–200
  alcohol withdrawal, 199
  average length of treatment, 214
  cocaine withdrawal, 199
  nicotine withdrawal, 199–200
  opiate withdrawal, 199, 214
  signs and symptoms, 214
Women
  African Americans. *See* Black
  Asian, 9
  as perpetrators of substance use related violence, 133–148
  as victims of substance use related violence, 33, 123–132

Index **349**

black, 9, 52–55, 66, 87, 94, 127–128, 156–157, 161, 180, 189, 206
brown, 9, 37, 44, 55, 56–58, 61, 66, 143
Caucasians. *See* White
crimes perpetrated by, 133–148
dependence on men, 10, 209
dual diagnosis, 182–190, 202
Dutch, 36. *See also* White
elderly, 29, 97–120, 169, 178, 179
fatal motor vehicle crashes, 5
gender role, 44–48
Haitian. *See* Black
Hispanic, 9, 44, 55, 66, 143, 189. *See also* Brown
homeless, 11
homemakers, 47–48
impaired driving, 5, 146
incarcerated, 34–35, 38–39, 88, 92, 134, 143, 148
incidence of substance use, 3–4
information sources for, 238–286
inner city, 11
Jamaican. *See* Black

Jewish, 9, 143. *See also* White
Latina, 37, 56–58, 61, 159. *See also* Brown
lesbian, 8, 37, 39–40, 56, 188t, 194, 206
murders, 5, 92–93, 95
Native American, 8, 11, 95, 143, 189, 198
North American, 11
nurses, 43
referral agencies for, 238–286
substance use related mortality, 4
suicide, 5, 13, 49, 124t, 128–130, 129t, 186, 190
treatment centers for, 238–286
treatment issues, 198, 209–210
white, 8–9, 31, 47, 50, 54, 55, 66, 100, 127–128, 157, 169, 171, 180
Women dimension, 8–9
Women for sobriety, 206, 207t
Women's biology, 43
Women's role, 45. *See also* Gender role
Woolie, 22

Zoloft® *See* Sertraline
Zyban®. *See* Bupropion